Lecture Notes in Computer Science 8842

Commenced Publication in 1973
Founding and Former Series Editors:
Gerhard Goos, Juris Hartmanis, and Jan van Leeuwen

Robert Meersman   Hervé Panetto
Alok Mishra   Rafael Valencia-García
António Lucas Soares   Ioana Ciuciu
Fernando Ferri   Georg Weichhart
Thomas Moser   Michele Bezzi
Henry Chan (Eds.)

On the Move to Meaningful Internet Systems: OTM 2014 Workshops

Confederated International Workshops:
OTM Academy, OTM Industry Case Studies Program,
C&TC, EI2N, INBAST, ISDE, META4eS, MSC,
and OnToContent 2014
Amantea, Italy, October 27-31, 2014
Proceedings

 Springer

Volume Editors

Robert Meersman, Austria, E-mail: rameersman@gmail.com

Hervé Panetto, France, E-mail: herve.panetto@univ-lorraine.fr

Alok Mishra, Turkey, E-mail: alok@atilim.edu.tr

Rafael Valencia-García, Spain, E-mail: valencia@um.es

António Lucas Soares, Portugal, E-mail: als@fe.up.pt

Ioana Ciuciu, France, E-mail: ioana.ciuci@gmail.com

Fernando Ferri, Italy, E-mail: fernando.ferri@irpps.cnr.it

Georg Weichhart, Austria, E-mail: georg.weichhart@metasonic.de

Thomas Moser, Austria, E-mail: thomas.moser@stina-global.com

Michele Bezzi, France, E-mail: michele.bezzi@sap.com

Henry Chan, China, E-mail: cshchan@comp.polyu.edu.hk

ISSN 0302-9743   e-ISSN 1611-3349
ISBN 978-3-662-45549-4   e-ISBN 978-3-662-45550-0
DOI 10.1007/978-3-662-45550-0
Springer Heidelberg New York Dordrecht London

Library of Congress Control Number: 2014953778

LNCS Sublibrary: SL 3 – Information Systems and Application, incl. Internet/Web and HCI

Typesetting: Camera-ready by author, data conversion by Scientific Publishing Services, Chennai, India

Printed on acid-free paper

Springer is part of Springer Science+Business Media (www.springer.com)

General Co-Chairs' Message for OnTheMove 2014

The OnTheMove 2014 event, held during October 27–31 in Amantea, Italy, further consolidated the importance of the series of annual conferences that was started in 2002 in Irvine, California. It then moved to Catania, Sicily in 2003, to Cyprus in 2004 and 2005, Montpellier in 2006, Vilamoura in 2007 and 2009, in 2008 to Monterrey, Mexico, to Heraklion, Crete in 2010 and 2011, to Rome 2012, and to Graz in 2013. This prime event continues to attract a diverse and relevant selection of today's research worldwide on the scientific concepts underlying new computing paradigms, which of necessity must be distributed, heterogeneous, and supporting an environment of resources that are autonomous yet must meaningfully cooperate. Indeed, as such large, complex, and networked intelligent information systems become the focus and norm for computing, there continues to be an acute and even increasing need to address the implied software, system, and enterprise issues and discuss them face to face in an integrated forum that covers methodological, semantic, theoretical, and application issues as well. As we all realize, email, the Internet, and even video conferences on their own are not optimal nor even sufficient for effective and efficient scientific exchange.

The OnTheMove (OTM) Federated Conference series has been created precisely to cover the scientific exchange needs of the communities that work in the broad yet closely connected fundamental technological spectrum of Web-based distributed computing. The OTM program every year covers data and Web semantics, distributed objects, Web services, databases, information systems, enterprise workflow and collaboration, ubiquity, interoperability, mobility, grid, and high-performance computing.

OnTheMove does *not* consider itself a so-called multi-conference event but instead is proud to give meaning to the "federated" aspect in its full title[1]: It aspires to be a primary scientific meeting place where all aspects of research and development of Internet- and intranet-based systems in organizations and for e-business are discussed in a scientifically motivated way, in a forum of loosely interconnected workshops and conferences. This year's 11th edition of the OTM Federated Conferences event therefore once more provided an opportunity for researchers and practitioners to understand, discuss, and publish these developments within the broader context of distributed, ubiquitous computing. To further promote synergy and coherence, the main conferences of OTM 2014 were conceived against a background of three interlocking global themes:

---

[1] On The Move Towards Meaningful Internet Systems and Ubiquitous Computing–Federated Conferences and Workshops.

- Trusted Cloud Computing Infrastructures Emphasizing Security and Privacy
- Technology and Methodology for Data and Knowledge Resources on the (Semantic) Web
- Deployment of Collaborative and Social Computing for and in an Enterprise Context

Originally the federative structure of OTM was formed by the co-location of three related, complementary, and successful main conference series: DOA (Distributed Objects and Applications, held since 1999), covering the relevant infrastructure-enabling technologies, ODBASE (Ontologies, DataBases and Applications of SEmantics, since 2002) covering Web semantics, XML databases and ontologies, and of course CoopIS (Cooperative Information Systems, held since 1993), which studies the application of these technologies in an enterprise context through, e.g., workflow systems and knowledge management. In the 2011 edition of DOA security aspects, originally started as topics of the IS workshop in OTM 2006, became its focus as secure virtual infrastructures. Subsequently these further broadened to include Cloud-based systems emphasizing aspects of trust and privacy. As these latter aspects came to dominate agendas in its own and overlapping research communities, we decided for 2014 to rename the event as the Cloud and Trusted Computing (C&TC) conference, and to organize and launch it in a workshop format to define future editions.

Both main conferences specifically seek high-quality contributions of a more mature nature and encourage researchers to treat their respective topics within a framework that simultaneously incorporates (a) theory, (b) conceptual design and development, (c) methodology and pragmatics, and (d) application in particular case studies and industrial solutions.

As in previous years we again solicited and selected additional quality workshop proposals to complement the more mature and "archival" nature of the main conferences. Our workshops are intended to serve as "incubators" for emergent research results in selected areas related, or becoming related, to the general domain of Web-based distributed computing. This year this difficult and time-consuming job of selecting and coordinating the workshops was brought to a successful end by Yan Tang, and we were very glad to see that some of our earlier successful workshops (EI2N, META4eS, ISDE, INBAST, OntoContent) re-appeared in 2014, in some cases with a sixth or even eighth edition, and often in alliance with other older or newly emerging workshops. The new MSC workshop is an initiative of the same proposers of the erstwhile SOMOCO workshop. The Industry Case Studies Program, started in 2011 under the leadership of Hervé Panetto and OMG's Richard Mark Soley, further gained momentum and visibility in its fourth edition this year.

The OTM registration format ("one workshop buys all") actively intends to stimulate workshop audiences to productively mingle with each other and, optionally, with those of the main conferences. In particular EI2N continues to so create and exploit a visible synergy with CoopIS.

We were most happy to see that in 2014 the number of quality submissions for the OnTheMove Academy (OTMA) increased for the third consecutive year.

OTMA implements our unique, actively coached, formula to bring PhD students together, and aims to carry our "vision for the future" in research in the areas covered by OTM. Its 2014 edition was managed by a dedicated team of collaborators led by Peter Spyns and Maria-Esther Vidal, and of course inspired by the OTMA Dean, Erich Neuhold. In the OTM Academy, PhD research proposals are submitted by students for peer review; selected submissions and their approaches are to be presented by the students in front of a wider audience at the conference, and are independently and extensively analyzed and discussed in front of this audience by a panel of senior professors. One will readily appreciate the effort invested in this by the OTMA Faculty.

As the main conferences and the associated workshops all share the distributed aspects of modern computing systems, they experience the application pull created by the Internet and by the so-called Semantic Web. For ODBASE 2014, the focus continues to be the knowledge bases and methods required for enabling the use of formal semantics in Web-based databases and information systems. For CoopIS 2014, the focus as before was on the interaction of such technologies and methods with business process issues, such as occur in networked organizations and enterprises. These subject areas overlap in a scientifically natural fashion and many submissions in fact also treated an envisaged mutual impact among them. For our new core event C&TC 2014, the primary emphasis was now squarely put on the virtual and security aspects of Web-based computing in the broadest sense. As with the earlier OnTheMove editions, the organizers wanted to stimulate this cross-pollination by a program of famous keynote speakers around the chosen themes and shared by all OTM component events. We were proud to announce for this year:

- Domenico Saccà
- Ernesto Damiani
- Henk Sol
- Johann Eder

The general downturn in submissions observed in recent years for almost all conferences in computer science and IT this year finally also affected OnThe-Move, but we were still fortunate to receive a total of 126 submissions for the three main conferences and 85 submissions in total for the workshops. Not only may we indeed again claim success in attracting a representative volume of scientific papers, many from the USA and Asia, but these numbers of course allow the respective Program Committees to again compose a high-quality cross-section of current research in the areas covered by OTM. Acceptance rates vary but the aim was to stay consistently at about one accepted paper for every two to three submitted, yet as always the rates are subordinated to professional peer assessment of proper scientific quality. As usual we have separated the proceedings into two volumes with their own titles, one for the main conferences and one for the workshops and posters, and we are again most grateful to the Springer LNCS team in Heidelberg for their professional support, suggestions, and meticulous collaboration in producing the files and indexes ready for downloading on the USB sticks.

The reviewing process by the respective OTM Program Committees was performed to professional quality standards: Each paper in the main conferences was reviewed by at least three referees (four for most ODBASE papers), with arbitrated e-mail discussions in the case of strongly diverging evaluations. It may be worthwhile to emphasize once more that it is an explicit OnTheMove policy that all conference Program Committees and chairs make their selections in a completely sovereign manner, autonomous and independent from any OTM organizational considerations. As in recent years, proceedings in paper form are now only available to be ordered separately.

The general chairs are once more especially grateful to the many people directly or indirectly involved in the set-up of these federated conferences. Not everyone realizes the large number of persons that need to be involved, and the huge amount of work, commitment, and in the uncertain economic and funding climate of 2014 certainly also financial risk that is entailed by the organization of an event like OTM. Apart from the persons in their roles mentioned above, we therefore wish to thank in particular our main conference PC co-chairs:

- CoopIS 2014: Michele Missikoff, Lin Liu and Oscar Pastor
- ODBASE 2014: Alfredo Cuzzocrea and Timos Sellis
- C&TC 2014: Michele Bezzi and Henry Chan

And similarly we thank the 2014 OTMA and Workshops PC (co-)chairs (in order of appearance on the website): Alexis Aubry, Georg Weichhart, Ronald Giachetti, Michele Dassisti, Rafael Valencia García, Ricardo Colomo Palacios, Thomas Moser, Alok Mishra, Jürgen Münch, Deepti Mishra, Ioana Ciuciu, Anna Fensel, Fernando Ferri, Patrizia Grifoni, Arianna D'Ulizia, Maria Chiara Caschera, António Lucas Soares, Carla Sofia Pereira, Peter Spyns, Maria Esther Vidal, Anja Metzner, Erich J. Neuhold, and Alfred Holl.

All of them, together with their many PC members, performed a superb and professional job in managing the difficult yet essential process of peer review and selection of the best papers from the harvest of submissions. We all also owe our sincere gratitude to our supremely competent and experienced conference secretariat and technical support staff in Guadalajara and Brussels, respectively, Daniel Meersman and Jan Demey.

Two of the general co-chairs also thankfully acknowledge the academic freedom, logistic support, and facilities they enjoy from their respective institutions, Université de Lorraine CNRS, Nancy, France, and Latrobe University, Melbourne, Australia, without which such a project quite simply would not be feasible. We do hope that the results of this federated scientific enterprise contribute to your research and your place in the scientific network. We look forward to seeing you at next year's event!

September 2014

Robert Meersman
Hervé Panetto
Tharam Dillon

Organization

OTM (On The Move) is a federated event involving a series of major international conferences and workshops. These proceedings contain the papers presented at the OTM Academy, the OTM Industry Case Studies Program, C&TC, EI2N, INBAST, ISDE, META4eS, MSC and OnToConten 2014 and the CoopIS and ODBASE'14 poster papers.

Executive Committee

General Co-chairs

Robert Meersman   TU Graz, Austria
Hervé Panetto   University of Lorraine, France
Tharam Dillon   La Trobe University, Melbourne, Australia

OnTheMove Academy Dean

Erich Neuhold   University of Vienna, Austria

Industry Case Studies Program Chairs

Hervé Panetto   University of Lorraine, France

C&TC 2014 PC Co-Chairs

Michele Bezzi   SAP Research, France
Henry Chan   Hong Kong Polytechnic University, China

EI2N 2014 PC Co-Chairs

Alexis Aubry   University of Lorraine, France
Georg Weichhart   Metasonic AG, Germany and Johannes Kepler
                         Universität, Austria
Ronald Giachetti   Naval Postgraduate School, Monterey, USA
Michele Dassisti   Politecnico di Bari, Italy

INBAST 2014 PC Co-Chairs

Rafael Valencia García   Universidad de Murcia, Spain
Ricardo Colomo Palacios Østfold University College, Norway
Thomas Moser   Stina Global, Austria

ISDE 2014 PC Co-Chairs

Alok Mishra   Atilim University, Turkey
Jürgen Münch   University of Helsinki, Finland
Deepti Mishra   Atilim University, Turkey

META4eS 2014 PC Co-Chairs

Ioana Ciuciu   Joseph Fourier University, France
Anna Fensel   STI Innsbruck and FTW Telecommunications
                           Research Center Vienna, Austria

MSC 2014 PC Co-Chairs

Fernando Ferri   IRPPS, National Research Council, Italy
Patrizia Grifoni   IRPPS, National Research Council, Italy
Arianna D'Ulizia   IRPPS, National Research Council, Italy
Maria Chiara Caschera   IRPPS, National Research Council, Italy

OnToContent 2014 PC Co-Chairs

António Lucas Soares   University of Porto and INESC TEC, Portugal
Carla Sofia Pereira   Polytechnics Institute of Porto and INESC
                           TEC, Portugal
Mustafa Jarrar   Birzeit University, Palestine

CoopIS 2014 PC Co-Chairs

Michele Missikoff   Università Politecnica delle Marche and CNR,
                           Italy
Lin Liu   Tsinghua University, China
Oscar Pastor   Universidad Politècnica de Valencia, Spain

ODBASE 2014 PC Co-Chairs

Alfredo Cuzzocrea   ICAR-CNR and University of Calabria, Italy
Timos Sellis   RMIT University, VIC, Australia

Logistics Team

Daniel Meersman
Jan Demey

OTM Academy 2014 Program Committee

Alfred Holl
Andreas Schmidt
Anja Metzner
Avigdor Gal
Christoph Bussler
Dejing Dou
Erich Neuhold
Erik Proper
Fatiha Saïs

Frédéric Le Mouël
Galia Angelova
Hervé Panetto
Marcello Leida
Maria Esther Vidal
Paolo Ceravolo
Peter Spyns
Philippe Cudré-Mauroux

Industry Case Studies 2014 Program Committee

Albert Fleischmann
Andres Garcia Higuera
Antoine Lonjon
Arturo Molina
Ayelet Sapir
Christoph Bussler
Dennis Brandl
Detlef Zühlke
Dimitrov Marin
Dominique Ernadote
Donald Ferguson
Ed Parsons
Florian Kerschbaum
Francesco Danza
François B. Vernadat
Georg Weichhart
Hervé Panetto
Ian Bayley
J. Cecil
Jean-Luc Garnier
Jorge Cardoso
Juan-Carlos Mendez
Laurent Liscia

Lawrence Whitman
Luis Camarinha-Matos
Martin Zelm
Mattew Hause
Michele Dassisti
Milan Zdravkovic
Peter Loos
Peter Benson
Ricardo Gonçalves
Richard Soley
Richard Martin
Serge Boverie
Sheron Koshy
Sinuhe Arroyo
Sobah Abbas Pertersen
Steve Vinoski
Ted Goranson
Tuan Dang
Vincent Chapurlat
Yannick Naudet
Yannis Charalabidis
Yasuyuki Nishioka

C&TC 2014 Program Committee

Alex Garthwaite
Alfredo Cuzzocrea

Andreas Thor
Anthony Sulistio

Aravind Prakash
Barzan Mozafari
Bhavani Thuraisingham
Changyu Dong
Charalabos Skianis
Cheng-Kang Chu
Ching Hsien (Robert) Hsu
Christoph Reich
David Chadwick
Florian Kerschbaum
Francesco Di Cerbo
Gregorio Martinez
Heng Yin
Iulia Ion
Jiannan Ouyang
Joe Loyall
Kai Kunze

Luwei Cheng
Marco Casassa Mont
Martin Jaatun
Nohhyun Park
Peter Pietzuch
Ramesh K. Sitaraman
Russell Sears
Ryan Ko
Scharam Dustdar
Siani Pearson
Smriti R. Ramakrishnan
Stefan Dešloch
Tim Kraska
Venkatanathan Varadarajan
Yuan Yu
Zhiqiang Lin

EI2N 2014 Program Committee

Alexis Aubry
Andres Garcia
Angel Ortiz Bas
Antonio Dourado Correia
Charlotta Johnsson
Claudia Diamantini
David Romero Diaz
David Chen
Duta Luminita
Eduardo Rocha Loures
Erik Proper
Esma Yahia
François B. Vernadat
Georg Weichhart
Gino Dini
Giuseppe Berio
Hamideh Afsarmanesh
Hervé Panetto
Istvan Mezgär
J. Cecil
Janusz Szpytko
John Krogstie
Juan-Carlos Mendez
Kamelia Stefanova

Lawrence Stapleton
Luca Settineri
Luis Camarinha-Matos
Marek Wegrzyn
Mario Lezoche
Martin Zelm
Michele Dassisti
Milan Zdravkovic
Miroslav Trajanovic
Nacer Boudjlida
Néjib Moalla
Osiris Canciglieri
Ovidiu Noran
Peter Loos
Peter Bernus
Prasad Calyam
Qing Li
Rafael Batres
Raul Poler
Ricardo Jardim Goncalves
Richard Soley
Roland Jochem
Ronald Giachetti
Shimon Nof

Ted Goranson
Thomas Knothe
Udo Kannengiesser
Vincent Chapurlat

Virginie Goepp
Yannick Naudet

INBAST 2014 Program Committee

Achim Hoffmann
Alejandro Rodríguez-González
Ana Muñoz
Antonio Alejandro Lopez-Lorca
Estefania Serral Asensio
Fajar Juang Ekaputra
Francisco Garcia-Sanchez
Francisco J. García-Peñalvo
Frederik Gailly
Ghassan Beydoun
Giner Alor-Hernández
Jesualdo Tomás Fernández-Breis

Jose Luis Ochoa
Juan Miguel Gómez-Berbís
Miroslav Minovic
Oscar Pastor Lopez
Rafael Valencia Garcia
Reza Zamani
Ricardo Colomo Palacios
Robert Brown
Sören Auer
Sergio de Cesare
Thomas Moser
Vladimir Stantchev

ISDE 2014 Program Committee

Adam Wojciechowsk
Adel Taweel
Alexander Norta
Alok Mishra
Amar Gupta
Cagatay Catal
Deepti Mishra
Deo Prakash Vidyarthi
Ian Allison

Juan Garbajosa
Juergen Muench
Jukka Kääriäinen
Liguo Yu
Luis Iribarne
Marco Kuhrmann
Nik Bessis
Srini Ramaswamy

META4eS 2014 Program Committee

Adrian Brasoveanu
Ana Roxin
Andrea Kö
Anna Fensel
Camelia Pintea
Christophe Debruyne
Christophe Roche

Constantin Orasan
Cosmin Lazar
Dia Miron
Doina Tatar
Dumitru Roman
Erik Mannens
Filip Radulovic

Fouad Zablith

Georgios Meditskos

Ioana Ciuci

Irene Celino

Juriy Katkov

Luz-Maria Priego-Roche

Magali Séguran

Maria Poveda Villalón

Marin Dimitrov

Mike Matton

Peter Spyns

Stamatia Dasiopoulou

Vikash Kumar

MSC 2014 Program Committee

Adam Wojciechowski

Anna Formica

Arianna D'Ulizia

Fernando Ferri

Frederic Andres

Juan De Lara

Karin Coninx

Kevin C. Almeroth

Maria Chiara Caschera

Nicola Santoro

Nikos Komninos

Nitendra Rajput

Patrizia Griffoni

Rajkumar Kannan

Rebecca Montanari

Riccardo Torlone

Richard Chbeir

Stephen Marsh

Tiropanis Thanassis

OnToContent 2014 Program Committee

Alan Ruttenberg

Alessandro Oltramari

Alex Borgida

Andreas Schmidt

Anna Fensel

Antonio Lucas Soares

Armando Stellato

Barry Smith

Boris Villazon-Terrazas

Carla Pereira

Christophe Roche

Cristina Ribeiro

Cristovão Sousa

Giancarlo Guizzardi

Giuseppe Pirrö

Guadalupe Aguado-de-Cea

Irene Celino

Luigi Selmi

Manuel Silva

Marco Rospocher

Mathias Brochhausen

Matteo Palmonari

Mauricio Almeida

Miguel-Angel Sicilia

Mustafa Jarrar

Nikos Loutas

Nuno Silva

Patrice Seyed

Renata Baracho

Roberta Cuel

Rute Costa

Stefan Schulz

William Hogan

Zoltan Miklos

OnTheMove 2014 Keynotes

Mining and Posting Big Data on the Web to Add Value to Information Contents

Domenico Saccà

University of Calabria, Italy

Short Bio

Domenico Saccà (http://sacca.deis.unical.it) is full professor of Computer Engineering at the University of Calabria since 1987 and he is presently chairing the School of Computer Engineering at that university.

Since 2009 he is also President of the Computing and Telecommunication Competence Center ICT-SUD, operating in five regions of Southern Italy: Calabria, Campania, Puglia, Sardegna and Sicilia.

From January 2002 to January 2009, he was Director of the CNR (the Italian National Research Council) Research Institute ICAR (Institute for High Performance Computing and Networking), located in Rende (CS) and branches in Naples and Palermo. Previously, from 1995 on, he was director of the CNR ISI (Institute on System and Computer Sciences).

In the past he was visiting scientist at IBM Laboratory of San Jose, at the Computer Science Department of UCLA and at the ICSI Institute of Berkeley; moreover, he was scientific consultant of MCC, Austin and manager of the Research Division of CRAI (a research institute in southern Italy).

His current research interests focus on advanced issues of databases such as: data and process mining, inverse data mining, data warehousing and OLAP on distributed platforms, compressed representation of datacubes, database query languages. Recently he has started some research activities on cyber security topics such as protection of systems, services and end users as well as on privacy issues.

His list of publications contains more than 200 papers on journals (including Journal of the ACM, SIAM Journal on Computing, ACM Transactions on Database Systems, Theoretical Computer Science, IEEE Transactions on Software Engineering, IEEE Transactions on Knowledge and Data Engineering, VLDB Journal, Information Systems, ACM Transactions on Knowledge Discovery from Data) and on proceedings of international conferences.

He has been member of the program committees of several international conferences and director of international schools and seminars.

Talk

"Mining and Posting Big Data on the Web to add value to information contents"

A multi-dimensional view of WEB Search is first presented to substantiate the speaker's position: a powerful search needs enriched information, which is to be published with additional discovered attributes (hidden dimensions).

Some classical DB theory tools (e.g., Data exchange and DATALOG) can be re-considered as powerful frameworks for creating multi-dimensional views for their flexible search without having to fight with SQL syntax.

Data mining can be used not only for discovering knowledge from WEB data but also for adding value to data to be published on the WEB.

An ambitious goal is to combine the strengths of both SQL and NOSQL approaches: the structural approach of SQL to enrich documents and the "unstructured" approach of NOSQL to free the search from join harassment and to enable scalable performance.

Cloud Assurance: The Notion and the Issues

Ernesto Damiani

Università degli Studi di Milano, Italy

Short Bio

Ernesto Damiani is a full professor at the Computer Science Department of Università degli Studi di Milano, Italy, the director of Secure Servcie-oriented Architectures (SESAR) lab and the Head of the University's Ph.D. program in Computer Science. His areas of interest include Cloud and SOA security, semi-structured information processing, business process analysis and discovery. He has published several books and more than 300 papers and international patents. His work has appeared, among many others, in the IEEE Trans. on Knowledge and Data Engineering, the IEEE Trans. on Service Computing, the ACM Trans. on Information and System Security, the IEEE Trans. on Fuzzy Systems, the ACM Trans. on Information Systems and the ACM Trans. on Software Engineering and Methodology. He is a senior member of the IEEE and ACM Distinguished Scientist.

Ernesto Damiani leads/has led a number of international research projects: he was the Principal Investigator of the ASSERT4SOA project (STREP) on the security certification of SOA; has led the activity of SESAR research unit within SecureSCM (STREP), ARISTOTELE (IP), ASSERT4SOA (STREP), CUMULUS (STREP) and PRACTICE (IP) projects funded by the EC in the 7th Framework Program.

Ernesto has been an Associate Editor of the IEEE Trans. on Service-Oriented Computing since its inception, and is an Associate Editor of the IEEE Trans. on Fuzzy Systems. Also, Prof. Damiani is Editor in chief of the International Journal of Knowledge and Learning (Inderscience) and of the International Journal of Web Technology and Engineering (IJWTE).

Talk

"Cloud Assurance: The Notion and the Issues"

Generating and handling assurance information on the cloud is an open challenge, as conflicting requirements (e.g., transparency vs. privacy) are emerging and the size of data involved is huge. Still, managing assurance is of paramount importance for guaranteeing the desired security and dependability properties of cloud-based computations. In this talk, we first discuss the conceptual framework to represent monitoring and test-based assurance, grounding assurance-based service-level agreements (SLAs) and certification models for cloud-based services. Then, we focus on:

(i) the definition of security and dependability properties to be negotiated and certified on the cloud (ii) the types of evidence underlying them and the mechanisms for generating evidence (iii) the phases of the assurance artifacts life-cycle.

eHealtheNough or pHealth: Providing COLLAGEN for Ennovations

Henk G. Sol

University of Groningen/Delft University of Technology, The Netherlands

Short Bio

Prof. dr. Henk G. Sol is over 40 years a driver of engaged scholarship in the field of information systems and decision enhancement. With his school of nearly 80 completed PhD dissertations supervised and some 25 PhD dissertations under way, he is a major contributor to building the foundations of design science research in management and information systems.

In addition, he is responsible for the graduation of over 700 Engineering MSc and MBA students. All dissertations are based on theory development applied to tackle issues that matter in practice and are relevant to both developing and developed countries.

As founding dean he was responsible for the establishment of the Faculty of Technology, Policy and Management at Delft University of Technology and of the Faculty of Economics and Business at the University of Groningen, the Netherlands.

Prof. Sol has organized numerous international conferences and workshops, of which the conference series on CRIS and Dynamic Modeling have been seminal. He has published widely in renowned journals, edited many books, and given many keynote presentations all over the world. He acted as a consultant to many governments and organizations worldwide. He was founding father of IFIP TC8, 8.1 and 8.3, AIS and many (inter)national doctoral consortia.

Henk G. Sol serves currently in various academic and professional roles: President of the Supervisory Board of Groningen Airport Eelde NV, Eelde; Director of Sol Information Management BV, Haren; Chairperson of the Board of Trustees, Uganda Technology and Management University, Kampala; Chairperson of Stichting PAO Informatica; Consulting Professor of PBLQ, The Hague; and Member of the Board of Trustees of the International Institute for Communication and Development, the Hague.

Talk

"eHealtheNough or pHealth: Providing COLLAGEN for Ennovations"

Enhancing issues that matter is a major challenge in our ambient society, especially in the health domain: we have to navigate in the sea of information to deliver shared value. Agile, analytic, big, intelligent, smart, sustainable data describe the potential for decision enhancement. Processes have to be engineered accordingly to deliver shared value.

Many initiatives are taken around eHealth, but what is the impact of the many projects in terms of usefulness, usability and usage?

Studies on the effectiveness of eHealth may lead to the conclusion that eHealth is eNough. Many examples indicate that the patient is often neglected, that physical and decision processes are not looked into and that the technology is pushed, despite great development funds for e.g. eInclusion and Ambient Assisted Living.

Delivering shared value calls for: conversations to collectively identify locally relevant problems, governance to make political, administrative and business decisions about tackling such problems and engaged innovations to develop localized solutions.

The COLLAGEN (Collective Learning and Agile Governance Environment) approach provides a set of services for scoping, facilitation and enhancement of business processes, packed into decision apps and providing guidelines for conversational inquiry. The approach supports smart governance for business engineering and engaged innovations, and delivers shared value to resolve issues that matter in society, especially in health care and cure.

It is posited that innovations in health care demand pHealth for delivering shared value based on patient focus, personal intervention, process anchoring and participatory design.

Managing the Execution of Business Processes

Johann Eder

Alpen-Adria Universität Klagenfurt, Austria

Short Bio

Johann Eder is full professor for Information and Communication Systems in the Department of Informatics-Systems of the Alpen-Adria Universität Klagenfurt, Austria. From 2005-2013 he was Vice President of the Austrian Science Funds (FWF). He held positions at the Universities of Linz, Hamburg and Vienna and was visiting scholar at AT&T Shannon Labs.

The research interests of Johann Eder are databases, information systems and data management for medical research. He successfully directed many funded research projects on workflow management systems, temporal data warehousing, application interoperability, information systems modelling, information systems for medical research, etc.

Johann Eder has contributed to workflow systems and business process management for 2 decades, in particular in the area of workflow systems languages and architectures, exception handling, time management, and data management. His research led to the development of the commercial workflow management systems altavistaWorks and @enterprise.

He published more than 150 papers in international journals and conference proceedings. He served in numerous program committees for international conferences and as editor and referee for international journals. He acted as general chair and/or PC chair for CAiSE, ADBIS, BPM, CoopIS, and DAWAK conferences.

Talk

"Managing the Execution of Business Processes"

Managing the execution of business processes requires many decisions: whom to assign to a task, when to execute a task, how to deal with exceptions, etc. Some of these decisions can be automated according to some policies. Some cannot be automated but can be supported by process technologies.

In this talk we will analyze which decisions have to be taken at the run-time of business processes by process participants and by process managers and discuss how these decisions can be supported by components of workflow management systems, in particular time management systems, resource management systems, scheduling systems, exception handling systems, and process warehousing.

Table of Contents

Industry Case Studies Program 2014

Industry Case Studies Program 2014 PC Chairs Message

Models for Interoperable Infrastructures

Applications

Cloud and Trusted Computing (C&TC) 2014

Cloud and Trusted Computing 2014 PC Co-Chairs Message

Privacy and Access Control

Reliability and Performance

Cloud and Configuration Management

Workshop on Enterprise Integration, Interoperability and Networking (EI2N) 2014

Interoperability in (System-of-) Systems

Applications

Workshop on Industrial and Business Applications of Semantic Web Technologies (INBAST) 2014

International Workshop on Information Systems in Distributed Environment (ISDE) 2014

ISDE 2014 PC Co-Chairs Message

Distributed Information Systems Applications

Architecture and Process in Distributed Information System

Distributed Information System Development and Operational Environment

Workshop on Methods, Evaluation, Tools and applications for the Creation and Consumption of Structured Data for the e-Society (META4eS) 2014

Ontology in Use for eSociety

Knowledge Management and Applications for eSociety

Workshop on Mobile and Social Computing for collaborative interactions (MSC) 2014

MSC 2014 PC Co-Chairs Message

Social Networks and Social Services

Social and Mobile Intelligence

Multimodal Interaction and Collaboration

Workshop on Ontology Content (OnToContent) 2014

Cooperative Information Systems (CoopIS) 2014 Posters

Ontologies, DataBases, and Applications of Semantics (ODBASE) 2014 Posters

The 11th OnTheMove Academy PC Chairs' Message

This OTMA edition focused on context-aware paradigms, and management and mining techniques to enhance the performance and behavior of complex process in different domains, e.g., business information systems or bioinformatics. Furthermore, community and semantically driven Information Technologies for business ecosystems and data science and governance applications were part of our topics of interest In the ten past editions, the OTM Academy has yearly innovated its way of working to uphold its mark of quality and excellence. OTMA Ph.D. students publish their work in a highly reputed publication channel, namely the Springer LNCS OTM workshops proceedings. The OTMA faculty members, who are well-respected researchers and practitioners, critically reflect on the students work in a positive and inspiring atmosphere, so that the students learn to improve not only their research capacities but also their presentation and writing skills. OTMA participants learn how to review scientific papers. They also enjoy ample possibilities to build and expand their professional network thanks to access to all OTM conferences and workshops. And last but not least, an ECTS credit certificate rewards their hard work.

Crucial for the success of OTM Academy is the commitment of our other OTMA faculty members whom we sincerely thank:

- Alfred Holl (University of Applied Sciences, Nuremberg, Germany)
- Josefa Kumpfmüller (Vienna, Austria), Student Communication Seminar
- Anja Metzner, University of Applied Sciences Augsburg, Germany
- Erich J. Neuhold (University of Vienna, Austria), OTMA Dean

The OTMA submissions were reviewed by an international programme committee of well-respected experts. We thank them for their effort and time:

- Galia Angelova (Bulgarian Academy of Science, Sofia, Bulgary)
- Christoph Bussler (Tropo Inc., USA)
- Paolo Ceravolo (Università degli Studi di Milano, Italy)
- Philippe Cudré-Mauroux (Massachusetts Institute of Technology, USA)
- Dejing Dou (University of Oregon, Oregon, USA)
- Avigdor Gal (Technion – Israel Institute of Technology, Haifa, Israell)
- Frédéric Le Mouël (University of Lyon, Lyon, France)
- Hervé Panetto (Nancy University, Nancy, France)
- Erik Proper (Public Research Centre - Henri Tudor, Luxembourg)
- Fatiha Saïs (Université Paris-Sud XI, France)
- Andreas Schmidt (Karlsruhe University of Applied Sciences, Germany)

We also express our thanks to Christophe Debruyne (Vrije Universiteit Brussel) who again volunteered to be the OTMA 2014 "social media master".

This year, nine papers were submitted by Ph.D. students. Three submissions are published as regular papers and four as short papers.

We hope that you find the papers of these upcoming researchers promising and inspiring for your own research.

September 2014   Peter Spyns
                                                          Maria Esther Vidal

A Literature Study on the State-of-the-Art of Contingency Research in Business Process Management

Tom Pauwaert and Amy Van Looy

Ghent University, Faculty of Economics and Business Administration,
Department of Business Informatics and Operations Management,
Tweekerkenstraat 2, B-9000 Ghent, Belgium
{Tom.Pauwaert,Amy.VanLooy}@UGent.be

Abstract. Business Process Management (BPM) gets increasing attention, both from practitioners and academics. However, studies recently start calling out the importance of a fit with the environment, which is called BPM contingency. This means that generic BPM principles and models do not always deliver the promised outcomes, as they fail to consider the specific environments in which certain organizations operate. Using a structured literature review, we present a state-of-the-art of contingency research on business processes.

Keywords: business process management, business process orientation, contingency, resource-based view, dynamic capability.

1   Introduction

Business Process Management (BPM) aims at improving business processes to enhance, among others, an organization's competitiveness and performance in pursuit of long-term sustained competitive advantage [1]. As from its rise in the 1990s, BPM continues to be a top priority for organizations [2]. This interest is partially driven by the need to improve business processes to face changing economic environments [3], e.g. in moderately dynamic and high velocity markets [4].

Although BPM is generally recognized as important to organizations, it needs to cope with two types of criticism, i.e. one-size-fits-all and path-dependency. First, the current one-size-fits-all approach of BPM is followed by many maturity models [5]. Their static roadmap is based on best practices to advance from a current level to the next desired level. The first criticism states that those best practices are generic, and do not fully consider the characteristics of a specific organization. This criticism is only valid to some extent, as the best practices are merely given as examples and not to be followed blindly. Secondly, criticism frequently states that BPM does not consider the path-dependent emergence of possible capabilities. This means that the development of capabilities within an organization depends on the organization's history, past experiences, knowledge, assets and resources. Path-dependency is related to the principle of equifinality, which indicates that even when (1) organizations develop their capabilities from different starting points and (2) take unique paths in their development, the end results might be similar [4]. In response to the criticism,

R. Meersman et al. (Eds.): OTM 2014 Workshops, LNCS 8842, pp. 3–7, 2014.
© Springer-Verlag Berlin Heidelberg 2014

scholars start recognizing the importance of a contingent BPM approach [1][6]. Therefore, this paper explores the extent to which the process literature introduces a contingency approach in the different domains of BPM, and where further research is required.

Subsequently, section 2 describes prior work on contingency research and BPM research. Section 3 explains our methodology to gain insight into how contingency has been handled in the context of BPM. The preliminary results are discussed in section 4, followed by the research limitations and future research avenues (section 5).

2   Prior Work

2.1   Theories Underlying a Contingency Approach

In the management literature, Teece [7] identified three paradigms for long-term sustained competitive advantage (i.e. one of the main goals of BPM) [1]. The first two paradigms are the structure-conduct-performance paradigm (e.g. the competing forces of Porter [8]) and the strategic conflict paradigm. These two paradigms take a more external approach, while the third paradigm - the **Resource-Based View (RBV)** - conceptualizes firms as bundles of (internal) resources [9]. Resources within the RBV are conceptualized as any asset of an organization, including but not limited to people, knowledge and capabilities. Following this line of thought, the **Dynamic Capability Theory (DCT)** [4][7] builds upon the RVB by proposing a distinction between: (1) operational capabilities, and (2) dynamic capabilities [6]. The operational capabilities gear towards the operational functioning of the organization and are, as such, closely related to business processes [6]. The dynamic capabilities, on the other hand, are those capabilities that help organizations restructuring their resources into new value-creating resource configurations [4][6][7]. Translated towards BPM, operational capabilities may be conceptualized as the business processes in BPM, while dynamic capabilities are more similar to those BPM capabilities concerned with optimizing and changing business processes.

One of the most important aspects of the dynamic capability theory is the recognition that organizations should adapt to their environment in order to sustain competitive advantage. This underlying philosophy is the cornerstone of **contingency theory** [10], which assumes that there is generally no 'best' way to organize an organization; there must be a good 'fit' with the environment. When translating these theories to BPM, the dynamic capability theory and the contingency theory may underlie BPM in an attempt to address the one-size-fits-all criticism mentioned in the introduction. Both theories also focus on the path-dependency of capabilities to influence the optimal areas for investment, and the equifinality of operational and dynamic capabilities.

2.2   Prior Work on Business Process Management

Two capability frameworks give an overview of the critical success factors in BPM, and summarize the different domains in the business process literature as such. The first capability framework was introduced by de Bruin and Rosemann [11], and is based on a literature review and Delphi studies. It distinguishes six main capability areas, which were input for a maturity model on BPM. On the other hand, the capability framework of Van Looy et al. [12] is based on theories underlying business processes and organization management, and is validated by a sample of 69 maturity models that focus on specific processes and/or BPM. This second framework also distinguishes six main capability areas, namely: (1) modeling, (2) deployment, (3) optimization, (4) management, (5) culture, and (6) structure. To our knowledge, the main difference is that the second framework can be considered as independent of any particular maturity model, while the first framework rather represents a single maturity model. Hence, the second framework will be used to structure our literature review.

3   Methodology

We conducted a structured literature review to find articles that deal with a contingency approach in the business process literature. The Web of Knowledge was used with predetermined search keywords in June 2014. An important requirement was that the papers focus on "business process(es)". This keyword was used in combination with either one of (1) "context*", (2) "contingen*", (3) "dynamic capab*" or (4) "environment*". All combinations of 'keyword in topic' (TS) or 'keyword in title' (TI) have been used. The sample sizes varied greatly with a sample of 2,327 results for the most permissive search query (TSxTS) and 81 results for the most restrictive one (TIxTI). After looking through the results of the different queries, the most restrictive search query (i.e. with 81 results) was selected to categorize the identified papers using the capability framework chosen in section 2.2 [12]. The reason for selecting the most restrictive query was to minimize the number of irrelevant papers, which were abundant when using the other search strategies. Based on their title and abstract, the 81 resulting papers were then analyzed by two coders (i.e. authors of this article). Even though the search query was already rather restrictive, the 81 results still contained papers that were not relevant to contingency for business processes, and thus the research question. Hence, four papers were removed. The 77 remaining papers were then classified into one or more main capability areas or BPM domains of the framework. The title and abstract of the selected papers were analyzed to reach consensus among the coders. In case of dispute, a further inspection of the article text provided the necessary clarification to reach consensus.

4   Preliminary Results

This section presents the preliminary results of our structured literature study by categorizing the 77 identified contingency studies in the respective BPM domains, i.e. by classifying them into Van Looy et al.'s capability framework [12]. Only one article could not be classified into a single capability, and encompasses all BPM domains.

Table 1 shows that most papers deal with contingency for process modeling, deployment and optimization. The modeling papers mainly focus on how to model contextual properties or events in process designs. Deployment contingency relates to how business processes can be deployed in a context-sensitive manner, while optimization contingency examines how processes can be optimized considering the context in which they operate. The management, cultural and structural domains of the framework are less represented, i.e. respectively 11, five and two contingency papers. A possible explanation is that those domains take a holistic, organizational view on BPM (called business process orientation), which is emerging in recent years. However, further examination of publication years does not fully support this explanation.

Table 1. Classification of the identified contingency papers in BPM domains

Classification	% of Papers	# of papers	Recurring Keywords
Modeling	42.9%	33	Modeling
Deployment	37.7%	29	BPEL, binding constraints, workflows, ERP
Optimization	29.9%	23	Analytics, process mining, improvement, reengineering (BPR), simulation, monitoring
Management	14.3%	11	n/a
Culture	6.5%	5	Knowledge management, national culture, sme
Structure	2.6%	2	Knowledge management
All	1.3%	1	n/a

Table 1 shows that articles on the management aspects of contingent BPM did not have common keywords (i.e. indicated by n/a in Table 1). On the other hand, the contingency papers on culture and structure mainly emphasize knowledge management practices. In addition, the 'culture' domain has one article on national culture, and one article that focuses on small and medium enterprises (i.e. organization size). For the more technical domains, Table 1 shows a few sets of keywords that commonly recur.

While a more in-depth content analysis of the contingency papers is required, the temporary results suggest that a lot of research is still to be done on the topic of contingent BPM (especially in the managerial, cultural and structural domains of BPM).

5   Conclusion

This review is a first attempt to shed light on contingent business process research. An underrepresentation in the literature was found for the 'softer' and more recent BPM domains, i.e. management, culture, and structure. On the other hand, the domains dealing with the traditional process lifecycle (i.e. modeling, deployment and optimization of business processes) seem to be more actively researched through a contingency lens. However, the current paper faces two important limitations. First, the sample was restricted to articles indexed by the Web of Knowledge. Consequentially, we may have missed some articles that are indexed in other academic databases. Secondly, our sample consists solely of articles that are retrievable through the predetermined search keywords. Hence, any paper that does not identify itself as being specifically geared towards business processes nor simultaneously towards some measure of contingency will not have been detected.

In future research, we will extend the scope of this review by using a constrained citation analysis [13], i.e. starting from a few of the most influential articles of the underlying theories discussed in section 2 (i.e. contingency theory, dynamic capability theory, RBV). This approach might provide us with a sufficiently large sample to identify the important contingency studies in other disciplines, i.e. beyond BPM (e.g. operations management, situational method engineering, etc.). Afterwards, we will verify to which degree the theories or contingency approaches in other disciplines can be used as the basis for a BPM contingency theory.

References

1. Trkman, P.: The critical success factors of business process management. Int. J. Inf. Manag. 30, 125–134 (2010)
2. McKinsey: Global Survey Results: IT's unmet potential, http://www.mckinseyquarterly.com
3. McCormack, K., Willems, J., Bergh, J., van den, D.D., Willaert, P., Štem-berger, M.I., Škrinjar, R., Trkman, P., Ladeira, M.B., Oliveira, M.P.V., de Vuksic, V.B., Vlahovic, N.: A global investigation of key turning points in business process maturity. Bus. Process Manag. J. 15, 792–815 (2009)
4. Eisenhardt, K.M., Martin, J.A.: Dynamic capabilities: what are they? Strateg. Manag. J. 21, 1105–1121 (2000)
5. vom Brocke, J., Schmiedel, T., Recker, J., Trkman, P., Mertens, W., Viaene, S.: Ten principles of good business process management. Bus. Process Manag. J. 20, 530–548 (2014)
6. Ortbach, K., Plattfaut, R., Poppelbuß, J., Niehaves, B.: A Dynamic Capability-Based Framework for Business Process Management: Theorizing and Empirical Application. Presented at the (January 2012)
7. Teece, D.J., Pisano, G., Shuen, A.: Dynamic capabilities and strategic management. Strateg. Manag. J. 18, 509–533 (1997)
8. Miller, D., Friesen, P.H.: Porter's Generic Strategies and Performance: An Em-pirical Examination with American Data Part I: Testing Porter. Organ. Stud. 7, 37–55 (1986)
9. Wernerfelt, B.: A resource-based view of the firm. Strateg. Manag. J. 5, 171–180 (1984)
10. Lawrence, P.R., Lorsch, J.W.: Organization and environment: managing differentiation and integration. R. D. Irwin (1969)
11. Rosemann, M.: The Six Core Elements of Business Process Management. In: vom Brocke, J., Rosemann, M. (eds.) Handbook on Business Process Management, vol. 1, pp. 107–122. Springer, Heidelberg (2010)
12. Van Looy, A., De Backer, M., Poels, G.: A conceptual framework and classification of capability areas for business process maturity. Enterprise Information Systems 8, 188–224 (2014)
13. Lecy, J., Beatty, K.: Structured Literature Reviews Using Constrained Snowball Sampling and Citation Network Analysis (2012)

Towards a Compliance-Aware Inter-organizational Service Integration Platform

Laura González and Raúl Ruggia

Instituto de Computación, Facultad de Ingeniería, Universidad de la República, Uruguay
{lauragon,ruggia}@fing.edu.uy

Abstract. Organizations are increasingly required to collaborate with each other in order to achieve their business goals. The service oriented paradigm is currently the preferred approach to carry out this collaboration as facilitates interconnecting the software systems of different organizations. More concretely, such integration is supported by integration platforms which are specialized middleware-based infrastructures enabling the provision, discovery and invocation of interoperable software services. On another hand, these integrated and collaborative environments (e.g. e-government, e-health, e-science, e-commerce and e-business) must comply with regulations originating in laws, sectorial regulations, service level agreements and standards, among others. This research aims at proposing solutions to monitor and enforce compliance requirements in inter-organizational service integration platforms. Particularly, this work addresses compliance requirements on services, information exchanged and the flow of interactions between organizations. The solutions, which are based on well-known enterprise integration patterns and other capabilities (e.g. adaptability and context-awareness), are then refined into specific middleware technologies, notably Enterprise Service Bus and Complex Event Processing engines.

Keywords: regulatory compliance, enterprise service bus, complex event processing, service-oriented computing, enterprise integration, middleware.

1 Introduction

Over the last decades organizations have become distributed and dynamically federated entities which increasingly need to collaborate with each other by integrating and composing business services [1]. To achieve this, integrated software systems that implement such business services have become a must, as they enable to exchange data and execute business functions across organizations. This trend has led to large scale information systems which interconnect the software systems of different, autonomous and geographically distributed organizations sharing common goals [2][3][4]. This kind of systems can be found in different application domains such as e-government, e-health, e-science, e-commerce and e-business, among others [5].

In this context, the service oriented paradigm is currently the preferred approach to carry out multi-organization collaboration by allowing the integration and composition of distributed software services [4]. Such service integration is supported by the

R. Meersman et al. (Eds.): OTM 2014 Workshops, LNCS 8842, pp. 8–17, 2014.

so-called integration platforms, which are specialized infrastructures including an intermediate processing layer that facilitates the provision, discovery and invocation of interoperable software services. This intermediate processing allows performing validations (e.g. on access control policies), monitoring service invocations (e.g. on response time) and solving integration issues (e.g. communication protocol mismatches). Integration platforms are based on advanced middleware technologies, notably Enterprise Service Bus (ESB) and Complex Event Processing (CEP) engines.

Examples of large scale software systems supported by service integration platforms (SIP) can be found in e-government [6] and e-health [7] initiatives. In particular, the Uruguayan E-government Platform [6] includes an Interoperability Platform (InP) which facilitates the implementation and usage of e-government services based on a statewide service-oriented architecture (SOA). Indeed, by leveraging the Web Services technology, public agencies can offer their functionalities through interoperable software services, which are usually hosted on agencies' servers and exposed through proxy services in the InP. This way, all service invocations pass through the InP allowing to apply on them security controls and mediation operations (e.g. intelligent routing, message transformation). Fig. 1 presents a general overview of the InP.

Fig. 1. Uruguayan E-Government Interoperability Platform

Furthermore, the advent of cloud computing introduced the need for cloud-based integration alternatives involving a trusted intermediary party which provides solutions for different cloud integration requirements (e.g. cloud to on-premise, cloud to cloud, on-premise to on-premise [8]). These cloud-based SIPs, which support integration scenarios within and across organizations, can take different forms (e.g. Internet Service Bus [9], Cloud Service Broker [10] and Integration Platform as a Service [8]).

On another hand, these integrated and collaborative environments have to satisfy regulatory compliance requirements, originating from laws (e.g. personal data protection laws), standards and code of practice (e.g. HL7, WS-Interoperability), sectorial regulations (e.g. Sarbanes-Oxley, HIPAA) and service level agreements (SLA), among others, that apply to each organization as well as to the entire system [11]. Furthermore, in recent years, enforcing such compliance requirements (i.e. taking actions to assure their fulfillment) has become increasingly important, particularly in scenarios involving inter-organizational interactions. This is due to the fact that the non-adherence to these requirements may lead to the malfunction of the whole system and even may face organizations to litigation risks and even criminal penalties [12].

In particular, in the previous e-government scenario there are many compliance requirements that public agencies have to fulfill. For example, in order to improve the interoperability level, the Web Services provided by the agencies have to adhere to various WS-I profiles (http://www.ws-i.org/). Also, the information interchanged between public agencies cannot infringe the Uruguayan personal data protection law (http://www.parlamento.gub.uy/leyes/AccesoTextoLey.asp?Ley=18331). Lastly, services have to be compliant with the SLAs (e.g. regarding response time, availability and throughput) that are established when they are registered in the platform.

Despite the relevance of these issues, current solutions addressing them are limited in terms of flexibility, agility and maintainability [12] and they do not address inter-organizational contexts [13][14]. In turn, given the mediation role of SIPs in inter-organizational interactions, these platforms are very suitable to perform the monitoring and enforcement of certain types of compliance requirements. Therefore, this work aims at proposing solutions to monitor and enforce compliance requirements based on SIPs and focusing on inter-organizational contexts. In particular, it addresses compliance requirements of services, information exchanged by organizations and the control flow of interactions between organizations. These solutions, which are based on well-known enterprise integration patterns (EIPs) and other specialized capabilities (e.g. adaptability and context-awareness), are then refined into specific middleware technologies (notably ESB and CEP Engines), types of regulations (e.g. data protection regulations) and application domains (e.g. e-health and e-government).

Then, the research questions for this work are: RQ1) Which are the most common families of compliance requirements in inter-organizational contexts?, RQ2) How can these compliance requirements be specified?, RQ3) Which capabilities should SIPs include to monitor and enforce these families of requirements? RQ4) How would a reference architecture for this platform be?, RQ5) How can the required capabilities be built by leveraging native features of middleware technologies like ESB and CEP?, RQ6) What are the potential and limitations of these technologies to carry out the required tasks, and how can they be extended or complemented?, and RQ7) Are current middleware products mature enough to implement the required tasks?

The expected contributions of this work are, firstly, academic, by proposing, specifying and evaluating novel integration technologies with specialized features to monitor and enforce compliance requirements in inter-organizational contexts. This is an open area [13] which is becoming more relevant with the advent of cloud-based integration solutions [8]. Also, the results of this work would be applied in real-world large-scale collaborative software systems (e.g. e-government, e-health) to allow a more efficient development and delivery of reliable public services.

The rest of the paper is organized as follows. Section 2 presents related work and Section 3 presents the research hypotheses. Section 4 presents the leveraged material and Section 5 describes the methods and work plan. Section 6 presents preliminary results and section 7 describes the evaluation methodology and contrasts the proposed solutions with existing work. Finally, Section 8 presents conclusions and future work.

2   Related Work

Various initiatives and projects have addressed regulatory compliance issues in service-based systems within organizations and, more recently, across them.

One of the most relevant projects in this area is the European project COMPAS [15] that proposes an integrated solution for runtime compliance governance in SOA which includes tools for modeling compliance requirements, linking them to business processes (BPs), monitoring process execution using CEP techniques, displaying the current state of compliance and analyzing cases of non-compliance [16][17]. However, the project mainly focuses on orchestrations (i.e. BPs managed within a single organization), while our solutions also address compliance requirements within a flow of interactions between organizations (e.g. choreographies). Also, although performing corrective actions is mentioned [17], the project mainly deals with monitoring tasks while our work also addresses enforcement tasks.

As the previous project, other proposals also focus on orchestrations and on monitoring tasks. In [18] an extension to a methodology called "architecture for BP optimization (aPro)" is proposed. This extension addresses the automatic generation of CEP rules to deal with the challenges of the runtime checking of compliance requirements in BPs. Also, in [19] a method for monitoring control-flow deviations during process execution is proposed. Its main contribution is a formal technique to derive monitoring queries from a process model, so that they can be directly used with CEP.

There are also proposals to deal with compliance requirements of choreographies. In [20] a Multi-source Monitoring Framework is proposed, through which the non-functional properties of choreographies can be monitored. Compared to our approach, this work only has detective purposes. Also, in [21] an architectural framework to verify the compliance of the overall sequence of inter-organizational choreography operations is proposed. Leveraging CEP, the solution uses event patterns to filter, monitor, and check for the incoming and outgoing calls. The solution performs preventive actions by filtering messages that do not comply with the requirements. Our proposal also deals with this kind of requirements, but it is not restricted to only that.

Other proposals focus on specific regulations. In [22], a proposal to enforce compliance with data privacy regulations in a health-related cross-organizational context is proposed. The authors propose an event-driven architecture based on an ESB and domain-specific languages (DSLs) to manage the elicitation and enforcement of data privacy rules. The paper characterizes the roles of Data Producer, Data Consumer and Policy Enforcer defining the events and message exchanges among them. However, compared to ours, this work does not address mechanisms to dynamically enforce non-complying interactions and it does not cover either other types of regulations.

More recently, compliance issues in cross-organizational BPs are being addressed. In [13][14] a property of "compliability" is defined to characterize interaction models consistent with a set of compliance rules. This work focuses on design time checking of compliance rules related to control flow, while ours deals with run-time checking and also covers other requirements (e.g. data-related).

Regarding middleware-based solutions, most of the previous proposals leverage these technologies. However, our work considers their mechanisms as first class citizens and not merely as tools. This allows: i) explicitly leveraging them, ii) identifying their limitations and complementing or enhancing them, and iii) refining the proposed solutions into different middleware technologies (e.g. ESB) and products (e.g. Esper).

3   Research Hypotheses

To address the research questions, we start from the following research hypotheses:

- **Hypothesis 1 (H1).** There are suitable mechanisms (e.g. DSLs) to specify the most common families of compliance requirements within inter-organizational contexts, in particular, regarding services, information exchanged by organizations and the control flow of interactions between organizations. (RQ1)(RQ2)
- **Hypothesis 2 (H2).** A SIP supporting the following characteristics is able to monitor and enforce these families of requirements: enterprise integration and connectivity patterns [23][24], adaptability [25], advanced monitoring and context-awareness [26]. (RQ3)
- **Hypothesis 3 (H4).** A reference architecture for a Compliance-aware Inter-organizational SIP can be specified to cover large-scale (e.g. e-health) as well as cloud-based (e.g. e-science) inter-organizational scenarios. (RQ4)
- **Hypothesis 4 (H4).** The capabilities in H2 can be built with native or extended mechanisms provided by middleware technologies (e.g. ESB, CEP). (RQ5)(RQ6)
- **Hypothesis 5 (H5).** Current middleware products (e.g. JBossESB) provide a suitable foundation to implement the required monitoring and enforcement tasks for the identified families of compliance requirements. (RQ7)

There are solid grounds for these hypotheses based on the related work described above. However, the research questions address extended issues on each of the items that have to be further analyzed.

4   Material

The material to evaluate the hypotheses presented in Section 4 comprises: i) existing knowledge on SIPs and middleware technologies: it mainly consists in our previous work which focused on proposing adaptive SIPs [25], context-aware SIPs [26] and domain-specific SIPs [27][28]; ii) existing knowledge on regulatory compliance: it mainly comes from the related work described in Section 2, in particular, we highlight the results obtained in the COMPAS project; iii) real application scenarios focusing on specific e-government [6] and e-health [7] integration platforms along with standards (e.g. SOAP, HL7), codes of practices (e.g. WS-I, IHE), laws (e.g. personal data protection laws) and agreements (e.g. SLAs); iv) Event-B [29] as a formal method to specify the proposed SIP as well as the compliance solutions. Event-B provides suitable characteristics (e.g. events and refinements support) to specify this kind of systems, there are various experiences of its usage in similar contexts [30] and we have already used in previous work [28]; and v) prototypes, leveraging existing middleware products, and prototypes from our previous work [31]. These prototypes will allow performing a functional and non-functional evaluation of the proposed mechanisms, evaluating the potential and limitations of current middleware technologies, and identifying / proposing enhancements or complementary components for them.

5 Methods / Work Plan

A successive refinement approach is being followed starting with the identification of relevant families of compliance requirements in inter-organizational contexts, continuing with the characterization of a compliance-aware inter-organizational SIP and its capabilities, and finishing with an incremental analysis and specification of solutions for monitoring and enforcing those families of requirements and specific regulations.

Event-B [29] will be used to specify the integration platform and the proposed solutions. This method is highly suitable to formally specify event-based systems in successive abstraction levels, which directly supports the proposed refinement-oriented methodology. Also, the practical application of the solutions will be discussed in the context of e-government and e-health domains, focusing on personal data protection laws and on standards and codes of practice suitable for these areas.

Based on this methodology, the work-plan consists of: i) identify common families of compliance requirements within inter-organizational contexts (e.g. interaction flow), ii) identify / propose suitable mechanisms to specify these families of requirements (e.g. domain-specific languages), iii) identify the required capabilities to monitor and enforce these requirements within SIPs, iv) define a reference architecture for a compliance-aware SIP which cover large-scale as well as cloud-based inter-organizational scenarios, v) specify the compliance-aware SIP and its capabilities through suitable mechanisms (e.g. Event-B), vi) propose and specify solutions to monitor and enforce the identified families of requirements based on these capabilities, vii) refine the reference architecture and the solutions to different type of regulations (e.g. data protection laws), viii) refine SIP capabilities into native or extended mechanisms provided by middleware technologies, notably ESB and CEP, and ix) prototype and evaluate the proposed solutions, using concrete middleware products and covering specific application domains (e.g. e-government, e-health).

6 Preliminary Results

This section describes the general architecture of the compliance-aware inter-organizational SIP and its envisioned refinement through different abstraction levels.

Fig. 2 presents the high-level architecture of the proposed platform which may be hosted within a trusted party (e.g. a supervisory agency).

As in any integration platform, the interactions (e.g. service requests / responses) between the interacting parties (i.e. organizations) pass through the platform in the form of messages (e.g. SOAP messages). In addition, the platform processes the messages to verify their compliance with the configured compliance requirements and, eventually, performs suitable actions to enforce them. To this end, it is equipped with traditional (e.g. EIP) and specialized (e.g. adaptability) capabilities. It also includes specific solutions, built over the former, to monitor (e.g. the exchanged information) and enforce (e.g. by blocking an interaction) common families of compliance requirements. Leveraging these specific solutions, higher-level solutions for specific types of regulations (e.g. personal data protection laws) can be built and refined into different domains (e.g. e-health).

Fig. 2. High Level Architecture of the Compliance-aware SIP

Fig. 3 shows the different abstraction levels in which the compliance requirements, as well as the actions to be taken when a violation to them is detected, can be seen.

Fig. 3. Different Abstraction Levels

At LEVEL 1 there are the laws and standards which are usually specified in natural language. Some parts of them may be specified, by domain experts, using the mechanisms (e.g. DSLs) provided at LEVEL 2. If suitable mappings are set (between LEVEL 2 and LEVEL 3) the specifications at the second level may be automatically transformed into monitoring and enforcement solutions built on top of the solutions at LEVEL 3. As stated before, the latter are based on the capabilities of traditional SIPs (LEVEL 4) which can be, in turn, supported by different middleware technologies, such as ESB and CEP (LEVEL 5). Finally, the concrete implementation of these middleware technologies is provided by different products, such as Esper (LEVEL 6).

Note that the first four abstraction levels, and the mappings between them, support the agile development of compliance solutions by leveraging the proposed capabilities of the compliance-aware SIP (LEVEL 3). In turn, the last three abstraction levels provide the flexibility to implement a concrete compliance solution using different middleware technologies and products according to the specific context of use (e.g. scale of the solution, available resources). As a final remark, this work mainly concentrates on providing solutions and specifications for the third and fourth abstraction levels, along with the corresponding mappings with the second and fifth level.

Next, three examples are presented in order to illustrate the envisioned operation of the platform, focusing on the third and fourth abstraction levels.

Example 1: Personal data protection laws usually state that organizations cannot share sensitive personal data unless the person gives an explicit consent for that. In this case, the solution to monitor exchanged information (LEVEL 3) can be used to check if some sensitive data is interchanged without the corresponding consent. If so, and enforcement action can be taken (LEVEL 3), for example, to filter (i.e. take out) the sensitive data from the interchanged information before leaving the platform. This last action can be implemented at LEVEL 4 by the message transformation EIP.

Example 2: Two organizations agreed an allowed set of interactions and the order in which they have to take place (e.g. using BPMN2 at LEVEL 2) with the aim of carry out a collaborative business process. In this case, the solution to monitor the order of interactions (LEVEL 3) can be used. At LEVEL 4, this monitoring solution may be implemented using the temporal characteristics of CEP. If the order of interactions is not the agreed, the enforcement action to block an interaction can be taken (LEVEL 3), which is supported by the validate pattern (at LEVEL 4). The re-sequencer pattern (LEVEL 4) can also be used to return messages in the correct order.

Example 3: Some e-health regulations require that individual's health information has certain levels of data quality, in particular, regarding completeness. In this case, the solution to monitor the exchanged information (LEVEL 3) can also be used to check if the health information has the required level of completeness. If not, the enforcement action to transform the information (LEVEL 3) can be taken in order to complete the missing data. This is supported at LEVEL 4 by the enricher EIP.

Note that the platform will provide configuration options to manage the monitoring and enforcement of the regulations covered by the platform as well as to establish the application scope (one or several services, one or several organizations, etc.). These configurations have to be performed by business experts who know which could be the enforcement actions for a given regulation (e.g. block the interaction, modify the exchanged information) and the business implications of performing them or allowing non-complying interactions. Finally, there may be end-to-end requirements between organizations (e.g. confidentiality) that prevent monitoring and enforcing some compliance requirement at the SIP. Such cases would be analyzed as part of our evaluation activities with the aim of identifying the limitations of our proposal.

7   Evaluation and Discussion

The evaluation and validation of the results will mainly focus on: i) the capacity of the mechanisms to monitor and enforce the compliance of the identified families of requirements, which will be evaluated through the formal specification by showing that the solution correctly treats these requirements, ii) the development productivity and run-time efficiency of the proposed approach, which will be evaluated by comparing our proposal with ad-hoc case-by-case implementations of regulatory compliance and by using execution indicators related to the overhead of the SIP, iii) the appropriateness to relevant application domains, notably e-government and e-health, which will be evaluated by applying the mechanisms to mainstream regulations.

On another hand, the main differences between our work and other existing proposals on regulatory compliance in service-based systems are: i) the focus on inter-organizational contexts, which is an open research area addressed by ongoing projects [14], (ii) the proposal of enforcement mechanisms and not only monitoring ones, iii) the formal specification of the integration platform using Event-B, iv) leveraging the capabilities of middleware technologies as first-class citizens to build the solutions.

8   Conclusions and Future Work

This work proposes solutions, at different abstraction levels, to monitor and enforce compliance requirements within inter-organizational SIPs. The solutions leverage well-known EIP and specialized capabilities of SIPs which are then mapped to specific middleware technologies (e.g. ESB). The proposed methodology aims at incrementally addressing the main issues by identifying the required capabilities as well as specifying and prototyping the proposed solutions in order to evaluate them.

Future work in this research line will include the detailed design of the proposed platform and a formal specification using Event-B. We will also address the identification and specification of relevant compliance requirements in selected application domains (e-government and e-health). Finally, it will also include developing prototypes to evaluate the proposed solutions. In the long term, future work will address other application domains and other types of requirements as well as using different middleware technologies and products to implement prototypes. Finally, this work will be a step forward on discussing strategies to efficiently implement regulatory compliance mechanisms in e-government taking advantage of existing platforms.

References

1. Di Nitto, E., Ghezzi, C., Metzger, A., Papazoglou, M., Pohl, K.: A journey to highly dynamic, self-adaptive service-based applications. Autom. Softw. Eng. 15, 313–341 (2008)
2. De Michelis, G., Dubois, E., Jarke, M., Matthes, F., Mylopoulos, J., Papazoglou, P., Pohl, K., Schmidt, J.W., Woo, C., Yu, E.: Cooperative information systems: a manifesto. Citeseer (1996)
3. Mylopoulos, J.: Cooperative Information Systems. IEEE Expert 12, 28–31 (1997)
4. Mecella, M., Scannapieco, M., Virgillito, A., Baldoni, R., Catarci, T., Batini, C.: Managing Data Quality in Cooperative Information Systems. On the Move to Meaningful Internet Systems. Springer, London (2002)
5. Call for Papers of the 22th International Conference on Cooperative Information Systems, CoopIS 2014 (2014),
   http://www.onthemove-conferences.org/index.php/coopis14
6. González, L., Ruggia, R., Abin, J., Llambías, G., Sosa, R., Rienzi, B., Bello, D., Álvarez, F.: A service-oriented integration platform to support a joined-up E-government approach: The uruguayan experience. In: Kő, A., Leitner, C., Leitold, H., Prosser, A. (eds.) EDEM 2012 and EGOVIS 2012. LNCS, vol. 7452, pp. 140–154. Springer, Heidelberg (2012)
7. Baru, C., Botts, N., Horan, T., Patrick, K., Feldman, S.S.: A Seeded Cloud Approach to Health Cyberinfrastructure: Preliminary Architecture Design and Case Applications. In: 2012 45th Hawaii International Conference on System Science (HICSS). IEEE (2012)
8. Pezzini, M., Lheureux, B.J.: Integration Platform as a Service: Moving Integration to the Cloud. Gartner (2011)
9. Ferguson, D.: The internet service bus. Move Meaningful Internet Syst. In: 2007 CoopIS DOA ODBASE GADA IS., p. 5 (2010)
10. Peter Mell, Timothy Grance: The NIST Definition of Cloud Computing. NIST
11. Papazoglou, M.P.: Making Business Processes Compliant to Standards and Regulations. In: Enterprise Distributed Object Computing Conference, EDOC (2011)

12. Turetken, O., Elgammal, A., van den Heuvel, W.-J., Papazoglou, M.: Enforcing Compliance on Business Processes through the use of Patterns (2011)
13. Knuplesch, D., Reichert, M., Mangler, J., Rinderle-Ma, S., Fdhila, W.: Towards compliance of cross-organizational processes and their changes. In: La Rosa, M., Soffer, P. (eds.) BPM Workshops 2012. LNBIP, vol. 132, pp. 649–661. Springer, Heidelberg (2013)
14. Knuplesch, D., Reichert, M., Fdhila, W., Rinderle-Ma, S.: On enabling compliance of cross-organizational business processes. In: Daniel, F., Wang, J., Weber, B. (eds.) BPM 2013. LNCS, vol. 8094, pp. 146–154. Springer, Heidelberg (2013)
15. COMPAS: COMPAS Project - Final Report (2011)
16. Birukou, A., D'Andrea, V., Leymann, F., Serafinski, J., Silveira, P., Strauch, S., Tluczek, M.: An integrated solution for runtime compliance governance in SOA. In: Maglio, P.P., Weske, M., Yang, J., Fantinato, M. (eds.) ICSOC 2010. LNCS, vol. 6470, pp. 122–136. Springer, Heidelberg (2010)
17. Holmes, T., Mulo, E., Zdun, U., Dustdar, S.: Model-aware Monitoring of SOAs for Compliance. Service Engineering, pp. 117–136. Springer, Vienna (2011)
18. Koetter, F., Kochanowski, M.: A model-driven approach for event-based business process monitoring. In: La Rosa, M., Soffer, P. (eds.) BPM Workshops 2012. Lecture Notes in Business Information Processing, vol. 132, pp. 378–389. Springer, Heidelberg (2013)
19. Weidlich, M., Ziekow, H., Mendling, J., Günther, O., Weske, M., Desai, N.: Event-Based Monitoring of Process Execution Violations. In: Rinderle-Ma, S., Toumani, F., Wolf, K. (eds.) BPM 2011. LNCS, vol. 6896, pp. 182–198. Springer, Heidelberg (2011)
20. Ben Hamida, A., Bertolino, A., Calabrò, A., De Angelis, G., Lago, N., Lesbegueries, J.: Monitoring Service Choreographies from Multiple Sources. In: Avgeriou, P. (ed.) SERENE 2012. LNCS, vol. 7527, pp. 134–149. Springer, Heidelberg (2012)
21. Baouab, A., Perrin, O., Godart, C.: An Event-Driven Approach for Runtime Verification of Inter-organizational Choreographies. In: International Conference on Services Computing (2011)
22. Armellin, G., Betti, D., Casati, F., Chiasera, A., Martinez, G., Stevovic, J.: Privacy preserving event driven integration for interoperating social and health systems. In: Jonker, W., Petković, M. (eds.) SDM 2010. LNCS, vol. 6358, pp. 54–69. Springer, Heidelberg (2010)
23. Wylie, H., Lambros, P.: Enterprise Connectivity Patterns: Implementing integration solutions with IBM's Enterprise Service Bus products
24. Hohpe, G., Woolf, B.: Enterprise Integration Patterns: Designing, Building, and Deploying Messaging Solutions. Addison-Wesley Professional (2003)
25. González, L., Ruggia, R.: Adaptive ESB Infrastructure for SBS. Adaptive Web Services for Modular and Reusable Software Development: Tactics and Solutions. IGI Global (2012)
26. González, L., Ortiz, G.: An ESB-Based Infrastructure for Event-Driven Context-Aware Web Services. In: Canal, C., Villari, M. (eds.) ESOCC 2013. CCIS, vol. 393, pp. 360–369. Springer, Heidelberg (2013)
27. Riezi, B., González, L., Ruggia, R.: Towards an ESB-Based Enterprise Integration Platform for Geospatial Web Services. In: The Fifth International Conference on Advanced Geographic Information Systems, Applications, and Services, Nice, France (2013)
28. Llambías, G., Ruggia, R.: A middleware-based platform for the integration of Bioinformatic services. XL Conferencia Latinoamericana en Informática, Uruguay (2014)
29. Abrial, J.-R.: Modeling in Event-B: System and Software Engineering. Cambridge University Press, Cambridge (2010)
30. Tounsi, I., Hadj Kacem, M., Hadj Kacem, A.: Building correct by construction SOA design patterns: Modeling and refinement. In: Drira, K. (ed.) ECSA 2013. LNCS, vol. 7957, pp. 33–44. Springer, Heidelberg (2013)
31. González, L., Laborde, J.L., Galnares, M., Fenoglio, M., Ruggia, R.: An adaptive enterprise service bus infrastructure for service based systems. In: Lomuscio, A.R., Nepal, S., Patrizi, F., Benatallah, B., Brandić, I. (eds.) ICSOC 2013. LNCS, vol. 8377, pp. 480–491. Springer, Heidelberg (2014)

Process Engine Selection Support

Simon Harrer

Distributed Systems Group, University of Bamberg, Germany
simon.harrer@uni-bamberg.de

Abstract. Nowadays, business processes and their execution are corner stones in modern IT landscapes, as multiple process languages and corresponding engines for these languages have emerged. In practice, it is not feasible to select the best fitting engine, as engine capabilities are mostly hidden in the engine implementation and a comparison is hampered by the large differences and high adoption costs of the engines. We aim to overcome these problems by a) introducing an abstract layer to access the functionality of the engines uniformly, b) by revealing the engine capabilities through automated and isolated tests for typical requirements, and c) support the user in their selection of a process engine by determining and explaining the fitness of the engines for a single process or a given set of processes using policy matching against previously revealed engine capabilities. Early results show the general feasibility of our approach for BPEL engines for a single capability.

Keywords: BPM, process engines, engine selection, execution requirements, testing.

1 Introduction

Today, process-centric information systems [11] are corner stones in the current IT landscapes in industry, creating a $6.6 billion dollar market of Business Process Management (BPM) solutions [1]. Within this market, at least 19 different business process modeling languages have emerged [6]. Typically, these languages define execution semantics, are implemented in process engines onto which processes are deployed, and instances of these processes are executed by interacting with the engines through message passing. In this work, we focus on such executable process languages, e.g., the OASIS standard BPEL [7] and the OMG standard Business Process Modeling and Notation 2.0 (BPMN) [8], as both are defined in a standard, widely used, executable, and have multiple implementations. There are at least 31 BPMN engines[1] and more than ten BPEL engines available on the market, which vary greatly in their feature set [2]. Hence, the selection of an engine for a given process is a real practical issue in various situations. A typical scenario is that a developer requires an engine with a small footprint which may have slow performance for development whereas the production server may use an engine with a large footprint but with high performance characteristics, hence, the best engine depends on more than functional properties of the process. And a company may use more than one engine, as having multiple runtimes is typical in

---

[1] See http://www.bpmn.org/#tabs-implementers

R. Meersman et al. (Eds.): OTM 2014 Workshops, LNCS 8842, pp. 18–22, 2014.

state-of-the-art practice and feasible with current cloud and virtualization techniques. In a typical web application, multiple programming languages, database systems and different cloud services are already used extensively.

To foster a constant improvement of processes in industry, it is standard practice to apply the Business Process Management (BPM) lifecycle, which consists of four steps within a closed loop. First, the process is modeled using the vocabulary of a process language. Second, the engine, i.e., the runtime environment, is selected, setup and configured in the *system configuration* step. Third, the process is deployed onto and its instances are executed on the previously provisioned engine, the so called *process enactment*. Fourth, the execution of the process instances is diagnosed via audit trails, which are used to model an improved process in the next iteration.

The issue of this BPM lifecycle is that while we design processes using a standardized process language, the selection of the best fitting engine for a given process is not feasible at the current status-quo. For both BPEL and BPMN, there are many engines that vary greatly in their capabilities, including the level of standard conformance, performance, robustness, installability, security, monitoring functionality, licensing cost and vendor support available. Hence, a *model once, run anywhere* paradigm does not hold here, requiring adaption costs. What is more, due to the complexity of these process languages and their engines, a comparison is very time intensive and requires detailed knowledge of the engines. Moreover, although these engines support standard conform and vendor-independent processes, the management of the engines is vendor-dependent, i.e., every engine has its custom installation, startup and shutdown routines, and different deployment methods as well as descriptors. Hence, an automated selection of an engine for a given process and its execution on the selected engine is not feasible to date, resulting in ill-informed selection decisions for engines with possible hidden costs.

In this work, we aim to overcome these problems by improving the *system configuration* step of the BPM lifecycle. Hence, we tackle the research question: *How to determine and explain the fitness of a set of engines for a set of processes?*

This work is structured as follows. In Sect. 2, related work is outlined. The research hypotheses are given in Sect. 3, and the approach is explained in Sect. 4. The preliminary results are given in Sect. 5, followed by an evaluation in Sect. 6. A discussion and future work is outlined in Sect. 7. Section 8 concludes this work.

2   Related Work

The selection or comparison of process engines is neglected in research so far, except for our preliminary work which is explained in Sect. 5. Engines have only been compared according to their support for workflow patterns. Such a pattern is a reusable solution to a reoccurring problem in a specific context and the support of a pattern is determined by the effort required to implement it. A plethora of pattern catalogs and corresponding evaluations exist[2], e.g., the control-flow [10] patterns. Such evaluations reveal helpful engine capabilities, but render only partially relevant for our case as this would require determining the used patterns in a given process. In addition, they only focus on the functionality of a process, neglecting non-functional aspects.

---

[2] See http://www.workflowpatterns.com/

Instead of selecting engines, there are studies to compare and select process languages which we aim to learn from. While Kopp et al. [4] distinguish between block- or graph-based process modeling languages, Lu et al. [5] categorize several business process modeling approaches as either rule-based or graph-based approaches, and then compare them with five different criteria. In [9], the fitness of a process language for a given set of requirements is evaluated.

3   Research Hypotheses

The research question formulated in Sect. 1 is translated into the following three research hypotheses which build on one another.

H1: Uniform Process Engine Management. The lifecycle and management functionality of different engines and their processes is vendor-dependent, but can be managed uniformly and vendor-independently.

H2: Revealing Engine Capabilities through Tests. Methodically created tests are suitable to reveal functional and non-functional capabilities of engines.

H3: Explained Engine Selection through Policy Matching. Policies are suitable to formalize the execution requirements of a process and the engine capabilities, and therefore can be used to determine and explain the fitness of process engines for a set of processes.

4   Approach

In this section, we elaborate the overall approach to support the hypothesis from Sect. 3 and how they build upon another.

We propose to support H1 by introducing a Uniform Process Management Layer (UPML) for managing engines uniformly. UPML provides mappings for the engines in different versions, different configurations (e.g., executing processes in-memory or not), and different environments (e.g., locally, in a virtual machine or in the cloud). Such a layer is required for the BPM lifecycle steps *system configuration* and *process enactment*, as both require that the selected engine has to be available (installed, configured and started) and the process has to be executed (deployed and instances of it executed). Hence, our layer includes lifecycle methods of the engine (install, start, stop, and uninstall) and of the process (deploy and undeploy).

To support H2, we use a methodical approach to determine engine capabilities through tests. For each typical process requirement, we create executable tests that are executed on top of the UPML via a testing tool. A test consists of a process, a list of messages the process that are going to be sent as requests along with expectations to the corresponding responses. This method consists of a generic part applicable for every requirement and a customized part which has to be fitted for each requirement. The produced test results are converted to engine capabilities which conform to the policy type that provides a mean to formalize different degrees of fulfillment of the typical process requirement. To ensure that we cover the right requirements, we conduct a literature study, create tests for the found requirements, and execute them reusing the UPML.

H3 is supported by providing a framework that allows formalizing the process requirements in terms of policies. A policy contains constraints, e.g., a specific language feature has to be available, or the engine must start in less than 5 seconds. By encoding all the engine capabilities and the process requirements as XML-based policies, we can determine the fitness of an engine for a process, as well as provide estimations on adaption costs for possible alternatives , e.g., portability costs to change a process for another engine. The latter is especially interesting in the cases of finding no or more than one engine that is considered fit, as well as finding a single one which is not acceptable for the user. When determining the fitness for a set of processes, we will aggregate the atomic fitness results to enable informed decisions as well. We use the policy serialization and matching algorithm of Web Services Policy 1.5 Framework [12] for our needs.

5 Preliminary Results

To validate the approach outlined in Sect. 4, we conducted a case study for BPEL engines in [3] which builds upon additional previous work cited there. We showed that it is possible to overcome the huge API differences of seven open source BPEL engines by means of a uniform management API (H1), to determine standard conformance capabilities of engines using automated tests (H2), to select the best fitting engine for a process using previously revealed standard conformance capabilities as well as to automatically execute the process on the selected engine (H3).

6 Evaluation

We use multiple methods to ensure the validity of the results. Regarding H1, we evaluate the correctness of UPML by checking whether both, the simplest possible process and the process that only uses features that are supported by every engine, can be deployed and executed on every of the supported engines. Regarding H2, we focus on ensuring that the tests *are correct* by checking syntax and semantics via XML and XML Schema validations automatically, *test the correct features* by conducting peer-reviews within our group and with engine experts, and *produce the correct results* by fully automating the test procedure for reproducible results, repeating the test procedure multiple times to prevent any alternations, providing a fresh engine instance for each single test to avoid side-effects between tests, and compare the results to one another to detect any anomalies, e.g., take the log files into account for tests that are not successful on any engine. Regarding H3, we evaluate the produced prototype with a large set of processes as training data to test the correctness of the selection procedure.

7 Discussion and Future Work

Instead of using only workflow patterns for a manual comparison of engines, we provide an approach that reveals the capabilities of engines and determines the fitness of a set of engines for a given set of processes, and can automatically execute them on the selected engine. In the future, we aim to complete the BPEL case study in Sect. 5 for multiple engine capabilities. Furthermore, we aim to conduct a second case study using BPMN, proving the applicability of our approach on processes and engines using another process language.

8 Conclusion

We have presented an approach to help in the selection of the best fitting engine for processes and their execution on selected engines, enabling to use the best available runtime for given processes, or provide guidance for process adaption to target other engines. Early results show the general feasibility of the approach for the process language BPEL, seven open source BPEL engines and the selection criteria standard conformance, hence, answering the research question partly.

References

1. Clair, C.L., Cullen, A., Keenan, J.: Prepare For 2013's Shifting BPM Landscape. Technical report, Forrester Research (January 2013)
2. Harrer, S., Lenhard, J., Wirtz, G.: BPEL Conformance in Open Source Engines. In: Proceedings of the 5th IEEE International Conference on Service-Oriented Computing and Applications (SOCA 2012), Taipei, Taiwan, December 17–19, pp. 1–8. IEEE (2012)
3. Harrer, S., Lenhard, J., Wirtz, G., van Lessen, T.: Towards Uniform BPEL Engine Management in the Cloud. In: INFORMATIK (to appear, September 2014)
4. Kopp, O., Martin, D., Wutke, D., Leymann, F.: The Difference Between Graph-Based and Block-Structured Business Process Modelling Languages. Enterprise Modelling and Information Systems Architectures 4(1), 3–13 (2009)
5. Lu, R., Sadiq, W.: A Survey of Comparative Business Process Modeling Approaches. In: Abramowicz, W. (ed.) BIS 2007. LNCS, vol. 4439, pp. 82–94. Springer, Heidelberg (2007)
6. Mili, H., Tremblay, G., Jaoude, G.B., Lefebvre, E., Elabed, L., Boussaidi, G.E.: Business Process Modeling Languages: Sorting Through the Alphabet Soup. ACM Comput. Surv. 4, 4:1–4:56 (2010)
7. OASIS. Web Services Business Process Execution Language, v2.0 (April 2007)
8. OMG. Business Process Model and Notation, v2.0. (January 2011)
9. Thöne, S., Depke, R., Engels, G.: Process-oriented, flexible composition of web services with UML. In: Olivé, À., Yoshikawa, M., Yu, E.S.K. (eds.) ER 2003. LNCS, vol. 2784, pp. 390–401. Springer, Heidelberg (2003)
10. van der Aalst, W.M.P., ter Hofstede, A.H.M., Kiepuszewski, B., Barros, A.P.: Workflow Patterns. Distributed and Parallel Databases 14(1), 5–51 (2003)
11. van der Aalst, W.M.P., ter Hofstede, A.H.M., Weske, M.: Business Process Management: A Survey. In: van der Aalst, W.M.P., ter Hofstede, A.H.M., Weske, M. (eds.) BPM 2003. LNCS, vol. 2678, pp. 1–12. Springer, Heidelberg (2003)
12. W3C. Web Services Policy Framework (WS-Policy), v1.5 (September 2007)

Context Enriched Patterns of Behavior
for Delivering Notifications in Ambient-Assisted Living

Paula Lago

Systems and Computing Engineering Department,
School of Engineering, Universidad de los Andes, Colombia
pa.lago52uniandes.edu.co

Advisor: Claudia Jiménez-Guarín, Universidad de los Andes
Co-Advisor: Claudia Roncancio, Grenoble INP - Ensimag

Abstract. Ambient Assisted Living (AAL) refers to ambient intelligent environments where health and personal care is monitored to help to ensure elder's health, safety, and well-being, detecting possible situations that should be watched over. To effectively reason about a current situation and determine its criticality, it should be compared to past patterns. Current systems that learn patterns do not take into account the context in which they occur and we believe adding contextual variables to the description of patterns could improve the reasoning about current situations. Moreover, it can help improve the notification process to dynamically select who and what should be notified, maintaining the privacy of the elder and avoiding spam. In this paper we detail our proposal for a system that adds context to behavior patterns in order to then create personalized messages to the different members of the network of care of an elder living alone.

Keywords: ambient assisted living, notification system, patterns of behavior, adaptation.

1 Introduction

The increasing rate and number of population ageing over the last and coming decades is becoming a challenge at the social, familiar and state levels. In particular, providing health-care for older adults can be costly both monetary and in terms of the changes of lifestyle for informal caregivers. Besides the common deterioration that comes from aging, elders express their preference for maintaining independence as long as possible and aging in place. Nonetheless, both caregivers and elders would like to know that care would arrive at the proper time when needed. Ambient assisted living (AAL), intelligent environments that keep track of its inhabitant's routines and health status to support maintaining health and functional capabilities of the elder and support carers among other objectives [1], can help senior people to maintain their independence and autonomy. However, in order to receive proper care, situations that need attention should be effectively identified and notified to right people in the network of care of the elder, avoiding spam and preserving privacy.

R. Meersman et al. (Eds.): OTM 2014 Workshops, LNCS 8842, pp. 23–29, 2014.
© Springer-Verlag Berlin Heidelberg 2014

Identifying situations that should be watched over requires the system to know and constantly update the routines or patterns of behavior of the elder, since these enable reasoning about the level of unusualness of the situation. This reasoning requires that the situation is described with all relevant contextual variables that might change its degree of abnormality. For example, waking up late might be more usual on Sundays than on weekdays or cooking at home might be unusual at night but not at midday. Additionally, routines change over time hence the system needs to adapt to these changes to maintain its performance and relevance. Learning and evolving the patterns of behavior with contextual variables that enable reasoning about current situations is one of the challenges of this work.

Besides reasoning about a situation, there should be an action in response to it. One important action is keeping all the important members of the network of care (doctors, carers, family) informed about the status of "quality of life" of the elder and notifying when an emergency or abnormal situation happens. These can be done by setting up rules on the different events so the proper information is send to each individual considering privacy issues, the desires and needs of the elder and avoiding spam. It is important that these rules are dynamic and can act based on uncertain knowledge about a situation since the reasoning process result may be a degree of belief and not an absolute truth.

Discovering patterns of behavior can be done using pattern mining and evolving classifiers [2,3]. However, the current techniques are not capable of describing patterns with different contextual variables such as day of the week, start times, durations nor expressing confidence intervals for such variables. In the same way, information flow processing systems use rules for defining actions on incoming data when a condition is met but they cannot handle uncertainty in the events [4] which, as we have said before, would be required in an ambient assisted living solution.

In this research, we propose a system that includes contextual variables to describe patterns of behavior and is able to reason on uncertain results based on rules to deliver adaptive notifications, reports, alarms, reminders or feedback so that the proper actions can be taken to preserve the quality of life of the elder. In this paper we detail our proposal and how it compares to current related work.

2   Proposal Approach

A smart home for elder care can be aware of different types of events that occur during the daily life of the elder through the information collected by sensors attached to the environment or worn by the user. Among others, these situations could be emergencies, changes in routines that are early signs of disease, routine compliance and special events that could start conversations with relatives (i.e. new restaurant tried by the elder, neighbor visiting). Each of these events should be acted upon differently but the action needed depends on the situation, the context and the concerns of the elder. An action in this work corresponds to a message delivered to either the elder or someone in the care network like the doctor, a relative, a neighbor or an emergency service. It is evident that not all situations should be treated or informed equally to all members of the care network. Plus, the policies that govern the notification process could evolve as the routines, needs and desires of the elder change, thus the system needs to adapt as well.

We identified six types of events in an ambient assisted living environment that could be notified: emergencies, subtle changes in behavior that could be a sign of disease, routine compliance, positive changes of behavior (i.e. more exercise) that should be encouraged, uncommon behavior that signifies no risk but could be interesting to share (i.e. going out for lunch) and uncommon behavior. Classifying a situation in one of these categories depends on the patterns of behavior of the elder. Not for everyone going out at 9pm would be an unusual event, but for some it might be considered an emergency. Similarly, going out at 9pm could be normal on Wednesdays but not on Sundays. Consequently, learning the patterns of behavior of the elder is an important feature for a notification system for AAL. Also, since routines and behavior pattern can change based on the day of the week, time, season or weather condition, we believe that these patterns should be described with all relevant contextual variables and confident intervals in order to improve the interpretation of events.

Finally, as not all of these events trigger the same action (the person notified is different, the information sent changes, etc.), different rules specifying what to do on each situation should be defined. These rules need to be dynamic as they could change as the concerns or routines change and they also need to take into consideration the fact that knowledge about the situation may be uncertain.

2.1 Research Challenges

The following research challenges have been identified for the development of a context-aware notification system for elder care at home settings:

- Learning and evolving patterns of behavior with their corresponding contextual variables such as day of the week, start time, duration, season among others and different tolerance intervals for those that need it.
- Creating a dynamic rule system that can act based on the uncertain knowledge that may result from the reasoning about a current situation. If the system beliefs that there is a chance of an emergency, or some interesting event it should be able to decide when, how and to whom send the corresponding notification without generating spam.

3 Related Work

Since population aging is a worldwide phenomenon, there are many initiatives and projects researching on ambient assisted living solutions all around the globe. For example, in Europe the Ambient Assisted Living Joint Program of the European Commission [1] finances projects in the use of information technologies for ageing well. For this thesis we are interested in two aspects of the ambient assisted living research topics: learning and evolving patterns of behavior with contextual variables and reasoning about current situations as critical, abnormal, interesting or routine for sending the right information to the right people in the network of care of the elder, using adaptive rules.

3.1   Learning and Evolving Patterns of Behavior in an Ambient Assisted Living Environment with Context

Learning patterns of behavior is an important feature for ambient intelligence in general and in particular in ambient assisted living because it enables the delivery of personalized services [5].   Patterns of behavior are discovered through pattern mining on the activities of the elder or on the sensor events [6]. A frequent behavior can be thought of as a sequence of actions or activities that is repeated frequently. As this, learning a frequent behavior can be thought of as a problem of sequential pattern mining, i.e. discovering all sequential patterns that have a minimum support [7].   Since events in a smart environment come in a streaming fashion and there is not a database to mine all the patterns from, incremental and progressive sequential pattern mining techniques are more suitable [8,9]. Also, since human behavior is not deterministic, sometimes a behavior can have some actions that do not correspond to it in the middle or actions could be done in different orders. For this, sequential pattern mining with gaps can help [2].

Even though sequential pattern mining may help in learning frequent behaviors, current techniques do not take into account the fact that, at least for human behaviors, some patterns may be frequent just in some contexts but not for the entire database of behaviors. Some work has been done in knowing which patterns are more relevant in a period of time based on the last time it was seen or the inter-item interval [10] and in learning temporal relationships on each of the sequences learned [11]. However, both works only learn temporal context on the sequences that have already been identified as frequent on the whole data but does not contemplate that some sequences may be frequent just on Mondays, for example. The temporal and other relevant context variables must be considered as the sequences are learned and not after.

Other technique that can be used for learning patterns of behavior that change with time is evolving classifiers [3]. Evolving refers to the ability of deleting patterns as they become less frequent and adding new frequent patterns as new events arrive. These classifiers represent behaviors as a sequence of events and learn the most frequent sequences. They are able to operate in real time systems [12]. Since the events in smart homes are sensor events, these approaches learn patterns which can change very quickly or not have the adequate semantics to be usable. Other drawback of these approaches is that they don't describe the duration of the pattern and changes in duration can be of interest for health applications.

3.2   Sending Notifications of the Events to the Network of Care

Keeping the network of care informed about the overall status and possible situations that need attention is important in ambient assisted living so proper care can be given at appropriate times. The notifications must be delivered in a personalized fashion to guarantee that there is no spam and the urgency of a notification depends on the criticality of the situation to be notified. It is a two-step process: reasoning about a current situation and notifying the appropriate persons. This process can be thought of as an information flow processing system [4] since events come in a streaming fashion and the rules from processing depend on the learned behaviors [13].

The reasoning step is a classification on the shift from frequent behavior of the current situation. Shifts of current situations compared to learned patterns can occur because there was a change in daily frequency, duration or sequence. However, the reasoning process can only give a probability or degree of criticality as a result. Current information flow processing systems do not support this kind of answer. Also, the rules that govern the notification process must consider these degree of belief to decide who, when and how should be notified about the situation.

Nava-Muñoz et al. [15] present a survey on notifications on elder care, taking into account different environments such as hospitals, nursing homes and homes. We are interested in notifications that are sent only on home assisted living and not medical environments.

4   Exploratory Results

We conducted an exploratory study using one dataset from the CASAS project [16] in order to study how routines differ from person to person and as time passes. The dataset consist of sensor events gathered in a real-life setting for a long-time period (six months approximately), annotated with 9 activities that happen during the day (sleeping, eating, bed to toilet, preparing a meal, work, wash dishes, housekeeping, relax and going out). It is an appropriate dataset for a study on behavior patterns and changes over time due to its length.

We were able to measure how changes in routine can affect the performance of a classifier. If the current situation cannot be correctly identified, then any reasoning about it i.e. classifying it as risky, normal or abnormal is likely flawed. In Fig. 1 we

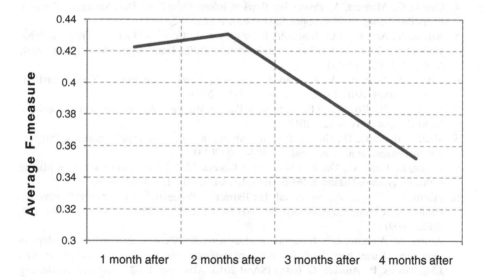

Fig. 1. Average F-measure of a HMM classifier on data collected time after the initial training data. The average F-measure drops significantly as time passes, supporting the need for adaptive learning of patterns of behavior.

show the average F-measure of an HMM trained with two-month data and the performance of this classifier when used with data collected one, two, three and four months after the initial train data. The F-measure drops significantly as time passes, supporting the need for adaptive systems that learn from the user as they are used.

5   Conclusions

We have identified in this paper some enhancement opportunities for ambient assisted living systems. First, patterns of behavior when learned should be contextualized to improve the reasoning about a current situation. Second, when sending notifications adaptive rules that act on uncertain knowledge must be configured to deliver personalized messages to every member in the network of care. The expected result of this work is to develop a system for AAL that takes into account both aspects and is implemented with affordable costs.

References

1. European Commission. Ambient Assisted Living Joint Programme (2008),
   http://www.aal-europe.eu/
2. Eltabakh, M.Y., Ouzzani, M., Khalil, M.A., Aref, W.G., Elmagarmid, A.: Incremental Mining for Frequent Patterns in Evolving Time Series Datatabases (2008),
   http://dx.doi.org/10.1.1.154.5991
3. Ordóñez, F.J., Iglesias, J.A., de Toledo, P., Ledezma, A., Sanchis, A.: Online activity recognition using evolving classifiers. Expert Syst. Appl. Mar. 40(4):1248–1255 (2013)
4. Cugola, G., Margara, A.: Processing flows of information: From Data Stream to Complex Event Processing. ACM Comput. Surv. 44(3), 1–62 (2012)
5. Aztiria, A., Augusto, J.C., Basagoiti, R., Izaguirre, A., Cook, D.: Learning Frequent Behaviors of the Users in Intelligent Environments. IEEE Trans. Syst. Man, Cybern. Syst. 43(6), 1265–1278 (2013)
6. Aztiria, A., Izaguirre, A., Augusto, J.: Learning patterns in ambient intelligence environments: a survey. Artif. Intell. Rev. 34(1), 35–51 (2010)
7. Mooney, C.H., Roddick, J.F.: Sequential Pattern Mining – Approaches and Algorithms. ACM Comput. Surv. 45(2) (2013)
8. Mallick, B., Garg, D., Grover, P.S.: Incremental mining of sequential patterns: Progress and challenges. Intell. Data Anal. 17, 507–530 (2013)
9. Huang, J., Tseng, C., Ou, J., Chen, M.: A General Model for Sequential Pattern Mining with a Progressive Database. IEEE Trans. Knowl. 20(9), 1153–1167 (2008)
10. Mhatre, A., Verma, M., Toshniwal, D.: Extracting Sequential Patterns from Progressive Databases: A Weighted Approach. In: 2009 Int. Conf. Signal Process. Syst., pp. 788–792. IEEE (2009)
11. Aztiria, A., Augusto, J.C., Basagoiti, R., Izaguirre, A.: Accurate temporal relationships in sequences of user behaviours in intelligent environments. In: Augusto, J.C., Corchado, J.M., Novais, P., Analide, C. (eds.) ISAmI 2010. AISC, pp. 19–27. Springer, Heidelberg (2010)
12. Iglesias, J. A., Angelov, P., Ledezma, A., Sanchis, A.: Creating Evolving User Behavior Profiles Automatically. IEEE Trans. Knowl. Data Eng. 24(5), 854–867 (2012)

13. Etter, R., Costa, P.D., Broens, T.: A Rule-Based Approach Towards Context-Aware User Notification Services. In: 2006 ACS/IEEE Int. Conf. Pervasive Serv., pp. 281–284. IEEE (2006)
14. Barbieri, D.F., Braga, D., Ceri, S., Della Valle, E., Grossniklaus, M.: Incremental Reasoning on Streams and Rich Background Knowledge. In: Aroyo, L., Antoniou, G., Hyvönen, E., ten Teije, A., Stuckenschmidt, H., Cabral, L., Tudorache, T., et al. (eds.) ESWC 2010, Part I. LNCS, vol. 6088, pp. 1–15. Springer, Heidelberg (2010)
15. Nava-muñoz, S., Moran, A.L.: A Review of Notifications Systems in Elder Care Environments: Challenges and Opportunities. In: Cruz Cunha, M.M., Miranda, I., Gonçalves, P. (eds.) Handb. Res. ICTs Human-Centered Healthc. Soc. Care Serv., pp. 407–429 (2013)
16. Cook, D. J., Crandall, A. S., Thomas, B. L., Krishnan, N.: CASAS: A Smart Home in a Box. IEEE Comput. 46(7), 62–69 (2013)

Developing a Service Oriented IT Platform
for Synchromodal Transportation

Prince Mayurank Singh

Services, Cyber Security and Safety Research Group
University of Twente, Enschede, The Netherlands
p.m.singh@utwente.nl

Abstract. Due to rapid global economic growth and competition, there is an increased pressure on logistic companies. On one hand, they have to be flexible and agile, to meet Service Level Agreements (SLA's) with clients, while on the other hand they have to comply with government regulations and environment protection laws. Better utilization of different modes of transport and improved decision making can contribute to solving both these challenges. This requires increased co-operation between logistic service providers (LSPs). Our aim is to develop an IT platform which facilitates increased cooperation between logistic partners and allows them to function in a synchromodal way. We use the principles of Service Oriented Architecture (SOA) to design the IT platform. Using this platform, a single consignment can be fulfilled using different modes of transport and unforeseen problems in transportation can be dealt with. A consortium of leading Dutch logistic companies will be the test bed for this research.

Keywords: Service Oriented Architecture, SOA, Synchromodal, IT platform, Logistics, Multimodal, Transportation.

1   Introduction

The core of all business depends on logistic. Raw materials have to be shipped in and products have to be shipped out to markets. These markets can be as near as the next village or as far as another continent. Customers are increasingly becoming more demanding and aware. They demand their goods as early as possible and in the best condition. Apart from this there are government restrictions on CO_2 emissions [3] and a constant increase in competition. Moreover, unexpected condition such as delays, traffic jams etc. can further make it difficult for a logistic company to fulfill an order in time. Business for logistic companies is not simple. In today's world a single consignment from source to destination involves many logistic companies having different modes of transport and using different IT systems.

3PLs (3rd party logistic service providers) are companies which have resources of their own and take orders from clients to fulfill a complete shipment. 4PLs [1][5,6] (4th party logistic service providers) are those LSPs which do not have resources for transportation but make use of their network, contacts and knowledge to fulfill an

R. Meersman et al. (Eds.): OTM 2014 Workshops, LNCS 8842, pp. 30–36, 2014.

entire shipment (see Fig. 1). Although logistic companies already cooperate for operations [1], there still is considerable scope of improvement.

Firstly, there should be increased usage of diverse modes of transport thereby reducing the pressure on roads [3]. Secondly, in case of an untoward incident or unexpected situation, LSPs should be able to change the current mode of transport. Thirdly, there is a lot of information available (like weather, real-time traffic condition etc.) which can be incorporated in logistic planning. Lastly, becoming more environment friendly. Efficient utilization and sharing of resources between logistic companies is required to reduce pressure on a single mode of transport and reduce CO_2 emissions [3][9].

Moving toward synchromodal transportation [4][9] can provide the above improvements. In synchromodal transportation the decision for the next part of transportation is made as late as possible to account for any unexpected situation and take advantage of the new information. As the name suggests, the synchronization of modalities of transport is the corner stone for synchromodal transportation.

Three major outputs are expected out of this research, firstly, an in-depth study of state-of-the-art techniques used by logistic companies for cooperation and day to day operations. Secondly, a SOA [7,8][10] inspired IT integration platform which facilitates synchromodal transportation and use of real time information. Lastly, a working prototype, as a proof of concept. The research plan and the preliminary results are explained in the following chapters.

2   Background

This research is a part of a bigger project. The other parts of the project are concerned with data management and efficient planning for synchromodal transportation. A consortium of small and medium sized Dutch logistic companies is involved in this research. All these companies are based in The Netherlands. University of Twente is also a part of the consortium and is responsible for the research on synchromodal transportation. The logistic companies in the consortium are responsible for facilitating the research by providing information and insight about their current way of working. Also, they are a crucial source of input for understanding challenges in the way of synchromodal transportation. Thus, the main stakeholder for this research are the consortium partner, logistic companies outside the consortium and vendors of various sensor devices. Other stakeholders include the European Union, environmentalists and the government. The terms logistic company and logistic service provider (LSP) are used interchangeably in the text.

3   Research Questions

The problem statement for this research is - *Design* a *Service Oriented IT platform* for *logistic companies* which *hides* their *internal business processes* and IT architecture and facilitates *better coordination* between them, thereby enabling them to operate in a *synchromodal* way.

1. *Design.* This is a design science research [11,12], as it involves the design and development of an IT integration platform (the artifact).

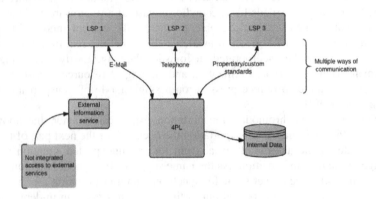

Fig. 1. A model showing current functioning of a 4PL and partner LSPs

2. *Service Oriented IT Platform.* The IT platform will be designed on the principles of SOA. This is a design criteria for the artifact.
3. *Logistic Companies.* The main stakeholder for this research.
4. *Hides, Internal Business Processes, Better Coordination.* The artifact (i.e. IT platform) should be at a higher level of abstraction and independent of the internal implementations [2] of different logistic companies. This is also a design criteria and follows directly from the 2nd point above.
5. *Synchromodal.* This is the desired effect of the artifact on the domain, i.e. by using the artifact the stakeholder must be able to function in a particular fashion (synchromodal way).

RQ1: Who are the stakeholders for this research, what are their goals and their priorities?

RQ1.1: How is the current logistic landscape and what are the current ways of working? How efficient are these w.r.t synchromodal transportation?
RQ1.2: What are the major challenges in the way of synchromodal transportation?
RQ1.3: What are the expectation of the stakeholders?

RQ2: What are the requirements of the artifact w.r.t. to the stakeholder?

RQ2.1: How will the stakeholders benefit from this platform?
RQ2.2: What are the desired results w.r.t. to these requirements? When are the requirements said to be met?
RQ2.3 What are the different treatments available?
RQ2.4 What is the justification for choosing a particular treatment?

RQ3: How can the artifact be validated?

RQ3.1 Which technologies and systems are currently being used? How good or bad is the performance of these systems?

RQ3.2 How good or bad is the performance of the artifact? Are the effects of the artifact in line with the goals of the stakeholders?

4 Resources

There is limited literature available in the field of synchromodal transportation. So, information has to be gathered via interaction with the consortium partners, different academic conferences and research groups working on similar topics. Yet, previous approaches for multimodal transport will be studied. Since a great degree of cooperation between LSPs is required for synchromodal transport, therefore the business models, process models and IT models of LSPs have to be studied in detail. Any previous approach involving the application of SOA [8] principle in developing an interaction platform will also provide useful guidelines. An important feature of this research is that it is very close to industry and involves frequent information exchanges.

5 Research Plan

This research follows the design science research methodology. Fig. 2 shows the steps in a design science research cycle. Currently, this research is in the first step, i.e. problem investigation. Thus, the focus is on understanding the problem and all its facets clearly. The next step is to choose the best treatment (a way of solving the problem), called the artifact. The third step is validation of the artifact followed by its specific implementation.

The implementation step may provide inputs for even better understanding of the problem, which were perhaps not evident during problem investigation. In context of this research, understanding the requirements of the different LSPs and their present way of working is an important part of the problem investigation. For this purpose a 4-step interaction scheme with different LSPs in the consortium has been formulated. The first step is to know the company, its stake in the research and an overview of its operations. The next step is for getting further information with the help of a questionnaire. The questionnaire will be filled by the LSPs employees which have a knowledge of the processes and technologies used by the company. Based on the result of Step 1 the questionnaire for different LSPs may be different. The third step involves making a generic process model based on communality analysis. In the final step, the design of the artifact is done in consultation and with further inputs from the LSPs.

6 Preliminary Results

The first step has been completed for 5 LSPs in the consortium. To better understand the operations and challenges being faced by the LSPs we present the profile of two of them. The real names of the companies have been suppressed because of privacy requirements.

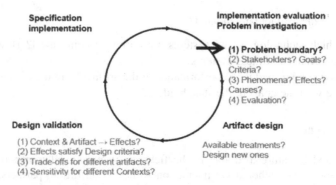

Fig. 2. Design Science Research Cycle [11,12]

ALPHA B.V: is a medium sized 4PL, having international operations, based in the eastern part of Netherlands. Its partners operate on road, rail and sea. Yet, logistic planning is done statically. Dynamic planning which is aided by weather or traffic information is not done. ALPHA doesn't get location data from deep sea vessels, trucks and trains that are involved in a particular shipment. Most of the communication with its partner LSPs is via email or telephone. A significant amount of human experience is involved in choosing the best combination of partners for particular SLA.

BETA B.V: is a small sized logistic company in the western part of Netherlands. Its operations are on road and in the sea. Most of the communication and data collection involved in fulfilling an SLA is manual. Raw data is collected from various sources and manually entered in excel sheets. A significant amount of human experience is involved in planning and forecasting since there is no real time data integration with planning of consignments. One of the biggest challenge in the way of synchromodal transportation is the absence of a common IT platform to integrate data from diverse sources and aid in planning. Planning is done statically and is largely non flexible in case of unforeseen circumstances.

We can conclude that logistic companies are different by their very nature and in different stages of development. Some are quite established, having much experience and a large market share. They have their own way of working and have fixed clients. Others are new, open to new technologies and trying to carve a market share for themselves. Considerable human intervention is involved in planning. There isn't a contingency plan for unexpected situations. An employee in a LSP was asked, *what happens when you know that there is high probability of delay in the shipment arriving at the port?* He replied, *"We just send the truck, and ask the truck to wait. May take a few minutes or even a full day"*. Planning data is derived from diverse sources and is scattered. Mostly, raw data is manually fed into systems. Most LSPs want to move to a synchromodal way of working and thus there is a strong impetus to incorporate real time data and be prepared for last minute changes and delays.

7   Evaluation

The evaluation of the artifact is an important part of design science research. RQ3 is concerned with the evaluation of the artifact. The working principle of the artifact will be used to develop a game. This game will be played by the different stakeholders and will help them to better understand the benefits provided by the artifact and the corresponding organizational, procedural and behavioral changes. The idea behind this research is to allows different logistic companies to do business together. Yet, the IT platform should not cause deadlock. This is to be proved mathematically. The artifact will be presented to stakeholders to know whether the artifact meets required goals. Moreover, experts in the field of logistics and SOA will also be involved in the evaluation of the artifact. A prototype of the IT platform will be developed as the part of this research. This prototype will be used to carry out case studies. The learnings from the case studies will be used to make improvements in the prototype. These case studies will serve as a proof of concept for the artifact. The stakeholders can use these case studies to analysis what more needs to be done to function in a synchromodal way.

Some assumption will have to be made for the evaluation of the prototype. These assumptions can't be stated now, but they will become clear as the research progresses.

8   Discussion

Each logistic company is unique in itself. When they are supposed to work together in a consortium, differences become apparent at various levels. There are difference in the usage of technology, desire to expand, concerns over data security, enterprise architecture maturity etc. Moreover, two LSPs which are partners in one consignment might be competitors in some other. So, a healthy relationship and trust has to be developed for a synchromodal way of working. This ensures that one strong partner doesn't overshadow a weaker partner. The results of this research will have important scientific and engineering contributions. *Generalizability,* the research method used in this research and the results are not necessarily case specific. They may be used in different contexts. Moreover, the artifact will also be reusable (with minor changes) in different contexts. *Innovativeness,* this research will deliver a new application, which did not exist yet. The results will guide future research in the domain of synchromodal transportation. *Application of SOA,* the engineering contribution of the research is that it serves as a proof of concept for SOA and its application for solving challenges in the field of logistics.

9   Conclusion

The road towards synchromodal transportation is not easy. It's always difficult to design systems for whom a fit-for-all approach is necessary. Yet, the benefits of synchromodal transportation are numerous and have positive effects not only on business but also on society and general well-being. In this paper we have introduced the research idea, presented a research plan and discussed the preliminary results. Many concepts will become more clear and new challenges might become apparent as the research progresses.

Acknowledgement. This research is funded by the Dutch Institute for Advanced Logistics, DINALOG. (www.dinalog.nl)

References

1. Augenstein, C., Ludwig, A.: Interconnected service models - Emergence of a comprehensive logistics service model. In: 17th IEEE EDOC Conference Workshops (EDOCW), pp. 239–245. IEEE Computer Society, Vancouver (2013)
2. Cardoso, J., Barros, A., May, N., Kylau, U.: Towards a unified service description language for the internet of services: Requirements and first developments. In: IEEE International Conference on Service Computing (SCC), pp. 602–609. IEEE Press, Miami (2010)
3. European Commission, White Paper: Roadmap to a Single European Transport Area - Towards a competitive and resource efficient transport system. Brussels (2011)
4. DINALOG. Synchromodal Transport. Retrieved from http://www.dinalog.nl/en/themes/synchromodal_transport
5. Mutke, S., Augenstein, C., Ludwig, A.: Model based integrated planning for logistic service contracts. In: 17th IEEE EDOC Conference Workshops (EDOCW), pp. 219–228. IEEE Computer Society, Vancouver (2013)
6. Mutke, S., Augenstein, C., Roth, M., Ludwig, A.: Real-time information acquisition in a model based integrated planning environment for logistic contracts. Journal of Object Technology, M:1–M:23 (2011)
7. Papazoglou, M.: Web Service and SOA. Pearson. England (2012)
8. Patig, S.: Design of SOA services: Experiences from industry. In: Cordeiro, J., Ranchordas, A., Shishkov, B. (eds.) ICSOFT 2009. CCIS, vol. 50, pp. 150–163. Springer, Heidelberg (2011)
9. Pleszko, J.: Multi-Variant configurations of supply chain in the context of synchromodal transport. LogForum- Scientific Journal of Logistics 8(4), 287–295 (2012)
10. Wang, H., Wang, S.: Ontological map of service oriented architecture for shared services management. Expert systems with applications 41, 2362–2371 (2014)
11. Wieringa, R.: Design Science as Nested Problem Solving. In: 4th International Conference, DESRIST 2007, pp. 1–12. ACM, Philadelphia (2009)
12. Wieringa, R., Heerkens, H.: Designing Requirement Engineering Research. In: CERE 2007, pp. 36–48. IEEE, New Delhi (2007)

Models in the Design of Context-Aware Well-Being Applications

Steven Bosems and Marten van Sinderen

University of Twente, Department of EECMS, Enschede, The Netherlands
{s.bosems,m.j.vansinderen}@utwente.nl

Abstract. Context-aware systems that make use of sensor information to reason about their context have been proposed in many domains. However, it is still hard to design *effective* context-aware applications, due to the absence of suitable domain theories that consider dynamic context and associated user requirements as a precursor of system development. In this paper, we discuss a theory for the *well-being* domain and propose a model-driven development process that exploits the proposed theory to build effective, i.e. user-centric, context-aware applications.

Keywords: Well-Being, Context-Aware, Model-Driven, Causal Reasoning.

1 Introduction

We define context-aware computing as the combination of sensor, reasoning and other technology that provides IT systems with real-time awareness of their environment and advanced analytics to offer services that address the varying requirements of their users (cf. [2]). Widely used alternative terms to describe this paradigm are smart, ambient, ubiquitous, and pervasive computing [6, 9].

Despite many technological advances in this area, the design of effective context-aware applications is hard because designers cannot always anticipate the dynamics of context and associated user requirements [8].

In this paper, we propose a theory to address this problem, albeit limited to the well-being domain. Furthermore, we present a model-driven development process that applies the proposed theory to establish user requirements for selected well-being goals and derive context-aware well-being applications to support these goals.

This paper builds on the research presented in [3]. The paper is further structured as follows: Section 2 introduces our theory of well-being; Section 3 presents a model-driven development process for context-aware well-being applications using the theory; Section 4 explains how validation of developed applications may lead to improvements to both the theory and these applications; Section 5 concludes the paper, mentioning related work, our contributions so far, and planned future research.

R. Meersman et al. (Eds.): OTM 2014 Workshops, LNCS 8842, pp. 37–42, 2014.

2   Theory of Well-Being

Our theory of well-being is intended to be used for the development of context-aware applications that support individual well-being. This is in contrast to most existing theories that try to answer philosophical questions about what is 'good for' a person [7, 15]. Our theory is based on the assumption that a person's well-being is influenced by interactions between health conditions and contextual factors (cf. [17]). Certain conditions and factors can be monitored by IT applications through sensors, and reasoning algorithms based on knowledge on the interactions can be used to decide on useful interventions (informing, advising, instructing a person, or controlling certain conditions or factors). We will only consider those conditions, factors and interactions that are proven by medical practice, which classifies our theory as objective [15].

Our theory is expressed as a causal loop diagram (a special directed graph) consisting of nodes and edges. Nodes represent variables for health conditions and contextual factors, and edges represent cause-effect relations between two variables. Nodes may have boundary values for the variables, including min and max values, and objective norms. Edges have a polarity to indicate whether a change of the 'source' variable causes a change in the same ('+') or opposite ('-') direction for the 'target' variable. Other attributes may be used to characterize the timing between cause and effect (e.g., immediate or delayed) and the strength of the effect (e.g., weak or strong).

We built our theory by studying literature and interviewing experts. This resulted in the identification of a set of relevant variables and their causal relations, all mapped into a single causal loop diagram, which we call the Dynamic Well-being Domain Model (DWDM) [5]. We realize that the knowledge that we have captured is still very limited. Therefore, we consider it as a 'living' model, which is subject to constant improvement based on our own new insights and other people's comments.

The modeling constructs used for the DWDM are simple but powerful. They allow to reason about the importance and effect of conditions and factors for well-being goals, where goals are statements that can be related to one or more of the variables. For example, a goal can be to improve one's physical condition, and a factor that has a (delayed) positive effect on this is physical exercise. One interesting phenomenon that is exposed by the model is that of feedback loops. A reinforcing loop exists if the loop contains an even number of causal relations with '-' polarity. These loops reinforce themselves in that a change in any variable will lead to a self-fueled increasing change in all variables in the loop (provided all remains the same outside the loop). A balancing loop exists if the loop contains an odd number of causal relations with '-' polarity. These loops are self-correcting as a change in any variable propagates and returns a change of that variable in the opposite direction. Both types of loops are illustrated in Fig. 1, showing an excerpt of our DWDM.

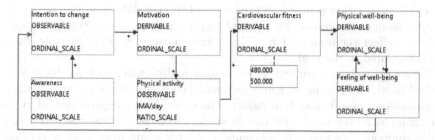

Fig. 1. Excerpt of DWDM relevant for improving well-being through physical exercise

3   System Development

The DWDM is system-independent, but it can be used to constrain and steer the development of context-aware applications [3]. We distinguish four development phases: (i) selection of relevant variables, (ii) design of a first system model, (iii) design of a refined system model, and (iv) deriving the application code. These phases follow the Model Driven Architecture (MDA) in the sense that they correspond with the CIM, PIM, PSM and code level, respectively, of MDA [11].

Selection of Relevant Variables. In order to develop an application that supports some well-being goal, we have to identify the variables (and relations) in the DWDM that are relevant to the selected well-being goal [14]. For example, Fig. 1 shows the variables that are relevant to the goal of improving physical well-being through physical exercise. This could be used to develop an application that monitors and gives advice on physical activity (in fact, the model was inspired by an existing application, called Activity Coach [13]). The model can be specialized by considering the characteristics and preferences of a target user group (e.g., athletes, elderly, or workers) or even an individual user.

Design of First System Model. Subsequently, we analyze the model from the previous phase to determine which variables can be directly measured through (affordable) sensors or through user interaction. For example, in Fig. 1, "Physical activity" can be measured by an accelerometer/gyroscope sensor and "Awareness" can be measured by querying the user. We call such variables observable. There are also variables that cannot be directly measured. To quantify these variables, we have to use the values of variables related to them. We call such variables derivable. These classifications are of course not fixed, but depend on available budgets and the technological state of the art.

   Further, we have to decide in what way the well-being goal will be supported, keeping in mind that components exist that correspond to observable variables. For example, the goal of improving physical well-being can be supported by providing monitoring information and advice on physical activity. In this case, the provided information is based on the interpretation of data from the accelerometer/gyroscope, and the advice is based on the variation in observable variables and what effect the propagation of this variation causes in other variables more directly related to the goal.

We adopt a general context-aware system architecture, such as the one described in [4], and use the decisions mentioned above to instantiate this architecture, resulting in a first system model. The model may comprise several views. For example, a structural view can show the accelerator/gyroscope and a user dialog component as well as other components that follow from a mapping of the expected support onto the generic structure of the architecture. Next to that, a behavioral view can show the interactions between or involving these components, partly based on the need for communication to realize the expected support to the well-being goal.

Design of Refined System Model. The next step is to decide how the components will be distributed and which technology platforms will be involved. Since the system handles personal and private information, the user must trust the system and all entities involved in the systems operation. To mitigate a potential distrust, the number of involved service providers can be limited. We identify three types of platforms/services: (i) smartphones, (ii) external storage providers, and (iii) web/application servers. A user might be more trusting if information is kept on the smartphone, rather than offloading storage and/or computation to external parties. On the other hand, limited power and storage resources on the smartphone have to be taken into account.

Once a strategy of distribution has been chosen, platform specific bindings can be defined. This entails adding information about technology choices and infrastructure services to run the previously identified components.

Deriving Application Code. The refined model can be translated to application code, the language of which depends on the platform(s) of choice. Code generation for specific platforms has become common practice, so we will not further discuss this step here.

4   Theory/System Co-evolution

Throughout the development process of a context-aware application, decisions are constrained or informed by the DWDM. Assuming that both our DWDM and the design decisions are correct, the application will provide the expected support to the chosen well-being goal. If either is incorrect, the application will likely not provide useful behavior for the well-being goal. If the latter is the case, the application and the system models need to evaluated for adherence to the DWDM. If a discrepancy is found, the application has to be modified. If no discrepancy is found, the DWDM is probably based on incomplete or faulty knowledge, and has to be modified. Next, the system development has to be repeated with the improved DWDM.

The means and content of the system-provided interventions to the user (in our example, information and advice) is crucial for user acceptance, and therefore also for the experienced support to the well-being goal. Since the DWDM cannot be used for these aspects of the system design, we need here involvement of behavioral scientist and HCI developers, the discussion of which is outside the scope of this paper.

5   Conclusions and Future Work

Context-aware systems have a clear potential to provide better user services in many domains. But it is hard to realize this potential. Often, developed applications are not effective in that they fail to support user goals in certain (unforeseen) contexts encountered by the user. Establishing and understanding user requirements in the design phase, and systematically developing an application from these requirements while applying design patterns and platform knowledge are recognized problems in this area [1, 6, 9, 10, 12, 16].

In this paper, we have introduced a theory of well-being and a Dynamic Well-being Domain Model (DWDM) to help understand user requirements for well-being goals and to constrain and steer the development of applications to support such goals. The proposed development process is an application of the Model Driven Architecture (i.e., model-driven development). The DWDM captures knowledge on cause-effect relations between health conditions and contextual factors, and makes it possible to reason how changes in these variables can contribute to a well-being goal. Understanding the nature of the variables and the effect of their variation at the user level can be translated to design decisions in the different phases of the development process.

We continuously try to improve our DWDM by considering new studies and experiences as well as input from experts. We are also investigating the possibility of automating parts of the development process. The proposed approach is currently evaluated through experiments, in which two groups of students (one using tools that support our process, the other a control group) design and document a context-aware application.

Acknowledgements. This publication was supported by the Dutch national program COMMIT (project P7 SWELL).

References

[1] Alférez, G.H., Pelechano, V.: Dynamic evolution of context-aware systems with models at runtime. In: France, R.B., Kazmeier, J., Breu, R., Atkinson, C. (eds.) MODELS 2012. LNCS, vol. 7590, pp. 70–86. Springer, Heidelberg (2012)

[2] Bartels, A.H.: Smart computing drives the new era of it growth. Forrester Inc. (2009)

[3] Bosems, S., van Sinderen, M.J.: Improving context-aware applications for the well-being domain: Model-driven design guided by medical knowledge. In: 3rd Int. Conf. on Sensor Networks (SENSORNETS 2014), pp. 397–403 (2014)

[4] Bosems, S. et al.: SWELL D1.2 Overall architecture. Tech. rep. (2013)

[5] Bosems, S. et al.: Dynamic domain model for well-weing (2014), http://wwwhome.ewi.utwente.nl/~bosemss/2014/OTMA/ddm.png

[6] Dey, A.K., Abowd, G.D.: The context toolkit: Aiding the development of context-aware applications. In: SIGCHI Conf. on Human Factors in Computing Systems, pp. 431–441 (1999)

[7] Easterlin, R.A.: Building a better theory of well-being. In: Economics & Happiness: Framing the Analysis, pp. 29–64 (2006)

[8] Greenberg, S.: Context as a dynamic construct (2001)

[9] Henricksen, K., Indulska, J.: Developing context-aware pervasive computing applications: Models and approach. Pervasive and Mobile Computing 2(1), 37–64 (2006)

[10] Kailas, A., et al.: From mobile phones to personal wellness dashboards. IEEE pulse 1(1), 57–63 (2010)

[11] Kleppe, A.G., et al.: MDA explained: The model driven architecture: Practice and promise. Addison-Wesley (2003)

[12] Lane, N.D., et al.: BeWell: A smartphone application to monitor, model and promote wellbeing. In: 5th Int. ICST Conf. on Pervasive Computing Technologies for Healthcare, pp. 23–26 (2011)

[13] op den Akker, H., et al.: Development and evaluation of a sensor-based system for remote monitoring and treatment of chronic diseases - the continuous care & coaching platform. In: 6th Int. Symposium on Ehealth Services and Technologies (2012)

[14] Soriano Perez, C.S.: Context aware systems in well-being: From user needs to software architecture. Master's thesis, Universitat Politecnica de Valencia (2014)

[15] Varelius, J.: Objective explanations of individual well-being. Journal of Happiness Studies 5, 73–91 (2004)

[16] Welsh, K., et al.: Towards requirements aware systems: Run-time resolution of design-time assumptions. In: 26th IEEE/ACM Int. Conf. on Automated Software Engineering, pp. 560–563 (2011)

[17] World Health Organization: Towards a common language for functioning, disability and health: ICF. International Classification 1149, 1–22 (2002)

Providing Proof of Trustworthiness Reconstructing Digital Objects' Custody Chain

Angela Di Iorio and Marco Schaerf

DIAG - Department of Computer, Control, and Management Engineering Antonio Ruberti - Sapienza University of Rome, Italy
{angela.diiorio,marco.schaerf}@uniroma1.it

Abstract. Providing proof of the trustworthiness of the digital contents, supported by digital objects, goes through the reconstruction of information which could address replication of preserving repositories, heterogeneity in the maintenance approaches, and differences of the technological applications. In this research will be investigated how to use Semantic Web technology for providing technological evidence, about custody chain, ensuring that the digital content is what it was purported to be at its creation time.

1 Problem Statement

The ever-growing digital deluge of the knowledge society products is demanding the availability of methods and tools, for ascertaining the trustworthiness of digital contents, in a flawless way.

The digital contents, or digital resources, can be represented by diverse types of digital objects, that can be supported by different kind of formats. Going deeply, digital formats are supported by consistent layers of technologies, ranging from the hardware environment, to the software(base and application) environment, necessary to render and to access their intellectual content[7]. The complexity of digital objects becomes harder, if we add the description layer about objects, known as metadata, that can be differently related, structured and aggregated.

Considering, the variety of digital objects in terms of supporting technologies, the problem of technological decays is concerning all user communities, involved in the process of management and production, interested in the fruition services ever more reliable, and dealing with huge amount of objects and data.

As the time passes and the supporting technology evolves, the digital resources can go under different transformations, like for example the format migration, which should be detected and recorded by their management systems. Likewise the management systems can maintain the integrity checking process information, for ensuring that the object files were integer until a certain point in time, hopefully back their creation. Moreover the owner of the digital objects could transfer them to other escrow agencies, in order to use third-party repository services.

R. Meersman et al. (Eds.): OTM 2014 Workshops, LNCS 8842, pp. 43–51, 2014.

In this scenario, providing proofs of trustworthiness, about digital resources, becomes far from to be done in a consistent manner, neutralizing opportunities of contents reuse, with the guarantees of trustworthiness.

The trustworthiness of contents implies the feasible reconstruction of the provenance information through the custody chain of the digital objects, the digital history of objects management. In other words it is necessary to retrieve the information about the events happened during its life-cycle (format migrations, integrity checks, changes in stewardship organizations...).

The information about custody chain of digital objects is obviously supported by machine processes, and usually serialized following standards focused on modelling entities involved in the processes of digital objects management.

Three models were designed for dealing with the digital provenance of information[20],[18],[22](detailed in sec. 3, that can be used for reconstructing the custody chain information.

Providing proof about the trustworthiness of the digital contents, involves to process these set of information that can be very challenging in terms of complexity and quantity. The feasible processing of said information needs the adoption of actual computing techniques ranging from data management, information integration, data mining, information retrieval, semantic web and knowledge representation technologies.

2   Relevance

The problem statement of the previous section is relevant to different use cases, in digital libraries world and digital repository systems, for preserving digital contents in the long term. The problem matters all agents involved in the management and production of the digital resources, as well as, all the fruition services based on the reuse of digital contents. The methodology, and the technology adopted in producing and managing digital resources has a strong impact on the future opportunity of reusing digital contents.

Considering that, mostly all actual scientific and cultural production of intellectual works is digital, and that huge amount of the past intellectual production has been reproduced in the digital world, there are high probabilities that it is necessary to find new methods and technologies useful to provide proofs about the trustworthiness of contents, which is supported by the trustworthiness of agents involved in the production and in the management of digital objects.

In addition, as the infrastructure initiatives grows (i.e. Data Intensive Cyber Environments (DICE)[1], DataNet Federation Consortium (DFC)[2], GIGAS initiative for the Data Harmonisation and Semantic Interoperability[3],[4]..), in size

---

[1] Data Intensive Cyber Environments (DICE), http://dice.unc.edu/

[2] DataNet Federation Consortium, http://datafed.org/

[3] GIGAS technical note, Data Harmonisation and Semantic Interoperability within INSPIRE, GEOSS and GMES,
http://www.thegigasforum.eu/project/project.html

[4] European research infrastructure (including e-Infrastructures),
http://cordis.europa.eu/fp7/ict/e-infrastructure/home_en.html

and number of disciplines, it becomes critically challenging to address the coherent and interoperable development of the metadata management, and the ability of searching relevant information and contents. The trustworthiness of existing contents in the big data scenario should be addressed, in order to improve the performance of the global digital infrastructures.

3   Related Work and Background

The literature around the trustworthiness of repository information is huge, as well as that related to the provenance information. Mainly all said literature it is derived by the reference model of digital repositories: the Open Archival Information System (OAIS)[5] defines "The Archive is responsible for creating and preserving Provenance Information from the point of Ingest; however, earlier Provenance Information should be provided by the Producer. Provenance Information adds to the evidence to support Authenticity."

Here we refer to some of the representative works related to the audit certification [4], [3] about the trustworthy of digital repository, and to self-auditing based on the risk assessment (DRAMBORA)[17]. Following this initiatives the ISO standard 16363:2012 - Audit and certification of trustworthy digital repositories[13], was released to the communities. The main purpose of this standard is to define a recommended practice as basement for audit and certification process, to assess the trustworthiness of digital repositories.

Nevertheless the certification of the trustworthiness of a repository is just one of the aspects involved in the trustworthiness of the digital contents, as specifically mentioned in the [11]. Even though the practices of audit and certification, widely tested by many repository systems[21], can support the evidence about the repository, it cannot certify that the managed resources are trustworthy.

Indeed, even though we have a shared methods for building and measuring the repository trustworthiness [16], the standards-based practice for producing the resources, supporting the trustworthiness of content has not been investigated, and developed.

In addition other aspects related to the overall management of the digital objects has to be considered in our research path.

As reported in[23] while the general management of repositories, aiming to maintain information about authenticity of data, are important and have been addressed under different perspective, the institutional reputation appears to be the strongest structural assurance indicator of trust. In [10] was underlined that more has to be done for finding the best business model for those organizations that serve as trusted digital repositories, appropriate formats for long-term preservation, and the copyright and intellectual property issues associated with migration and emulation.

The cross-cut approach, connecting agents (persons, organizations and software) and rights information and documentation, ruling the actions that could be performed, by authorized agents, on digital objects, is the set of information necessary for reconstructing the custody chain.

An implementation model for dealing with all those aspects is the PREMIS[20] standard, which is widely adopted, and is based on well structured semantics. If completely adopted, PREMIS can support the proof of trustworthy of the digital contents, reconstructing their custody chain, by means of processing information about the maintenance practices of the digital objects and connecting information about the entities defined in the data model: objects, events, agents, and rights.

Similarly the Provenance data model[22], and the related ontology, describes the use and production of entities by activities, which may be influenced in various ways by agents. The model's core structure are: entity, activity, and agent.

The third data model related is the Open Provence Model[18] where the needs of provenance by the research community had been substantiated as a better understanding of the "capabilities of the different systems, the representations they used for provenance, their similarities, their differences, and the rationale that motivated their designs". The nodes defined by the model are: artifact, process, and agent.

4   Research Hypotheses

The main research question in our work is:

How can we provide proof about the trustworthiness of digital
contents, supported by the provenance information related to
the digital objects?

To answer this question, we will further answer to other emerging questions like:

- *How can we reconstruct the provenance information through the event's chain and audit trails records of the holding repository?*
- *How can we check and classify the flaws in the custody chain and reconstruct it?*
- *How can we enforce provenance information through the related rights documentation, identifying agents eligible to the preservation actions?*
- *How can we relate the trustworthiness of the repository, with the trustworthiness of the agents (persons, organizations, and software)?*
The research question had led to the following hypothesis:
- *The trustworthiness of agents managing the repository has influence on the trustworthiness of contents and repository.*
- *Consequently the trustworthiness of contents depends on the possibility of retrieving information about their provenance, through heterogeneous sources of information.*
- *In presence of lack, inconsistency or incompleteness of the provenance information it should be possible to recover information by reasoning about the related information, if the management of the digital objects has been performed with a reasonable level of curation.*

5 Material

In order to retrieve information about custody chain of the digital resources, we will be using a set of existing digital resources, containing standard metadata related to images and books, digitized by two different Organizations, that here we will refer as **S** and **G**.

These Organizations, even adopting the same standard PREMIS, for provenance information, have defined specific structures for their own needs, and consequently they have produced digital resources, with different processes and respecting their own metadata structures, and standards.

The set of digital resources originally produced by the Organization **G** are produced by digitization of real books, owned by the Organization **S**. The Organization **S** has been transforming the digital resources produced by the Organization **G**, into its own metadata structure, embedding also PREMIS standard, for provenance information.

This conversion process is managed by a system, that uses a dark repository based on a relational database. The digital resources, built by the massive conversion system(MASSCONV) and respecting metadata structure and standards adopted by the Organization **S**, are transferred in a third repository deputed to the management of the long term digital preservation Organization **C**. The dataset that will be used is the relational database of the Organization **S**, used for producing digital resources digitized in house, and for transforming the digital resources, produced by the Organization **G**, in the its own conforming metadata structure.

Actually the number of resources that we provide to be used are 20,000, while the number of contained digital objects it is not possible being precisely estimated, at this stage of work. The process of transformation from the metadata framework of **G** to the target **S**, regarding the mass digitization project is under development, and verification. The foreseen number should be over two millions of objects, while for the in-house digitized books, the number of objects should be over 300,000.

6 Proposed Approach and Work Plan

Providing evidence about the trustworthiness of digital contents relies strongly on the feasibility of reconstructing the source of information in an interoperable manner, evaluating the consistency of data for ascertain the custody chain, even rebuilding the feasible interruption or inconsistency of data, concerning the custody chain.

In our case scenario, mainly described in the previous section, we will rebuild the history of the digital objects starting by the MASSCONV database information and tracing back the events, matching rights information about the eligibility of agents to perform action on it or having specific restrictions. Because the system had gathered also information about objects coming from the repository of the Organization **G**, the approach will deal with the change of custody of the objects. Considering that the system for processing MASSCONV is based on relational database for performance reason, while the metadata serialized respects semantics defined by XML schema (PREMIS), available also in Web Ontology Language (OWL)[5], in draft version by the end of 2011[6], we will use the Semantic Web Technologies for dealing with the task of tracing back the provenance information.

The system MASSCONV has adopted for mapping data from the local relational database with different schemas, toward the semantics of PREMIS schema, the Global As View approach of the Information integration[2],[15],[14], we actually are evaluating the feasible adoption of an Ontology Based Data Access system(OBDA), for reasoning over data.

The OBDA [19][1][12] is able to deal with the integration of the conceptual layer defined by the ontology and the data layer managed by the relational database, or by noSQL database[6].

7   Evaluation

At the best of our knowledge there isn't tool for evaluating our Hypothesis, in addition because the work-flow of management is under control of the same Organization **S**, it shouldn't be found lack of information about the custody chain, and the Organization **S** trusts in Organization **G** for the objects management.

Consequently, to evaluate our hypothesis we will primarily use our own dataset as ground truth, considering that we know the provenance of resources as primary source of information, for determining the reconstruction of the custody chain of the digital objects. Evaluation of the hypothesis will involve realizing process mining and reasoning, that can support the detection of lack or incompleteness of information about the custody chain, and how the information is maintained in the transfer of resources from one repository to another. The verification of the results will be done tracing back the metadata produced by the different management processes of the holding repository. If every objects it will be consistently self-documented, retrieving the correct information that we know in advance, we will provide failed information in order to check if the system is able to find lack, inconsistency or incompleteness in the information.

8   Discussion

Looking at the long term, even in 5 years, we have to consider how much events had occurred to the digital objects and how much information related to them is produced by events connecting agents (humans and software), and rights for checking the eligibility to perform action over objects. These information, known as metadata, is the core business for preserving access to the intellectual content.

---

[5] OWL Web Ontology Language Primer (Second Edition),
http://www.w3.org/TR/owl-primer/
[6] PREMIS Ontology,
http://www.loc.gov/standards/premis/owlOntology-announcement.html

Consequently the preservation metadata infrastructure is the basement for the reliability of access services to the intellectual products, and for ensuring the trustworthiness of the contents.

Our approach combines different aspects coming from Digital Libraries and Preservation metadata management and the emerging use of Semantic Web tools like the ontology-based knowledge management systems for reasoning over metadata and recovering inconsistency.

We believe that the trustworthiness of digital resources is based on an orchestration of trustworthiness, which involves not only the archiving repository, but also all the other agents involved in the production and management process of the digital resources.

As consequence we will address the further step over the repository's trustworthiness, retrieving the liability of agents involved in the custody chain (provenance). Our idea is to use reasoning systems for evaluating information managed at different level: archiving repository (log files, audit trails records...), digital resources related information (involving events, changes in rights actions or restrictions, agents responsible in the management...). The reasoning over provenance information implies to reason over the different source of information, involving also problem of interoperability.

As similar works about provenance information we found [9] and [8] that cannot be compared to ours because they are focused on different kind of materials. They access to the provenance information respectively about the Web pages and the digital publishing, while our material's provenance information is supposed to be reliably preserved in its digital history. The digital history of materials is not bordered to its web life, which can be part of its history.

We know that digital contents' repository systems will have layered amount of metadata information, about the management of digital objects, recording events that had impacted on them, and agents involved in the events.

The contents' migration processes, from one file format to new one, and other business rules could also imply changes of storage and changes of rights' management. Furthermore, the semantics evolution, coming from the reference community, and the dissemination of resources in other contexts, probably will challenge the digital management of the preservation systems.

We believe that it will be an increasing need of reasoning services over this amount of data and supported by the relevant ontologies. In our research we will start to use semantic web technologies, for retrieving relevant information for proving the trustworthiness of contents, by means of the reasoning over the digital objects management information and over the information about the status and the change in the custody chain.

The last aspect to consider is the concept of trust, which is largely based on a lack of deception[24]. Referring to the data repositories, the study says that "trust in data itself plays a distinctive and important role for users to reuse data, which may or may not be related to the trust in repositories". Furthermore as other influencing factors, like organizational attributes, user communities (recommendations and frequent use), past experiences, repository processes (documentation, data cleaning, and quality checking), matters to the creation of a trust relationship between users and the repository.

9 Conclusions

We believe that over the contingency of the technologies supporting digital contents, the long-term requirement for the digital preservation is essential for maintaining access to the managed digital contents. The trust consensus building for the repositories, maintaining the management of the resources in the long term, must be substantiated, by the transparent possibility of measuring the strategies and processes adopted for the management system, by the responsible agents.

Providing proofs of the trustworthiness about the digital contents, managed in the long term, will determine the successful establishment of the trust relationship between the trustor (user) and the trustee (management repository).

References

1. Calvanese, D., De Giacomo, D., Lembo, D.: The Mastro System for Ontology-based Data Access. Semantic Web 2(1), 43–53 (2011)
2. Calvanese, D., De Giacomo, G., Lenzerini, M., Nardi, D., Rosati, R.: Information Integration: Conceptual Modeling and Reasoning Support. In: Proceedings fo the 3rd IFCIS International Conference on Cooperative Information Systems, pp. 280–289 (1998)
3. Center for Research Libraries, OCLC Online Computer Library Center: Trustworthy repositories audit & certification: Criteria and checklist (2007)
4. Center for Research Libraries and RLG Programs: Trustworthy repositories audit and certification checklist (2007),
   http://www.crl.edu/sites/default/files/attachments/pages/trac_0.pdf
5. Consultative Committee for Space Data: Reference Model for an Open Archival Information System (OAIS), Recommended Practice CCSDS 650.0-M-2 Magenta Book (2012), http://public.ccsds.org/publications/archive/652x0m1.pdf
6. Curé, O., Kerdjoudj, F., Duc, C.L., Lamolle, M., Faye, D.: On the potential integration of an ontology-based data access approach in nosql stores. In: 2012 Third International Conference on Emerging Intelligent Data and Web Technologies (EIDWT), pp. 166–173. IEEE (2012)
7. Dappert, A., Peyrard, S., Chou, C.C., Delve, J.: Describing and preserving digital object environments. New Review of Information Networking 18(2), 106–173 (2013)
8. De Nies, T.: Assessing content value for digital publishing through relevance and provenance-based trust. In: Alani, H., et al. (eds.) ISWC 2013, Part II. LNCS, vol. 8219, pp. 424–431. Springer, Heidelberg (2013)
9. De Nies, T., Coppens, S., Verborgh, R., Sande, M.V., Mannens, E., Van de Walle, R. Michaelides, D., Moreau, L.: Easy access to provenance: an essential step towards trust on the web. In: 2013 IEEE 37th Annual Computer Software and Applications Conference Workshops (COMPSACW), pp. 218–223. IEEE (2013)
10. Dryden, J.: Measuring trust: Standards for trusted digital repositories. Journal of Archival Organization 9(2), 127–130 (2011)
11. Giaretta, D.: Oais model and certification of trusted digital repositories (2013)

12. Haase, P., Horrocks, I., Hovland, D., Hubauer, T., Jimenez-Ruiz, E., Kharlamov, E., Pinkel, J.K.C., Rosati, R., Santarelli, V., Soylu, A., et al.: Optique system: Towards ontology and mapping management in obda solutions. In: Second International Workshop on Debugging Ontologies and Ontology Mappings-WoDOOM 2013, p. 21 (2013)
13. ISO (the International Organization for Standardization): Iso 16363:2012 - space data and information transfer systems – audit and certification of trustworthy digital repositories (2012), https://www.iso.org/obp/ui/#iso:std:iso:16363:en
14. Katzis, Y., Papakonstantinou, Y.: View-based Data Integration. In: Encyclopedia of Database Systems, pp. 3332–3339. Springer (2009), http://www.springerreference.com/docs/html/chapterdbid/64034.html
15. Lenzerini, M.: Data integration: a theoretical perspective. In: Proceedings of the Twenty-First ACM SIGMOD-SIGACT-SIGART Symposium on Principles of Database Systems, pp. 233–246 (2002), 10.1145/543613.543644
16. McGovern, N.Y.: Trust in repositories: Building and measuring trustworthiness using trac (2013)
17. McHugh, A., Ruusalepp, R., Ross, S., Hofman, H.: Digital repository audit method based on risk assessment. Digital Curation Centre (DCC) and DigitalPreservationEurope, DPE (2007)
18. Moreau, L., Clifford, B., Freire, J., Futrelle, J., Gil, Y., Groth, P., Kwasnikowska, N., Miles, S., Missier, P., Jim, Myers, o.: The open provenance model core specification (v1. 1). Future Generation Computer Systems 27(6), 743–756 (2011)
19. Poggi, A., Lembo, D., Calvanese, D., De Giacomo, G., Lenzerini, M., Rosati, R.: Linking Data to Ontologies. In: Spaccapietra, S. (ed.) Journal on Data Semantics X. LNCS, vol. 4900, pp. 133–173. Springer, Heidelberg (2008)
20. PREMIS Editorial Committee: PREMIS Data Dictionary for Preservation Metadata version 2.2 (2012), http://www.loc.gov/standards/premis/v2/premis-2-2.pdf
21. Rodrigues, E., Ferreira, M., Carvalho, J., Faria, L., Silva, H., Príncipe, P., Moreira, J.: Large scale repository auditing to iso 16363. Open Repositories 2014 (2014)
22. World Wide Web Consortium and others: Prov-dm: the prov data model (2013)
23. Yakel, E., Faniel, I., Kriesberg, A., Yoon, A.: Trust in digital repositories. International Journal of Digital Curation 8(1), 143–156 (2013)
24. Yoon, A.: End users trust in data repositories: definition and influences on trust development. Archival Science 14(1), 17–34 (2014)

Industry Case Studies Program 2014 PC Chairs Message

Cloud computing, service-oriented architecture, business process modelling, enterprise architecture, enterprise integration, semantic interoperabilitywhat is an enterprise systems administrator to do with the constant stream of industry hype surrounding him, constantly bathing him with (apparently) new ideas and new "technologies"? It is nearly impossible, and the academic literature does not help solving the problem, with hyped "technologies" catching on in the academic world just as easily as the industrial world. The most unfortunate thing is that these technologies are actually useful, and the press hype only hides that value. What the enterprise information manager really cares about is integrated, interoperable infrastructures that support cooperative information systems, so he can deliver valuable information to management in time to make correct decisions about the use and delivery of enterprise resources, whether those are raw materials for manufacturing, people to carry out key business processes, or the management of shipping choices for correct delivery to customers.

The OTM conference series have established itself as a major international forum for exchanging ideas and results on scientific research for practitioners in fields such as computer supported cooperative work (CSCW), middleware, Internet/Web data management, electronic commerce, workflow management, knowledge flow, agent technologies and software architectures to name a few. The recent popularity and interest in service-oriented architectures & domains require capabilities for on-demand composition of services. Furthermore, cloud computing environments are becoming more prevalent, in which information technology resources must be configured to meet user-driven needs. These emerging technologies represent a significant need for highly interoperable systems.

As a part of OnTheMove 2014, the Industry Case Studies Program on "Industry Applications and Standard initiatives for Cooperative Information Systems for Interoperable Infrastructures", supported by OMG, IFAC TC 5.3 "Enterprise Integration and Networking" and the SIG INTEROP Grande-Région, emphasized Research/Industry cooperation on these future trends. The focus of the program is on a discussion of ideas where research areas address interoperable information systems and infrastructure. 9 short papers have been presented, focusing on industry leaders, standardization initiatives, European and international projects consortiums and discussing how projects within their organizations addressed software, systems and architecture interoperability. Each paper has been reviewed by an international Programme Committee composed of representatives of Academia, Industry and Standardisation initiatives. We thank them for their dedication and interest.

We hope that you find this industry-focused part of the program valuable as feedback from industry practitioners, and we thank the authors for the time and effort taken to contribute to the program.

September 2014   Hervé Panetto

Flexibility Requirements
in Real-World Process Scenarios
and Prototypical Realization in the Care Domain

Georg Kaes[1], Stefanie Rinderle-Ma[1], Ralph Vigne[2], and Juergen Mangler[1]

[1] University of Vienna, Faculty of Computer Science, Austria
[2] CERN, Switzerland
{georg.kaes,stefanie.rinderle-ma,juergen.mangler}@univie.ac.at,
ralph.vigne@cern.ch

Abstract. Flexibility is a key concern in business process management and mature solutions and systems have been developed during the last years. What can be observed is that the approaches mostly consider process instances that are executed based on a process schema reflecting a process type, e.g.,'an order process. The process instances might be adapted during runtime in an individual manner (ad-hoc changes) or the process schema evolves due to, for example, new regulations. We studied cases from four different domains for their requirements on flexibility. These use cases are characterized by long running, highly adaptive, and individual instances, i.e., instances that are not based on a common process schema, but develop during runtime based on context and process-relevant data. The requirements analysis shows that can only part of them can be met by existing approaches. To illustrate an initial solution meeting the identified requirements, a prototypical implementation of the care domain use case is demonstrated, followed by a discussion of lessons learned and a research agenda.

1 Introduction

Flexibility is a key topic in business process research [1–4]. Some business processes require a high degree of flexibility, but still follow a predefined schema, which can be repeatable reused for multiple instances [3]. A different set of processes describe situations that require a high degree of flexibility regarding the instance design. They are based on a standardized, but very minimalistic process skeleton, and adapted on-the-fly according to constantly changing requirements. Domain-specific solutions that support individually developed processes (plans) have been already developed in health care [5][1]. Another study from the logistics domain stating similar requirements was presented in [6]. Further business domains that are investigated in this paper are:

- **Care Planning:** The *ACaPlan* project[2], developed at the University of Vienna, aims at supporting nurses in care centers who are adapting therapy

---

[1] See Section 4 for a discussion.
[2] http://cs.univie.ac.at/project/acaplan

R. Meersman et al. (Eds.): OTM 2014 Workshops, LNCS 8842, pp. 55–64, 2014.

plans based on a patients symptoms. The inherent human-centered process structure requires a highly adaptive and individualisable approach.

- **Manufacturing:** *Azevedos*, which participated in the FP7 project[3], is one of the leading manufacturers of machines for cork transformation. They plan and produce machines which are tailored according to the demands of one specific customer, thus leading to a very adaptive and individual production process.
- **Software Development:** *Mesonic*[4] develops Electronic Resource Planing and Customer Relationship Management technology. Their *Support Net* is a central access point where support cases of retailers and customers are distributed to the support team. For each user there exists a highly adaptive process instance, containing each interaction with the system and all resulting consequences.
- **Hotel and Event Management:** Schlosspark Mauerbach[5] (SPM) is a seminar location and a hotel close to Vienna. Based on wishes, suggestions and complaints by hotel guests, customer specific process instances have to be adapted.

Although these four applications differ in their business area, they have one thing in common: All implement at least one type of long running process based on a minimalistic standardized process schema, which has to be continuously adapted according to individually changing requirements. These adaptations eventually lead to highly individual, customized, and long running process instances which have to be supported accordingly.

Though several generic approaches regarding process flexibility have already been discussed [1–4], the following challenges are not yet (fully) supported:

- **Adaptation and Management of Highly Individual Process Instances:** This refers to the on-the-fly creation and adaptation of highly adaptive process instances. All relevant data related to the process instance, including the structure of the instance itself, have to be managed through the whole life cycle and made available to the person in charge when required.
- **Maintenance and Support of Changes to Adapt Highly Individual Process Instances:** Since these highly adaptive and individual process instances are not based on a common schema, known similarity checks based on a process schema like [7] or classical process life cycle support [8] cannot be utilized for determining which situations are similar, and which are not. This circumstance leads to the utilization of other data sources describing the process instance and its environment. These data sources will be used for assessing and analyzing the current situation, and recommending suitable adaptations to the person in charge.
- **Support and Application of Data Driven Process Changes:** Based on changes of certain data items - for example the body temperature of a

---

[3] http://fp7-adventure.eu
[4] http://www.mesonic.com/
[5] http://www.schlosspark.at/

patient - new adaptations of a certain process instance can be triggered or recommended to the person in charge.

In order to address these above mentioned research gaps, the methodology depicted in Figure 1 is applied in this work.

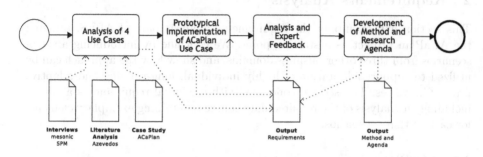

Fig. 1. Research Methodology

1. We started with an analysis of the different use cases from distinct business domains, revealing the basic requirements. For the use cases of *Mesonic* and *Schlosspark Mauerbach* interviews with domain experts were conducted. The requirements of Azevedos have been analyzed based on documents from the ADVENTURE FP7 project. In cooperation with domain experts from two nursing centers in Lower Austria, we developed the basic concepts of the ACaPlan prototype, which also serves as a use case.
2. Based on our findings, we developed a first prototype of the ACaPlan Use Case. Since this prototype is a good representative for such a use case, we focused our efforts mostly on this project. During the implementation phase, we discovered additional requirements for such a system.
3. After the first version of the ACaPlan prototype has been finished, we analyzed the results with the domain experts and implemented their feedback to the requirements.
4. Based on this feedback round, we were able to define a certain set of requirements, as well as to develop a road-map for our future research.

The contribution of this paper is threefold: First, we define the basic requirements for highly adaptive, individual, long-running process instances. Second, we have developed a methodology to support users and data-driven process adaptation, which we name **APES** (**A**daptive **P**rocess **E**nvironment **S**upport). Third, by developing and enhancing our ACaPlan prototype, we provide a testing environment, where the results of this methodology can be demonstrated and tested.

The rest of this paper is organized as follows: Section 2 describes the setting of the process. After a short introduction into the ACaPlan prototype and the three other use cases, a description of the general and data-source related requirements (Section 2.3) is given. Section 3 describes the overall approach for providing support in adaptive process environments. Based on our prototypical implementation of the nursing case study, necessary steps and required information are illustrated. The paper concludes with an overview over related work (Section 4), followed by our research agenda and conclusion (Section 5).

2   Requirements Analysis

This section will exemplify the requirements analysis part of APES, utilizing the ACaPlan project as a starting point. We continue by introducing a set of scenarios from three other business domains, and show how the approach can be utilized to support adaptation of highly individual, long-running and adaptive process instances. The section concludes with a general requirements analysis, including an analysis of the required data sources containing exemplary elements for each of these scenarios.

2.1   ACaPlan

ACaPlan (Adaptive Care Planning) is an adaptive process application which aims at supporting nurses in geriatric nursing homes at their daily work. The ACaPlan project implements the central processes and data sources necessary for taking care of each patient in an optimal, individualized way. Based on the symptoms a patient shows and related data the nurse is supported in finding the correct diagnoses, and in further consequence in designing optimal therapy plans, which lead to a better situation for the patient as effectively as possible. This therapy plan is inserted into a patient-specific, long running, highly adaptive process instance, which includes all of his therapy plans.

Based on the data available about each patient and the environment, APES can provide decision support for nurses who have to set up a therapy plan for a patient: Starting with information about prior conditions and related therapies, therapy plans can be suggested or not. When it is unknown if a certain treatment may help a patient, the basic informations about the patient can be used for finding comparable ones which already had this kind of therapy, and suggest the therapies which proved being successful first.

2.2   Further Use Cases

This section illustrates three other scenarios, where APES can be used to provide support during the adaptation of a long running, highly adaptive and individual process instance.

Business Field Manufacturing – Scenario Azevedos: The company could profit from APES in the adaptation of the production and documentation process of its products. Based on informations about the requirements of customers, process patterns which have been used for customers with comparable requirements can be suggested and reused. With the APES approach in place, if suppliers have bottlenecks, or Azevedos needs to optimize its production processes, adaptations to the processes can be carried out in standardized way.

Business Field Software Development – Scenario Mesonic: Information about how to solve problems of comparable users or of the same user in the past can be utilized to help the supporter to interact with one specific customer.

Business Field Hotel and Event Management – Scenario Schlosspark Mauerbach: At Schlosspark Mauerbach, the *Customer Process*, which encompasses all interactions with one specific customer, is the central process for incident management. Based on information about the customer and comparable guests, future events and stays at the hotel can be optimized.

2.3   General Requirements and Required Data Sources

Based on our experiences from the ACaPlan prototype, we were able to conduct several general, and data-source related requirements for a supportive adaptive process environment. The general requirements are as follows:

- creation of general process stubs serving as a basis for later adaptations, which will individualize the process.
- on-the-fly adaptation of instances, based on information from multiple data sources
- supporting multiple process patterns as defined in [4] including insertion, deletion, moving and replacing.
- alerting persons in charge of adaptations when certain data sources change (e.g. a change in the patients body temperature can trigger certain adaptations)
- utilization of every data source available for assessing the current situation from multiple vantage points.

One of the key issues is to identify and analyze data sources, that (1) help in building and adapting the individual process instances which are not based on a common schema and (2) help in determining the similarity of the processes instances. The following list summarizes the data sources which are relevant for a comprehensive view on a single process instance:

- **Subject Data:** Who or what individual element is directly related to the process instance and thus affected by the adaptation?
- **Environmental Data:** Which other data elements, which are not directly related to the subject can be relevant for planning and executing an adaptation?
- **Goals:** What are possible goals which could be reached by an adaptation?
- **Trigger Conditions:** What are the events and data sets which make planning and executing an adaptation necessary? This includes requirements for optimization as well as any other data or event which makes an adaptation necessary.
- **Process Fragments:** What elements are provided for possible adaptations? This source contains the items APES can suggest for adapting the process instance.

These data elements are important for support during the adaptation of process instances, as they provide comprehensive information regarding the process instance and its environment. The more data about a process instance can be gained and categorized, the better the understanding of how the process in real life works is, thus leading to an improved support during adaptation.

Table 1 outlines exemplary allocations of the data sources in the four scenarios as described in Section 2.2.

Table 1. Data Source Allocation in the different Use Cases

Subject Data	Care Planning	Manufacturing	Software Dev	Hotel
	Patient	Product	Customer	Guest
Environmental Data	Nursing home information	supplier information, employee workload, factory information	employee workload, other projects	hotel information (occupied rooms etc.), upcoming events
Goals	cure the symptoms, make him happy	produce the machine, react to the customer	satisfy customer, solve bugs	satisfy guest
Trigger Conditions	new symptoms arise, the patient expresses desires	the customer has new requirements	the customer has a problem	the guest has a special wish for his next stay
Process Fragments	solutions for a diagnosis, as defined in the repository	work steps for planning and producing	tasks for the support / development / other teams	measures taken by the various hotel employees

3   The ACaPlan Prototypical Implementation

The approach for generating good recommendations for adaptations of a highly adaptive, long running process instance is divided into several distinct steps. The ACaPlan prototype, which is based on the *Cloud Processing Execution Engine*[6], is comprised of several REST web services, which can be called from multiple environments, allowing the development of custom interfaces. Over a web interface, which can be accessed by mobile devices and standard browsers, nurses use our approach for assessing which therapy is optimal for a patient given the environmental data, his basic data, current symptoms and goals.

The steps are:

1. Assess the situation: How can issues which have to be changed be described?
2. Find possible diagnoses which match the current symptoms.
3. Based on these diagnoses, generate a therapy plan and set the goals.
4. Adapt the process instance by inserting the new therapy plan and goals.

The first step is covered by our nursing interface, a website which can be opened from multiple devices. Over an input mask as depicted in Figure 2, the nurse can describe the current symptoms of the patient.

The relevant nursing knowledge is described in a repository which is based on the nursing knowledge standards NANDA, NIC and NOC [9]. Here, each diagnosis is described in detail, including possible symptoms, risk factors, things that can be done to solve the issue (i.e., therapy steps) and possible outcomes.

Currently, the diagnoses are matched with the nurses inputs by using a simple pattern matching technique: If the words the nurses has typed in are found in

---
[6] cpee.org

the relevant sections of the diagnosis, the diagnosis is added. Additionally, each element which matches the search parameters can be supplied with a score, which will be added to the overall score of the diagnosis. The result of this step is shown to the nurse, who can now select relevant diagnoses (cf. Figure 3).

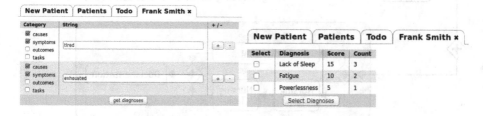

Fig. 2. Input Screen for symptoms in ACaPlan

Fig. 3. Selection Screen for diagnoses in ACaPlan

Each diagnosis includes the therapy tasks which can be executed and goals which can be achieved. Additionally, a set of possible solutions is defined for each diagnosis, including a predefined set of tasks and goals. These solutions are the process fragments, which in further consequence will be added into the specific therapy plan, as depicted in Figure 4. If no solution applies to the current situation, a new process fragment has to be generated. In similar situations, this new process fragment can be reused for the process instance.

This prototype utilizes the different data sources on a preliminary level. Given the inputs of a nurse, diagnoses are selected containing the possible adaptations, which are suggested to the user. In Section 5 we describe how this process can be enhanced.

4   Related Work

Due to constant changes in the process environment, process flexibility, i.e. adapting process instances as well as schemata, has emerged as a crucial challenge [10] [3].

The imperative approach of defining processes defines one explicit sequence of steps that solve the intention behind the business process [11], resulting in a process model which is hard to understand for highly adaptive processes. During many years of research, powerful solutions at the technical level to develop changes on instance level and evolve process schemes have emerged [10]. However, except few approaches [12] [13], little attention has been spent on how to support users when defining and applying changes.

The declarative approach defines all relations between process steps [11] [14], thus allowing for multiple solutions to solve the intention behind the business process. Imagine an adaptive process containing all therapies for a patient in a care center: there is the potential to conduct hundreds of therapies with hundreds of thousands of steps in total. The sheer number of possibilities, with no explicit

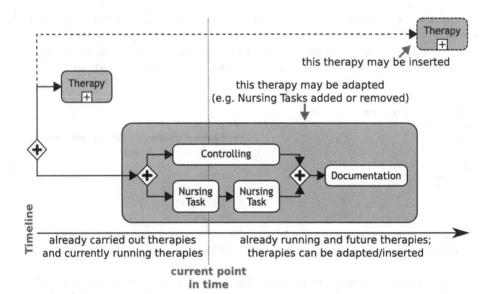

this therapy may be inserted

this therapy may be adapted
(e.g. Nursing Tasks added or removed)

Fig. 4. Exemplary Adaptive Process Instance

sequences but just dependencies is recognized to be very confusing for users of the system [11]. Thus the imperative approach is generally easier to comprehend for related personnel.

For a real-world process, data connected to the process as a whole, or to certain steps, plays a key role when executing the process. Standing in contrast to traditional workflow paradigms, data-driven processes aim at putting the control flow of the process in the background, and instead using data related to the process for the definition of the control flow at instance level. The process structure itself is only defined at a very coarse level, and the resulting skeletons evolve dynamically based on the data provided for the current instance [15].

Especially in the field of medicine, specialized solutions such as *K4Care* [5] have been developed. They utilize independent agents for the different tasks and users. In general, agent-based solutions are flexible, but the scalability of the solutions is questionable. The approach employs SDA* [16] models, where all possible *s*tates, *d*ecisions and *a*ctions have to be defined at the creation of a therapy, including "follow-up actions in which the state of the patient is checked" [5]. Thus, it remains unclear what happens in case of unforeseen situations. As they are not included in any process model, the system cannot provide recommendations. Here, flexible process engines such as the CPEE provide the option to dynamically adapt the concerned process instances in order to resolve the exceptional situation.

Generating knowledge out of past experiences is a central feature necessary for providing recommendations for the user when adaptations become necessary. The purpose of Process Mining is to extract this information [17]. Generally, there are three ways of utilizing the results of log mining [18], i.e., process discovery, conformance checking, and model enhancement.

Log files, which are utilized for process mining can have a multitude of formats. A well known representative is MXML, which is based on XML and among others used by the process mining suite *ProM*. XES (*Extensible Event Stream*), which can be seen as a successor of MXML, impresses with a high degree of flexibility.

5   Research Agenda and Conclusion

Long running, highly adaptive and individual process instances occur in a variety of business fields. Since control flow related similarity checking algorithms cannot be utilized to find comparable process instances, other data sources have to be used for this task. Based on our experience from the ACaPlan project, such data sources are defined and evaluated with three other possible applications from different business domains. Secondly, the basic methodology of how we utilize the available information for providing adaptation support is outlined. Although the first ACaPlan prototype already illustrates basic functionality, the following concepts must be developed in order to close the above mentioned research gaps:

- **Support of Change Patterns:** In this stage of our prototype the adaptation of the therapy process only supports adding new therapies as a whole into the process instance. [4] defines several change patterns of process instances and schemata. In addition to the insertion deletion, updating and skipping therapies or parts of them would be desirable.
- **Utilization of the Data Sources for Generating Recommendations:** We can utilize the above mentioned data sources for analyzing the current situation and answering among others the following questions:
  - Do the symptoms the patient currently suffers from appear for the first time, or have they occurred before?
  - If they occurred before, which therapy has been used to treat them, and has it been successful?
  - Are there any other patients who had comparable symptoms before, and which therapies have been used on them successfully?
  - Have there been any situations before where the same goals should be reached?
- **Data Driven Process Changes:** Based on certain changes in data, adaptations of the respective process instances have to be triggered and either carried out automatically, or recommended to the person in charge.

We focused our efforts on the ACaPlan project as a first representative use case, but will continue to implement the other presented use cases in the future. Thus, the general applicability of the presented methodology will be evaluated.

References

1. van der Aalst, W.M.P.: A decade of business process management conferences: Personal reflections on a developing discipline. In: Barros, A., Gal, A., Kindler, E. (eds.) BPM 2012. LNCS, vol. 7481, pp. 1–16. Springer, Heidelberg (2012)

2. Schonenberg, H., Mans, R., Russell, N., Mulyar, N., van der Aalst, W.: Process flexibility: A survey of contemporary approaches. In: Dietz, J.L.G., Albani, A., Barjis, J. (eds.) CIAO and EOMAS 2012. LNBIP, vol. 10, pp. 16–30. Springer, Heidelberg (2008)
3. Rinderle, S., Reichert, M., Dadam, P.: Correctness criteria for dynamic changes in workflow systems a survey. Data & Knowledge Engineering 50, 9–34 (2004)
4. Weber, B., Reichert, M., Rinderle-Ma, S.: Change patterns and change support features enhancing flexibility in process-aware information systems. Data & Knowledge Engineering 66, 438–466 (2008)
5. Isern, D., Moreno, A., Sánchez, D., Hajnal, A., Pedone, G., Varga, L.: Agent-based execution of personalised home care treatments. Applied Intelligence 34, 155–180 (2011)
6. Bassil, S., Keller, R.K., Kropf, P.G.: A workflow-oriented system architecture for the management of container transportation. In: Desel, J., Pernici, B., Weske, M. (eds.) BPM 2004. LNCS, vol. 3080, pp. 116–131. Springer, Heidelberg (2004)
7. Dijkman et al.: Similarity of business process models: Metrics and evaluation. Information Systems 36, 498–516 (2011)
8. Weber, B., Reichert, M., Rinderle-Ma, S., Wild, W.: Providing integrated life cycle support in process-aware information systems. International Journal of Cooperative Information Systems 18, 115–165 (2009)
9. Georg, K., Jürgen, M., Stefanie, R.M., Ralph, V.: The NNN formalization: Review and development of guideline specification in the care domain. abs/1404.2162, technical report, arXiv (2014)
10. Reichert, M., Weber, B.: Enabling Flexibility in Process-Aware Information Systems: Challenges, Methods, Technologies. Springer (2012)
11. Pichler, P., Weber, B., Zugal, S., Pinggera, J., Mendling, J., Reijers, H.A.: Imperative versus declarative process modeling languages: An empirical investigation. In: Daniel, F., Barkaoui, K., Dustdar, S. (eds.) BPM Workshops 2011, Part I. LNBIP, vol. 99, pp. 383–394. Springer, Heidelberg (2012)
12. Günther, C.W., Rinderle, S., Reichert, M., van der Aalst, W.: Change mining in adaptive process management systems. In: Meersman, R., Tari, Z. (eds.) OTM 2006. LNCS, vol. 4275, pp. 309–326. Springer, Heidelberg (2006)
13. Rinderle, S., Weber, B., Reichert, M., Wild, W.: Integrating process learning and process evolution – A semantics based approach. In: van der Aalst, W.M.P., Benatallah, B., Casati, F., Curbera, F. (eds.) BPM 2005. LNCS, vol. BPM, pp. 252–267. Springer, Heidelberg (2005)
14. Pesic, M., Schonenberg, H., Van der Aalst, W.M.P.: Declare: Full support for loosely-structured processes. In: EDOC, pp. 287–287 (2007)
15. Rinderle, S., Reichert, M.: Data–driven process control and exception handling in process management systems. In: Martinez, F.H., Pohl, K. (eds.) CAiSE 2006. LNCS, vol. 4001, pp. 273–287. Springer, Heidelberg (2006)
16. Riano, D.: The SDA model: A set theory approach. In: CBMS, pp. 563–568 (2007)
17. van der Aalst, W., et al.: Process mining manifesto. In: Daniel, F., Barkaoui, K., Dustdar, S. (eds.) BPM Workshops 2011, Part I. LNBIP, vol. 99, pp. 169–194. Springer, Heidelberg (2012)
18. Rozinat, A., Zickler, S., Veloso, M., van der Aalst, W.M., McMillen, C.: Analyzing multi-agent activity logs using process mining techniques. In: Distributed Autonomous Robotic Systems, vol. 8, pp. 251–260. Springer (2009)

Adapting the Fact-Based Modeling Approach in Requirement Engineering

Yan Tang Demey

European Space Agency/ESTEC,
Keplerlaan 1, P.O. Box 299, NL-2200 AG Noordwijk, The Netherlands
yan.tang@esa.int

Abstract. Requirement Engineering plays a key role in developing complex space systems successfully. How to achieve efficient and effective information exchange during the whole life cycle of a space system is a challenge, which can be tackled by realizing *semantic interoperability* between involved partners (as presented in ECSS-E-TM-10-23A [1]). Using academic works related to fact based modelling (FBM), the European Space Agency (ESA) has initiated the development of a new knowledge management system (called Fact-based Modeling Unifying System or FAMOUS) to provide means to tackle semantic interoperability. The Agency has also organized an international working group of FBM experts to support this objective. In this paper, two Requirement Engineering use cases currently developed at ESA will be presented: one related to requirement analysis for spacecraft on-board software and the other one to requirement management for human spaceflight missions.

Keywords: Fact-based Modeling, Information modelling, Requirement Engineering, Semantic Interoperability and Ontology Engineering.

1   Introduction

The Fact-based Modeling (FBM, www.factbasedmodelling.org) approach, originated in Europe in the 1970s, is a "conceptual approach for modelling, transforming and querying information where all facts of interest are represented in terms of attribute-free structures known as fact types" [2].

FBM is a formal language based on First Order Logic. It combines *graphical* notation, which makes it easy for modelers to express and visualize information and textual *verbalization* for depicting models into formal requirements that can be validated by the domain experts (not expert in conceptual modelling) prior to constitute the specification baseline of any customer/supplier contracts.

FBM is *conceptual*, addressing the semantics without precluding any implementation issues. Using FBM, modelers capture the needs from the stakeholders (i.e. the Customer) without constraining the resulting model to any technologies or solutions (e.g. UML or relational).

Though FBM marks a line between conceptual and implementation issues, the latter is not neglected either. FBM includes methods of transforming conceptual

R. Meersman et al. (Eds.): OTM 2014 Workshops, LNCS 8842, pp. 65–69, 2014.

models to lower-level structures for implementation. Suppose we want to have an information system containing a relational database management system (RDBMS) and exchange its content with others using XML in compliance with an interface control document (ICD) expressed as a XML schema (XSD), one can transform the FBM conceptual model into 1) a relational logical model and related SQL DDL for instantiation, and 2) a hierarchical logical model and related XSD, for exchanging.

Following the classical three-layer structure suggested in [3] (i.e. conceptual, logical and physical layers), FAMOUS provides the means to model in FBM and transform, in both directions, a conceptual model into the following two sets of models: 1) logical models (e.g relational, hierarchical, object oriented; 2) physical models (e.g. SQL and XMI for data repositories, but also XSD or man machine interface (MMI) specifications for users (humans or computers).

In addition, FBM also provides methods for transforming conceptual models to procedural programming code (e.g. in C++ and C#).

In the remaining of this paper, we will illustrate two use cases: one is about ontology-based requirement analysis for spacecraft on-board software in Sec. 2 and the other is requirement management for human spaceflight missions. Sec. 3. Conclusion and vision will be illustrated in Sec. 4.

2   Use Case 1: Ontology-Based Requirement Analysis for Spacecraft On-Board Software

Following the ECSS-E-ST-40C standards [4] [5], software resides at all levels of a space system, ranging from system functions to firmware. The standards can be viewed as a process model of software development in different project phases (i.e. 0, A, B, C, D, E and F). The customer derives requirements, which (in case they are not the requirements at the lowest level) break down at various levels in different phases. Every time when new requirements are derived, we shall ensure the *completeness* and *consistency* of the requirement and the requirement breakdown. Moreover, according to [6], we shall also ensure the *unambiguity, verifiability, modifiability* and *traceability* of requirements.

In order to achieve requirements of high quality, we first need to look into the source of a requirement, which is the set of semantic elements used by the functions of space system software. Since a decade ago, a reference on-board software architecture called OSRA has been discussed intensively in ESA's annual workshop on Avionics Data, Control and Software Systems (ADCSS, http://adcss.esa.int). This reference architecture is based on the definition of software architecture given by Bass et al. [7] – "The software architecture of a program or computing system is the structure or structures of the system, which comprises software components, the externally visible properties of those components, and the relationship among them..." Precisely speaking, OSRA is to realize the "visible properties" and the "relationship" in this definition.

OSRA consists of two sub-structures – *static* and *dynamic*. The static structure describes how functions, components (also called 'parts') and assemblies of software system are structured and dependent on each other. System hierarchy, interfaces and usage are modeled in the static structure. The dynamic structure involves active objects, such as tasks, processes and threads. A mapping between the static and dynamic structures needs be established.

Since FBM is capable of modeling both static and dynamic domain concepts, it provides an excellent tailoring facility of establishing this mapping. Taking into an account that FBM is conceptual, we can ensure the *unambiguity, consistency* and *completeness* of requirements realized by FBM's formalism methods, constraints checksum methods and derivation rules.

Another important characteristic provided by FBM to OSRA is the textual verbalization, with which we can map the requirements written in a natural language to formal expressions that can be defined using First-Order Logic or Description Logic, and vice versa. It ensures a requirement to be *verifiable*. The *Modifiability* and *traceability* are ascertained by the versioning methods in FBM.

Furthermore, the vision is to provide the engineers in charge of writing requirements with a toolset guiding them towards the elicitation of verified requirements, i.e. semantically correct with regard to the domain and knowledge of space systems.

3 Use Case 2: Requirement Management for Human Spaceflight Missions

A challenge in ESA's projects concerning human spaceflight missions beyond Low Earth Orbit (LEO) is to deal with nominal and *off-nominal* situations *autonomously*. The idea of involving ePartners (i.e. personalized crew support systems that are ubiquitous and maybe wearable) in astronaut-automation teams has been introduced and gradually getting mature in the campaigns of MARS-500[1], Mission Execution Crew Assistant project (MECA[2]), and now Human ePartner Agent Robot Teaming project (HEART).

In MECA-HEART, ePartners help a crew on a spaceflight mission with more effective collaborative operations by a social and cognitive solution based on a rich knowledge base. With the support of ePartners, the crew can understand contextualized constraints in a better way in order to cope with unexpected, complicated and potentially hazardous events.

The knowledge base of MECA-HEART contains the following components:

- Ontologies at different levels (i.e. an infrastructure ontology at a global level and domain ontologies) that are modeled in FBM. The ontology at the global level can contain, for instance, user and user-task context model. A domain ontology can be, e.g., a shared cognitive system infrastructure model or a requirements baseline model.

---

[1] http://www.esa.int/Our_Activities/Human_Spaceflight/Mars500
[2] http://www.esa.int/Our_Activities/Human_Spaceflight/
Concordia/Experiments_2012-2013

- Data models, that are derived from the ontologies. For example, logical relational database models can be generated from the requirements baseline model.
- Datasets, which are the population of the data models, or, comply with the data models. Furthermore, the data from a dataset that complies with a data model can as well be annotated with domain ontologies.
- Process models (e.g. business process models, FBM derivation rules) that are properly annotated with the ontologies.

FBM is used to model the MECA-HEART ontologies and data models. Following the three-level FBM triangle architecture (i.e. meta-model level, model/schema level and instance/data level), instances in one triangle can be at the schema level of another. In MECA-HEART, this principle is applied to deal with complicated domains, such as requirements management.

The design specification of MECA-HEART requirements management consists of core functions and requirements that elaborate on these core functions [8]. Each design specification is derived, iteratively evaluated and refined accordingly. A cognitive system shall satisfy a set of requirements, each of which belongs to one or more *requirements baseline*s that are contextualized and organized by *use case*s. A requirement is justified by some *claim*s, which can be measured.

Together with this social, iterative and human-centric cognitive method of design specification, FBM provides methods of establishing relations between these key concepts, which can be further developed as linked models, each of which corresponds to a concept definition. Moreover, how to deal with semantics under the Open World Assumption in FBM tackles the challenge of coping with unexpected, complicated and potentially hazardous events.

4   Conclusion

In this paper, we have illustrated two use cases currently developed at ESA that are:

- used to demonstrate the power of FBM for capturing the stakeholder needs, transforming them into a formal specification that can be validated prior to contracting any suppliers;
- used to support the development of FAMOUS by acknowledging the ESA needs and ensuring that all required capabilities are implemented within FAMOUS.

Acknowledgement. Mr J.L. Terraillon is responsible for the OSRA development; Mr M. Wolff for the MECA-HEART; Mr S. Valera for FBM and FAMOUS. The work is supported by the internal research fellowship financed by the European Space Agency.

References

1. ECSS: Space System Data Repository ECSS-E-TM-10-23A. ESA/ECSS, Noordwijk (2011)
2. The FBM Working Group: Fact-Based Modelling Metamodel: Exchanging Fact Based Conceptual Data Models. Standardization Internal Report, European Space Agency, Nederlands (2014)
3. Abiteboul, S., Hull, R., Vianu, V.: Foundations of Databases. Addison-Wesley (1995)
4. The S/W Working Group: Space Engineering - Software ECSS-E-ST-40C. ECSS, Noordwijk (2009)
5. The S/W Working Group: Space Product Assurance - software product assurance ECSS-Q-ST-80C. ECSS, Noordwijk (2009)
6. IEEE: IEEE Recommended Practice for Software Requirements IEEE Std 830-1993. IEEE (1993)
7. Bass, L., Clements, P., Rick, K.: Software Architecture in Practice, 3rd edn. Addison-Wesley (2012)
8. Westera, M., Boschloo, J., van Diggelen, J., Koelewijn, L., Neerincx, M., Smets, N.: Employing Use-Cases for Piecewise Evaluation of Requirements and Claims. In: Proceedings of the 28th Annual European Conference on Cognitive Ergonomics, New York, pp. 279–286 (2010)

Model-Based LCA for Sustainable Energy-Production from Olive-Oil Production: An Italian Agricultural-District Case

Francesca Intini[1,*], Gianluca Rospi[1], Silvana Kuhtz[1],
Luigi Ranieri[2], and Michele Dassisti[3]

[1] Dipartimento delle Culture Europee e del Mediterraneo (DiCEM),
Università degli Studi della Basilicata, Matera, Italy
{francesca.intini,gianluca.rospi,silvana.kuhtz}@unibas.it
[2] Dipartimento di Ingegneria dell'Innovazione DII, Università del Salento, Lecce, Italy
luigi.ranieri@unile.it
[3] Dipartimento di Meccanica Management e Matematica, Politecnico di Bari, Bari, Italy
michele.dassisti@poliba.it

Abstract. Renewable energy sources will play in the years to come a central role in moving the world onto a more secure, reliable and sustainable energy path. In this paper the case of an Italian power plant fed from biomass (de-oiled pomace and waste wood) is discussed for an agricultural district. The optimal operating conditions are addressed by setting up an information model for the improvement of accuracy of estimation of the potential of biomass from the sustainability perspective. Criticalities of data consistency and coherence are highlighted too as a function of the systemic problem introduced by the several sources within the agricultural district.

Keywords: model based LCA, Biomass, Systems Sustainability and Thrivability.

1   Introduction

Bioenergy is a promising renewable energy option, both at present, as well as in the near- and medium-term future. It is doomed to play a crucial part in integrated systems of energy supply and to be a valuable element of a new energy mix in the near future[1].   The focus of this study is the LCA assessment to evaluate the effectiveness to use one of the most available biomass in the south of Italy, the dry olive pomace, to produce electricity. Provided the mess and the heterogeneity of data necessary, the approach adopted required to fix an informational model to assure consistency on the final results. Spain, Greece and Italy are the three main producers of olive oil amounts to about 80% of the world production [2]. The information model developed is based on a systemic approach, and it tries to finalise the data necessary to the sustainability assessment using am incremental information approach.

---

* Corresponding author.

R. Meersman et al. (Eds.): OTM 2014 Workshops, LNCS 8842, pp. 70–79, 2014.

That means, the simple database available is not enough to have an accurate estimation of sustainability of a solution: the incremental approach requires an increment of local information concenrning several aspects, in order to improve the accuracy of the analysis. In our case we will see how it has been done to evaluate the potential of biomass production form two Italian agricultural districts, namely Puglia e Basilicata, taking into account several critical factors to align information and assess the sustainability of the investment in a power plant. The model is illustrated in the following figure where there are interactions between the production system, local authorities, environmental and economic variables from specific company.

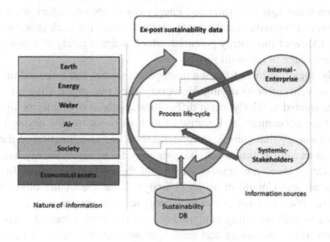

Fig. 1. Information model

2   Olive Oil Extraction Systems and Wastes Produced

2.1   State of the Art

The life cycle of extra-virgin olive oil is as follows:

i) olive trees are planted.;

ii) the soil around the roots of the trees is periodically ploughed, irrigated and fertilized and the trees and olives are also protected from pests [3];

iii) once a year, olives are harvested and transported into the processing unit where they are washed, milled and finally olive oil is extracted through centrifugation. Again, no specific tracing system is adopted so far in the traditional regions addressed: by-products energy potentials is rarely available but in statistical form. The traditional pressing system generates olive oil and two kinds of by-products: wastewater and pomace (olive husk) [4];

iv) there are two ways of extracting the oil: traditional pressing, used for many centuries with only minor modifications, and centrifugation, that the olive oil industry has taken over in the last decades. There are also two centrifugation systems, called three-phase and two-phase systems [5]. Depending on the system, waste represent different biomass nature and energy potential. Again a specific information is required from a bioenergy point of view.

v) after the extraction by pressing, a solid fraction, called olive husk, is obtained as by-product along with an emulsion containing the olive oil that is separated by decantation from the remaining olive mill wastewater. The three-phase system generates three fractions at the end of the process: a solid (olive husk or olive pomace) and two liquids (oil and wastewater). In spite of the advantages of this system compared to pressing (complete automation, better oil quality, smaller area needed) it also presents some inconveniences (greater water and energy consumption, higher wastewater production and more expensive installations). Accurate data for each process is required to have a clear view of the energy potential, which is again rarely available due to non industrialization stage of olive-oil production.

vi) tipically, the olive husk from the three-phase system had a second oil extraction with organic solvents after its drying. However, when two-phase olive mill waste was intended to be treated similarly, great difficulties appeared owing to its high moisture and carbohydrate concentration. Because of its high moisture, the drying process demands a lot of energy that significantly increases costs as a function of the nature of the crops. Such an information would be greatly useful to assess energy balances.

In the literature there are several studies on the de-oiled pomace. In particular, Masghouni et al. and Caputo et al. [6-7] analyzed the use of the olive oil industry waste as fuel to obtain thermal or electric energy through combustion.

The interest in understanding comprehensively the environmental costs and benefits of biomass use is increasing and for this reason several studies based on the life cycle assessment (LCA) approach have been published [8]. But to our knowledge none of them gives results for olive waste to energy recovery from a systemic point of view for an agricultural district .

The paper intend to provide an assessment of the environmental consequences of the energy production from de-oiled pomace in each stage of life cycle for the district addressed, utilizing the LCA methodology.

3   LCA Application to the Specific Case

3.1   LCA Study Performed

The potential environmental benefits, in terms of GHG savings that can be obtained from replacing fossil fuels with biomass sources, are one of the main driving forces for the promotion of bioenergy. Life Cycle Assessment (LCA) is an appropriate method for evaluating the GHG performance of bio-energy compared to that of fossil alternatives. The GHG balance of bio-energy systems differs depending on the type of feedstock, carbon stock changes due to land use change, transport, processing of the feedstocks and conversion technologies to produce heat or electricity.

In this study, the methodology used is the LCA technique, based on ISO 14040 and ISO 14044 (2006) to make comparisons and choose among alternatives. This assessment methodology is based on the identification of information concerning energy and materials used as well as emissions released to the environment.

The LCA study performed focuses on the environmental impacts (both direct and indirect) of the electric power plant fuelled by biomass. The plant, located in Italy, produces a gross electrical power equal to 12 MWe and the exhaust gases are utilized for the production of the steam in a closed cycle.

In this LCA study, the chosen functional unit is 1 kWh - in order to be independent of the kind of biomass and to simplify the comparison of results for different energy sources - against the other units such biomass (kg), hectare of dedicated agricultural land (ha), or km driven for transportation biofuels (km) [9].

The impact categories considered has been as follows:

• Global Warming Potential (GWP100);
• Stratospheric Ozone Depletion Potential;
• Acidification;
• Eutrophication.

The system boundary has been selected so as to take into account the phases of treatment and processing of fuel burned in the power plant. The system boundary has been defined taking into account that the input of recycled materials to a product system was included in the data set by adding the data on environmental impacts caused in earlier life cycles of the district, in the case they are considered as co-products.

The inputs are allocated on the various production steps according to defined procedures. Allocation between different grades, such as organic/non organic or extra virgin/virgin olive oil, shall be based on product volume or mass [10]. Allocation for the co-product pomace has been made by value because it is destined for further process by a pomace factory for the production of pomace oil and dry pomace (fuel).

SimaPro 7.2.3 was used as a supporting tool in order to implement the LCA model and carry out the assessment [11]. The analysis uses the database Ecoinvent 2.2 [12].

As reference processing cycle, the virgin pomace, co-product of the olive oil mill production, undergoes drying and extracting pretreatment, is then transformed in the de-oiled pomace: this is qualified as a renewable fuel according to the Italian normative Decree 152/06. As district strategy scenario, the virgin pomace is produced in the plant near the site of energy plant, so that the impact of the transport is zero. With the extraction process of virgin pomace, the products are:

• olive-pomace oil obtained from olive pomace previously dried by extraction with solvent;
• exhausted pomace, which consists of dry pomace, residue of the extraction process of olive-pomace oil.

3.2   From Residues to Energy

The phase of the olive oil production involves the extraction of oil from olives; this process is carried out in mills that use the traditional method for pressure or the method of extraction by centrifugation. This process produces the olive pomace, olive oil and wastewater to recycling. In Table 1 the inventory per 1 kg of the olive pomace is illustrated.

Table 1. Input-output table of the milling process

INPUT	Unit	Quantity
Olive	kg	1
Water	kg	0.4
Electricity	kWh	2.6
OUTPUT		
Olive oil	kg	0.15
Virgin pomace	kg	0.35
Wastewater	kg	0.7
Olive Waste	kg	0.2

For the application of the allocation principle the following prices are considered:

- olive pomace: 70,00 €/t
- olive oil: 12,00 €/kg;
- vegetable water: 0 €/t.

According to this, the allocation is equal to 99% for the olive oil.

The pomace drying process reduces the humidity to about 10% by applying a hot air current. The objective of the drying is to block the fermentation processes in the virgin pomace and further allow the extraction of pomace oil. Table 2 shows values per kg of the dry pomace.

Table 2. Input-output table per 1 kg of the dry pomace

INPUT	Unit	Quantity
Virgin pomace	kg	2
Fuel	kg	0.15
Electricity	kWh	0.03
OUTPUT		
Steam	kg	1
Exhaust gases	kg	0.14
Ash	kg	0.006
Dry pomace	kg	1

Hexane is used for the extraction of oil contained in dry pomace. Before the extraction process, the process of distillation of the pomace oil separates the hexane from the oil and allows the sale of the pomace oil in the market. Table 3 shows the inventory per kg of the finished product.

Table 3. Input-output table of the oil extraction process

INPUT	Unit	Quantity
Dry pomace	kg	1
Heat	kWh	0.18
Electricity	GWh	0.03
Hexane	kg	0.001
OUTPUT		
Steam	1	kg
Exhaust gases	0.14	kg
Ash	0.006	kg
Dry pomace	1	kg

The biomass energy recovery plant includes some non-hazardous waste. In particular energy recovery (heat or electricity) from residues of oil production represents a step towards to the environmental objectives of reducing wastes of the agriculture sector. The exhausted pomace is characterized by a low calorific value of 4000 kcal/kg and by a low content of nitrogen and sulphur. The advantages of products with high energy content are: the reduction of mass and volume of solid waste, the reduction of pollutants and the potential recovery of energy that can be sold. It is clear that the quality of the energy content and waste pollution is strongly dependent on the process above the final treatment. Information on these elements are critical to the final process as well as on the amount of energy derivable.

In the process in analysis the impact of the wood waste transport was measured. In one year there are 1335 trips with an average distance of 100 km. The data were obtained from the company for the year 2009 and shown in Table 4 together with the inventory per MWh of produced electricity. In the energy plant, the low process temperature avoids the post-heating of the exhaust gases.

Table 4. Input-output table of the biomass energy recovery plant

INPUT	Unit	Quantity
De oiled pomace	kg	541
Waste wood	kg	342
Air	Sm^3	4224
Urea	kg	1
water	m^3	0.1
transport	km	1.36
OUTPUT	Unit	Quantity
Electricity	MWh	1
exhaust gases	kg	796
water	m^3	0.097
Ash	kg	88

The impact assessment is reported in Table 5, in term of functional unit of 1kWh.

Table 5. Life Cycle Assessment: the indicators of principal environmental impact categories, with 1 kWh as functional unit

Impact category	Unit	Total (1 kWh from de oiled pomace)
Acidification	g SO_2 eq	0.342
Eutrophication	g PO_4^{3-} eq	0.126
Global warming (100-year)	kg CO_2 eq	0.0748
Ozone layer depletion (20-year)	mg CFC-11 eq	0.0117

4   Information Model for Assessing the Sustainability of Biomass in the Apulia Area

4.1   The Methodological Approach

The methodological approach used is divided into the following stages following the information model developed:

- selection of crop species which, from a preliminary analysis of available data from agriculture department, seem to be of most interest for the Apulia Region and for the assessment of the related agronomic requirements;
- collecting the data from local sources needed to characterize the specific land (soil characteristics, climate, use and land cover, topography, administrative boundaries). The information model take cares of coherence of these local data with regional one to improve the estimation process;
- based on previous data, development of land suitability maps for each energy crops with preliminary estimate of the areas considered most suitable and possible amount of biomass available.

There are two principal types of organic fraction of MSW, each with physical, chemical and biological processes that influence the energy transformation: one coming from unsorted waste by mechanical separation; one coming from the separate collection of large users; one coming from the separate collection of households.

The calculation of the biogas will be made available with the following logic:

- the tables ISTAT (5° general census of agriculture) will read the area planted with olive trees for each municipality affected by our analysis;
- in practice is considered, given the structure of the land and trees, planted about 120 trees/ha knowing that you get a productivity of about 30 kg olive/tree* year. It is therefore known that the productivity of olive groves in the area in question is about 3600 kg olive/ha*year;
- the virgin pomace is about 45% of the olive harvest;

- as regards the pomace (humidity 17%), its availability is equal to 1.17 of olive pomace.

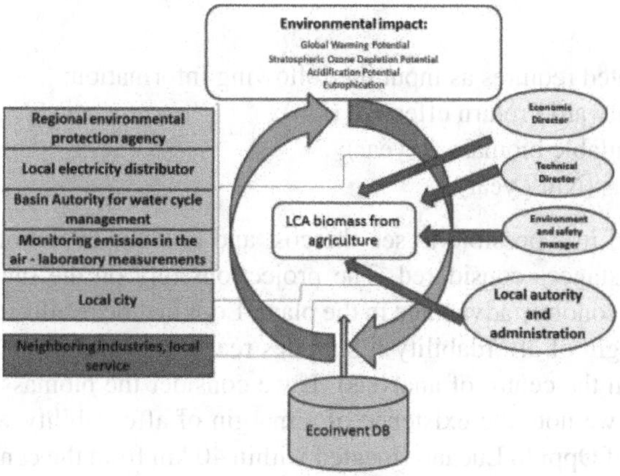

Fig. 2. Information model – case study

The value of the constant kinetics of degradation, which measures the speed with which the material decomposes, has been chosen equal to 0.8 whereas the pomace as putrescible organic material. This constant allows us to calculate, along with the efficiency of uptake, the amount of biogas producible in one year. The first of the coming out from the information model phase is consists in estimating the energy that can be produced from the amount of biomass available and therefore the layout of the anaerobic digestion. Obviously, the dimensioning will be influenced by the type of biomass considered (that influence the producibility of biogas) and by technology in analysis. The model is based on the following data: availability of biogas, net calorific value of biogas, net calorific value of natural gas (kWh / Nm ^{3}), cogeneration electrical efficiency, cogeneration thermal efficiency, hours of operation per year (h / year). From this information it is possible to size the CHP needed to production of electrical and thermal energy at district level. Note this information, determine the flow of biogas and methane necessary to ensure continuous operation and thus allows to set the strategy at district level to determine out how much methane will need to purchase to compensate for any lack of biogas.

4.2   System Design

To structure the model of economic analysis, it is necessary to size the entire anaerobic digestion plant in order to assess the potential costs and revenues. In our application case, we sized the anaerobic digestion plants with a minimum size of 2000 m^3 for biogas from manure beef and buffalo, 4000 m^3 of the residue from biogas, and 1500 m^3 for biogas from biowaste. These data were derived from a systemic analisys at distric level.

The economic data selected for the model are as follows (excluding governmental incentives):

- Revenues;
- Cost;
- Investment.

The model created requires as input the following information:
- the distance outward / return effective (km);
- quantity of available biomass (t/ year);
- available biogas (Nm³/ year).

From the model it is possible to see the cost and revenue evolution projections in function of the distances considered. The projections rely on the range of distances where there is an economic advantage in the plant. Looking the results it is clear that the manure has a margin of affordability if supplies reach the town of Garaguso (located within 35 km from the centre of analysis). If we consider the biomass represented by pomace olive oil, we note the existence of a margin of affordability when the supply reaches the town of Oppido Lucano (located within 40 km from the centre of analysis). Considering the organic fraction of municipal solid waste, we realize that there is a degree of convenience for the first two municipalities surrounding the centre of analysis.

Obviously these evaluations are substantially affected by the amount of biomass that each common adds to the considered cumulative.

5   Conclusions

LCA methodology was applied to evaluate the environmental performance of the recovery of olive oil sector residuals and wood waste at district level trhough an ad-hoc information model to improve the efficiency of the sustainability analysis performed.

Bioenergy chains which have residues as raw materials show the best LCA performances, since they avoid both high impacts of dedicated crop production and the emissions from waste management.

The estimation approach proposed could be useful to public decision-makers with an higher degree of accuracy than the classical LCA approach. In particular in our case this was done to understand the areas in which the conditions are favourable for the development of a chain of biogas based on local biomass.

References

1. Ladanai, S., Vinterbäck, J.: Global Potential of Sustainable Biomass for Energy, SLU. Swedish University of Agricultural Sciences Department of Energy and Technology, Uppsala (2009)
2. Ioannis, S.A., Aikaterini, K.: Olive Oil Waste Management: Treatment Methods and Poten-tial Uses of Treated Wast. In: Waste Management for the Food Industries, pp. 453–568. Academic Press, Amsterdam (2008)
3. Avraamides, M., Fatta, D.: Resource consumption and emissions from olive oil production: a life cycle inventory case study in Cyprus. Journal of Cleaner Production 16(3), 809–821 (2008), doi:10.1016/j.jclepro.2007.04.002

4. Allegra, C.: Audit energetico-ambientale della filiera olivicola: applicazione in campo ad un frantoio. In: Graduation Thesis, Private Communication (2005)
5. Roig, A., Cayuela, M.L., Sanchez-Monedero, M.: The use of elemental sulphur as organic alternative to control pH during composting of olive mill wastes. Chemosphere 57(9), 1099–1105 (2004), doi:10.1016/j.chemosphere.2004.08.024
6. Masghouni, M., Hassairi, M.: Energy applications of olive-oil industry by-products: I. The exhaust foot cake. Biomass and Bioenergy 18(3), 257–262 (2000), doi:10.1016/S0961-9534(99)00100-2
7. Caputo, C., Scacchia, F., Pelagagge, P.M.: Disposal of by-products in olive oil industry: waste-to-energy solutions. Applied Thermal Engineering 23(2), 197–214 (2003), doi:10.1016/S1359-4311(02)00173-4
8. Hennig, C., Gawor, M.: Bioenergy production and use: Comparative analysis of the eco-nomic and environmental effects. Energy Conversion and Management 63, 130–137 (2012), doi:10.1016/j.enconman.2012.03.031
9. Carpentieri, M., Corti, A., Lombardi, L.: Life cycle assessment (LCA) of an integrated biomass gasification combined cycle (IBGCC) with CO2 removal. Energy Conversion and Management 46(11-12), 1790–1808 (2005), doi:10.1016/j.enconman.2004.08.010
10. Environdec: Product Category Rules Virgin Olive Oils and its Fraction (2010), http://www.environdec.com/PCR/Detail/?Pcr=5934
11. PRè Consultants: SimaPro 7.2.3, Database manual – methods library (2010), http://www.pre.nl/
12. Ecoinvent: The Swiss Centre for Life Cycle Inventories, Ecoinvent V2.2 (2010)

Forecasting Industry Big Data with Holt Winter's Method from a Perspective of In-Memory Paradigm

Sudipto Shankar Dasgupta[*], Prabal Mahanta,
Rupam Roy, and Ganapathy Subramanian

SAP Labs India Pvt. Ltd., EPIP Zone, Brookefield, Bangalore, KA 560066, India
{sudipto.shankar.dasgupta,p.mahanta,
rupam.roy,ganapathy.subramanian}@sap.com

Abstract. Industrial data in time series exhibit seasonal behavior like demand for materials for any Industry and this call for seasonal forecasting which is of considerable importance for any planning for an industry as the business profitability revolves around the decisions based on the results of forecasting. This paper tries to explore the situations in the business industry domain which concentrates on the analysis of seasonal time series data using Holt-Winters exponential smoothing methods and along with this exploration the paper tries to optimize most of the intermediate stage for detailed analysis using in-memory database and sql techniques.

Keywords: Holt-winters, exponential smoothing, principal component analysis, ARIMA, periodic AR, in-memory, sql, SAP-HANA®.

1 Introduction

Analysis of data starts with selection of a model after time series data has been captured, this makes it very crucial as there are several statistical models available for this particular step which basically is followed by the technique where graph sequence plots of the time series is done and forecasted and this steps provides the visual impression of the nature of the time series alongside depicting the behavioral components in the series. The model selection step includes the selection of input variables, equation of relationship and estimating the parameter values in the equation and the verification of the model using measures such as MAPE (Mean Absolute Percentage Error), RSE (Relative Square Error), and MSE (Mean Square Error). Now overall the general assumption of time series would be a combination of a certain pattern and some random error [8][9][10][15].

From an analyst perspective, this task is very cumbersome and due diligence is required to accurately measure and come up with the seasonal and daily patterns wherever applicable but the task is bound to be error prone due to human intervention that is introduced. This paper will present a way to come around this problem and will

---

[*] Corresponding author.

R. Meersman et al. (Eds.): OTM 2014 Workshops, LNCS 8842, pp. 80–85, 2014.

help the analyst to reach his numbers accurately specifically for businesses exploring their data using Holt-Winter's Algorithm [1].

2   Concept Discussion

Most of the business domain experts generally deal with data for the intention of finding seasonality pattern of sales of the products and this is represented as time series data which is assumed to repeat after a certain period say N [11][12][13][14].

For an industry dealing with the sales of woolen garments would see seasonal spike during winter season in any region and so would a paint manufacturing company would see rise in sales during non-rainy season. So basically depending on the industry in case study the seasonality would be defined and this may be additive or multiplicative. In this paper we concentrate on the most popular multiplicative model which can be represented as:

$$Data_t = T_t \times S_t \times R_t \tag{1}$$

Here T_t , S_t and R_t are called the trend, seasonal and residual effects respectively.

Now if we realize for a visualization perspective for any time series data we can crunch for monthly tourist arrivals in Bangalore from Period X to Period Y if represented as the figure 1 would suggest the model required would be multiplicative.

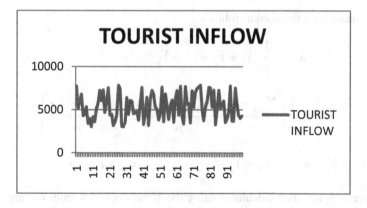

Fig. 1. Tourist inflow in Bangalore for Period X=1 to Period Y=100

Another important parameter that we have to consider is the Seasonality Index of a period which indicates how much this period typically deviates from the annual average. At least one full season of data is required for computation of SI.

The stage of performing forecasting requires stationary conditions to be configured and this can be done via First Order where expected value of X(t) remains same for all t and Second Order Stationary where if it is first order stationary and covariance is between X(t) and X(s) and is function of length (t-s) only [3].

Exponential smoothing technique is a procedure for continually revising a forecast in the context of recent events and in this technique it assigns exponentially decreasing weights as the events become aged [2].

The Holt-Winters model uses a modified version of exponential smoothing where it applies triple exponential smoothing formulae to the time series which can be local average value for the series, trend smoothing and lastly seasonal sub series smoothing which are represented by the following equations:

$$a_t = \alpha(Y_t - s_{t-p}) + (1-\alpha)(a_{t-1} + b_{t-1}) \tag{2}$$

$$b_t = \beta(a_t - a_{t-1}) + (1-\beta)b_{t-1} \tag{3}$$

$$s_t = \gamma(Y_t - a_t) + (1-\gamma)s_{t-p} \tag{4}$$

where:
α, β and γ are the smoothing parameters
a_t is the smoothed level at time t
b_t is the change in the trend at time t
s_t is the seasonal smooth at time t
p is the number of seasons per year

Initial values are calculated as follows:

$$a_p = \frac{1}{p}(Y_1 + Y_2 + \ldots + Y_p) \tag{5}$$

$$b_p = \frac{1}{p}\left[\frac{Y_{p+1} - Y_1}{p} + \frac{Y_{p+2} - Y_2}{p} + \ldots + \frac{Y_{p+p} - Y_p}{p}\right] \tag{6}$$

$$s_1 = Y_1 - a_p, \quad s_2 = Y_2 - a_p, \quad \ldots, \quad s_p = Y_p - a_p \tag{7}$$

The forecasts are then calculated using the latest estimates from the appropriate exponential smooth output that have been applied to the series [5][6][7].

3   Methodology

We analyzed sales data from a top product manufacturing company where the data had upward trend together with seasonal variation and this size is proportional to the local mean level and this suggested for the multiplicative approach.

Now we could have analyzed the data using fixed power transformation value by a manual process but instead we pushed the data in the table into the memory and on top of the in-memory table we applied heuristics to calculate the optimal power transformation where variance of the transformed data stabilized the parameter value.

Now the issue of the performance of the approach also requires evaluation and observation for the out-of-sample forecasts and the coverage in terms of prediction intervals for the sales data set. We choose to use SAP-HANA® [16][17] database which offers both column store, in-memory paradigm and in built Prediction libraries for this study.

Now we know that both multiplicative and additive models with variations can be used to model the data in non-adaptive and adaptive techniques so we developed a sql procedure that parses the data and tries to fit the data to both the models and the respective techniques and outputs the result in the form of the optimal technique and model to be used.

For the non-adaptive technique data of the first two years is used for building the model and the criterion used for selection of parameters is MAPE and the past data is not required in the memory while for the adaptive technique, where original parameters are defined using the data of the first two years and parameters are adjusted after every two years.

The objective of the exercise was to find the unique values of alpha, beta and gamma based on the product and location hierarchy. The feature of the method is to automate the values of the smoothing parameters i.e. α, β and γ to vary in steps of 0.1 with the condition of varying the smoothing parameters while keeping one of the parameters constant. So we will have a lookup tables for each combination of smoothing parameters for each product-location hierarchy.

After we configure the lookup tables, we push the same to in-memory and then we compute the demand output for all the combinations. This way we have an exhaustive list of demand output values for various combinations of smoothing parameters in a specific product-location hierarchy and out of which we choose the best trend and seasonality combination and this helps us to plan better.

SAP-HANA® [17] provides us with the opportunity to explore the row and column store perspective of the database and itself being an engine provides us with the pre-dictive libraries and a complex computation calculation engine.

To explore the architecture we start feeding seasonal data into the algorithm and then the calculation engine using the predictive algorithm in this case Holt Winters computes the seasonality and applies smoothing utilizing the input parameters like periodicity and smoothing parameters α, β and γ. The calculation engine then calculates the demand output using combination of smoothing parameters which is used as a lookup for the calculation engine and the output is recorded and archived for further analysis.

4   Observation and Conclusion

As a part of the exercise we performed the optimization using SAP-HANA® [16] column store in memory parallelization on a custom hierarchy data. The following were the exercise observation:

- Data Points: 121 * 7 for the location based profit center hierarchy
- Iteration: 729 for combination of smoothing parameters

For smoothing parameters, the step size was 0.1 varying from 0.1 to 0.9.

The lookup for iteration was designed with the intention of keeping two smoothing parameters constant and varying one for the specified step size of 0.1 from the value of 0.1 to 0.9 so forming the 729 iterations.

Now the data set for profit center is prepared with location specific which is a custom SAP hierarchy and for this the dataset had 121 specific centers each for 7 different locations.

We feed this data into the calculation engine to the Holt winter's method algorithm and for a specific center and region combination we get the forecasted sales value at 39 seconds flat for average runs.

The experiment reveals that after using the methodology and the in-memory technique for parallelization we can perform the operations within seconds and for the same purpose the industry domain experts suggested that it takes up to 20-25 days to come up with the best sales prediction for combination of smoothing parameters.

This will help the industry to scale out their solutions for larger data sets and get better insights to their data. To extend this research we have begun to research on the datasets that are non-SAP formats and minimize the data cleaning, formatting and calculation in the process of computing predictive values for different business domains and using different techniques.

Acknowledgement. The authors would like to thank their colleagues for the immense support and motivation during this research and they would like to convey their regards to Abdul Razack for his guidance throughout the research.

References

1. Yar, M., Chatfield, C.: Prediction intervals for the Holt-Winters forecasting procedure. International Journal of Forecasting 6, 127–137 (1990)
2. Bote, D.: Exponential smoothing with missing observations and outliers. In: Šafránková, J. (ed.) Proceedings of the 6th Annual Conference of Doctoral Students, Part I. Faculty of Mathematics and Physics, pp. 30–36. Charles University of Prague (1997)
3. Cipra, T.: Some problems of exponential smoothing. Apl. Mat. 34, 161–169 (1989)
4. Gardner, E.S.: Exponential smoothing: the state of the art. Journal of Forecasting 4, 1–28 (1985)
5. Montgomery, D.C., Johnson, L.A.: Forecasting and Time Series Analysis. McGraw-Hill, New York (1976)
6. Ratinger, T.: Seasonal time series with missing observations. Appl. Math. 41, 41–55 (1996)
7. Wright, D.J.: Forecasting data published at irregular time intervals using an extension of Holt's method. Manage. Sci. 32, 499–510 (1986)
8. Bowerman, B.L., O'Connell, R.T., Koehler, A.B.: Forecasting. Time Series, and Regression. Thomson Books Cole (2005)

9. Brockwell, P.J., Davies, R.A.: Introduction to Time Series and Forecasting. Springer, New York (2002)
10. Brubacher, S.R.: Time series outlier detection and modeling with interpolation. Bell Labatories Technical Memo, Murray Hill, NJ (1974)
11. Kotsialos, A., Papageorgiou, M., Poulimenos, A.: Long-term sales forecasting using Holt-Winters and neural network methods. Journal of Forecasting 24 353-368 (2005)
12. Makridakis, S., Wheelwright, S.C., Hyndman, R.J.: Forecasting, Methods and Applications, 3rd edn. Wiley (1998)
13. Siegel, A.F.: Robust regression using repeated medians. Biometrika 68 242-244 (1982)
14. Winters, P.R.: Forecasting sales by exponentially weighted moving averages. Management Science 6, 324-342 (1960)
15. Yohai, V.J., Zamar, R.H.: High breakdown estimates of regression by means of the minimization of an efficient scale. Journal of the American Statistical Association 83, 406-413 (1988)
16. Franz, F., et al.: SAP HANA database: data management for modern business applications. ACM Sigmod Record 40(4), 45–51 (2012)
17. Vishal, S., et al.: Efficient transaction processing in SAP HANA database: the end of a column store myth. In: Proceedings of the 2012 ACM SIGMOD International Conference on Management of Data. ACM (2012)

Routing in OPC-UA with Rosa Overlay Network[*]

Tuan Dang[1], Dragutin Brezak[2], and Patrick Bellot[2]

[1] EDF Research, Chatou, France
[2] Telecom ParisTech, Paris, France
tuan.dang@edf.fr, {brezak,bellot}@telecom-paristech.fr
http://www.cluster-connexion.fr

Abstract. We present a new Transport mechanism for the OPC-UA middleware. This mechanism, based on an overlay network, allows to find a new route for OPC-UA packets in case of routing failure.

1 The Middleware OPC-UA

In 1995, a standard technique was proposed to enhance the interoperability of industrial systems. This technique was named OPC (OPC means OLE for Process Control) and is now a trademark of the OPC Foundation. OPC describes architectures and communications between a client and a server processing data from instrumentation devices. This specification is named OPC-DA (Data Access). It was bound to Microsoft Windows since it requires OLE (Object Linking and Embedding) combined with COM and DCOM (COM: Component Object Model, DCOM: Distributed COM). Several other standard techniques such as OPC-A&E (Alarm & Events) or OPC-HDA (Historical Data Access) followed. Thanks to the need for industrial standards at that moment and to the pervasive use of Microsoft Windows in plant floor, the world of automation and process industry has widely accepted these specifications.

In 2006, the OPC Foundation begins to release the new OPC-UA [1] standard. OPC-UA (UA means Unified Architecture) is not restricted to a single operating system such as Windows or Linux. OPC-UA is based on W3C standards and uses TCP/IP to be compatible with Ethernet environments. It is interoperable, designed to operate between different operating systems provided they implement the same profile. The OPC-UA specifications have been unified with a single server having a unique address space containing all objects of an OPC-UA server. We will not give the description of objects [1, Part 3] nor the way they are used to implement the information model [1, Part 5]. Let us just say that the address space may contain variables which values are bound to an external device acting as a server for input (such as a sensor) or for output (such as an actuator) or both.

---

[*] This work is founded by the *Cluster CONNEXION* project, a French *Investissement d'avenir* project running from march 2012 to march 2016. The goal is to make nuclear power plants more competitive and sustainable with advanced technologies.

R. Meersman et al. (Eds.): OTM 2014 Workshops, LNCS 8842, pp. 86–90, 2014.

The server proposes many base services classified into service categories. The first categories allow the client to open a session to the server. Then, other categories of services can be requested when we are in a session to provide:

- OPC-DA (Data Access) that allows the client to read and write attributes of all variables (and other objects) in the address space;
- OPC-HDA (Historical Data Access) that allows the client to maintain and consult the history of any attributes of any objects in the address space;
- OPC-A&E (Alarms & Events) that allows the client to set conditions and alarms and to subscribe to them through a Publish-Subscribe scheme, it uses the notion of monitored items and subscriptions that are first-class objects;
- OPC-UA Methods that can be seen as software routines linked to some *Method* objects;
- and finally, there are query services that allow the client to explore the address space in many ways; this can be used, for instance, by automatic configuration management tools.

2 The Layered Architecture of OPC-UA

In OPC-UA specifications, the messages corresponding to all these services, either request or response messages, are abstractly specified. They can be implemented in many programming language. In the architecture of OPC-UA, the server/client softwares assume they get the messages written in their programming languages. The client software builds its request message and it gives it to the so-called stack. The stack takes the message, serialises it, secures it and sends it to the server. On the server side, the message is processed by the stack: it is received, its security is checked and it is deserialised to get a message to be processed by the server software. What is important in this architecture is that only the stack is concerned with serialisation, security and transport.

The specifications define two ways for serializing. The message can be translated in binary (UA-Binary) or in a dialect of XML (UA-XML). The specifications define several ways for securing messages. Messages can be encrypted, signed or both of them, or none. And the algorithms for encrypting and signing, as the length of the keys for that, are also specified. Finally, the specifications define two ways for transporting the messages : UA-TCP and HTTP/SOAP. Theoretically, we can replace each of these layers by an equivalent one.

3 The Overlay Network Rosa

Rosa [2], Robust Overlay network with Self-Adaptive topology, is a distributed overlay network developed at Telecom ParisTech. The primary purpose of Rosa is to automatically recover from underlying network failures and to route messages even if the path between two nodes is interrupted. If the usual routing path between two nodes is interrupted, Rosa automatically finds another route if such a route exists, all without interference of the end user.

Used in its routing algorithm, a Distributed Hash Table (DHT) is built over Rosa. This DHT is resilient in the sense that an association is stored in all the nodes of what is called a lump (this term is defined later). By taking advantage of the features from both Rosa and DHT, new services like resilient routing service and distributed file storage service can be implemented. Consequently, this makes Rosa competitive. It could be put right next to the other well known overlay networks with similar characteristics such as Chord and Kademlia.

Rosa consists of mutually connected nodes, directly or indirectly, representing physical elements and paths from the underlying network. They are organized in clusters called lumps. Every node is a part of at least one lump and all nodes within one lump form a complete graph. That means that each node within one lump is interconnected with all others nodes of the lump. Rosa can be represented as an entanglement of lumps. One of the most spectacular aspect of Rosa is its automatic management of lumps.

To allow an efficient routing and searching in Rosa, lumps are arranged into a chain structure, also known as chain of lumps (CoL), that allocates subintervals of interval $I_{init} = [0, 2^{64}[$. If compared to a real chain, each lump always has at least two neighbours, one predecessor and one successor. Moreover, lumps can have additional neighbour lumps if one of its member node is also a member of another lump, that is neither predecessor nor successor. These neighbours are considered to be shortcuts in the chain of lumps. The last lump in the chain of lumps is connected to the first one to complete a circle.

The structure of Rosa is shown in Fig. 1. We see at the bottom the underlay IP network. Then above, we see the lumps grouping nodes together. And at the top, we see the CoL. Note that the first and last lumps have a node in common.

Every lump has what is called a resilient threshold and nodes leave or join other lumps to maximise the overall resilient threshold. The resilient threshold of a lump is defined as as the minimal number of failures on the elements of the virtual links of the lump that are mandatory to isolate a node of the lump from the others. If the number of failures is less than the resilient threshold, there exists a path between any two nodes of the lump. The management of lumps will tend to increase the thresholds of lumps.

During Rosa's operations, the order of lumps in the chain structure might change due to the automatic reconfiguration process or due to network failures. Bigger lumps could absorb smaller lumps or could separate into two lumps. To ensure a stable operation of Rosa, we enforce the following constraints: all subintervals from interval I_{init} are allocated; every lump has at least one common node with its predecessor and at least one common node with its successor; and finally each lump has allocated at least one subinterval. It is mandatory that first two conditions are met all the time, whereas the third condition ensures efficiency and load-balancing over the lumps.

Rosa overcomes several limitations that often come with overlay networks. First, it has been proven that it is scalable. It is able to cope with any number of nodes without loosing any relevant data and without overloading the network. The complexity of the routing algorithm in Rosa is $O(N)$ where N is the number

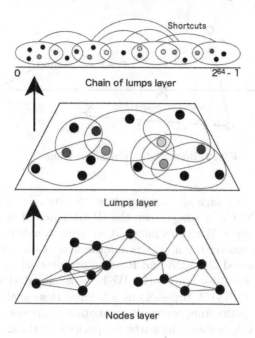

Fig. 1. Rosa structure

of lumps. Due to a Small Worlds phenomenon, it is probable that an efficient number of shortcuts per nodes will lead to an extremely fast routing of $O(1)$. In order for this to work, there should approximately be 2.3 shortcuts per lump, though a mathematical proof has not been made. As often in the case of the Small Worlds paradigm, only simulations have been made.

The current implementation of Rosa is totally new. We have reimplemented the resilient threshold with a more efficient algorithm [3]. We have also reimplemented lumps joining, splitting and absorption operations with new strategies. With this implementation, we have overcomed some of the current limitations [2].

4   A New Transport Layer for OPC-UA

We consider only UA-TCP. Messages are described in [1, Part 6]. For interoperability reasons, there is no sender nor receiver information in messages. This is clearly because OPC UA does not want to be bound to a type of network. When using socket over an IP network, the sender can be taken from the socket itself. And the receiver is of course the node that receives the messages.

Now, let us assume that the Transport layer of OPC UA failed to send a message to the destination. Then the message has to be transported using Rosa. That means that the packet will go through some relays to bypass the failures, see Fig. 2. With such a path, not handled using IP routing, we will have no information about the sender at the receiving node and no information about the receiver at any intermediate node. Thus, we have to add this information (sender

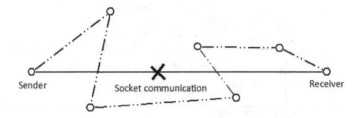

Fig. 2. Rosa roads to bypass a failure

and receiver) to the message and to drop it at the arrival. The Rosa message will contain the OPC UA message, then the IP address and port of the sender and those of the receiver. With this information, Rosa is able to route the OPC UA message and to recover the necessary information at the arrival.

We have implemented OPC-UA and Rosa on our network at Telecom Paris-Tech with nodes on several sub-networks. We have measured what happens with a generic 5 minutes OPC-UA transactions set. Since Rosa is always reconfiguring itself, the Rosa paths from one node to another is always changing. When we switch to OPC-UA routing, the paths for packets go through 3 to 5 nodes. Moreover, the time for executing the 5 minutes transactions set becomes 25 minutes with Rosa routing on. Using the emergency Rosa routing takes around five times more than UA-TCP. That is the price we have to pay for robustness.

5   Conclusion

Because of licensing concerns, we have implemented our own but still incomplete C++ version of OPC-UA using the OPC Foundation specifications [1]. The merge with Rosa, as described above, has been made. The result is an OPC-UA implementation which security and safety of routing are higher than an ordinary OPC-UA over IP. It can be used in critical environments where the continuity of operations is crucial. Of course, the continuity of operations is done at the expense of any kind of QoS since the message has to go through an unknown path to reach its destination.

References

1. OPC UA Specification, Part 1 to Part 12, Release 1.01 (February 2009)
2. Baud, L.: ROSA: un réseau de recouvrement adaptable, auto-organisant et extensible. PhD thesis, Telecom ParisTech, Paris (France) (2010)
3. Stoer, M., Wagner, F.: A Simple Min-Cut Algorithm. Journal of the ACM 44(4), 585–591 (1997)

Reporting Optimizations with Bill of Materials Hierarchy Traversal in In-Memory Database Domain Using Set Oriented Technique

Sudipto Shankar Dasgupta[*], Prabal Mahanta,
S. Pradeep, and Ganapathy Subramanian

SAP Labs India Pvt. Ltd., EPIP Zone, Brookefield, Bangalore, KA 560066, India
{sudipto.shankar.dasgupta,p.mahanta,pradeep.s,
ganapathy.subramanian}@sap.com

Abstract. Customers with production environment with massive customization in their logic leads to the challenge of traversing the Bill of Materials data hierarchy and its effective management for real time reporting which is required to accommodate diverse operations. There are various techniques to streamline the process of reporting but in present scenario, customers are doing it in batch processing manner and the reports are generated for past data and the tools and techniques used require human intervention. This paper comes up with effective in-memory database technique to traverse the complex BOM data hierarchy and facilitate in real time reporting. This not only helps the customer to customize their databases and have complex hierarchies but also helps in real time reporting which facilitates the customers to have insights to their business in real time with the advantage of streamlining their past and present performances and predict the future performances to edge the competition. The experiment was done with a top FMCG company data which provided us with the insights of de-complicating the traversal stage in an in-memory database paradigm leading to faster reporting times.

Keywords: Algorithms, SQL, Column Store, using SAP-HANA®, Optimization.

1   Introduction

Data warehousing has been one of the most crucial applications of any of the databases in existence and with the vast expansion of the data in the open world and also in the enterprise domain, it has become important to find new techniques to accelerate reporting. The fundamental data structure which prevents accelerated operations is hierarchy [1] and recursion which in enterprise data management is considered fundamental.

From manufacturing and supply chain management perspective, where planning process is heavily dependent on traversal of Bill of Material, it becomes a necessary

---

[*] Corresponding author.

R. Meersman et al. (Eds.): OTM 2014 Workshops, LNCS 8842, pp. 91–95, 2014.

optimization requirement to traverse the data structure efficiently enough to facilitate responsive reporting mechanism. The hierarchy data structure which comprises of parent child relationship is also one of the major forms of representation in the area of human capital management [6], project management where optimal scheduling [1] requirement exists. If we represent the hierarchy data structure then to a general extend it can illustrated as done in Fig.1.

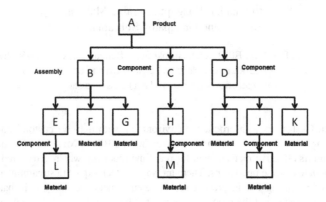

Fig. 1. Example for Structure of Bill of Materials [1]

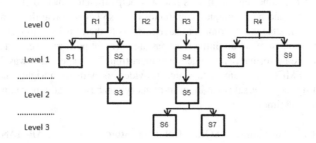

Fig. 2. Bill of Materials with multiple root node

Algorithms like Adjacency list, Path enumeration, Nested sets, Transitive closure are the generic methods to exploit the problem of hierarchical data traversal. When we explore the sql domain, then we can find that direct algorithms like Warshall's Algorithm [2] and Warren's algorithm [3] are explored where we have to choose the optimal processing order but with the study by Agarwal et al [9] this mode of execution can be excluded and there are also multiple studies on optimization of set based recursive queries by Carlos Ordonez [6]. The room for improvement exists using SQL recursion in columnar database where there are limited work done including Christian Tinnefeld et al , where they propose that the data representation is with pre order and post order encoding[1] which proposes a data model different from parent child data representation. This paper involves study of parent child hierarchy data traversal in column store with set based sql recursions in column store. For the study, SAP

HANA in memory database has been used which provides the option to persist data in both row store and in memory column store [7].

2   Discussion

According to Garwood,1988, BOM defines "items or raw materials that go into the product" and from referring to Cox et al.(1992) BOM (Bill of Materials) is emphasized as a "list of all subassemblies, intermediate parts, and raw materials that go into a parent assembly showing the quantity of each required to make an assembly" [3][4][5]. Material Requirement Planning and detailed scheduling involves computation of material requirements for each of the sub assembly and components for the requirement at a top level material [8]. The process of BOM explosion computes the total quantity requirement on each material based on a single unit requirement of all the individual materials. Now this calls for optimally traverse the hierarchy so that reduce the computation time and in turn accelerate the reporting mechanism so as to have a greater and in-depth insights on the business data and take management decisions or financial investments. To prove that reporting time can be reduced significantly experiments were done in a SAP-HANA® SP7 system installed in SUSE Linux 11 with a hardware configuration of 1 TB RAM and 40-core processor on a top FMCG company data where there were 6 levels with input sizes varying from 250k to 1 million records and output size varying from 1000 to 10000 for each input size. For the set based traversal linear recursive algorithm (set based hierarchy traversal) is used. This involves queries of the form where R and T can be considered as tables with j and i rows respectively:

$$R = R \cup (R \bowtie T) \qquad (1)$$

The result of $R \bowtie T$ gets added to R itself. Since R is joined once with T recursion is linear. Table R is joined with T based on some comparison between R:j and T:i. [10]. In this paper equi-join (R: j = T:i) predicate is considered.

The number of iteration passes would be same as the navigation level (λ). Hence the execution time T can be represented as:

$$T \propto \lambda \qquad (2)$$

The results are compared with tuple based direct access algorithm.

3   Experiment Results

With different values of level, for row store the execution time is consistently higher compared to column store. The execution time for level 3 it is almost double in row store compared to column store. For column store the execution time linearly increases with increase in level.

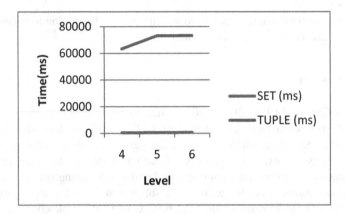

Fig. 3. Average Execution time in ms for Set Based algorithm and Tuple based algorithm for different Levels with fixed input size and output size

The execution time for Set based algorithm is significantly less compared to Tuple based algorithm for the same input size and output size.

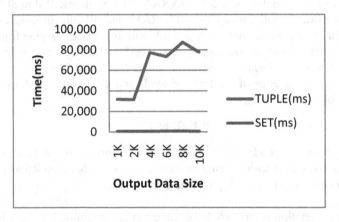

Fig. 4. Average Execution time in ms for Set Based algorithm and Tuple based algorithm for different output sizes with fixed input size and level (6)

The execution time for Set based algorithm is significantly less compared to Tuple based algorithm for the same level and output size.

4   Observation

The figures 3 and 4 reveal that the set based algorithm as explained in previous sections is considerably faster compared to when it comes to handling the BOM hierarchy traversal in SAP-HANA® column store. On an average the execution times is more than 100 times faster for the same input size , output size and levels in Set based approach compared to Tuple based approach. Hence it can be concluded that set based algorithm is more effective for hierarchical BOM data traversal in enterprise data. This allows faster reporting times and near real time reporting.

Acknowledgments. The authors would like to thank their colleagues for the immense support and motivation during this research and they would like to convey their regards to Dr. Vishal Sikka, Abdul Razack for their guidance throughout the research.

References

1. Tinnefeld, C., Wagner, B., Plattner, H.: Operating on Hierarchical Enterprise Data in an In-Memory Column Store
2. Papadimitriou, C.H., Sideri, M.: On the Floyd–Warshall algorithm for logic programs. The Journal of Logic Programming 41(1), 129–137 (1999)
3. Adam Drozdek's Data Structures and Algorithms in C++, p. 173. PWS Publishing (1996)
4. Ordonez, C.: Optimization of linear recursive queries in SQL. IEEE Transactions on Knowledge and Data Engineering 22(2), 264–277 (2010)
5. Abadi, D.J., Samuel, R., Madden, N.: Column-Stores vs. Row-Stores: How different are they really? In: Proceedings of the 2008 ACM SIGMOD International Conference on Management of Data. ACM (2008)
6. Data in an In-Memory Column Store, Carlos Ordonez Optimization of Linear Recursive Queries in SQL
7. Knolmeyer, G., Mertens, P., Zeier, A., Dickersbach, J.: The SAP HANA Database – An Architecture Overview
8. Supply chain management and advanced planning-—basics, overview and challenges
9. H Stadtler - European journal of operational research–Elsevier (2005)
10. Agarwal, R.C., Aggarwal, C.C., Prasad, V.V.V.: A tree projection algorithm for generation of frequent item sets. Journal of Parallel and Distributed Computing 61(3), 350–371 (2001)
11. Carlos Ordonez, Optimization of Linear Recursive Queries in SQL

Cloud and Trusted Computing 2014 PC Co-Chairs Message

Welcome to the Cloud and Trusted Computing 2014 (ex-DOA), the fourth International Symposium on Cloud Computing, Trusted Computing and Secure Virtual Infrastructures, held in Amantea, Italy.

This year the conference extends its scope, explicitly incorporating Cloud Computing. Cloud Computing is establishing itself as "the" paradigm for software consumption, boosted by low-entry barriers, and economic convenience. At the same time, with users losing of control of infrastructure, Cloud Computing is raising major trust, security and privacy challenges such managing user personal information, verifying secure configurations or assuring reliable performances.

This conference provides an ideal forum for discussion between these two, diverse, but interconnected communities: Cloud Computing and Security and Trust. All submitted papers passed through a rigorous selection process. In the end, we decided to accept 6 regular papers and 2 short papers, with a good mix of contributions from academic and industrial researchers.

Organizing a conference like C&TC is a team effort, and many people need to be acknowledged: First, we would like to thank the authors, whether or not their papers were accepted, for having chosen C&TC to present their work. They provided the high-quality content and the discussion topics, which are the essence of our event. Second, we would like to acknowledge the dedicated work of the experts in the field from all over the world who served on the Program Committee. Thirdly, we would like to thank our keynote speaker Ernesto Damiani from University of Milano. Finally, we would like to thank the whole OTM team for its support, patience and guidance. These proceedings are the result of the hard work that everyone has put into C&TC14. We hope that you enjoy them.

September 2014

Michele Bezzi
Henry Chan

Re-Identification Risk Based Security Controls

Francesco Di Cerbo* and Slim Trabelsi

Product Security Research, SAP Labs France
805, Av. du Docteur Maurice Donat
06250 Mougins, France
francesco.di.cerbo@sap.com

Abstract. Companies are taking more and more advantage of cloud architectures for their IT systems. By combining private and public cloud resources, it is possible to facilitate data submissions by customers and processing with third parties, among other advantages. But this represents also a potential threat to personal data's privacy and confidentiality. Even if legal obligations regulate the usage of personal data, for example requiring to disclose them in anonymised form, users do not have any visibility or control on data disclosure operations, nor on anonmymisation policies used by companies. To this extent, we propose a solution to establish and enforce data-centric security policies, in order to enable secure and compliant data processing operations. Our proposal is particularly fit for cloud architectures as it supports multiple actors with different roles, responsibilities and obligations. We also present a use case to demonstrate the peculiarities of our proposition.

Keywords: Privacy, Re-identification Risk Assessment, Anonymisation, Access Control, Usage Control.

1 Introduction and Motivation

Large organizations store and process huge quantities of personal data about their customers or collected during their activities. They often have to disclose datasets containing users' private information to third parties for data analysis, application testing or support. Cloud services are often used for data collection, processing and sharing operations, as part of their growing importance in enterprise IT architectures. Besides the recognised technical advantages of cloud services [7,3], their adoption poses a number of questions about the privacy and legitimate use of personal data. The multi-tenancy of cloud infrastructures as well as complex cloud service composition paradigms (e.g. a PaaS cloud provider that makes use of the services of a IaaS provider) may lead to a difficult understanding of actors involved in data processing and thus to an uncertain accountability and doubts about the privacy of user's personal information.

To preserve data confidentiality and comply with privacy regulations, as legally prescribed for many markets [1,19], specific guidelines must be followed by

---

* Corresponding author.

R. Meersman et al. (Eds.): OTM 2014 Workshops, LNCS 8842, pp. 99–107, 2014.
© Springer-Verlag Berlin Heidelberg 2014

companies and their associates. For instance, personal data disclosures may require specific anonymisation operations.

However, users do not have means to verify that such guidelines are indeed applied, neither by companies nor by their associates and cloud providers/operators.

To address this situation, we propose a security mechanism focussed on enforcing on each single piece of information, specific security policies consisting of access and usage control directives. Our mechanism lies on the cloud, thus regulating data accesses from any party, be them users, companies or their partners and could operators. In particular, our proposal takes advantage of a quantitative evaluation of the re-identification risk (privacy metrics) that may help to estimate the privacy exposure of users' information associated to data disclosure operations. Users are then empowered to indicate specific risk thresholds for allowing the usage of their data. Our mechanism is able to enforce this constraint against any requester, on top of other possibly applicable prescriptions.

Access and usage control policies are required in our mechanism to make machine readable and enforceable the considered privacy prescriptions; for example by expressing the anonymisation constraints related to a data release or sharing. These policies should express access control restrictions based on re-identification risk thresholds and limit but also express 'after-the-fact' usage conditions, for example authorising and regulating subsequent sharing operations performed by data recipients, imposing to notify the data owner on certain circumstances and so on. Without such policies, shared datasets can escape from the controls imposed by privacy regulation policies and expose individuals data to re-identification by correlating several data sources. Associating re-identification risks to the access and usage control policy constraints may help to prevent against data leakage.

With this strong association it becomes possible for users to maintain a certain control on the usage of their data and personal identifiable information (PII [1]), and for companies to increase the accountability of their associates and cloud providers.

The paper is structured as follows: Sect. 2 introduces the main concepts connected to usage control and data anonymisation, Sect. 3 details the mechanism's architecture, Sect. 4 depicts a use case scenario involving medical data and finally 5 concludes the paper.

2 Related Work

2.1 Usage Control

Usage Control can be defined as an extension and generalization of standard access control, introducing concepts such as continuity of control or mutability of subjects and objects attributes. Compared to access control, usage control has a broader scope as it applies not only on the access time but through the whole period of object usage. Moreover, in terms of the type of information being protected, UCON covers the scopes traditionally assigned to access control models or DRM, but also adds means of privacy protection. This allows to employ it in situations where a central entity needs to protect sensitive information, as well as in reversed scenarios, where the users provide personal data to a service provider and want to control how their data is used.

Among the different usage control model definitions, the UCON ABC model, proposed by Park and Sandhu [10] is worth of mention, for the important number of papers it influenced. Pretchner et al. [11] propose an advancement of the usage control model to comprise distributed architectures and their associated threats, using a centralist approach to control resource utilisation.

2.2 Privacy through Data Anonymisation

The HIPAA Privacy Rule [19] establishes three means for publishing confidential medical records, called Safe Harbor, Limited Dataset and Statistical Standard. The Safe Harbor prescribes a set of attributes (identifiers, quasi- identifiers and traceable information) that must not be transmitted to any third party. The Limited Dataset standard foresees an agreement with two institutions for sharing patients data, with specific obligations for the receiving party for excluding any patient re-identification activity. The Statistical standard permits data sharing operations in any format, provided an expert certifies that the risk is very small that the information could be used by the recipient, alone or in combination with other reasonably available information, to identify an individual . Similarly, the European Data Protection Directive[1] permits the use of personal data in anonymous form, implying that "'account should be taken of all the means likely reasonably to be used either by the controller or by any other person to identify the said person"' (the data subject).

Malin et al.[6] analyse HIPAA Privacy Rule, underlining its openness to re-identification risks, and suggesting a number of strategies and measures to diminish it, like for instance the adoption of anonymisation methods like k- anonymity. However, no concrete guidelines are provided for adopting them, also in consideration of the very diverse medical data that may be shared and their many different usages (e.g. DNA sequences are complex to anonymise preserving individuals privacy but at the same time avoiding ambiguities or errors in subsequent data analysis phases).

Murphy and Chueh[8] propose an anonymisation mechanism based on addition or subtraction of small random values to the results of aggregative operations on dataset attributes. However, such method can be prone to re-identification attacks based on repeated requests of the same aggregated information of the same dataset to estimate the mathematical characteristics of the anonymisation function, and thus to reconstruct the true results of anonymised operations. In a subsequent work, Murphy et al. [9] use the anonymisation mechanism described before as part of an infrastructure for sharing medical data among medical entities (i2b2) and performing data analysis. While such infrastructure allows data sharing operations in a controlled way, no access control mechanisms or policies are part of the proposed infrastructure.

Kamateri et al.[4] propose a Linked Data solution (LiMDAC) for sharing medical data among different organizations while at the same time enacting access control directives on datasets. Such solution relies on different models for describing access control directives defined by data providers, and for representing data client profiles. Access control decisions are made by analysing the different pieces of information provided by means of the two models. However, patients do not have any control on prescribing the robustness of any anonymisation methods to be applied on their data, and LiMDAC requires medical records to be already anonymised by data provider entities before entering the solution.

3   Architecture

A simplified architecture diagram of our mechanism is depicted in Fig. 1. Only the main actors have been indicated: users, a dataset owner and a dataset requester.

The mechanism receives two sets of input:

- Recordsets from users, submitted together with specific security policies (called '*sticky policies*', as they are always bound to their data).
- Anonymisation policies (P) for the dataset composed by all user-submitted recordset; anonymisation policies are defined by dataset owners.

The mechanism aggregates all received recordsets in a dataset X and can return an anonymised dataset $P(X)$ in response to a request submitted by the dataset requester.

Our mechanism relies on two main components, one responsible for the enforcement of access and usage control directives on data (the PPL Engine or Data Handling [13]) and the other for computing the re-identification risk and executing data anonymisation operations (the DB Anonymizer[14]). Both components have been developed and made available under the umbrella of the EU initiative FI-WARE[1] as Open Source Software. The mechanism also comprises a database/storage service (referred as 'DB' in the figure).

The enforcement component relies on the PPL Engine [17]. Besides offering traditional access control characteristics (RBAC), it is responsible for applying usage control measures on protected data, for example by enforcing obligations stated in sticky policies when certain triggers like temporal intervals or information accesses occur. More details on PPL Engine and Data Handling are presented and discussed in the previously referenced documents. Sticky policies are defined by means of XACML[2] and PPL[15,18], two specifications relying on XML.

The current mechanism supports sticky policies (expressed using XACML and PPL specifications) able to specify an arbitrary threshold for re-identification risk as part of XACML rule and functions. Listing 1.1 provides an example of such policy: the AuthzDownstreamUsage element permits to distribute further the data protected by the sticky policy (identified by XACML Resource

---

[1] http://www.fi-ware.org

tags, not shown here) provided that they are anonymised with a maximum re-identification risk of 0.2 (defined using function reidentificationrisk).

Listing 1.1. Extension to XACML and PPL to consider re-identification risk

```
<sp:Attribute ...>
...
 <ppl:AuthzDownstreamUsage allowed="true" matching="true">
  <ppl:Policy PolicyId="RB66KbOBef5apYwFZrJ6"
   RuleCombiningAlgId="...">
  <xacml:Target>
   <xacml:Rule Effect="Permit" RuelId="Rule_ReIdentification_Risk">
    <xacml:Condition>
     <xacml:Apply
      FunctionId="function:double-less-than-or-equal">
      <xacml:AttributeValue
       DataType="http://www.w3.org/2001/XMLSchema#double">0.2
      </xacml:AttributeValue>
      <xacml:EnvironmentAttributeDesignator
       AttributeId="sap:usagecontrol:attributeid:reidentificationrisk"
       DataType="http://www.w3.org/2001/XMLSchema#double"/>
     </xacml:Apply>
    </xacml:Condition>
   </xacml:Rule>
...
```

The re-identification risk and anonymisation component implements an algorithm [16] to evaluate statistically the re-anonymisation risk, combining k-anonymity [12] and the Shannon entropy uncertainty estimation. A deeper discussion of the algorithm and its characteristics can be found in the referenced paper. The component is also in charge of anonymising datasets according to a policy. Anonymisation policies essentially describe semantically a dataset structure and express for each attribute whether it will be anonymised (and how) or not. A simple anonymisation policy is presented in [14].

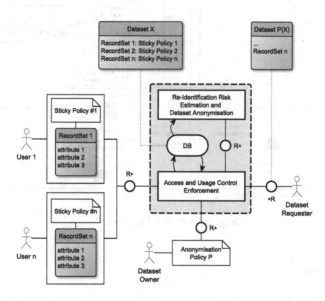

Fig. 1. High-level Architectural View

The business logic of the mechanism can be described as for the following Fig. 2. As a first step, users define a data security policy for submitting their data to an entity (for this reason referred as "'dataset owner"'). When requesters ask to access the dataset records, they specify one of the anonymisation policies P made available by the dataset owner. Access to protected data can be granted to requesters only in accordance with directives stated in each recordset's sticky policy. Therefore, the re-identification risk for policy P is computed, and this value is used in evaluating the sticky policy conditions. Subsequently, all sticky policies of concerned recordsets are evaluated in order to create a response for a requester. As part of the conditions to be verified, users can state in their policy specific re-identification risk thresholds for permitting access to their data. Other conditions are related for instance to the access purpose specified by a requester or specific obligations to be fulfilled. The mechanism decides for each recordset whether it will be part of the response dataset. After the policy evaluation activity, the filtered dataset $P(X)$ is obtained as result of the anonymisation operation using policy P.

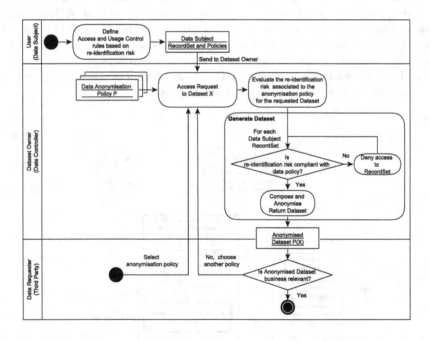

Fig. 2. Activity Diagram

4   Use Case

For exemplifying the usage of our mechanism, let us consider the following scenario, illustrated in Fig. 3. The patients of an hospital submit their personal

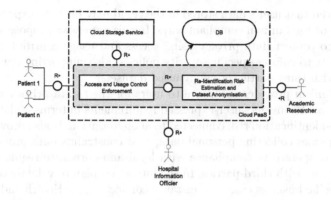

Fig. 3. Use Case

data (identity but also medical information) for the purpose of receiving medical cares. The hospital can legitimately use these data according to such purpose. However, it can also be in the need of sharing them with third parties, like other hospitals and academics for participating to a research project; it is possible for the hospital to do so, provided that personal data are 'adequately' anonymised, as seen in previous Sect. 2.2. The hospital uses the services of a cloud PaaS provider to host a part of its software. In our example, the PaaS provider offers also storage and database service on top of its application execution facilities[2].

Our mechanism permits to provide an increased privacy assurance to patients and at the same time, to ensure a compliant information consumption of hospital's data. Patients can specify a threshold for the re-identification risk in the case their data are used for other purposes than those initially approved, thus complementing with an objective criterion the legal protection guarantees. The hospital can ensure that datasets given to third parties are appropriately anonymised also with respect to privacy requirements expressed by patients.

The mechanism can protect data privacy also without relying on specific cloud provider privacy assurances. It is possible for instance to encrypt patients' data (not necessarily the sticky policies) before storing them on the cloud, and this can be done also for database data (see for instance [5]). It is to remark that with these measures, mechanism stakeholders can be protected also in the case of complex cloud compositions that can be used by the cloud PaaS provider to deliver its services.

5 Conclusions

Cloud services offer valuable services for companies to simplify, extend and improve their offering to end users and with business partners. However, concerns

---

[2] An example of such PaaS provider can be for instance SAP HANA Cloud,
http://www.sap.com/pc/tech/cloud/software/
hana-cloud-platform-as-a-service/index.html

may arise given that user's data stored in the cloud may be more exposed to privacy threats or used in non compliant ways. In this paper, we propose a security mechanism to protect data privacy using access and usage control functionalities. It permits to enforce specific security policies, also supporting data sharing operations with third parties of anonymised datasets.

Our mechanism provides assurance to users for their data privacy and compliant usage, as it considers user-expressed requirements in terms of data access, usage and re-identification risk connected to anonymisation. It also provides benefits to companies collecting personal data, as it constraints data processes and treatments to operate in compliance with legal and corporate regulations also when interacting with third-parties. In the future, we plan to validate our mechanism in specific business cases, for instance connected to e-Health and business intelligence applications. That would allow for considering and evaluating possible support tools, for instance to help users in choosing their re-identification risk thresholds according to best practices and/or legal requirements for specific use cases and situations.

Acknowledgements. This work is partially supported by project Coco Cloud (FP7-ICT-2013-10, grant no: 610853, URL:www.coco-cloud.eu).

References

1. European Parliament. Directive 95/46/EC of the european parliament and of the council of 24 october 1995 on the protection of individuals with regard to the processing of personal data and on the free movement of such data. Technical Report EUR-Lex - 31995L0046, European Parliament (November 1995)
2. Godik, S., Anderson, A., Parducci, B., Humenn, P., Vajjhala, S.: OASIS eXtensible access control 2 markup language (XACML) 3. Technical report, OASIS (2002)
3. Jansen, W., Grance, T.: Guidelines on security and privacy in public cloud computing. Technical Report NIST SP 800-144, National Institute of Standards and Technology (December 2011)
4. Kamateri, E., Kalampokis, E., Tambouris, E., Tarabanis, K.: The linked medical data access control framework. Journal of Biomedical Informatics 50, 213–225 (2014)
5. Kerschbaum, F.: Searching over encrypted data in cloud systems. In: Conti, M., Vaidya, J., Schaad, A. (eds.) SACMAT, pp. 87–88. ACM (2013)
6. Malin, B., Karp, D., Scheuermann, R.H.: Technical and policy approaches to balancing patient privacy and data sharing in clinical and translational research. Journal of Investigative Medicine: The Official Publication of the American Federation for Clinical Research 58(1), 11–18 (2010), 00046 PMID: 20051768
7. Mell, P., Grance, T.: The NIST definition of cloud computing. Technical Report NIST SP 800-145, National Institute of Standards and Technology (September 2011)
8. Murphy, S.N., Chueh, H.C.: A security architecture for query tools used to access large biomedical databases. In: Proceedings of the AMIA Symposium, pp. 552–556 (2002), 00059 PMID: 12463885

9. Murphy, S.N., Weber, G., Mendis, M., Gainer, V., Chueh, H.C., Churchill, S., Kohane, I.: Serving the enterprise and beyond with informatics for integrating biology and the bedside (i2b2). Journal of the American Medical Informatics Association 17(2), 124–130 (2010)
10. Park, J., Sandhu, R.: The UCON ABC usage control model. ACM Transactions on Information and System Security (TISSEC) 7(1), 128–174 (2004), 00158
11. Pretschner, A., Hilty, M., Basin, D.: Distributed usage control. Communications of the ACM 49(9), 39–44 (2006), 00784
12. Samarati, P., Sweeney, L.: Protecting privacy when disclosing information: k-anonymity and its enforcement through generalization and suppression. Technical report, Technical report, SRI International, 00705 (1998)
13. SAP. the FI-WARE Data Handling Generic Enabler, http://wiki.fi-ware.org/FIWARE.OpenSpecification.Security.Data_Handling_Generic_Enabler (accessed on June 25, 2014)
14. SAP. the FI-WARE Database Anonymizer Generic Enabler, http://wiki.fi-ware.org/FIWARE.OpenSpecification.Security.Optional_Security_Enablers.DBAnonymizer (accessed on June 25, 2104)
15. Trabelsi, S., Njeh, A., Bussard, L., Neven, G.: The ppl engine: A symmetric architecture for privacy policy handling. In: W3C Workshop on Privacy and data usage control, vol. 4 (2010)
16. Trabelsi, S., Salzgeber, V., Bezzi, M., Montagnon, G.: Data disclosure risk evaluation. In: Kalam, A.A.E., Deswarte, Y., Mostafa, M. (eds.) CRiSIS, pp. 35–72. IEEE (2009)
17. Trabelsi, S., Sendor, J.: Sticky policies for data control in the cloud. In: 2012 Tenth Annual International Conference on Privacy, Security and Trust (PST), pp. 75–80. IEEE (2012)
18. Trabelsi, S., Sendor, J., Reinicke, S.: Ppl: Primelife privacy policy engine. In: 2011 IEEE International Symposium on Policies for Distributed Systems and Networks (POLICY), pp. 184–185. IEEE (2011)
19. U.S. Department of Health and Human Services. Standards for privacy of individually identifiable health information, final rule. Technical Report 67(157), 53182–53273, Federal Register (2002)

Obligation Based Access Control

Laurent Gomez and Slim Trabelsi

SAP Product Security Research
Mougins, France
{laurent.gomez,slim.trabelsi}@sap.com

Abstract. Access control systems can be categorized in two classes:
stateless or stateful. While stateless access control systems consider only
current state of the system for access decision, stateful access control
integrates past and current state of the system. The state of the system can change depending on the way how resources were used. We also
observe that stateful access control systems strongly rely on centralised
state monitoring infrastructure. In the context of distributed systems,
state monitoring is very difficult to achieve, both for security and technical reasons. In this paper, we propose to use obligation execution proof
to evaluate current distributed system state. Data usage conditions are
defined as obligations expressing the actions that must be executed before or after granted access. In this paper, we aim at fostering distributed
access control enforcement relying on certified obligations.

Keywords: Access control, obligation, distributed systems.

1 Introduction

Access control rules or policies specify the conditions that must be fulfilled by
a subject (e.g., user, service, machine) in order to access a resource (e.g., file)
to perform an action (e.g., read). In the context of distributed systems, such as
mobile network, access control represents a major security challenge. Considering the lack of trust in distributed entities, enforcement of access control on is a
crucial security issue. Access control systems can be categorized in two classes:
stateless or stateful. Stateless access control systems consider only current state
of the system for access decision, while stateful access control integrates past
accesses. Even though stateless access control systems prevail, stateful access
control remains crucial and mandatory for environments where the access and
the usage control are complementary to comply with security and privacy regulations and laws. Stateful firewall is the most popular stateful access control
system. Based on the traffic to a machine (e.g., number of access, access attempt), stateful firewall identifies malicious traffic and block it. Least privilege
access control also falls under the stateful model. Following the least privilege
paradigm, access control engine grants subject access only to resources required
for its legitimate purpose. It keeps track of granted access, and continuously
checks if the subject reaches its maximum resource knowledge threshold. The

R. Meersman et al. (Eds.): OTM 2014 Workshops, LNCS 8842, pp. 108–116, 2014.
© Springer-Verlag Berlin Heidelberg 2014

drawback of stateful access control relies on centralised monitoring of current state of the system. In the context of distributed systems, centralised monitoring is a difficult task. It implies the establishment of a trust relationship between the access control engine and the distributed entities. In addition, in distributed systems, stateful access control systems do not monitor the use of granted resources on respective distributed entities. The way resources are used once access granted is out of its scope, and does not have any influence on future access control decisions. For example, access is granted to a confidential file, and the subject shares it with an untrusted third party. It will not impact future access control decision. In fact, usage condition on a resource once access granted is not considered as valuable information in stateful access control systems. Regarding usage condition on accessed resources, access control security policy can contains usage control rules so called obligations [1]. Obligations express the actions that must be executed before or after granted access. For example, in the case of a data sharing, retention period after which a file has to be deleted is an example of obligation. We distinguish pre-obligation from post-obligation. Pre-obligation are actions to be performed before requesting access to a new resource, while post-obligation are meant to be executed once access is granted [5]. In order to cope with the lack of decentralised monitoring of system state, we propose the integration of proof of execution of obligations in a stateful access control model. We introduce the concept of obligation based access control model where a subject has to proof the proper execution of past obligations. We propose to consider obligation execution in access control rules. For that purpose, we collect and verify proof of obligation execution before granting access to resources. In the context of distributed systems, obligation based access control is a way to foster execution of obligations where the access control engine do not have any information about the past behaviour of the requesting entity. Our solution relies on the certification of obligation executions by signing proofs insuring that obligations have been properly executed. The paper is organized as follows: in section 2, we introduce our approach for obligation based access control. The latter is illustrated in section 3 in a mobile and nuclear use cases. State of the art related to obligation based access control is discussed in section 4. We then conclude this paper in section 5.

2   Our Approach

In order to foster the proper execution of obligations in distributed systems, we propose an obligation based access control. Based on executed obligations, a subject would have access to additional resources (services or data). Our proposition is to reward obligation execution. The overall process of obligation access control is illustrated in Figure 1. Following this process, once access granted to a resource, a subject has to execute several obligations. Their execution are monitored, and certified by an Obligation Certification Service. For any further request to the subject for additional resource, proof of obligations might be requested by the Access Control Engine. Request for proof of obligation execution

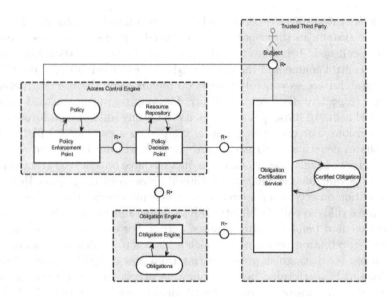

Fig. 1. Architecture

Fig. 2. Obligation based access control process

are integrated into access control rules. Therefore, a subject sends a request to an Access Control Engine to perform an action on a given resource. The Access Control Engine grants access to the subject. In addition the subject is requested to execute a set of obligations associated to the granted resource. The subject delegates the execution of the obligation to the Obligation Engine. When the Obligation Engine executes an obligation, it notifies the Obligation Certification Service in order to certify the obligation execution. When the subject requests access to a new resource to the Access Control Engine, the latter retrieves from the Certification Obligation Service proofs of proper execution of past obligations.

The overall architecture of this approach is depicted in Figure 2. The Access Control Engine is in charge of the enf orcing predefined access control policies. The Obligation Engine enforces the execution of obligations. And the Obligation Certification Service has the role to certify the execution of obligations enforced by the obligation engine. The proper enforcement of obligation based access control in distributed environment raises a major challenge: generation of obligation execution proof. The question is how to proof the execution of an obligation. In order to solve this issue, we need to establish a trust relationship between the Access Control Engine, the Obligation Engine, and the Obligation Certification Service component. Following our approach, we identify a trust domain, including the subject, the Obligation Certification Engine and its repository.

2.1   Obligation Certification

As depicted in Figure 2, obligation certification process is decomposed into three sub-steps: obligation execution, and obligation execution proof, and obligation signature. Obligation execution and execution proof are the duties of the Obligation Engine, while the certification is delegated to the Obligation Certification Service. For sake of clarity, we denote obligations as follows:

$$Obligation = \{subject,\ trigger,\ action\}$$

An obligation is an action that a subject is required to take after an event defined as a trigger. For example, the resource has to be deleted after 2 days, or the resource cannot be shared. The Trigger is based on detected events. This event can be temporal (e.g., due at a specific point of time), contextual (e.g., based on mobile device location), or any action executed on the resource (data access, modification, deletion, etc.). For further detail on obligation definition, you can refer to PPL policy definition [1].

Obligation Execution. Whenever the Access Control Engine grants access to a resource, a set of obligation is extracted from the access control policy. Those obligations are pushed to the Obligation Engine. It then monitors for any event triggering the execution of obligation stored its obligation repository. Once a trigger is reached, the obligation action has to be executed by the Obligation Engine. In the case of data retention period, the trigger is the end of period, and the action is the deletion of the resource.

Obligation Execution Proof. The Obligation Engine has to bring the proof to the Certification Obligation Engine of the proper execution of the obligation. To that respect, the Obligation Engine might have several options to proof the proper execution of an obligation on the system. Associated to the description of the obligation, the Obligation Engine might rely on snapshot of file system, application operating system log (e.g., file deleted, file not sent by an email client). To that respect, we are limited by the type of proof of execution. We denote an Obligation proof as follows:

$$Obligation\ Proof = \{Obligation,\ Proof\}$$

Obligation is the description of the obligation (including subject, action and trigger); while the Proof brings evidence that the obligation has been properly executed.

Obligation Certification. Once a proof of obligation execution is generated, it is pushed to the Obligation Certification Engine. The Obligation Certification Service is then in charge of certifying and storing the proof of obligation. After the authentication of the Obligation Engine, the Obligation Certification Service signs the obligation proof, following regular signature scheme. The latter implies the distribution of a key pair (public/private) to the Obligation Certification Service. The distribution and revocation of key pair amongst the distributed system is out of the scope of this paper. The topic has been largely addressed, and we rely on existing solutions for key distribution and revocation [2]. Once signed, the certified obligations are then stored by the Certified Obligation Repository, maintained by the Certification Obligation Service.

2.2 Obligation Based Access Control

The subject sends a request to the access control engine. The Access Control Engine evaluates the request, and finds the matching security policy with the request. If an the execution of a specific obligation is required, the Access Control Engine contacts the Certification Obligation Service or requests to the subject certified obligation proofs. After Access Control Engine authentication, the Certification Obligation Service retrieves the required obligation from the Certification Obligation Repository. The Access Control Engine checks the validity of the certified obligation. If all the access conditions are validated, subject is granted access to the resource. In this case, we update again the Obligation Engine with the associated obligation with the new granted access. Anytime, obligation triggers is raised, the matching obligation action is executed, a proof is generated and certified by the Certification Obligation Service.

3   Use Case

3.1 Mobile Data Sharing Use Case

We illustrate our approach with a mobile data sharing service. This service enables mobile user to get access to file stored on a cloud based file sharing service. This service is in charge of maintaining files, based on an access control policy defined by the file owner. A data subject shares two files:

FileA, on which the following policy is defined

```
Policy{
    Subject = ANY
    Action= ANY
    Resource = FileA.pdf
    Obligation = {after 20 minutes, DeleteFile}
    Condition (None)
}
```

With this policy, the cloud based service grants access to fileA, and the file must be deleted after 20 minutes.

```
FileB, on which the following policy is defined
Policy{
  Subject = ANY
  Action= ANY
  Resource = FileB.pdf
  Condition (CertifiedObligation(FileA.pdf deleted)
              OR (Not access to fileA.pdf))
}
```

With this access control policy, the access to fileB is restricted only to subjects that can proof that, if previously accessed, fileA has been deleted from their file system. As a proof, we use a log produced by the mobile operating system where all operations on the file system are logged. That information, together with the obligation description is certified by the Certification Obligation Service, and then store in the Certified Obligation Repository. In this use case, a user requests access to fileA. The file is stored on a her mobile phone. After 20 minutes, fileA is deleted, according to the obligation defined by fileA subject. The deletion of fileA is certified by the Certification Obligation Engine. Then, the same mobile user sends a new request for fileB. The cloud based service needs to have to guarantee that FileA has been deleted from the mobile phone. Before granting access to FileB, the cloud based service checks to the Certification Obligation Service for the following certification: CertifiedObligation(FileA.pdf deleted). In this case, the deletion of FileA has been certified by the Obligation Certification Service. As a consequence, access to FileB is granted to the mobile user.

3.2   Nuclear Plant Use Case

Nuclear plants are high sensitive and very restricted areas that require very strict and strong security controls on the data stored and processed within the buildings. In some cases, and for compliance and transparency reasons, the nuclear plans can require work with external companies for maintenance or security and safety audit. Lets assume that one of the companies is in charge of collecting radiation measures from different sensors dispatched in different areas of the building. Its role is to evaluate whether or not the radiation values are compliant with the security and safety regulations. Collecting such information represents a risk of data leakage. It can potentially give critical information related to secret procedures and technology. For that reason, before having access to radiation sensor measures, external companies agents have the obligation to delete all the data related to past security and safety audits. They can keep only final decision of the report (compliant or not). They also have to proof that they deleted all the data collected during previous audits. Then, when they proceed for a new compliance verification mission in the same nuclear plant or another one belonging to the same company, before accessing to any data, they have to provide the certified proofs that they have already deleted all the data related to past measurements. Lets assume now that the nuclear plant is divided in many areas, for every area there is a set of sensor measuring the radiation. Every day for each area the average measured value of the radiation is securely stored in a data base. The third party audit company can have access to this value but for specific areas. We can have for example a policy expressing the authorization for the Audit Company to read the radiation mean value of the day 19/05/2014 for the area L 52. Once the value accessed it should be deleted after 1 hour.

```
Policy{
    Subject = AuditCompany
    Action= Read
    Resource= AreaL52.RadiationMeasure#19052014
    Obligation = {after 1 hour, DeleteData}
    Condition (None)
}
```

Now in order to access to another measure value related to another area L 66 or to another date 19/06/2015 , the Audit Company has to proof that the data AreaL52.RadiationMeasure#19052014 he accessed in the past is deleted.

```
Policy{
    Subject = AuditCompany
    Action= Read
    Resource = AreaL52.RadiationMeasure#19062015
                    AreaL66.RadiationMeasure#19052014
    Condition(
CertifiedObligation(
        AreaL52.RadiationMeasure#19052014 deleted
)
    )
}
```

4 State of the Art

4.1 Contextual Privacy Management in Extended Role Based Access Control Model

In [2], the authors propose the integration of consent context, purpose and provisional obligation in access control enforcement. According authors definition, provisional obligations are some actions following resource access. To that extend, access is granted to the resource only when the binding obligations are executed. The authors define an obligation that specifies that location data deletion must be notified. To that respect, no access decision is based on proper execution of obligation. Rather, the authors express obligations that have to be executed before or after the access to a resource. On the contrary, we focus on the use of former obligation execution proof for access decision. In addition, we propose the certification of such obligation proof, which give some guarantee to the access control engine on the validity of this obligation proof.

4.2 An Obligation Model Bridging Access Control Policies and Privacy Policies

In [3], the authors propose an obligation model for Privacy aware Role based access control. In this paper, obligation is defined as obligation requirements specifying some other actions that must be performed sometime in order to allow a certain action to be executed now. The authors understand obligation as legal constraints (e.g., age) in order to get access to resources. While in our approach, obligation is an action that the subject is required to take after the triggering of an event. The authors provide an example of obligation. In a healthcare scenario, a physician requests access for information on a child. In order to access to that information, the physician needs consent of her parents within the next 6 days. After this period, the access to the file is rejected. While we propose to base our access control enforcement based on certified execution obligation, the authors propose to an integration of legal constraints into a role based access control model.

4.3 Obligations in Risk-Aware Access Control

In [4], authors propose a risk based access control system based on post-obligation evaluation. In their stateless access control model, the requested resource is granted only if the requestor or the context of the request is evaluated as low risk. In order to perform this risk evaluation the authors propose to ask the requestor to perform some obligation before granting him the access to the resource. The obligation is a risk evaluation challenge and the access grant is the reward when the obligation is correctly executed. In our solution we only rely on pre-obligations that happened in the past and the main advantage is the access delays. In [5], the requested has to fulfil obligations in order to access the resource, in ours the obligation are already executed and certified, the Access control engine has just to verify the proofs.

5 Conclusion

In this paper we introduced the notion of obligation based access control as an innovative way to use obligation executions proofs as authorization credentials. Our concept relies on the notion of rewarding a proper execution of obligations associated to past accessed data in order to have access to a new resource. The behaviour during the data usage is therefore regulated with obligations. These obligations are mandatory actions that must execute a data controller after accessing a data or a resource. Certified obligation execution offers a compliance proof that can be used as access token that can be used to access new resources. To the difference with other state of the art solutions we focus on pre-obligations and not post-obligations in order exploit all the past behaviour of the user as guarantee of trust used to unlock new resources. We proposed in this paper a new architecture model recommended for obligation based access control. We then detailed the certification process used to certify past obligations and use them as access control tokens. Our future work focuses on the secure enforcement mechanisms. Currently we assume that the engine is trusted enough to properly enforce policies. This assumption is of course strong and not realistic. To cope with this issue we are exploring two paths; the first one is based on a new encryption scheme supporting the obligation certification during the encryption and decryption phases of the data. The second path relies on trusted computing. The idea is to host Obligation Engine and Certification Obligation Service. The goal is to have a guarantee on obligation execution in addition to the integrity of obligation proof. Trusted computing also eases the establishment of trust relationship amongst distributed entities for further monitoring of current state of the system.

Acknowledgements. This paper is done in the context of the FP7 EU COCO Cloud Project, referenced as FP7-ICT-2013-10-610853.

References

1. Trabelsi, S., Sendor, J., Reinicke, S.: PPL: PrimeLife Privacy Policy Engine. POL-ICY (2011)
2. Ben-Ghorbel-Talbi, M., Cuppens, F., Cuppens-Boulahia, N., Bouhoula, A.: An extended role-based access control model for delegating obligations. In: Fischer-Hübner, S., Lambrinoudakis, C., Pernul, G. (eds.) TrustBus 2009. LNCS, vol. 5695, pp. 127–137. Springer, Heidelberg (2009)
3. Ni, Q., Bertino, E., Lobo, J.: An Obligation Model Bridging Access Control Policies and Privacy Policies. In: Proceedings of the 13th ACM Symposium on Access Control Models and Technologies, SACMAT 2008 (2008)
4. Chen, L., Cramptony, J., Kollingbaum, M.J., Norman, T.J.: Obligations in Risk-Aware Access Control. In: Proceedings of the 13th ACM Symposium on Access control Models and Technologies, SACMAT (2008), Proceedings of the 2012 Tenth Annual International Conference on Privacy, Security and Trust, PST 2012 (2012)
5. Bettini, C., Jajodia, S., Wang, X.S., Wijesekera, D.: Provisions and Obligations in Policy Management and Security Applications. In: Proceedings of the 13th ACM Symposium on Access Control Models and Technologies, SACMAT 2008 (2008), Proceedings of the 28th International Conference on Very Large Data Bases, VLDB 2002 (2002)

A Comprehensive Theoretical Framework
for Privacy Preserving Distributed OLAP

Alfredo Cuzzocrea[1] and Elisa Bertino[2]

[1] ICAR-CNR and University of Calabria, Italy
[2] CERIAS and Purdue University, IN, USA
cuzzocrea@si.deis.unical.it, bertino@cs.purdue.edu

Abstract. This paper complements the *privacy preserving distributed OLAP framework* proposed by us in a previous work by introducing *four major theoretical properties* that extend models and algorithms presented in the previous work, where the experimental validation of the framework has also been reported. Particularly, our framework makes use of the *CUR matrix decomposition technique* as the elementary component for *computing privacy preserving two-dimensional OLAP views effectively and efficiently*. Here, we investigate theoretical properties of the CUR decomposition method, and identify four theoretical extensions of this method, which, according to our vision, may result in benefits for a wide spectrum of aspects in the context of privacy preserving distributed OLAP, such as *privacy preserving knowledge fruition schemes and query optimization*. In addition to this, we also provide a widespread experimental analysis of the framework, which fully confirms to us the major practical achievements, in terms of both efficacy and efficiency, due to our framework.

1 Introduction

Privacy Preserving Distributed OLAP [2,31,19,24,4,23] is crucial in today's world as organizations need to collaboratively harness the potential of "big data" analytics for decision making while at the same time assuring the privacy and confidentiality of their own data sets. This is referred in literature as *privacy preserving OLAP* [10,8] *in distributed environments* [2,31,19,24,4,23]. In scenarios adhering to the privacy preserving distributed OLAP paradigm, analysts working at different companies federated to the same main organization perform OLAP on business data extracted from their own respective legacy databases. To this end, analysts build and query data cubes made available in the other companies' sites, thus exposing them to *privacy breaches*. Assume that each company within the same main organization has the policy that the company's sale data is strictly confidential and not to be shared with other company. On the other hand, the organization encourages companies to collaboratively work on enhancing common *Business Intelligence* (BI). It should be noted that the respective OLAP tasks performed by analysts against their own data cube are private, as each of them uses only data belonging to her/his company. By

R. Meersman et al. (Eds.): OTM 2014 Workshops, LNCS 8842, pp. 117–136, 2014.

contrast, when analysts *aggregate* their respective data cubes into one common *SUM-based data cube* for BI purposes, data privacy breaches arise as analysts can easily *infer* data cells of other analysts' data cubes starting from data cells stored in the common data cube and her (his, respectively) proper data cube, via simple *linear interpolation techniques* [11,12].

Our reference scenario example adheres to the *Secure Multiparty Computation* (SMC) [28] model, which is well-known in the context of *Privacy Preserving Distributed Data Mining research* [5,21], with respect to which Privacy Preserving Distributed OLAP can be considered a major, yet-independent, research area. In order to solve the challenging problem of *computing and managing privacy preserving data cubes in distributed environments*, in [9] we introduced an innovative privacy preserving distributed OLAP framework that relies on the novel concept of *secure distributed OLAP aggregation task*.

Basically, this framework is based on the idea of performing OLAP across multiple distributed *SUM-based two-dimensional OLAP* views extracted from data cubes under the SMC requirements [9]. To this end, we introduced and experimentally assessed the *Secure Distributed OLAP aggregation protocol* (SDO) [9]. Briefly, the SDO protocol works as follows. Having fixed a certain node ordering (e.g., DNS-based), the *first* node N_0 in the distributed environment computes a *privacy preserving version* V_0^{PP} of its proper OLAP view, denoted by V_0, and sends V_0^{PP} to the second node N_1 in the distributed environment. N_1 in turn: (*i*) combines V_0^{PP} with its proper local view, denoted by V_1, in order to perform the target OLAP operation; (*ii*) sends the local OLAP result, which is again represented by a view, denoted by V_1^{PP}, to the "following" node according to the fixed node ordering, and so forth. It should be noted that, since V_0^{PP} is privacy preserving, V_1^{PP} is also privacy preserving. This step is iterated until the local OLAP result computed at node N_{n-1} in the distributed environment, denoted by V_{n-1}^{PP}, is returned to the node N_0, which derives from V_{n-1}^{PP} the *exact* global OLAP result of the target OLAP task, denoted by V^{GLOBAL}, on the basis of the local view V_0, which is hidden to the other nodes of the distributed environment, and its privacy preserving version V_0^{PP}. The final global OLAP result V^{GLOBAL} is sent to the external application that finally forwards V^{GLOBAL} to all the other nodes in the distributed environment.

In this proposal, the core method exploited to obtain privacy-preserving two-dimensional OLAP views is given by the *CUR matrix decomposition* [14], which, as argued by Drineas *et al.* [13], can be used for privacy preservation purposes. In more detail, CUR is a matrix decomposition method for computing *approximate representations* of large matrices. It can be applied to several application contexts ranging from classification problems to similarity search problems, from analysis of biological data to compression of hyper-spectral data for image processing, and so forth [14].

Formally, given a large $m \times n$ matrix $\mathbf{A}$, a CUR matrix decomposition is a *low-rank approximation* of $\mathbf{A}$, denoted by $\mathbf{A}'$, that represents $\mathbf{A}$ *in terms of a small number of columns and rows of* $\mathbf{A}$, as follows: $\mathbf{A} \approx \mathbf{C} \cdot \mathbf{U} \cdot \mathbf{R} \equiv \mathbf{A}'$, where: (*i*) $\mathbf{C}$ is an $m \times c$

matrix *that* stores $O(1)$ columns of **A**; (*ii*) **R** is an $r \times n$ matrix that stores $O(1)$ rows of **A**; (*iii*) **U** is a $c \times r$ carefully-chosen matrix. In particular, the number of columns of **C** consists of $c = \theta(1/\varepsilon^2)$ columns of **A**, and the number of rows of **R** consists of $r = \theta(1/\varepsilon^2)$ rows of **A**, respectively, with $\varepsilon > 0$ arbitrarily small. **C** and **R** are built by means of *adaptive sampling* [30], via c (r, respectively) trials by picking a column (a row, respectively) of **A** with probability p_j defined as follows: $p_j = \dfrac{|A[\bullet][j]|^2}{\sum_j |A[\bullet][j]|^2}$, whereas the probability p_i for rows is defined as follows: $p_i = \dfrac{|A[i]|^2}{\sum_j |A[i]|^2}$, respectively.

In the previous work [9], we have specifically focused on the class of *SUM-based distributed OLAP aggregation tasks*, being SUM a popular aggregate operator for OLAP applications (e.g., [19]). Despite this, the framework [9] is general enough to deal with more sophisticated distributed OLAP aggregation tasks that embed complex OLAP aggregations (e.g., [18]) rather than conventional ones (e.g., SUM, COUNT, AVG). Also, while the framework [9] is general enough to deal with OLAP views computed over any arbitrary kind of data sources, in [9] we considered the specialized case represented by data cubes computed on top of *distributed collections of XML documents*, which are increasingly relevant for BI applications. The core of the framework [9] is represented by the *CUR matrix decomposition technique* [14], which allows us to compute privacy preserving two-dimensional OLAP views effectively and efficiently, *at a provable approximation error* [9].

In this paper, we further extend the proposed privacy preserving distributed OLAP framework [9] by providing a number of theoretical results that nicely extend the capabilities of the framework. We believe that these theoretical results result in benefits for a wide spectrum of aspects, such as *privacy preserving knowledge fruition schemes* and *query optimization*. More specifically, we provide theoretical contributions on the following aspects of the framework [9]: (*i*) *re-construction capabilities of the CUR decomposition method*, where we prove that the privacy preserving two-dimensional OLAP views can be used for re-constructing the original OLAP views in a theoretically-sound manner; (*ii*) *independence capabilities of the CUR decomposition method*, where we prove that the final two-dimensional OLAP view obtained from the target distributed OLAP aggregation task can be obtained from the two-dimensional OLAP views of the first and the last node of the reference environment, respectively, without dependency on the OLAP views of the remaining nodes, still in a theoretically-sound manner; (*iii*) *differential privacy notions*, where we introduce significant notions of *differential privacy* [15] for the framework [9] – as widely known, differential privacy represents a useful tool for representing and managing privacy preserving databases; (*iv*) *a widespread experimental analysis of the proposed privacy preserving distributed OLAP framework*, which fully confirms to us the major practical achievements, in terms of both efficacy and efficiency, due to this framework. A preliminary study that is the theoretical basis of this work appears in the workshop paper [42].

2   Related Work

Distributed Privacy Preserving OLAP techniques solve the problem of making distributed OLAP data cubes (i.e., OLAP data cubes populating a distributed environment) able to preserve the privacy of data during common (data) management tasks (e.g., computing data cubes, querying data cubes etc) or, under an alternative interpretation, generating a privacy preserving OLAP data cube from distributed data sources. With respect to the first problem, to the best of our knowledge, no approaches exist addressing this problem, beyond the framework [9], whereas concerning the second problem, the approach by Agrawal *et al.* [2] is the state-of-the-art approach. The approach [9] belongs to the second privacy preserving distributed OLAP scientific context, as it aims at solving the problem of supporting privacy preserving OLAP over distributed two-dimensional OLAP views, but, under a broader meaning, it also encompasses some characteristics of the first distributed privacy preserving OLAP scientific context.

By looking at the recent literature, while a plethora of initiatives focusing on Privacy Preserving Distributed Data Mining [5,21] exist, to the best of our knowledge, only [2,31,19,24,4,23] deal with the problem of effectively and efficiently supporting privacy preserving OLAP over distributed data sources. Agrawal *et al.* [2] define a privacy preserving OLAP model over data partitioned across multiple clients using a *randomization approach*, which is implemented by the so-called *Retention Replacement Perturbation* algorithm, on the basis of which (*i*) clients perturb tuples which they contribute to the partition in order to achive *row-level privacy*, and (*ii*) the server is capable of evaluating OLAP queries against perturbed tables via *reconstructing* the original distributions of attributes involved by such queries. Agrawal *et al.* prove that the proposed distributed privacy preserving OLAP model is safe against privacy breaches. The approach by Tong *et al.* [31] is another distributed privacy preserving OLAP approach that is reminiscent of ours. More specifically, they [31] propose the idea of obtaining a privacy preserving OLAP data cube from *distributed data sources across multiple sites* via applying perturbation-based techniques on *aggregate data* that are retrieved from each single site as a baseline step of the main (distributed) OLAP computation task. Other approaches [19,4,24] focus on the significant issue of providing efficient data aggregation while preserving privacy over *Wireless Sensor Networks* (WSN). In more details, He *et al.* [19] propose a solution based on two privacy-preserving data aggregation schemes that make use of innovative *additive aggregation functions*. These schemes are called *Cluster-based Private Data Aggregation* (CPDA) and *Slice-Mix-AggRegaTe* (SMART), respectively. The proposed aggregation functions fully-exploit topology and dynamics of the underlying wireless sensor network, and bridge the gap between collaborative data collection over such networks and data privacy needs. Chan and Castelluccia [4] focus on a formal treatment of a *Private Data Aggregation* (PDA) security model over WSN; this contribution is general enough to cover most cases of security-demanding scenarios over WSN and from a practical perspective allow one to execute privacy preserving data aggregation operations over WSN. The work by Lin *et al.* [24] is an incremental contribution aiming at improving security and saving energy consumption of the privacy preserving data aggregation task over WSN; the main idea of such an approach consists in integrating the super-increasing sequence and perturbation techniques into compressed data aggregations in order to gain efficiency. Li *et al.* [23] propose a novel incremental method for supporting secure and privacy preserving information aggregation over smart grids; this method introduces a novel scheme according to which data aggregation is performed at all smart meters involved in routing the data from the source meter to the collector unit, and the user privacy is provided by the use of *homomorphic encryption* on the transmitted data. Finally, there are more recent efforts that clearly confirm the interest from the research community for the issues investigated in this paper. Among others, Jurezyk and Xiong [22] propose a fully-decentralized anonymization protocol over horizontally-partitioned distributed databases, which supports privacy-preserving aggregate query answering in a distributed fashion, whereas Mohammed *et al.* [26] propose *LKC-privacy*, a new privacy model for achieving anonymization over distributed high-dimensional *healthcare data*, which is perfectly compliant with the privacy preserving distributed OLAP scenario we investigate in our research, as high-dimensional data smoothly resemble data cube cells.

3   From Privacy-Preserving Views to the Original Data Sets

A critical property that is central to theoretical aspects of the CUR decomposition method is related to assessing the capabilities of the method in re-constructing the original matrix **A** from the approximating matrix **A'** that is retrieved by the method itself. In fact, beyond playing a central role in the effectiveness of the proposed privacy preserving distributed OLAP framework, the re-construction property also ensures the theoretical convergence of conceptual constructs and theory tools of the framework.

In order to prove the re-construction property ensured by the CUR decomposition method, we provide Theorem 2 (see next) whose proof is characterized by a structure inspired by the theoretical model proposed by Agrawal *et al.* [2]. In more detail, with respect to the re-construction property ensured by the proposed *Retention Replacement Perturbation* algorithm [2], Agrawal *et al.* provide rigorous probabilistic bounds over aggregates that are re-constructed from a relational table that has been perturbed by means of their algorithm. These aggregates are defined in terms of input range queries over the perturbed relational table, and their values are compared with the values of aggregates retrieved by the same queries over the original relational table. Here, we follow a similar approach, i.e. we study the re-construction property of the CUR decomposition method by considering the aggregate values of range queries over the approximating matrix **A'** in comparison with the aggregate values of the same queries over the original matrix **A**.

Before introducing Theorem 2, some definitions are necessary. First, we define a two-dimensional range query Q over the $m \times n$ matrix **A** (**A'**, respectively) as follows:

$$Q = [\langle l_1 : u_1 \rangle; \langle l_2 : u_2 \rangle] \tag{1}$$

where: (*i*) l_1 denotes a lower bound on the dimension d_1 of **A** (**A'**, respectively); (*ii*) u_1 denotes an upper bound on the dimension d_1 of **A** (**A'**, respectively); (*iii*) $l_1 < u_1$; (*iv*) l_2 denotes a lower bound on the dimension d_2 of **A** (**A'**, respectively); (*v*) u_2 denotes an upper bound on the dimension d_2 of **A** (**A'**, respectively); (*vi*) $l_2 < u_2$. On the basis of well-understood matrix algebra [17] principles, the evaluation of Q over **A** (**A'**, respectively) can be expressed as follows:

$$\mathbf{x}^T \cdot \mathbf{A} \cdot \mathbf{y} = z \qquad (2)$$

where: (*i*) **x** models an *m*-dimensional vector whose elements **x**[*i*], with $0 \leq i \leq m - 1$, are defined as follows:

$$\mathbf{x}[i] = \begin{cases} 1 & \text{if } l_1 \leq i \leq u_1 \\ 0 & \text{otherwise} \end{cases} \qquad (3)$$

(*ii*) **y** models an *n*-dimensional vector whose elements **y**[*j*], with $0 \leq j \leq n - 1$, are defined as follows:

$$\mathbf{y}[j] = \begin{cases} 1 & \text{if } l_2 \leq j \leq u_2 \\ 0 & \text{otherwise} \end{cases} \qquad (4)$$

and (*iii*) z models the answer to Q (z' models the approximate answer to Q, respectively).

For the sake of clarity, Theorem 2 proves that the approximate answer to Q, z', is *probabilistically-close* to the exact answer to Q, z, or, in other words, the re-construction property of the CUR decomposition method.

Second, we introduce the concept of *re-constructible function*, also inspired by [2], whose formal definition is provided in Definition 1. Intuitively, a numeric function γ is said to be re-constructible iff it allows us to "invert" the transformation of the original matrix **A** (cell partitions of **A**) in the perturbed matrix **A'** (cell partitions of **A'**) due to the CUR decomposition method, in our case. In our theoretical analysis, we interpret numeric functions γ as the data distributions associated with elements of the original matrix **A** (the approximating matrix **A'**, respectively). A relevant property of a re-constructible function γ is that of verifying whether it is $\langle n, \varepsilon, \delta \rangle$-*re-constructible* by means of the so-called *re-constructing function* γ', such that n is the number of items in γ, and ε and δ are positive integer arbitrarily small. In other words, this corresponds to verifying whether an *unbiased estimator* [27] γ' for γ exists. If this is the case, γ' gives us theoretically-proofed probabilistic bounds on the error we commit in reconstructing the function γ (by means of γ').

Definition 1. *Let* $\alpha : \mathbb{R}^m \rightarrow \mathbb{R}^n$ *be a perturbation function converting a matrix* **A** *into the approximating matrix* **A'***; a numeric function* γ *on* **A** *is said to be* $\langle n, \varepsilon, \delta \rangle$-*re-constructible by means of a re-constructing function* γ'*, such that n is the number of items in* γ*, and* ε *and* δ *are positive integers arbitrarily small, iff* γ' *can be evaluated on* **A'** *and the following condition holds:* $|\gamma - \gamma'| = max\{\varepsilon, \varepsilon \cdot \gamma\}$*, such that* $max\{I\}$ *denotes the operator max over a given item set* I*.*

Based on these theoretical constructs and concepts, we now focus on re-constructing the answer z to a given range query $Q = [\langle l_1{:}u_1 \rangle; \langle l_2{:}u_2 \rangle]$ over $\mathbf{A}$ from the approximating matrix $\mathbf{A'}$ (or, equally, retrieving the approximate answer to Q, z') and the probabilities p_i and p_j (see Section 1) exploited by the CUR decomposition method to obtain $\mathbf{A'}$ from $\mathbf{A}$. For this theoretical setting, the re-constructing function γ' we adopt is defined as follows:

$$\gamma'(Q = [\langle l_1 : u_1 \rangle; \langle l_2 : u_2 \rangle]) = \sum_{i=l_1}^{u_1} \sum_{j=l_2}^{u_1} \left[\mathbf{A'}[i][j] - \frac{(1-p_i)\cdot p_j}{p_i \cdot (1-p_j)} \cdot b \right] \tag{5}$$

where: (i) $\mathbf{A'}[i][j]$ denotes an element of $\mathbf{A'}$; (ii) p_i (see Section 1) denotes the probability of picking the i-th row of $\mathbf{A}$ during the CUR decomposition method; (iii) p_j (see Section 1) denotes the probability of picking the j-th column of $\mathbf{A}$ during the CUR decomposition method; (iv) b is defined as follows:

$$b = \frac{max\{\mathbf{A'}\} - min\{\mathbf{A'}\}}{max\{\mathbf{A}\} - min\{\mathbf{A}\}} \tag{6}$$

such that $max\{\mathbf{B}\}$ denotes the operator max over the elements of $\mathbf{B}$, with $\mathbf{B}$ in $\{\mathbf{A}, \mathbf{A'}\}$, and $min\{\mathbf{B}\}$ denotes the operator min over the elements of $\mathbf{B}$, with $\mathbf{B}$ in $\{\mathbf{A}, \mathbf{A'}\}$, respectively. Theorem 2 states that the re-constructing function γ' (5) is an unbiased estimator for the function γ determined by the CUR decomposition method, under the following condition:

$$n \geq 4 \cdot \log(\frac{2}{\delta}) \cdot (p_i \cdot p_j \cdot \varepsilon)^{-2} \tag{7}$$

where: (i) n denotes the number of elements of $\mathbf{A}$ involved in the evaluation of Q; (ii) ε and δ are positive integers arbitrarily small; (iii) p_i and p_j are the probabilities, exploited by the CUR decomposition method, respectively (see Section 1).

Theorem 2. *Let the value* $\mathbf{A}[i][j]$ *in* $[min\{\mathbf{A'}\}, max\{\mathbf{A'}\}]$ *be estimated by the re-constructing function* γ'; *then* γ' *is a* $\langle n, \varepsilon, \delta \rangle$-*unbiased-estimator for* γ *if the following condition holds:* $n \geq 4 \cdot \log(\frac{2}{\delta}) \cdot (p_i \cdot p_j \cdot \varepsilon)^{-2}$.

Proof. Let $\mathcal{X}_{ij}$ denote a *random variable* [27] for the event that element $\mathbf{A}[i][j]$ of $\mathbf{A}$ is perturbed, and the perturbed element $\mathbf{A'}[i][j]$ is contained by the interval $[min\{\mathbf{A'}\}, max\{\mathbf{A'}\}]$. It should be noted that the collection of random variables $\mathcal{X}_{ij}$ are i.i.d. [27], and that the probability that element $\mathbf{A}[i][j]$ of $\mathbf{A}$ is perturbed is given by the following expression:

$$P(\mathcal{X}_{ij} = 1) = (1 - p_i) \cdot (1 - p_j) \cdot b \tag{8}$$

As a consequence, the following equality holds:

$$P(\mathcal{X}_{ij} = 0) = 1 - P(\mathcal{X}_{ij} = 1) = 1 - (1 - p_i) \cdot (1 - p_j) \cdot b \tag{9}$$

Likewise, let $\mathcal{Y}_{ij}$ denote a random variable for the event that element $\mathbf{A}[i][j]$ of $\mathbf{A}$ is *not* perturbed, and it is contained by the interval $[min\{\mathbf{A'}\}, max\{\mathbf{A'}\}]$. Similarly to the case of random variables $\mathcal{Y}_{ij}$, it should be clear that the collection of random variables

y_{ij} are i.i.d. and that the probability that element $A[i][j]$ of A is not perturbed is given by the following expression:

$$P(y_{ij} = 1) = p_i \cdot p_j \tag{10}$$

In turn, the following expression holds:

$$P(y_{ij} = 0) = 1 - P(y_{ij} = 1) = 1 - p_i \cdot p_j \tag{11}$$

Now, let Z_{ij} denote a random variable for the event that, during the CUR decomposition method, element $A[i][j]$ of A falls within the interval $[min\{A'\}, max\{A'\}]$. It follows that Z_{ij} can be defined in terms of the previous random variable X_{ij} and y_{ij}, as follows:

$$Z_{ij} = X_{ij} + y_{ij} \tag{12}$$

due to the fact that, during the CUR decomposition method, an arbitrary element $A[i][j]$ of A may be contained (i.e., $X_{ij} = 1$ and $y_{ij} = 0$) or not (i.e., $X_{ij} = 0$ and $y_{ij} = 1$) by the interval $[min\{A'\}, max\{A'\}]$. From (12), it follows that the collection of random variables Z_{ij} are i.i.d. and that the probability that element $A[i][j]$ of A falls within the interval $[min\{A'\}, max\{A'\}]$ is given by the following expression:

$$P(Z_{ij} = 1) = P((X_{ij} + y_{ij}) = 1) = P(X_{ij} = 1) + P(y_{ij} = 1) \tag{13}$$

From (8) and (10), (13) we finally obtain the following expression:

$$P(Z_{ij} = 1) = (1 - p_i) \cdot (1 - p_j) \cdot b + p_i \cdot p_j \tag{14}$$

As a consequence, the following formula holds:

$$P(Z_{ij} = 0) = 1 - P(Z_{ij} = 1) = 1 - (1 - p_i) \cdot (1 - p_j) \cdot b + p_i \cdot p_j \tag{15}$$

Furthermore, let Δ_1 denote the range of Q on the dimension d_1 of A (A', respectively). From (1), it clearly follows that the cardinality of Δ_1, $\|\Delta_1\|$, is given by the following expression:

$$|\Delta_1\| = u_1 - l_1 \tag{16}$$

Similarly, let Δ_2 denote the range of Q on the dimension d_2 of A (A', respectively). From (1), it clearly follows again that the cardinality of Δ_2, $\|\Delta_2\|$, is given by the following expression:

$$\|\Delta_2\| = u_2 - l_2 \tag{17}$$

Also, let $\|Q\|$ denote the *volume* (or *selectivity* [6,7]) of Q. Based on (1), (16) and (17), $\|Q\|$ is given by the following expression:

$$\|Q\| = \|\Delta_1\| \cdot \|\Delta_2\| \tag{18}$$

such that $\|\Delta_1\|$ denotes the cardinality of Δ_1, and $\|\Delta_2\|$ denotes the cardinality of Δ_2, respectively.

Now, let U_{ij} denote a random variable defined as the *summation of random variables* Z_{ij} [P] over the two-dimensional domain of A (A', respectively) modeling the range of Q, i.e. $[\langle l_1:u_1 \rangle; \langle l_2:u_2 \rangle]$ that is defined as follows:

$$\mathcal{U}_{ij}(\Delta_1,\Delta_2) = \sum_{h=i}^{i+\Delta_1-1}\sum_{k=j}^{j+\Delta_2-1} Z_{hk} \cdot \mathbf{A'}[h][k] \qquad (19)$$

It should be noted that random variables $\mathcal{U}_{ij}$ are those associated with the evaluation of the approximate answer to Q, z', and they underlie the definition of the re-constructing function γ' (5). The number of elements of $\mathbf{A'}$ involved in the Q's evaluation process, n (or, equally, the number of items of $\gamma' - \gamma$, respectively), is given by the following expression:

$$n = \|Q\| = \|\Delta_I\| \cdot \|\Delta_2\| \qquad (20)$$

How to model the approximate evaluation of Q over $\mathbf{A'}$ *in a probabilistic manner?* In order to answer this critical question, first note that each one among the n elements $\mathbf{A'}[i][j]$ of $\mathbf{A'}$ may contribute (i.e., $\mathcal{U}_{ij} = 1$) or not (i.e., $\mathcal{U}_{ij} = 0$) to the approximate answer to Q, z'. Our final aim is to find probabilistic bounds for the probability $P(\mathcal{U}_{ij} = 1)$. Since the random variables Z_{ij} are i.i.d. and the random variables $\mathcal{U}_{ij}$ are defined as the summation of Z_{ij}, then $\mathcal{U}_{ij}$ are *independent Bernoulli random variables* [27]. Under the condition (7), by applying the well-known *Chernoff bound* [27], the following inequality holds:

$$P\left[\left|\mathcal{U}_{ij}(\Delta_1,\Delta_2) - n\cdot t\cdot \mathbf{AVG}(\Delta_1,\Delta_2)\right| > n\cdot\theta\right] < 2e^{\frac{-n\cdot\theta^2}{4\cdot t}} \leq \delta \qquad (21)$$

such that (*i*) $t = P(Z_{ij} = 1)$ (14); (*ii*) $\mathbf{AVG}(\Delta_1,\Delta_2)$ denotes the average value of elements $\mathbf{A'}[i][j]$ of $\mathbf{A'}$ contained by the two-dimensional range of Q, $[\langle l_1:u_1\rangle; \langle l_2:u_2\rangle]$; (*iii*) θ is defined as follows:

$$\theta = \prod_{i=l_1}^{u_1}\prod_{j=l_2}^{u_2} p_i \cdot p_j \cdot \varepsilon \qquad (22)$$

where p_i and p_j are the probabilities exploited by the CUR decomposition method (see Section 1), respectively, and ε is a positive integer arbitrarily small; (*iv*) δ is a positive integer arbitrarily small. From (21), it follows that, with probability greater than $1 - \delta$, the following inequality holds:

$$\gamma - \varepsilon < \sum_{i=l_1}^{u_1}\sum_{j=l_2}^{u_1}\left[\mathbf{A'}[i][j] - \frac{(1-p_i)\cdot p_j}{p_i\cdot(1-p_j)}\cdot b\right] < \gamma + \varepsilon \qquad (23)$$

from which it follows that $|\gamma - \gamma'| < \varepsilon$ with probability $1 - \delta$, and that re-constructing function γ' (5) is an unbiased estimator for the function γ determined by the CUR decomposition method.

4   Breaking the Dependency from Local Views: Towards Theoretically-Sound Privacy-Preserving Distributed OLAP

Based on the results in [9] and the fact that SUM-based OLAP aggregation is a *non-holistic* operator [16], it is easy to demonstrate that the final global result of the target distributed **OLAP** aggregation task, i.e. the view V^{GLOBAL}, can be reconstructed as follows (as formally stated by Theorem 3):

$$V^{GLOBAL} = V_0 + \left(V_{n-1}^{PP} - V_0^{PP} \right) \tag{24}$$

Theorem 3. *The final global* **OLAP** *view* V^{GLOBAL} *obtained from any arbitrary* **SUM**-*based secure* **OLAP** *aggregation task over a distributed environment populated by n nodes can be retrieved from combining the local* **OLAP** *view* V_0 *at node* N_0, *the privacy preserving* **OLAP** *view* V_0^{PP} *at node* N_0 *and the privacy preserving* **OLAP** *view* V_{n-1}^{PP} *at node* N_{n-1} *without dependency on the* **OLAP** *views located at other nodes* N_i, *with* $1 \le i \le n - 2$, *of the reference distributed environment, i.e.* $V^{GLOBAL} = V_0 + \left(V_{n-1}^{PP} - V_0^{PP} \right)$.

Proof. Take as reference a distributed environment populated by n nodes. First, note that, given two consecutive nodes N_{i-1} and N_i in the fixed node ordering, such that $1 \le i \le n - 2$, since we focus on **SUM**-based **OLAP** aggregations, the privacy preserving view V_i^{PP} at node N_i is obtained by combining the local view V_i at node N_i with the privacy preserving view V_{i-1}^{PP} returned to node N_i from node N_{i-1}, as follows (see Section 1):

$$V_i^{PP} = V_i + V_{i-1}^{PP} \tag{25}$$

By contrast, for the *sole* instance represented by the first node N_0, the privacy preserving view V_0^{PP} is directly obtained from the local view V_0 via the **CUR**-based approximation method (see Section 1). Hence, with respect to privacy preserving views located at nodes of the reference distributed environment, the following equalities hold:

$$\begin{aligned} V_0^{PP} &= \mathsf{CUR}(V_0) \\ V_1^{PP} &= V_1 + V_0^{PP} \\ V_2^{PP} &= V_2 + V_1^{PP} \\ &\cdots \\ V_{n-1}^{PP} &= V_{n-1} + V_{n-2}^{PP} \end{aligned} \tag{26}$$

Based on (25), by applying simple mathematical substitutions, (26) can be re-written as follows:

$$\begin{aligned} V_0^{PP} &= \mathsf{CUR}(V_0) \\ V_1^{PP} &= V_1 + V_0^{PP} \\ V_2^{PP} &= V_2 + V_1^{PP} = V_2 + V_1 + V_0^{PP} \\ &\cdots \\ V_{n-1}^{PP} &= V_{n-1} + V_{n-2} + ... + V_1 + V_0^{PP} \end{aligned} \tag{27}$$

Based on (27), (24) can be expanded as follows:

$$\begin{aligned} V^{GLOBAL} &= V_0 + \left(V_{n-1}^{PP} - V_0^{PP} \right) \\ &= V_0 + \left(\left(V_{n-1} + V_{n-2} + ... + V_1 + V_0^{PP} \right) - V_0^{PP} \right) \end{aligned} \tag{28}$$

i.e.:

$$V^{GLOBAL} = V_0 + V_1 + V_2 + ... + V_{n-1} \qquad (29)$$

which, from Section 1, represents the (exact) final result of the target distributed OLAP aggregation task.

Theorem 3 is another relevant theoretical result of our research. It allows us to obtain the final global result of the target secure distributed OLAP aggregation task, V^{GLOBAL} from the OLAP views stored at the first node N_0 of the reference distributed environment, V_0 and V_0^{PP}, respectively, one exact (i.e., V_0) and one privacy preserving (i.e., V_0^{PP}), and from the privacy preserving OLAP view V_{n-1}^{PP} returned to node N_0 from node N_{n-1}, *without dependency on the OLAP views* (local and privacy preserving) *of other nodes* N_i, with $1 \le i \le n - 2$, of the reference distributed environment. Intuitively, this phenomenon opens interesting theoretical as well as query-optimization opportunities for enhancing our privacy preserving distributed OLAP framework.

As a useful corollary deriving from Theorem 3 (Corollary 1), it follows that our proposed framework is *orthogonal* to the specific method used for obtaining the privacy preserving view V_i^{PP} at node N_i (CUR, in our case). Hence our framework maintains its validity and generality with any arbitrary privacy preserving method (e.g., [11,20,29,32,33,34,12,25,3]). This gives further merits to our research.

Corollary 1. *The proposed privacy preserving distributed OLAP framework is orthogonal to the method used to compute privacy preserving two-dimensional OLAP views.*

Proof. A direct consequence from Theorem 3.

5   Innovative Differential Privacy Notions for Privacy Preserving Distributed OLAP

We now focus on other theoretical properties of our privacy preserving distributed OLAP framework that are related to the well-understood notion of differential privacy [15]. Based on the non-holistic nature of SUM-based OLAP aggregations [16], given a local view V_i at node N_i, we introduce two different differential privacy notions for the privacy preserving process over V_i (i.e., $V_i^{PP} = V_i + V_{i-1}^{PP}$). The first one, formally introduced by Definition 2, is referred to as *full-differential privacy* and denoted by ΔP_i^F. It is modeled as a (two-dimensional) view that makes V_i^{PP} different from V_i (or, equally, that makes V_i^{PP} privacy preserving with respect to V_i).

Definition 2. *Given a two-dimensional OLAP view V and its privacy preserving version V^{PP}, the full-differential privacy between V^{PP} and V, denoted by ΔP^F, is a two-dimensional view defined as follows: $\Delta P^F = V^{PP} - V$.*

The second differential privacy notion, formally introduced by Definition 3, is referred to as *marginal-differential privacy* and denoted by ΔP_i^M.

Definition 3. *Given a two-dimensional OLAP view V and its privacy preserving version V^{PP}, the marginal-differential privacy between V^{PP} and V, denoted by ΔP^M, is a partition of two-dimensional cells whose elements are defined as follows:*

$$\Delta P_i^M[m][c] = \begin{cases} V_i[m][c] & \text{if } V_i^{PP}[m][c] = V_i[m][c],\ 0 \le m \le \| d_{i,0} \| \wedge 0 \le c \le \| d_{i,1} \| \text{ where } d_{i,0} \text{ and } d_{i,1} \\ V_i^{PP}[m][c] & \text{otherwise} \end{cases}$$

denote the dimensions of V.

Let $d_{i,0}^{PP}$ and $d_{i,1}^{PP}$ denote the dimensions of V_i^{PP}. It follows that $\| d_{i,0} \| = \| d_{i,0}^{PP} \|$ and $\| d_{i,1} \| = \| d_{i,1}^{PP} \|$. It should be noted that, while full-differential privacy ΔP_i^F defined according to Definition 2 conforms to the classical notion of differential privacy [15], the marginal-differential privacy ΔP_i^M defined according to Definition 3 plays a relevant role with respect to the critical problem of maintaining privacy under the occurrence of *updates* on the target data sources which affects Privacy Preserving Data Mining [1].

Starting from the basic differential privacy notions, their *global versions* are derived in our framework as follows. First, from Section 1, the following two critical aspects of our privacy preserving distributed OLAP framework should be clear enough: (*i*) the full-differential privacy ΔP_i^F that propagates across pairs of consecutive nodes N_{i-1} and N_i (in the fixed node ordering) of the reference distributed environment is originated by the "first" full-differential privacy ΔP_0^F at node N_0; (*ii*) ΔP_0^F represents the differential privacy that, by propagating node by node, makes each local view V_i at node N_i, with $1 \le i \le n - 1$, privacy preserving (i.e., V_i^{PP}), in consequence of the secure OLAP aggregation routine performed at node N_i as a baseline step of the whole secure distributed OLAP aggregation task. Hence, at the last node N_{n-1} of the reference distributed environment, *the full-differential privacy ΔP_{n-1}^F at node N_{n-1} globally embeds all the contributions of the "previous" full-differential privacies* ΔP_0^F, ΔP_1^F, ..., ΔP_{n-2}^F. This leads to the concept of *global full-differential privacy*, formally introduced by Definition 4, that is associated with the target secure distributed OLAP aggregation task $\mathcal{T}$, denoted by $\Delta P_{\mathcal{T}}^F$.

Definition 4. *Given an arbitrary SUM-based secure OLAP aggregation task $\mathcal{T}$ over a distributed environment populated by n nodes, the global full-differential privacy associated to $\mathcal{T}$, denoted by $\Delta P_{\mathcal{T}}^F$, is defined as follows:*

$$\Delta P_{\mathcal{T}}^F = \sum_{i=0}^{n-1} \Delta P_i^F = \Delta P_0^F + \Delta P_1^F + ... + \Delta P_{n-1}^F, \quad \text{where} \quad \Delta P_i^F \quad \text{denotes the full-}$$

differential privacy at node N_i.

Intuitively like Theorem 3, Definition 4 can be exploited for further theoretical analysis as well as for query-optimization opportunities. At the same time, we derive, with similar insights, the concept of *global marginal-differential privacy*, formally introduced by Definition 5, that is associated with the target secure distributed OLAP aggregation task $\mathcal{T}$, denoted by $\Delta P_{\mathcal{T}}^{M}$.

Definition 5. *Given an arbitrary SUM-based secure OLAP aggregation task $\mathcal{T}$ over a distributed environment populated by n nodes, the global marginal-differential privacy associated to $\mathcal{T}$, denoted by $\Delta P_{\mathcal{T}}^{M}$, is defined as follows:*

$$\Delta P_{\mathcal{T}}^{M} = \sum_{i=0}^{n-1} \Delta P_i^{M} = \Delta P_0^{M} + \Delta P_1^{M} + ... + \Delta P_{n-1}^{M}, \quad such \quad that \quad \Delta P_i^{M} \quad denotes \quad the$$

marginal-differential privacy at node N_i.

Like the other differential privacy notions introduced in this paper, both the global full- and marginal-differential privacy can be used as baseline operators to devise more sophisticated privacy-preserving protocols with SMC features (like SDO [9]) over distributed OLAP settings more complex than the one assumed in this paper. In these settings, participant nodes may belong to *different classes* (e.g., classes of nodes with different behavior), or may hold *disjoint partial knowledge* on the overall environment. By combine such "pieces" of knowledge nodes can enhance their ability to infer additional knowledge which leads to increased data privacy risks.

6   Experimental Evaluation and Analysis

In order to assess the effectiveness and the efficiency of our privacy preserving distributed OLAP framework [9], we conducted a comprehensive experimental campaign on distributed collections of synthetic, benchmark and real-life XML documents stored in (synthetic, benchmark and real-life) XML data sets, against which we tested the performance of the proposed secure distributed OLAP aggregation protocol SDO [9] under the ranging of several experimental parameters. This finally allowed us to achieve a wide and reliable experimental evaluation and analysis. We selected XML data sets as the reference ones for our experimental assessment as XML is widely known as the *de facto* standard for OLAP over distributed environments.

First, we provide a description about the XML data sets adopted in our experimental campaign. For what regards synthetic XML data sets, element values of the synthetic XML documents have been generated according to three distinct data distributions, namely *Uniform* [6], *Gauss* [27], and *Zipf* [35]. In more detail, Uniform data sets have been generated by means of a Uniform distribution on the interval [75, 125]; Gauss data sets have been generated by means of a *normal* Gauss distribution; Zipf data sets have been generated by means of a Zipf distribution whose parameter z ranges on the interval [0.5, 0.9]. As regards benchmark XML data sets, we considered

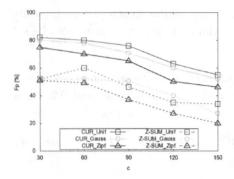
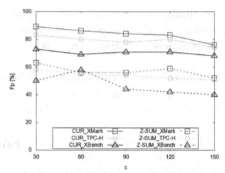

Fig. 1. Variation of F_P w.r.t. the number of columns c (number of blocks, respectively) on 2,000 × 2,000 **OLAP** views extracted from synthetic **XML** data sets for the **CUR** decomposition method and *Zero-Sum*

Fig. 2. Variation of F_P w.r.t. the number of columns c (number of blocks, respectively) on 2,000 × 2,000 **OLAP** views extracted from benchmark **XML** data sets for the **CUR** decomposition method and *Zero-Sum*

the popular data sets *XMark* [36], the **XML**-*version of TPC-H* [37] and *XBench* [38]. In particular, for the data set *TCP-H*, we considered the **XML** document extracted from the table *Lineitem*, which is the biggest one among those composing the whole data set. Finally, as regards real-life **XML** data sets, we considered the well-known data sets *Treebank* [39], *SwissProt* [40] and *NASA* [41]. In turn, from each one of these **XML** data sets, we extracted a 2,000 × 2,000 two-dimensional **OLAP** view, whose (two-dimensional) data cells follow the same distribution of the underlying (**XML**) data set.

We defined four kinds of experiment. In the first kind of experiment, we analyze the privacy preserving capabilities of the **CUR** decomposition method on a *singleton* two-dimensional **OLAP** view with respect to the ranging of the number of columns c exploited by the method itself to compute privacy preserving **OLAP** views (see Section 1). In the second kind of experiment, we conducted a similar experience but focused to study the **CUR**-decomposition's privacy preserving capabilities with respect to the ranging of the probability p_j (see Section 1) of picking the j-th column of the target **OLAP** view during the decomposition process (see Section 1). In the third kind of experiment, we analyze the privacy preserving capabilities of our distributed **OLAP** framework, by studying how the "privacy degree" of distributed **OLAP** views, stored at nodes of the target experimental setting, varies across the nodes under the execution of a **SUM**-based distributed **OLAP** aggregation task (see Section 1). In all the first three kinds of experiment, we considered *Zero-Sum* [29] as the comparison method. This because of three main reasons: (*i*) *Zero-Sum* makes use of a *matrix-like* formalism to face-off and solve the privacy preserving of **OLAP** data cubes, like ours; (*ii*) *Zero-Sum* can be reasonably considered as one of the state-of-the-art perturbation-based approach for centralized privacy preserving **OLAP**; (*iii*) due to its simplicity, *Zero-Sum* can be easily extended as to deal with the more probing case of distributed privacy preserving **OLAP**, like the one addressed and solved by our proposed framework (in this extended implementation, the "original" method *Zero-Sum* plays the same role of the one played by the CUR decomposition method in our framework, i.e. dealing with the privacy preservation of a singleton two-dimensional OLAP view). Finally, in the fourth kind of experiment, we stressed the *sensitivity* of the CUR decomposition method by studying the variation of the probability $P(e^E)$ of the event of $e^E = \mathbf{A} \equiv \mathbf{A}'$, which models the case of obtaining the approximate matrix $\mathbf{A}'$ as *equal* to the input matrix $\mathbf{A}$ (see Section 1), with respect to the ranging of the probability p_j (see Section 1), like in the second kind of experiment.

As regards the metrics of evaluating our privacy preserving distributed OLAP framework, we considered the *privacy factor F_P* introduced by Sung *et al.* in [29], which gives a reliable measure of how much a privacy preserving OLAP data cube (OLAP view, respectively) $\mathcal{D}'$ preserves the privacy of the original OLAP data cube (OLAP view, respectively) $\mathcal{D}$ by inspecting the privacy of cells of $\mathcal{D}'$ with respect to cells of $\mathcal{D}$. In more detail, let (*i*) $\mathcal{D}$ be the input data cube, (*ii*) $\mathcal{D}'$ be the privacy preserving data cube computed by means of a given (privacy preserving) method, (*iii*) $X\{\mathbf{k}\}$ be a data cube cell having $\mathbf{k}$ as multidimensional index, with X in $\{\mathcal{D}, \mathcal{D}'\}$, the privacy factor F_P is defined as follows [29]:

$$F_P(\mathcal{D}, \mathcal{D}') = \frac{1}{\|\mathcal{D}\|} \cdot \sum_{k=0}^{\|\mathcal{D}\|-1} \frac{|\mathcal{D}'\{\mathbf{k}\} - \mathcal{D}\{\mathbf{k}\}|}{|\mathcal{D}\{\mathbf{k}\}|} \tag{30}$$

Figure 1 shows the results obtained from the first kind of experiment, i.e. the percentage variation of the privacy factor F_P with respect to the number of columns c on 2,000 × 2,000 two-dimensional OLAP views extracted from the synthetic XML data sets. Similarly to this, Figure 2 and Figure 3 show the same experimental pattern on benchmark and real-life XML data sets, respectively. With respect to the comparison approach *Zero-Sum*, the parameter c models the *number of blocks* of the partition used to compute the final privacy preserving OLAP view [29]. As shown by Figure 1, Figure 2 and Figure 3, privacy factor values ensured by the CUR decomposition method are high so that obtained (perturbed) OLAP views are privacy preserving accordingly. Also, it turns that the CUR decomposition method outperforms *Zero-Sum* . Note that, with respect to the synthetic XML data sets, the CUR decomposition method works well on Uniform data sets rather than on Gauss and Zipf data sets (for which the performance is still high), because of the sampling phase introduced by the method (as widely-known, sampling works well on Uniform data sets [7] rather than other kinds of data sets).

Figure 4 shows the results obtained from the second kind of experiment, i.e. the percentage variation of the privacy factor F_P with respect to the probability p_j (see Section 1) on the target OLAP views over synthetic XML data sets considered in our experimental assessment. Similarly to this, Figure 5 and Figure 6 show the same experimental pattern on benchmark and real-life XML data sets, respectively. With respect to the comparison approach *Zero-Sum*, the parameter p_j models the *probability of perturbing data cube cells belonging to the j-th block of the partition used to*

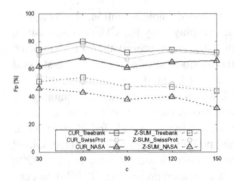
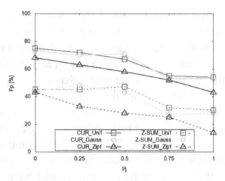

Fig. 3. Variation of F_P w.r.t. the number of columns c (number of blocks, respectively) on $2,000 \times 2,000$ **OLAP** views extracted from real-life **XML** data sets for the **CUR** decomposition method and *Zero-Sum*

Fig. 4. Variation of F_P w.r.t. the number of columns c (number of blocks, respectively) on $2,000 \times 2,000$ **OLAP** views extracted from real-life **XML** data sets for the **CUR** decomposition method and *Zero-Sum*

compute the final privacy preserving **OLAP** view [29]. Like for the case of the first kind of experiment, as confirmed by Figure 4, Figure 5 and Figure 6, we again observed a good performance of the **CUR** decomposition method.

Figure 7 shows the results obtained from the third kind of experiment, i.e. the percentage variation of the privacy factor F_P with respect to the position i of nodes populating a target experimental distributed environment composed by 20 nodes, such that each node stores one singleton **OLAP** view over synthetic **XML** data sets among those considered in our experimental assessment. Similarly to this, Figure 8 and Figure 9 show the same experimental pattern on benchmark and real-life **XML** data sets, respectively. In more detail, in this experiment we inspected the "privacy degree" of each new local **OLAP** view generated in each node by a singleton aggregation step of the whole distributed **OLAP** aggregation task. As shown by Figure 7, Figure 8 and Figure 9, the privacy factor F_P increases with the node position, i.e. each new local **OLAP** view achieves a *higher* privacy degree than the degree of previous views (in the fixed node ordering). The latter is a nice property confirming that our proposed privacy preserving distributed **OLAP** framework fully satisfies the rigorous requirements and constraints posed by the **SMC** model. Also, Figure 7, Figure 8 and Figure 9 demonstrate that the proposed privacy framework, beyond ensuring a good privacy preservation effect on singleton two-dimensional **OLAP** views as confirmed by the previous two kinds of experiment, exposes a good performance even over the target experimental distributed environment, hence it perfectly fulfills the initial goals (i.e., effectively and efficiently supporting secure distributed **OLAP** aggregation tasks – see Section 1), yet outperforming the comparison approach *Zero-Sum* in a distributed setting as well as in a centralized one.

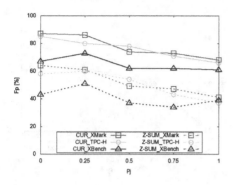

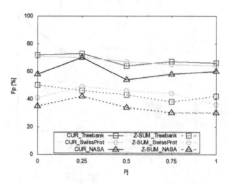

Fig. 5. Variation of F_P w.r.t. the probability p_j on 2,000 × 2,000 OLAP views extracted from benchmark XML data sets for the CUR decomposition method and *Zero-Sum*

Fig. 6. Variation of F_P w.r.t. the probability p_j on 2,000 × 2,000 OLAP views extracted from real-life XML data sets for the CUR decomposition method and *Zero-Sum*

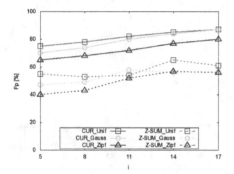

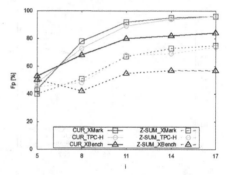

Fig. 7. Variation of F_P w.r.t. the node position i of a 20-node distributed environment on 2,000 × 2,000 OLAP views extracted from synthetic XML data sets for the CUR decomposition method and *Zero-Sum*

Fig. 8. Variation of F_P w.r.t. the node position i of a 20-node distributed environment on 2,000 × 2,000 OLAP views extracted from benchmark XML data sets for the CUR decomposition method and *Zero-Sum*

Finally, Figure 10 shows the results obtained from the fourth kind of experiment, i.e. the variation of the probability $P(e^E)$ with respect to the ranging of the probability p_j (see Section 1), both being critical model parameters of the CUR decomposition method, again on the target OLAP views over synthetic XML data sets considered in our experimental assessment. Similarly to this, Figure 11 and Figure 12 show the same experimental pattern on benchmark and real-life XML data sets, respectively. As shown in Figure 10, Figure 11 and Figure 12, we observe an initial increase of $P(e^E)$ as p_j increases (as expected), but then $P(e^E)$ makes stable to around under the value 0.5. This further confirms to us the benefits of the CUR decomposition method in computing effective privacy preserving OLAP views.

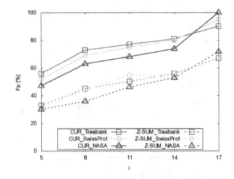

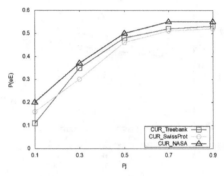

Fig. 9. Variation of F_P w.r.t. the node position i of a 20-node distributed environment on $2{,}000 \times 2{,}000$ **OLAP** views extracted from real-life **XML** data sets for the **CUR** decomposition method and *Zero-Sum*

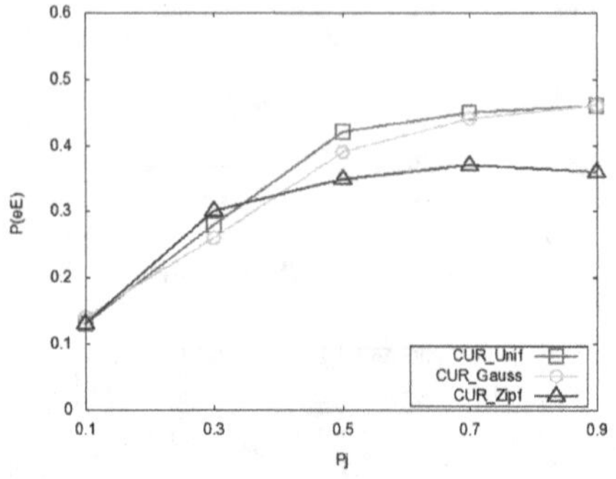

Fig. 10. Variation of $P(e^E)$ w.r.t. the probability p_j on $2{,}000 \times 2{,}000$ **OLAP** views extracted from synthetic **XML** data sets for the **CUR** decomposition method

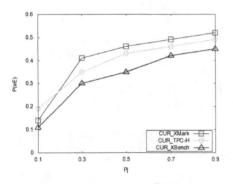

Fig. 11. Variation of $P(e^E)$ w.r.t. the probability p_j on $2{,}000 \times 2{,}000$ **OLAP** views extracted from benchmark **XML** data sets for the **CUR** decomposition method

Fig. 12. Variation of $P(e^E)$ w.r.t. the probability p_j on $2{,}000 \times 2{,}000$ **OLAP** views extracted from real-life **XML** data sets for the **CUR** decomposition method

Concluding, our comprehensive experimental campaign conducted on distributed collections of synthetic, benchmark and real-life **XML** data sets, has clearly demonstrated, under the stressing of a wide variety of experimental parameters, the effectiveness and the efficiency of the proposed privacy preserving distributed **OLAP** framework, even in comparison with the performance of the state-of-the-art perturbation-based method *Zero-Sum*.

7   Conclusions and Future Work

Starting from the results of our previous research [9], which defined a privacy preserving distributed **OLAP** framework, in this paper we have introduced a number of theoretical results that nicely extend the capabilities and the potentialities of this framework. These theoretical results are mainly related to some relevant capabilities of the **CUR** matrix decomposition method, which is the core tool for computing privacy preserving two-dimensional OLAP views in the framework [9]. In order to further support our framework [9], in this paper we have also provided a widespread experimental analysis that fully confirms to us the major practical achievements, in terms of both efficacy and efficiency, due to this framework. Future work is mainly oriented to extend the theoretical results presented here as to make them more robust in order to cover two "difficult" privacy preserving distributed OLAP scenarios of the main framework [9], i.e. (*i*) the need for *multi-resolution OLAP analysis across suitable dimensional hierarchies*, and (*ii*) the presence of *coalition of attackers* that may share *partial knowledge* in order to magnify the capabilities of sensitive data cell inference tasks.

References

[1] Agrawal, S., Haritsa, J.R., Prakash, B.A.: FRAPP: A Framework for High-Accuracy Privacy-Preserving Mining. Data Mining and Knowledge Discovery 18(1), 101–139 (2009)

[2] Agrawal, R., Srikant, R., Thomas, D.: Privacy-Preserving OLAP. Proc. of SIGMOD, 251–262 (2005)

[3] Barak, B., Chaudhuri, K., Dwork, C., Kale, S., McSherry, F., Talwar, K.: Privacy, Accuracy, and Consistency Too: A Holistic Solution to Contingency Table Release. In: Proc. of PODS, pp. 273–282 (2007)

[4] Chan, A.C.-F., Castelluccia, C.: A Security Framework for Privacy-Preserving Data Aggregation in Wireless Sensor Networks. ACM Transactions on Sensor Networks 7(4), art. 29 (2011)

[5] Clifton, C., Kantarcioglu, M., Lin, X., Vaidya, J., Zhu, M.: Tools for Privacy Preserving Distributed Data Mining. SIGKDD Explorations 4(2), 28–34 (2002)

[6] Colliat, G.: OLAP, Relational, and Multidimensional Database Systems. SIGMOD Record 25(3), 64–69 (1996)

[7] Cuzzocrea, A.: Accuracy Control in Compressed Multidimensional Data Cubes for Quality of Answer-based OLAP Tools. In: Proc. of SSDBM, pp. 301–310 (2006)

[8] Cuzzocrea, A.: Privacy Preserving OLAP: Models, Issues, Algorithms. In: Proc. of MIPRO, pp. 1538–1543 (2011)

[9] Cuzzocrea, A., Bertino, E.: A Secure Multiparty Computation Privacy Preserving OLAP Framework over Distributed XML Data. In: Proc. of SAC, pp. 1666–1673 (2010)

[10] Cuzzocrea, A., Russo, V.: Privacy Preserving OLAP and OLAP Security. In: Wang, J. (ed.) Encyclopedia of Data Warehousing and Mining, 2nd edn., pp. 1575–1581. IGI Global (2009)

[11] Cuzzocrea, A., Russo, V., Saccà, D.: A robust sampling-based framework for privacy preserving OLAP. In: Song, I.-Y., Eder, J., Nguyen, T.M. (eds.) DaWaK 2008. LNCS, vol. 5182, pp. 97–114. Springer, Heidelberg (2008)

[12] Cuzzocrea, A., Saccà, D.: Balancing Accuracy and Privacy of OLAP Aggregations on Data Cubes. In: Proc. of DOLAP, pp. 93–98 (2010)

[13] Drineas, P., Kannan, R., Mahoney, M.W.: Computing Sketches of Matrices Efficiently and Privacy Preserving Data Mining. In: Proc. of DIMACS PPDM (2004), http://dimacs.rutgers.edu/Workshops/Privacy/

[14] Drineas, P., Kannan, R., Mahoney, M.W.: Fast Monte Carlo algorithms for Matrices III: Computing a Compressed Approximate Matrix Decomposition. SIAM Journal on Computing 36(1), 184–206 (2006)

[15] Dwork, C.: Differential privacy: A survey of results. In: Agrawal, M., Du, D.-Z., Duan, Z., Li, A. (eds.) TAMC 2008. LNCS, vol. 4978, pp. 1–19. Springer, Heidelberg (2008)

[16] Gray, J., Chaudhuri, S., Bosworth, A., Layman, A., Reichart, D., Venkatrao, M., Pellow, F., Pirahesh, H.: Data Cube: A Relational Aggregation Operator Generalizing Group-By, Cross-Tab, and Sub-Totals. Data Mining and Knowledge Discovery 1(1), 29–53 (1997)

[17] Golub, G.H., Van Loan, C.F.: Matrix Computations. Johns Hopkins University Press (1989)

[18] Han, J., Pei, J., Dong, G., Wang, K.: Efficient Computation of Iceberg Cubes with Complex Measures. Proc. of SIGMOD, 1–12 (2001)

[19] He, W., Liu, X., Nguyen, H., Nahrstedt, K., Abdelzaher, T.: PDA: Privacy-Preserving Data Aggregation for Information Collection. ACM Transactions on Sensor Networks 8(1), art. 6 (2011)

[20] Hua, M., Zhang, S., Wang, W., Zhou, H., Shi, B.-L.: FMC: An approach for privacy preserving OLAP. In: Tjoa, A.M., Trujillo, J. (eds.) DaWaK 2005. LNCS, vol. 3589, pp. 408–417. Springer, Heidelberg (2005)

[21] Jiang, W., Clifton, C.: A Secure Distributed Framework for Achieving k-Anonymity. Very Large Data Bases Journal 15(4), 316–333 (2006)

[22] Jurczyk, P., Xiong, L.: Distributed anonymization: Achieving privacy for both data subjects and data providers. In: Gudes, E., Vaidya, J. (eds.) Data and Applications Security XXIII. LNCS, vol. 5645, pp. 191–207. Springer, Heidelberg (2009)

[23] Li, F., Luo, B., Liu, P.: Secure and Privacy-Preserving Information Aggregation for Smart Grids. International Journal of Security and Networks 6(1), 28–39 (2011)

[24] Lin, X., Lu, R., Shen, X.: MDPA: Multidimensional Privacy-Preserving Aggregation Scheme for Wireless Sensor Networks. Wireless Communications and Mobile Computing 10(6), 843–856 (2010)

[25] Liu, Y., Sung, S.Y., Xiong, H.: A Cubic-Wise Balance Approach for Privacy Preservation in Data Cubes. Information Sciences 176(9), 1215–1240 (2006)

[26] Mohammed, N., Fung, B.C.M., Hung, P.C.K., Lee, C.-K.: Centralized and Distributed Anonymization for High-Dimensional Healthcare Data. ACM Transactions on Knowledge Discovery from Data 4(4), art. 18 (2010)

[27] Papoulis, A.: Probability, Random Variables, and Stochastic Processes. McGraw-Hill (1984)

[28] Pinkas, B.: Cryptographic Techniques for Privacy-Preserving Data Mining. SIGKDD Explorations 4(2), 12–19 (2002)

[29] Sung, S.Y., Liu, Y., Xiong, H., Ng, P.A.: Privacy Preservation for Data Cubes. Knowledge and Information Systems 9(1), 38–61 (2006)

[30] Thompson, S.K., Seber, G.A.F.: Adaptive Sampling. John Wiley & Sons (1996)

[31] Tong, Y., Sun, G., Zhang, P., Tang, S.: Privacy-Preserving OLAP based on Output Perturbation Across Multiple Sites. In: Proc. of PST, p. 46 (2006)

[32] Wang, L., Jajodia, S., Wijesekera, D.: Securing OLAP Data Cubes against Privacy Breaches. In: Proc. of SP, pp. 161–175 (2004)

[33] Wang, L., Wijesekera, D., Jajodia, S.: Cardinality-based Inference Control in Data Cubes. Journal of Computer Security 12(5), 655–692 (2004)

[34] Zhang, N., Zhao, W., Chen, J.: Cardinality-based Inference Control in OLAP Systems: An Information Theoretic Approach. In: Proc. of DOLAP, pp. 59–64 (2004)

[35] Zipf, G.K.: Human Behaviour and the Principle of Least Effort: an Introduction to Human Ecology. Addison-Wesley (1949)

[36] Schmidt, A., Waas, F., Kersten, M.L., Carey, M.J., Manolescu, I., Busse, R.: XMark: A Benchmark for XML Data Management. In: Proceedings of the 28th International Conference on Very Large Data Bases, pp. 974–985 (2002)

[37] Transaction Processing Performance Council (2004), http://www.tpc.org/tpch/default.asp

[38] Yao, B.B., Özsu, M.T., Khandelwal, N.: XBench Benchmark and Performance Testing of XML DBMSs. In: Proceedings of the 20th IEEE International Conference on Data Engineering, pp. 621–632 (2004)

[39] University of Pennsylvania, The Penn Treebank Project (2002), http://www.cis.upenn.edu/~treebank/

[40] Swiss Institute of Bioinformatics, Swiss-Prot Protein Knowledgebase (2005), http://www.expasy.ch/sprot/

[41] GSFC/NASA XML Project, NASA (2003), http://xml.gsfc.nasa.gov

[42] Cuzzocrea, A., Bertino, E., Saccà, D.: Towards A Theory for Privacy Preserving Distributed OLAP. In: Proceedings of the EDBT/ICDT Workshops, pp. 221–226 (2012)

A Template-Based Policy Generation Interface for RESTful Web Services

Philip Raschke and Sebastian Zickau

Service-centric Networking
Technische Universität Berlin, Berlin, Germany
philip-raschke@mailbox.tu-berlin.de,
sebastian.zickau@tu-berlin.de

Abstract. Cloud computing solutions imply chances for economic advantages concerning investment, administration and maintenance costs. On the downside these advantages are paid with a loss of autonomy; the service providers often predetermine configuration and authorization functionalities. The increase of participating actors represents recent privacy, security and legal issues for service providers and users. The different interests of all involved stakeholders raise a need for distributed access control functionalities, which consider the various restrictions of the stakeholders. The presented work designs and realizes a web interface, service users can use to express fine-grained access control policies concerning their resources. The increase of RESTful online services is addressed by a template approach that serves as a basis for the policy interface. A particular focus is set on the eXtensible Access Control Markup Language (XACML), a standard for distributed access control. Following the XACML standard the web interface is realized within the XACML component model. Users' requirements are retrieved via the web interface and translated into a complete XACML policy. The generated policies are tested for syntactic and semantic correctness as well as usability.

Keywords: Cloud Computing, Distributed Access Control, REST, Policy Administration, Policy Creation Interface.

1   Introduction

A recent growth of software as a service (SaaS) offers and a continual increase of SaaS users are observable. The possibilities of cloud computing solutions are broad and users accustom to new paradigms of accessing private data regardless of the device they use or the place they are located. Further, cloud computing solutions imply new possibilities for optimizing internal work processes by enhancing communication and resource sharing.

Despite all advantages of applying cloud computing solutions a crucial drawback of SaaS offers arise. The private resources are stored within the service providers' domain. Access restrictions to these resources can only be expressed if the service providers take these desires into account within the development and

R. Meersman et al. (Eds.): OTM 2014 Workshops, LNCS 8842, pp. 137–153, 2014.

deployment of the service. In current implementations of access control solutions the service users' requirements are sometimes not taken into account. Functionalities giving the users control over their resources need to be implemented by the service providers. Furthermore, specific rules can not be formulated by the service providers due to lack of knowledge about the users' requirements, e.g., their user management realized with a Lightweight Directory Access Protocol (LDAP) server or Active Directory (AD) service. Additionally access control functionalities are complex to implement and therefore expensive. Shifting this complexity to other service providers requires open standards and trustful partners.

Service users are not offered enough configuration settings to achieve optimal access control. More functionalities or a complete list of operations performed by the service on their resources are desirable in certain scenarios. The decisions to whether use a cloud computing solution or not is attached to the shortness of management capabilities [24]. These additional management capabilities should give the service users the possibility to configure, e.g., who can access the data complying with a set policy, with the integration of location and time restrictions as well as device constraints. These restrictions in particular are relevant for facilities that handle highly sensitive data, e.g., facilities in the healthcare domain such as hospitals, health centers, and medical practices.

The article is structured into six sections. Following the introduction and motivation, Section 2 provides an overview of related work and used technologies, including an XACML overview. Section 3 presents the conceptual work on the interface together with the RESTful template approach. Implementation and evaluation results are represented in Section 4 and 5. The article concludes with a summary and an outlook.

1.1   Motivation

The presented work targets to offer a service for cloud computing users to regain management capabilities by expressing access control restrictions in a simplified way. The presented solution focuses exemplary on dynamic attributes regarding time and location. Further this article aims to deploy a standardized distributed access control technology enabled by a single interface to specify access control restrictions. As a positive side effect service providers can neglect complex implementations of access control functionalities since these are provided by a trusted third party (see Fig. 1).

The presented solution follows the Representational State Transfer (REST) architectural style [1] for web services, which is a popular technology for modern cloud computing services. Within RESTful web services the usage of annotations provide additional information about resources and actions. Based on this information an XML template is generated which functions as a basis for the web interface. Service users have the possibility to explicitly permit or prohibit the users' access to certain resources or actions by including local directory servers into the access control architecture (see Fig. 1). Furthermore, the web interface eases the process of policy creation concerning the XACML features by utilizing maps on which polygons can be drawn specifying in which areas access is granted or denied. In the best case the service users are able to control every action performed on their resources. The service provider has no overhead by outsourcing access control implementations. The solution is realized within the TRESOR project[1] in which a trusted third party ecosystem is deployed [24].

2 Related Work and Technologies

To give an overview of state-of-the-art technologies concerning the main problem of the work, it is of relevance to take a look at existing distributed authorization techniques, which are mostly realized by defining a policy language to enable interchangeability. Within the variety of policy languages [3] two of them stick out, namely the eXtensible Access Control Markup Language (XACML) [4] proposed by the Organization for the Advancement of Structured Information Standards (OASIS) [18] and the Enterprise Privacy Authorization Language (EPAL) [5] first introduced by IBM later advanced by the World Wide Web Consortium (W3C) [26]. Due to a high number of XACML implementations an overview of software using XACML for access control is given.

EPAL. EPAL is an authorization language similar to XACML specified as markup language in XML. IBM first published it as Research Report in March 2003 later advanced by the W3C. The language was designed to easily describe and exchange authorization policies. It only describes a policy language, neither a component model nor a request-response format are specified. EPAL is one of a few completely standardized policy languages although due to a lack of implementations, employing EPAL is not feasible.

2.1 XACML

XACML is a representative of the attribute-based access control solutions and was first released in February 2003 by OASIS. XACML defines a component model, a request-response model and a policy language. The current version is 3.0, which was released in January 2013. XACML enables fine-grained access control [6] and due to the defined component model access control solutions can be shifted from the actual application to a third party, which is in charge of the compliance of defined access control policies. Since a policy is represented by an XML file stored at the Policy Retrieval Point (PRP) [8] rules within a policy can be defined by the service provider as well as by the service user.

WSO2 Identity Server. The WSO2 Identity Server [27] is an open source identity management and security tool for enterprise web applications. It was also developed by the WSO2 Inc. and published under Apache2 license. It uses XACML for access control requirements and supports XACMLv2 and XACMLv3. It provides an interface for policy creation and editing and therefore addresses a simplification of the policy creation process. It further includes a tool called TryIt for exploring policy impact.

---

[1] **T**rusted **E**cosystem for **S**tandardized and **O**pen cloud-based **R**esources
http://www.cloud-tresor.de/

ALFA. ALFA [2] is a policy language developed by Axiomatics Inc. It is a free closed source plugin for the Java IDE Eclipse, which can be obtained by registering at the Axiomatics website. The language was developed to ease the process of building XACML policies. Axiomatics claims that ALFA is syntactically similar to Java and C#. ALFA policies are converted to XACMLv3 policies, which can be directly used and applied.

NoXACML. NoXACML is an open source project of independent developer Brad Cox published on code.google.com [17] first announced in June 2012 under Apache2 license. NoXACML targets the complexity of policy creation and editing similar to ALFA and the WSO2 Identity Server. Like ALFA, NoXACML defines a policy language, which is syntactically similar to Java. A complete XACMLv3 policy can be generated and used for access control.

2.2 XACML Engines

There are a number of implementations regarding different aspects of XACML. Some implementations offer a full functional XACML engine, which is designed to cover the whole functionality from formulating an incoming request, over the evaluation to the response formulation. Other implementations focus on the aspect of creating XACML policies and especially simplifying this process.

Sun's XACML implementation. Sun's XACML implementation [23] (in the following also referred as Sun engine) is a XACML engine developed by Sun Microsystems and was last updated in June 2006. The Sun engine is an open source product, which supports XACMLv2. The engine contains the main implementation of XACMLv2 as well as tests. The engine can be used to evaluate XACML requests and policies, it formulates the response and transmits it back to the requesting entity.

Balana. Balana [7] is an open source XACML engine implemented in Java, which supports XACMLv3 as well as XACMLv2. Balana is a derivative of Sun's XACML implementation and was released by WSO2 Inc. under Apache2 license. The engine is composed of the different packages. The package balana-core is the actual implementation of the XACML standard. Noteworthy is that the package balana-utils provides utility methods to easily create XACMLv3 policies. The engine similar to the Sun engine is capable of retrieving and evaluating XACML requests, it subsequently formulates the respective XACML response.

XEngine. The XEngine was developed by the Michigan State University in cooperation with the North Carolina State University [9]. It was released in 2008 under GNU General Public License. The XEngine is open source and written in Java. Similar to the other XACML engines the XEngine retrieves XACML requests and evaluates these by matching it against a set of XACML policy files. The response is returned to the requesting entity. The engine's focus is exclusively on performance concerning the request processing. The XEngine uses techniques like conversion, normalization and tree structures to improve performance [9].

2.3   GeoXACML

GeoXACML [10] is an extension to the XACML standard. It was standardized by the Open Geospatial Consortium (OGC) [19] and first released in June 2005. The current version of GeoXACML is 1.0.1 released in May 2011. It extends the functionality of XACML by providing functions and data types for geospatial information to enable, e.g., location-based access control (LBAC). Some applications need to take the location of the requesting device into account to make an access control decision. Therefore, the Geography Markup Language (GML) [11] is used which was also formulated by the OGC in cooperation with the International Organization for Standardization (ISO) and was first released in May 2000. GML is used to define coordinates, polygons and shapes in two- and three-dimensional space. GeoXACML enhances the features of XACML by enabling the formulation and evaluation of location information in XACML policies and requests.

3   Concept and Design Overview

Distributed architectures require standards to enable interoperability and interchangeability. The last section gave a few options for distributed access control standards in which XACML exposed as the currently most advanced standard available inasmuch as a variety of XACML realizations exist and the standard is constantly developed further. As much as users can benefit from the deployment of XACML with a web interface that is supposed to give them the feasibility to express precise policies to govern access to their resources. Service providers receive chances to save costs when outsourcing sophisticated authorization functionalities and mechanisms to a third party. To accomplish an advantage on the service providers' side, a trusted third party is assumed whose focus is solely on authorization. As stated in the last section another benefit of XACML is that an XACML policy can represent both the users' and the providers' access restrictions and requirements. Yet an instance is needed that conflates the requirements of both sides and merges them into an XACML policy. Therefore an XML template is used that constitutes the service listing, the operations the service performs on the respective resources.

Since this article targets in particular RESTful web services [1] the operations can be smartly mapped to the established methods of the Hypertext Transfer Protocol (HTTP) operations, i.e., GET for read, POST for write, PUT for create, and DELETE for delete. A resource is usually expressed as a Uniform Resource Identifier (URI), consequently the tuple containing an operation and a resource is declared as an action. For each action the web interface offers service users a possibility to specify a subject that is permitted to conduct a respective action. One service user is assumed to be an administrator of a larger enterprise or organization, hence a possibility to interconnect the web interface of the Policy Administration Point (PAP) to an LDAP server or to an Active Directory (AD) server. Owing to the capability of expressing precise policies with XACML the administrator furthermore can specify a time frame in which an access is permitted, e.g., only for two weeks or daily between 9am and 5pm). Using the GeoXACML extension the policy administrator can define an area (or multiple areas, using polygons) from which an access is allowed, e.g., only within the facilities of the enterprise. An omitted statement is interpreted as no restriction. With the help of these two information sources (template and user input) a complete GeoXACML policy is generated.

3.1   Architecture Overview

The involved parties are the *Service Provider*, the *Trusted Third Party* and the *Enterprise (Service User Domain)*. The service provider develops one or many web services and for each web service one *template* is generated listing each action of the service. The creation or generation and authenticity of named template is not in the scope of this work.

Figure 1 gives an overview of the stakeholders and involved components. As stated above the presented work addresses enterprises or organizations with a set of employees with different roles and responsibilities ordinary connected within the same network (Service User Domain). Moreover a policy administrator is assumed who is in charge of the user management and the role assignment. Therefore an LDAP server is supposed to be in place, from which a list of employees and their roles can be retrieved. It is connected to the PAP web interface. Requests from the network proceed through the trusted third party's Policy Enforcement Point (PEP) where an XACML compliant request is formulated and transmitted to the Policy Decision Point (PDP). The XACML conformable response is retransmitted to the PEP, which either proceeds or aborts the request. Besides the PEP the trusted third party runs a PDP at which a policy shall be evaluated. Generated policies can be delivered from the PAP to the PDP usually stored in a PRP. Generated policies contain user and service identifiers. A connection between the PAP and the LDAP of the service user is required to enable access to the service users' information. The architecture of the service itself is open to the service providers' restrictions and needs. Figure 1 generically outlines a typical service architecture.

3.2   Interface Procedure

The web interface is located at the PAP to create and modify existing policies. The use case *Create Policy* is performed by the administrators of the respective enterprise. They express the enterprise's restriction via the web interface and generate the policy. The service providers are in charge of the use case *Generate Template*, which involves the creation of the template file and the transmission to the PAP. To summarize the main functions of the web interface enterprises need to be authenticated so policies created within a certain session can be related to them, the template file of a certain service must be parsed and converted into a web form and input of the user has to be verified and processed to a valid XACML policy.

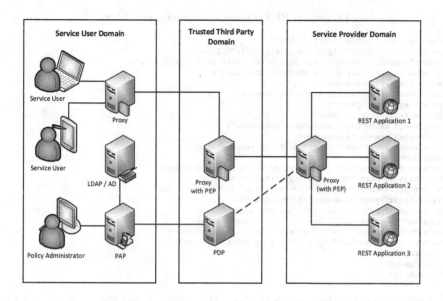

Fig. 1. Architecture Overview

At first the users authenticate at the login page. If the provided credentials are correct the users are redirected to the service overview page. Within the service overview page the booked services are presented. From here they are able to logout again, switch to the LDAP configuration page, or select a service for which they intend to generate a policy. On the LDAP configuration page the users are asked to provide their enterprise's LDAP information. In case of a logout, the users are directed to a blank page where their current session is destroyed.

When selecting a specific service, the users are redirected to the service page where the template of the service is parsed and an appropriate form is generated (see Fig. 2). Nevertheless, if the users did not provide any LDAP information, they are immediately redirected to the LDAP configuration page without printing any content of the service page. The users are able to get back to the service overview page. After expressing their restrictions with the help of the provided form, they can start the process of generating the policy. A success page showing the generated policy is presented to the users.

3.3   REST Template Structure

Each service generates an XML template file listing all actions the service performs. As already stated the creation and authenticity of this file are not within the scope of this article.

Listing 1. REST Template Schema (simplified)

```xml
<?xml version="1.0" encoding="UTF-8"?>
<xs:schema xmlns:xs="http://www.w3.org/2001/XMLSchema"
elementFormDefault="qualified" attributeFormDefault="unqualified">
<xs:element name="service" maxOccurs="unbounded">
<xs:complexType><xs:sequence>
<xs:element name="description"></xs:element>
<xs:element name="paths">
<xs:complexType><xs:sequence>
<xs:element name="path" maxOccurs="unbounded">
<xs:complexType><xs:sequence>
<xs:element name="desc" type="xs:string"></xs:element>
</xs:sequence>
<xs:attribute name="methods" type="xs:string"></xs:attribute>
<xs:attribute name="url" type="xs:string"></xs:attribute>
<xs:attribute name="params" type="xs:string"></xs:attribute>
</xs:complexType></xs:element></xs:sequence>
</xs:complexType></xs:element></xs:sequence>
<xs:attribute name="id" type="xs:int"></xs:attribute>
<xs:attribute name="name" type="xs:string"></xs:attribute>
<xs:attribute name="url" type="xs:string"></xs:attribute>
</xs:complexType>
</xs:element>
</xs:schema>
```

Listing 1 shows the schema of the XML service templates. The root of the XML file is the `<service>` element, which defines the three attributes id, name and url. The attribute id must be a unique numerical identifier. The attribute name simply gives the name of the service whereas the attribute url specifies the URL of the service. It is to note that the url attribute has to be given as regular expression starting with the character ˆ and ending with the $ sign.

The `<service>` element contains a `<description>` element and a `<paths>` element. The `<description>` element compromises a service description; the `<paths>` element contains a sequence of `<path>` elements.

A `<path>` element specifies a methods attribute of type string, an attribute url of a regular expression type and an attribute params of type string. Further, the `<path>` element contains a `<desc>` element, which describes the semantic meaning of the `<path>` element. Listing 2 shows a REST example template for a simplified patient management service.

Listing 2. REST Template Example (simplified)

```xml
<service id="00001" name="Patient Management System" url="http://www.pms.med">
<description>
The Patient Management System (PMS) is a central system to manage patients and
their treatment during their stay in your facility.
</description>
<paths>
<path methods="get" url="http://www.pms.med/patient/*" params="">
<desc>View a patients file and diagnosis.</desc>
</path>
<path methods="post" url="http://www.pms.med/patient/*" params="">
<desc>Edit a patients file.</desc>
</path>
<path methods="put post" url="http://www.pms.med/bloodpressure/*" params="">
<desc>Add or modify a patient's list of blood pressures.</desc>
</path>
<path methods="put post" url="http://www.pms.med/medication/*" params="">
```

```
<desc>Add or modify a medicament to a patient's medication.</desc>
</path>
</paths>
</service>
```

methods contains one or many operations separated by whitespace, e.g. methods="GET POST".

url specifies a URL given as regular expression, e.g.,

$$\text{^http://www.example.com/resource/*\$}$$

params specifies one or many HTTP GET parameters separated by whitespace, e.g. **params="id query"**. The **params** attribute can be useful to involve the service provider's restrictions and requirements. It can express that an operation performed on a certain resource is permitted or denied if a particular parameter is provided or matches a specific value.

The following maps the REST template information to the XACML policy elements, such as *actions, subjects, roles, time, dates,* and *locations.*

Action. To retrieve the essential information from a services template an *action* is defined as a single operation on a specific resource. All *actions* are aggregated in a set. For each **<path>** element the cross product of the **methods** and **url** attribute is built, so a **<path>** element defines as many *actions* as it lists operations within the **methods** attribute.

User input. Each *action* is expanded by the three fields *subject, time* and *location.* These attributes are specified by the service user via the web interface.

Subject and Role. To express that a certain person of the enterprise is permitted to execute a particular *action,* the service users (the enterprise's administrators) are able to search their local LDAP server for the preferred employee (by **uid**). A set of employees can be stated. Further, the LDAP server can be searched for roles to express that a specific employee type is allowed to perform respective operation on the corresponding resource. The subject field is separated into roles and users. Both subfields can contain information, which are combined into a disjunction.

Time. The time field is segmented into the subcategories *date* and *time.* The date field contains two dates whereby the second value is never situated in the past when compared to the first date. A further constraint is that either both values are empty or both have to be given. The date field can be used to express that a particular *action* is permissible within a period. The subfield *time* is analogously given to express that an *action* is permitted at specific hours (e.g. between 9 am and 5 pm). Limitations for the date field apply to the subfield *time.* The subfields do not exclude each other, information of both are conjunct.

Location. The *location* field expresses that a specific action is feasible to conduct within a single or multiple areas. An area (or polygon) is defined as a set of points whereas a point consists of a *latitude* and *longitude* field. Multiple areas are merged into a disjunction (see Fig. 3).

3.4   XACML Rule

To finally transform the information into a valid GeoXACML policy, the information of the *subject*, *time* and *location* fields are merged into a single conjunction forming a predicate (see logic expression 1 below).

$$(role \lor users) \land (date \land time) \land (location_1 \lor location_2 \lor ... \lor location_k) \quad (1)$$

As shown in Listing 3 a `<Rule>` element contains at least a `<Target>` and a `<Condition>` element whereas the `<Condition>` element is the predicate, which must be satisfied to assign the rule's decision its *Effect* attribute. The `<Target>` element is defined as the respective action including its operation and resource. Therefore a rule expresses that a specific access to a resource is permitted if the predicate is satisfied by the response context.

A complete GeoXACML policy can be generated at this point since all relevant information is gathered. The policy then is used at runtime to control access to resources.

Listing 3. XACML Rule Example (simplified)

```
<!-- Rule to see if we should allow the Subject to login -->
<Rule RuleId="LoginRule" Effect="Permit">
<!-- Only use this Rule if the action is login -->
<Target>
<Subjects><AnySubject/></Subjects>
<Resources><AnyResource/></Resources>
<Actions>
<ActionMatch MatchId="...:function:string-equal">
<AttributeValue DataType="...string">login</AttributeValue>
<ActionAttributeDesignator DataType="...string" AttributeId="ServerAction"/>
</ActionMatch></Actions>
</Target>
<!-- Only allow logins from 9am to 5pm -->
<Condition FunctionId="...:function:and">
<Apply FunctionId="...:function:time-greater-than-or-equal"
<Apply FunctionId="...:function:time-one-and-only">
<EnvironmentAttributeSelector DataType="...time"
AttributeId="...:environment:current-time"/>
</Apply>
<AttributeValue DataType="...">09:00:00</AttributeValue>
</Apply>
<Apply FunctionId="...:function:time-less-than-or-equal"
<Apply FunctionId="...:function:time-one-and-only">
<EnvironmentAttributeSelector DataType="...time"
AttributeId="...:environment:current-time"/>
</Apply>
<AttributeValue DataType="...">17:00:00</AttributeValue>
</Apply>
</Condition>
</Rule>
```

4   Implementation

The web interface was programmed with the script language PHP Hypertext Preprocessor (PHP) to cover the functionalities of parsing XML documents, connect to a LDAP server and generate an XML file. Nevertheless, the web interface easily could have been implemented by the use of other programming languages such as Ruby, Java or Python.

Each instance of the *action class* represents an operation the service performs on a particular *URL*, hence the class specifies the two attributes *resource* and *method*. In addition, to these the attributes *id, params* and *desc* are defined. In case both *subjects* and *roles* are defined by the service user, the two predicates are merged into a single disjunction. If the service user already generated a policy for the chosen service, the state of the input fields would be restored by loading the serialized data.

4.1 Interface

Figure 2 shows the interface of the service detail page, with *Resources, Methods, Parameters, Subjects, Time* and *Location*.

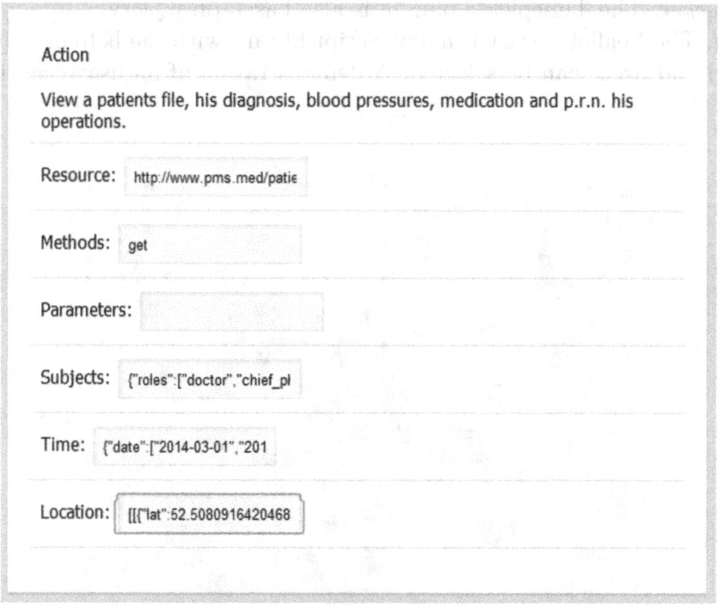

Action

View a patients file, his diagnosis, blood pressures, medication and p.r.n. his operations.

Resource: http://www.pms.med/patie

Methods: get

Parameters:

Subjects: {"roles":["doctor","chief_pl

Time: {"date":["2014-03-01","201

Location: [[["lat":52.5080916420468

Fig. 2. Service detail page

Figure 3 represents the process of specifying a certain area from which a request is permitted to proceed, in this case the premises of the Paulinen Hospital in Berlin, Germany. OpenStreetMap is used to present the map information[2] to the policy creator.

---

[2] ©OpenStreetMap contributors.

4.2   Used Technologies

Below a list of technologies is provided which were used to build the interface and realize particular components of the web interface.

PHP. As stated above, PHP was used in version 5.3.8, additionally the PHP extensions php_ldap and php_curl have been used for LDAP connection handling and executing HTTP POST requests via curl.

jQuery. The JavaScript library jQuery is used by several plug-ins that were used to build the web interface. Especially the Leaflet API requires loading the jQuery library before.

jQueryUI. The JavaScript library jQueryUI provides several useful functionalities such as the auto-complete function or the date-picker to ease the process of filling HTML forms.

Colorbox. Colorbox is a jQuery plug-in, therefore requires loading jQuery before. The plug-in is used to visualize content within a box apart from the page's structure. It is useful to load content on users demand simultaneously not overloading the page with too much input fields.

Timepicker. The Timepicker plug-in is also based on jQuery.

Leaflet. The Leaflet library is a JavaScript library with the help of a map can be loaded and areas can be selected. A demonstration of its usage can be seen in Fig. 3.

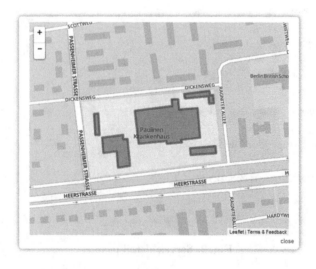

Fig. 3. GPS-Polygons around Hospital Premises

4.3   Problems and Solutions

During the process of implementation problems occurred especially with the XacmlPolicyGenerator class. The generation of the XACML policies was planed to be realized by taken the respective XSD schema file of the XACML standard into account. Therefore the PHP class SDO DAS XML [21] was preferred to use, yet the SDO extension seemed to be not compatible with newer PHP versions. The problem was solved by using the XMLWriter class of PHP with the drawback that XML documents were created with the help of this class without taking the XSD schema into account. Therefore a syntax test needed to be done to test the generated policies for syntactic validity. The serialization of the form's state at the moment of submission, to enable later modifications, originally was not considered as necessary since the XACML policies follow a strict pattern. Therefore it is possible to parse these XACML policies to recover users' input. Nevertheless, the performance and complexity of the web interface can be significantly improved by serializing the data. Further performance improvements were made when the content of the Colorboxes was created only once.

5 Evalution

In this section the evaluation of the web interface and the generated policies is presented. These two main components have to be treated differently in concern of testing. The generated policies need to be tested for syntactic and semantic validity. Subsequently the processes of testing the semantic and syntactic validity of the policies are discussed.

5.1 Test Scenario

For the test scenario two enterprises were defined. Respective information was provided in a MySQL database to enable a login at the web interface. Further, four web services were specified, each web service offers a template file as described in Section 3. One hospital used two web services; the other one used three web services. The web interface presented only the services used by the respective users. In total five policies were generated. The five web services specified 34 actions in total. To stress the variety of possible policies that can be made with the help of the web interface, one hospital mainly expressed role based access control restrictions by not limiting the use of services by time or location. Whereas the other hospital strictly restricted the use of services to the time between 8:00 a.m. and 8:00 p.m. Furthermore, it only allowed access to services from the premises of the hospital. The policies were generated and to ease the process of evaluation, aggregated into a single policy set.

5.2 Requests

The appropriate requests were generated during the process of policy creation. Therefore for each rule generated within a policy one valid request was generated specifying exactly the attributes the rule defines. This valid request was generated for XACMLv2 and XACMLv3. Further, for each rule as many requests were generated as the rule defines attributes (i.e. *subjects, roles, hours, date, location*). These requests were expected to evaluate to *deny*, hence each of them was falsify a single attribute. For the test scenario 162 XACMLv2 and XACMLv3 requests were generated, which were saved into particular files. The contents of those were sent to the respective GeoXACML engine via a HTTP POST requests. The result of each request was matched against the expected outcome value, which is contained in the filename of the respective XACML request. The described algorithm was performed by a PHP script, which also visualizes the results of the matching of expected and actual response.

5.3   GeoXACML Engines

To test the generated policies a GeoXACML engine was needed, that is capable of retrieving a policy, accepting and evaluating a request and then formulates the decision, which are transmitted to the requesting entity. To test the generated GeoXACML policies, the engine, which was built within the TRESOR project, was used.

5.4   Semantic Validation

The core of the generated policies is their content, which is supposed to represent the service users' access restrictions. It is therefore unalterable that invalid requests evaluate to *deny* and valid requests evaluate to *permit*. To test the generated policies for semantic validity it is of importance to define a test scenario in which policies are created. These are tested with valid and invalid requests. The desired result is that any requests evaluates to the expected outcome otherwise an error must have been made during the transformation of the users' input to the XACML policy. The responses show that all requests are evaluated to their expected outcomes. Interestingly calling the PHP scripts between 8:00 p.m. and 8:00 a.m. leads to errors of rules, which specified a time restriction. These errors occur, since the valid requests specify the correct attributes, their expected outcome naively should be *permit*, yet the time is not specified within the request context. Actually their expected response should dynamically change to *deny* if they are transmitted between 8:00 p.m. and 8:00 a.m. On the other hand this inconsistency shows the equivalence of the policies in the version XACMLv2 and XACMLv3, since the exact same requests lead to errors, during the same time period.

5.5   Syntactic Validation

The most precise way to evaluate the syntactic validity of the generated policies is to check those against the specified schema, which is defined by an XSD file. For the syntactic validation the Notepad++ plugin XML Tools were used. The tests were run consecutively for each policy starting with the policies in version XACMLv2, followed by the policies in version XACMLv3. It is to mention that the results of a policy are not distinct from another policy in the same version. All policies in XACMLv2 showed the syntactic error in Listing 4.

Listing 4. Error Message during Syntax Validation

```
ERROR: Element {urn:oasis:names:tc:xacml:2.0:policy:schema:os}Subjects:
This element is not expected. Expected is one of
({urn:oasis:names:tc:xacml:2.0:policy:schema:os}Actions,
{urn:oasis:names:tc:xacml:2.0:policy:schema:os}Environments).
```

This error is caused by the *target* definition of each policy. The root of the error remains unknown, yet investigations show that the use of the `<Subjects>` element in the policy target leads to this error. The identifier is used to map an access from a particular domain (i.e. a certain enterprise) to a specific policy. Tests without the `<Subjects>` element were evaluated to valid. Remarkable is also that the syntax checks for the policies in version XACMLv3 showed no errors, although the same identifier was used. Generally it is to say, that the generated policies are syntactical correct and therefore can be applied within real scenarios.

5.6 Usability Tests

It is observable that the current state of the web interface needs improvement in respect of what the user is expected to fill out and what his input semantically means. Information the user is not meant to edit should be presented as text and not in input fields. Further, the three input fields *subjects*, *time* and *location* should be highlighted. The user should get a feedback by expressing a restriction, for instance when selection a certain role an overlay can be presented to the user, stating that this role is now permitted to perform respective action. Besides the test subjects confirmed that the web interface is usable yet it needs further improvements concerning the usability to ease the process of policy generation.

6 Summary and Outlook

This work presents a web interface to generate precise and fine grained Geo-XACML policies by service users to protect their cloud-based resources. The web interface requires a template file, which describes the REST functionalities of the service. The template files hold information about all operations (represented by HTTP methods), which are performed on a particular resource (represented by URLs). This article addresses service users such as hospitals or other facilities that handle sensitive data and aggregate commonly more service users with different roles. The web interface was designed to be used by an administrator who represents the facility and who is in charge of the user management of the facility. The policies were tested for semantic and syntactical validity.

A possibility for service users to dynamically chose the level of granularity for a certain action can be discussed and implemented. This leads to another aspect of the web interface, the current attributes that the interface specifies may not be suitable for certain use cases. It is therefore useful to think of features to manipulate or alter the attributes. Section 5 also shows that usability improvements can be made. Also the realization of recurring events in XACML policies is not trivial and need to be investigated as a stand-alone research topic. As stated in Section 3, the *parameters* attribute of the template file can represent the service providers' restrictions. Further, it would be useful to automate the process of generating the service template files out of given source code.

Acknowledgement. The work presented in this paper was performed in the context of the TRESOR project. TRESOR is funded by the German Federal Ministry of Economics and Technology (BMWi).

References

1. Fielding, R.T.: Architectural Styles and the Design of Network-based Software Architectures University of California. Irvine, USA (2000)
2. Axiomatics Language for Authorization (ALFA),
   https://www.axiomatics.com/solutions/products/
   authorization-for-applications/developer-tools-and-apis/
   192-axiomatics-language-for-authorization-alfa.html
3. Kumaraguru, P., Lobo, J., Cranor, L.F., Calo, S.B.S.: A survey of privacy policy languages In: Workshop on Usable IT Security Management. In: Proceedings of the 3rd Symposium on Usable Privacy and Security, USM 2007, ACM (2007)
4. OASIS: eXtensible Access Control Markup Language (XACML) Version 3.0 (2013),
   http://www.oasis-open.org/committees/xacml
5. W3C: The Enterprise Privacy Authorization Language, EPAL (2004),
   http://www.w3.org/2003/p3p-ws/pp/ibm3.html
6. Anderson, A.: A Comparison of Two Privacy Policy Languages: EPAL and XACML. Sun Microsystems Inc. (2005)
7. Balana Engine, https://github.com/wso2/balana
8. Vollbrecht, J., Calhoun, P., Farrell, S., Gommans, L., Gross, G., de Bruijn, B., de Laat, C., Holdrege, M., Spence, D.: AAA Authorization Framework IETF (2000)
9. Liu, A.X., Chen, F., Hwang, J., Xie, T.: XEngine: A Fast and Scalable XACML Policy Evaluation Engine (2008)
10. Open Geospatial Consortium: Geospatial eXtensible Access Control Markup Language (GeoXACML) Version 1, Corrigendum Open Geospatial Consortium (2011),
    http://www.opengeospatial.org/standards/geoxacml
11. Open Geospatial Consortium: OpenGIS Geography Markup Language (GML) Encoding Standard (2007), http://www.opengeospatial.org/standards/gml
12. Mazzoleni, P., Crispo, B., Sivasubramanian, S., Bertino, E.: XACML Policy Integration Algorithms ACM Trans. Inf. Syst. Secur. 11, 4:1-4:29 (2008)
13. Abi Haidar, D., Cuppens-Boulahia, N., Cuppens, F., Debar, H.: An Extended RBAC Profile of XACML. In: Proceedings of the 3rd ACM Workshop on Secure Web Services, pp. 13–22. ACM (2006)
14. Hu, V., Martin, E., Hwang, J., Xie, T.: Conformance Checking of Access Control Policies Specified in XACML. In: 31st Annual International Computer Software and Applications Conference, COMPSAC 2007, vol. 2, pp. 275–280 (2007)
15. Lorch, M., Kafura, D., Shah, S.: An XACML-based Policy Management and Authorization Service for Globus Resources. In: Proceedings of the 4th International Workshop on Grid Computing. IEEE Computer Society (2003)

16. Lorch, M., Proctor, S., Lepro, R., Kafura, D., Shah, S.: First Experiences Using XACML for Access Control in Distributed Systems. In: Proceedings of the 2003 ACM Workshop on XML Security, pp. 25–37. ACM (2003)
17. NoXACML, https://code.google.com/p/no-xacml/
18. Organization for the Advancement of Structured Information Standards, OASIS, https://www.oasis-open.org/
19. Open Geospatial Consortium, OGC, http://www.opengeospatial.org
20. Rao, P., Lin, D., Bertino, E., Li, N., Lobo, J.: An Algebra for Fine-grained Integration of XACML Policies. In: Proceedings of the 14th ACM Symposium on Access Control Models and Technologies, pp. 63–72. ACM (2009)
21. PHP SDO XML Data Access Service,
    http://php.net/manual/en/sdo-das-xml.examples.php
22. Seitz, L., Rissanen, E., Sandholm, T., Firozabadi, B.S., Mulmo, O.: Policy Administration Control and Delegation Using XACML and Delegent. In: Proceedings of the 6th IEEE/ACM International Workshop on Grid Computing, pp. 49–54. IEEE Computer Society (2005)
23. Sun's XACML implementation, http://sourceforge.net/projects/sunxacml/
24. Thatmann, D., Slawik, M., Zickau, S., Küpper, A.: Towards a federated cloud ecosystem: Enabling managed cloud service consumption. In: Vanmechelen, K., Altmann, J., Rana, O.F. (eds.) GECON 2012. LNCS, vol. 7714, pp. 223–233. Springer, Heidelberg (2012)
25. Turkmen, F., Crispo, B.: Performance Evaluation of XACML PDP Implementations. In: Proceedings of the 2008 ACM Workshop on Secure Web Services, pp. 37–44. ACM (2008)
26. World Wide Web Consortium, W3C, http://www.w3.org/
27. WSO2 Identity Server, http://wso2.com/products/identity-server/
28. Xu, M., Wijesekera, D., Zhang, X., Cooray, D.: Towards Session-Aware RBAC Administration and Enforcement with XACML. In: IEEE International Symposium on Policies for Distributed Systems and Networks, POLICY 2009, pp. 9–16 (2009)
29. Zhang, N., Ryan, M., Guelev, D.P.: Synthesising Verified Access Control Systems in XACML. In: Proceedings of the 2004 ACM Workshop on Formal Methods in Security Engineering, pp. 56–65. ACM (2004)

Energy-Efficient Data Processing
at Sweet Spot Frequencies

Sebastian Götz[1], Thomas Ilsche[1], Jorge Cardoso[2], Josef Spillner[1],
Uwe Aßmann[1], Wolfgang Nagel[1], and Alexander Schill[1]

[1] Technische Universität Dresden, Germany
[2] University of Coimbra, Portugal
{sebastian.goetz1,thomas.ilsche,josef.spillner,
uwe.assmann,wolfgang.nagel,alexander.schill}@tu-dresden.de,
jcardoso@dei.uc.pt

Abstract. The processing of Big Data often includes sorting as a basic operator. Indeed, it has been shown that many software applications spend up to 25% of their time sorting data. Moreover, for compute-bound applications, the most energy-efficient executions have shown to use a CPU speed lower than the maximum speed: the CPU *sweet spot* frequency. In this paper, we use these findings to run Big Data intensive applications in a more energy-efficient way. We give empirical evidence that data-intensive analytic tasks are more energy-efficient when CPU(s) operate(s) at sweet spots frequencies. Our approach uses a novel high-precision, fine-grained energy measurement infrastructure to investigate the energy (joules) consumed by different sorting algorithms. Our experiments show that algorithms can have different sweet spot frequencies for the same computational task. To leverage these findings, we describe how a new kind of self-adaptive software applications can be engineered to increase their energy-efficiency.

1 Introduction

Electricity used in global cloud data centers likely accounts for between 1.1% and 1.5% of total electricity use. IDC[1] estimates that the digital universe of Big Data will double every two years, reaching 40,000 exabytes in 2020. This large volume of data will require complex analytics processing applications, which will necessitate massive processing power.

This state of affairs calls for the development of new approaches to reduce energy consumption [1], which has already led researchers to develop new hardware and software architectures, virtual machine migration strategies, and water cooling mechanisms.

Since analytical applications for Big Data rely heavily on the performance of data-intensive tasks such as data aggregation, data sorting, and data formatting,

---

[1] http://www.emcchannel.com/collateral/analyst-reports/
idc-the-digital-universe-in-2020.pdf

R. Meersman et al. (Eds.): OTM 2014 Workshops, LNCS 8842, pp. 154–171, 2014.
© Springer-Verlag Berlin Heidelberg 2014

in this paper we look into new techniques to make these tasks more energy-efficient. While making, e.g., the task of data sorting 5% more energy-efficient seems a marginal achievement, this value needs to be contextualized (see [2]). Facebook generates more than 5 petabytes of new data on a daily basis; LinkedIn generated more than 5 billion searches in 2012; Twitter generates more than 500 million tweets a day; and Cisco forecast for global mobile data traffic (2013-2018)[2] estimates that traffic will grow at a compound annual growth rate of 78% to 2016, reaching 10.8 exabytes per month. Clearly, reducing in 5% the required energy of a data-intense sorting task translates into large savings.

Our approach involves executing sorting algorithms under various configurations (e.g., the number of elements to sort and the CPU frequency) and evaluating which *sweet spots* of the underlying hardware architecture enables a more energy-efficient execution. The data obtained was used to construct a task profile, which then resulted in a predictive model to determine at which frequency a CPU should be clocked to run a specific data-intensive sorting task most efficiently. We show how to automate the detection of sweet spots and their use to develop self-adaptive software, which automatically selects the CPU frequency to execute algorithms based on sweet spots and energy objectives to reach. Our approach is based on two previous findings:

1. It has been shown that for certain computational applications, the most energy-efficient execution is achieved using the CPU sweet spot frequency, a CPU frequency setting that is often between the minimum and maximum.
2. It has been shown that software applications spend up to 25% of their time sorting data.

1) It is already known from previous academic and industrial research that processors do not follow a proportional path. Single processors have power states and associated frequencies for which the energy-efficiency, i.e., the ratio between utilization and energy consumption is maximized in so-called sweet spots [3] and often minimized in high-performance *turbo mode* [4, 5]. Furthermore, in multiprocessor systems, additional overlap effects result from using the turbo mode as a gap-filler before switching on the next core when the utilization increases [6]. This effect, in particular the sweet spot, translates into time-dependent energy efficiency due to Dynamic Voltage Frequency Scaling (DVFS; a commonly used power-management technique).

2) More than 25% of the running time of many applications has at some point been spent on sorting [7]. While more recent results are missing from the literature, it is expected that the processing of Big Data will place an even greater emphases on sorting. In their approach, Herodotou et al. [8] also use sorting algorithms to evaluate the performance of systems for Big Data analytics since "they are simple, yet very representative". Other data-intensive tasks of interest, but not explored in our work, include search and indexing over large volumes of data.

---

[2] http://www.cisco.com/c/en/us/solutions/collateral/service-provider/
visual-networking-index-vni/white_paper_c11-520862.html

Among our results, we determined that the automated detection and use of sweet spot frequencies reduces energy consumption by up to 25% and that data-intensive tasks can be designed as self-adaptive applications to exploit the benefits of sweet spots. Our findings can contribute to the development of energy-efficient analytics applications and databases for Big Data, since they operate on large amounts of data and heavily rely on the task of sorting to process data.

This paper is structured as follows. Sect. 2 enumerates three central research questions that are addressed throughout this paper. Sect. 3 describes our approach and the methodology we have followed to experimentally analyze the energy-efficiency of data-intensive processing tasks. We discuss the results of our experiments in Sect. 4 and show in Sect. 5, how these findings can be used, to build self-adaptive software, able to leverage this knowledge to save energy. Finally, Sect. 6 and 7 present related work and our conclusions, respectively.

2   Research Questions

The energy-efficiency of data-intensive processing tasks looks into how software, the underlying computing system and the environment affect energy consumption. Our research questions (RQ) are the following:

- RQ1 (Measurement Setup). How to instrument a computing system with measurement devices to obtain fine-grained measurements for its individual parts (e.g., fan, disk, power supply, and CPU sockets)? (Sect. 3.1).
- RQ2 (Sweet spots). How can sweet spot frequencies contribute to improve the energy-efficiency of data processing tasks? Which mathematical functions characterize them? (Sect. 4).
- RQ3 (Dynamic Software Adaptation). How to explore sweet spots to dynamically adapt software to achieve a higher energy-efficiency? (Sect. 5).

In this paper, we study how different implementations of algorithms typically used by data-intensive tasks affect differently the energy efficiency of a computing system. We take the computational task of sorting n numbers, as it represents a common use case for Big Data analytics.

While research has looked into how to make information and communication technologies more energy-efficient, it is rather hard to find a precise definition for *software energy-efficiency*. Thus, to remove any possible ambiguity on the results of our research, we define the concept as follows:

Definition 1 (Software energy-efficiency). *Energy is defined as the amount of joules, required by a full or partial computing environment, to execute a software application. A software application S_1 is said to be more energy-efficient than an application S_2, if it requires less energy to accomplish the same computational task.*

Definition 2 (Computing environment). *A full computing environment includes all the devices that, directly or indirectly, consume energy to enable a software application to be executed. For example, it typically includes CPUs, fans, and disks. A partial computing environment only includes a subset of those devices.*

3   Approach and Methodology

Computational complexity (i.e., big O notation) is often a first step in assessing the performance of an algorithm. However, in practice, the best big O algorithm may perform worse due to, e.g., physical memory constraints. Quicksort is such an example since is often used even though it does not have the best big O (worst case) performance. It is common practice to optimize implementations for run-time and, in most cases, optimizations will also reduce energy consumption. However, in recent hardware with increasing energy-efficiency features, such as DVFS, the fastest algorithm is often no longer the most energy-efficient one.

Our approach to gain insights is experimental. We use energy as a main optimization goal and vary the algorithm and hardware configuration for comparison. The methodology has the following activities:

- Measurement environment (Sect. 3.1).
  - Instrument server with energy sensors.
  - Determine static power consumption of the server.
  - Setup software infrastructure to conduct the experiments.
- Software under test (Sect. 3.2).
  - Select the data-intensive computational task to be tested experimentally.
  - Select different software implementations for the task.
- Experimental results analysis (Sect. 4).
  - Determine resources affected by task.
  - Interpret measurement results.
- Generalization and application of the results (Sect. 5).

3.1   Measurement Setup: Energy Monitoring

Hardware. The system under test is a dual socket system with Intel Xeon E5-2690 processors. Several layers of power measurement instrumentation are required. The complete AC input is measured with a calibrated ZES Zimmer LMG450 power analyzer. Several custom-built, shunt-based sensors are added to the system. All sensors are pluggable via Molex connectors used in many standardized systems. For this paper, we monitor the 12 V input of the two individual sockets separately. They supply power for the CPUs and their attached memory. The voltage drop over the measurement shunt is amplified with calibrated amplifiers and digitally captured by a National Instruments PCI-6255 data acquisition board with 7541 samples per second. The power consumption is computed digitally from individual readings for current and voltage. During the experiment, all data processing happens on a separate system to avoid perturbation of the system under test. This measurement infrastructure serves as an answer to RQ1, but requires significant effort, as described in [9].

The processors provide 15 different frequencies from 1.2 to 2.9 GHz and the turbo mode with frequencies up to 3.8 GHz, depending on thermal and power budget. Both, frequency and voltage are set uniformly for all cores of a socket by the hardware. As demonstrated in [10], the available memory bandwidth

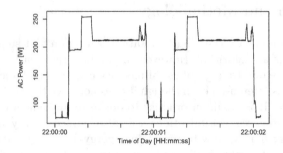

Fig. 1. Energy trace of two succeeding sorting invocations with idle phase

depends on the core frequency for the Sandy Bridge-EP architecture. Earlier Intel architectures, such as the one used in [3], provided a constant memory bandwidth independent of the selected frequency. The variable memory bandwidth did not allow for a straight-forward selection of the optimal frequency for applications that become memory-bound at a certain frequency. However, our approach does not require specific bottleneck analysis, because it uses the energy measurement results to select among different settings instead.

Measurements. To investigate the energy consumption of data-intensive tasks, we run different sort algorithms for different input sizes multiple times. Prior to each invocation, we randomly generate integer lists to be sorted. Across all invocations, we used lists of sizes between 10 and 50 million elements, always containing integers with a value range of 6 million (i.e., $0 \leq x < 6 \times 10^6$). Each invocation is preceded by a pause of 1 second to "cool down" the CPU and other resources (i.e., let them switch to idle mode).

Measurements of sort invocations utilizing a single core of a multi-core machine are not representative, due to the static power consumption of other devices besides the CPU, which does not change, regardless of how many cores are used. Hence, we fully utilized all cores of the machine with a separate sort invocation operating on a copy of the same list. By using MPI barriers [11], we ensure that all sort invocations are started at the same time. As execution time, we measured the longest duration of the parallel sort invocations and ensured that variation of durations among parallel processes was less than 5%.

Fig. 1 visualizes the invocation scheduling by AC power consumption (i.e., at the wall) over time for two consecutive sort invocations. The spikes at the beginning and end of each invocation are due to (MPI) synchronization. The short period of 250 W in each run denotes the list generation.

As shown in Table 1, the static power consumption of the server originates from the power supply, the fan, the motherboard, the disk, and the sockets.

For the investigation of the effect of different CPU frequencies on the timing and energy-efficiency of sorting, we used the *userspace* CPU governor of Linux to explicitly set the frequency of the CPU. Linux also offers the governors *performance* and *powersave* that statically select the highest/lowest frequency within

Table 1. Static idle power consumption of the server

Power supply & Fans	Board	SSD	Sockets	Total
≈26W	≈7W	≈1W	≈20W × 2	≈74W

the borders of a setting. The *ondemand* governor changes the frequency based on CPU usage. In our use case of continuously sorting, the CPU usage will be at 100% for the active cores. Therefore, the *ondemand* governor will eventually select the highest frequency.

We executed list generation and sorting for three algorithms with different list sizes for all possible frequencies of the CPU and the turbo mode. We collected the total energy consumption of the server per execution, the energy consumption of the sockets, and the response time. This enables to investigate whether a sweet spot frequency exists and if static power consumption leads to a shift of the sweet spot frequency for sockets, only compared to the whole server.

3.2   Software Setup: Sorting Algorithm

As mentioned before, data analytics over Big Data are a key target for energy efficiency with huge absolute savings, even for small percentages in relative savings. These systems are very complex and rely heavily on computational tasks such as data cleansing, data aggregation, data sorting, and data formatting. We suggest to study a well-known and representative algorithm: sorting. In many applications, more than 25% of the running time of computers has at some point been spent on sorting [7].

We selected two stable sort implementations: counting sort and radix sort. We also looked at the non-stable sorting of the C++ Standard Library: std::sort. Counting sort is a stable sorting algorithm with a linear time complexity of $O(n)$. Radix sort performs $O(n \times log_2(n))$ comparisons [12]. Our implementation (GNU libstdc++) uses a combination of intro sort and insertion sort.

Based on this knowledge about the time complexity of sorting algorithms, we investigated the energy consumption of the three algorithms. Since sorting is compute bound, one could assume the CPU to be the predominant consumer of energy amongst all other resources in a server. We collected empirical support for this hypothesis and, in addition, determined further resources consuming energy due to sorting. It is important to know that the frequency of a CPU affects timing, power and, consequently, the energy consumption of algorithms. In general, we will give empirical support for the following claims:

1. The highest frequency of a CPU does not necessarily lead to the lowest energy consumption (power integrated over time).
2. Each algorithm has a detectable frequency at which the resulting energy consumption is lowest (sweet spot frequency).
3. Different algorithms can have different sweet spot frequencies.

AC Power Consumption of Sort for 50mio Elements

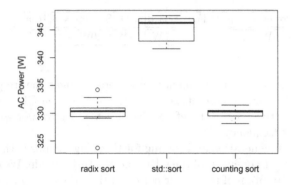

Fig. 2. AC power consumption for sorting 50 million elements

4   Results of the Experiments

Before investigating the impact of different frequencies on energy-efficiency in Sect. 4.2, we analyze in Sect. 4.1[3] whether algorithms differ in their power consumption and show that algorithms with low power consumption are not necessarily the best in terms of energy consumption.

4.1   On the Power Consumption Level of Software

The weighted moments, among them the mean value, quartiles, minimum and maximum excluding extreme outliers, are shown in Fig. 2 for a sorting task on 50 million elements where both CPUs of the server operate in turbo mode.

From the figure, one can infer that using radix or counting sort leads to a lower power consumption than std::sort. The former two have an almost equal level. The savings compared to std::sort amount to 4.6%. Yet, radix sort is clearly the fastest algorithm and, hence, the best when combining both metrics without prioritization of one over the other. Counting sort is, despite its low power consumption, the worst in terms of energy consumption. From this so-called *sweet spot perspective*, which will be further elaborated on in the following section, the savings for radix sort amount to 77.6% compared to counting sort. Table 2 summarizes the key numbers from the experiments: Duration including range, power consumption per time unit and overall energy consumption for the mean duration. All power values include 74 W idle consumption.

4.2   On the Sweet Spots of Software

In this section, we investigate and prove wrong the common misconception that software energy-efficiency equates directly to CPU performance. For this purpose, we have collected evidence that executing software applications at high

---

[3] All raw measurements retrieved from the experiments were processed with the statistics software R.

Table 2. Sorting algorithms comparison for 50mio elements (in turbo mode)

Algo.	t_{min} (s)	t_{max} (s)	t_{range} (s)	P (W)	E (J)
radix	1.880	1.901	0.021	330.4	626.9
std::sort	4.226	4.230	0.004	346.3	1464.1
count.	8.444	8.516	0.072	330.3	2801.5

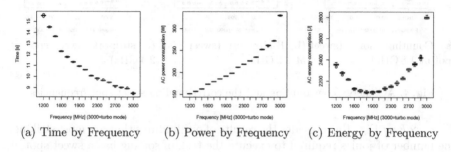

(a) Time by Frequency   (b) Power by Frequency   (c) Energy by Frequency

Fig. 3. The sweet spot of counting sort to sort 50mio elements

CPU frequencies may lead to lower software energy-efficiency. Therefore, we re-fine research question RQ2 into:

- RQ2a (Effectiveness). Can we increase software energy efficiency by changing the clock frequency of the CPU executing a software task?
- RQ2b (Determinability). Can the clock frequency of the CPU executing a software task, which makes the software more energy efficient, be determined?

For the three different algorithmic implementation, radix sort, std::sort and counting sort, we measured the energy consumed to sort 10, 20, . . . , 50 million integers. Fig. 3 shows the results obtained for sorting 50 million elements using counting sort. Measurement results for all other list sizes and algorithms are shown in Fig. 4. The figure shows three charts: time per frequency, power per frequency, and energy per frequency. Note that turbo mode frequency varies over time, depends on different factors and can be between 2.9 and 3.8 GHz. Very high frequencies are unlikely as we fully use all cores.

Time× Freq Fig. 4(a) shows that as the clock frequency of the CPU increases from 1.2 GHz to 2.9 GHz and turbo mode, the mean time required to execute the software task of sorting decreases in a non-linear form. What should be noticed is that at 1.4 GHz the mean time to complete the task drops significantly.

Power× Freq Fig. 4(b) shows the power consumed based on the CPU clock fre-quency selected. The results could be considered foreseeable, since the power consumption of the CPU increases by its frequency. Nonetheless, up to 2 GHz the power consumption is more modest and has visible increments at 1.5 GHz, 2.2 GHz, 2.7 GHz and for the turbo mode.

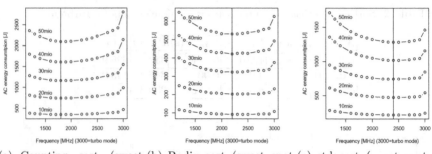

(a) Counting sort (sweet (b) Radix sort (sweet spot (c) std::sort (sweet spot at spot at 1.8 GHz) at 2.2 GHz) 2.4 GHz)

Fig. 4. AC energy consumption and the corresponding sweet spot frequencies

Energy× Freq Fig. 4(c) provides the results of our findings that are most striking: the number of joules required to execute the task of sorting has a sweet spot at 1.8 GHz. The energy consumption declines by approximately 25% (708 J) when the CPU frequency is changed from turbo mode to 1.8 GHz.

For the other algorithms, the results are also interesting. std::sort is more energy efficient at 2.4 GHz. This corresponds to energy savings of approximately 12% (or 176 J) compared to the turbo mode, which leads to the shortest response time. Running the CPU at a low frequency, i.e., 1.2 GHz, increases the energy consumed by 25% (427 J) compared to the sweet spot frequency. Radix sort is more energy-efficient at 2.2 GHz, which corresponds to energy savings of approximately 15% (or 96 J) compared to the turbo mode and 18% (119 J) compared to the lowest frequency.

Fig. 4 clearly shows the different sweet spot frequencies (vertical dotted line), in ascending order, for counting, radix and std::sort. The lines in the diagram correspond to list sizes of 10..50 million elements.

Table 3 provides an overview of the results and identifies the sweet spots for each algorithm (sweet spots are marked with a star '*'), and the energy savings that can be achieved when the most energy-efficient CPU clock frequency is selected compared to using the maximum frequency (i.e., turbo mode).

In order to gain more insights, we calculate the energy savings from running the algorithms at the sweet spot frequency compared to the maximum frequency

Table 3. The energy-efficient sweet spot of sorting algorithms

Algorithm	E (J)	Freq. (MHz)	t (s)	P (W)
radix	530.8	*2200	2.6	204.2
radix	626.9	turbo	1.9	330.4
std::sort	1282.3	*2400	5.9	216.9
std::sort	1464.1	turbo	4.2	346.3
count.	2093.8	*1800	11.3	184.9
count.	2801.5	turbo	8.5	330.3

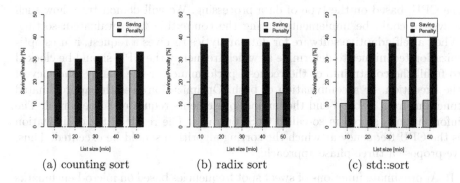

Fig. 5. AC energy saving compared with time penalty

(AC energy saving) and the associated loss of performance (time penalty). The penalty is always higher than the savings. Fig. 5 compares AC energy savings and time penalties for all three algorithms and all list sizes.

While researchers have already found that energy-efficiency can be achieved by redesigning software code, by making better use of memory and, by using more efficient hardware components (see [13]), it is not well known that the energy-efficiency of software is also affected by the frequency of the CPU at very precise frequencies other than the maximum frequency. Namely, our findings provide an answer (A) to our two research questions:

- A2a (Effectiveness). Software energy efficiency can be improved by choosing the most adequate CPU clock frequency. CPU clock frequency leads to a considerable variability of the energy needed to complete a data-intensive computational task.
- A2b (Determinability). The CPU clock frequency which makes software more energy efficient can be determined. In the case of counting sort for 50mio elements, reducing the clock frequency by ≈60% of its maximal speed can lead to an energy reduction of 25%.

These results entail not only that for data analytics tasks the sweet spot of CPU frequency can, and should be determined, but it also shows that data-intensive tasks with the same algorithmic complexity can have a different energy efficiency. Therefore, it seems natural to consider developing energy-efficiency benchmarks for software applications. While ISO software quality parameters include over 50 metrics [14], SPEC CPU2006 provides comparative studies on hardware performance and SPECpower for hardware energy efficiency[4], the same does not happen to software energy efficiency.

5   Dynamic Software Adaptation

Our idea to implement a new kind of self-adaptive software for data analytics and business intelligence is to enable data-intensive tasks to select the frequency of

---

[4] https://www.spec.org

the CPU, based on the type of data processing. We will demonstrate how such a system could be implemented using the computing task evaluated: sorting. When a self-adaptive software for data analytics receives a request, it uses optimization techniques to determine at which frequency the CPU should be clocked to fulfill the constraints of the request: performance or the energy efficiency of the execution, or a combination of both. Optimization uses the approximated functions from Table 4 and the number of elements requested to be sorted. The information is stored in so-called QoS contracts. The result of the optimization is the CPU frequency at which the sorting algorithm should be executed. Thus, we propose a three-phase approach:

1. Approximate functions of sweet spot frequencies based on micro-benchmarks to determine a server's individual sweet spot frequency.
2. QoS contracts to capture the assessed non-functional behavior.
3. Optimization to compute the optimal frequency and algorithm for a given user request at runtime.

We extend previous work (see [15]) by incorporating hardware reconfiguration by means of explicit frequency scaling.

5.1   Approximate Functions

It is possible to predict the sweet spot frequency by approximating a function of the energy consumption depending on the frequency using multiple linear regression and searching the minimum value of this function for a given list size. Fig. 4 depicts the energy consumption across all possible frequencies for sort invocations of the three investigated sort algorithms. For each algorithm a sweet spot frequency can be determined independently of the list size.

For the measurements of radix sort, fourth grade polynomial functions approximate the measured values very precisely as shown in Table 4. The first five rows show functions for 10..50 millions elements, whereas the last row represents the generic function $E(freq, size) = a \times freq + b \times freq^2 + c \times freq^3 + d \times freq^4 + e + f \times listsize$ with an adjusted R^2 of more then 99%. The minimum of this general function is at 2.4 GHz for all list sizes, which is not the measured mean sweet spot at 2.2 GHz, but is less than 1% distant from it. The cause of this difference is the (small) deviation of the approximated function and the closeness of the frequencies around the sweet spot frequency.

Thus, to automatically determine a sweet spot frequency on a target platform (unknown at design time), a developer has to provide a (micro) benchmark for different algorithmic implementations. Using the approach described above, the system can compute the sweet spot frequency automatically.

5.2   QoS Contracts

The Quality Contract Language (QCL) [15] allows to capture the non-functional behavior of an implementation. A contract in QCL specifies for an implementation of a data analytics task (e.g., radix sort) pairs of non-functional provisions

Table 4. Fourth grade polynomial functions for radix sort on 10 to 50 million elements (ars = adj.r.squared)

e (intercept)	$a \times freq$	$b \times freq^2$	$c \times freq^3$	$d \times freq^4$	$f \times listsize$	ars
98.558887	-17.000578	24.473429	1.497380	5.577048	1.00E+07 (fixed)	0.93990
214.645925	-30.237388	45.255654	2.977515	10.231982	2.00E+07 (fixed)	0.96998
344.115647	-43.960454	78.485585	1.588671	15.814538	3.00E+07 (fixed)	0.95190
450.068206	-49.751193	103.690842	0.926805	21.180903	4.00E+07 (fixed)	0.96550
564.112603	-51.629321	131.365326	6.015857	26.856475	5.00E+07 (fixed)	0.95546
-15.65866	-86.12392	171.4039	5.816562	35.62546	1.16653E-05	0.9942

and requirements. If the requirements are fulfilled, the provisions are guaranteed to hold. Listing 1.1 depicts an example of a QCL contract for the radix sort implementation used in this paper. It specifies 2 modes, which are alternative pairs of requirements and provisions. The two modes represent the most energy efficient and the fastest way to execute the algorithm. Thus, for the first mode, the sweet spot frequency determined in the previous phase is specified as a requirement on the CPU. The second mode specifies the highest possible frequency as a requirement. In addition, the runtime and energy consumption on the CPU are specified as functions depending on the list size. They are determined analogously to the sweet spot functions in the first phase. All modes specify which guarantees are given if a set of requirements is fulfilled. In the example contract, a specific maximum response time, which is equal to the time required on the CPU and a small overhead (x1 and x2, respectively), is guaranteed.

```
1  contract Radixsort implements Sort.sort {
2    mode efficient {
3      requires resource CPU {
4        frequency = 2.400 [MHz]
5        max time = f1<list_size> [ms]
6        max energy = f2<list_size> [J] }
7      provides max response_time = time + x1
8    }
9    mode fastest {
10     requires resource CPU {
11       frequency = 3.000 [MHz]
12       max time = f3<list_size> [ms]
13       max energy = f4<list_size> [J] }
14     provides max response_time = time + x2
15   }
16 }
```

Listing 1.1. Example of a QCL contract for radix sort

Contracts, like the discussed example, can then be used to generate problem formulations for off-the-shelf constraint satisfaction and optimization problem solvers.

5.3   Optimization

To determine the service with a particular CPU frequency an algorithm should be run on, we use an integer linear program (ILP) as shown in Listing 1.2. For clarity, we only show an ILP example for the decision whether radix sort shall be executed on one of two servers with different CPU frequencies in either the most energy-efficient or the fastest way. In the example, all values referring to server $N1$ correspond to the measurement values shown in the last section for a sort request of 30 million elements. The values referring to server $N2$ are not based on measurements, but introduced to show the general applicability of the approach to multiple servers.

```
 1 min: energy#N1 + energy#N2;
 2 //decide for one server and variant
 3 b#rdx#eff#N1 + b#rdx#fast#N1 + b#rdx#eff#N2 + b#rdx#fast#N2
 4 = 1;
 5 //approximated runtime per decision
 6 time#N1 =            1620b#rdx#eff#N1 + 1164b#rdx#fast#N1;
 7 //base load + decision-induced consumption
 8 energy#N1 =      97 +  324b#rdx#eff#N1 +  376b#rdx#fast#N1;
 9 //min frequency + sweet spot-min frequency
10 frequency#N1 = 1200 + 1000b#rdx#eff#N1 + 2000b#rdx#fast#N1;
11 time#N2 =            1120b#rdx#eff#N2 +  940b#rdx#fast#N2;
12 energy#N2 =     100 +  420b#rdx#eff#N2 +  530b#rdx#fast#N2;
13 frequency#N2 = 1200 + 1000b#rdx#eff#N2 + 2000b#rdx#fast#N2;
14
15 bin b#rdx#eff#N1,b#rdx#fast#N1,b#rdx#eff#N2,b#rdx#fast#N2;
```

Listing 1.2. Example of an Integer Linear Program for self-adaptive software

The ILP example comprises 4 decision variables and 3 usage variables per server. The decision variables of the optimization problem have the form:

$$b\#algorithm\#variant\#server$$

The prefixing b denotes the Boolean type of the variable, which is explicitly stated as constraint on lines 22 and 23, and *algorithm*, *variant* and *server*, delimited by pounds (#), denote the respective algorithm, variant (energy efficient or fast) and server. The meaning of $b\#rdx\#eff\#N1 = 1$ is the decision to use radix sort in its energy-efficient variant on server $N1$. Thus, each decision is represented by a variable. Each server is characterized by the variables *time*, *energy* and *frequency*, which include the name of the server separated by a pound. They denote the time required on, the energy spent by and the CPU frequency used for the respective server.

The objective function of the ILP is a linear combination of the problem's variables. In the example, the objective function specifies the goal to minimize the energy consumption of both servers for user requests to sort n elements.

Then, two types of constraints are generated for a specific request (e.g., the invocation of sort for a list of 30 million elements as in the example above).

First, a structural constraint to ensure the selection of at least one variant is generated (cf. line 3 and 4). Second, for each server variable (time, energy and frequency) a constraint, reflecting the impact of a decision on them is generated. For example, the constraint in line 6 and 7 specifies that deciding for radix sort in efficient mode on server N1 will require 1620 ms, whereas using fast mode will require only 1164 ms. For energy consumption, the idle consumption has to be considered in addition. The constraint on line 9 and 10 reflects an idle consumption of 97 J and the respective consumption of radix sort in the most efficient and fastest mode. Considering the idle consumption is important if the servers are always powered. The frequency constraint on line 12 and 13 reflects the minimum possible frequency (1200 MHz), the sweet spot frequency (1000+1200 MHz), and the maximum possible frequency (1000+2000 MHz).

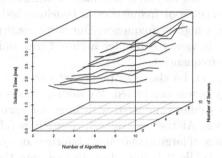

Fig. 6. Time to Compute Adaptation Decision

To solve this optimization problem, standard solvers like LP Solve [16] can be applied. The time required to solve problems as shown in the example, depends on the number of modes (i.e., execution variants) for which we used $m = 2$ representing the most efficient and the fastest variant, the number of algorithms for the same task A (e.g., different sort algorithms) and the number of servers N. Fig. 6 shows the time required to solve ILPs with $A = [1..10]$ algorithms with 2 modes each on $N = [2..10]$ servers. As can be seen, the time to derive the decision is negligible. It took ≈3.1 ms to identify which algorithm out of 10 to run on which of 10 servers.

5.4   Limitations

The approach we presented is feasible for Big Data intensive tasks since the processing of one single task can take several minutes. For tasks with a short duration (typically less that 2 seconds), managed by multi-process operating systems, the approach is generally not, or at least not easily, applicable. If two distinct data-intensive tasks have different sweet spot frequencies and the tasks are multi-tasked, the operating system needs to switch the sweet spot frequencies rapidly or choose the frequency that minimizes the overall energy consumption.

Nonetheless, the future generation of processors will most likely enable setting the frequency of individual cores, making the sweet spot approach valid for a broader type of tasks beyond data-intensive ones.

6 Related Work and Future Work

The closest existing research to our work was conducted by Livingston et al. [3]. Their work classifies software applications as memory- and compute-bound. For memory-bound applications, they demonstrate that a higher energy-efficiency is achieved at lower CPU frequencies since memory behaves as a bottleneck. For compute-bound applications, a higher energy-efficiency is achieved at higher CPU frequencies since finishing work quickly is the best approach for efficiency. For algorithms which cannot be purely classified as memory- or compute-bound, they propose to use sweet spot frequencies, a benchmarked optimal frequency between the lowest and highest frequency. Our work confirms the findings by Livingston et al. also in newer computer architectures and makes a detailed analysis of sweet spot frequencies.

Other related work can be classified taking into account the level at which energy-efficiency analysis was conducted. We use the terms macro-, meso-, and micro-level to express studies conducted with large software applications, algorithms, and instructions. At the macro-level, researchers (cf. [13]) have looked into the energy-efficiency of large management information systems such as ERP, CRM, and databases. While it is important to look into the efficiency of such systems to identify fields of improvements, the approach taken does not allow to gather insights on how software could be re-engineered differently to obtain energy reductions. At the meso-level, Bunse et al. [17] evaluate various sorting algorithms in battery powered mobile communication using smartphones. The results indicate that insertion sort is most efficient. Rivoire et al. [18] investigate system-level benchmarks for sorting. Nonetheless, the work does not explore the effect of CPU frequency on software energy-efficiency. At the micro-level, Ong and Yan [19] use an abstract machine to study the energy consumption of search and sorting algorithms. The energy requirement of each instruction was estimated and, e.g., an ALU access consumes 8×10^{-12} joule per 32 bits. Their findings indicate that the energy consumption can differ in orders of magnitude between algorithms, and, also, that faster algorithms can sometimes consume more energy than slower ones. In [20], the authors propose a first-order, linear power estimation model that uses performance counters to estimate CPU and memory consumption. The accuracy of the model estimates consumption within 4% of the measured CPU consumption.

Our long-term research goal is to study how energy-efficient mechanisms can be implementation as part of self-adaptive software and service systems that change their behavior and implementation, and affect the computing environment to reduce energy consumption. Fig. 7 shows relevant dimensions of research in this field.

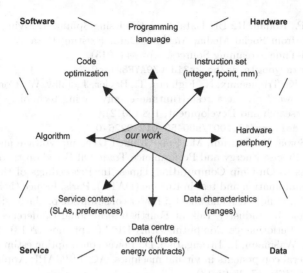

Fig. 7. Dimensions and directions of energy-efficient software research

7 Conclusion

Software applications for data analytics over Big Data typically have a high energy consumption. In this paper we studied a mechanism to make data-intensive processing tasks more energy efficient. Our findings indicate that the existence of CPU sweet spots can be explored in three ways: 1) by adapting the CPU frequency to sweet spots, the maximum power used by data analytics tasks can be established; 2) the use of sweet spots leads to effective energy gains of up to 25% ; and 3) sweet spots enable the design of new and more efficient self-adaptive software architectures. Our results are important, especially for large cloud data centers (e.g., Facebook, LinkedIn, and Twitter), since they can lead to the design of new software and scheduling policies to reduce energy consumption of data analytics and business intelligence applications.

Acknowledgements. This work has been partially funded by the German Research Foundation (DFG) under project agreements SFB 912/1 2011 and SCHI 402/11-1.

This is an "executable" paper. All measurement results, executable source code used for the experiments, logs and traces can be found online at the experimental results platform Areca[5].

References

[1] Koomey, J.: Growth in Data center electricity use 2005 to 2010. Analytics Press (2011), http://www.analyticspress.com/datacenters.html

---

[5] http://areca.co/26/The-Cost-of-Sorting

[2] Zadrozny, P., Kodali, R.: Big Data Analytics Using Splunk: Deriving Operational Intelligence from Social Media, Machine Data, Existing Data Warehouses, and Other Real-Time Streaming Sources. Apress (2013), http://books.google.de/books?id=CK9AYF8WTsoC

[3] Livingston, K., Triquenaux, N., Fighiera, T., Beyler, J., Jalby, W.: Computer using too much power? give it a rest (runtime energy saving technology). Computer Science - Research and Development, 1–8 (2012), http://dx.doi.org/10.1007/s00450-012-0226-0

[4] Choi, K., Soma, R., Pedram, M.: Fine-Grained Dynamic Voltage and Frequency Scaling for Precise Energy and Performance Trade-Off Based on the Ratio of Off-Chip Access to On-Chip Computation Times. In: Proceedings of the conference on Design, automation and test in Europe (DATE), Paris, France (February 2004)

[5] Brochard, L., Panda, R., Thomas, F.: Power consumption of clusters: Control and Optimization. In: Industry Talk at Fourth International Conference on Energy-Aware High Performance Computing, EnA-HPC (September 2013)

[6] Versick, D., Waßmann, I., Tavangarian, D.: Power consumption estimation of CPU and peripheral components in virtual machines. ACM SIGAPP Applied Computing Review 13(3), 17–25 (2013)

[7] Knuth, D.E.: The Art of Computer Programming, 2nd edn. Sorting and Searching. Addison-Wesley (1998)

[8] Herodotou, H., Lim, H., Luo, G., Borisov, N., Dong, L., Cetin, F.B., Babu, S.: Starfish: A self-tuning system for big data analytics. In: CIDR, vol. 11, pp. 261–272 (2011)

[9] Hackenberg, D., Ilsche, T., Schone, R., Molka, D., Schmidt, M., Nagel, W.E.: Power measurement techniques on standard compute nodes: A quantitative comparison. 2013 IEEE International Symposium on Performance Analysis of Systems and Software (ISPASS), 194–204 (2013)

[10] Schöne, R., Hackenberg, D., Molka, D.: Memory performance at reduced cpu clock speeds: an analysis of current x86_64 processors. In: Proceedings of the 2012 USENIX conference on Power-Aware Computing and Systems, HotPower 2012, p. 9. USENIX Association, Berkeley (2012)

[11] M. P. I. Forum, Mpi: A message-passing interface standard - version 3.0 (September 2012) http://www.mpi-forum.org/docs/mpi-3.0/mpi30-report.pdf

[12] ISO/IEC, ISO/IEC 14882:2011: Programming languages – C++, Tech. Rep (1998)

[13] Capra, E., Francalanci, C., Slaughter, S.A.: Measuring application software energy efficiency. IT Professional 14(2), 54–61 (2012)

[14] ISO/IEC, ISO/IEC 25010: Systems and software engineering - Systems and software Quality Requirements and Evaluation (SQuaRE) - System and software quality models, Tech. Rep (2010)

[15] Götz, S., Wilke, C., Richly, S., Aßmann, U.: Approximating quality contracts for energy auto-tuning software. In: Proceedings of First International Workshop on Green and Sustainable Software, GREENS 2012 (2012)

[16] Eikland, K., Notebaert, P.: LP Solve, 5.5 reference guide, http://lpsolve.sourceforge.net/5.5/ (access on December 26, 2012)

[17] Bunse, C., Höpfner, H., Roychoudhury, S., Mansour, E.: Choosing the best sorting algorithm for optimal energy consumption. In: Proceedings of the International Conference on Software and Data Technologies (ICSOFT), pp. 199–206 (2009)

[18] Rivoire, S., Shah, M.A., Ranganathan, P., Kozyrakis, C.: Joulesort: A balanced energy-efficiency benchmark. In: Proceedings of the ACM SIGMOD Intl. Conference on Management of Data, SIGMOD (2007)

[19] Ong, P.-W., Yan, R.-H.: Power-conscious software design-a framework for modeling software on hardware. In: IEEE Symposium on Low Power Electronics, Digest of Technical Papers, pp. 36–37 (October 1994)

[20] Contreras, G., Martonosi, M.: Power prediction for intel xscale reg; processors using performance monitoring unit events. In: Proceedings of the 2005 International Symposium on Low Power Electronics and Design, ISLPED 2005, pp. 221–226 (2005)

A Novel Heuristic Scheme for Modeling and Managing Time Bound Constraints in Data-Intensive Grid and Cloud Infrastructures

Alfredo Cuzzocrea[1] and Guandong Xu[2]

[1] ICAR-CNR and University of Calabria, Italy
[2] University of Technology, Australia
cuzzocrea@si.deis.unical.it, Guandong.Xu@uts.edu.au

Abstract. Inspired by the emerging *Cloud Computing* challenge, in this paper we provide *a comprehensive framework for modeling and managing time bound constraints in data-intensive Grid and Cloud infrastructures*, along with its experimental assessment and analysis. We provide both conceptual and theoretical contributions of the proposed framework, along with a *heuristic scheme*, called RGDTExec, that solves all possible instances of the problem underlying the proposed framework by exploiting a suitable *greedy algorithm*, called RGDTExecRun. As we demonstrate throughout the paper, the framework keeps several aspects of research innovations that are beneficial in a wide range of application scenarios.

1 Introduction

Among modern recent technological innovations, *Clouds* [16], without doubts, are the most prominent ones of recent years, even because the are strictly related to emerging research challenges, such as *Service-oriented Architectures* (SOA) (e.g., [27, 28]), *Resource Virtualization frameworks* (e.g., [17, 18]), *Big Data* (e.g., [1, 6, 9, 15]), and so forth. A special class of Clouds infrastructures is represented by so-called *data-intensive Cloud infrastructures*, where services that elaborate in the Clouds are mostly devoted to perform data-intensive processing (e.g., against Big Data repositories). This, indeed, represents an interesting class of applications, with a wide range of examples borrowed from real-life scenarios [7, 19]. *Grid infrastructures* (e.g., [17, 18]) are the "natural" ancestors of Cloud infrastructures and, similarly to the case of Clouds, it is possible to identify a clear and well-understood class of *data-intensive Grid infrastructures* as well (e.g., [11–14]), having similar characteristic of actual data-intensive Cloud infrastructures.

Grid Data Warehouses (GDWH) represent a well-known examples of data-intensive Grid infrastructures (e.g., [5, 22, 24–26, 30]), and, similarly, recent research initiatives are focusing their attention to *Cloud Data Warehousing* as

R. Meersman et al. (Eds.): OTM 2014 Workshops, LNCS 8842, pp. 172–191, 2014.

well (e.g., [4]). In GDWH, data-intensive services are oriented to implement typical Data Warehousing services, such as [20] *ETL, indexing, view materialization* and so forth, against node-distributed and large-in-size data repositories, which well-capture actual trends of Big Data storages. In this context, *Data Transformation* (DT) services (e.g., [3]), which are oriented to transform large-scale volumes of data, e.g., from a semi-structured nature to a relational nature for analytics-aware processing [9,15], represent a classical instance of data-intensive services that may populate both Grid as well as Cloud infrastructures.

Still under the wider umbrella of SOA architectures, the *Real-Time SOA* (RTSOA) initiative (e.g., [29]) pursues the idea of defining a novel class of SOA architectures where services, which are governed by fixed *service level constraints*, must be executed under well-defined *time bounds*, hence opening the door to innovative research experiences as well as novel applications and systems in this area. With a straightforward vision, in our research we introduce the so-called *Grid- and Cloud-based data-intensive RTSOA frameworks*, where data-intensive services against Big Data repositories must be executed within a temporal scheduling that is defined by application-oriented requirements.

Focusing in the so-delineated context, in this paper we provide *a comprehensive framework for modeling and managing time bound constraints in data-intensive Grid and Cloud infrastructures*, along with its experimental assessment and analysis. In more details, we provide both conceptual and theoretical contributions of the proposed framework, along with a *heuristic scheme*, called RGDTExec, that solves all possible instances of the problem underlying the proposed framework by exploiting a suitable *greedy algorithm*, called RGDTExecRun. Although models and algorithms presented in this paper are focused on data-intensive Grid infrastructures, they are straightforwardly extended to data-intensive Cloud infrastructures as well.

This paper complements and substantially extends the previous workshop paper [8]. In particular, the contributions of this paper with respect [8] are the following ones: (*i*) we provide a complete theoretical framework for modeling and managing time bound constraints in data-intensive Grid and Cloud infrastructures, with substantial much more theoretical findings and contributions – in particular, we capture service level constraints as well as time bounds constraints finer, and we develop a more sound theoretical model; (*ii*) we provide an improved version of greedy algorithm RGDTExecRun; (*iii*) we provide a comprehensive and deeply-developed experimental assessment and analysis of the proposed framework.

2 Capturing Service Level and Time Bound Constraints in Grid- and Cloud-Based Data-Intensive RTSOA Frameworks

We are giving a Data Grid G composed by N Grid nodes and M Grid DT services. The whole set of Grid nodes in G is denoted by $N(G)$, whereas $S(G)$ denotes the whole set of DT services available in G. Services in $S(G)$ can be composed by external data-intensive consumer applications in order to define even-complex DT processes, denoted by $P_{DT}(G)$, over massive amounts of data located across Grid nodes in $N(G)$. A DT process over G is in turn defined as a collection of DT tasks, denoted by $T_{DT}(G)$, whose input/output and temporal execution ordering are a-priori determined and scheduled by consumer applications. From classical Grid-based RTSOA application scenarios, recall that a DT process $P_{DT}(G)$ ends with a success if all the DT tasks $T_{DT}(G)$ composing $P_{DT}(G)$ end with a success within their respective time bounds. Otherwise, $P_{DT}(G)$ evolves towards an abort state.

We assume that each Grid node N_k in $N(G)$ makes available a set of M_k DT services $S(N_k) = \{S_{k,0}, S_{k,1}, \ldots, S_{k,|M_k|-1}\}$, such that $S(N_k) \subseteq S(G)$. Therefore, given a Grid node N_k in $N(G)$, and a DT service S_j in $S(G)$ belonging to a DT task $T_{DT}(G)$ over G to be executed on N_k, S_j can alternatively be *locally available* at N_k or *remotely available* at another node N_h in $N(G)$, with $h \neq k$. Without any loss of generality, we admit that Grid nodes in $N(G)$ could expose DT services that are also replicated in other Grid nodes in $N(G)$ (e.g., to load balancing and fault tolerance purposes). As a consequence, the *effective* set of DT services available in G is given by the following formula:

$$S(G) = \bigcup_{k=0}^{N-1} S(N_k) \tag{1}$$

such that $S(G)$ has an effective cardinality given by the following formula:

$$|S(G)| = \sum_{k=0}^{N-1} M_k \tag{2}$$

In order to fix a significant case study in the context of Grid-based RTSOA frameworks we are interested in, here we focus on a GDWH scenario where *Grid nodes are populated with multidimensional data repositories stored in the form of OLAP data cubes, and external applications define DT services over these Grid nodes.* The latter can be reasonably considered as an emerging GDWH scenario suitable to a wide spectrum of data-intensive *e*-science Grid applications focused on analyzing and mining multidimensional data, such those ranging from scientific and statistical data sets to biological data sets and sensor network data repositories. On the basis of this application scenario, the set of services $S(G)$ available in G encompasses, as a consequence, specific *DW-oriented DT services*, such as data transportation among Grid nodes by means of *range queries* over data cubes [21], or materialization of *snapshot OLAP views* in remote Grid nodes to query and data management efficiency purposes [11,13].

Despite this particular instance of the main problem, the model for supporting Grid-based RTSOA frameworks we propose in this paper is general enough to deal with any kind of data formats over the Grid (e.g., XML, RFID etc), thus realizing an *orthogonal* solution that can be easily customized to different and heterogeneous GDWH scenarios. Under a broader vision, the latter is a strength point of the proposed Grid-based RTSOA frameworks.

For instance, *SensorGrid* [11,13] represents the case of a GDWH for efficiently managing and querying summarized sensor network readings over the Grid. In *SensorGrid*, summarized sensor network readings modeled in terms of data cubes are *compressed across the Grid nodes at different levels of approximation*. Also, replicas of compressed data cubes are distributed across the Grid, to query and data management efficiency purposes. The query performance of *SensorGrid* has been experimentally assessed in [14], which clearly confirms the benefits deriving from embedding the data compression/approximation paradigm into high-performance data management activities performed in the core layer of GDWH. Hence, the scenario defined by *SensorGrid* denotes a typical running environment for Grid-based RTSOA frameworks introduced in this research.

Given a DT process $P_{DT}(G)$ over G, a *DT process instance* of $P_{DT}(G)$ (i.e., a *realization* of $P_{DT}(G)$), denoted by $W_{DT}(G)$, is formally defined as a set of the so-called *DT task instances*, denoted by $Q_{DT}(G)$ (i.e., *realizations* of DT tasks $T_{DT}(G)$), as follows:

$$W_{DT}(G) = \{Q_{DT,k_0}(G), Q_{DT,k_1}(G), \ldots, Q_{DT,k_{m-1}}(G)\} =$$
$$\{\langle N_{k_0}, I_{k_0}, s_{k_0}(G), \ell_{k_0}, \Delta t_{k_0}, O_{k_0}\rangle, \tag{3}$$
$$\ldots, \langle N_{k_{m-1}}, I_{k_{m-1}}, s_{k_{m-1}}(G), \ell_{k_{m-1}}, \Delta t_{k_{m-1}}, O_{k_{m-1}}\rangle\}$$

At a higher level of abstraction, given a DT process instance $W_{DT}(G)$ over G, the ordering of the DT task instances of $W_{DT}(G)$, $Q_{DT,k_j}(G)$, determines the temporal ordering in which these task instances are executed.

In every DT task instance $Q_{DT,k_j}(G) = \langle N_{k_j}, I_{k_j}, s_{k_j}(G), \ell_{k_j}, \Delta t_{k_j}, O_{k_j}\rangle$, (i) N_{k_j} denotes the Grid node in $N(G)$ on which the task $Q_{DT,k_j}(G)$ is executed; (ii) I_{k_j} denotes the input of the task $Q_{DT,k_j}(G)$, which, without any loss of generality, can be a data cube or a data cube partition; (iii) $s_{k_j}(G)$ denotes the set of DT services in $S(G)$ implementing the task $Q_{DT,k_j}(G)$; (iv) ℓ_{k_j} denotes the *service level bound* on the set of DT services $s_{k_j}(G)$; (v) Δt_{k_j} denotes the time bound within which the set of DT services $s_{k_j}(G)$ must be completed; (vi) O_{k_j} denotes the output of the task $Q_{DT,k_j}(G)$, which, without any loss of generality, can be again a data cube or a data cube partition. In our proposed Grid-based RTSOA frameworks, a DT task instance $Q_{DT,k_j}(G)$ ends with a success if a percentage $\gamma\%$ of DT service $S_{k_j,i}$ in $s_{k_j}(G)$ end with a success, being γ an input parameter of our theoretical model.

According to the consolidated QoS paradigm, for each DT service $S_{k_j,i}$ in $s_{k_j}(G)$ *different provisioning levels for $S_{k_j,i}$ are available*, namely the set $Levels(S_{k_j,i}) = \{S_{k_j,i}^0, S_{k_j,i}^1, \ldots, S_{k_j,i}^{P_{k_j,i}-1}\}$, which, without any loss of generality, are assumed to be sorted by provisioning level, i.e. $QoS(S_{k_j,i}^0) < QoS(S_{k_j,i}^1) < \ldots < QoS(S_{k_j,i}^{P_{k_j,i}-1})$, such that $QoS(S_{k_j,i}^p)$ denotes the QoS of $S_{k_j,i}^p$. Also, we assume that the following property holds: $QoS(S_{k_j,i}) \equiv QoS(S_{k_j,i}^{P_{k_j,i}-1})$. For what regards time, the complete execution of each DT service $S_{k_j,i}$ in $s_{k_j}(G)$ requires an amount of time, denoted by $\Delta T(S_{k_j,i})$, which, without any loss of generality, can be modeled in terms of a *fraction* of the whole quantity Δt_{k_j} available to $s_{k_j}(G)$, i.e. $\Delta T(S_{k_j,i}) = \lfloor \frac{\Delta t_{k_j}}{F_{k_j,i}} \rfloor$, being $F_{k_j,i}$ a positive integer such that $F_{k_j,i} \geq 1$ (it should be noted that, when $F_{k_j,i} = 1$, then $\Delta T(S_{k_j,i}) = \Delta t_{k_j}$, i.e. the complete execution of $S_{k_j,i}$ consumes the *whole* amount of time Δt_{k_j} available to *all* the DT services in $s_{k_j}(G)$). Contrary to QoS of services, due to typical *unpredictably* of Grid service executions of Grid environments [17, 18], here we do not assume any ordering relation among execution times $\Delta T(S_{k_j,i})$ of services $S_{k_j,i}$ in $s_{k_j}(G)$. In our proposed Grid-based RTSOA frameworks, a DT service $S_{k_j,i}$ ends with a success if it completes its execution with a success within a fraction of Δt_{k_j} (we better discuss this critical aspect in Section 4). Causes of failure for a DT service $S_{k_j,i}$ are the following: (*i*) *applicative failures*, which occur when $S_{k_j,i}$ does not complete its execution due to external errors (e.g., code exceptions, data access failures, and so forth); (*ii*) *violation of the time bound*, which occurs when $S_{k_j,i}$ does not complete its execution within its time bound. For the sake of simplicity, without any loss of generality in the remaining part of the paper we assume to deal with the second class of DT service failures only, hence we admit that applicative failures do not occur in our target Grids. This allows us to focus the attention on DT service failures deriving from violations of real-time bound constraints, which is the main goal of our research.

According to the Grid-based RTSOA paradigm we introduce in this paper, each DT task instance $Q_{DT,k_j}(G) = \langle N_{k_j}, I_{k_j}, s_{k_j}(G), \ell_{k_j}, \Delta t_{k_j}, O_{k_j} \rangle$ over G is constrained to two classes of constraints. The first one is about the level of DT services in $s_{k_j}(G)$, bounded by ℓ_{k_j}, and the second one is about the time required by the complete execution of *all* the DT services in $s_{k_j}(G)$, bounded by Δt_{k_j}. In the following, we separately investigate these two constraints.

3 Service Level Constraints: Theoretical Model

For what regards the service level constraint, given a DT task instance $Q_{DT,k_j}(G)$ having service level bound ℓ_{k_j}, for each DT service $S_{k_j,i}$ in $s_{k_j}(G)$ a service level bound is consequently superimposed on the QoS of $S_{k_j,i}$, $QoS(S_{k_j,i})$. *How to model $QoS(S_{k_j,i})$?* We can answer this fundamental question by focusing the attention on how the *computational complexity* of a given *data-intensive algorithm* algorithm $\mathcal{A}$ (i.e., an algorithm that processes massive data sets), denoted by $O(\mathcal{A})$, can be modeled. Without any loss of generality, $O(\mathcal{A})$ can be formally expressed as the result of the following complexity contributions: (*i*) the *data complexity* of $\mathcal{A}$, denoted by $O_D(\mathcal{A})$, which models the complexity of parts of $\mathcal{A}$ that directly elaborate data (e.g., query evaluation, update operations etc); (*ii*) the *algorithmic complexity* of $\mathcal{A}$, denoted by $O_A(\mathcal{A})$, which models the complexity of parts of $\mathcal{A}$ that implement specific routines (e.g., merging, sorting etc). Therefore, $O(\mathcal{A}) = O_D(\mathcal{A}) \oplus O_A(\mathcal{A})$.

For the specific case of a data-intensive algorithm $\mathcal{A}$, since $O_A(\mathcal{A}) \ll O_D(\mathcal{A})$, $O(\mathcal{A})$ can be *asymptotically reduced* to $O_D(\mathcal{A})$, i.e. $O(\mathcal{A}) \approx O_D(\mathcal{A})$. In addition to this, since in any data-intensive routine $\mathcal{R}$ the higher complexity is the one due to *data access costs*, denoted by $Cost(\mathcal{R})$, as large volumes of data are typically stored in secondary memory, *we can reasonably assume $O_D(\mathcal{A})$ to be equal to the cost of accessing data involved by data-intensive routines in $\mathcal{A}$, denoted by $Cost(\mathcal{A})$*, i.e. $O(\mathcal{A}) \approx O_D(\mathcal{A}) \approx Cost(\mathcal{A})$.

Therefore, based on the latter theoretical tools, since in the reference GDWH scenario DT services $S_{k_j,i}$ in $s_{k_j}(G)$ process massive amounts of multidimensional data stored in data cubes, *we can meaningfully model the QoS of $S_{k_j,i}$, $QoS(S_{k_j,i})$, in terms of the (data access) cost needed to execute $S_{k_j,i}$, $Cost(S_{k_j,i})$.*

Note that, in general, *several* services $S_{k_j,i}^p$ in $Levels(S_{k_j,i})$ can satisfy the service level constraint. Similarly to DT services $S_{k_j,i}$ in $s_{k_j}(G)$, the QoS of services $S_{k_j,i}^p$ in $Levels(S_{k_j,i})$, fixed $S_{k_j,i}$, can be modeled in terms of that data access costs needed to execute $S_{k_j,i}^p$, $Cost(S_{k_j,i}^p)$. By combining the above-introduced complexity tools and the multiple-level service provisioning scheme, a higher level of service means a higher computational cost and, similarly, a lower level of service means a lower computational cost. Upon this service-oriented complexity model, we introduce the whole cost needed to execute *all* the DT services in $s_{k_j}(G)$, denoted by $Cost(s_{k_j}(G))$, as follows:

$$Cost(s_{k_j}(G)) = \sum_{i=0}^{|s_{k_j}(G)|-1} Cost(S_{k_j,i}) \tag{4}$$

since data access costs are clearly *summarizable*.

As a consequence, the whole service level constraint over $s_{k_j}(G)$ can be formally modeled as follows:

$$Cost(s_{k_j}(G)) \le \ell_{k_j} \tag{5}$$

From (4), the following constraint follows:

$$\sum_{i=0}^{|s_{k_j}(G)|-1} Cost(S_{k_j,i}) \le \ell_{k_j} \tag{6}$$

which finally models the service level constraint in our proposed Grid-based RTSOA frameworks.

It should be noted that, apart from nice theoretical formulations, the above-introduced complexity tools allow us to achieve other amenities. For instance, given a service $S_{k_j,i}$ in $s_{k_j}(G)$, we can elegantly model the cost needed to execute $S_{k_j,i}$, $Cost(S_{k_j,i})$, in terms of *closed data access cost complexity formulas* via exploiting previous theoretical results available in active literature. To give an example, consider a query service $S_{k_j,i}^Q$ in $s_{k_j}(G)$ executing an M_1-dimensional range query [21] over an N_1-dimensional data cube $\mathcal{D}_1$. The cost of $S_{k_j,i}^Q$, $Cost(S_{k_j,i}^Q)$, is given by: $O(\prod_{k=0}^{N_1-1} |d_k|)$, such that d_k denotes a dimension of $\mathcal{D}_1$, with $k \in \{h_0, h_1, \dots, h_{M_1-1}\}$, being $h_m \in \{0,1,\dots,N_1-1\}$. Now, consider another query service $S_{k_j,u}^Q$ in $s_{k_j}(G)$, such that $u \ne i$, executing an M_2-dimensional range query over an N_2-dimensional data cube $\mathcal{D}_2$ still belonging to the Grid G. Similarly to $Cost(S_{k_j,i}^Q)$, the cost of $S_{k_j,u}^Q$, $Cost(S_{k_j,u}^Q)$, is given by: $O(\prod_{k=0}^{N_2-1} |d_k|)$, with $k \in \{h_0, h_1, \dots, h_{M_2-1}\}$, being $h_m \in \{0,1,\dots,N_2-1\}$. Thanks to complexity tools above, the total cost needed to execute both the DT services $S_{k_j,i}^Q$ and $S_{k_j,u}^Q$ in $s_{k_j}(G)$, $Cost(s_{k_j}(G))$, is given by the following formula: $Cost(s_{k_j}(G)) = O(\prod_{k=0}^{N_1-1} |d_k|) + O(\prod_{k=0}^{N_2-1} |d_k|)$.

4   Time Bound Constraints: Theoretical Model

For what regards the time bound constraint, given a DT task instance $Q_{DT,k_j}(G)$ having time bound Δt_{k_j}, for each DT service $S_{k_j,i}$ in $s_{k_j}(G)$ a time bound is consequently superimposed on the (complete) execution time of $S_{k_j,i}$, $\Delta T(S_{k_j,i})$. Let $Time(S_{k_j,i})$ denote the *model time* in our proposed theoretical model for supporting Grid-based RTSOA frameworks. It should be noted that, conceptually, $Time(S_{k_j,i})$ is different from $\Delta T(S_{k_j,i})$, meaning that the first one is a model construct allowing us to express the time bound constraint, whereas the second one is a variable model recording the amount of time consumed by the complete execution of $S_{k_j,i}$. Since each DT task instance $Q_{DT,k_j}(G)$ is modeled in terms of a collection of DT services $s_{k_j}(G)$, without any loss of generality, in order to satisfy the time bound constraint the following two properties must *simultaneously* hold: (i) $Time(S_{k_j,i}) \leq \Delta t_{k_j,i}$, being $\Delta t_{k_j,i}$ a fraction of Δt_{k_j}, which models the time bound within which all the DT services in $s_{k_j}(G)$ must be completed, i.e., $\Delta t_{k_j,i} = \lfloor \frac{\Delta t_{k_j}}{G_{k_j,i}} \rfloor$, with $G_{k_j,i} \geq 1$; (ii) $\sum_{i=0}^{|s_{k_j}(G)|-1} \Delta t_{k_j,i} \leq \Delta t_{k_j}$. Now, focus the attention on the relation between the parameters $G_{k_j,i}$ and $F_{k_j,i}$ (see Section 2) for a given DT service $S_{k_j,i}$ in $s_{k_j}(G)$. In order to the previous two properties on time bounds hold, the following property on parameters $G_{k_j,i}$ and $F_{k_j,i}$ must hold: $F_{k_j,i} \geq G_{k_j,i} \forall S_{k_j,i} \in s_{k_j}(G)$. As highlighted in Section 2, if the execution time of $S_{k_j,i}$ exceeds $\Delta t_{k_j,i}$, then $S_{k_j,i}$ ends with a failure.

How to model $Time(S_{k_j,i})$? Contrary to the service level constraint, where suitable complexity tools (see Section 3) allow us to elegantly model the QoS of $S_{k_j,i}$, $QoS(S_{k_j,i})$, in terms of data access costs, $Cost(S_{k_j,i})$, for the actual case we cannot rely on similar complexity tools, hence we have to *pragmatically* consider the effective execution time of $S_{k_j,i}$, $\Delta T(S_{k_j,i})$, in order to model the time needed to execute $S_{k_j,i}$, $Time(S_{k_j,i})$. In fact, it should be noted that in highly-dynamic environments like Grids, given a Grid service S, the effective execution time of S, denoted by $\mathcal{T}(S)$, depends on several and disparate parameters such as load balancing issues, actual availability and reliability of Grid nodes etc [17, 18]. As a consequence, given a Grid service S, *it is not possible to a-priori deterministically predict the value of $\mathcal{T}(S)$*. Indeed, only an *estimate* of $\mathcal{T}(S)$, denoted by $\rho(\mathcal{T}(S))$, can be provided, for instance based on *statistics* on service execution times gathered across the target Grid (e.g., [23]). At a theoretical level, we can estimate $\rho(\mathcal{T}(S))$ based on somewhat *closed time complexity formulas* available in literature. For instance, in the case of compressed data cubes, some of such formulas are available in [12].

Therefore, based on the latter main observation, since in the reference GDWH scenario DT services $S_{k_j,i}$ in $s_{k_j}(G)$ are Grid services by definition, *we can meaningfully model the model time needed to execute $S_{k_j,i}$, $Time(S_{k_j,i})$, in terms of an estimate of the effective execution time required by $S_{k_j,i}$, $\Delta T(S_{k_j,i})$, denoted by $\widetilde{\Delta T}(S_{k_j,i})$, still based on somewhat closed time complexity formulas and statistics on service execution times across the target Grid.*

Upon this temporal model driven by estimates of service execution times, we introduce the whole amount of time needed to execute *all* the DT services in $s_{k_j}(G)$, denoted by $Time(s_{k_j}(G))$, as follows:

$$Time(s_{k_j}(G)) = \sum_{i=0}^{|s_{k_j}(G)|-1} Time(S_{k_j,i}) \tag{7}$$

since amounts of time are clearly *summarizable*.

As a consequence, the whole time bound constraint over $s_{k_j}(G)$ can be formally modeled as follows:

$$Time(s_{k_j}(G)) \leq \Delta t_{k_j} \tag{8}$$

From (7), the following constraint follows:

$$\sum_{i=0}^{|s_{k_j}(G)|-1} Time(S_{k_j,i}) \leq \Delta t_{k_j} \tag{9}$$

which finally models the time bound constraint in our proposed Grid-based RTSOA frameworks.

5 Overall Theoretical Model Formulation

Here we formally provide the theoretical model supporting the execution of a given DT process $P_{DT}(G)$ having instance $W_{DT}(G)$ in Grid-based RTSOA frameworks. To this end, first we introduce a *global constraint* bounding the cost of *all* the DT services in $W_{DT}(G)$, denoted by C_{MAX}, and a *global constraint* bounding the amount of time within which *all* the DT services in $W_{DT}(G)$ must be completed, denoted by T_{MAX}, respectively. In our proposal, these global constraints are modeled in terms of the service level bound and the time bound that are *globally* defined on the whole DT process instance $W_{DT}(G)$ starting from the service level bounds ℓ_{k_j} and the time bounds Δt_{k_j} that are *locally* defined on the set of DT task instances $Q_{DT,k_j}(G)$ in $W_{DT}(G)$, respectively. C_{MAX} is defined as follows:

$$C_{MAX} = argmax_{Q_{DT,k_j}(G) \in W_{DT}(G)} \{\ell_{k_j}\} \tag{10}$$

whereas T_{MAX} is defined as follows:

$$T_{MAX} = argmax_{Q_{DT,k_j}(G) \in W_{DT}(G)} \{\Delta t_{k_j}\} \tag{11}$$

All considering, the theoretical model for supporting the execution of a given DT process $P_{DT}(G)$ having instance $W_{DT}(G)$ in Grid-based RTSOA frameworks under the global constraint C_{MAX} that bounds the overall cost of services implementing DT task instances $Q_{DT,k_j}(G)$ in $W_{DT}(G)$, and the *global constraint* T_{MAX}, which bounds the overall execution time of services implementing DT task instances $Q_{DT,k_j}(G)$ in $W_{DT}(G)$, can be formally modeled by the *simultaneously accomplishment* of both the constraints (6) and (9) over *all* the task instances $Q_{DT,k_j}(G)$ in $W_{DT}(G)$, as follows:

$$\begin{cases} \sum_{j=0}^{|W_{DT}(G)|-1} Cost(s_{k_j}(G)) \leq C_{MAX} \\ \sum_{j=0}^{|W_{DT}(G)|-1} Time(s_{k_j}(G)) \leq T_{MAX} \end{cases} \tag{12}$$

i.e.:

$$
\begin{cases}
\sum_{j=0}^{|W_{DT}(G)|-1} \sum_{i=0}^{|s_{k_j}(G)|-1} Cost(S_{k_j,i}) \leq \\
\quad argmax_{Q_{DT,k_j}(G) \in W_{DT}(G)} \{\ell_{k_j}\} \\
\sum_{j=0}^{|W_{DT}(G)|-1} \sum_{i=0}^{|s_{k_j}(G)|-1} Time(S_{k_j,i}) \leq \\
\quad argmax_{Q_{DT,k_j}(G) \in W_{DT}(G)} \{\Delta t_{k_j}\}
\end{cases}
\tag{13}
$$

which represents the final formulation of the theoretical model supporting Grid-based RTSOA frameworks proposed in this paper. From (13), it clearly follows that the formal conditions under which the DT process instance $W_{DT}(G)$ ends with a failure are the following: (*i*) the data access cost required by the complete execution of $W_{DT}(G)$, denoted by $Cost(W_{DT}(G))$, does not satisfy the global service level constraint, i.e. $Cost(W_{DT}(G)) > C_{MAX}$; (*ii*) the amount of time required by the complete execution of $W_{DT}(G)$, denoted by $\Delta T(W_{DT}(G))$, does not satisfy the global time bound constraint T_{MAX}, i.e. $\Delta T(W_{DT}(G)) > T_{MAX}$.

6   Complexity Analysis

Running of a given DT process $P_{DT}(G)$ having instance $W_{DT}(G)$ in Grid-based RTSOA frameworks under the global constraints C_{MAX} and T_{MAX} according to (13), determines an *optimization problem*, which is characterized by an *exponential complexity*. We next demonstrate this complexity. Consider a DT task instance $Q_{DT,k_j}(G)$ to be executed on a Grid node N_{k_j} in $N(G)$ within the time bound Δt_{k_j} by means of the related set of DT services $s_{k_j}(G) = \{S_{k_j,0}, S_{k_j,1}, \dots, S_{k_j,|s_{k_j}(G)|-1}\}$. For each DT service $S_{k_j,i}$ in $s_{k_j}(G)$, we have $P_{k_j,i}$ available service levels of $S_{k_j,i}$, $Levels(S_{k_j,i}) = \{S_{k_j,i}^0, S_{k_j,i}^1, \dots, S_{k_j,i}^{P_{k_j,i}-1}\}$, with likely different costs, which, without any loss of generality, can be assumed to be sorted as follows: $Cost(S_{k_j,i}^0) < Cost(S_{k_j,i}^1) < \dots Cost(S_{k_j,i}^{P_{k_j,i}-1})$, being $Cost(S_{k_j,i}) \equiv Cost(S_{k_j,i}^{P_{k_j,i}-1})$ (see Section 2). Among all the services in $Levels(S_{k_j,i})$, we have to finally select that service that *globally* (i.e., in *conjunction* with the other services of $W_{DT}(G)$) satisfies the constraint C_{MAX}, while also not violating the constraint T_{MAX}. Let $S_{k_j,i}^*$ denote the latter service. To simplify, assume that each DT service $S_{k_j,i}$ in $s_{k_j}(G)$ has the *same* number of available service levels, denoted by P. Under this assumption, for each DT task instance $Q_{DT,k_j}(G)$ in $W_{DT}(G)$, the complexity of selecting the service $S_{k_j,i}^*$ is $O(P^{|s_{k_j}(G)|})$. For the whole DT process instance $W_{DT}(G)$, which is defined as a set of m DT task instances $Q_{DT,k_j}(G)$ (see Section 2), the complexity of running the related process $P_{DT}(G)$ is $O(m \times P^{|s_{k_j}(G)|})$.

This complexity analysis confirms to us that *heuristic schemes* are necessary in order to find *sub-optimal solutions* to the optimization problem deriving from (14). In turn, these schemes are implemented in the vest of *greedy algorithms*, which are able to find sub-optimal solutions at a likely *sub-polynomial cost*.

7   The RGDTExec Heuristic Scheme

We solve the optimization problem deriving from (13) by means of the innovative heuristic scheme RGDTExec. This scheme finally allows us to efficiently support real-time Grid DT services over Grid-based RTSOA frameworks. Since we focus on Grid-based RTSOA frameworks in GDWH scenarios whose Grid nodes are populated by multidimensional data cubes, compressed versions of these data cubes and their replicas (like in *SensorGrid* [11, 13] for the case of sensor network readings high-performance management), the main intuition underlying RGDTExec consists in *exploiting the data compression/approximation paradigm in support of the greedy criterion*. We next describe in detail how RGDTExec works.

Consider a DT task instance $Q_{DT,k_j}(G)$ to be executed on a Grid node N_{k_j} in $N(G)$ within the time bound Δt_{k_j} by means of the related set of DT services $s_{k_j}(G) = \{S_{k_j,0}, S_{k_j,1}, \ldots, S_{k_j,|s_{k_j}(G)|-1}\}$. Focus on the actual DT service $S_{k_j,i}$ in $s_{k_j}(G)$, for which $P_{k_j,i}$ service levels are available, $Levels(S_{k_j,i}) = \{S_{k_j,i}^0, S_{k_j,i}^1, \ldots, S_{k_j,i}^{P_{k_j,i}-1}\}$. Also, let $\widetilde{\Delta T}(S_{k_j,i})$ be the estimate of the effective execution time of $S_{k_j,i}$, $\Delta T(S_{k_j,i})$. In our proposal, the estimate $\widetilde{\Delta T}(S_{k_j,i})$ is "inherited" by the $P_{k_j,i}$ service levels of $S_{k_j,i}$, $S_{k_j,i}^0, S_{k_j,i}^1, \ldots, S_{k_j,i}^{P_{k_j,i}-1}$, via assigning to each service $S_{k_j,i}^p$ in $Levels(S_{k_j,i})$ an estimate of the effective execution time of $S_{k_j,i}^p$, denoted by $\widetilde{\Delta T}(S_{k_j,i}^p)$, which is defined in dependency on $\widetilde{\Delta T}(S_{k_j,i})$ as follows:

$$\widetilde{\Delta T}(S_{k_j,i}^p) = \frac{Cost(S_{k_j,i}^p)}{\sum_{h=0}^{|Levels(S_{k_j,i})|-1} Cost(S_{k_j,i}^h)} \cdot \Delta T(S_{k_j,i}) \tag{14}$$

such that the following property holds:

$$\sum_{p=0}^{|Levels(S_{k_j,i})|-1} \widetilde{\Delta T}(S_{k_j,i}^p) \leq \Delta T(S_{k_j,i}) \tag{15}$$

According to our heuristic scheme RGDTExec, among all the $P_{k_j,i}$ service levels of $S_{k_j,i}$ in $s_{k_j}(G)$, *we greedily select that service* $S_{k_j,i}^p$ *that satisfies the service level constraint* $Cost(S_{k_j,i}^p) \leq \ell_{k_j}$ *and, simultaneously, can satisfy the time bound constraint* $Time(S_{k_j,i}^p) \leq \Delta t_{k_j,i}$, *i.e.* $\widetilde{\Delta T}(S_{k_j,i}^p) \leq \Delta t_{k_j,i}$.

This also means that RGDTExec selects, among all the available multidimensional data sets involved by the DT service $S_{k_j,i}$ (i.e., original data cubes, compressed data cubes, and replicas) that compressed representation allowing both the constraints to be satisfied, by discarding those multidimensional data sets for which the constraints cannot be satisfied (even though these data sets could ensure a higher degree of accuracy than the former ones).

Both two parameters, i.e. costs of services and execution times, can be a-priori estimated. First ones thanks to closed data access cost complexity formulas (see Section 3) and second ones thanks to closed time complexity formulas plus service execution time statistics (see Section 4). The difference relies in the fact that estimates on service costs are highly releasable (thanks to the asymptotical reduction of the complexity of data-intensive DT services to the data complexity – see Section 3), whereas estimates on service execution times introduce a great variance due to the unpredictable nature of Grid environments (see Section 2). Therefore, the effective execution time of DT services must be considered (see Section 4).

Now, focus the attention on temporal aspects of DT services in great detail. Consider a service $S^p_{k_j,i}$ in $Levels(S_{k_j,i})$ selected by the greedy criterion of RGDTExec. Let $\widetilde{\Delta T}(S^p_{k_j,i})$ be the estimate of the effective execution time of $S^p_{k_j,i}$. Let $\Delta T(S^p_{k_j,i})$ be the effective execution time of $S^p_{k_j,i}$. If $\Delta T(S^p_{k_j,i}) \leq \widetilde{\Delta T}(S^p_{k_j,i}) \leq \Delta t_{k_j,i}$, then $S^p_{k_j,i}$ ends with a success and the "next" DT service $S_{k_j,i+1}$ in $s_{k_j}(G)$ is processed by RGDTExec. In this case, if $\Delta T(S^p_{k_j,i}) < \widetilde{\Delta T}(S^p_{k_j,i})$, then the exceeding amount of time $\Delta T^+(S^p_{k_j,i}) = \widetilde{\Delta T}(S^p_{k_j,i}) - \Delta T(S^p_{k_j,i})$ is invested to "enlarge" the estimate of the effective execution time of services $S^p_{k_j,i+1}$ in $Levels(S_{k_j,i+1})$, by correcting formula (14) as follows:

$$
\widetilde{\Delta T}(S^p_{k_j,i+1}) = \Delta T^+(S^p_{k_j,i}) + \\
\frac{Cost(S^p_{k_j,i+1})}{\sum_{h=0}^{|Levels(S_{k_j,i+1})|-1} Cost(S^h_{k_j,i+1})} \cdot \Delta T(S_{k_j,i+1})
\tag{16}
$$

This implies that an *higher* provisioning level $S^p_{k_j,i+1}$ for $S_{k_j,i+1}$ can be selected by RGDTExec.

Contrary to the latter case, if $\Delta T(S^p_{k_j,i}) > \widetilde{\Delta T}(S^p_{k_j,i})$ and $\Delta T(S^p_{k_j,i}) \leq \Delta t_{k_j,i}$, then $S^p_{k_j,i}$ ends with a success and the "next" DT service $S_{k_j,i+1}$ in $s_{k_j}(G)$ is processed by RGDTExec. Since in this case $\Delta T(S^p_{k_j,i}) > \widetilde{\Delta T}(S^p_{k_j,i})$, then the estimate of the effective execution time of services $S^p_{k_j,i+1}$ in $Levels(S_{k_j,i+1})$ is lowered by the defecting amount of time $\Delta T^-(S^p_{k_j,i}) = \Delta T(S^p_{k_j,i}) - \widetilde{\Delta T}(S^p_{k_j,i})$, by correcting formula (14) as follows:

$$
\widetilde{\Delta T}(S^p_{k_j,i+1}) = \frac{Cost(S^p_{k_j,i+1})}{\sum_{h=0}^{|Levels(S_{k_j,i+1})|-1} Cost(S^h_{k_j,i+1})} \cdot \\
\Delta T(S_{k_j,i+1}) - \Delta T^-(S^p_{k_j,i})
\tag{17}
$$

This implies that a *lower* provisioning level $S^p_{k_j,i+1}$ for $S_{k_j,i+1}$ can be selected by RGDTExec.

Finally, if $\Delta T(S^p_{k_j,i}) > \widetilde{\Delta T}(S^p_{k_j,i})$ and $\Delta T(S^p_{k_j,i}) > \Delta t_{k_j,i}$, then $S^p_{k_j,i}$ ends with a failure and, in turn, this causes the failure of the DT service $S_{k_j,i}$, and the "next" DT service $S_{k_j,i+1}$ in $s_{k_j}(G)$ is processed by RGDTExec.

Without going into details, it is a matter of fact to understand that effective execution times depend on the ordering in which DT services $S_{k_j,i}$ in $s_{k_j}(G)$ are executed, which in our model is a-priori fixed. It should be noted that more complicated schemes can be devised, such as choosing the "next" DT service

$S_{k_j,i+1}$ in $s_{k_j}(G)$ in dependence on load balancing issues and chancing topologies that are typical of Grid environments. These models are outside the scope of this paper and left as future work.

The above-illustrated approach of RGDTExec on DT task instances $Q_{DT}(G)$ is exploited as baseline operation for supporting the execution of the whole DT process instance $W_{DT}(G)$, via iterating that operation for m steps, under the global service level bound C_{MAX} and the global time bound T_{MAX}, respectively (see Section 5). Finally, Figure 1 shows greedy algorithm RGDTExecRun, which implements RGDTExec, by focusing on the whole DT process instance $W_{DT}(G)$. To this end, RGDTExecRun makes use of greedy algorithm RGDTExecRunQDT (see Figure 2), which focuses on a singleton DT task instance $Q_{DT}(G)$, as baseline operation. The meaning of the pseudo-codes shown in Figure 1 and Figure 2, respectively, can be easily inferred from the detailed description of RGDTExec above, thus they do not deserve further details.

Algorithm RGDTExecRun

Input: The GDWH G; a DT process instance $W_{DT}(G)$ over G;
service execution time statistics on G, *Stats*; the model parameter γ.

Output: TRUE if the complete execution of $W_{DT}(G)$ ends with a success;
FALSE otherwise.

Begin
```
    success ← TRUE;
    DTTaskSet ← W_DT(G).getDTTaskSet();
    C_MAX ← computeArgMax(DTTaskSet, 0);
    T_MAX ← computeArgMax(DTTaskSet, 1);
    DTTS_Size ← DTTaskSet.size();
    k ← 0;
    while(k < DTTS_Size&&success == TRUE){
        Q_DT(G) ← W_DT(G).getDTTask(k);
        serviceLevelBound ← Q_DT(G).getServiceLevelBound();
        timeBound ← Q_DT(G).getTimeBound();
        success ← RGDTExecRunQDT(G, Q_DT(G), serviceLevelBound, timeBound, Stats, γ);
        if(success == TRUE){
            effectiveExecCost ← Q_DT(G).getEffectiveExecCost();
            C_MAX ← C_MAX − effectiveExecCost;
            if(C_MAX < 0){
                success ← FALSE;
            }
            if(success == TRUE){
                effectiveExecTime ← Q_DT(G).getEffectiveExecTime();
                T_MAX ← T_MAX − effectiveExecTime;
                if(T_MAX < 0){
                    success ← FALSE;
                }
            }
        }
        k ← k + 1;
    }
    return success;
```
End

Fig. 1. Algorithm RGDTExecRun

8   Experimental Assessment and Analysis

In order to assess the performance of RGDTExec (thus, the one of algorithm RGDTExecRun), we developed an experimental framework on top of *Sensor-Grid* [11,13], where specific real-time Grid DT processes have been devised and developed. In particular, we designed three kinds of such processes, which are compliant with a typical GDWH environment, and embed arbitrary

Algorithm RGDTExecRunQDT

Input: The GDWH G; a DT task instance $Q_{DT}(G)$ over G; the service level bound C;
the time bound T; service execution time statistics on G, $Stats$;
the model parameter γ.

Output: TRUE if the complete execution of $Q_{DT}(G)$ ends with a success;
FALSE otherwise.

Begin

```
success ← TRUE;
N ← Q_DT(G).getCurrentGridNode(G);
D ← Q_DT(G).getInputDataCube(G);
succededLevelServiceCounter ← 0;
DTServiceSet ← Q_DT(G).getDTServiceSet();
DTSS_Size ← DTServiceSet.size();
h ← 0;
while(h < DTSS_Size){
    S ← Q_DT(G).getDTService(h);
    levelServiceSet ← S.getLevelServiceSet();
    levelServiceCostEstimateVector ←
        buildLevelServiceCostEstimateVector(levelServiceSet, S, N, D);
    levelServiceExecTimeEstimateVector ←
        buildLevelServiceExecTimeEstimateVector(levelServiceSet, S, N, D, Stats);
    L ← matchLevelService(S. levelServiceSet, C, T, levelServiceCostEstimateVector,
        levelServiceExecTimeEstimateVector);
    threadController ← createThreadController(L);
    startingTime ← threadController.start();
    while(threadController.isRunning(L) == TRUE ||
        timeBoundNotExceeded(threadController, System.getCurrentTime() −
        startingTime) == TRUE){
        effectiveExecTime ← threadController.getExecTime(L);
        L_Index ← levelServiceSet.indexOf(L);
        execTimeEstimateL ← levelServiceSet.getExecTimeEstimate(L_Index);
        if(effectiveExecTime ≤ T){
            succededLevelServiceCounter ← succededLevelServiceCounter + 1;
            exceededTime ← execTimeEstimateL − effectiveExecTime;
            if(exceededTime > 0){
                L_Next ← levelServiceSet.getNextlevelService(L);
                L_Next_Index ← levelServiceSet.indexOf(L_Next);
                levelServiceSet.setExecTimeEstimate(
                    L_Next_Index, execTimeEstimateL_Next + exceededTime);
            }elseif(exceededTime < 0){
                L_Next ← levelServiceSet.getNextlevelService(L);
                L_Next_Index ← levelServiceSet.indexOf(L_Next);
                levelServiceSet.setExecTimeEstimate(
                    L_Next_Index, execTimeEstimateL_Next− Math.abs(exceededTime));
            }
        }
    }
    h ← h + 1;
}
if(⌊⌊((succededLevelServiceCounter/DTSS_Size) ∗ 100)⌋ < γ){
    success ← FALSE;
}
return success;
```

End

Fig. 2. Algorithm RGDTExecRunQDT

synthetically-generated DT tasks and, in turn, DT services. First Grid DT process focuses on simple data cube transferring across a set of Grid nodes, and is called *Data Cube Materialization Service* (DCMS). In this case, the final goal is that of materializing a data cube from a Grid node to another one. In a Grid OLAP architecture, this process could be used for query and data management efficiency purposes. Specifically, in order to stress the performance of RGDTExec under the ranging of a scaling-up input, we made use of two different experimental parameters for DCMS, namely (i) the number of Grid nodes N of the underlying (Grid) infrastructure and (ii) the data cube size K. Without going into details, it is a matter of fact to note that both parameters have a critical impact over the performance of RGDTExec.

The second kind of Grid DT process deals with another important challenge that one can find in a Grid OLAP architecture, the so-called *Long-Running Data Cube Query Service* (LRDCQS). This process realizes a (range) query that *explores several Grid nodes during its evaluation,* and is very useful for a wide spectrum of data-intensive e-science Grid applications (e.g., biological data management). On the basis of this query paradigm, the input query computes intermediate results over data cubes stored in Grid nodes, and the final answer is obtained by combining the intermediate results according to some given strategy (e.g., view-based, pipe-based and so forth). The most significant characteristic of such queries with respect to conventional ones just relies in the *duration* of queries, which is several orders of magnitude greater than the one of queries occurring in conventional paradigms. In LRDCQS, we considered the following experimental parameters to be ranged: (i) the number of Grid nodes N (like in the first case), and (ii) the *selectivity* of queries L. In particular, as widely-recognized, the latter parameter plays a key role in assessing the performance of any query engine. In our experiments, selectivity of queries has been modeled as a percentage value with respect to the whole volume of target data cubes.

The third kind of Grid DT process considers *fragmentation aspects* [10] that are still relevant in Grid OLAP architectures for both data management and query efficiency purposes. The resulting service is called *Data Cube Fragmentation Service* (DCFS). Given a data cube $\mathcal{D}$ and a partitioning scheme $\mathcal{P}$ that represents $\mathcal{D}$ in terms of a collection of B *buckets* [2], such that $B > 0$, DCFS fragments $\mathcal{D}$ in B sub-cubes and disseminates these sub-cubes across the Grid nodes, given an arbitrary *fragmentation plan* $\mathcal{F}$. We assessed the capabilities of RGDTExec when running DCFS under the ranging of the following experimental parameters: (i) the number of Grid nodes N (like in the previous cases), and (ii) the *bucketization degree* of $\mathcal{P}$, B.

In order to finally obtain a *comprehensive* experimental framework, services, service levels, data loads and service loads across the target Grid have been modeled according to two different-in-nature *synthetic distributions*, the *Uniform distribution* and the *Zipf distribution*, respectively, which well-capture two opposite configurations one can find in real-life Grid settings. In particular, the Uniform distribution describes a Grid setting where Grid nodes have "similar" data and service loads (the most significant factors among the previous ones), whereas the Zipf (also called *Skew*) distribution models a Grid setting where Grid nodes have asymmetric data and services loads.

As regards the experimental environment, each Grid node of the experimental architecture was run *Gnu/Linux Fedora Core 6 OS* with *Globus Toolkit 3*, and has been equipped with *Intel Pentium IV* at 2 GHz processor and 1 GB RAM. As regards the metrics, we engineered the so-called *Percentage Temporal Gain* (PTG), which models the percentage reduction of time required to completely execute DT services of experimental DT processes over the Grid embedding RGDTExec with respect to the case that considers the *same* Grid not running our heuristic scheme (i.e., a version of the same Grid that does not implement RGDTExec in its middleware layer). As regards other settings of our theoretical model, the most significant parameters to be discussed are the following: (i) C_{MAX}, which globally bounds the whole cost of DT services; (ii) T_{MAX}, which globally bounds the whole execution time of DT services (see Section 2); (iii) γ, which models the percentage of DT services ending with a success with respect to the total number of DT services in a DT given task (see Section 2). Setting adequately these parameters in the experimental framework is a non-trivial engagement. For what regards C_{MAX} and T_{MAX}, to the sake of simplicity, we devised an experimental model where these parameters are modeled in terms of *percentage reductions* with respect to the corresponding values of total cost of services and total execution time, respectively, due to the complete execution of the *same* DT services over the *same* Grid not running RGDTExec. This leads to the definition of the experimental parameters C_{MAX}^R and T_{MAX}^R, respectively. Furthermore, we considered two different scenarios deriving from the combined values of these parameters, since they have a significant influence on RGDTExecRun runs (see Section 7). According to the first scenario, *loose model constraints* are introduced in consequence of "low" values of both combined parameters C_{MAX}^R and T_{MAX}^R. Contrary to this, according to the second scenario, *tight model constraints* are introduced in consequence of "high" values of both combined parameters C_{MAX}^R and T_{MAX}^R. For what regards γ, we experimentally tuned this parameter in order to *always* ensure the success of DT tasks in DT processes considered in our experimental assessment.

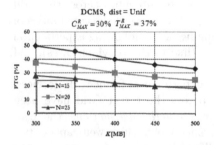 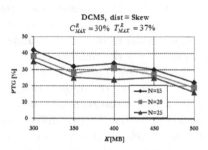

Fig. 3. Experimental results for the Grid DT process DCMS in the case of loose model constraints with Uniform (left) and Skew (right) data and service loads

Figure 3 shows the experimental results for the Grid DT process DCMS in the case of loose model constraints with Uniform (left) and Skew (right) data and service loads, under the ranging of the respective experimental parameters introduced above. In particular, we notice that the temporal gain decreases as the size of the data cube increases. This is reasonable, as a big-in-size data cube requires a relevant amount of time to be materialized from a Grid node to another one.

Figure 4 shows instead the experimental results for the Grid DT process LRDCQS under similar experimental scenario and configuration. In this case, the more is the selectivity of queries the more is the time required by query evaluation. This observation is in line with previous results, as evaluating highly-selective queries requires a higher amount of time with respect to the case of evaluating lowly-selectivity queries.

Figure 5 shows the experimental results for the Grid DT process DCFS under similar experimental scenario and configuration. In this case, the more is the

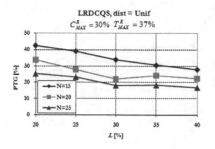
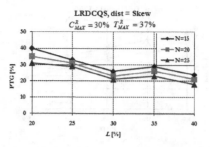

Fig. 4. Experimental results for the Grid DT process LRDCQS in the case of loose model constraints with Uniform (left) and Skew (right) data and service loads

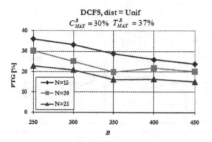
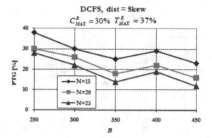

Fig. 5. Experimental results for the Grid DT process DCFS in the case of loose model constraints with Uniform (left) and Skew (right) data and service loads

number of buckets of the input partitioning scheme the more is the time required by the fragmentation process.

Beyond the previous obvious experimental evidences, for all kinds of experiment we observe an *effective* reduction of time required to complete the respective Grid DT service for the target Grid running RGDTExec with respect to the same Grid not running RGDTExec, under the satisfaction of the input model constraints. This confirms to us the benefits deriving from embedding RGDTExec within the core layer of Grid architectures adhering to the Grid-based RTSOA paradigm introduced in this paper.

Finally, Figure 6, Figure 7 and Figure 8 show the same collection of previous experiments in the case of tight model constraints, respectively. As expected, we observe a general performance decrease with respect to the case of loose model constraints.

Finally, an interesting aspect that derives from the experimental results above is represented by the fact that Grid size, i.e. the number of (Grid) nodes composing the target Grid, has a significant impact on the performance of RGDTExec. Ranging the number of Grid nodes allows us to stress the *scalability* of RGDTExec. In particular, we observe that performance decreases as the number of Grid nodes increases, i.e. we obtain a lower percentage reduction of time required to completely execute the DT services over the Grid. This suggests us that a higher number of Grid nodes does not ensure a better performance in all cases, as

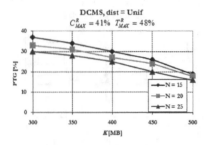
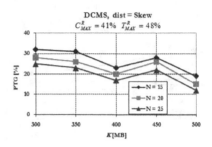

Fig. 6. Experimental results for the Grid DT process DCMS in the case of tight model constraints with Uniform (left) and Skew (right) data and service loads

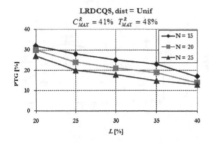
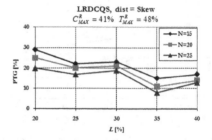

Fig. 7. Experimental results for the Grid DT process LRDCQS in the case of tight model constraints with Uniform (left) and Skew (right) data and service loads

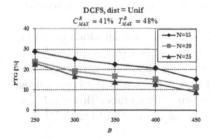
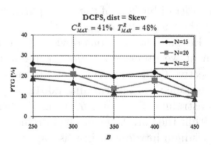

Fig. 8. Experimental results for the Grid DT process DCFS in the case of tight model constraints with Uniform (left) and Skew (right) data and service loads

RGDTExec could require a higher amount of time to perform each greedy choice. On the other hand, typical real-life Grid settings incorporate a relevant number of nodes to high availability and reliability purposes, so that both the aspects (i.e., performance and availability/reliability) should be traded-off in real-life Grid-based RTSOA application scenarios.

9 Conclusions and Future Work

In this paper, we have provided a comprehensive framework for modeling and managing time bound constraints in data-intensive Grid and Cloud infrastructures. Main contributions of the proposed framework are a heuristic scheme and the deriving greedy algorithm which both allow us to solve all possible instances of the problem underlying the proposed framework. We have also provided a comprehensive experimental evaluation of the framework which has finally confirmed to us the benefits due to the framework in modern data-intensive application scenarios.

Future work is mainly devoted to further enhance our proposed framework in order to make it capable of dealing with novel metaphors of actual research challenges such as *uncertain and imprecise data management* and *streaming data processing*.

References

1. Agrawal, D., Das, D., El Abbadi, A.: A Big Data and Cloud Computing: Current State and Future Opportunities. In: Proceedings of EDBT 2011, pp. 530–533 (2011)
2. Barbará, D., DuMouchel, W., Faloutsos, C., Haas, P., Hellerstein, J.M., Ioannidis, Y.E., Jagadish, H.V., Johnson, T., Poosala, V., Ross, K.A., Sevcik, K.C.: The new jersey data reduction report. IEEE Data Engineering Bullettin 20(4), 3–45 (1997)
3. Bowers, S., Ludäscher, B.: An Ontology-Driven Framework for Data Transformation in Scientific Workflows. In: Rahm, E. (ed.) DILS 2004. LNCS (LNBI), vol. 2994, pp. 1–16. Springer, Heidelberg (2004)
4. Cao, Y., Chen, C., Guo, F., Jiang, D., Lin, Y., Ooi, B.C., Vo, H.T., Wu, S., Xu, Q.: ES2: A cloud data storage system for supporting both OLTP and OLAP. In: Proceedings of IEEE ICDE 2011, pp. 291–302 (2011)
5. de Carvalho Costa, R.L., Furtado, P.: An SLA-enabled grid data warehouse. In: Proceedings of IEEE IDEAS, pp. 285–289 (2007)
6. Cohen, J., Dolan, B., Dunlap, M., Hellerstein, J.M., Welton, C.: MAD Skills: New Analysis Practices for Big Data. PVLDB 2(2), 1481–1492 (2009)
7. Costan, A., Tudoran, R., Antoniu, G., Brasche, G.: TomusBlobs: Scalable Data-intensive Processing on Azure Clouds. Concurrency and Computation: Practice and Experience (2013) (in press)
8. Cuzzocrea, A.: Data transformation services over grids with real-time bound constraints. In: Meersman, R., Tari, Z. (eds.) OTM 2008, Part I. LNCS, vol. 5331, pp. 852–869. Springer, Heidelberg (2008)
9. Cuzzocrea, A.: Analytics over Big Data: Exploring the Convergence of Data Warehousing, OLAP and Data-Intensive Cloud Infrastructures. In: Proceedings of IEEE COMPSAC 2013, pp. 481–483 (2013)
10. Cuzzocrea, A., Darmont, J., Mahboubi, H.: Fragmenting very large XML data warehouses via K-means clustering algorithm. International Journal of Business Intelligence and Data Mining 4(3-4), 301–328 (2009)
11. Cuzzocrea, A., Furfaro, F., Greco, S., Mazzeo, G.M., Masciari, E., Saccà, D.: A distributed system for answering range queries on sensor network data. In: Proceedings of IEEE PerSeNS 2005, pp. 369–373 (2005)

12. Cuzzocrea, A., Furfaro, F., Masciari, E., Saccà, D., Sirangelo, C.: Approximate query answering on sensor network data streams. In: Stefanidis, A., Nittel, S. (eds.) GeoSensor Networks, pp. 53–72. CRC Press (2004)

13. Cuzzocrea, A., Furfaro, F., Mazzeo, G.M., Saccá, D.: A grid framework for approximate aggregate query answering on summarized sensor network readings. In: Meersman, R., Tari, Z., Corsaro, A. (eds.) OTM-WS 2004. LNCS, vol. 3292, pp. 144–153. Springer, Heidelberg (2004)

14. Cuzzocrea, A., Kumar, A., Russo, V.: Experimenting the query performance of a grid-based sensor network data warehouse. In: Hameurlain, A. (ed.) Globe 2008. LNCS, vol. 5187, pp. 105–119. Springer, Heidelberg (2008)

15. Cuzzocrea, A., Song, I.-Y., Davis, K.C.: Analytics over Large-Scale Multidimensional Data: The Big Data Revolution. In: Proceedings of ACM DOLAP, pp. 101–104 (2011)

16. Dean, J., Ghemawat, S.: MapReduce: Simplified Data Processing on Large Clusters. Communications of the ACM 51(1) (2008)

17. Foster, I., Kesselman, C., Nick, J.M., Tuecke, S.: Grid services for distributed system integration. IEEE Computer 35(6), 37–46 (2002)

18. Foster, I., Kesselman, C., Tuecke, S.: The anatomy of the grid: enabling scalable virtual organizations. International Journal of High Performance Computing Applications 15(3), 200–222 (2001)

19. Fox, G.: Data Intensive Applications on Clouds. In: Proceedings of ACM DataCloud 2011 (2011),
http://grids.ucs.indiana.edu/ptliupages/publications/
data311gf-fox.pdf

20. Gray, J., Chaudhuri, S., Bosworth, A., Layman, A., Reichart, D., Venkatrao, M., et al.: Data cube: a relational aggregation operator generalizing group-by, cross-tab, and sub-totals. Data Mining and Knowledge Discovery 1(1), 29–53 (1997)

21. Ho, C.-T., Agrawal, R., Megiddo, N., Srikant, R.: Range queries in OLAP data cubes. In: Proceedings of ACM SIGMOD 1997, pp. 73–88 (1997)

22. Iqbal, S., Bunn, J.J., Newman, H.B.: Distributed heterogeneous relational data warehouse in a grid environment. In: Proceedings of CHEP 2003 (2003),
http://www.slac.stanford.edu/econf/C0303241/proc/papers/THAT007.pdf

23. Kiran, M., Hashim, A.-H.A., Kuan, L.M., Jiun, Y.Y.: Execution time prediction of imperative paradigm tasks for grid scheduling optimization. International Journal of Computer Science and Network Security 9(2), 155–163 (2009)

24. Lawrence, M., Dehne, F.A., Rau-Chaplin, A.: Implementing OLAP query fragment aggregation and recombination for the OLAP enabled grid. In: Proceedings of IEEE IPDPS 2007, pp. 1–8 (2007)

25. Lawrence, M., Rau-Chaplin, A.: The OLAP-Enabled Grid: Model and Query Processing Algorithms. In: Proceedings of IEEE HPCS 2006, vol. 4 (2006)

26. Nguyen, M., Tjoa, A.M., Weippl, E., Brezany, P.: Toward a grid-based zero-latency data warehousing implementation for continuous data streams processing. International Journal of Data Warehousing and Mining 1(4), 22–55 (2005)

27. Papazoglou, M.P., Georgakapoulos, G.: Service-oriented computing. Communications of the ACM 46(10), 24–28 (2003)

28. Papazoglou, M.P., van den Heuvel, W.-J.: Service-oriented architectures: approaches, technologies and research issues. VLDB Journal 16(3), 389–415 (2007)

29. Tsai, W.-T., Shao, Q., Sun, X., Elston, J.: Real-Time Service-Oriented Cloud Computing. In: Proceedings of IEEE SERVICES 2010, vol. 1, pp. 473–478 (2010)

30. Wehrle, P., Miquel, M., Tchounikine, A.: A grid services-oriented architecture for efficient operation of distributed data warehouses on globus. In: Proceedings of IEEE AINA 2007, pp. 994–999 (2007)

Network and Storage Latency Attacks to Online Trading Protocols in the Cloud

Claudio A. Ardagna and Ernesto Damiani

Università degli Studi di Milano, Dipartimento di Informatica, Italy

Abstract. Online trading protocols enable participants to trade, barter, or sell goods and services over a private network or the global Net. Due to diversity of network and computational resources at their disposal, participants communicate and carry out their trading with different latencies. This scenario may give rise to *latency attacks*, where malicious parties (a.k.a. *fast traders*) exploit lower latency to attack trading protocols' fairness and increase their income. With the advent of the cloud, the problem of identifying and preventing latency attacks is exacerbated by the fact that cloud providers and privileged users could collude to make latency attacks simpler and more effective. In this paper, we give an overview of network and storage latency attacks in multi-party trading protocols, focusing on cloud peculiarities and providing some empirical recommendations for protocol design.

Keywords: Cloud, Multi-party online trading protocol, Network latency attack, Storage latency attack.

1 Introduction

Today, billions of users have adopted an "always connected" lifestyle: they are continuously surrounded by sensors, carry mobile devices like smartphones or tablets, and work by interacting with remote, cloud-based services via a network infrastructure. While everybody is aware that different users have access to different network, computing, and storage technologies with different latency and throughput, fewer realize that differences in latency can be weapons in the hands of attackers [4]. The impact of latency and performance variations in traditional trading systems has been recognized and analyzed since long [9]; but the advent of online trading systems has created an entirely new situation. If the price of a security varies every 10ms, traders located at more than $3 \cdot 10^7$m (30000km: the distance the light travels in 10ms) will have no possibility of taking the most recent price into account in their buy-or-sell decisions. Once a price reaches them, a more recent one has already been generated at the source. This may not seem a big deal (the radius of the Earth is around $6,371$km), until we remark that very few customers have a direct, fiber-optic connection to the price formation site. The other customers will then experience higher network latencies, giving to the ones enjoying lower latency a clear *price sampling* advantage:

R. Meersman et al. (Eds.): OTM 2014 Workshops, LNCS 8842, pp. 192–201, 2014.

the knowledge of more (and more recent) prices than their fellow traders. *High-frequency traders*, who use sophisticated computer algorithms to rapidly trade securities, are known to pay high hosting costs to deploy their automatic trader agents "close" to price formation sites. Taking into account latency differences when formulating a strategy is in principle possible: for instance Wah and Wellman [19] analyzed the impact of latency arbitrage on efficiency and liquidity in fragmented financial markets. They proposed an elegant, simple model of latency across two markets with a single traded security, very far from actual trading systems covering thousands of securities. Other researchers focused on building a fair (same latency) network environment on the top of existing networks. Cheng and Wang [7] considered latency-sensitive applications, analyzed the problem of predicting network latency, and presented a solution to network performance isolation. Lobo et al. [13] analyzed the impact of IPv6 on high-frequency trading systems, while Cheng et al. [6] the impact of latency on cloud pricing variations. Tomanek and Kencl [18] proposed a cloud-latency auditing platform based on global probes to measure service latency at various cloud layers.

In the following, we will not cover legitimate exploitation of low latency to improve buy-or-sell decision making, like the *price sampling* advantage. Rather we focus on *latency attacks*, where latencies are used to purposefully undermine the ability of fellow traders to get the best price. Latency attacks have been known for several years, and several reports of their taking place on commodity markets worldwide have been published [12]. However, achieving lower latency than fellow traders on the physical network requires a huge investment in technology (high-speed network or computational devices), whose deployment cannot easily escape audit and forensics analysis. Today, cloud architectures are giving to cloud providers a much finer-grained control of network and storage latencies experimented by users. The cloud environment makes it easier to get away with latency attacks, since it permits to reduce the attack upfront costs and to hide the attacker's tracks from audit and forensics analysis.

In this paper, we describe some additions to the attack surface of multi-party trading protocols due to cloud hosting and the corresponding latency scenario. Based on our empirical analysis, we identify some areas where protocol checking is needed to prevent latency attacks based on collusion between cloud providers and privileged users. The remaining of this paper is organized as follows. Section 2 presents network latency attacks, discussing their application in the cloud and possible countermeasures. Similarly, Section 3 presents storage latency attacks, discussing their application in the cloud and possible countermeasures. Section 4 gives our concluding remarks.

2   Network Latency Attacks

We first discuss in detail the notion of network latency attack in physical networks (Section 2.1). We then focus on its possible enactment in cloud environments (Section 2.2) and on possible countermeasures (Section 2.3).

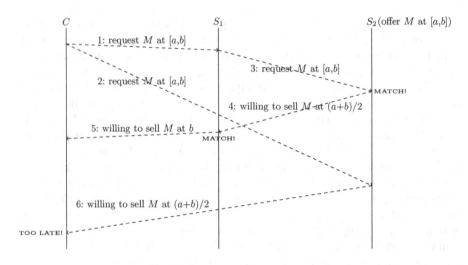

Fig. 1. An example of network latency attack

2.1   Network Latency Attacks in Physical Networks

A network latency attack to a multi-party protocol takes place whenever an attacker can exploit a temporary information asymmetry among parties, due to differences in information propagation speed over the network. To gain full understanding of this notion, let us consider a simple protocol where a customer C announces (*broadcasts*) to the market its interest in buying a good M in the price bracket $[a,b]$, with $b \geq a$. Let us also assume the market is composed of two suppliers S_1 and S_2 only. We denote by $\mathcal{L}(X,Y)$ the network latency time between any two parties X and Y. The protocol's window of information asymmetry is the (*wallclock*) time interval during which one of the two suppliers knows the request, while the other does not it yet. Formally, the window can be expressed as:

$$\Delta\mathcal{L} = |\mathcal{L}(C,S_1) - \mathcal{L}(C,S_2)| \qquad (1)$$

Let us now assume S_1 to enjoy low network latency to both interlocutors, that is, $\mathcal{L}(C,S_1) \ll \mathcal{L}(C,S_2)$ and $\mathcal{L}(S_1,S_2) \ll \mathcal{L}(C,S_2)$. Whenever a request and the corresponding offer have overlapping price intervals, some kind of price arbitration takes place and identifies a price that lies somewhere within the intersection between the request and the offer price intervals. For the moment, we shall not describe the price arbitration algorithm, which will become relevant to our analysis only in Section 3. Here, we concentrate on network latency attack and specifically on the case where the computation time T_{pa} required for price arbitration is much lower than network latency (*fast price arbitration*), that is, $T_{pa} \ll \min(\mathcal{L}(S_1,S_2),\mathcal{L}(C,S_1))$. Figure 1 presents an example of network latency attack to our simple protocol. We note that, for the sake of simplicity, our example assumes demand price brackets to coincide with the initial offer by S_2.

Figure 1 shows the interaction between a customer C requesting a good M and a supplier S_2 selling M in a price bracket $[a,b]$. A competitor S_1, knowing the existence of S_2 and receiving the request *broadcast* by C, tries to increase its revenue by exploiting its reduced network latency compared to the one of S_2. In other words, S_1 responds to C's request in the window of information asymmetry (see Equation 1). C requests to buy M at $[a,b]$ to both S_1 (Step 1) and S_2 (Step 2). S_1, building on its higher network performance, requests to buy M at $[a,b]$ to S_2 (Step 3). Since the sale transaction is accepted by S_2 if the max price b proposed by S_1 is greater than/equal to the min price a offered by S_2 ($b \geq a$), S_2 accepts the request by S_1 and sells M to it at $(a+b)/2$ (Step 4). After concluding the transaction, S_1 can resell M to C at a price of b (Step 5), well before C receives the reply by S_2 accepting to sell M at $(a+b)/2$ (Step 6).

The inflicted damage consists in: *i)* C buying at overprice from S_1 (M is sold by S_1 to C at price b, while C could have bought it from S_2 at the lower price $(a+b)/2$;[1] *ii)* S_2 underselling to S_1 for the same amount. Two interesting questions that arise regarding this attack are:

- how does S_1 get to know the existence of S_2?
- How does S_1 get to know the window of asymmetry (which is also its window of opportunity) without owning the network?

The empirical answers are: by *shilling* and *sampling*. S_1 can first act as a *shill*, that is, a fake buyer requesting small quantities of M just to lure S_2 into responding. Once S_2 has made an offer, revealing information on its price bracket, S_1 keeps on measuring the network latency between itself and S_2. When a real customer C comes online and S_1 notices that C is much closer to itself in term of latency, the attack can start.

2.2   Network Latency Attacks in the Cloud

The advent of cloud computing and Software Defined Networks (SDNs) has given to cloud providers full control over virtual network latencies, for instance, via the configuration of virtual switches in the cloud [14]. A cloud provider can then easily introduce a suitable delay in the communication channel between C and S_2, making S_1 an "instant fast trader" without any need for S_1 to sample network delays, as would be needed in a physical network.[2] Introducing virtual network delays is not illegal – if they may even be compatible with the Service Level Agreement (SLA) between the cloud provider and S_2 – because binding differences in network latency *w.r.t.* other customers (or in general, any *relative QoS guarantee* [8]) is not an usual request in cloud SLAs [2,3,5,10,15,20].

2.3   Countermeasures

Metric-based detection of latency attacks can be attempted. From the point of view of customer C, the onset of a latency attack could be guessed from a high

---

[1] We remark that in case $a=b$, the selling price of S_1 and S_2 are the same for C.

[2] We note that for protocols different from the one in this paper, the cloud provider may need to introduce a delay also in the communications from S_2 to S_1.

number of convenient offers coming in too late; from the point of view of an auditor sitting within the price arbitration mechanism, the latency attack could be detected when seeing a high number of price arbitrations that come close to the higher boundary of the requester's price bracket. However, in both cases, attack detection based on auditing may be impaired by the background noise of similar events taking place, for instance, due to "physiological" network latency oscillations and to market variability.

As an alternative to metric-based approaches, machine-learning techniques can be deployed to detect latency attacks. However, research in this area is still in its infancy.

Empirical protocol checking to prevent the attack also suggests to avoid FIFO acceptance of offers in favor of *i)* a random deadline and *ii)* best or second best offer selection. These precautions could make increasingly difficult for the colluding cloud provider to insert the "right" delays.

3   Storage Latency Attacks

Similarly to Section 2, we first discuss the notion of storage latency attack in physical networks (Section 3.1). We then focus on its possible enactment in cloud environments (Section 3.2) and on possible countermeasures (Section 3.3).

3.1   Storage Latency Attacks in Physical Networks

We start by discussing the impact of computation time T_{pa} on the robustness of our sample multi-party protocol. Let us assume that T_{pa} required for price arbitration is much higher than network latency (*slow price arbitration*). Formally, $T_{pa} \gg \min(\mathcal{L}(S_1, S_2), \mathcal{L}(C, S_1))$. In this case, we can disregard network latency completely and concentrate on computation time. In fact, the only enabling condition for the attack is S_1 to enjoy a much faster arbitration service than S_2, expressed as:

$$T_{pa}(C, S_1) \ll T_{pa}(C, S_2) \tag{2}$$

with $T_{pa}(X,Y)$ the computation time for price arbitration between any two parties X and Y. It is important to remark that the effect in Equation 2 can be due to arbitrages involving S_1 using a faster CPU and/or enjoying a lower latency access to local storage than the other arbitrages. Let us analyze these causes in more detail. In principle, price arbitrage requires computing a function whose arguments are the request and offer price brackets. For the sake of simplicity, given a party X with a demand price bracket $[r,s]$ and a party Y with offer price bracket $[u,v]$ for the same good M, we consider an arbitrage agent that takes the upper boundary s of the request bracket of X, the lower boundary u of the offer bracket of Y, verifies that $s \geq u$, and computes the average. The arbitrage service pseudo-code goes as follow:

Table 1. An example of data structure for demand and offer brackets

Trader	Good	Demand bracket	Offer bracket
C	M	$[r,s]$	—
S_1	M	—	$[u_1,v_1]$
S_2	M	—	$[u_2,v_2]$

ARBITRAGE(X:customer, Y:supplier, Z:good)
$[r,s]$:= **demandbracket**(X,Z);
$[u,v]$:= **offerbracket**(Y,Z);
if ($s \geq u$)
  return$((u+s)/2)$
else return(FAIL)

Table 1 shows an example of data structure containing demand and offer brackets, which are used by function **ARBITRAGE**. We note that Table 1 only shows the entries for a single good M, but a real table would in principle include all goods any trader (customer or supplier) in the market is prepared to trade. This type of data structure, whose anonymized form was patented by Google [16], is a core conceptual component of online trader systems.

The latency attack can involve providing a faster computation of $(u_1+s)/2$ when $Y=S_1$ (*computation speed attack*), faster reads from the table of **demandbracket**(X,Z) and **offerbracket**(Y,Z) when $Y=S_1$ (*storage attack*), or both. Diagrammatically, it can be outlined as presented in Figure 2. Figure 2 shows the interaction between a customer C requesting a good M and a supplier S_2 selling M in a price bracket $[a,b]$. A competitor S_1, knowing the existence of S_2 and receiving a request *broadcast* by C, tries to increase its revenue by exploiting its reduced computation time T_{pa} compared to the one of S_2. More in detail, C requests to buy M at $[a,b]$ to both S_1 (Step 1) and S_2 (Step 2). S_1 building on its higher T_{pa} requests to buy M at $[a,(a+b)/2]$ to S_2 (Step 3) and, at the same time, notifies C that is willing to sell M at a price of b (Step 4), though it does not own M yet. In fact, given that *i)* a selling transaction is executed by S_2 if the max price $(a+b)/2$ proposed by S_1 is greater than/equal to the min price a offered by S_2 $((a+b)/2 \geq a)$, and *ii)* S_1 knows the arbitration price to be calculated by S_2 as the mean of the two price values, S_1 also knows S_2 will accept its request and sell M to it at $(3a+b)/4$ (Step 6). In the meantime, S_2 will reply to the request at Step 1, though it is too late (Step 5).

Figure 2 shows how the difference $T_{pa}(C,S_1) \ll T_{pa}(C,S_2)$ can create a window of opportunity for S_1. S_1 can make an offer to C, while counting on a later buy, and then obtain the offered good M at a lower price from S_2. In the meanwhile, S_2 is kept busy obtaining a much slower price arbitrage on C's original offer. Again, the inflicted damage consists in: *i)* C buying at overprice from S_1 (M is sold by S_1 to C at price b, while C could have bought it from S_2 at the lower

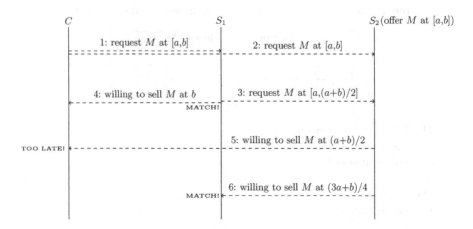

Fig. 2. An example of storage latency attack

price $(a+b)/2$;[3] *ii)* S_2 underselling to S_1 for the same amount. An interesting question arising in this scenario is:

– how is it possible to provide an arbitration service that is fast when the arbitration is requested by some privileged users (the attacker S_1 in our example) and slow for all the others, *without changing neither the service's code nor the data structure implementation?*[4]

Empirical answers to this question include using *i)* multiple copies of the data structure and *ii)* different concurrency control policies.

To discuss the first answer, let us go back to our example. The hosting service carrying out the arbitration could use two copies of Table 1, one for arbitrations requested by S_1 and another one for the rest of the traders (S_2 in our example). To appreciate the difference between latencies involved in using different copies of the same data structure hosted on different storage technologies, we refer to the quantification of storage latency for advanced technologies recently published in different research works (e.g., [1,11]), which show storage access times in the order of μs. The access time of advanced storage is therefore about two orders of magnitude smaller than the access time of modern Solid State Drives (SSDs), which boast random data access times around 0.1ms. Assuming that the decision on which copy of the table to use (and, consequently, which storage to access) is made at runtime (e.g, via dynamic linking), inspecting the source code of the hosted arbitration service (see our pseudo-code above) would not reveal any reason for the latency difference.

The second answer does not involve using multiple copies of the data structure or different storage technologies; rather, it introduces a difference in storage

---

[3] Again, we note that in case $a=b$, the selling price of S_1 and S_2 are the same.
[4] The part of the question in italics is very relevant, because traders or regulatory authorities may well require the arbitration service implementation to be transparent.

latency simply by giving different, user-dependent priorities to the low-level operations on the data structure. Runtime prioritization of operations on data has been used for improving performance limiting write contention in parallel and concurrent programs [17]. In our case, run-time prioritization is used to introduce a delay. For instance, read operations made for computing arbitrations involving S_1 could be given higher priority than updates, while the contrary could hold for reads involving S_2. Once these priorities are in place, a malicious hosting service can make a table read by S_2 much slower simply by matching it with a fake update (which would be executed first) on the same row of the table. In this case, even step-by-step debugging the arbitration service execution would not reveal the reason of the difference in latency between arbitrations involving the two traders.

3.2 Storage Latency Attacks in the Cloud

Again, let us now assume our trading protocol is hosted in cloud. If the cloud provider colludes with one of the suppliers, the storage attack described above can be brought about much more easily, as the physical location of the data structures used by the arbitrage service and the prioritization of data access operations are under full control of the cloud provider [17]. In particular, even when all traders enjoy the same SLA *w.r.t.* computing performance and the same absolute upper boundary on storage access, differences in physical storage technology used for the underlying data or different concurrency control policies could result in huge differences in access time and high variance of the execution time of arbitrage, while remaining within the boundaries of a given SLA.

3.3 Countermeasures

Countermeasures to cloud-supported storage latency attacks require external auditing of cloud configurations to make sure that ad hoc reconfiguration was not used to disrupt fairness. Unfortunately auditing techniques and components are still in their infancy, although standards like ISO 27k started defining cloud auditing procedures.

4 Conclusions

In this paper, we described some additions to the attack surface of multi-party online trading protocol implementations due to cloud hosting. Based on our analysis, we identified two mechanisms, namely, latency control on virtual switches and virtualized storage, and runtime prioritization of access operation to virtualized storage, which allow a cloud provider to implement a complex latency attack (e.g., usually requiring direct fiber routes and network delay sampling) in a straightforward way. As a first result of our analysis, it is clear that in some domains protocol checking is needed to prevent latency attacks based on collusion between cloud providers and privileged users. In addition, the importance of cloud transparency clearly emerges. If a customer has the possibility of verifying mean latency or anonymized latencies of other customers (e.g., via a trusted third party), its trust in the fairness of a trading would increase. This discussion points to the need of an independent *certification process* that underwrites properties like fairness of cloud-hosted trading. In our future work, we will study latency testing and monitoring techniques suitable for online certification of trading systems and set up concrete examples of latency attacks on different cloud protocol stacks.

Acknowledgments. This work was partly supported by the EU-funded project CUMULUS (contract n. FP7-318580) and by the Italian MIUR project SecurityHorizons (c.n. 2010XSEMLC).

References

1. Akerson, D., Onufryk, P.: NVM Express: Optimizing for PCIe SSD Performance. Storage Networking Industry Association (2013), (accessed in date September 2014)
2. Amazon: Amazon EC2 Service Level Agreement (June 2013), http://aws.amazon.com/ec2/sla/, (accessed in date September 2014)
3. Anisetti, M., Ardagna, C.A., Damiani, E., Bonatti, P.A., Faella, M., Galdi, C., Sauro, L.: e-Auctions for multi-cloud service provisioning. In: Proc. of the 11th IEEE International Conference on Services Computing (SCC 2014), Anchorage, AL, USA (June–July 2014)
4. Arnuk, S., Saluzzi, J.: Latency Arbitrage: The Real Power Behind Predatory High Frequency Trading. Themis Trading LLC White Paper (2009), (accessed in date September 2014)
5. Casalicchio, E., Silvestri, L.: Mechanisms for SLA provisioning in cloud-based service providers. Computer Networks 57(3), 795–810 (2013)
6. Cheng, H.K., Li, Z., Naranjo, A.: Cloud Computing Spot Pricing Dynamics: Latency and Limits to Arbitrage (2012), (accessed in date September 2014)
7. Cheng, L., Wang, C.-L.: Network performance isolation for latency-sensitive cloud applications. Future Generation Computer Systems 29(4), 1073–1084 (2013)
8. Chua, K.C., Gurusamy, M., Liu, Y., Phung, M.H.: Relative QoS differentiation (chapter 3). In: Quality of Service in Optical Burst Switched Networks, pp. 73–90. Springer, US (2007)
9. Hasbrouck, J., Saar, G.: Low-latency trading. Journal of Financial Markets 16(4), 646–679 (2013)
10. Hewlett Packard (HP): Service Level Agreements for All Products, http://www.hpcloud.com/sla, (accessed in date September 2014)
11. Kim, H., Seshadri, S., Dickey, C.L., Chiu, L.: Phase change memory in enterprise storage systems: Silver bullet or snake oil? In: Proc. of the 1st Workshop on Interactions of NVM/FLASH with Operating Systems and Workloads (INFLOW 2013), Farmington, PA, USA (November 2013)
12. Lewis, M.: Flash Boys: A Wall Street Revolt. W. W. Norton & Company, New York (2014)

13. Lobo, N., Malik, V., Donnally, C., Jahne, S., Jhaveri, H.: Evaluating the Latency Impact of IPv6 on a High Frequency Trading System (2012), http://morse.colorado.edu/~tlen5710/12s/LatencyImpact.pdf, (accessed in date September 2014)
14. Phemius, K., Bouet, M.: Monitoring latency with openflow. In: Proc. of the 9th International Conference on Network and Service Management (CNSM 2013), Zürich, Switzerland (October 2013)
15. Sakr, S., Liu, A.: SLA-based and consumer-centric dynamic provisioning for cloud databases. In: Proc. of the 5th IEEE International Conference on Cloud Computing (CLOUD 2012), Honolulu, HI, Hawaii (June 2012)
16. Sernet, P.: Online commodities trading system with anonymous counter bid/offer function. Patent US US 09/731,542 (March 2002)
17. Shun, J., Blelloch, G.E., Fineman, J.T., Gibbons, P.B.: Reducing contention through priority updates. In: Proc. of the 18th ACM SIGPLAN Symposium on Principles and Practice of Parallel Programming (PPoPP 2013), Shenzhen, China (February 2013)
18. Tomanek, O., Kencl, L.: Claudit: Planetary-scale cloud latency auditing platform. In: Proc. of the 2nd IEEE International Conference on Cloud Networking (Cloud-Net 2013), San Francisco, CA, USA (November 2013)
19. Wah, E., Wellman, M.P.: Latency arbitrage, market fragmentation, and efficiency: A two-market model. In: Proc. of the 14th ACM Conference on Electronic Commerce (EC 2013), Philadelphia, PA, USA (June 2013)
20. Zhao, L., Ren, Y., Li, M., Sakurai, K.: Flexible service selection with user-specific qos support in service-oriented architecture. Journal of Network and Computer Applications 35(3), 962–973 (2012)

A Configuration-Management-Database Driven Approach for Fabric-Process Specification and Automation

Florian Bär[1], Rainer Schmidt[1], Michael Möhring[2],
Alfred Zimmermann[3], and Dierk Jugel[3]

[1] Faculty of Computer Science and Mathematics, Munich University of Applied Sciences,
Lothstr. 64, 80335 Munich, Germany
{Florian.Baer,Rainer.Schmidt}@hm.edu
[2] Faculty of Business Administration, Aalen University of Applied Sciences
moehring@htw-aalen.de
[3] Faculty of Computer Science, Reutlingen University of Applied Sciences,
Alteburgstraße 150, 72762 Reutlingen
{Alfred.Zimmermann,Dierk.Jugel}@reutlingen-university.de

Abstract. In this paper we describe an approach that integrates a Configuration-Management-Database into fabric-process specification and automation in order to consider different conditions regarding to cloud-services. By implementing our approach, the complexity of fabric-processes gets reduced. We developed a prototype by using formal prototyping principles as research methods and integrated the Configuration-Management-Database Command into the Workflow-Management-System Activiti. We used this prototype to evaluate our approach. We implemented three different fabric-processes and show that by using our approach the complexity of these three fabric-processes gets reduced.

Keywords: Business Process Management, Workflow Management, Resource Perspective, IT-Service-Management, Cloud-Computing, Self-Service.

1 Introduction

In order to create and configure a cloud-service, a fabric-process [1] has to consider conditions arising from a functional-, correctness- and governance-perspective. Traditional process modeling approaches [2,3,4] embed these conditions in the control-flow of the fabric-process. However, this increases the complexity of the fabric-process significantly. This is due to the fact, that in order to consider these special conditions in the control-flow of the fabric-process, a bunch of additional process tasks and branches are required.

In this paper we present an approach that integrates a Configuration-Management-Database (CMDB) [5] into fabric-process specification and automation in order to handle such conditions separately from the control flow of the fabric process. By this,

R. Meersman et al. (Eds.): OTM 2014 Workshops, LNCS 8842, pp. 202–209, 2014.

it is possible to streamline the control-flow of the fabric-process. Furthermore these conditions can be managed centrally and without redundancies.

In order to evaluate our approach we developed a prototype for the presented approach by using formal prototyping principles [6] as research methods and integrating the CMDB Command [7] into the open-source Workflow-Management-System (WFMS) [8] Activiti [9]. By evaluating the prototype we are able to show, that the presented approach reduces the complexity of the three specified fabric-processes.

The remainder of this paper is organized as follows. First, we argue that it is necessary to capture all the complex relationships between cloud-services and virtual resources within a cloud-environment in order to specify and automate fabric-processes properly. In section 3 we describe an approach that integrates a CMDB into a WFMS. In section 4 we describe a prototype of the presented approach that is integrating the CMDB Command into the open-source WFMS Activiti. In section 5 we evaluate the prototype. Related work is discussed in section 6. Section 7 concludes this paper.

2 Configuration-Management-Database for Fabric-Process Support

A CMDB stores information about the IT-infrastructure of an enterprise. It stores so-called Configuration Items (CIs), e. g. cloud-services and virtual resources such as virtual machines, as well as their inter-relationships [5]. So, a CMDB can be considered as a labeled graph representing the IT-infrastructure and its inner-relationships [10]. A CMDB is described by a triple G=(V, E, L). The set of vertices is denoted V. The vertices represent the different CIs. The set of edges is $E \subseteq V \times V$. Both the vertices and the edges of the graph are labeled. The labels of the vertices are defined by the function L(v). The labels of the edges are defined as L(e) = L(x,y) with x and y being vertices. The labeling of the vertices represents the status of the CIs: L(v) $\in$ {s0, s1, ..,sn }. The labeling of the edges L(e) $\in$ {r0, r1, ..,rn } represents the relationships of the CIs, such as part-of, connected, precondition etc. Fig. 1 illustrates an exemplary CMDB-graph in the form of an UML-Object-Diagram.

Fig. 1 illustrates an example for the complex relationship structures that can exist in cloud-environments. A mediawiki-service requires an already installed and configured webserver, database-server and php-environment. So, the mediawiki-service depends on these three virtual resources. If only one of these three virtual resources is missing, the mediawiki-service cannot be provided. Instead, first the missing virtual resource has to be installed and configured. However, there are also dependencies among the virtual resources. For example, the php-environment should only be installed and configured when the webserver is already installed and configured. So, whether it is at design-time or at run-time these relationships that can be seen as some kind of requirements have to be checked. If some of these relationships / requirements are not fulfilled, the missing ones have to be established.

The example described above points out that in order to create and provide a cloud-service, first its relationships / requirements have to be checked for fulfillment. In Fig. 2 the lifecycle of a cloud-service is illustrated as an UML-State-Machine-Diagram regarding to [11,12]. We extended this lifecycle by adding a guard-constraint to the transition between the defined-state and the created-state. This added guard-constraint requires all the requirements of the cloud-service to be fulfilled. If the requirements of the cloud-service are not fulfilled, the cloud-service cannot be created and has to stay at the defined-state.

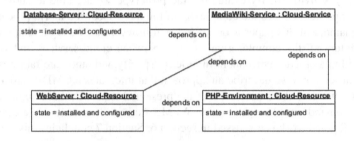

Fig. 1. An example for the complex relationship structures in cloud-environments

In section 3 we provide an approach for implementing the added guard-constraint. This approach integrates a CMDB into fabric-process specification and automation. With this approach it is possible to check the requirements of a cloud-service that has to be create without the need to increase the complexity of the appropriate fabric-process.

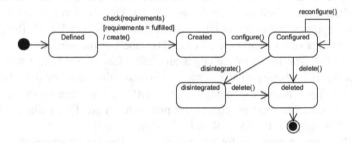

Fig. 2. An extended service-lifecycle regarding to [11,12]

3   Integrating a Configuration-Management-Database into Fabric-Process Specification and Automation

As described in section 2, a cloud-service can only be created if its requirements are already fulfilled. Due to this fact, it is necessary to check this requirements for fulfillment when specifying and automating the fabric-process that is needed in order to create the cloud-service. If the requirements of the cloud-service are not already fulfilled, the fabric-process has to install and configure the missing components and relationships. To check the requirements of a cloud-service when specifying and automating the appropriate fabric-process, an extensive resource meta-model, such as the Fabric-Resource-Meta-Model (FRMM) [1], is needed. Though, when implementing such a resource meta-model directly into an existing WFMS, the requirements of the cloud-service have to be checked in the control-flow of the process. An approach like this would increase the complexity of the fabric-process. An example for a fabric-process that creates a mediawiki-service by installing a mediawiki and its requirements in cloud-environment is depicted in Fig. 3 in Form of a BPMN-Diagram. It is shown that several additional process task and branches are needed in order to consider all the requirements of the mediawiki-service. By this, the complexity of the appropriate fabric-process is increased.

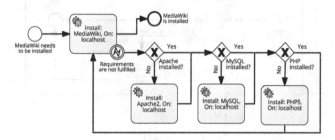

Fig. 3. Considering the special conditions of the mediawiki-service in the control-flow of the appropriate fabric-process

But, like described in section 2, a CMDB already allows to capture the complex relationship structures that can exist between virtual resources. Therefore it is not necessary to implement a resource meta-model directly into a WFMS, but rather to integrate an already running CMDB. By this, the CMDB and its data represent the resource perspective [8,13] of the fabric-processes that are specified with the WFMS. So, the consideration of the conditions of the cloud-service that has to be created or configured can be outsourced to the CMDB. By this, it is not necessary to consider the conditions in the control-flow of the fabric-process. Hence, this approach would not increase the complexity of the fabric-process. This fact is depicted in Fig. 4.

A CMDB can be integrated into fabric-process specification and automation by providing it as an external service [14] and integrating it with a WFMS by providing a cloud-based information system [15]. Cloud-based information systems can be seen as successors of component-based information systems [16]. In Fig. 4 a cloud-based information system is shown, that integrates a WFMS and a CMDB. The cloud-based information system is illustrated as a BPMN-Choreography-Diagram. The fabric-process that is shown in Fig. 4 creates the same mediawiki-service that is created by the fabric-process shown in Fig. 3. However, as it is shown in Fig. 4, by integrating the CMDB into fabric-process specification, the fabric-process is less complex.

4   Prototype

To evaluate the CMDB-driven approach for fabric-process specification and automation described in section 3, we developed a prototype. According to [6] prototyping an information system depends on different steps. In the previous section of the paper, we described and identify the basic requirements as the first step of prototyping. The next step is to develop a prototype to the state of a working prototype. Therefore, we develop the prototype as a cloud-based information system. By this, the prototype integrates two separate cloud-services: the WFMS Activiti and the CMDB Command. While Activiti can be used in order to specify and automate the relevant fabric-processes, Command and its provided web-service were integrated in order to check the requirements of the cloud-services we wanted to create.

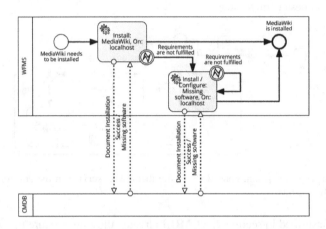

Fig. 4. Integrating a WFMS and a CMDB by defining a cloud-based information system

In Fig. 4, the integration of Activiti and Command is depicted in the form of a BPMN-Choreography-Diagram. Command provides several web-services within its REST-API. One of these web-services can be used in order to document the installation of a certain virtual resource in the CMDB. When this web-service has completed its work, it returns a JSON-string. If the documentation of the installation was successful, this JSON-string contains a success-message. In case of an unsuccessful documentation of the installation due to missing requirements of the virtual resource, the JSON-string lists these missing requirements. The interaction between Activiti and Command is depicted in Fig. 4 exemplary for a mediawiki-service.

In order to integrate Command into fabric-process specification and automation, we implemented several java classes that provide methods in order to invoke the described web-service provided by command and that can be executed by Activiti. These java classes were implemented for each virtual resource that has to be installed and configured in order to create the cloud-services that were evaluated. Each of these java classes provides methods for installing and configuring the appropriate virtual resource as well as an operation for documenting this installation in Command. The java classes were provided to Activiti as .jar-files.

In order to invoke the installation and configuration methods of the implemented java classes, we implemented a separate java class called Automate. This java class has to be attached to the service-tasks of the fabric-processes. The Automate class is able to invoke the installation and configuration methods of the implemented java classes based on the names of the service-tasks it is attached to. In order the java class is able to interpret the names of the service-tasks it is attached to, they have to match the following regular expression: [A-Z][a-z]+:\s[A-Za-z\d]+,\s[A-Z][a-z]+:\s[A-Za-z\d]+. An example for a service-task name that is matching this regular expression is: Install: MediaWiki, On: localhost. In order to install and config a certain virtual resource, we made use of the Ubuntu system commands.

5   Evaluation

The use of the prototype as well as the evaluation for revising and enhancing are the next steps for prototyping an information system according to [6]. To evaluate our approach, we implemented three different fabric-processes into the prototype. The first fabric-process is creating a mediawiki-service in the provided cloud-environment by installing a mediawiki on a specified virtual machine running in the provided cloud-environment. The second fabric-process creates a camunda-service by installing the camunda workflow-engine. The third fabric-process provides a phpBB-board. We specified all of these fabric-processes by using Activiti. All of these fabric-processes only consist of service-tasks. To each of these service-tasks we attached the Automate java class implemented by us. By this, we were able to automate the specified fabric-processes. Fig. 4 depicts the fabric-process that creates the mediawiki-service. Due to limited space, the other two fabric-processes are not illustrated in this paper. However, these two fabric-processes are similar to the process shown in Fig. 4. The implemented fabric-processes only differ in the name of the first process task. While the fabric-process depicted in Fig. 4 installs a mediawiki instance, the other fabric-processes install the camunda workflow-engine and a phpBB instance. Also, the camunda-service relies on less virtual resources. So, the appropriate fabric-process is less complex due to the fact that there are less pre-conditions that have to be checked for fulfillment.

Each of the implemented fabric-processes has to create its appropriate cloud-service on three different virtual machines. We provided three different test-environments in form of three different virtual machines: a test-environment that already provides all requirements of the appropriate cloud-service, a test-environment that already provides two requirements of the appropriate cloud-service and a test-environment that does not provide any requirement of the appropriate cloud-service.

After we ensured that the presented approach and the implemented prototype is working, we measured the complexity of the implemented fabric-processes by measuring their appropriate number of activities, joins and splits (NOAJS) [17]. For each of the implemented fabric-processes, we also specified an appropriate fabric-process that creates the same cloud-service but considers the special conditions of this cloud-service in its control-flow. One of these also specified fabric-processes is depicted in Fig. 3. Due to limited space and due to the fact that the fabric-processes that consider the conditions of the phpBB- and camunda-service in their control-flow are very similar to the fabric-process depicted in Fig. 3, these two other fabric-processes are not illustrated in this paper.

We measured the complexity of these fabric-processes as well. So, we were able to compare the complexity of a fabric-process specified by using the presented approach with its appropriate fabric-process considering the conditions of the cloud-service in its control-flow. The results are shown in Table 1.

Table 1. The complexity of the specified fabric-processes

	Our approach	Traditional approach
MediaWiki / phpBB	4	8
Camunda	4	6

6   Related Work

Fundamental decisions for the data model and the architecture of CMDBs are discussed in [18]. Design considerations for CMDBs are developed in [19]. In [10] algorithms for discovering infrastructure patterns in CMDBs are developed. This research could help to support the evaluation of complex conditions in fabric-processes. The configuration of services from sub-ordinated services and resources is also the theme of other areas of research. E.g. the configuration of business services is analyzed in [20]. In [17] a number of process complexity metrics were introduced and discussed.

7   Conclusion

We developed a CMDB-driven approach for fabric-process specification and automation. We showed that by using our CMDB-driven approach, the complexity of a fabric-process can be reduced. By reducing the complexity of a fabric-process, it is easier to re-redesign it and so to become more flexible and competitive. As a result, academics and practitioners can benefit from this approach both. For example, practitioners can use this approach to improve and evaluate available fabric-processes as well as the competitiveness of the IT-departments and enterprises. There are some limitations to discuss. By implementing our approach, the check for pre-condition fulfillment is outsourced to a CMDB. By this, the CMDB has to provide information about the relevant CIs and their inter-relationships to the WFMS. However, there might be the case where the CMDB is not able to provide the relevant information by default. So, additional enhancements have to be made to the CMDB. However, the resulting additional effort would not increase the fabric-process complexity using existing process complexity metrics like we did in our evaluation.

References

1. Bär, F., Schmidt, R., Möhring, M.: Fabric-Process Patterns. In: Bider, I., Gaaloul, K., Krogstie, J., Nurcan, S., Proper, H.A., Schmidt, R., Soffer, P. (eds.) BPMDS 2014 and EMMSAD 2014. LNBIP, vol. 175, pp. 139–153. Springer, Heidelberg (2014)

2. Scheer, A.-W., Nüttgens, M.: ARIS Architecture and Reference Models for Business Process Management. In: van der Aalst, W.M.P., Desel, J., Oberweis, A. (eds.) Business Process Management. LNCS, vol. 1806, pp. 376–389. Springer, Heidelberg (2000)

3. Lu, R., Sadiq, W.: A Survey of Comparative Business Process Modeling Approaches. In: Abramowicz, W. (ed.) BIS 2007. LNCS, vol. 4439, pp. 82–94. Springer, Heidelberg (2007)

4. Green, P., Rosemann, M.: Integrated process modeling: An ontological evaluation. Inf. Syst. 25, 73–87 (2000)

5. AXELOS Ltd.: ITIL glossary and abbreviations (2011), http://www.itil-officialsite.com/nmsruntime/ saveasdialog.aspx?lID=1180&sID=242

6. Naumann, J.D., Jenkins, A.M.: Prototyping: the new paradigm for systems development. Mis Q., 29–44 (1982)

7. GmbH, F.N.T.: FNT Command, http://www.fntsoftware.com/en/products/fnt-command/

8. Jablonski, S., Bussler, C.: Workflow Management: Modeling Concepts, Architecture and Implementation. International Thomson Computer Press (1996)

9. Activiti Committer: Activiti BPM Platform, http://www.activiti.org/

10. Anchuri, P., Zaki, M.J., Barkol, O., Bergman, R., Felder, Y., Golan, S., Sityon, A.: Graph mining for discovering infrastructure patterns in configuration management databases. Knowl. Inf. Syst. 33, 491–522 (2012)

11. Schmidt, R., Möhring, M.: Two-Phase Composition of Complex Business Services in Cloud-Environments. In: Proceedings of the 17th IEEE International Enterprise Distributed Object Computing Conference Workshops (EDOCW), Vancouver, Canade, pp. 63–70 (2013)

12. Schmidt, R.: Requirements for the Service Process Lifecycle. Presented at the BPMDS 2008 (2008)

13. Bussler, C., Jablonski, S.: Policy resolution for workflow management systems. In: Proceedings of the Twenty-Eighth Hawaii International Conference on System Sciences, vol. 4, pp. 831–840 (1995)

14. Leymann, F., Roller, D., Schmidt, M.-T.: Web services and business process management. IBM Syst. J. 41, 198–211 (2002)

15. Schmidt, R.: Conceptualisation and Lifecycle of Cloud Based Information Systems. In: 2012 IEEE 16th International Enterprise Distributed Object Computing Conference Workshops (EDOCW), pp. 104–113 (2012)

16. Brown, A.W., Wallnan, K.C.: Engineering of component-based systems. In: Proceedings of the Second IEEE International Conference on Engineering of Complex Computer Systems, pp. 414–422 (1996)

17. Cardoso, J., Mendling, J., Neumann, G., Reijers, H.A.: A discourse on complexity of process models. In: Eder, J., Dustdar, S. (eds.) BPM Workshops 2006. LNCS, vol. 4103, pp. 117–128. Springer, Heidelberg (2006)

18. Madduri, H., Shi, S.S.B., Baker, R., Ayachitula, N., Shwartz, L., Surendra, M., Corley, C., Benantar, M., Patel, S.: A configuration management database architecture in support of IBM service management. IBM Syst J 46, 441–457 (2007)

19. Brenner, M., Garschhammer, M., Sailer, M., Schaaf, T.: CMDB-Yet Another MIB? On Reusing Management Model Concepts in ITIL Configuration Management. Large Scale Manag. Distrib. Syst., 269–280 (2006)

20. Becker, J., Beverungen, D., Knackstedt, R., Matzner, M.: Configurative Service Engineering - A Rule-Based Configuration Approach for Versatile Service Processes in Corrective Maintenance. In: 42nd Hawaii International Conference on System Sciences, HICSS 2009, pp. 1–10 (2009)

Increasing Trust in the Cloud through Configuration Validation[*]

Matteo Maria Casalino[**], Henrik Plate, and Serena Elisa Ponta

SAP Product Security Research, 805 Avenue Dr. M. Donat, 06250 Mougins, France
matteocasalino@gmail.com, {henrik.plate,serena.ponta}@sap.com

Abstract. Cloud scenarios are a flexible and scalable solution for the creation, provisioning and consumption of services. Service providers and consumers typically decide and negotiate requirements for their services. However, as these are operated by the cloud platform, consumers have a reduced visibility on the actual fullfillement of the requirements. To increase their trust in the cloud, this paper proposes an approach for configuration validation that relies on a standard based language and adapts to the dynamic nature of cloud environments.

1 Introduction

The correct configuration of software components is a critical requirement of any running system to ensure not only the correct behavior of applications, but also compliance with, e.g., regulations, policies, laws. When consumers outsource services to the cloud, their functional and security requirements are to be enforced by the cloud provider. Configuration validation aims at providing assurance about system security and compliance against regulatory requirements, Service Level Agreements (SLA), etc. Several works [1,2] and initiatives like the Security Content Automation Protocol [3] (SCAP) propose languages and approaches for automating configuration validation by using (extensions of) standard languages. SCAP and proprietary tools only focus on single hosts and [1,2] consider distributed environments. In particular they do not consider the challenges of cloud environment [4,5]. The dynamic nature of cloud scenarios, where new services may be deployed at any point in time, requires a continuos monitoring of configurations to enforce the requirements. Moreover, as clearly stated in [6], an important challenge of cloud computing is the lack of trust that stems from the lack of transparency.

In this paper we propose an approach for configuration validation in the cloud that considers the dynamic nature of cloud solutions where new instances of software components may be deployed at any point in time, and increases the stakeholders' trust in the correctness of the systems' operation.

---

[*] This work was partially supported by the FP7-ICT-2011-8 Project A4CLOUD (no. 317550, http://www.a4cloud.eu/).

[**] Currently at University Claude Bernard Lyon 1.

R. Meersman et al. (Eds.): OTM 2014 Workshops, LNCS 8842, pp. 210–216, 2014.

This paper is structured as follows. Section 2 describes the usage and benefits of configuration validation in the cloud and Section 3 shows the solution we propose to technically realize it. In Section 4 we discuss related works and we conclude in Section 5 with some final remarks.

2   Use Cases

The benefits of performing configuration validation in cloud scenarios can be illustrated straight-forwardly when looking at the typical combination of Platform as a Service (PaaS) and Software as a Service (SaaS) delivery models. The platform provider (PP) offers a runtime environment with a variety of features to application developers. Such features comprise, e.g., dynamic application instantiation to scale according to demand, datastore management (for data replication and backup), or the possibility to use TLS for server-side authentication and communication protection. The developer, in turn, offers an application service to its customers, whereby the latter commonly ignores details about the actual runtime environment, e.g., whether it is owned and operated by the application service provider or other parties. Hence the application developer is the Service Provider (SP) for the End Users (EUs) of its service.

Service properties of both the application service and the platform service are in parts configurable, in parts defined in SLAs. The former are maintained through the use of dedicated interfaces, e.g., the Google App Engine Administration Console, and then translated into low-level settings of possibly multiple distributed components. Using TLS for a Java-based Web application service, for instance, concerns both the application's deployment descriptor as well as the container's configuration. SLA-defined service properties are agreed upon at service subscription time and their enforcement is typically transparent to consumers. In either case, the service consumer is interested in getting assurance that (agreed-upon or configured) properties are correctly enforced. In fact, since number and location of service instances change dynamically, e.g., in response to increasing demand, every new instance as well as related platform components must be correctly configured as part of deployment and provisioning processes.

Increasing Service Providers' Assurance. Configuration validation allows to check the configuration settings of software components. A set of checks (a.k.a. a checklist) can be executed at any point in time to report on the actual configuration settings. If the PP implements such functionality, given a checklist focusing on the configuration settings mandated by the SLA, the PP can automatically check the configurations upon every new deployment of application instances and/or periodically. The same functionality can be used for additional platform checks that the SP can negotiate with the PP (though not included in the SLA), e.g., to make sure that the PP follows common security configuration best practices. For instance the SP may want to check that the Tomcat security guide from OWASP [7] has been followed for configuring every application server instance where its applications are running. By providing reports on the executed checks, configuration validation allows the PP to provide the SP with a greater level of assurance about the fullfillment of the SLA and the correct runtime behavior.

Increasing End Users' Assurance. In order to use a service, the EUs establish a SLA with the SP. Such document states the requirements of the EU that the SP has to meet. As the service is made available by the PP (SaaS), the SLA between the SP and the EU has to be met when the application is run by the PP. Notice that the fact that the service is available through the cloud is transparent for the EU who only interacts with the SP. In such a scenario, the SP can require the PP to perform application- and EU-specific checks to ensure that the application and the application server are correctly configured whenever the application is deployed. By providing the EU with the report on the validation performed on the service he is using, configuration validation increases the EU assurance.

3   Configuration Validation

In this section we describe how the configuration validation activities for the cloud scenario introduced in Section 2 can be technically implemented. To do so, we need two main ingredients: (i) a language to specify declarative configuration checks and (ii) a software architecture comprising an interpreter for such a language as well as a framework to collect the to-be-checked configurations.

As multiple stakeholders have to agree on the meaning of the checks, it is important to rely as much as possible on standards. As such, the MITRE's OVAL specification [8] represents a good starting point as it allows the specification of unambiguous checks (the so-called *OVAL definitions*), i.e., arbitrary boolean combinations of *OVAL tests*. An important limitation of OVAL, though, is that it does not allow a single check to span over the configurations of several software components distributed across a multi-host environment, as it is likely the case of a generic cloud platform provider. To overcome this issue, we make use of the extension to the OVAL language defined in [1] that introduces the concept of *target definitions*, i.e., expressions describing the characteristics of the software components that are to be subject to a given OVAL test. The mapping between target definitions and OVAL tests is given by the so-called *check definition*. With the help of these constructs, not only can we bind configuration checks to generic software components (say, e.g., every web application deployed in a JEE container), but we are also able to specialize their scope to match only the components belonging to a specific SP or, even further, that are used by one of its EUs. Configuration checks can be authored not only by the PP, but by SPs and EUs as well. As illustrated at the beginning of the sequence diagram in Figure 1, this happens at service subscription time. A possible outcome of this phase is partially represented in Figure 2, where an OVAL definition composed of two tests is defined (lines 2–7) to check the correct configuration of the encryption parameters of an application server.[1] Next, a target definition is

---

[1] The check logic, encoded in OVAL tests, can be expressed with standard OVAL constructs and is omitted for the sake of brevity.

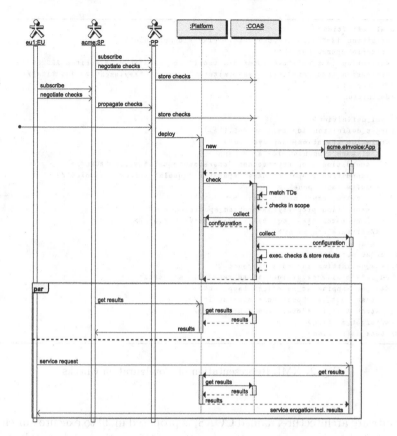

Fig. 1. Configuration Validation in PaaS/SaaS

specified (lines 10–21) that matches to any web application developed by ACME and deployed in a JEE container supporting the Java Servlet 3.0 specification. Finally a check definition (lines 22–27) binds the tests of the OVAL definition to their target, i.e., the application server where ACME's applications are deployed. Similarly, a check specific to an EU, say eu1, testing, e.g., the correctness of its access control configuration, would be mapped to an analogous target definition where the software component `sc:webapp` contains the additional condition `<condition property="consumer" operator="equal" value="eu1" />`.

Once negotiated, the configuration checks shall be executed periodically by the PP and the results made available to the relevant stakeholders. Depending on the system details and on the nature of the delivered services, the validation can be performed more or less frequently and upon certain events. Within our running example, we focus on a prototypical event-triggered validation. At any point in time, depending on PP's strategies, a new deployment of one SP's application can be needed. As this process involves a change in the runtime systems' configuration and potentially manual, hence error-prone, activities, it surely constitutes a candidate trigger for configuration validation.

```
1   <oval_definition>
2   <definition id="oval:acme.sla:def:1" class="compliance">
3    <criteria operator="AND">
4     <criterion test_ref="oval:acme.sla:tst:1" comment="Encr. algorithm AES256"/>
5     <criterion test_ref="oval:acme.sla:tst:2" comment="keylenght >= 128 bits"/>
6    </criteria>
7   </definition>
8   ...
9   </oval_definition>
10  <target_definition id="td:acme:def:1">
11   <relation operation="deployed_in">
12     <software_component id="sc:webapp">
13       <condition property="vendor" operator="equals" value="ACME"/>
14       <condition property="name" operator="equals" value="e-invoice"/>
15     </software_component>
16     <software_component id="sc:webappcont">
17       <condition property="supported_specification"
18         operator="less_eq" value="Java_Servlet_3.0" />
19     </software_component>
20   </relation>
21  </target_definition>
22  <check_definition id="cd:acme:check:2"
23    od_ref="oval:acme.sla:def:1" td_ref="td:acme:def:1">
24    <target_mapping sc_ref="sc:webappcont">
25      <test test_ref="oval:acme.sla:tst:1" />
26      <test test_ref="oval:acme.sla:tst:2" />
27    </target_mapping>
28  </check_definition>
```

Fig. 2. XML Representation of Configuration Checks

A software architecture, named COAS, is proposed in [9] to execute our checks in distributed environments; in the remainder of this section we discuss its use to support configuration validation in the cloud. COAS, operated by the PP, stores all the configuration checks in an XML database. When a new deployment is triggered, a dedicated component named *target definition evaluator* determines which are the target definitions (and corresponding checks) that are relevant to the new environment (by relying on the formal semantics given in [1]). For instance, when deploying the ACME's "eInvoice" web application the OVAL definition `oval:acme.sla:def:1` would be executed on the application container. Depending on the consumer of the application being deployed, all the EU-specific checks will also be considered. Once all the relevant checks have been executed, the results are stored.

As visible at the bottom of Figure 1, at any point in time the SPs are allowed to query the platform for the check results they are concerned with. Since we assumed that EUs are unaware of the platform, it is responsibility of the SPs to provide them with the results. To do so, the platform offers an API that the SP's applications can use to retrieve EU-specific results. Then, the behavior of the service delivered by the application may adapts according to such results in a way that depends on the SP's policies. For instance the application could abort the execution in case of failure of some critical checks. Otherwise, the results would be simply attached to the rest of the delivered content.

4   Related Work

An approach for the validation of configuration of cloud services is provided in [10]. The paper overviews the process for the provisioning of cloud servers and proposes an architecture and workflow for carrying out the validation by executing scripts on newly deployed OS and middleware and relying on existing back-end management tools and databases for collecting additional evidence. However, checking application- and EU-specific configurations by the means of such scripts, would require instance-specific customization, which we avoid by separating the check logic (OVAL definitions) from the declarative specification of check targets (Target Definitions) and from the actual fetching of the to-be-checked configurations (Target Definition Evaluation and Collection). By relying on a standard-based language, the approach we propose not only supports the validation of application's configurations, but also allows the different stakeholders to author their own checks.

The language we rely on [1] is an extension of the OVAL standard (part of the SCAP family of standards). In particular OVAL checks work on the granularity of machines (computer systems), and it is difficult, sometimes impossible, to write fine-granular configuration checks for combinations of software components independently from their computing environment (container). On the contrary, the language defined in [1] allows to bind checks to targets that match to distributed components. This is a key feature of the approach presented in this paper as it allows the different stakeholders to author and execute customized configuration checks without the need to directly access the platform.

One could choose to achieve our same objectives by using plain OVAL together with a state-of-the-art OVAL interpreter. Although possible, this approach would be highly inconvenient. In fact, as discussed in [9], using OVAL in a distributed environment would require maintaining host-specific replicas of the same checklists and installing dedicated software (interpreters) on each host. Furthermore, its adoption in cloud solutions would pose additional challenges as hosts are shared among multiple consumers, and the ownership of the different checks performed on each host would have to be considered.

5   Conclusion and Future Work

We proposed an approach for validating software configurations tailored to platform and software as a service scenarios. By featuring such a configuration validation service, platform providers are able to provide their customers with more assurance on the correct operation of their infrastructure. Of course, as stated in [5], consumers might not fully trust the evidence provided by the platform provider alone. Therefore, it is essential to complement our approach with auditing activities aimed at verifying the correct execution of the configuration validation process. Indeed having such an automated process in place would allow auditors to provide better assurance to customers, as it is generally preferable to audit the process itself rather than manually checking the correctness of potentially many configuration files scattered across a distributed system — an activity that, due to budget constraints, most often requires sampling [11].

As future work, we plan to develop automated assessment techniques to provide consumers with semantically richer results, e.g., metrics to help them better judge the impact and severity of failed checks.

References

1. Casalino, M.M., Mangili, M., Plate, H., Ponta, S.E.: Detection of configuration vulnerabilities in distributed (Web) environments. In: Keromytis, A.D., Di Pietro, R. (eds.) SecureComm 2012. LNICST, vol. 106, pp. 131–148. Springer, Heidelberg (2013)
2. Barrere, M., Badonnel, R., Festor, O.: Towards the assessment of distributed vulnerabilities in autonomic networks and systems. In: 2012 IEEE Network Operations and Management Symposium (NOMS), pp. 335–342 (2012)
3. NIST: (Security content automation protocols) http://scap.nist.gov.
4. Subashini, S., Kavitha, V.: Review: A survey on security issues in service delivery models of cloud computing. J. Netw. Comput. Appl. 34(1), 1–11 (2011)
5. Takabi, H., Joshi, J., Ahn, G.J.: Security and privacy challenges in cloud computing environments. IEEE Security Privacy 8(6), 24–31 (2010)
6. Khan, K., Malluhi, Q.: Establishing trust in cloud computing. IT Professional 12(5), 20–27 (2010)
7. OWASP: (Securing Tomcat) https://www.owasp.org/index.php/Securing_tomcat.
8. Baker, J., Hansbury, M., The, D.H.: oval language specification (version 5.10.1). MITRE Corporation (2012), http://oval.mitre.org/language/version5.10.1/OVAL_Language_Specification_01-20-2012.pdf
9. Casalino, M.M., Plate, H., Ponta, S.E.: Configuration assessment as a service. In: Di Pietro, R., Herranz, J., Damiani, E., State, R. (eds.) DPM 2012 and SETOP 2012. LNCS, vol. 7731, pp. 217–226. Springer, Heidelberg (2013)
10. Chieu, T., Singh, M., Tang, C., Viswanathan, M., Gupta, A.: Automation system for validation of configuration and security compliance in managed cloud services. In: Proceedings of the e-Business Engineering (ICEBE), pp. 285–291 (2012)
11. Hall, T.W., Hunton, J.E., Pierce, B.J.: Sampling practices of auditors in public accounting, industry, and government. Accounting Horizons 16(2), 125–136 (2002)

EI2N 2014 PC Co-Chairs Message

After the successful eighth edition in 2013, the ninth edition of the Enterprise Integration, Interoperability and Networking workshop (EI2N2014) has been organised as part of the On The Move Federated Conferences (OTM'2014) in Amantea, Calabria, Italy.

The workshop is co-sponsored by the IFAC Technical Committee 5.3 "Enterprise Integration and Networking" (main sponsor) and IFAC TC 3.1, 3.2, 3.3, 5.2, 5.4 and 9.5, the IFIP Work Group 8.1 "Design and Evaluation of Information Systems", the SIG INTEROP Grande-Région on "Enterprise Systems Interoperability", the French CNRS National Research Group GDR MACS and the Italian Pole INTEROP-Vlab.it.

Todays rapidly evolving global economy has reiterated the urgent industrial need to achieve dynamic, efficient and effective cooperation of partner organizations within networks of larger enterprises. Enterprises must collaborate in order to prosper in the dynamic and heterogeneous business environment meeting sustainability constraints of present times. This in turn requires a substantial improvement of existing frameworks and technologies along with the exploration of innovative theories and the development of breakthrough technologies. Such innovations will serve as the foundation for more productive and effective collaborative global partnerships, and is a driver for sustainable businesses.

Enterprise integration, interoperability and networking are major disciplines studying collaborative, communicative enterprise systems. Enterprise Modelling Techniques, Next Generation Computing Architectures and Socio-technical Platforms along with Semantic Interoperability approaches are essential pillars supporting the achievement of sustainable enterprise systems.

The international program committee has reviewed 15 papers. After a rigorous review process 6 papers have been accepted (40%). Every submitted paper was evaluated by at least three members of the program committee. It has been a great pleasure to work with these experts, who played a valuable role in providing feedback to the authors that allows the overall scientific field to evolve. We thank them for their precious voluntary contribution and continued interest.

We have divided this year's workshop in three sessions. The first two sessions consist of presentations of accepted papers, the third session is an interactive discussion called "Workshop Café. This special session is an integral part of the workshop since several years. The outcomes of these discussions will be reported during a plenary session jointly organized with the CoopIS'2014 and the OTM Industry Case Studies Program 2014, in order to share topics and issues for future research with a larger group of experts and scientists.

We would like to thank the authors, reviewers, sponsors and other colleagues who have together contributed to the continuing success of this workshop. We welcome all attendees and participants and look forward to an enthusiastic exchange of ideas and thoughts for the progress of science at the workshop.

September 2014

Alexis Aubry
Georg Weichhart
Ronald Giachetti
Michele Dassisti

Ontology of Enterprise Interoperability
Extended for Complex Adaptive Systems

Georg Weichhart[1,2] and Yannick Naudet[3]

[1] Metasonic AG, Pfaffenhofen, Germany
Georg.Weichhart@metasonic.de
[2] Dept. of Communications Engineering - Business Informatics,
Johannes Kepler University Linz, Austria
Georg.Weichhart@jku.at
[3] Centre de Recherche Public Henri Tudor, Luxembourg
yannick.naudet@tudor.lu

Abstract. Collaborating business organisations have to face the challenge of being interoperable despite the growing complexity of products and services, and despite the increasing agility requirements. Changes to products and services and to supply network configurations occur frequently and require to maintain interoperability constantly in a dynamic way. Designed to formalize and handle interoperability issues, the Ontology of Enterprise Interoperability lacks means to capture the dynamics of modern business. We propose in this paper an extension based on the Complex Adaptive Systems theory. A use-cases is discussed by applying the ontology within a knowledge life cycle framework.

Keywords: Enterprise Interoperability, Ontology of Interoperability, Complex Adaptive Systems.

1 Introduction

Research in Enterprise Interoperability has taken a systems science approach to interoperability in recent years [6]. Systems science is grounded in General Systems Theory (GST), which originates from works of *von Bertalanffy* [2]. GST is based on the observation and modeling of biological systems, and provides a general framework facilitating communication between disciplines.

Following GST a system is a distinguishable whole which is placed in an environment. "The decomposition of the system leads to the notion of 'element' a unity whose properties and functions may be determined by its place within the whole. ... The element can be appreciated as such only with respect to the system under study, representing itself either a minimal (further indivisible) component of the system or the maximal decomposition limit within the range of the objective of investigation." [3, p. 256]. Systems have (typed) connections, with typological characteristics, leading to a "systems organisation" and in case of "vertical connections" eventually to the organisational form of a "systems level hierarchy". GST assigns systems to have goals (objectives), which are inherently regulating ("controlling") the (purposive) systems behavior [3].

R. Meersman et al. (Eds.): OTM 2014 Workshops, LNCS 8842, pp. 219–228, 2014.

In this view, Supply Chains, Enterprises and Departments are represented as *Enterprise Systems*. The enterprise systems's elements are to varying degree independent, yet need to operate together in order to deliver some value to customers. This need of having both, independence and a functioning collaboration, makes interoperability in general, and Enterprise Interoperability a major concern.

Designed to model interoperability in enterprise systems, The Ontology of Enterprise Interoperability (OoEI) includes concepts from the domain of GST and highlights the systemic core of enterprise interoperability research [9,11].

Building on the GST's theoretical body, a sub-class of systems with special attention to dynamic behaviours are Complex Adaptive Systems (CAS) [13]. Research in this domain shows that Enterprise Systems exhibit behaviour so that these systems may be classified as CAS. Enterprise Systems modelled as CAS on different levels of abstraction. Typical systems levels are supply network level [4] and enterprise level [7].

In the presented theoretical work, we coalesce these two streams of research to identify missing conceptualisations, amd facilitating the semantically grounded exchange of information with respect to interoperability of systems.

The article is structured as follows. First the systemic core of the Ontology for Enterprise Interoperability is presented. It highlights important concepts and relationships, to describe enterprise interoperability. This is followed by a discussion of selected properties of complex adaptive systems. The then following part discusses the combined ontology. Its use is shown by making use of an organisational knowledge framework. Finally main insights and future research is discussed.

2   Ontology of Enterprise Interoperability

Interoperability is usually defined as the ability of systems to exchange and act together. The Ontology of Enterprise Interoperability (OoEI) is based on the notion of *interoperability problem*, stating that such issues appear when incompatible systems are put in relation.

Its purpose is to support decision-making in interoperability related problem solving. It has been applied to use-cases to demonstrate added value in supporting negotiations for establishing interoperability [9]. It includes a systemic core centred on the notion of system and its properties.

It has to be stressed that from the GST point of view, the individual systems elements of a super system are on the one hand *independent*, and allow on the other hand that the parent system *provides aggregated functionalities* emerging through the interaction of the individual systems. These are two important aspects for systems that want to sustainable and evolve over time. Neither integrated systems nor compatible systems cover these aspects. The one aspect is important since the aggregation of functionalities allows a system to provide more functionality than just the sum of its element's functions. The other aspect is important as system elements may only be exchanged during adaptation when there is some independence.

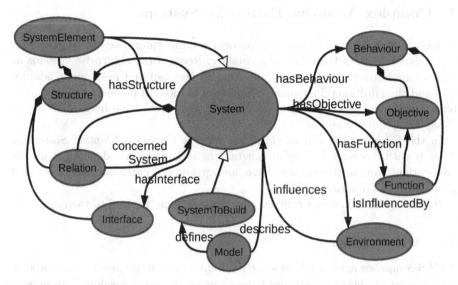

Fig. 1. Conceptual diagram of the systemic core of the OoEI [11,9]
Legend: Empty triangle ... subClass; Diamond shaped arrows ... hasPart

Integrated systems show a functional dependence where the overall system is not fully functioning when one element fails [12,5]. To the other extreme, two systems are "just" compatible if these do not interfere with each other. Compatible and not interoperable systems, show isolated functionality that can not be combined due to the missing interoperability [12,5].

Figure 1 shows the main elements of the systemic core of the OoEI as described in [11,9]. Taking the systems paradigm to the extreme, everything is modelled as a system. Most importantly the system element is a system. The OoEI models a system as a whole composed of a structure of system elements, relation between them and interfaces through which interactions occur. A system is distinguishable from its environment, where an environment is anything outside that system including other systems. Systems interact with the environment and other systems through interfaces. The environment influences the behaviour and potentially the structure of a system, which influences that environment in turn. Finally, the behaviour of a system is determined by the functions it executes in order to meet its objective.

OoEI has been implemented in OWL and allows formalizing enterprises together with interoperability problems and their solutions, and reasoning to detect those problems. However in its current state, the teleological part of systems is only represented through the concepts of behavior and function, which is not enough to represent systems' dynamic. Additionally, it was not design originally to formalize complex adaptive systems, which modern enterprises are, definitively (if not already the case before).

3   Complex Adaptive Enterprise Systems

Dynamics and changes in the environment require enterprises to continuously act in order to keep their business running. Recognising enterprise systems as "static" systems is not sufficient [4]. Due to the required permanent adaptation and the additional increasing complexity of modern business products, Enterprise Systems (e.g. Organisations, Supply networks) have been modelled as *Complex Adaptive Systems* [4,1].

In the following we aim at clarifying what a *Complex Adaptive System* is. As it is with Systems Theory in general, the definitions are dependent on the application domain. Researchers have not agreed on a particular list of selected properties that describe a CAS.

However, the following properties are commonly attributed to them.

3.1   Active Agents

A CAS comprises agents, which sense their environment, memorize observations, communicate to other agents and have a certain degree of freedom / autonomy. Depending on the Enterprise System observed, different agent types may be identified. Agents in supply networks are the enterprises taking part in these organisational networks [4]. Within organisations, the agents are the organisational units, which themselves consist of human agents [1]. Agents are sensing their environment in which they are acting. Environment here includes not only the larger system environment but also other agents. Agents are capable of establishing a (communicative) relationship with their environment.

By definition, agents have a certain degree of freedom, which allows them to consider several dimensions of the observed environment before choosing an alternative [4]. Reasoning of (intelligent) agents is supported by their capabilities to memorize observed facts. This memory may influence future behaviours, making agents non-linear inter-dependent [10].

"Very" intelligent agents may also be able to learn, adapting actively to the environment.

3.2   Non-linear Relationships and Feedback Loops

The above described active agents interact with each other and the environment forming relationships. Interactions are non-linear, because of uncertainties in the environment, and agents considering different, heterogeneous variables sensed within their vicinity. Additionally relationships may be indirect where agents leave messages in the environment that are picked up by other agents in the future.

Agents may receive feedback for their doing. Feedback-loops where agents are influenced by their environment, and in turn influencing the environment are one source of non-linearity. In particular feedback may amplify or dampen a certain behaviour which in the former case may lead to unexpected results and to some sort of path-dependence. As the relationships bear non-linearities, the behaviour of the overall system is not predictable from the individual agent's behaviour, but emerges over time

3.3   Dynamism in the Environment, Co-Evolution, and Emergence

In addition to the dynamics "created" by active agents and feedback-loops, the environment itself is dynamic. Non-linearities and many agents evolving over time in parallel lead to co-evolution. The evolution is dependent on the paths take by the agents over time. Agents are actively evolving together with the dynamic environment. For example the inability of natural agents to react to a changed environment may lead to their death. On the other hand, this adaptation might include potentially of the generation of new agents. Hence the number of agents in a system is also changing dynamically.

As agents are active, a group of agents might be actively organising their relationships within the larger environment. This activity is called self-organisation, as it is not possible to control this from the outside due to the freedom granted to agents. One mechanism to influence agents, is to make use of attractors. Attractors do not control agents but influence their behaviour. Agents close to attractors may stay close, where agents far away from attractors may not feel any influence at all.

Finally, in a CAS it is neither possible to predict a single agent's behaviour, nor the collaborative behaviour of multiple agents. The system's structure evolves over time and its behaviour emerges out of the agents individual behaviour in an manner that can not be predicted from its elements. However, while its not predictable how a CAS evolves, it does not have a random future.

A CAS can be defined as a set of agents, A, system elements other than agents, SE, and relationships between all those elements, R: $CAS = \{A, SE, R\}$. At time t, the behaviour of the CAS is a function of its past behaviours that are mainly a consequence of its agents' behaviour, of its previous structure, and of the environment (at $t-1$ since the behaviour is also a reaction to the environment influence):

$$Behaviour_{CAS}(t) = f_t(Behaviour_A(t-1, ..., t-n),$$
$$Structure_{CAS}(t-1), Environment_{CAS}(t-1)).$$

This function f_t changes over time, to account for the unpredictability of the CAS behaviour. A CAS structure is like for any other system, the set of its subsystems, relations and interfaces, except that subsystems comprise agents and potentially attractors: $Structure_{CAS} = \{A, SE, R, I\}$, where the set of attractors AT can comprise elements from A or SE: $\forall at \in AT, at \in A \cup SE$. Then the agents are in turned influenced by attractors in the system, so that we have:

$$Behaviour_A(t) = g_t(Behaviour_A(t-1),$$
$$Structure_A(t-1), Behaviour_{AT}(t-1)).$$

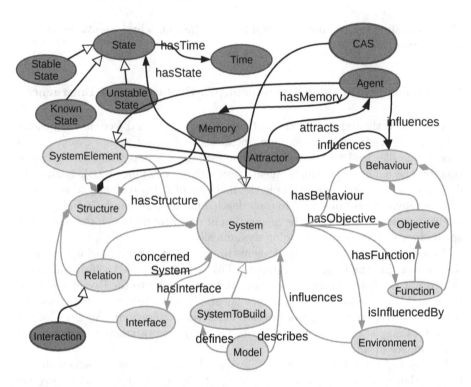

Fig. 2. Elements of the Ontology of Enterprise Interoperability, extended with CAS related concepts. (notation follows fig.1)

4   Extending OoEI with CAS

The preceding section shows that adapting OoEI to CAS implies introducing new elements, in particular to represent the system' dynamics. The proposed extensions are illustrated in fig.2.

We first add the notion of system's *State*, linked to a temporal element (*Time*). It represents not only the values of a system properties at a time t but also all facts about it at this moment. In particular, it should record the system's structure (*i.e.* the number and kind of existing relations / interactions and system elements) and behaviour. Assuming a system evolves from a given state to another one in the course of time, this is enough to account for the adaptive feature of CAS and globally for the dynamics of any system.

It is important to distinguish between a *Stable State* and an *Unstable State*: In the latter case, agents need to adapt to bring the system to a stable state again. In decision making, unstable states are identified as problems. Formalising these allows better detection, and supports ensuring that interoperability solutions do not introduce instability. A list of acceptable or known states should be formalised, which requires the concept of *Known State*.

Then the concept of *Agent* must be introduced, as a subclass of *System Element*. It is obviously itself a system and possesses its properties, like in particular a specific structure and a specific behaviour with its own objective. According to the meaning given in the CAS context, an agent is a specific kind of system that exhibits a list of specific properties that distinguish it from other system elements in a system.

First an agent is autonomous, meaning even as a part of a system, it keeps some freedom of behaviour. In an enterprise system in particular (see e.g. [9]), this means that the decisional system keeps only a partial control on agents. With this freedom to act, agents are capable of self-organisation through their interactions, they can have unpredictable behaviour and can generate unpredictable behaviour of the system they are part of.

It is then important to formalise the *Interaction* concept as a specific kind of *Relation*, because interactions are at the heart of CAS.

Last, agents can self-adapt and transform, meaning in particular that their structure, function, objective and behaviour can change over time. Structurally, they can have a *Memory* helping them learning and adapting accordingly. This feature is particular to agents and is part of their *Structure*. As part of a system, agents are part of its structure. As autonomous entities they have an influence not only on this structure (e.g. self-organisation, changing number of agents...) but most importantly on the system's behaviour (formalised by a *influences* link). More than other subsystems, agents are responsible of emerging behaviour in a system. A last important element is the concept of *Attractor*, which is a special kind of subsystem that the system uses to influence the agents' behaviour. When such attractors are instantiated, new relations appear in the system between attracted agents and attractors.

Finally, the concept of CAS itself can be formalised as a subclass of *System*. What distinguishes it from another system is that some of its elements are agents. A true CAS behaviour is expected from a system when it contains enough agents to actually "produce" some emerging behaviour (usually a big number, but there is no minimum threshold...). Although this is not shown in fig.2, this kind of property can be formalized as a dedicated rule in the ontology.

5   Enterprise Interoperability Applied in the Knowledge Life Cycle

Knowledge management and organisational learning are key issues for today's organisations, providing means for organisational agility and resilience within changing business environments.

In the following we use the *Knowledge Life-Cycle* (KLC) approach [8] to show how the CAS Extended OoEI may be used for collaborative decision making to overcome an organisational interoperability barrier concerning the process level (fig.3). The KLC divides learning and the management of knowledge in two parts: *single loop learning* and *double loop learning*.

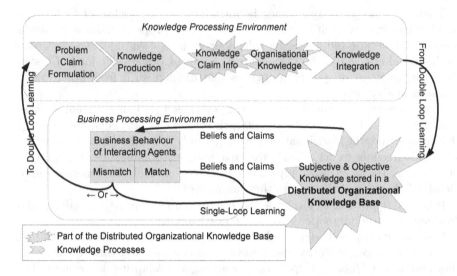

Fig. 3. Simplified representation of the knowledge life cycle [8]

Human Agents are independently processing their business processes, based on organisation wide beliefs and claims. Information is stored in the *distributed organisational knowledge-base*. In KLC this knowledge-base is a "general" concept that includes technical means ranging from private cloud storage systems to the memory of human agents.

Individual agents work within their local *business processing environment*. During the execution of tasks, agents run into situations conflicting with their beliefs. Sometimes small, situation specific, changes to the tasks and processes are sufficient for fixing problems. Small adaptations by individual agents are termed *single loop learning*.

In fig.3 single loop learning is shown at the bottom. Observed situations are compared with the information in the knowledge-base to detect exceptions.

The CAS extended Ontology supports single loop learning, by providing means to articulate problems in a semantically unambiguous manner. Such descriptions support information retrieval (from the knowledge-base) and knowledge exchange. Informally (using concepts from the CAS extended OoEI) an agent compares an observed system with the model stored in the knowledge base. Identifying an unstable state, the agent adapts her/his behaviour to transfer the system back to a stable state. In simple cases no interaction with other agents on the organisational level is needed and the behavioural change does not impact the organisational system's stability.

More dramatic situations exist where claims or beliefs, being fundamental to the organisational system, appear to be wrong. Intervention is needed at the organisational system level. The overall enterprise enters an unstable state, and multiple agents are needed to find a solution. This is done in the *knowledge processing environment* depicted on top of fig.3. A *double loop learning* process is started in order to update/change claims and beliefs in the distributed organisational knowledge base.

In the knowledge processing environment, and therefore on organisational level, a problem-claim is formulated. The CAS extended Ontology facilitates formulation of unstable states of systems, unfulfilled functions of systems, unexpected behaviours of systems, etc.

Problems that trigger double loop learning may be formulated as conceptual, technological or organisational *interoperability barriers* using concepts from the original OoEI. Within the knowledge processing environment it is important to have a vocabulary that allows all agents to communicate using a common semantics.

Problem claims formulated by one or more agent need to be analysed and clarified, having multiple agents contribute from multiple perspectives. Semantic unambiguity of information makes double loop learning more efficient and effective. At this stage the process might be stopped when the claim is not understood as a problem any more. Or, in order to overcome the, now accepted, problem, new knowledge is produced. Information about problem and solution has to be *integrated* back into the business processing environment to be available to other agents. Using the CAS extended Ontology descriptions of changed behaviours, modified interfaces, new attractors, etc. is stored in the *distributed organisational knowledge base*. Methods of transfer include teaching, sharing, broadcasting.

When transferring solutions from the knowledge-processing environment to the business processing environment, the Ontology allows to model learning material as attractors influencing learning and business processing behaviours of agents [14].

6 Conclusions

Today's business environment requires agile and collaborative organisations. The existing Ontology of Enterprise Interoperability facilitated the negotiation about interoperability problems in order to support collaborations to overcome interoperability barriers. However, we found the need to extend the ontology to allow the modelling of dynamic aspects and active agents that are placed in a complex adaptive business ecosystem.

We described the application of the Complex Adaptive Systems extended Ontology of Enterprise Interoperability in the Knowledge Life Cycle framework. It enables agents in a dynamic systems to communicate semantically unambiguously to solve interoperability related problems.

In a first step a Multi Agent System (MAS) based decision support system might use the ontology to support human decision makers, by retrieving existing documents referenced using concepts of the ontology. More research is needed to implement the CAS extended OoEI in a Multi Agent System to negotiate in order to bridge interoperability barriers.

Acknowledgement: The research leading to these results has received funding from the European Commission within the IAPP programme under grant agreement n° 286083. See http://www.ianes.eu.

References

1. Anderson, P.: Complexity theory and organization science. Organization Science 10(3), 216–232 (1999)
2. von Bertalanffy, L.: General System Theory - Foundations, Development, Applications, 17th edn. George Braziller, New York (1969)
3. Blauberg, I., Sadovsky, V., Yudin, E.: Some problems of general systems development. In: Gray, W., Rizzo, N.D. (eds.) Unity Through Diversity. Current Topics of Contemporary Thought, vol. 9, Gordon and Breach (1973)
4. Choi, T.Y., Dooley, K.J., Rungtusanatham, M.: Supply networks and complex adaptive systems: control versus emergence. Journal of Operations Management 19(3), 351–366 (2001)
5. Dassisti, M., Jardim-Goncalves, R., Molina, A., Noran, O., Panetto, H., Zdravković, M.M.: Sustainability and interoperability: Two facets of the same *gold medal*. In: Demey, Y.T., Panetto, H. (eds.) OTM 2013 Workshops 2013. LNCS, vol. 8186, pp. 250–261. Springer, Heidelberg (2013)
6. Ducq, Y., Chen, D., Doumeingts, G.: A contribution of system theory to sustainable enterprise interoperability science base. Computers in Industry 63(8), 844–857 (2012), special Issue on Sustainable Interoperability: The Future of Internet Based Industrial Enterprises
7. van Eijnatten, F.M., Putnik, G.D.: Chaos, complexity, learning, and the learning organization: Towards a chaordic enterprise. The Learning Organization 11(6), 418–429 (2004)
8. Firestone, J.M., McElroy, M.W.: Doing knowledge management. The Learning Organization 12(2), 189–212 (2005)
9. Guédria, W., Naudet, Y.: Extending the ontology of enterprise interoperability (ooei) using enterprise-as-system concepts. In: Mertins, K., Bénaben, F., Poler, R., Bourrières, J. (eds.) Enterprise Interoperability VI. Proceedings of the I-ESA Conferences, 7th edn., pp. 393–403. Springer International Publishing Switzerland (2014), http://dx.doi.org/10.1007/978-3-319-04948-9_40
10. Holland, J.H.: Hidden Order: How Adaptation Builds Complexity. Basic Books, New York (1996)
11. Naudet, Y., Latour, T., Guedria, W., Chen, D.: Towards a systemic formalisation of interoperability. Computers in Industry 61, 176–185 (2010)
12. Panetto, H.: Towards a classification framework for interoperability of enterprise applications. International Journal of Computer Integrated Manufacturing 20(8), 727–740 (2007)
13. Warren, K., Franklin, C., Streeter, C.L.: New directions in systems theory: Chaos and complexity. Social Work 43(4), 357–372 (1998)
14. Weichhart, G.: The learning environment as a chaotic and complex adaptive system. Systems. Connecting Matter, Life, Culture and Technology 1(1), 36–53 (2013), http://www.systems-journal.eu/article/view/130/138

Towards a Conceptual Framework for Requirements Interoperability in Complex Systems Engineering

Anderson Luis Szejka[1,2,3], Alexis Aubry[1,2], Hervé Panetto[1,2],
Osiris Canciglieri Júnior[3], and Eduardo Rocha Loures[3]

[1] Centre de Recherche en Automatique de Nancy (CRAN),
University of Lorraine, Vandoeuvre-lès-Nancy Cedex, France
[2] CRAN UMR 7039, CNRS, France
{anderson-luis.szejka,alexis.aubry,
herve.panetto}@univ-lorraine.fr
[3] Graduate Program in Production Engineering and Systems,
Pontifical Catholic University of Parana, Curitiba, Brazil
{osiris.canciglieri,eduardo.loures}@pucpr.br

Abstract. Requirements Engineering (RE) is an important activity in system engineering and produces, from the users' needs, specifications related to what the final system must be. This process in complex systems engineering is extremely intense, because there is a large number of stakeholders involved, with expertise deriving from heterogeneous domains. Moreover, requirements' improvements and variations are common during system life cycle phases. Thus, there is a risk of inconsistency of requirements during the engineering of a system. This paper provides a contribution in requirements engineering as it explores requirements interoperability in complex systems when multiples dimensions are involved. It discusses requirement management according to the cross-domains dimension, the cross-systems life cycle dimension, the cross-requirements dimension and the risk of inconsistency when three dimensions are involved simultaneously during the life cycle phases. The main result is an overview of the existing gaps in one and/or more dimensions allowing a discussion on the possibilities to cope with the problem of requirements inconsistency in multiples dimensions.

Keywords: Requirements Engineering, Requirements Interoperability, Complex Systems Engineering, Requirements Consistency.

1 Introduction

Enterprises have been specializing in specific domains and establishing partnerships with other companies to complement their initial skills to face globalization and consequently its intensified competition. This approach resulted in the so-called collaborative network that allows the development of complex systems and collaborative activities in many industrial domains like aeronautics, nanotechnology, aerospace, bioengineering, etc. According to [1], for succeeding in these collaborative engineering processes, it is important to formalize how different partners can work

R. Meersman et al. (Eds.): OTM 2014 Workshops, LNCS 8842, pp. 229–240, 2014.
© Springer-Verlag Berlin Heidelberg 2014

together and, through their interactions, how a common objective can be achieved within different perspectives. These engineering processes follow best practices generally defined in the so-called systems engineering domain.

System Engineering (SE) is "an interdisciplinary approach and means to enable the realization of successful systems" [2]. It focuses on holistically and concurrently understanding stakeholder needs; exploring opportunities; documenting requirements; and, synthesizing, verifying, validating and evolving solutions while considering the complete problem, from system concept exploration throughout all phases until system disposal. One of the SE processes is dedicated to analysing users and systems requirements, denominated Requirement Engineering (RE). RE refers to activities of formulating, documenting and maintaining systems requirements [3] to produce, from the users' needs, a set of specification related to what the final system must be.

Requirements provide the basis for all phases of the system development and must be controlled inside all these phases and domains to avoid misinterpretation and mistakes that would compromise the final results [2,4,5]. While approaches such as model-based systems engineering (MBSE) have been studied in [6,7,8], for improving the definition of requirements based on models, there is still a semantic gap between all requirements definitions when they are defined in different domains for the same engineering project and requirement consistency management in different systems life cycle phases. In order to cope with this challenge, we are working to define a conceptual framework that aims to formally model requirements interoperation in term of impact and semantic equivalence or subsumption. This formal definition will facilitate the verification of the system requirements coherence taking into account the technical constraints defined by appropriate experts along the systems life cycle phases.

The paper is structured as follow: Section 2 addresses the problem statement regarding to the management of requirements when multiple information come from multiple stakeholders' needs during the system life cycle phases. Section 3 presents a literature review concerning the main issues on system requirements considering the cross-domains dimension, the cross-systems life cycle dimension and the cross-requirements dimension. Section 4 is devoted to discuss the main drawbacks and existing gaps in related works. Finally, section 5 concludes and presents perspectives for the research continuation.

2   Problem Statement

RE is a key activity in the process of engineering a system. Indeed, complex systems with multidisciplinary perspectives require special attention to ensure that all requirements are fulfilled and misinterpretation and mistakes do not occur during phase's evolution of the system life cycle [9]. In fact, the misinterpretation and mistakes may cause significant *a posteriori* system refactoring, which result in scheduling overruns and increasing the projects costs [10].

The traditional system requirement approach does not support [11,12,13]:

- the cascading impacts of frequent changes or updates of requirements;
- the dispersion of responsibility and the risk of non-consistency of requirements due to the number of stakeholders involved in the development process.

Specialists normally define each requirement using different expertise from heterogeneous domains focused on a single domain and a single life cycle phase. This fact leads to risk of misunderstanding among specialists due to semantic gaps. However, it is important to enhance the system requirements engineering activity that identifies the potential risk for the system-of-interest if one requirement is not satisfied. RE standards, approaches and tools are not able to deal with the risk if the non-satisfied requirement affects other life cycle phases and/or others domains.

For analysing these issues, the authors intend to consider three dimensions of the requirements analysis process as illustrated in Figure 1: (i) the domains dimension; (ii) the system lifecycle phase's dimension; and (iii) the requirements dimension. The first dimension concerns the set of domains involved in system engineering process, for instance mechanical domain, electrical domain, computer science domain. For this particular case, each expert in these domains must define specific requirements based on their particular skills. The second dimension is related to different phases of the systems life cycle, where each phase has its proper constraints represented by specific requirements. The last dimension represents different requirements as basic elements defined by the requirements analysis process, which this requirement will represent accurately the stakeholder's needs. Each one of these requirements is associated to a single domain and a single life cycle phase.

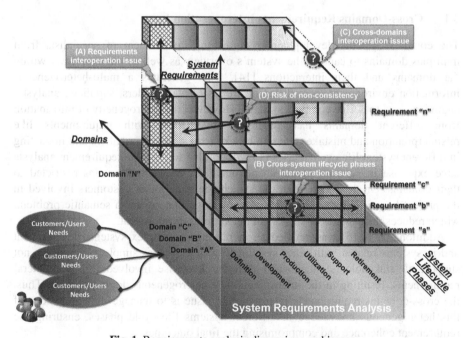

Fig. 1. Requirements analysis dimensions and issues

For each dimension, an interoperation issue can be identified. Within the requirements dimension there are problems of completeness, coherency, uniqueness, univocity, feasibility, traceability and verifiability (Detail A – Figure 1). The dimension related to the systems life cycle phases may have some issues concerning the impact analysis between all phases (Detail B – Figure 1). Finally, the main scientific issue comes from the heterogeneity of the domains, which imposes some knowledge representation and analysis for managing requirements and their semantic relationships (Detail C – Figure 1).

The authors also identified a fourth issue that illustrates the interrelationships among the three dimensions presented (Detail D – Figure 1). This last issue, which takes also into account dynamical, interactive and recursive properties of the requirement analysis process, is the most critical one. For example, if a specific requirement in one particular domain for a single phase is added or updated, it may impact other requirements already defined in other domains and/or other phases.

3   Related Works

The related works were structured according to the three issues of this research: (i) cross-domains requirement interoperation, (ii) cross-systems life cycle requirement interoperation and (iii) cross-requirement interoperation in a single domain/systems life cycle phases.

3.1   Cross-Domains Requirements Interoperation Issue

The complex systems development requires the involvement of specialists from multiples domains to capture the system's overview as well as the overviews within the domains and their interactions [14]. This generates a multi-heterogeneous information environment from different groups of stakeholders, suppliers, analysts' engineers, etc., to define complex systems. However, the heterogeneity of information from different domains has generated divergences with requirements like misinterpretation and mistakes due to a lack of requirements formalism and impacting in different system life cycle phases [15]. According to [16], the requirement analysts have expertise in systems development, but their knowledge remains restricted to their domains. On the other hand, the stakeholders and other customers involved in the project have different expertise and knowledge that creates a semantic problem, which reduces the chances of success of the systems development.

Additionally, in [6] was verified an increasing in complex systems development and in systems related with other system. It occurs because simple system does not support all stakeholders' needs and different expertise involved in stakeholders' requirements, resulting in the intensification of heterogeneous domains issues. Thus, the cross-domains requirements interoperation issue is to manage the complexity of this heterogeneous knowledge in different systems life cycle phases, ensuring the requirement coherence and compromising the final outcomes.

Thereby, in [17], the authors designed a conceptual multiple view approach model using object oriented model and UML (Unified Modelling Language) to structure information relationships between mechanical and manufacturing domain. Translating mechanisms propitiated the relationship between different domains. Each mechanism dealt with a specific knowledge, which is responsible for translating the information from product view to manufacturing view. Despite the cross-domain approach/solution presented in this research, the mechanisms were restricted to specific domains. In [18], it was proposed the integration between Model-Driven Engineering (MDE) and Domain Specific Language (DSL), creating a common language and a reasoner to analyse information in multiple domains. DSL formalizes the application structure, behaviour and requirements in a single domain and MDE structures the link between information through reasoning mechanisms in multiples domains. This allowed the exchanging information between heterogeneous domains. However, this approach did not present how to model the domains knowledge in different phases of the system life cycle and the impact of environment changes, which the domain is associated.

In [19], a model-driven domain was proposed and described as part of ontology without axioms and rules. This model provides a common reference point and is used to manage objects development of the system and automatically supports the discovery dependency link. It was limited to early system development life cycle phases (definition and concept) and did not have a mechanism to ensure the consistency of the requirements after the automatic discovery of dependency links. [20] employed MBSE to structure requirements from multiples domains during the system life cycle phases to ensure the requirement consistency. This approach adapted the Vee-model to specific driven to MBSE models supporting the system building. However, this approach did not address the model performance in systems that suffer from frequent requirement changes. In [21], the authors proposed a model-based design (MBD) methodology adapted from MBSE, integrated to the W model proposed by [22] to support the complex system development in multiples domains. For each domain the methodology created a model with their requirements and specific information allowing in a SysML environment the interaction between different domains. The information follows the W model that ensures the consistency of requirements, verification and validation. However, this methodology worked with early phases of the systems life cycle and did not address the requirements control and management in different phases of the systems life cycle.

3.2   Cross-Systems Life Cycle Requirements Interoperation Issue

The systems life cycle phases relate all activities of engineering of system, from definition until retirement as well as rules or verifications to confirm the system maturity [2]. According to [23], there are standards and models (ISO/IEC/IEEE 29148:2011 [24], ISO/IEC/IEEE 15288:2002 [25], etc.) that standardize each phase of systems life cycle and rules that define the evolution and verification of the system. However, for [5] a single view model of the system does not explicitly fit all situation of the system life cycle. According to [5,7,26], these models or standards can be used to determine all phases of the life cycle, but they contain particular characteristics that make them more suitable for specific phases. For instance, the waterfall is suitable for defining phases, because this model uses the feedback concept ensuring and revising the information integrity during a single phase [27]. Moreover, the traditional models ensure the information consistency in the direct flow according to representative life cycle model proposed by ISO/IEC TR 24748-1:2010 [28], i.e., if it is necessary to change some information in previous phases, these models are not able to manage the new information [29]. Nevertheless, the systems life cycle does not follow a linear progression, i.e., iteration and recursion will occur modifying the life cycle flow as illustrate in Figure 2.

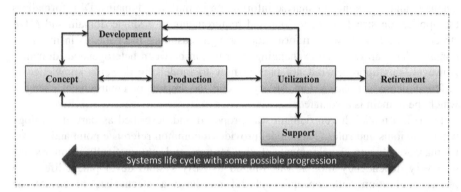

Fig. 2. Life cycle model representation adapted from ISO/IEC TR 24748-1:2010 [28]

In this context, [7] proposed a framework for a model-based requirements engineering to structure the system requirements in a SysML modelling. Moreover, they extend this approach to system life cycle, proposing solutions to integrate requirement in different phases of the system life cycle. However, this approach did not depict the evolution of the requirement in different phases and if the framework is able to analysis the change impact in different phases of the system life cycle. In [30] a methodology to verify the requirement consistency during the system life cycle phases in a dynamic manner is proposed. The methodology, named vVDR (virtual Verification of System Design against System Requirement), contributed to three main steps in the system life cycle phases: system requirement analysis, system design and system testing. Although, the methodology covered different system life cycle phases and analysed the requirements consistency, it did not report if there are consistency checking when the requirements are replaced or if there are impact analyses in different requirements occasioned by their replacement.

In [31], the authors proposed a formalization of semantic annotation for system interoperability from different domains views in a Product Life Cycle Management (PLM) environment. The formalization made explicit the tacit knowledge intrinsic in application models and act to support all activities during the product life cycle. Nevertheless, this approach did not depict the annotations in requirements that change frequently along the life cycle and how to ensure the semantic of these requirements. [32] proposed a model-driven ontology, which integrate the model-driven architecture (MDA) and an ontology, to create a manufacturing system interoperable between design domain and manufacturing domain. The solution emphasized the need of designing the knowledge in a common-logic-based ontology language to allow information exchange between domains. But this solution was limited to two heterogeneous domains and there was no evidence of possibilities to expand information exchange to multi-domains and integrate them.

3.3   Cross-Requirements Interoperation Issue in a Single Domain/System Life Cycle Phases

Requirements are necessary attribute in a system, a statement that identifies capabilities, characteristics and quality factor of a system to ensure its value and utility for a customer or a user [2,4,5]. Based on literature and standards, there are two main types of requirements: Functional Requirements and Non-Functional Requirements (Quality requirements, Constraints, etc.) [2,5,33]. It is necessary to certify that among requirements will not have problems with completeness, coherency, uniqueness and univocity, as well as the traceability between requirements.

In [12], the complexity of translating customer needs in functional or non-functional requirements is demonstrated, because the customers or stakeholders environment was associated with a different requirement environment than the requirements analyst (RA). Thus, RE emerges as a cooperative, interactive and incremental process to elicitation, negotiation and documentation of the requirements and constraints of complex systems. The RE aims to solve the requirements problem in early stages of the requirements process [3,5,34]. Within RE, beyond elicitation and negotiation, the traceability stands for a relevant problem. Requirements traceability is responsible for tracking information from stakeholder to all level of the engineering of the system as well as providing an understanding about any requirement change [5]. However, requirements traceability relations are not automatic generated and maintained [35, 44] and the identification typically occurs manually [36, 43] making traceability relations susceptible to errors, if changes occur during the engineering of the system [37].

According to [37], the lacks of automated traceability become a prominent problem in complex systems once there is a need to establish traceability between large collections of requirements and other systems documentation. To [38], changes can be required in any phases of the system life cycle (design, implementation or use). However, in Dynamic Adaptive Systems (DAS) a large numbers of requirements are faced changes of environment. Thus, the traditional traceability approach, which works with static and simple system, does not support this new system development once it is necessary to analyse simultaneously the changed requirements, identifying them and tracing the impact of the change in other requirements.

In [39], the authors advocate that if the traceability is consistently maintained it would prevent a dissemination of potential requirements inconsistencies into different system life cycle phases. Thus, according to the authors further researches are necessary to ensure the requirement traceability, making sure that the requirements information is complete, coherent, unique and univocal. According to [40], consistency of requirements can be ensured through validation and verification methods. In this context, [41] proposed an interoperation meta-model to structure the information transforming from stakeholder requirements (problem space) to specifications (solution space). This meta-model was responsible to control the exchange information in collaborative domains, ensuring their consistency and traceability during all this process. However, this meta-model was limited to early phases of the system life cycle and did not ensure the requirement exchange in different phases.

In [35], the authors presented a systematization approach to ensure the requirement consistency in different phases of system life cycle. This approach consists of some mechanisms: (i) mechanism to formalize the requirements and its features, (ii) mechanisms to consistency checking and (iii) mechanisms to correct the inconsistency problems. Moreover, the authors proposed a mechanism to manage the variability of information in different phases of the system life cycle, its consistency in all system life cycle. The authors did not depict if there are consistency impacts with requirements changing during the system life cycle and if this systematization is able to identify these impacts. In [42], the authors proposed a model to integrate the goal-oriented approach to RELAX, based on KAOS (Knowledge Acquisition in automated specification) and DSL (Domain Specific Language). This model supports the constant requirements changing, but it does not support the requirements evolution during different life cycle phases.

4   Discussion

This research is working to evidence the relevant issues to the requirements engineering in order to ensure all requirements coherency and consistency in all systems life cycle phases. These issues provided support to a conceptual framework proposal that aims to formally model requirements interoperation in term of impact and semantic equivalence or subsuming. Therefore, the authors proposed three dimensions to investigate the related issues: the cross-domain, the cross-systems life cycle phases' and the cross-requirements dimensions.

Related works were found for each dimension regarding requirements engineering and particular solutions proposals. Thus, based on the related works issues/solutions, the Table 1 is proposed, which shows specific analysis by categorization, positioning each paper according to their subjects and degree of importance for the research. The adopted classification criteria were:

— (D1) *Particular cases* – Papers/articles concerning the requirements exchange limited to two specific domains;
— (D2) *Ability to be generic* – Papers/articles concerning the requirements exchange among different domains and that can be adapted to other domains;
— (D3) *Generality of the approach* – Papers/articles concerning the requirements exchange among different domains whose approaches do not need any adaptation;
— (LC4) *Yes* – For papers/articles that concerns the requirement exchange among one or more phases of the system life cycle;
— (LC5) *No* – For papers/articles that do not concern the requirement exchange among one or more phases of the system life cycle;
— (R6) *Requirements Traceability* - Papers/articles regarding the requirements traceability in one or more system life cycle phases and different domains;
— (R7) *Requirements Interoperability* – Papers/articles regarding the exchange of requirements between one or more systems lifecycle phases and different domains. This interoperability issue does not consider any requirements changes during the systems life cycle phases;
— (R8) *Requirements Impacts* - Papers/articles regarding the exchange of requirements between one or more systems lifecycle phases and different domains. This interoperability issue considers the impacts caused by any requirements changes during the systems life cycle phases.

Table 1. Related works classification according to each research issue

Authors and Publication Year	Cross-Domains issue			Cross-Systems Life Cycle issue		Cross-Requirements issue		
	(D1)	(D2)	(D3)	(LC4)	(LC5)	(R6)	(R7)	(R8)
ADELSON and SOLOWAY, 1985 [45]	✔				✔			
RAMESH and JARK, 2001 [35]					✔	✔		
EGYED and GRÜNBACHER, 2002 [44]					✔	✔		
CLELAND-HUANG et al., 2002 [36]					✔	✔		
CANCIGLIERI JR. and YOUNG, 2003 [17]	✔	✔		✔			✔	
SPANOUDAKIS et al., 2004 [37]					✔	✔		
RATCHEV, URWIN, MULLER, PAWAR and MOULEK, 2003 [12]				✔			✔	
KECECI, GARBAJOSA and BOURQUE, 2006 [43]					✔	✔	✔	
SCHMIDT, 2006 [18]	✔	✔			✔			
STECHERT and FRANKE, 2008 [46]	✔	✔			✔	✔	✔	
WELSH AND SAWYER, 2009 [38]					✔	✔		✔
HOLT and PIERRY, 2010 [7]				✔		✔		
SCHAMAI et al., 2010 [30]				✔		✔	✔	
MONEVA, HAMBERG AND PUNTER, 2011 [15]	✔	✔			✔			
AHMAD and BRUEL, 2012 [42]					✔	✔	✔	✔
BOUFFARON et al., 2012 [41]	✔			✔			✔	
CMYREV et al., 2012 [39]				✔		✔	✔	
STRASUNSKAS and HAKKARAINEN, 2012 [19]	✔	✔			✔	✔		
OERTEL and JOSKO, 2012 [40]					✔	✔	✔	
LIAO et al., 2012 [31]	✔	✔		✔				
CHANDLER and MATTHEWS, 2013 [26]	✔	✔		✔				
CHUNGOORA et al., 2013 [32]	✔	✔		✔			✔	
HAVEMAN and BONNEMA, 2013 [20]	✔	✔	✔	✔				
BARBIERI et al., 2014 [21]	✔	✔		✔				

It is observed in Table 1 that there are some poorly explored gaps: in cross-domain issue, items (D2) and (D3) and in cross-requirement issue, item (R8). In cross-domain issue, it was verified that existing approaches proposed by the literature solve specific information exchange between domains. But, when this approach is extended to multiples domains (more than three), there are strict and/or limited solutions. This issue makes evident the problem with the semantic gap in multiples domains as well as the risk of mistakes and misinterpretation. In cross-requirement issue was noticed that there are researches addressing the requirement traceability and interoperability. Nevertheless, these researches did not consider the impact, which frequents requirements improvements and variations may cause to the consistency and coherency among requirements as well as ensuring the requirement consistency during different systems life cycle phases.

These results represent a preliminary evaluation about the models, frameworks and methodologies found in the literature, concerning the three dimensions. However, it is important to consider that requirements are not static, i.e. requirements' variations, advances and improvements may occur during the system life cycle phases' evolution. Although, the three dimensions consider the inherent relationship to each of them, it is important address all three issues simultaneously. Therefore, it is necessary explore or develop methodologies to support the systems-of-system, focusing on the three dimensions concurrently. The authors consider this approach as the fourth issue in order to ensuring the system requirements consistency and coherence.

5   Conclusion

This research points towards a conceptual framework for requirements interoperability in complex system engineering in order ensure the system requirements consistency and coherence in all life cycle phases. Requirements are not static, i.e., they may suffer changes, updates or removals during the system life cycle phase's evolution. Thus, it is necessary to manage these relationships to avoid misinterpretation and mistakes with requirements.

The authors proposed four issues to be investigated. Three of them are directly generated from the different presented dimensions (cross-domain, cross-systems life cycle phases and cross-requirements). The last one is the interrelationship among these issues. From these issues, an extensive literature review has been provided and the related works has been classified in order to identify the gaps that were not explored and/or need further researches. Whilst, the literature review and its classification highlighted the gaps in the same issue and/or the relationship among them such as: the need of requirement's language formalization or standardization in order to avoid misinterpretation and mistakes in multiples domains and the impact that frequent requirement changes/updates cause in the system requirements during system life cycle.

The continuity of the research should therefore identify and determine scientific methods identification and determination that are able to conceptually represent these 3 dimensions and the dependencies existing among them. It should also explore how to cope with the impact of requirements changes can cause among requirements in multiples domains during the system life cycle phases.

References

1. Mallek, S., Daclin, N., Chapurlat, V.: The application of interoperability requirement specification and verification to collaborative process in industry. Computers in Industry 63, 643–658 (2002)
2. Haskins, C.: INCOSE, INCOSE Systems Engineering Handbook: A Guide for Life Cycle Processes and Activities. The International Council on Systems Engineering, 3rd edn (2006)
3. Young, R.R.: The Requirements Engineering Handbook, 1st edn. Artech House, Boston (2004)
4. Afis, C.: Guide Bonnes Pratiques en Ingénierie des Exigences, 1st edn. Cépadules, Paris (2012)
5. Sebok, Guide to the Systems Engineering Body of Knowledge (SEBoK), version 1.2 (2013), http://www.sebokwiki.org

6. Haskins, C.: INCOSE, INCOSE Systems Engineering Vision 2020, The International Council on Systems Engineering, 2nd edn. (2007)
7. Holt, J., Perry, S., Brownsword, M.: Model-Based Requirement Engineering, 1st edn., p. 340. The Institution of Engineering and Technology, London (2011)
8. OBJECT MANAGEMENT GROUP (OMG): MDA Guide, Version 1.0.1 (2003)
9. Colombo, P., Khendek, F., Lavazza, L.: Bridging the gap between requirements and design: An approach based on Problem Frames and SysML. Journal of Systems and Software 85(3), 717–745 (2012)
10. Flanigan, D., Brouse, P.: System of Systems Requirements Capacity Allocation. Procedia Computer Science 8, 112–117 (2012)
11. Brooks, R.T., Sage, A.P.: System of System Integration and Test. Information Knowledge and Systems Management 5, 261–280 (2006)
12. Ratchev, S., Urwin, E., Muller, D., Pawar, K.S., Moulek, L.: Knowledge based requirement engineering for one-of-a-kind complex systems. Knowledge-Based Systems 16(1), 1–5 (2003)
13. Bernard, Y.: Requirements management within a full model-based engineering approach. Systems Engineering 15, 119–139 (2012)
14. Bjørner, D.: From domain to requirements. In: Degano, P., De Nicola, R., Meseguer, J. (eds.) Montanari Festschrift. LNCS, vol. 5065, pp. 278–300. Springer, Heidelberg (2008)
15. Moneva, H., Hamberg, R., Punter, T.: A Design Framework for Model-Based Development of Complex Systems. In: 32nd IEEE Real-Time Systems Symposium and 2nd Analytical Virtual Integration of Cyber-Physical Systems Workshop, Vienna, pp. 1–8 (2011)
16. Vitharana, P., Jain, H., Zahedi, F.M.: A knowledge based component/service repository to enhance analysts' domain knowledge for requirements analysis. Information & Management 49(1), 24–35 (2012)
17. Canciglieri Jr., O., Young, R.I.M.: Information sharing in multiviewpoint injection moulding design and manufacturing. International Journal of Production Research 41(7), 1565–1586 (2003)
18. Schmidt, D.C.: Model-Driven Engineering. IEEE Computer 39(2), 25–31 (2006)
19. Strasunskas, D., Hakkarainen, S.E.: Domain model-driven software engineering: A method for discovery of dependency links. Information and Software Technology 54(11), 1239–1249 (2012)
20. Haveman, S.P., Bonnema, G.M.: Requirements for High Level Models Supporting Design Space Exploration in Model-based Systems Engineering. Procedia Computer Science 16, 293–302 (2013)
21. Barbieri, G., Fantuzzi, C., Borsari, R.: A model-based design methodology for the development of mechatronic systems. Mechatronics (in press, 2014)
22. Nattermann, R., Reiner, A.: Approach for a data-management-system and a proceeding-model for the development of adaptronic systems. In: International Mechanical Engineering Congress and Exposition (ASME), pp. 1–10 (2010)
23. Schneider, F., Berenbach, B.: A Literature Survey on International Standards for Systems Requirements Engineering. Procedia Computer Science 16, 796–805 (2013)
24. International Organization for Standardization: ISO/IEC/IEEE 29148:2008 – Systems and software engineering – Life cycle processes and Requirement Engineering (2011)
25. International Organization for Standardization: ISO/IEC/IEEE 15288:2002 – Systems and software engineering – System life cycle processes, ISO/IEC (2002)
26. Chandler, S.R., Matthews, P.C.: Through-Life Systems Engineering Design & Support with SysML. Procedia CIRP 11, 425–430 (2013)
27. Ruparelia, N.B.: Software Development Lifecycle Models. ACM SIGSOFT Software Engineering Notes 35(3), 8–13 (2010)

28. International Organization for Standardization: ISO/IEC TR 24748:2010 – Systems and software engineering – Life cycle management – Part 1: Guide for life cycle management, ISO/IEC (2011)
29. Gausemeier, J., Gaukstern, T., Tschirner, C.: System Engineering Management Based on a Discipline-Spanning System Model. Procedia Computer Science 16, 303–312 (2013)
30. Schamai, W., Helle, P., Fritzson, P., Paredis, C.J.J.: Virtual Verification of System Designs against System Requirements. In: Models 2010 ACES-MB Workshop Proceedings, vol. 1, pp. 53–67 (2010)
31. Liao, Y., Lezoche, M., Loures, E.F.R., Panetto, H., Boudjlida, N.: Formalization of Semantic Annotation for System Interoperability in a PLM environment. In: Proceeding of OTM Federated conferences and workshops and 2nd Workshop on Industrial and Business Application of Semantic Web Technologies (INBAST), Rome, vol. (1), pp. 1–7 (2002)
32. Chungoora, N., Young, R.I., Gunendran, G., Palmer, C., Usman, Z., Anjum, N.A., Cutting-Decelle, A.F., Harding, J.A., Case, K.: A model-driven ontology approach for manufacturing system interoperability and knowledge sharing. Computers in Industry 64(4), 392–401 (2013)
33. Insitute of Electrical and Electronics Engineers, IEEE Std 830-1998 - Recommended Practice for Software Requirements Specifications. IEEE Computer Society, New York (1998)
34. Pohl, K.: The three Dimensions of Requirements Engineering: A framework and its applications. Informatic Systems 19(3), 243–258 (1994)
35. Ramesh, B., Jarke, M.: Toward reference models for requirements traceability. IEEE Transactions on Software Engineering 27, 58–93 (2001)
36. Cleland-Huang, J., Chang, C.K., Sethi, G., Javvaji, K., Haijian, H., Jinchun, X.: Automating speculative queries through event-based requirements traceability. In: Proceedings of IEEE Joint International Conference on Requirements Engineering, pp. 289–296 (2002)
37. Spanoudakis, G., Zisman, A., Pérez-Miñana, E., Krause, P.: Rule-based generation of requirements traceability relations. Journal of Systems and Software 72(2), 105–127 (2004)
38. Welsh, K., Sawyer, P.: Requirements tracing to support change in dynamically adaptive systems. In: Glinz, M., Heymans, P. (eds.) REFSQ 2009 Amsterdam. LNCS, vol. 5512, pp. 59–73. Springer, Heidelberg (2009)
39. Cmyrev, A., Noerenberg, R., Hopp, D., Reissing, R.: Consistency Checking of Feature Mapping between Requirements and Test Artefacts. CESAR Project 1, 1–12 (2012)
40. Oertel, M., Josko, B.: Interoperable Requirements Engineering: Tool Independent Specification, Validation and Impact Analysis. In: Embedded World 2012 Exhibition and Conference, pp. 3–7. Nuremberg (2012)
41. Bouffaron, F., Gouyon, D., Dobre, D., Morel, G.: Revisiting the interoperation relationships between System Engineering collaborative processes. In: 14th IFAC Symposium on Information Control Problems in Manufacturing, INCOM 2012, Romania, pp. 1–6 (2012)
42. Ahmad, M., Bruel, J.M., Laleau, R., Gnaho, C.: Using RELAX, SysML and KAOS for Ambient Systems Requirements Modeling. Procedia Computer Science 10, 474–481 (2012)
43. Kececi, N., Garbajosa, J., Bourque, P.: Modelling functional requirements to support traceability analysis. In: IEEE International Symposium on Industrial Electronics, vol. 4, pp. 3305–3310 (2006)
44. Egyed, A., Grunbacher, P.: Automating requirements traceability: Beyond the record & replay paradigm. In: 17th IEEE International Conference on Automated Software Engineering, pp. 163–171. IEEE Press, New York (2002)
45. Adelson, B., Soloway, E.: The Role of Domain Expenence in Software Design. IEEE Transactions on Software Engineering 11, 1351–1360 (1985)
46. Stechert, C., Franke, H.J.: Managing requirements as the core of multi-disciplinary product development. CIRP Journal of Manufacturing Science and Technology 1(3), 153–158 (2009)

Bigraph-Ensured Interoperability
for System(-of-Systems) Emergence

Dominik Wachholder and Chris Stary

Communications Engineering, Department of Information Systems
Johannes Kepler University Linz
Altenberger Straße 69, 4040 Linz, Austria
{dominik.wachholder,christian.stary}@jku.at
http://ce.jku.at/en

Abstract. Today's complexity of distributed application systems, such as dynamic supply networks, requires a system-of-systems (SoS) perspective for effective adaptation and sustainable use. Those systems not only need to be operated as separate systems (e.g., optimizing each transport modality in supply networks), but also are required to capture complex situations as interconnected entity (e.g., adapting a transport chain involving different modalities according to weather conditions). SoS can handle such challenges through emerging behavior, while letting each of the involved systems operate separately. The latter property requires interoperability of systems that can be preserved even in dynamically changing environments applying the theory of bigraphs. Abstract relationships allow not only the representation of dynamic interaction but also the respecification of these systems through behavior adaptations. This abstraction supports cross-system decomposition as well as composition of interaction patterns for the purpose of emergent behavior. We demonstrate the potential of this approach by orchestrating two distributed and independent systems. SoS behavior orchestration enables to directly respond to changes in the application system context.

Keywords: context-sensitive interoperability, cross-system interaction, behavior orchestration, emergent behavior.

1 Introduction

Distributed application systems have become increasingly ubiquitous and are claimed to survive in highly dynamic settings serving a broad range of requirements today. In many cases, however, such systems are not compiled to an inseparable entity, but rather are composed of various operationally and managerially independent (sub-)systems that are interconnected to serve a common objective [10]. This particular class of systems is referred to as system-of-systems (SoS). Consider a supply network that integrates different transport modalities, such as air cargo, sea freight, and road freight transport. The involved systems for managing these transport modalities operate autonomously, but are interconnected to provided additional functionality. For example, the integration of air cargo

R. Meersman et al. (Eds.): OTM 2014 Workshops, LNCS 8842, pp. 241–254, 2014.

and sea freight transport might allow a decrease in transport time and costs by optimizing delivery routes.

In literature there is no consensus on a distinct definition of SoS[1]. However, it appears that the inherent characteristics of *operational independence of elements, managerial independence of elements, evolutionary development, emergent behavior*, and *geographic distribution* remain constant [16]. A more recent but similar taxonomy, proposed by [6], introduces the characteristics of autonomy, belonging, connectivity, diversity, as well as emergence. The first three characteristics are considered as core properties and therefore fundamental to SoS [3]. Accordingly, systems are described and represented as being autonomous in terms of functionality and operation, while being interconnected with each other in order to contribute to the goal of a system at a higher level (cf. Fig. 1).

Interoperability as an inherent part of system connectivity is crucial when it comes to system interaction and collaboration [5]. This is especially true when taking into account the autonomous nature of systems. In the case of systems not being interoperable, neither connectivity nor diversity or emergence is enabled. In other words, interoperability is essential to not only overcome system autonomy, but also to enable systems to be diverse and emergent in behavior. As a consequence, both the static representation of interaction patterns as well as the representation of behavior in terms of structural changes is necessary (cf. Fig. 1). Changes that are related to the overall system behavior might become visible on this basis ($B_1 = \{b_1, b_2, b_3\}$ vs. $B_2 = \{b_1, b_3, b_4\}$).

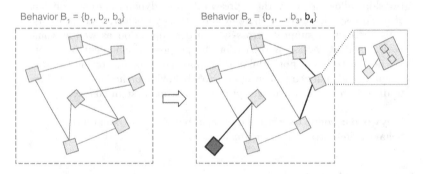

Fig. 1. Evolving Interaction Pattern

System interoperability is required for SoS behavior to be emergent (cf. [3] and [6]). Bigraphs, in that context, allow preserving interoperability among systems, both from a structural and behavior perspective (cf. [8] and [11]). Hence, SoS behavior can emerge in a concerted way. We explore this bigraph capacity in the following. Section 2 outlines the idea of bigraphs after briefly reviewing shortcomings of existing approaches to modeling distributed application systems in highly dynamic environments. Bigraph-based interoperability is then introduced

---

[1] A more detailed discourse on the definition of SoS is given in [10] and [24].

as representation approach (cf. Section 3) enabling concerted emergence of SoS based on modeling the structure and behavior of cross-system interaction (cf. Section 4). The paper concludes with a final discussion on the potential of this approach and further research directions.

2   Bigraphs in the Context of Emergent SoS Behavior

Emergent behavior not only requires distributed application systems to be interoperable and flexible in terms of interaction, but also expects these systems to adapt to changing circumstances, such as contextual conditions. Extensive research has been done already addressing interoperability in the context of system collaboration.

Traditional approaches require a common communication standard (e.g., protocol) in order to achieve interoperability among heterogeneous systems (cf. RPC [17], CORBA [21], DCOM [12], WSDL [25], etc.). Interoperability, however, is given only when systems can agree on a standard prior to their implementation. In dynamic environments where no common standard is defined, interoperability cannot be guaranteed (cf. [18]). Similar limitations exist for software bridges (cf. [9,15]), due to predefined sets of rules allowing the translation of requests from one standard to another (cf. [20] and [19]). The CORBA to WSDL/SOAP interworking standard [20], for instance, defines how CORBA constructs need to be mapped to XML-based structures in order to conform the WSDL/SOAP specification. Research within the scope of service identification and orchestration (cf. [14]) brings in the notion of system dynamics, but lacks in supporting emergence in system behavior.

Architecture description languages (ADLs), such as ACME [7] or AADL [1], allow the formal representation of system components and connectors. Such languages promote interoperability by means of well-defined representation formats, but are rather limited when it comes to system dynamics. Similar to the approaches mentioned above, interoperability cannot be guaranteed once multiple architecture description languages are used. [4] has addressed this limitation, saying that ADLs need to allow the dynamic insertion and removal of elements in order to support emergence in system behavior. However, no specific extension to ADLs is provided.

In order to overcome these limitations, formal approaches, such as process calculi for concurrent systems based on independent systems (agents) (cf. [2]), progressed towards representing systems including location awareness. Bigraphs [13] model systems by means of these properties, representing an agent's structure, behavior, and its environment. Intended to model ubiquitous systems, the theory captures the respective concepts of *agent*, *locality*, *connectivity*, *motion*, and *interaction*. The selection is attributed to the development rationale not only to implement computing tasks but also to reflect informing activities, interaction, and communication. Grouping these concepts, the theory introduces two domains – *space* and *motion* – with respect to the structure and dynamics of systems. The concepts of linking (connectivity) and placing (locality) of agents are central in terms of space, where agents represent independent components of systems. Motion and interaction are considered explicitly in the context of dynamics allowing bigraphs reconfiguring and adapting themselves by means of bigraphical reactive systems.

2.1   The Notion of Space

The theory of bigraphs represents the constituents of a physical space by means of agents. The nesting of agents describes their locality while edges represent the interlinking between those agents (cf. Fig. 2). In order to be able to integrate information on both the agents' placing as well as linking, bigraphs are composed of two independent graph structures on the same set of nodes (e.g., $N = \{n_0, n_1, n_2, n_3\}$). On the one hand, a forest (set of rooted trees[2]) describes the agents' placing by depicting their hierarchy. A hypergraph on the other hand describes their network of relationships. These structures are termed *place graph* (G^P) and *link graph* (G^L), forming together a bigraph G, so that $G = \langle G^P, G^L \rangle$.

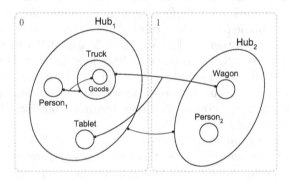

Fig. 2. Concrete Bigraph $\breve{G}$

A place-graph is a collection of rooted trees consolidated to a forest. Each tree depicts a region in the bigraph indicating an independent sub-structure of agents that are not part of others. The place graph $\breve{G}^P$ derived from the bigraph $\breve{G}$ is characterized by two rooted trees based on the regions $\{1, 2\}$ serving as roots (cf. Fig. 3a). All agents are subordinated to these roots describing their hierarchical structure as it is determined by their placing (nesting). The tablet, for instance, is subordinated to the hub which is placed in region 0. For the place graph $\breve{G}^P$, an outer face $2 = \{0, 1\}$ and, as there are no sites, an empty inner face $0 = \{\}$ is defined, resulting in $\breve{G}^P : 0 \rightarrow 2$.

A link-graph exhibits the same characteristics as an ordinary graph having nodes that are linked by edges. In contrast to an ordinary graph, however, a

---

[2] A rooted or oriented tree is a tree that has a designated root. Every node except the root has a unique parent.

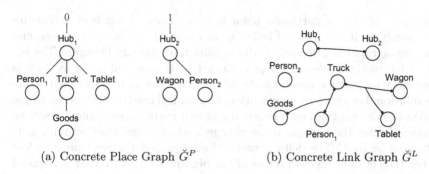

(a) Concrete Place Graph $\check{G}^P$ (b) Concrete Link Graph $\check{G}^L$

Fig. 3. Bigraphical Structures

link graph allows edges to connect any number of nodes[3]. In other words, a single edge e_0 might not only connect two (e.g., $N = \{n_0, n_1\}$), but a set of nodes (e.g., $N = \{n_0, n_1, n_2\}$). The link graph $\check{G}^L$ derived from the bigraph $\check{G}$ describes the network of relationships existent between agents (cf. Fig. 3b). A hyperedge connecting multiple nodes, for instance, is shown among the agents representing the truck, the wagon, and the tablet. For the link graph $\check{G}^L$, the outer as well as inner face is defined as empty set $\emptyset$, resulting in $\check{G}^L : \emptyset \to \emptyset$.

2.2   Dynamics of Bigraphs

Concrete bigraphs allow representing static structures of physical spaces based on the concepts of agent, placing, and linking (cf. Fig. 2). In order to allow these structures to evolve, distinct roles have to be assigned to edges connecting agents. In this manner, agents are equipped with so called *ports* defining the roles of edges. Fig. 4 gives a detailed view on the bigraph $\check{G}$ showing an agent representing a truck. The black blobs where the edges impinge on the agent are ports and define the roles as of type *Ethernet* or *person*.

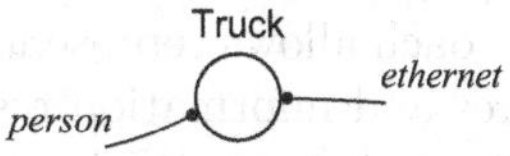

Truck

person   *ethernet*

Fig. 4. Ports

The concept of ports allows the definition of abstract bigraphs and, therefore, their composition. Areas where other bigraphs are allowed to be inserted are defined by sites. Edges crossing these sites indicate the bigraph's *inner face*. An abstract bigraph H (cf. Fig. 5) provides flexibility in terms of concrete agents

---

[3] Graphs that allow edges (hyperedges) to connect any number of nodes are referred to as hypergraphs.

that are part of H at a particular point in time. Thus, H can host various bigraphs satisfying its interface. Flexibility in order to be able to compose and decompose bigraphs is provided by the definition of abstract bigraphs. The behavior of interactive systems, however, cannot be represented so far as there is no possibility to describe the dynamics of these systems in terms of their structural evolution. For behavior specification, bigraphical reactive systems allow the definition of reaction rules each consisting of two parts, a *redex* and a *reactum*. The redex defines the bigraph to be changed, whereas the reactum represents the changed bigraph. The delta between the redex and the reactum therefore describes the set of changes in terms of the bigraph's structure that is required to be performed upon the system. A reaction rule can be performed whenever the system's bigraphical structure conforms the structure of the rule's redex. Upon execution, the system is transferred into the bigraphical state described by the corresponding rule's reactum.

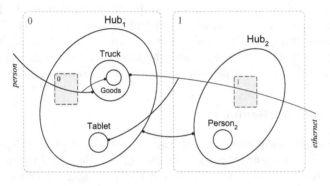

Fig. 5. Abstract Bigraph H

3   Bigraph-Ensured Interoperability

In the previous section, bigraphs have been introduced based on the concepts of space and motion. This approach allows representing application systems and their constituents (e.g., features and information resources) by means of agents having a certain structure and behavior. With respect to the structure, the representational characteristics of bigraphs are twofold. First, the structure of interaction is reflected by the concept of linking. Consider a system for optimizing transport chains that retrieves local weather conditions from external service providers. Secondly, the concept of locality allows describing the contextual conditions in which these systems operate. The same transport chain system, for instance, might optimize routes differently when snow-covered roads are being reported.

The behavior and therefore structural changes in system interaction is reflected by the bigraphical reactive system. Using the same concepts as for representing interaction, reaction rules allow describing changes in interaction by means of adaptations in the structural interaction pattern. Each transition is encapsulated in a reaction rule that, when applied on the bigraph, transforms it to a defined end state.

3.1 Representing Structure

Let us take as an example the case of an air cargo information system (IS) that is planing and managing the routes of cargo aircrafts considering surrounding weather conditions. The information system itself is represented as agent having ports that describe its interfaces allowing links to available routes, users, and weather alerts. Accordingly, not only the IS but all other (sub-)systems can be represented by means of bigraphical structures as well. In the example, two routes ($Route_1$ and $Route_2$), an external weather alert system ($Weather\ Alert\ System$), a specific weather alert ($Weather\ Alert$), and the system administrator ($Admin$) is represented. In terms of linking (cf. Fig. 6a), the information system is directly connected to the first route, the weather alert, as well as the system administrator. The weather alert exhibits links to the weather alert systems and the second route. Consequently, the air cargo information system's link graph is formally described as $\breve{F}^L : \emptyset \to \emptyset$.

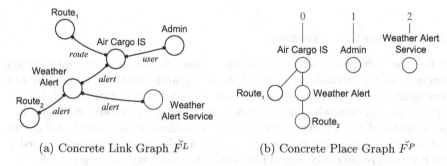

(a) Concrete Link Graph $\breve{F}^L$ (b) Concrete Place Graph $\breve{F}^P$

Fig. 6. Bigraphical Structures of an Air Cargo Information System

In addition to the mapping of agents and their correlations in the link graph (cf. Fig. 6a), the place graph $\breve{F}^P$ depicts the placing of agents that are involved in the air cargo information system (cf. Fig 6b). In contrast to the original idea, the placing does not describe an agent's situation in terms of its physical location but rather defines the environment in the sense of its contextual surrounding. For instance, the second route itself represents the originally planned route. Considered from the viewpoint of its surrounding environment, however, it adapts its behavior. In other words, the weather alert influences the way how the route is finally carried out and might cause the cargo aircraft to take a detour in order to avoid thunder clouds. Fig. 6b illustrates the example's place graph $\breve{F}^P : 0 \to 3$ and shows the second route that is subordinated to the weather alert and, in combination with the first route, part of the air cargo information system. Both, the system administrator as well as the weather alert system are depicted separately, meaning there is no contextual surrounding defined.

Based on the place graph $\check{F}^P$ and link graph $\check{F}^L$ (cf. Fig. 6a and 6b), a bigraph $\check{F}$ (cf. Fig. 7) can be constructed incorporating both structures. The bigraph $\check{F}$, therefore, has three regions $\{0, 1, 2\}$ including the IS as well as the system administrator and the weather alert system. The bigraph does neither exhibit any sites nor an inner or outer face as it is the representation of the concrete IS. On this basis, the bigraph $\check{F}$ is represented as $\check{F} : \langle \check{F}^P, \check{F}^L \rangle \Rightarrow \check{F} : \langle 0, \emptyset \rangle \rightarrow \langle 3, \emptyset \rangle \Rightarrow \check{F} : \epsilon \rightarrow \langle 3, \emptyset \rangle$.

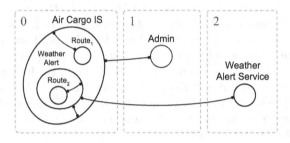

Fig. 7. Concrete Bigraph $\check{F}$

3.2   Representing Dynamics

So far, the bigraphical structure merely represents the air cargo information system from the example as it is. Abstract bigraphs might be derived to add more flexibility in terms of composition, however, do not make structural changes explicit, for instance, when new routes or weather alerts become available. The specification of a bigraphical reactive system addresses this aspect and allows encoding IS functionality by means of reaction rules, each composed of a redex and reactum, respectively. Fig. 8 illustrates an exemplary reaction rule showing the bigraph's structural modification involved when a new route which is put into the context of a specific weather alert becomes available. In order to apply this rule, a bigraph containing a specific weather alert as well as a route, each located in a separate region, is required. Both of the nodes are expected to offer broken links as of type *route* so that the nodes can be interlinked with each other in a later step. The site that is assigned to the weather alert indicates that other bigraphs satisfying the required interface can be inserted. Once a bigraph or a part of a bigraph matches this pattern, it can be transformed according to the rule's reactum. In the example, the route that has been located outside the weather alert now moves into the alert's context and establishes a relationship with it. The site remains in a state allowing further routes to be included in and associated with the weather alert.

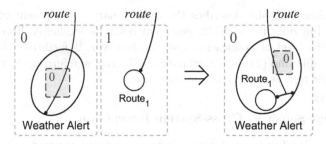

Fig. 8. Reaction Rule

3.3 Cross-System Interaction

Both, structural and dynamic aspects of bigraph-based representation have been discussed in the previous two sections. An air cargo information system including different routes that are handled in accordance with their contextual conditions (i.e., weather alerts) were shown. The example illustrates the abstraction mechanisms used to depict involved systems as agents having ports as facilitator for interaction. This abstraction not only allows the decomposition of systems into its constituents having a certain interaction pattern, but also enables cross-system interaction. Consider an air cargo information systems with routing functionality. The information system only provides the framework conditions, namely the infrastructure to calculate and manage routes. By means of the proposed representation approach, however, data and functionality is not only locally available, but rather can be access from other systems also. Accordingly, one system provides the framework conditions while the actual route is made available by a second one. In this matter, available ports can be matched and combined with each other in order to represent interaction. At this level, the distributed nature of the involved agents is of no importance, as system interaction can arise by simply matching the respective interfaces (inner and outer face). Fig. 8 therefore not only shows two agents that have broken links to be connected, but also describes the structural change that happens once the two systems start interacting.

4 Concerted Emergence of S(oS) Behavior

Bigraph-based representation fosters a systemic perspective on (distributed) application systems which considers them as interacting set of autonomous systems and sub-systems. Interoperability among the involved systems is addressed by the concept of connectivity, supporting the dynamic interaction of systems via typed connectors, so-called ports. The structure of interaction therefore is not required to be known a priori, but can evolve at run time. Emergent behavior, however, is not yet addressed as the representation of dynamic interaction merely involves structural changes in terms of the interconnections of agents.

This mechanism basically describes the evolutionary development of application systems but does not consider emergent behavior explicitly. Emergence of behavior at the level of application systems, however, is facilitated by (1) the concept of locality and (2) the formal nature of bigraphs, referring the rule-based abstraction for representing dynamic changes.

4.1   Context-Sensitive Cross-System Interaction

System interaction has been discussed from a cross-system perspective (cf. Section 3.3). In most cases, however, system interaction is also tied to contextual conditions, meaning that system behavior adapts to its surrounding. Consider a supply network that optimizes delivery routes by means of combining two systems for managing sea freight and air cargo. In case that a handover point for goods between the two systems is not in operation due to bad weather (contextual condition), system interaction is concerned while expected to handle the incident appropriately. The proposed approach allows representing these conditions by combining the concepts of locality and connectivity. In this matter, system interaction is still represented as links between agents, but includes the respective contextual conditions, too.

Imagine a specific transport route that has been defined for carrying goods from one location to another. The route itself is highly dependent on prevailing weather conditions. In other words, if the weather changes an alternative route might be necessary in order to keep the scheduled delivery time. Applying the proposed bigraph-based modeling approach, the route as well as both weather conditions are represented as agents (cf. Fig. 9). The situation's initial configuration shows the route as being located within the context of the first weather alert. In case the route only involves air cargo, weather alerts concerning driving conditions are not going to affect the actual shipping of the products. This means that the route remains the same no matter if it is considered from the perspective of the weather alert or not. If the situation changes with respect to the weather alert, however, it might become necessary to discard the original route. For instance, a tornado warning might affect the planned route when the highway is blocked.

This particular way of representing system interaction with respect to its contextual conditions allows for emergent behavior. As agents (e.g., *Route*) are not bound to their environment (e.g., *WeatherAlert*$_1$) and can be relocated as a result of reaction rules, it does not matter whether a system is known before or not. In the example, the system *WeatherAlert*$_2$ has appeared at a later stage but is available to be used as host, too, as long as the interfaces (inner and outer face) match with each other. Once the agent is relocated, not only the interaction pattern changes, but also the agent behavior adapts to the surrounding conditions.

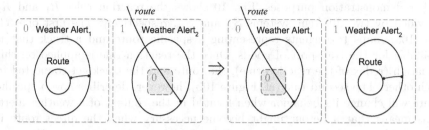

Fig. 9. Context-sensitive Interaction

4.2 Reaction-Rule Orchestration

In addition to context-sensitive system interaction, novel behavior can also emerge when bigraphical structures and reaction rules are orchestrated across systems. In this case, interaction patterns evolve that are not provided by a single system, but rather are combined results of interaction. Consider a supply system including its sub-system that appear during run time in order to optimize delivery routes. In this way, federated systems can optimize their behavior with the aid of currently available systems without having knowledge of these systems beforehand.

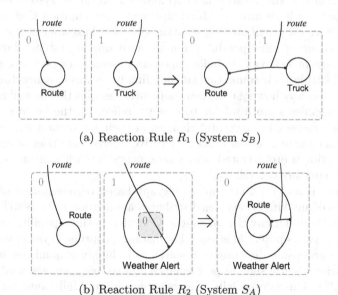

(a) Reaction Rule R_1 (System S_B)

(b) Reaction Rule R_2 (System S_A)

Fig. 10. Reaction Rule Orchestration

For demonstration purposes, Fig. 10 shows the reaction rules R_1 and R_2 provided by two different systems S_A and S_B, respectively. The first one (cf. Fig. 10a) maps two agents representing a specific route and a truck that is available for the transport of goods. Once the reaction rule is applied on this situation (redex of the reaction rule), the route and the truck get connected to each other. The second rule (cf. Figure 10b), however, describes how a specific route will change its behavior when located in the context of a weather alert. This means that a detour might become necessary when the direct route is unavailable due to bad weather conditions, such as thunderstorms. No novel behavior can emerge for either system when the respective rules are applied. For instance, a specific route might get connected to a truck, but will never consider bad weather conditions during delivery. The same holds true for the second system. However, SoS behavior can emerge when both rules are orchestrated. Consequently, a specific route not only gets connected to a truck but is able to consider bad weather conditions also.

5   Conclusions

Today, distributed application systems are expected to adapt to changing circumstances in order to maintain their quality of operation over time. In this context, the interoperability of such systems is crucial and provides the basis for both structural and behavioral adaptability in terms of system emergence. In this paper, we have proposed bigraph-based representation that suggests a SoS perspective on distributed application systems. This approach is not only capable of ensuring interoperability among autonomous systems, but also allows for emergent behavior. It builds upon an abstract perspective on systems represented within their contextual surrounding by means of connectors (ports) determining the way how systems can cooperate. Composition as well as decomposition mechanisms are available to directly reflect on the behavior of these systems with respect to structural changes in their interaction pattern. Novel behavior can emerge as either context-sensitive interaction arises or application system behavior is orchestrated across various systems without any knowledge of these systems any beforehand.

This paper is an initial attempt to bigraph-based representation of application systems of any kind. It enables distributed application systems to be flexible and sustainable under any circumstances. Considering the capabilities of the approach, however, its potential is huge. For instance, continual system verification represents a promising direction of research as in highly dynamic environments quality characteristics, such as performance and security, are essential (cf. [22], [23], and [26]). This is especially true when considering fully automated verification processes which are particularly crucial for application systems with high complexity due to their interaction patterns. Future research will investigate these questions and further impact of bigraph-ensured interoperability on SoS emergence.

References

1. AS5506, SAE Standard: Architecture Analysis & Design Language (AADL). Embedded Computing Systems Committee, SAE (2004)
2. Baeten, J.C.M.: A Brief History of Process Algebra. Theoretical Computer Science 335(2), 131–146 (2005)
3. Baldwin, W.C., Sauser, B.: Modeling The Characteristics of System of Systems. In: IEEE International Conference on System of Systems Engineering, SoSE 2009, pp. 1–6 (2009)
4. Batista, T.: Challenges for SoS Architecture Description. In: Proceedings of the First International Workshop on Software Engineering for Systems-of-Systems, USA, pp. 35–37. ACM Press, New York (2013), http://doi.acm.org/10.1145/2489850.2489857
5. Bezerianos, A., McEwan, G.: Presence Disparity in Mixed Presence Collaboration. In: Proceeding of the Twenty-sixth Annual CHI Conference Extended Abstracts on Human Factors in Computing Systems - CHI 2008, pp. 35–37. ACM Press, New York (2013), http://dl.acm.org/citation.cfm?id=1358628.1358845
6. Boardman, J., Sauser, B.: System of Systems - The Meaning of Of. In: 2006 IEEE/SMC International Conference on System of Systems Engineering, p. 6 (2006)
7. Garlan, D., Monroe, R., Wile, D.: Acme: An Architecture Description Interchange Language. In: CASCON First Decade High Impact Papers, CASCON 2010, pp. 159–173. IBM Corp., Riverton (2010), http://dx.doi.org/10.1145/1925805.1925814
8. Huai-Guang, W., Guo-Qing, W., Li, W.: Bigraphical Model of Service Composition in Ubiquitous Computing Environments. In: 2010 International Conference on Environmental Science and Information Application Technology (ESIAT), vol. 2, pp. 658–662 (July 2010)
9. IBM: Ibm integration bus (2013), http://www-03.ibm.com/software/products/us/en/integration-bus
10. Jamshidi, M.: Systems of Systems Engineering: Principles and Applications. CRC Press (2010)
11. Krishna, R., Wakeman, I., Chalmers, D.: Investigating Bigraphs to Model Dynamic Service Substitution in Pervasive Computing Scenarios. In: Proceedings of Workshop on Formal Approaches to Ubiquitous Systems (FAUS 2009), London, UK (2009)
12. Microsoft: Microsoft DCOM (2013), http://msdn.microsoft.com/library/cc201989.aspx
13. Milner, R.: The Space and Motion of Communicating Agents, vol. 20. Cambridge University Press (2009)
14. Mohammadi, M., Mukhtar, M.: A Review of SOA Modeling Approaches for Enterprise Information Systems. Procedia Technology 11(0), 794–800 (2013), http://www.sciencedirect.com/science/article/pii/S2212017313004143
15. Mule ESB: Mule esb (2013), http://www.mulesoft.com/mule-esb-open-source-esb
16. Nakagawa, E.Y., Gonçalves, M., Guessi, M., Oliveira, L.B.R., Oquendo, F.: The State of the Art and Future Perspectives in Systems of Systems Software Architectures. In: Proceedings of the First International Workshop on Software Engineering for Systems-of-Systems, SESoS 2013, pp. 13–20. ACM, New York (2013), http://doi.acm.org/10.1145/2489850.2489853
17. Nelson, B.J.: Remote Procedure Call (1981)

18. Nundloll, V., Grace, P., Blair, G.S.: The role of ontologies in enabling dynamic interoperability. In: Felber, P., Rouvoy, R. (eds.) DAIS 2011. LNCS, vol. 6723, pp. 179–193. Springer, Heidelberg (2011), http://dx.doi.org/10.1007/978-3-642-21387-8_14

19. OMG: WSDL/SOAP-CORBA Interworking (WSDL2C) (2004), http://www.omg.org/spec/WSDL2C/1.0/ (last accessed: August 27, 2014)

20. OMG: CORBA to WSDL/SOAP Interworking (C2WSDL) (2008), http://www.omg.org/spec/C2WSDL/1.2.1/ (last accessed: August 27, 2014)

21. OMG: Corba - wsdl/soap interworking specification (2013), http://www.omg.org/spec/C2WSDL/1.2.1

22. Perrone, G., Debois, S., Hildebrandt, T.T.: A Model Checker for Bigraphs. In: Proceedings of the 27th Annual ACM Symposium on Applied Computing, SAC 2012, pp. 1320–1325. ACM, New York (2012), http://doi.acm.org/10.1145/2245276.2231985

23. Perrone, G., Debois, S., Hildebrandt, T.: A Verification Environment for Bigraphs. Innovations in Systems and Software Engineering 9(2), 95–104 (2013), http://dx.doi.org/10.1007/s11334-013-0210-2

24. Sharawi, A., Sala-Diakanda, S., Dalton, A., Quijada, S., Yousef, N., Rabelo, L., Sepulveda, J.: A Distributed Simulation Approach for Modeling and Analyzing Systems of Systems. In: Proceedings of the Winter Simulation Conference, WSC 2006, pp. 1028–1035 (December 2006)

25. W3C: Web Services Description Language, WSDL (2007), http://www.w3.org/TR/wsdl20/ (last accessed: August 26, 2014)

26. Xu, D.Z., Xu, D., Lei, Z.: Bigraphical Model of Context-Aware in Ubiquitous Computing Environments. In: 2011 IEEE Asia-Pacific Services Computing Conference (APSCC), pp. 389–394 (2011)

The Need for Second Order Interoperation
A View Beyond Traditional Concepts[*]

Wided Guédria[1] and Henderik A. Proper[1,2]

[1] CRP Henri Tudor, Luxembourg
[2] Radboud University Nijmegen, The Netherlands EE-Team[**]
wided.guedria@tudor.lu, e.proper@acm.org

Abstract. Modern day enterprises need to be continuously "on the move" to deal with the many challenges and opportunities that confront them. The resulting changes can take shape as top-down and premeditated efforts, but are more likely to also take the form of numerous small changes that emerge bottom-up in a seemingly spontaneous fashion. Additionally, fixed organizational structures are being replaced by more dynamic networked enterprises, also blurring borderlines between existing enterprises within the same value web/chain.

We argue that the change processes of modern day enterprises are a key business process, next to the regular business processes involved in the operational activities. We therefore suggest to refer to the change processes as *second order* business processes, as they essentially change the regular (*first order*) business processes and their supportive structures. Second order business processes need the supported of information systems that capture, manipulate and disseminate information concerning different structural aspects (e.g. from value propositions, via business processes and supporting applications, to the underlying IT infrastructures) of a networked enterprise and its environment. We refer to such information systems as *second order information systems*.

In this position paper, we specifically zoom in on the need for interoperation of such second order information systems within networked enterprises that are "on the move". This is what we will refer to as *second-order interoperation*.

1 Introduction

To deal with the many challenges and opportunities that confront them, modern day enterprises need to be continuously "on the move". Socio-economic challenges, such as the financial crisis, mergers, acquisitions, innovations, novel technologies, new business models, servitisation of the economy, reduced protectionism, increased global competition, etc., provide key drivers for change. These challenges are fuelled even more by advances in (information) technology. The resulting changes can materialise in different forms. They might, for example, take shape as top-down and premeditated efforts,

---

[*] This work has been partially sponsored by the *Fonds National de la Recherche Luxembourg* (www.fnr.lu), via the PEARL and CORE programmes.

[**] The EE-Team is a collaboration between CRP Henri Tudor, the Radboud University Nijmegen, the HAN University of Applied Sciences, the Utrecht University of Applied Sciences, and the University of Luxembourg (www.ee-team.eu).

R. Meersman et al. (Eds.): OTM 2014 Workshops, LNCS 8842, pp. 255–264, 2014.
© Springer-Verlag Berlin Heidelberg 2014

but might also occur as numerous small changes that emerge bottom-up in a seemingly spontaneous fashion.

Operating in such environment requires flexibility and cooperation between enterprises, sharing their core competencies in order to exploit the market opportunities. Exchanges are needed for both operational control, solving interoperation problems and to a larger extent for the decision making process during the establishment of cooperation, including opportunity exploration, planning and implementation. These developments have also prompted enterprises to re-structure themselves in terms of more flexible network structures [11, 15, 9]. Traditional fixed organizational structures are being replaced by more dynamic networked enterprises [8, 26], also blurring the borderlines between existing enterprises within the same value chain/web.

In our view, change processes should be regarded as a key business process in an enterprise, next to the regular business processes involving in the operational activities. More specifically, we suggest to consider the change processes as a *second order* business processes. This will be elaborated upon in Section 2, which is based on earlier work as reported in [19, 18].

Furthermore, in fast moving networked enterprises, it is important for senior management, as well as the workers in the enterprise and other participants in the value web in and around the enterprise, to have insight in the workings of the enterprise as a whole. This insight might be needed to e.g. coordinate change, manage compliance, manage risks, assess performance, etc. As a result, information concerning different structural aspects (e.g. from value propositions, via business processes and supporting applications, to the underlying IT infrastructures) of the different elements of the networked enterprise and its environment is needed. We refer to such information systems as *second order information systems*.

In the case of a networked enterprise, the *second order information systems* are likely to run across multiple nodes in the associated network of organizations. This leads to a major challenge for the interoperation between these second order systems. It is acknowledged that one of the major issues in global collaboration and cooperation is the development of interoperability between enterprises. Hence, interoperability has become a key factor to success of enterprises and thus requires considerable attention. In this position paper, we specifically zoom in on the need for interoperation of the second order information systems within dynamic networked enterprises. This is what we will refer to as *second order interoperation*. We will elaborate on the concept of second order interoperation in Section 3, while Section 4 will connect it more explicitly into the need to steer the motion of enterprises.

2   Enterprises in Motion

In line with [6], we consider an enterprise to primarily be a social system, in particular a social system with a purpose. The social individuals, i.e. humans, making up the enterprise will typically use different technological artefacts to (better) achieve their purpose. As a result, enterprises are generally regarded as being socio-technical systems. In using the term enterprise we will therefore also refer to the used technological artefacts.

As a result of the socio-economical and technical challenges, enterprises need to change continuously. Different kinds of, and views on, change in enterprise exist. Some examples include:

- *Enterprise transformation* [21, 12], concerned with pre-meditated and fundamental changes to an enterprise's relationships with one or more key constituencies, e.g., customers, employees, suppliers, and investors.
- *Business innovation* [7], dealing with continuous innovation of the business, its products and/or services.
- *Continuous process improvement* and other forms of *business process reengineering* [5, 20].

These different flavours of change in enterprises are generalized as "*enterprises in motion*", where the word *motion* refers to "*an act, process, or instance of changing place*" [16].

It is important to note that enterprises do not just change by means of pre-meditated change programs. We even go as far as to argue that small changes actually make up the bulk of an enterprise's motion. As such, these seemingly small changes should be taken into due consideration as well. For example, it is quite common that business processes are *not* executed as designed. People working in an enterprise are likely to make changes to the design of business processes just 'to make it work'. Either to make it work for the individual worker, or because the designers did not realize all the variety and complexity one has to deal with in the day to day operations of the enterprise. One might even argue that business processes only work, because people will *make* them work, even if they are not designed well enough.

Given the needs of modern day enterprises to be constantly in motion to meet ever changing challenges, we argue that the continuous motion of an enterprise is actually one of its primary business processes, next to the 'normal' operational business processes. As such, the business process for continuous motion deserves careful design and management. They are 2nd order business processes, and as such, will require the support of 2nd order information systems.

3   The Need for Second Order Interoperation

We now turn to the need of enterprise interoperability, and do so more specifically in the context of steering the motion of a *networked* enterprise.

3.1   Enterprise Interoperability

Interoperability is defined as the "*ability of two or more systems or components to exchange information and to use the information that has been exchanged*" [14]. Having this ability, allows enterprises, organizations and more generally systems to interoperate. In line with this definition, interoperability begins with a theoretical idea of the following structures having symmetry: software components, hardware components, the interaction between software and hardware components, and the communication between systems exchanging information. Being interoperable means that the system is able to avoid/solve interoperability problems and interoperate with its partner. According to [4, 25], there are three kinds of interoperability problems:

- *Conceptual* problems are mainly concerned with the syntactic and semantic incompatibilities of information to be exchanged or to be used during an interoperation.
- *Technological* problems refer to the use of computer or ICT (Information and Communication Technologies) to communicate and exchange information (i.e. language, architecture & platforms, infrastructure, . . .). These problems concern the standards to use, store, exchange, processes or computerized data.
- *Organizational* problems relate to the definition of responsibilities and authorities so that interoperability can take place under good and well-established conditions.

In order to quickly overcome these interoperability problems and thus support enterprises to better interoperate with their partners, clients, providers, etc. Enterprise Interoperability (EI) requires continuous assessment and improvement.

3.2   Second-Order Interoperation

Preparing, maintaining and improving interoperability should be considered as a business process that should be designed (to prepare interoperability), assessed (e.g. using maturity models), improved (i.e. by reaching higher levels of interoperability) and maintained.

In line with the terminology used for aspect systems in an enterprise in motion [19], the running-producing system can be regarded as a first order interoperation. This requires the running system, to have the 'ability to interoperate' before interoperating, we refer to as 1st order interoperability. On the other hand, the motion-steering system can be regarded as a second order interoperation that needs also second order interoperability. These are illustrated in Figure 1. First order interoperation is an operational process within organizations (1st order business process). Motioning interoperation, by solving problems or improving it is a 2nd order business process that should be steered and supported. Consequently, enterprise interoperation focuses on those properties of an enterprise that are necessary and sufficient to meet its essential requirements for interoperability. This includes, in principle, all aspects of Figure 3, in particular the running, motioning, producing, and steering aspect systems.

3.3   Steering Areas of Interoperability

The establishment or diagnosis of enterprise interoperability leads to identify the different operational levels that are concerned. Four areas of interoperability, called Enterprise Interoperability (EI) concerns, have been defined, namely business, process, service and data [4].

- Interoperability of data aims to make work together different data models with different query languages to share information coming from heterogeneous systems.
- Interoperability of services aims at making it possible for various services or applications (designed and implemented independently) to work together by solving the syntactic and semantic differences.

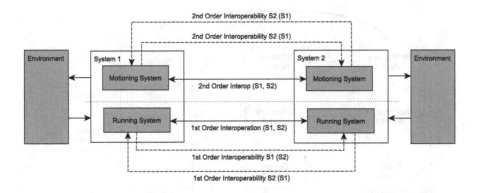

Fig. 1. Second order Interoperability and Interoperation

- Interoperability of processes aims to make various processes work together. In the interworked enterprise, the aim will be to connect internal processes of two companies to create a common process.
- Interoperability of business aims to work in a harmonized way to share and develop business between companies despite the difference of methods, decision making, culture of the enterprises or, the commercial making.

Given the needs to be constantly in motion to meet ever changing challenges, we argue that the continuous motion of each one of these interoperability concerns is actually one of its primary business processes, next to the normal operational business processes. As such, each business process for continuous motion deserves careful design and management.

3.4 Levels of Steering

Given the fact that an enterprise architecture forms a bridge between strategy and design [17], it follows that the motion-steering system actually involves (at least) three levels of steering. These are illustrated in Figure 2 [19]. At the top level we find the steering of strategically relevant issues. This concerns the definition and evolution of the enterprise's strategy. Depending on the goals and concerns that are involved in the strategic thinking level, the border between the strategic level and the architectural level would need to be adjusted. Needless to say, that this border cannot be fixed a priori. It will depend on the situations and concerns as they evolve.

At the next level, we find the architectural level. There the same applies. Depending on the essential requirements that follow from the strategic level, as well as the goals and concerns of the stakeholders, the border between the architectural level and design level can be adjusted. Again, this border cannot be fixed *a priori* as well. For example, a shifting societal focus towards e.g. the carbon footprint of the production of services and goods, may all of a suden trigger the architectural need to study the carbon impact of the enterprise's business processes. This would entail the need to, at an architectural level, now consider and design business processes at a finer level of detail then before.

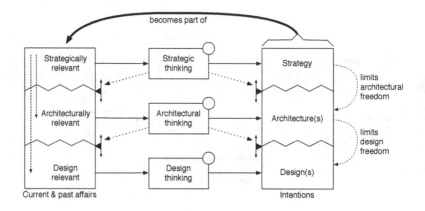

Fig. 2. Steering-Levels, taken from [19]

The last level of the steering system involves the design level. This design level is filled in by e.g. system development projects and/or decisions by self-steering teams on how they plan/organize their work.

The left hand side of Figure 2 shows the input, i.e. the abstraction (typically in terms of models) of the sensing activities, to the thinking activities. To stress the fact that this should not just involve the current state, but rather a historical perspective and current trends of the entire enterprise, we refer to this input as the *current & past affairs*[1]. The dotted arrows on the left side of Figure 2 illustrate that the lower levels can take the the higher levels of information as (contextual) input.

The right hand side of Figure 2, represents the results of the thinking activities. In other words, the intentions/plans for action. The dotted arrows illustrated the fact that the lower levels need to be compliant to the higher levels. As such, the (higher level) intentions are also a part of the input for the at the lower level. This is signified by the fat arrow running across the top of the diagram.

3.5   2nd Order Interoperability and Systemic Properties

Systems theory is a way to view the world [10]. It can be used as a paradigm to understand interoperability: interoperating systems, systems interoperation and interoperability problems as well as solutions. This is particularly relevant since interoperability is about relations between systems. This section proposes that 2nd order interoperability can also benefit from a systemic approach. Several characteristics of a system can influence its ability to interoperate. Based on [27], the main ones are the following:

- The openness of a system refers to the relationship between the system and its environment. Open systems affect and are affected by their environment [10]. The opposite of an open system is a closed system that does not have any interaction

---

[1] http://en.wikipedia.org/wiki/Current_affairs_(news_format)

with its environment. As a result of being closed, such a system cannot be interoperable.
- The stability of a system should be considered. An unstable system will be prone to create interoperability problems due to its changing nature.
- The adaptability of a system is an important factor. A system that can react to changes and adapt its structure or behaviour accordingly while keeping its original objective has a greater interoperability potential.
- The reversibility is one of the properties that interoperable system should have: even if the implementation of the interoperability between two systems leads to their adaptation or modification, these systems have to be able to come back to their initial state when interoperation ends (both from the point of view of structure and behaviour).

4   Steering the Motion of Enterprises

Given the potential impact which the challenges may have on an enterprise, and that as a consequence enterprise are continuously in motion, we argue that there is a need to steer this motion. It needs to be ensured that the motion is in line with the overal purpose and strategy of the enterprise, while also staying within the bounds of e.g. external regulations.

4.1   Steering

Based on the view that enterprises are continiously in motion and given the need to steer this motion, a distinction between four aspects systems is needed : the *running* aspect system, the *motioning* aspect system, the *producing* aspect system and the *steering* aspect system. The production aspect is concerned with the actual performance of activities of e.g. the motioning system (i.e. making changes) or the running system (e.g. producing products or delivering services). The steering aspect is concerned with the overall steering of the activities of the production system, such as ensuring their mutual alignment, efficiency and contribution to the overall goals (e.g. the purpose of the enterprise), as well as compliance to external regulations. According to the dictionary [16], to *steer* specifically means:

1. *to control the direction in which something (such as a ship, car, or airplane) moves;*
2. *to be moved or guided in a particular direction or along a particular course.*

We consider this to be applicable to the motion of an enterprise as well. Depending on the enterprise, its purposes, context, and concerns, the steering system can use different styles of steering. For example, a restrictive top-down style of control approach, or a more laissez-faire based care-taking/stewarding approach. It may also apply different rhythms towards steering the activities in the producing system. For example, a regular planning-based approach or a more evolutionary/agile approach.

4.2   The Sense-Think-Act Paradigm

The role of the steering system can be illustrated more specifically in terms of the control paradigm from management science. From a theoretical point of view, the control paradigm is based on the more general notions of cybernetics [2] and feedback systems [3]. The field of robotics has developed a variation of the control paradigm in the form of the Sense-Think-Act paradigm [22]. In terms of the requirements on a controlling system, we would have the following correspondence:

1. *Sense*: (1) the current & anticipated coordinative goals and constraints, (2) the state & motion of the object's environment, (3) the state & motion of the object itself and (4) the impact of earlier coordinative interventions.
2. *Think*: (1) perform a SWOT analysis of the motion of the object and its environment, in relation to the coordinative goals and constraints, as well as earlier intervention actions, and (2) formulate (when needed/desired) an intervention plan to influence the object and/or its environment.
3. *Act*: perform an intervention plan.

We argue that *sensing*, *thinking* and *acting* are actually more specific aspect systems of the *steering* system. For enterprises in motion, this leads to the situation as shown in Figure 3. The *sensing* aspect system observes the environment, the performing of motioning system, as well as the running system as a whole. It *acts* by influencing the performance part of the motioning system.

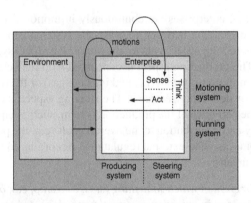

Fig. 3. Sense, Think and Act aspect systems added

4.3   Second Order Information Systems

The motion-steering system can be regarded as a second order information system [13]. As such, it is actually to be regarded an information system in the broad sense, as it involves both human and computerised actors. Needless to say, that IT can play an important role in this information system [18].

In this vein, techniques such as process mining [1], software cartography [24, 23] and enterprise cartography [24] are examples of IT based techniques that can support the sensing activities of the motion-steering system. Similarly, IT based techniques can be used to support the thinking and acting activities.

5   Conclusion

Operating in a dynamic environment requires flexibility and cooperation between enterprises. This needs the ability to be continuously "on the move" and the need to steer this motion. In this postion paper, we have focused on interoperation and defined second order interoperation/interoperability. We argued that the motion-steering system of an enterprise is essentially a second order information system, yielding several future challenges for the field of information systems [18]. We defined the change/motioning interoperation processes as second order interoperation, as it essentially changes the regular (first order) interoperation and its supportive structures. Based on this, we also identified different levels of steering enterprises in motion, positioning architectural steering (and thinking) in between strategic level steering and design level steering. Finally, we suggested the key ingredients of enterprise architecture as being: an engagement framework, a motivation framework, a design framework, a communication framework, and a process framework.

References

1. van der Aalst, W.M.P.: Process Mining: Discovery, Conformance and Enhancement of Business Processes. Springer, Heidelberg (2011)
2. Ashby, W.R.: An Introduction to Cybernetics. Chapman & Hall, London (1956)
3. Åström, K.J., Murray, R.M.: Feedback Systems: An Introduction for Scientists and Engineers. Princeton University Press (2008)
4. Chen, D.: Enterprise interoperability framework. In: Missikoff, M., Nicola, A.D., D'Antonio, F. (eds.) EMOI-INTEROP. CEUR Workshop Proceedings, vol. 200, CEUR-WS.org (2006)
5. Davenport, T.H.: Process Innovation: Reengineering work through information technology. Harvard Business School Press, Boston (1993)
6. Dietz, J.L.G., Hoogervorst, J.A.P., Albani, A., Aveiro, D., Babkin, E., Barjis, J., Caetano, A., Huysmans, P., Iijima, J., van Kervel, S.J.H., Mulder, H., Op't Land, M., Proper, H.A., Sanz, J., Terlouw, L., Tribolet, J., Verelst, J., Winter, R.: The discipline of enterprise engineering. International Journal Organisational Design and Engineering 3(1), 86–114 (2013)
7. Drucker, P.F.: Innovation and Entrepreneurship. Harper Collins (2006)
8. Friedman, T.L.: The World is Flat: A Brief History of the Twenty-first Century. Farrar, Straus and Giroux, New York (2005)
9. Galbraith, J.R.: Designing the Global Corporation. Jossey-Bass, San Fransisco, California (2000)
10. Giachetti, R.E.: Design of Enterprise Systems: Theory, Architecture, and Methods, 1st edn. CRC Press, Inc, Boca Raton (2010)
11. Hagel III, J., Singer, M.: Unbundling the Corporation. Harvard Business Review (March 1999)
12. Harmsen, F., Proper, H.A.E., Kok, N.: Informed governance of enterprise transformations. In: Proper, E., Harmsen, F., Dietz, J.L.G. (eds.) PRET 2009. Lecture Notes in Business Information Processing, vol. 28, pp. 155–180. Springer, Heidelberg (2009)

13. Hoppenbrouwers, S.J.B.A., Proper, H.A.: A Communicative Perspective on Second Order Information Systems. In: Lasker, G.E. (ed.) Proceedings of the 16th International Conference on System Research, Informatics and Cybernetics, Baden–Baden, Germany, IIAS (2004)

14. Institute of Electrical and Electronics Engineers. IEEE standard computer dictionary: A compilation of IEEE standard computer glossaries (1990)

15. Malone, T.: Making the Decision to Decentralize. Harvard Business School – Working Knowledge for Business Leaders (March 2004)

16. Meriam–Webster. Meriam–Webster Online, Collegiate Dictionary (2003)

17. Op't Land, M., Proper, H.A., Waage, M., Cloo, J., Steghuis, C.: Enterprise Architecture – Creating Value by Informed Governance. Enterprise Engineering SeriesGermany. Springer, Heidelberg (2008)

18. Proper, H.A.: Business informatics for enterprise transformations. In: 2013 IEEE 6th International Conference on Service-Oriented Computing and Applications (SOCA), pp. 251–251 (December 2013)

19. Proper, H.A.: Enterprise Architecture – Informed steering of enterprises in motion. In: Proceedings of the 15th International Conference, ICEIS 2013, Angers, France - Revised Selected Papers. LNBIP, Springer, Heidelberg (to appear, 2014)

20. Pyzdek, T.: The Six Sigma Handbook: The Complete Guide for Greenbelts, Blackbelts, and Managers at All Levels, Revised and Expanded Edition, 2nd edn. McGraw–Hill, New York (2003)

21. Rouse, W.B.: A theory of enterprise transformation. Systems Engineering 8(4), 279–295 (2005)

22. Siegel, M.: The sense-think-act paradigm revisited. In: 1st International Workshop on Robotic Sensing, ROSE 2003, pp. 5–10 (June 2003)

23. Sousa, P., Lima, J., Sampaio, A., Pereira, C.: An approach for creating and managing enterprise blueprints: A case for IT blueprints. In: Albani, A., Barjis, J., Dietz, J.L.G. (eds.) CIAO! 2009. LNBIP, vol. 34, pp. 70–84. Springer, Heidelberg (2009)

24. Sousa, P., Gabriel, R., Tadao, G., Carvalho, R., Sousa, P.M., Sampaio, A.: Enterprise transformation: The serasa experian case. In: Harmsen, F., Grahlmann, K., Proper, E. (eds.) PRET 2011. LNBIP, vol. 89, pp. 134–145. Springer, Heidelberg (2011)

25. Ullberg, J., Chen, D., Johnson, P.: Barriers to Enterprise Interoperability. In: Poler, R., van Sinderen, M., Sanchis, R. (eds.) IWEI 2009. LNBIP, vol. 38, pp. 13–24. Springer, Heidelberg (2009)

26. Umar, A.: IT infrastructure to enable next generation enterprises. Information Systems Frontiers 7(3), 217–256 (2005)

27. Walliser, B.: Systemes et modeles, introduction critique a l'analyse des systemes. Editions du Seuil (1977)

Enterprise Networks Integration in a Sensing Environment: A Case Study

Qing Li, Hao Luo, Pei-Xuan Xie, and Xiao-Qian Feng

Department of Automation, Tsinghua University, Beijing 100084, P.R. China
liqing@tsinghua.edu.cn

Abstract. Internet of things, mobile Internet, cloud computing and big data technologies build a sensing environment for all kinds of businesses. Inter enterprise collaboration is meeting new challenges of omni-channel marketing, closed-loop supply chain and enterprise networks integration. A data convergence oriented enterprise networks integration architecture is developed in the paper. How to use the developed technologies to solve problems of product lifecycle management and omni-channel marketing management are discussed in detailed cases studies.

Keywords: Enterprise network, data convergence, product lifecycle management, omni-channel marketing.

1 Introduction

With the process of globalization and the development of management models and information technologies, enterprises collaboration and cooperation is facing new business requirements in a sensing environment. Internet of things, mobile Internet, cloud computing and big data technologies are forming the new technical environment for all kinds of enterprises and business operations.

The new developing trends of enterprise operation are shown in Fig.1, including three directions:

(1) The scope of enterprise integration is extending to enterprise network integration. The topology of supply chain networks becomes more dynamic.

(2) The product lifecycle management, especially the closed-loop supply chain management for product recycling and disposal becomes a more and more important business issue.

(3) The market policies are developed from retail, e-commerce to the omni-channel marketing.

In order to overcome challenges in the sensing environment, the authors' team develop the architecture of the Enterprise Network Integration Platform (ENI-P) for the data oriented product lifecycle management and omni-channel marketing management challenges of enterprise networks [1]. The new concepts "Collaboration Agent" and "Data Portal" are introduced into system integration as well as their realization methods. In the paper, an industrial experiment system is deployed to illustrate how to realize the product whole life-cycle and omni-channels data convergence oriented enterprise networks integration in a sensing environment.

R. Meersman et al. (Eds.): OTM 2014 Workshops, LNCS 8842, pp. 265–274, 2014.

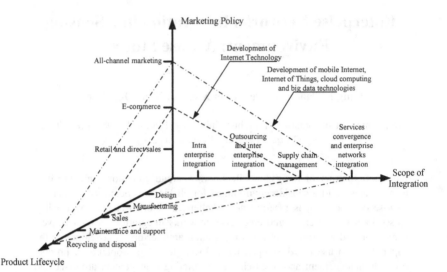

Fig. 1. Environment of enterprise network integration with business and technology development

2   Data Convergence Oriented Enterprise Networks Integration Framework

An enterprise network is built and operated based on integrated ISs, which can help to link business processes and local information systems one by one. Based on the understanding of business demands of enterprise networks, an integration framework or solution for the integration among intra ISs of member companies in a sensing environment must meet the following criteria:

(1) Member companies' ISs should be accessible through the framework. There shall include a mechanism to publish selected functions of intra ISs as services that can be accessed by its partners.

(2) Certain mechanism should be built up to support the intercommunication between the framework and different intra ISs.

(3) The member companies' IS services should be organised to support the enterprise's business processes and the processes should be accessible through the framework.

(4) The member companies' IS services, business processes and others applications should be well managed and under monitoring. They should be dynamically enabled or disabled.

(5) Users should be free of multiple logins, which means the framework will automatically deal with the services authorisation.

(6) Through the framework, data from different data sources can be collected and transferred in enterprise networks.

(7) The structure and operation logic of the framework shall be simple. It shall be realized as a light weight platform.

In order to satisfy with above criteria, as shown in Fig.2, the scheme of enterprise networks integration framework based on collaboration agents (CAs) and data portals (DPs) is developed.

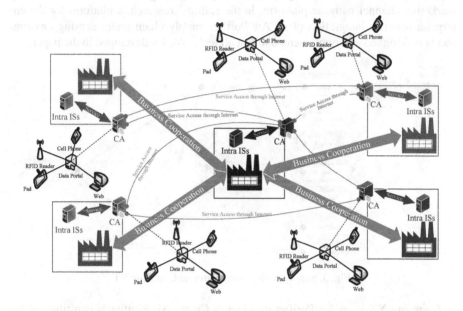

Fig. 2. Scheme of Collaboration Agent (CA) based enterprise network integration

In Fig.2, Collaboration Agents (CAs) are introduced into to solve the problem of inter enterprises integration. CA is implemented in every member enterprise. These CAs can access each other so as to structure a bridge to link the whole enterprise network. A CA consists of different APIs designed to connect applications on intra ISs of different companies. The CA can also encapsulate selected intra ISs functions as web services; therefore, all intra ISs in the enterprise network can be connected.

In order to collect and transfer data in a sensing environment, Data Porters (DPs) are developed. DPs present a mechanism to collect data from different sensors or data sources, collate original data, encapsulate and transfer data to targets.

Based on the integration framework, The Enterprise Network Integrating Platform (ENI-P) between a company's intra ISs and its partner companies' IS services in a sensing environment with CAs and DPs is developed. CA is the media of communication between outside services and intra enterprise ISs. DP is the media of communication between outside environment and relative enterprise networks. The platform also realizes single logins to intra enterprise ISs and outside ISs [1-5].

3   Cases Studies

The author's team developed the ENI-P framework for enterprise network integration in a sensing environment [1-5]. On one hand, it can be used to realize data integration for whole product lifecycle management; on the other hand, the omni-channel marketing management can also be highly realised by integrating data generated from every marketing channel with the platform. In the authors' research, a platform for the enterprise network integration of an Air Purifier supply chain under sensing environments is designed and implemented to test all technologies developed in the paper.

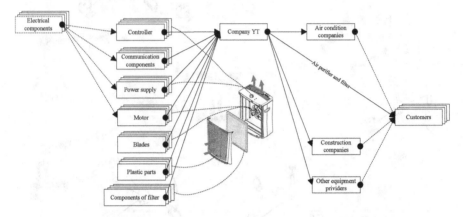

Fig. 3. Supply chain network around Company YT

Company YT is an Air Purifier provider in China. Air Purifier is constitute of filter, plastic parts and several different electronic components. Company YT purchases air purifier components from different suppliers and sales air purifiers to different downstream companies or directly to end customers via physical stores or electric commerces. Company YT has seven main kinds of suppliers classified by the type of their products, which include controllers, communication components, power supplies, motors, blades, plastic parts, and components of filter. There are multiple suppliers for every part. For the complexity and long manufacturing process of an air purifier, these seven types of suppliers also have their upstream suppliers, which provide electrical components. Company YT sales its product to end users via several different channels, including its own physical stores and online store, B2C online trading platforms such as Tmall.com and JD.com, mass-market retailers such as Carrefour and Wal-Mart, air condition companies, construction companies and some other business customers. As a result, company YT has a complex supply chain network in its upstream relationships and several downstream business partners, as shown in Fig.3. The supply chain network is a typical enterprise network.

On the other hand, the explosive growth of sensing and mobile Internet technology has made company YT under a sensing environment where the company can obtain amount of data from heterogeneous data sources. On this condition, company YT faces two main challenges:

(1) The sustainable development of information technology enriches the channels through which customers interact with the company.

(2) CLSC is a key issue for cost reduction and environment protection of company YT.

To verify technologies developed in the paper and solve omni-channel marketing management and whole product lifecycle management issues faced by Company YT, an industrial experimental system is deployed in Company YT and the typical parts of its partner companies and customers.

3.1 Omni-Channel Marketing Management

Realizing the trend of ever-increasing omni-channel shoppers, Company YT is about to integrate public e-business services, its own online business platform and all its physical channels for requirement of customers. Company YT has mainly four types of marketing channels: B2C, including online self-shop and third-part B2C platform such as Tmall.com, Amazon.cn, and JD.com; Retail, which includes self-supported shop and shops in supermarkets like Wal-Mart; Whole sale and B2B, including downstream business customers such as air condition companies and construction companies. One of the most typical examples of omni-channel marketing of Company YT is known as "showroom", which means customers test the products in an offline shop and place orders online via websites, QR codes, cell phones, pads, and so forth.

To satisfy the requirement of ever-increasing omni-channel shoppers, Company YT expects to implement omni-channels marketing management. One typical model of omni-channels marketing management concentrates on integrating online e-commerce and offline physical stores, and aims at delivering goods to customers from the nearest physical stores or warehouses. Company YT with omni-channels marketing management collects orders from all its online sales channels, inquiries location and distance information from Google Map, acquires inventory information from its offline business partners, and selects a nearest offline stores or warehouse to deliver goods for each order. Furthermore, several analyses can be done based on data collected by Company YT. By summarizing the sale distribution of its product, Company YT can take precision delivery from warehouses to physical stores before the products are sold.

However, Company YT is currently faced with the following problems when implementing the omni-channel marketing management:

(1) The sales staffs are not able to update the type and quantity of finished products in real time due to the unavailability of automatic information upload. It is now done by human power.

(2) When an order comes from one online channel, such as Tmall.com®, the status of inventory cannot be synchronised among all other marketing channels.

(3) The intra system cannot integrate order information from every channel for further analysis and provide support for decision-making of goods distribution decision.

(4) When a sales staff logs on to any online platforms, the intra enterprise systems are actually connected to the internet, which results in potential risks in information security.

Typical heterogeneous systems integration solutions, such as SOA with web service, cannot meet Company YT's specific requirements for omni-channel marketing management due to the following reasons:

(1) Introducing of every online platform partner's e-commerce system would break the unity of Company YT's own intra system, probably resulting in an isolated system since the intra system is specially designed for Company YT and the company is accustomed to its operating system, Company YT expects to retain all current business processes and operating behaviours. E-commerce platforms are only used as a source of data and a release of media- and business- related information.

(2) Each platform partner also has its standard business processes. It will not adjust the processes to meet Company YT's requirements. Traditional process analysis and process interoperating methods are therefore no longer applicable.

In order to solve the problem of integrating multiple marketing channels, it is necessary for Company YT to complete cross-computing environments processes modelling, analysis and design. Meanwhile, an integration platform is needed to manage omni-channel marketing. Omni-channel inventory synchronisation and logistical coordination would be realized.

In this case, Taobao.com®, JD.com®, and several physical stores are selected to illustrate how to achieving omni-channel marketing management. Integrating solutions for other e-business platforms using ENI-P would follow a similar process. Taobao.com® and JD.com® are the biggest and most famous e-business platform in China. Most companies with online business choose these two as their e-business platform.

Focus on the CP that how to shares inventory data in Taobao.com® with Company YT, it could be realized by three steps, namely inventory extraction, inventory standardisation and inventory import, as shown in Fig. 4. Other CPs are similar. Corresponding web services are developed and named as Taobao_Inventory_Extract, Inventory_Standardization, and Inventory_Import. Taobao_Inventory_Extract extracts inventory data from the Taobao.com® cloud and puts them into the input layer of a temporary database. Inventory_Standardization translates the data from an input layer into the format that intra system adopts and puts the result into the output layer of the Temporary database. Inventory_Import will finally import the standardised data into the intra system.

Taobao_Inventory_Extract is an API service. It is encapsulated into a web service by choosing an API from API library. This service is a dedicated interface for Taobao.com® and is the key of the whole process. Inventory_Import is similar to Taobao_Inventory_Extract and is the API with the intra system. Inventory_Standardization is an ordinary web service and could be used in many similar processes. It is encapsulated by the ENI-P encapsulation module.

After these web services are registered in ENI-P, they could be orchestrated into a new web service, named Taobao_Inventory_Synchronization. This process is generated with a mapping mechanism by the service orchestration module in ENI-P. It could be deployed on the CA as a web service and could provide a user interface for invocation [1-5].

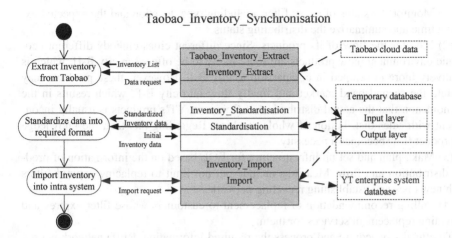

Fig. 4. Inventory synchronisation process

3.2   Whole Product Lifecycle Management

Due to increasing awareness of deteriorating air quality in China, demand for air purifier has risen sharply recent years. For Company YT, the efficiency of the CLSC of filter, which is critical part of product, has directly effect to the company's core competitiveness. However, one key challenge during the operation of CLSC is that information flow almost breaks down after products are delivered to customers. The uncertainty of the quantity, quality and timing of product in CLSC is caused by the unavailability of information and by the lack of control in the returning supply chain.

When considering traditional forward supply chain of air purifier, an intuitive solution to acquire information of products is set up a RFID network to collect data. However, once an air purifier is delivered to customers, its area of operations is expanding to the extent that amounts of RFID readers are needed to identify RFID tags, which is not cost-effective.

A new recycling strategy is proposed for Company YT, considering the unique characteristic of filters' life cycle. During the process of CLSC's operation, the whole machine and filter follow different life cycles. The whole machine extends its life span via maintenance, while the filters are recycled and reused for manufacturing of new products. Generally speaking, the filter of an air purifier expires before the whole machine does. Customers, thus, can continue to use an air purifier by replacing the expired filter. This characteristic of lifecycle makes it possible for Company YT to collect data about filters when it is used and recycle the expired filter when customers replace it with a new one. Therefore, the proposed strategy integrates sale and recycling processes of filters, which means Company YT provides the timely replacement service of filters to achieve sale and recycling simultaneously. A small geographic region – State B is selected as pilot region to verify this strategy. In order to implement the recycling strategy at high efficiency, Company YT has to complete some tasks as follows:

(1) Monitor the status of every filter, including type, location and the expected expiring time and summarize the distributing status.

(2) Monitor the flow of its products. Since different cities embody different economic environment, new products are more likely to be offered in city B-H, which is relatively more developed in comparison to city B-F. However, these products may go into the second hand market and finally flow into city B-F, which results in the phenomenon that the actual distribution of Company YT's products is usually inconsistent with sales distribution of whole machine. Regarding this fact, the knowledge of product flow becomes a necessity.

(3) Make plan and set up infrastructure for EOL based on the information of product distribution and flow. Measures include but not limit to replacing expired filters with new ones and establishing recycling network.

(4) Pulling recommendation of replacement to customers whose filter expires and providing replacement services for them.

To effectively acquire and process the required information, RFID network is used in forward supply chain where products are limit to areas under control of Company YT; Sensor in air purifier is taken as a tool to detect operation status of filters in reverse supple chain. In reverse supply chain, customers use cell phone or pad to get data collected by sensors via Bluetooth and transmit them to data portal via wireless network. The framework of ENI-Platform is shown in Fig.5. The components involved are as follows:

(1) Passive RFID tag is selected due to the simplicity of product tracking. It is small-sized and contains its own ID, product type and configuration parameters like producing data and expected expiring date. It is supposed to be detected by a RFID reader automatically when it goes into the interrogation zone.

(2) RFID reader is a fixed reader built in data collecting point in areas under control of Company YT, etc. With a RFID reader, product information from each product at each site can be gathered at a fast speed and then be written to the data portal.

(3) Sensor is installed in every air purifier to monitor the status of filter. With a sensor, information about the filters of air purifier can be gathered at a fast speed and used for further analysing.

(4) Cell Phone or Pad app is a media that collects data from sensors in air purifier via Bluetooth and transmit these data to data portals via Mobile Internet.

(5) Data Portal is installed in either a cell phone, a personal computer, or a processing server. Data Portal collects data from different sensors or channels, identifies the collected data, and transfers it to a standard format.

(6) Collaborate Agent is deployed in its partner companies for communication between Company YT and its partners. It also can provide services that integrate different business process.

(7) Internet plays the role of communication media.

(8) ENI-Platform based collecting network consists of both hardware and software and mainly completes the task of collecting data from field data portals. According to different requirements, it could be organized in different structure, which offers the whole product lifecycle management system a reliable and flexible framework in real application. User interface is available at every centre node in ENI-Platform for user interaction.

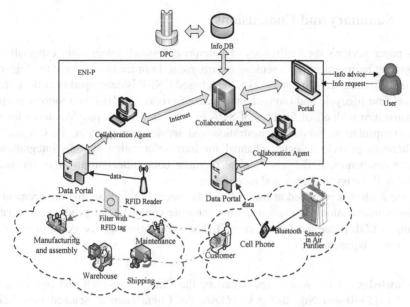

Fig. 5. Product lifecycle data collecting system

(9) Information database keeps the data collected from the field data portal database by ENI-Platform. The data could be further manipulated and analyzed by Data processing centre. Every physical node in ENI-Platform other than data portal node owns an information database.

(10) Data processing centre (DPC) acquires data from the information database and accomplishes several operations step by step. Firstly, it decides the location of a specific product based on a series of tracking information by finding its latest appearance. Secondly, it analyses sensor data from the specific product and decides whether the filter needs to be replaced. Then, it pushed notifications for customers whose filter need to be replaced and offers a report to portal for decision making.

With all hardware and software mentioned above ready, here is a typical application scenario how Company YT could implement whole product lifecycle management and recycle expired filters in state B.

Week by week, similar product tracking information accumulates and finally a statistic analysis is available to provide a clear view of what is going on in state B. A manager named M-B at headquarters logs into the portal and reads analyzing report formed by DPC. Therefore, by introducing ENI-Platform, Company YT can see a whole picture of its product distribution all over state B.

Usually to achieve such a good performance would need to spend a lot for traditional solution. However, Company YT found cost is significantly lower and can meanwhile promote sales of filters. All in all, ENI-Platform helps Company YT achieve all expected missions with a friendly maintenance environment at a reasonable cost.

4   Summary and Conclusions

This paper reviews the challenges of enterprise network integration, especially the integrating requirements in a sensing environment. In order to overcome the high cost barrier of special real-time networks, SOA based ENI-P is developed to collect, transfer and fuse lifecycle and omni-channel data of products. ENI-P is a loosely coupled infrastructure with all of features of SOA and web service. It provides tools for service encapsulation, service orchestration and service management. Its CA and DP mechanisms provide a secure channel for intra information systems integration of partner companies. ENI-P also realise products data collection and transformation. ENI-P is also easy to deploy and reconfigure.

Case studies is provided at the end of this paper. In this case, the requirement for business information integration among multiple channels and product information tracing at EOL phase are further cleared. The information service system can satisfy all of these requirements.

Acknowledges. This work is sponsored by the China High-Tech 863 Program, No. 2001AA415340 and No. 2007AA04Z1A6, the China Natural Science Foundation, No. 61174168, the Aviation Science Foundation of China, No. 20100758002 and 20128058006.

References

[1] Li, Q., Zhou, J., Peng, Q.R., Li, C.Q., Wang, C., Wu, J., Shao, B.E.: Business processes oriented heterogeneous systems integration platform for net-worked enterprises. Computers in Industry 61(2), 127–144 (2010)

[2] Li, Q., Wang, C., Wu, J., Li, J., Wang, Z.Y.: Towards the business–information technology alignment in cloud computing environment: anapproach based on collaboration points and agents. International Journal of Computer Integrated Manufacturing 24(11), 1038–1057 (2011)

[3] Li, Q., Wang, Z., Li, W., Cao, Z., Du, R., Luo, H.: Model-based ser-vices convergence and multi-clouds integration. Computers in Industry 64(7), 813–832 (2013)

[4] Li, Q., Wang, Z.Y., Cao, Z.C., Du, R.Y., Luo, H.: Process and data fragmentation-oriented enterprise network integration with collaboration modelling and collaboration agents. Enterprise Information Systems, 1-31 (2014) (ahead-of-print)

[5] Li, Q., Wang, Z.Y., Li, W.H., Li, J., Wang, C., Du, R.Y.: Applica-tions integration in a hybrid cloud computing environment: modelling and platform. Enterprise Information Systems 7(3), 237–271 (2013)

A Virtual Reality Based Simulation Environment for Orthopedic Surgery

J. Cecil[1], P. Ramanathan[2], Miguel Pirela-Cruz[3], and M. Bharathi Raj Kumar[1]

[1] School of Industrial Engineering, Oklahoma State University
[2] University of Wisconsin, Madison, WI 53706 USA
[3] Texas Tech Health Sciences Center, El Paso, Texas

Abstract. Virtual reality simulators in medicine are becoming more widely used to train residents and interns. In this paper, we discuss the design of a Virtual Surgical Environment (VSE) for performing a class of orthopedic surgeries. The VSE focuses on providing training to residents in LISS plating based surgeries (for addressing fractures of the femur). Using such virtual environments enables medical residents to develop a better understanding of the various surgical steps along with enabling them to practice specific surgical steps involving surgical instruments as well as other components. A brief discussion of the network based implementation is also provided; such an approach enables multiple users from different geographical locations to interact with an expert surgeon at another location. This network based approach was demonstrated as part of Next Generation Internet activities related to the GENI and US Ignite projects.

Keywords: Virtual Surgical Environment, Orthopedic, GENI.

1   Introduction

Current trends for medical/health related education include the use of simulations in a range of areas such as heart surgery, dermatologic surgery, etc. There have been a limited number of research efforts which have explored the use of Virtual Reality technology in developing simulation environments to facilitate various medical procedures including surgery. In general, the creation of virtual surgical environments will enable students to learn the appropriate way of managing various conditions with safety considerations to the residents and patients.

Such virtual environments are essential to educating/training young budding surgeons. The traditional way of surgical teaching involves students first merely observing a 'live' surgery and then gradually progressing to assisting experienced surgeons. Developing such virtual environments for educational and training purposes will accelerate and supplement existing approaches used to educate and train medical doctors. Using computer based simulations allows for medical students to be better prepared to serve the surgical needs of the general public. They have the potential benefit of providing more surgical training opportunities which in turn will facilitate a larger pool of better trained medical doctors who can serve the general public.

R. Meersman et al. (Eds.): OTM 2014 Workshops, LNCS 8842, pp. 275–285, 2014.

2   Literature Review of VR in Surgery

A brief literature review of relevant research efforts is presented in this section.

Qin et al. [1] developed a framework for simulating the soft tissue deformation in an orthopedic surgery. The experimental results showed the practicability of their model in providing interactive and realistic modeling of human tissue deformations. Delp and Loan [2] created graphical software, called SIMM (Software for Interactive Musculoskeletal Modeling), which can be used to develop and analyze musculoskeletal models. Once a model is defined by the user, the functions of each muscle can be analyzed by computing its length, forces, moment arms, and joint moments. The user can develop, alter, and evaluate models of many different musculoskeletal structures, which quantify the effects of musculoskeletal geometry, joint kinematics, and muscle-tendon parameters on muscle-tendon lengths, moment arms, muscle forces and joint moments. Tsai et al [3] developed a virtual reality orthopedic simulator which can simulate different orthopedic procedures including arthroplasty, corrective and open osteotomy, fusion, and open reduction. Peters [4] discussed the development of a virtual reality environment to assist surgeons in minimally invasive cardiac surgery. In [5], a virtual fixture technique was developed to support robotic cardiac catheter manipulation tasks. In [6], a simulation based approach is outlined to assist in pre-operative planning related to invasive cardiology. The overall emphasis of their research was to translate 2D imaging data into 3D visualization based environments which in turn could promote better understanding of cardiac morphology. In [7], the use of a virtual environment with haptic interface to train new surgeons in heart myoblast processes is discussed. In [7], a haptic enhanced virtual environment is outlined which can be used to train surgeons to improve hand-eye coordination as well as used to enhance a surgeon's teleoperation robot-assisted surgery skills. In [8], the use of 3D virtual fixtures to augment the visual guidance system with haptic feedback during minimally invasive heart surgery is detailed. In [9], an interactive simulator is described for real-time and tactile catheter navigation. The authors acknowledge that realistic simulation of cardiac intervention is still very challenging because of the complex and dynamic nature of the cardiac intervention process.

One of the most important aspects of simulating a virtual orthopedic simulator is modeling the drilling procedure. Vankipuram et al. [10] outlined their new drilling simulator which can be utilized for orthopedic surgery, and later reviewed the realization of the simulator using an experimental methodology by a group of surgery residents, experts, and beginners. Tsai et al [11] represented their model on calculating the drilling forces and modeling a real-like drilling procedure for an orthopedic surgery simulator. They used a 6DoF PHANTOM haptic device for the user's input concerning the drill angle, position, and speed. Sourina et al [12] developed a virtual orthopedic surgery simulator, called Virtual Bone Setter, capable of running on typical PCs, which can be used to train the surgery residents in correcting bone fractures. In [13], the development of a distributed virtual environment for orthopedic surgery is detailed. An information model of the LISS surgical process was first developed by closely interacting and interviewing orthopedic surgeons [14]. In [15], a virtual reality based training system for arthroscopic surgery is elaborated. The authors investigated the mechanical design, kinematics, dexterity measure, and control loop of haptic devices. They also discussed the organ mesh generation, tissue deformation simulation, and collision detection techniques. The manipulator mechanism with four degrees of freedom was developed and kinematic analysis of the manipulator was performed using direct and inverse kinematics analysis. The usable workspace of the manipulator was identified using Jacobian matrix and dexterity measures. A control system for the haptic device was developed for tracking the arthroscopic and the surgical instrument. They also further developed a knee model from visible human project (VHP), color images, and 3D meshes for finite element analysis to simulate a series of actions in the surgery. They also used a complex Finite Element Model (FEM) to deal with non-linear tissue deformation and topology changes. An advanced collision detection algorithm was used to detect virtual collisions between arthroscopic instruments and organs, and arthroscopic instruments and the arthroscopic during inspection or surgery

Laproscopic Surgery is another surgical field in which VR based simulators have been introduced. Azzie et al [16] developed and validated a pediatric laparoscopic simulator (PLS) subsequent to its adult laparoscopic counterpart. Makiyama et al [17] developed a virtual surgery simulator with the use in laparoscopic renal surgery. The simulator is patient specific; using the CT images of each individual person to build the volume model of the organ under consideration. The simulator enables the surgeon to perform the pre-operative rehearsal processes. The simulator discussed in [17] has been used by surgeons in ten cases in clinic centers and was reported as a useful tool for performing pre-operative rehearsal. Grantcharov et al [18] examined the impact of virtual reality (VR) surgical simulation on improvement of psychomotor skills relevant to the performance of laparoscopic cholecystectomy. Their research objective was to validate the role of VR simulation in surgical training by assessing the possibility of improvement and revision of surgical skills obtained through training in a VR simulation module and its replication in the physical operations. Aggarwal [19] et al. performed a survey about the attitude and willingness of the senior and junior surgeons toward the virtual reality laparoscopic simulators.

Other literature have discussed the attitude of surgeons towards the role of VR-based simulators and their use as training and planning tool in surgeries [20, 21]. Blyth et al [21] obtained feedback on two related aspects: (i) the first are the perceived requirements of a surgical simulator (ii) the second are the types of tasks which would benefit from the use of a surgical simulators. The results showed surgeons supported the use of simulators in general for surgery.

3   Design of the Virtual Surgery Environment (VSE)

Less Invasive Stabilization System (LISS) plating based surgery is an orthopedic surgery process which is used to address fractures on the human femur and other bones in the human body. Figure 1 depicts the use of LISS plating instruments used for surgery.

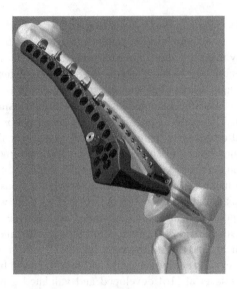

Fig. 1. View of an inserted LISS plate [9]

In this paper, we discuss the development of a virtual environment for LISS plating based surgery using a non-haptic environment. The virtual environments can be used in different modules such as training or evaluating the performance of surgery students.

The Virtual Surgery Environment (VSE) is a non-haptic environment which has been created using the Unity software engine. In this environment, the various steps of the LISS procedure have been simulated to enable medical residents to become more familiar with these surgical procedures. There are 2 basic windows in the Unity environment; the first window consists of the scene, and 3 other sub windows: hierarchy, project, and inspector (where the actual simulation modules are developed). The second window is the game window where the user can visualize and interact with the 'built' environment. Unity's intuitive workspace, and rapid productive workflow assists users to reduce the time, effort and cost of building interactive content. It is a fully integrated development engine that provides interactive 3D content. It is used to assemble the design and assets into scenes and environments. In addition, we can add lighting, audio, special effects, physics and animation in the model[22].

The Simulation based Environment has 2 segments for LISS plating related surgical training: (i) Training where the emphasis is on assembling the LISS plate (ii) Using the LISS plate and completing the surgery

3.1   Learning to Assemble the LISS Plate

The first part involves a medical resident or intern becoming familiar with the components and the assembly of the LISS plate itself. Our interest is to ensure that residents have a basic vocabulary and knowledge of the various components as well as know gain understanding of how to assemble this LISS plate used in the surgery. The first part of this module involves a resident being given an overview of the various surgical steps using both voice and text cues. Figure 2 provides a view of this virtual environment. The second part of the training module focuses on simulating the steps involved in assembling the LISS plate prior to use in the surgical process.

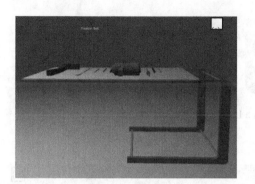

Fig. 2. View of the VSE showing the LISS Assembly process (text descriptions and cues are also provided as seen in this figure)

Unity software has a capability to accommodate various types of scripts to unite the assembling sequences in the real time environment. Some of the special scripts were applied on this surgical and LISS assembly simulation, namely textures, colors, appearance and audio. These scripts are used to improve the appearance and quality of the components and objects in the VSE. Control scripts were also placed on the model to support interaction with the virtual environment using mouse and keystrokes.

3.2   Virtual Surgery with Use of Assembled LISS Plate

The second module is an environment that allow users to practice the various surgery steps. The various steps include pre-operative planning, choice of implant (LISS), reduction, assembling of LISS insertion instrument, LISS plate insertion using hand, screw insertion, detach the insertion guide, and close the wounds. Users are provided both text and voice cues (figure 2 b). The key steps involving a LISS plate based surgical procedure are shown in Figure 3.

After performing the preoperative steps and choosing the proper implants for the observed fracture, the surgeon needs to attempt reduction of the fracture. This procedure usually is performed using hands or other specific reduction methods [23]. The next step in the surgery is the insertion of the LISS plate into its proper position under the skin while supporting the femur. The surgeon does this using the insertion guide which is assembled to the LISS plate before this step (figure 1). The next important step is to screw the LISS plate to the bone using different types of surgical screws. After the LISS plate is placed properly over the femur, the insertion guide can be detached from the LISS plate (figure 1).

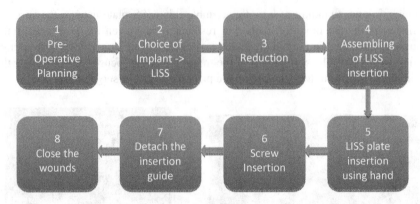

Fig. 3. Key Steps in a LISS plating based surgery

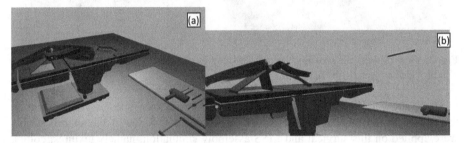

Fig. 4. View of the virtual environment built using Unity for the LISS plating based surgery process

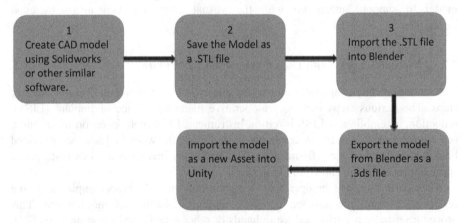

Fig. 5. Process of Importing 3D Model into Surgery Environment

Figure 4 (a) and (b) provides different views of the VSE. In figure 4 (a), a surgical table can be seen (on the left) with a model of the femur based on the age and sex of the patient; in the same figure, the surgical instruments can be seen on the right. Figure 4 (b) shows the automated view of the complete simulation process showing the LISS plating based surgical procedure. Figure 5 shows the process of creating and importing a 3D model into the virtual surgery environment. 3D modeling software can be used to design the object (exported as an .STL file). Subsequently, the .STL file was imported into a software called Blender. In Blender, the object or model can be exported as a .3DS file which is then imported into Unity (where the virtual surgery environment has been developed). The target objects (or design models) can be edited and scaled both in Blender and in Unity.

3.3   Virtual Surgery Interfaces

In [14], the authors had discussed a detailed information model of the LISS plating surgical process; this information model was built using eEML (the engineering Enterprise Modeling Language). This model was used as the basis to understand the LISS plating based surgical process which in turn served as the foundation to build the VSE.

Automated and practice (manual) modes of surgery environment can observe the desired steps in the surgery in a semi-automated manner; once he or she becomes familiar with the general steps. Then they can attempt to perform the surgical steps by themselves. The student can practice the LISS assembly and surgery procedures by using simple mouse and keystrokes in the VR Environment.

Both voice and text based instructions are used to guide beginner surgeons or residents when they practice the assembly of the LISS plate. Using basic navigation capabilities, a user can reposition a specific component in the LISS assembly to any location, navigate around an axis to see how a component is positioned or zoom in at a specific angle to have a closer look at an assembled set of components; as this is a network based simulation environment, an expert surgeon can gain control during a practice session and show a beginner surgeon or resident how complete a specific step in the desired manner. The text based descriptions of each component is also provided when the mouse hovers over a component is also provided (as seen in figure 2).

3.4   Network Based Interaction

The virtual environment can be linked using the emerging next generation Internet between a master surgeon and a medical student who may be in geographically distributed locations. This network based implementation is part of a US Ignite initiative which uses Global Environment for Network Innovations (GENI) networking concepts. GENI is a virtual laboratory at the frontiers of network science and engineering for exploring future internets at scale [24]. The networking architecture implemented enables users from different locations with separate instances of the virtual environment to control the simulation at one particular location [13]. Users placed at different remote locations have to connect to the main simulation over the Internet (Emulab). Each of the users has their own instance of the virtual environment, but the state of this environment is the same as the original one i.e., the display is the same. Initially, the control of the simulation lies with the

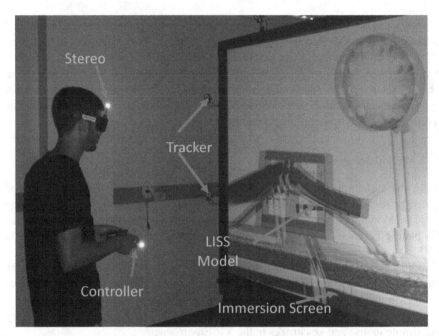

Fig. 6. An user interacting with the Virtual Surgical environment for LISS plating based surgery (the image appears a bit blurry as the models are projected in stereo; the user is wearing a stereo eyewear to see in 3D)

Fig. 7. Dr. Cruz (an orthopedic surgeon) using the VSE through a collaborative network

original user and this can be passed around to the other users. Consider the context of several users controlling the simulation over the Internet. It can be thought of as a token based approach. The token enables the user to control the simulation using the local virtual environment. The results of the user interaction will be reflected by the changes in the display of all the other users connected. Once the token has been passed to another user, the control of the simulation is also passed. All the end users that are participating in the simulation are connected to a server via the Internet (in this case EmuLab). A sensing and feedback module within the VSE enables the interaction with the software modules of the simulation and allows the simulation to be controlled from either the local input or the input over the network.

Using such a networked approach, the surgeon and his/her students do not have to be at the same physical location during the training. Each user is presented with his or her own instance of VSE. At any given instant, only one of the participants holds the control of VSE. The controlling participant may use his/her mouse (or potentially a haptic device) to carry out different surgical steps. The results of these steps are almost immediately visible in the VSE instance of every user (surgeon or resident). The user (who has control) can 'pass' the control to any other user b appropriate mouse commands.

Figure 7 shows a view of a surgeon interacting with the virtual surgical environment through the GENI framework. Our initial demonstrations with distributed users successfully highlighted the capabilities of using the VSE involving multiple users.

There are 2 versions of this surgical environment: non immersive running on PCs and an immersive environment that can be run on a Virtual Reality Powerwall (figure 6). In the immersive environment, a user can interact using 3D eyewear and a controller. The large screen has sensors and trackers with a back projector. This allows multiple users to interact while proposing surgical alternatives as well. Figure 6 shows a view of this environment.

The non-immersive version of the VSE was used in a pilot study with 6 orthopedic interns. A pre-test was administered prior to any instructions on performing the surgery. The interns then interacted with the virtual environment (focusing on the LISS plate assembly process). A post-test was then administered to evaluate the learning. Of the 6 interns, 3(or 50%) failed to demonstrate any significant improvement in the knowledge using the VSE. 3 (or 50%) of the 6 interns showed a dramatic improvement in their understanding and knowledge of the LISS plating based surgical process after interacting with the VSE. The semi immersive environment was not used in this pilot study. Additional modifications and tests are continuing involving the VSE.

4   Conclusion

This paper discussed the preliminary development of a virtual reality based environment for orthopedic surgery. The virtual environment can be accessed through a Next Generation network infrastructure which will enable surgeons and residents to interact from different locations. The initial implementation was demonstrated between surgeons and their staff interacting using haptic interfaces. Such a framework holds significant potential to impact medical education involving expert surgeons at distributed locations being able to teach and interact with medical residents (students) at other locations. It also lays the foundation for more advanced tele operation procedures where high gigabit information exchange is a necessity between collaborators at different locations.

Acknowledgments. We would like to acknowledge funding received from the National Science Foundation through grant number CNS 1257803 and the

Interdisciplinary Planning Grant program from Oklahoma State University (Office of the Provost). We would also like to acknowledge network resources provided by the GENI project (GPO) and US Ignite (as part of the GENI and US Ignite initiatives and demonstrations).

References

1. Qin, J., Pang, W., Chui, Y., Wong, T., Heng, P.: A Novel Modeling Framework for Multilayered Soft Tissue Deformation in Virtual Orthopedic Surgery. J. Med. Syst. 34, 261–271 (2010)
2. Delp, S.L., Loan, J.P.: A Graphics-Based Software System to Develop and Analyze Models of Musculoskeletal Structures. Comput. Biol. Med. 25(1), 21–34 (1995)
3. Tsai, M., Hsieh, M., Jou, S.: Virtual reality orthopedic surgery simulator. Computers in Biology and Medicine 31, 333–351 (2002)
4. Peters, T.M., Linte, C.A., Moore, J., Bainbridge, D., Jones, D.L., Guiraudon, G.M.: Towards a medical virtual reality environment for minimally invasive cardiac surgery. In: Dohi, T., Sakuma, I., Liao, H. (eds.) MIAR 2008. LNCS, vol. 5128, pp. 1–11. Springer, Heidelberg (2008)
5. Park, J.W., Choi, J., Park, Y., Sun, K.: Haptic Virtual Fixture for Robotic Cardiac Catheter Navigation. Artificial Organs 35(11), 1127–1131 (2011) ISSN 0160-564X
6. Sorensen, T.S., Therkildsen, S.V., Makowski, P., Knudsen, J.L., Pedersen, E.M.: A new virtual reality approach for planning of cardiac interventions. Artificial Intelligence in Medicine 22(3), 193–214 (2001)
7. Le, V.T., Nahavandi, S.: A Haptic Training Environment for the Heart Myoblast Cell Injection Procedure. In: Proceedings of the11th International Conference on Control, Automation, Robotics and Vision, Singapore, December 7-10, pp. 448–452 (2010)
8. Ren, J., Patel, R.V., McIsaac, K.A., Guiraudon, G., Peters, T.M.: Dynamic 3-D Virtual Fixtures for Minimally Invasive Beating Heart Procedures. IEEE Transactions on Medical Imaging 27(8), 1061–1070 (2008)
9. Yu, R., Zhang, S., Chiang, P., Cai, Y., Zheng, J.: Real-Time and Realistic Simulation for Cardiac Intervention with GPU. In: Proceedings of the 2010 Second International Conference on Computer Modeling and Simulation, vol. 3, pp. 68–72 (2010)
10. Vankipuram, M., Kahol, K., McLaren, A., Panchanathan, S.: A virtual reality simulator for orthopedic basic skills: A design and validation study. J. Biomed. Inform. 43(5), 661–668 (2010)
11. Tsai, M., Hsieh, M., Tsai, C.: Bone drilling haptic interaction for orthopedic surgical simulator. Computers in Biology and Medicine 37, 1709–1718 (2007)
12. Sourina, O., Sourin, A., Howe, T.S.: Virtual Orthopedic Surgery Training on Personal Computer. International Journal of Information Technology 6(1), 16–29 (2000)
13. Cecil, J., Ramanathan, P., et al.: Collaborative Virtual Environments for Orthopedic Surgery. In: Proceedings of the 9th Annual IEEE International Conference on Automation Science and Engineering (IEEE CASE 2013), Madison, WI (2013)
14. Cecil, J., Pirela-Cruz, M.: An information model for designing virtual environments for orthopedic surgery. In: Demey, Y.T., Panetto, H. (eds.) OTM 2013 Workshops 2013. LNCS, vol. 8186, pp. 218–227. Springer, Heidelberg (2013)
15. Zhang, G., Zhao, S., Xu, Y.: A virtual reality based arthroscopic surgery simulator. In: Proceedings of the 2003 IEEE International Conference on Robotics, Intelligent Systems and Signal Processing, vol. 1, pp. 272–277 (2003)

16. Azzie, G., Gerstle, J.T., Nasr, A., Lasko, D., Green, J., Henao, O., Farcas, M., Okrainec, A.: Development and validation of a pediatric laparoscopic surgery simulator. Journal of Pediatric Surgery 46, 897–903 (2011)
17. Makiyama, K., Nagasaka, M., Inuiya, T., Takanami, K., Ogata, M., Kubota, Y.: Development of a patient-specific simulator for laparoscopic renal surgery. International Journal of Urology 19, 829–835 (2012)
18. Grantcharov, T.P., Kristiansen, V.B., Bendix, J., Bardram, L., Rosenberg, J., Funch-Jensen, P.: Randomized Clinical Trial of Virtual Reality Simulation for Laparoscopic Skills Training. British Journal of Surgery 91, 146–150 (2004)
19. Aggarwal, R., Balasundaram, I., Darzi, A.: Training Opportunities and the Role of Virtual Reality Simulation in Acquisition of Basic Laparoscopic Skills. Journal of Surgical Research 145, 80–86 (2008)
20. Aggarwal, R., Balasundaram, I., Darzi, A.: Training Opportunities and the Role of Virtual Reality Simulation in Acquisition of Basic Laparoscopic Skills. Journal of Surgical Research 145, 80–86 (2008)
21. Blyth, P., Anderson, I.A., Stott, N.S.: Virtual Reality Simulators in Orthopedic Surgery: What Do the Surgeons Think? Journal of Surgical Research 131, 133–139 (2006)
22. Unity 3D game engine software for interactive design, http://unity3d.com/pages/create-games
23. LISS web site, http://www.synthes.com/MediaBin/International%20DATA/036.000.235.pdf
24. Global Environment for Network Innovations (GENI) networking concepts, http://www.geni.net

INBAST 2014 PC Co-Chairs Message

Semantic and knowledge-based technologies are steadily gaining momentum and they are currently achieving a certain degree of maturity. They provide a consistent and reliable basis to face challenges for the organization, manipulation and visualization of data and knowledge, thus playing a crucial role as the technological foundation for the development of a large number of Computational Intelligence systems.

INBAST 2014 is the third edition of the Industrial and Business Applications of Semantic Technologies and Knowledge-based information systems workshop series. The goal of the workshop series is the feasibility investigation of advanced Semantic and Knowledge-based methods and techniques, as well as their application in different domains such as in the run time of safety-critical live systems or in the design time engineering disciplines like software and systems engineering.

The workshop attracted a number of submissions, of which a total of 7 papers was accepted for presentation. The topics of the accepted papers cover a wide range of interesting application areas of semantic web technologies, such as Interoperability Assessment, Information Retrieval, Requirement Specification, Business Process Modeling, Customer Relationship Management, Opinion Mining and Fact-based modeling.

We would like to take this opportunity to thank the Program Committee members who agreed to review the manuscripts in a timely manner and provided valuable feedback to the authors. Finally, we want to thank the authors for their valuable contributions and insights.

September 2014

Rafael Valencia Garca
Ricardo Colomo Palacios
Thomas Moser

Referencing Modes and Ease of Validation within Fact-Based Modeling

Peter Bollen

Department of Organization & Strategy,
SBE, Maastricht University
p.bollen@maastrichtuniversity.nl

Abstract. In this article we will evaluate the different referencing modes in fact-based modeling and we will investigate to what extent the application of the fact based modeling methodology in a specific domain context has an impact on the choice of a referencing mode and under what conditions one referencing mode is preferred over another.

Keywords: Reference Mode, Nesting, Co-referencing, Flattening.

1 Introduction

Fact-based modeling (FBM) is a conceptual modeling approach for knowledge representation that has its roots in Falkenberg's 'Object-Role Model' [1, 2]. It was originally developed to overcome conceptual remodeling necessitated by the changing data base implementation technology in the 1960s and 1970s (i.e. hierarchical, network, relational) [3]. Researchers at Control Data Corporation [4] pioneered a modeling procedure together with a 'role-box' notation that could be used to instantiate the modeling constructs in any application area, by precisely applying the steps in the procedure (CSDP). The first-generation of fact-based modeling dialects, i.e. ENALIM [4, 5] and NIAM [6] were restricted to *binary* fact types. Another essential property of the earlier fact-based dialects was the distinction into Lexical Object Types (LOTs) and Non-Lexical Object types (NOLOTs). Two NOLOT's were associated in an *idea type* [6]. A referencing association between a NOLOT and a LOT was called a *bridge type* [6]. This distinction has lead to a referencing mode that is still available in a number of today's fact-based dialects: *co-referencing*. Subsequent fact-based dialects have incorporated the modeling construct of *nesting* (or *objectification*).

The objective of this article is to investigate the extent in which co-referencing and other referencing modes still exist in the current fact-based modeling dialects and how this effects the extent in which fact-based conceptual models can be validated by using a conceptual modeling procedure that guarantees semantic verification [7].

R. Meersman et al. (Eds.): OTM 2014 Workshops, LNCS 8842, pp. 289–298, 2014.

1.1   The Conceptualization Principle

In [8] the conceptualization principle is defined as follows:

'The conceptual schema must refer exclusively to rules of the UoD. Rules which govern the implementation of the information system must not be allowed to become part of the conceptual schema.'

In this article we will use the conceptualization principle as the first yard-stick to assess the quality of modeling constructs in a given fact-based modeling dialect.

2   Binary NIAM

In NIAM [6] a non-lexical objects is defined as: 'Real or abstract things in the object system which are non-utterable'. A lexical object is defined as:' Strings that can be uttered and which refer to an object'. NIAM distinguishes among 2 deep structures (or association types): *idea types* and *bridge types*. An idea type is an association between non-lexical objects and a bridge type is an association between a non-lexical object (NOLOT) and a lexical object (LOT). We will illustrate the modeling concepts in this article by a running example (based on [9]) that we will introduce here.

2.1   The Running Example: University Staff Languages Spoken Abroad

In this example we are interested in the language that university staff members have spoken abroad. We will give examples of instances of ground facts in this domain:

```
Staff member Peter B. has spoken English in the United States
      Staff member Peter B. has spoken English in Canada
Staff member Peter B. has spoken Spanish in the United States
Staff member Thijs M. has spoken English in the United States
```

These four ground facts constitute a significant set of instances with respect to the permitted states of the fact base. The communication pattern for this example can be generalized as follows:

```
AT1: Staff member <staff member name> has spoken <language>
                in <country>
```

In combination with the following naming convention fact types:

```
AT2: Staff member name <staff member name> identifies a
            member of the University staff
AT3: Language name <language name> identifies a language
            among the group of all languages
AT4: Country name <country name> identifies a country among
            the group of all countries
```

In (the 1982 version of) NIAM [6] the modeler needs to introduce a 'non-suspected' lexical object type to be able to express a ternary association (type) or a N-ary (N>2) association type in general. We will call this 'non-suspected' non-lexical object type in this example: *communication experience*. We must remark that this is a violation of the conceptualization principle. However, by introducing this additional object type in binary NIAM it will be possible to model the ternary association type AT1 as three binary fact types:

```
       FT5: Staff member <staff member name> took part in
  Communication experience <communication experience code>
FT6:Language <language name> is spoken during Communication
         experience <communication experience code>
 FT7:Communication experience <communication experience code>
          took place in Country <country name>
```

In order to populate association types FT5, FT6 and FT7 we need to introduce artificial identifiers in the form of 'communication experience codes'. The concept of communication experience is a 'non-suspected' lexical object type and is introduced because of the limitations of the (binary) NIAM conceptual modeling language. The limitation to binary fact types: '.. will sometimes lead to the specification of new non-lexical object types, not suspected at first..' [6]. The resulting NIAM 1982 conceptual schema is shown in figure 1.

In NIAM 1982 it is allowed to incorporate NOLOT's without an accompanying identifying LOT. Identification takes place by using the external uniqueness constraint and the total role constraints defined on the 'co-referenced' roles of the fact types (see figure 1). It should also be noted that the naming convention fact types AT2, AT3 and AT4 from our running example are modeled in NIAM 1982 using the 1:1 shortcut for the bridge types in which we have used the concentric circle symbols in which the outer circle is hyphenated: *Staff member* and *staff-member-name*, *Language* and *language-name*, *Country* and *country-name*.

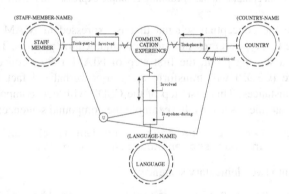

Fig. 1. Conceptual schema of running example expressed in NIAM 1982

This reliance on artificial entity types and 'phoney' naming conventions was considered a major inhibitor for the application of NIAM in industrial-scaled modeling projects, fact-based modeling evolved into a N-ary fact type modeling approach in the mid eighties [10, 11].

3   Nesting, Co-referencing and Flattening

In 1989 the first text book on N-ary NIAM was published:[12]. In this version of NIAM no longer a distinction was made into *idea types* and *bridge types*, but the abbreviated reference scheme that uses parentheses was given instead. However, the method describes how a 1:1 naming convention explicitly can be modeled as a *reference type* using label types. The main advancement of the NIAM 1989 text book was that the 'binary fact type only' restriction was removed and hence the resulting conceptual schemas could reflect the domain semantics to a higher extent. There was no longer a necessity to introduce 'non-suspected' NOLOT's or entity types let alone to introduce 'artificial naming conventions' for those non-suspected entity types. In figure 2 we have given the conceptual schema of our running example using the N-ary fact modeling conventions from NIAM 1989 [12]. We will call this way of referencing 'flat', since we will implicitly use the abbreviated referencing scheme for every entity type that plays (a) role(s) in the fact type.

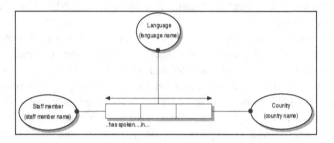

Fig. 2. Conceptual schema of running example expressed in NIAM 1989

If we analyze the conceptual schema that is expressed in NIAM 1989 we can conclude that the fact types represent atomic communication patterns. Taking the user verbalization as a starting point, the first step of NIAM 1989's conceptual schema design procedure (CSDP) will transform these user verbalized fact instances into elementary fact instances. This first step of the CSDP will 'cut' compound sentences into two or more atomic assertions, for example the compound sentence:

```
Staff member Peter B. has spoken English in the United States
            and has spoken English in Canada.
```

Will be split into two elementary sentences:

```
Staff member Peter B. has spoken English in the United States.
Staff member Peter B. has spoken English in Canada
```

Note that this transformation does not need the introduction of a 'non-suspected' entity type and an accompanying naming convention and therefore complies to the conceptualization principle [8].

Another modeling feature that was introduced in NIAM 1989 was the concept of *nesting* (or *nominalization*). An example of nesting is the situation in which the initial user verbalization is as follows:

```
Staff member Peter B. has visited the United States.
During that (those) visits he has spoken English.
```

In figure 3 we will illustrate how nesting (or nominalization) is expressed in a NIAM 1989 conceptual schema.

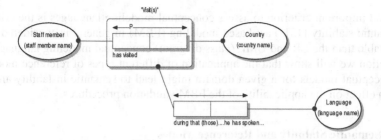

Fig. 3. Conceptual schema of running example expressed in NIAM 1989 using nesting

In NIAM 1989 the default constraint for an entity type that only plays one role in a conceptual schema is that such role is mandatory (even with the mandatory role symbol omitted). We note that the application of the nesting modeling construct is user-driven, i.e. the domain user explicitly acknowledges the existence of the nested or nominalized concept in the domain. So the application of the nesting concept in this way is in line with the conceptualization principle. It should also be noted that the nested 'object type' is information-bearing, e.g. it can be phrased as a sentence, e.g. *Staff member Peter B. has visited the United States.* In another fact-based dialect: FCO-IM [13] the concept of nesting is generalized into the nesting of unary fact types as 'existence-postulation' fact types for every object type.

In binary NIAM 1982 [6] all ternary or higher order association types need to be co-referenced. This implies that an analyst is forced to introduce entity types and naming conventions that were not conceptually contained in the Universe of Discourse. In [14] the term co-referencing was coined and was presented as one of three ways of representing objects and their identification: *nesting, co-referencing* and *flattening.* In [14] it is stated that the former three approaches to represent objects and their identification all map to the same relational schema.

In figure 4 we have given the co-referenced representation of our running example. Note that the conceptual schema in figure 4 is practically identical with the conceptual schema in figure 1, which contained the NIAM 1982, binary version of the model.

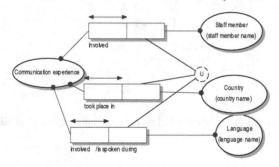

Fig. 4. Conceptual schema of running example expressed in NIAM 1989 using co-referencing

4   Semantic Stability, Validation Mechanisms and Referencing Modes

A second important criterion to assess conceptual modeling languages is the criterion of semantic stability [15]. Fact-based modeling (FBM) in general is considered to be more stable than the ER and UML (class diagram) conceptual modeling languages. In this section we will show that the application of different types of reference modes in the conceptual models for a given domain might lead to semantic instability and can have an effect on the applicability of the FBM validation procedures.

4.1   Semantic Stability and Reference Modes

Let's assume that we want to extend our Universe of Discourse (underlying figure 2) with the following communication patterns:

```
AT8: Staff member <staff member name> has visited <country>
AT9: That <visit> took place <number of times>
```

The integrated conceptual schema in NIAM 1989 of this extended UoD is given in figure 5, it now includes the new fact type and the objectification plus it shows the new (implied) mandatory role constraints that govern the extended UoD plus a subset constraint that states that each role combination of staff member and country in the 'language spoken' fact type must be a subset of the staff member, country pairs in the 'has visited' fact type. Let us now consider a situation in which our initial model has been modeled using co-referencing (figure 4) furthermore, the UoD is once again extended with the communication patterns AT8 and AT9 (see figure 6).

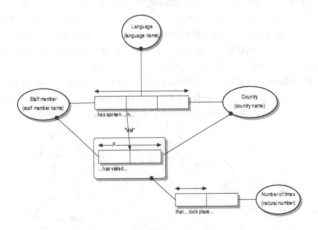

Fig. 5. Conceptual schema of extended running example expressed in NIAM 1989 I

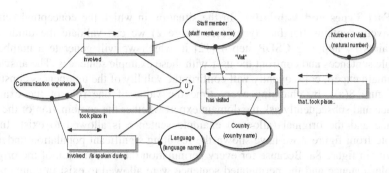

Fig. 6. Conceptual schema of extended running example expressed in NIAM 1989 II

The conceptual schema in figure 6 now includes the new fact type and the objectification plus it shows the new mandatory role constraints that govern the extended UoD. However, due to the choice for co-referencing it is not possible to use a sub-set constraint that enforces that a visit of a staff member to a country is a superset of the combination of *staff member in country has spoken language.*

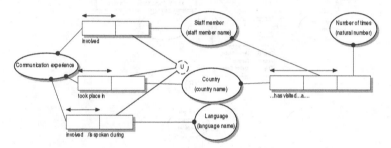

Fig. 7. Conceptual schema of extended running example expressed in NIAM 1989 III

As a third example to illustrate how the different reference modes interact we will once again consider the 'co-referenced' model from our running example in figure 4 and we will assume that our extended UoD is modeled using a flat fact type for the following communication pattern;

```
AT8': Staff member <staff member name> has visited <country>
                   a <number of times>
```

The integrated model is given in figure 7. Due to the choice for co-referencing the 'non-domain' entity type communication experience, it is not possible to use a sub-set constraint that enforces that a visit of a staff member to a country is a superset of the combination of *staff member in country has spoken language.*

4.2   Validation Mechanisms and Reference Modes

In this section we will investigate the relationship between the choice of reference mode and the extent in which we can use the conceptual schema design procedure to validate every outcome of a modeling (sub)step by confronting the domain expert with the in-between results in the language of the domain expert.

Flat Fact Types and Validation. In the situation in which the conceptual schema exclusively contains flat fact types (see figure 2) we can validate the uniqueness constraints by applying CSDP step 4 [12] in which we will generate a number of example sentences and confront the user with these example sentences. The answer of the domain expert, consequently will confirm the validity of the uniqueness constraint (see figure 8(a)), by changing every time the value of one role of the example sentence and subsequently ask the domain expert whether the combination of the new sentence and the original (allowed) example sentence is allowed to exist. In the example from figure 2 we have shown the resulting significant population under the fact type in figure 8a. Because for every permutation the combination of the original example sentence and the permutated sentence were allowed to exist in combination we have derived the 'default' uniqueness constraint that spans all N (=3) roles of the fact type (see figure 2). So flat fact types allow us to apply the CSDP in a straight-forward manner and thereby validate the conceptual schema at all times.

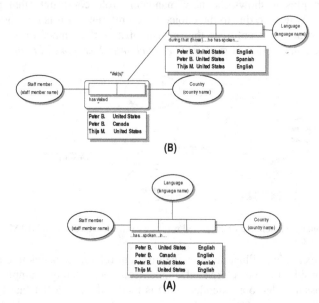

Fig. 8. Conceptual schema of extended running example expressed in NIAM 1989 IV

Nesting and Validation. When the nesting reference mode is used in the process of conceptual modeling we will substitute the N values of the objectification in the role that is played by the objectification by one 'concatenated value'. In figure 8(b), we have illustrated this application of the CSDP step 4 for our example from figure 3. In figure 8b we have shown the significant population for the nested version. In this case we have 2 significant populations, one for the population of the objectification itself and the other for the population of the association fact type. We note that in this situation we need to confront the user 2* 2= 4 times with pairs of example sentences to be able to derive the uniqueness constraints that govern the UoD. As a rule of thumb in a number of fact-based modeling dialects, the mere verbalization in the form of a nominalization implies a uniqueness constraint that spans all roles of the objectified fact type. However in FCO-IM nominalizations are allowed for which uniqueness constraints having an arity < N are allowed [16].

Co-referenced Object Types and Validation. In order to be able to model ternary or higher order communication patterns NIAM 1982 had to apply the concept of co-referencing in which 'non-obvious' domain concepts were introduced in tandem with 'artificial naming conventions'. We will now illustrate how the application of 'non-obvious' co-referenced object types will create validation problems when it comes to validating the uniqueness constraints. Let's consider the NIAM conceptual schemas in figure 1 and figure 4. What we notice right away is that the initial user verbalizations no longer are directly traceable in the schemas. Between CSDP step 1 (transform familiar information examples into elementary facts) and CSDP step 2 (draw a first draft of the conceptual schema diagram, and apply a population check) the NIAM analyst has to violate the conceptualization principle by introducing an artificial entity type *communication experience* and an artificial naming convention *communication experience code*. How can domain users validate the (proposed) uniqueness constraints in which an analyst permutates example sentences and from there draws conclusions with respect to the existence of non-existence of proposed uniqueness constraints, when the 'binarized' fact types do not directly reflect the actual domain semantics ? A domain expert can never validate such a model. The only way that validation can be done is by taking the N-ary flat fact types as a starting point and applying an explicit CSDP procedure [17, 18] and transform these results onto the co-referenced version of the conceptual schema.

Table 1. Summary reference modes

Criterion\mode	Flat	Nesting	Co-referencing
Conceptualization principle	*Complies*	*Complies, as long as objectifications are not forced upon users that communicate in a 'flat' way*	*Violates*
Semantic stability	*Complete additivity*	*Remodeling (nesting in retrospect might be required), when some domain experts adapt the objectified concept and some domain experts do not.*	*complete additivity*
Ease of validation	*Very good: efficient*	*Good (less efficient than flat fact types)*	*Not possible (only after transformation to flat form)*

5   Conclusion

We have shown that the 'flat' mode for referencing in which the entity types have an abbreviated referencing scheme will fully respect the conceptualization principle and will in general lead to models that are semantically stable. Only in those situations in which in another part of the domain a nominalization or objectification is made visible it might lead to remodeling, by 'splitting off' the objectified entity or nominalization from the initially modeled 'flat' fact types.

The nested reference mode basically allows us to treat 'compound' object types, i.e. entity types that have a multi-valued naming convention as entity types that have a simple naming convention. On the other hand when an integrated conceptual schema is created it will be possible that in a given fact type a concept is either modeled as a predicate (flat form) or as an objectification.

The co-referencing reference mode, however is a redundant modeling construct for the creation of conceptual schemas. We have seen that in order to validate, for example uniqueness constraints we have to use the flat or nested form in order to confront domain experts with real-life examples that they can accept or reject. In this situation, therefore, conceptually there is no need to transform such a N-ary fact type into a co-referenced format. In table 1 we have summarized our main findings.

References

1. Falkenberg, E.: Significations: the key to unify data base management. Information Systems 2, 19–28 (1976)
2. Falkenberg, E.: Concepts for modelling information. In: Modelling in Database Management Systems, North-Holland (1976)
3. Durchholz, R., Richter, G.: Information Management Concepts for use with DBMS interfaces. In: Modelling in Database Management Systems, North-Holland (1976)
4. Nijssen, G.: On the gross architecture for the next generation database management systems. In: Information Processing. IFIP (1977)
5. Nijssen, G.: A gross architecture for the next generation Database Management Systems. In: Nijssen, G. (ed.) Modelling in Database Management Systems, pp. 1–24. North-Holland (1976)
6. Verheijen, G., van Bekkum, J.: NIAM: An Information Analysis method. In: IFIP TC-8 CRIS-I Conference, North-Holland, Amsterdam (1982)
7. Bollen, P.: Enterprise resource planning requirements process: the need for semantic verification. LNCS (2013)
8. Griethuysen, J.: ISO, Concepts and terminology for the conceptual schema (1982)
9. Nijssen, G.: The first increment of the SIMF (2012)
10. Leung, C., Nijssen, G.: From a NIAM conceptual schema onto the optimal SQL relational database schema. Australian Computer Journal 19(2), 69–75 (1987)
11. Leung, C., Nijssen, G.: Relational Database design using the NIAM conceptual schema. Information Systems 13, 219–227 (1988)
12. Nijssen, G., Halpin, T.: Conceptual schema and relational database design: a fact oriented approach. Prentice-Hall, New-York (1989)
13. Bakema, G.P., Zwart, J.P., van der Lek, H.: Fully communication oriented NIAM. In: Nijssen, G., Sharp, J. (eds.) NIAM-ISDM 1994 Conference, pp. L1–L35. Albuquerque, NM (1994)
14. Halpin, T.: Conceptual Schema & Relational Database Design, 2nd edn. Prentice-Hall, Sydney (1995)
15. Halpin, T., Morgan, T.: Information Modeling and Relational Databases; from conceptual analysis to logical design, 2nd edn. San-Francisco, Morgan-Kaufman (2008)
16. Bakema, G., Zwart, J.P., van der Lek, H.: Fully Communication Oriented Information Modeling (FCO-IM) 2002: FCO-IM consulting
17. Bollen, P.: On the applicability of requirements determination methods. In: Management and Organization 2004. University of Groningen, Groningen. p. 219 (2004)
18. Bollen, P.: The natural language modeling procedure. In: Halevy, A.Y., Gal, A. (eds.) NGITS 2002. LNCS, vol. 2382, pp. 123–146. Springer, Heidelberg (2002)

Feature-Based Customer Review Summarization

Alessandro Maisto and Serena Pelosi

University of Salerno
Fisciano (SA), Italy
{maisto.ale,serenapalosi}@gmail.com

Abstract. To systematically monitor the online customer satisfaction means to deal with a large amount of non-structured data and with many Natural Language Processing challenges. The purpose of the present research is to automatically identify the benefits and the drawbacks expressed by internet users in Italian customer reviews in free text format. The work is grounded on Italian lexical and grammatical resources that, together, are able to investigate the semantic relation between the product features and the opinions expressed on them. On the base of these resources we built DOXA, a linguistic-based application that gives a feedback of statistics about the positive or negative nature of the opinions and about the semantic categories of the features.

Keywords: Sentiment Analysis, Opinion Mining, Feature Extraction.

1 Introduction

Internet offers the opportunity to build interactive relationships between firms and customers by empowering the exchange of information between these actors. The availability on the Web of a large quantity of information let the corporations direct their services and products to the appropriate targets with a greater precision [1]. Therefore, the increasing impact of the online word-of-mouth [2] and the growth of the user generated contents make it necessary a constant monitoring of the customer satisfaction expressed on the Web. This large amount of data is often non-structured and, as a result, its monitoring requires sophisticated NLP tools that must be able to pre-process it from its linguistic point of view and, then, automatically summarise its semantic content. The purpose of the present research is to provide companies with customer opinions overviews, automatically summarising the strengths and the weaknesses of their products and services.

Our contribution focuses on the automatic opinion feature extraction and summa-rization, which represents a task of the more general Sentiment Analysis research field. The features of a product (e.g. hotels) can be brand names (e.g. Artemide, Milestone), properties (e.g. cleanness, location), parts (e.g. rooms, apartments), related concepts (e.g. city), or parts of the related concepts (e.g. city centre, tube, museum, etc...) [3].

It is essential to discover not only the overall polarity of an opinionated document, but also its topic and features in order to discern the aspect of a product

R. Meersman et al. (Eds.): OTM 2014 Workshops, LNCS 8842, pp. 299–308, 2014.

that must be improved, or whether the opinions extracted by the Sentiment Analysis applications are relevant to the product or not. For example, (1), an extract from a hotel review, expresses two opinions (**O**) on two different kinds of features (**F**): the behaviour of the staff, and the beauty of the city in which the hotel is located.

(1)   [[Personale]**F** meravigliosamente accogliente.]**O** [[Roma] **F** è bellissima.]**O**
       "Staff wonderfully welcoming. Rome is beautiful."

It is crucial to distinguish between the two topics, because just one of them, the first one, refers to an aspect that can be influenced or improved by the company.

In this paper, Section 2 concisely recapitulates the most used techniques for the opinion features extraction and pruning. Section 3 introduces our approach, thanks to which we understand the relation between the features and the opinion expressed on them. Section 4 refers to the experimentation made up on a corpus of hotel reviews and presents the results achieved by our Sentiment application. The last Section summarises the future lines of action that our research will take.

2   State of the Art

The most used techniques aiming to find and summarise opinion features in costumer reviews anchor their extraction on opinion indicators. In general, most product features indicators are supposed to be nouns or noun phrases, while the words indicating the presence of opinions, adjectives among others, are often taken from opinion lexicons. The extraction is usually performed using both statistical and pat-tern-based techniques. Every kind of conceptual organization of the information extracted strongly reduces the redundancies by grouping together identical features and by organising the information on the base of their semantic relations. Ontologies are used by [4–8]. A pioneer work on feature-based opinion summarization is represented by [9]. Its average Precision of 72% and Recall of 80% have been enhanced in [10] eaching a Precision of 80% and a Recall of 89% thanks to the algorithm ClassPrefix-Span, which is based on the sequential pattern mining. [11] uses the Subsumption Hierarchy method and represents the features with Ngrams and lexico-syntactic extraction Patterns. By performing subsumption prior to feature selection, he achieved the best accuracy results ever: 99% on the [12] dataset. [3] uses the Web as a corpus to identify explicit and implicit features and Relaxation-labelling methods to infer the Semantic Orientation (SO) of words. In the opinion phrase polarity extraction task his software OPINE reached a Precision of 86% and a Recall of 89%. [7], using a dependency and semantic based approach, achieved a Precision of 73 % and a Recall of 79%. Double Propagation is another method that focuses on the natural relation between opinion words and features. The work proposed by [13] is based on part-whole patterns (meronymy) and "no" patterns. The systems results on 2000 sentences from every domain are 67% Precision and 60% Recall. [14] uses word relation features, such as unigrams, bigrams, and dependency relations. His best accuracy result (89%) has been reached with ensemble strategies. Concordance based feature extraction is the technique chosen by [15], that, thanks to hybrid patterns, obtained an average Precision of 79%, and a Recall of 72%. Candidate product features are selected employing noun phrases that appear in texts close to subjective adjectives. This intuition is shared with [16] and [17], who both propose a semantic method based on a list of positive and negative adjectives.

3 Method and Resources

In order to give our contribution to the resolution of the opinion feature extraction and selection tasks, performing them on a low-resourced language, like the Italian, we both exploited some pre-existing Italian lexical resources and built brand new resources on their base. The NLP software that has been chosen for the present work is Nooj(www.nooj4nlp.net), which allows both the language formalisation and the corpus processing. Electronic Dictionaries and Local Grammars are the resources that linguists can build with it, in order to parse texts and analyse their semantic content.

As concerns the lexical resources designed for the present work, we built two different kinds of dictionaries of simple words and a local grammar that, together, are able to recognise the simple sentences or the noun phrases that in costumer reviews are expression of sentiment. The first dictionary is what is commonly called an opinion lexicon; with it our software can extract different kinds of opinion expressions. The second one is an objective dictionary that describes its lemmas with appropriate semantic properties; it has been used to define and summarise the features on which the opinion holder expressed his opinions.

In order to identify the relations between opinions and features, the lexical items contained in the just mentioned dictionaries have been systematically recalled into a Nooj local grammar, that provides, as feedback, annotations about the (positive or negative) nature of the opinion and about the semantic category of the features. The Nooj resources created for the feature-based sentiment analysis and DOXA, our sentiment application, will receive an exhaustive description in the next paragraphs.

3.1 Subjective and Objective Lexical Resources

In this work the feature identification is anchored on the subjective expressions indicating opinions. Because the Italian language is not equipped with evaluated and freely available wordlists, a Sentiment Lexicon has been built from scratch by read-ing the Nooj Italian dictionaries of simple words, by excluding the words with a neutral meaning and by weighting the Prior Polarity [19] of the words endowed with a positive or negative Semantic Orientation. Every sentiment word has been weighed combining the labels POS "positive", NEG "negative", FORTE "intense" and DEB "weak". That produced an evaluation scale that goes from -3 (intensely negative) to +3 (intensely positive) and a strength scale from -1 (weak) to +1 (intense). While the dictionaries of adjectives (5000+ entries), verbs (600+ entries) and nouns (1000+ entries) have been manually annotated, the polarity of the adverbs (3600+ entries) has been automatically derived from the adjectives of sentiment that had a morpho-phonological relation with them (e.g. *vigoroso* "vigorous" → *vigoros-a-mente* "vigorous-ly"). In the end, 500+ Italian frozen sentences containing adjectives have been evaluated and then formalised with a pair of dictionary-grammar that is able to describe expressions that can reach high levels of variability[1]. An example of the Sentiment Lexicon, written with the Nooj formalism is reported in Figure 1(a).

S-Lemma	Category	FLX	DRV	Sent	Int
divertente	A	N79	ISSIMO:N88	POS	
accettabile	A	N79	ISSIMO:N88	POS	DEB
sommessamente	AVV				DEB
vigorosamente	AVV				FORTE
rammollimento	N	N5		NEG	DEB
biasimare	V	V3		NEG	
angosciare	V	V4		NEG	FORTE
amare	V	V3		POS	FORTE

S-Lemma	Category	FLX	SynSem
accappatoio	N	N12	Conc+Nindu
camera	N	N41	Conc+Nedi
colazione	N	N46	Conc+Ncibo
hotel	N	N165	Conc+Nedi
materasso	N	N5	Conc+Narr
piscina	N	N41	Conc+Nedi
televisione	N	N46	Conc+Ndisp
vino	N	N5	Conc+NliqBev

(a) *Extract of the Opinion Lexicon.*   (b) *Extract of the Dictionary of Concrete Nouns.*

Fig. 1. Extract of Dictionaries

Every lemma, classified on the base of its Part of Speech, is associated with inflec-tional ("FLX"), derivational ("DRV") and semantic (in this case polarity "Sent" and intensity "Int") properties. The objective lexicon consists in a Nooj dictionary of concrete nouns (Figure 1(b)), that has been manually built and checked by seven linguists; it counts almost 22.000 nouns described from a semantic point of view by labels ("Hyper") that specify every lemmas hyperonym.

3.2   Grammatical Resources

Thanks to the functionalities of Nooj, it has been possible to create a connection between these dictionaries and a Nooj syntactic grammar that takes the shape of a Finite State Transducer, a graph that represents specific patterns of texts and associates the recognised sequences with specific analysis results [20].

As shown in Figure 2, in the Feature Extraction phase the sentences or the noun phrases expressing the opinions on specific features are found in free texts. The annotations regarding their polarity (benefit/drawback) and their intensity (score, from -3 to +3) are attributed to each sentence on the base of the opinion words on which they are anchored.

---

[1] Among the idioms considered we count the *N0 Agg come C1* (e.g. Mary è bella come il sole, "Mary is as beautiful as the sun"); *N0 essere (Agg + Ppass) Prep C1* (e.g. Max è matto da legare, "Max is so crazy he should be locked up"); *N0 essere Agg e Agg* (e.g. Max è bello e fritto, "Max is cooked"); *C0 essere Agg (come C1 + E)* (Mary ha la coscienza sporca ↔ La coscienza è sporca, "Mary has a guilty conscience" ↔ "The conscience is guilty"), *N0 essere C1 Agg* (Mary è una gatta morta, "Mary is a cock tease").

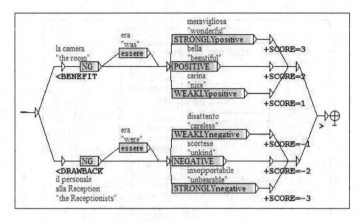

Fig. 2. Feature Extraction grammar

The graph reported in Figure 3 represents just an extract of the more complex Recursive Transition Network [20] built to perform the task, which includes more than 100 embedded graphs and thousands of different paths able to describe not only the sentences and the phrases anchored on sentiment adjectives, but also the ones that contain sentiment adverbs, nouns, verbs, idioms and other lexicon-independent sentiment expressions (e.g. *essere un (aspetto + nota + cosa + lato) negativo* "to be a negative side").

The Contextual Valence Shifters [21] that have been considered are Intensification, Negation, Modality and Comparison [22].

Differently from the other approaches proposed in Literature, the Feature Pruning task (Figure 3), in which the features extracted are grouped together on the base of their semantic nature, is performed in the same moment of the Extraction phase, just applying once the dictionaries-grammar pair to free texts. That happens because the grammar shown in Figure 4 is contained into the metanode "NG" (Nominal Group) of the feature extraction grammar.

The nouns that have been described in our objective dictionary as belonging to the same hyperonym receive the same annotation thanks to the instructions contained in this subgraph. The words labelled with the tags "Narr" (furniture, e.g. "bed") and "Nindu" (article of clothing, e.g. "bath towel") are annotated as "furnishings" (first path); the words labelled with the tags "Ncibo" (food e.g. "cake") and "NliqBev" (potable liquid substance, e.g. "coffee") receive the annotation "foodservice" (second path), and so on.[2]

In order to perfect the results we also included directly in the nodes of the grammar the words that were important for the feature selection, but that were not contained in the dictionary of concrete nouns (abstract nouns e.g. *pranzo* "lunch", *vista* "view"); and the hyperonyms themselves that, in general,

---

[2] Clearly, also the graph of Figure 3 is a simplification of the more detailed one incorporated in the real grammar, that in its complete version includes feature classes reported in Figure 3.

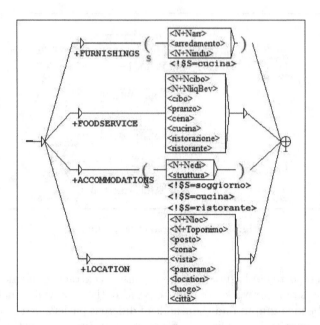

Fig. 3. Feature Selection grammar

correspond with each feature class name (e.g. *arredamento* "furnishings", *luogo* "location").

Finally, we disambiguated terms that in the objective dictionary were associated to more than one tag by excluding the wrong interpretations from the corresponding node. For example, in the domain of hotel reviews, if one comments the *cucina* "cooking" (first path) he is clearly not talking about rooms (in Italian *cucina* means also "kitchen"), but, respectively, about the food service and the whole holiday experience.

4   Experiment and Evaluation

The annotations provided by Nooj, once the lexical and grammatical resources are applied to texts written in natural language, can be on the form of XML tags. For this reason, they can be effortlessly recalled into an application that automatically applies the Nooj *ad hoc* resources and makes statistical analyses on them. So, we built DOXA a linguistic-based Sentiment application written in JAVA. It has been applied on a corpus composed of 1000 hotel reviews collected from websites like www.tripadvisor.it, www.expedia.it and www.booking.com. An extract[3] of the automatically annotated corpus is reported below.

---

[3] "I happened to be in this hotel after an accident and I must admit that if it hadnt been for the willingness, the kindness and the competence of Mario, Pino and Rosa I couldnt have solved a number of things. The hotel is fantastic, silent and definitely clean. Great the breakfast and very kind the responsible of the breakfast room"

Sono stato in questo albergo quasi per caso, dopo aver subito un incidente e devo ammettere che se non fosse stato per ⟨BENEFIT TYPE = "ATTITUDES" SCORE = "2"⟩la disponibilità⟨/BENEFIT⟩ , ⟨BENEFIT TYPE = "ATTITUDES" SCORE = "2"⟩la cortesia⟨/BENEFIT⟩ e ⟨BENEFIT TYPE = "ATTITUDES" SCORE = "2"⟩la professionalità⟨/BENEFIT⟩ di Mario, Pino e Rosa non avrei potuto risolvere una serie di cose. ⟨BENEFIT TYPE = "ACCOMMODATIONS" SCORE = "3"⟩L'hotel fantastico⟨/BENEFIT⟩, ⟨BENEFIT TYPE = "LOCATION" SCORE = "2"⟩silenzioso⟨/BENEFIT⟩ e ⟨BENEFIT SCORE = "3" TYPE = "CLEANLINESS"⟩decisamente pulito⟨/BENEFIT⟩. ⟨BENEFIT TYPE = "FOODSERVICE" SCORE = "3"⟩La colazione ottima⟨/BENEFIT⟩ ed ⟨BENEFIT TYPE = "ATTITUDES" SCORE = "3"⟩il responsabile della sala colazione gentilissimo⟨/BENEFIT⟩.

The evaluation presented in Table 1 shows that the method proposed in the present work performs very well with the hotel domain. We manually calculated, on a sample of 100 documents from the original corpus, the Precision on the Semantic Orientation Identification task (are the sentences polarity and intensity evaluated in the right way?) and on the Feature Classification task (is the type of the feature correctly annotated?).

Table 1. Evaluation of the tool

%	Precision		Recall	F-measure
	SO identification	Classification		
No residual category	93,3	92,4	72,3	81,1
Residual category	92,9	82,6	78,3	80,4

Because the classes used to group the features have been identified *a priori* in our grammar, we also checked the results of our tool with the introduction of a residual category to annotate the features that do not belong to these classes. Even though that causes an increase on the Recall, a commensurate decrease of the Precision in the Classification task makes the value of the F-measure similar to the one reached when the residual category is not taken into account. Significant examples of the sentences that have been automatically annotated in our corpus are given below:

(2)   Il responsabile della sala colazione gentilissimo (BENEFIT TYPE="ATTITUDES" SCORE="3")
       "Very kind the responsible of the breakfast room"

(3)   Le camere erano sporche (DRAWBACK TYPE="CLEANLINESS" SCORE="-2")
       "The rooms were dirty"

(4)   L'hotel è vicinissimo alla metro (BENEFIT TYPE="LOCATION" SCORE="3")
       "The hotel is really close to the tube"

In (2) the subjective adjective *gentilissimo* "very kind", recognised by the grammar as the superlative form (score 3) of the positive adjective *gentile* (score 2), makes the grammar recognise the whole sentiment expression and provides the in-formation regarding its polarity and intensity. That is why the Finite State Transducer associates the tag "benefit" and the higher score to the feature that, in that case, is represented by a noun.

In (3) is shown that the "type" of the features can be indicated not only by names, but also by specific adjectives, as happens with sporche "dirty", that is both an opin-ion word that specifies that the whole expression is negative, and a feature class indicator that let the grammar classify it in the group of "cleanliness" rather than in the group of "accommodations" (that, instead, would be selected by the noun camera "room", described in our objective dictionary with the tags Conc "concrete" and Nedi "building").

In the end, sentence (4) attests the strength of the influence of the review domains: sometimes the lexicon is not enough to correctly extract and classify the product features. Domain-specific lexicon independent patterns are often required in order to make the analyses adequate [23, 24].

4.1 Multi-document Opinion Visual Summarization

Doxa is a prototype able to analyse opinionated documents from their semantic point of view. It automatically applies the Nooj resources to free texts, it sums up the values corresponding to every sentiment expression, standardizes the results for the total number of sentiment expressions contained in the reviews and, then, provides statistics about the opinions expressed.

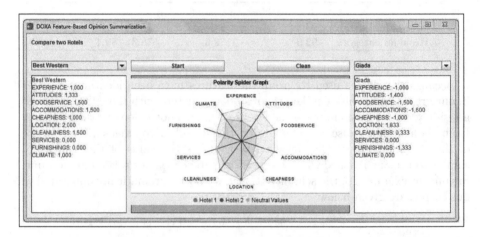

Fig. 4. Opinion Visual Summarization with Doxa

In its basic version Doxa performs both the sentence-level and the document-level Sentiment Classification reaching an average F-measure of 71,4% on the first task and of the 84,1% on the second task on a multi-domain corpus [22].

In this paper we improve the functionalities and the performances of the software by introducing the sentiment analysis based on the opinion features. In the Hotel domain, this deeper analysis considerably increases the Precision on the sentences-level SO identification task, that goes from 81,3% to 93,3%, without any loss in the Recall, that holds steady, just rising of 0,2 percentage points (from 72,% to 72,3%). The feature-based module of Doxa, completely grounded on the automatic analysis of free texts, allows the comparison between more than one object on the base of different kinds of aspects that characterize them.the regular decagon in the centre of the spider graphs of Figure 3 represents the threshold value (zero) with which every group of opinion on the same object is compared: when a figure is larger than it, the opinion is positive; when it is smaller the opinion is negative; when a features value is zero it means that the consumers did not express any judgement on that topic.

5 Conclusion and Future Work

The automatic transformation of non-structured reviews in structured visual summaries has a strong impact on the work of company managers that must ground their marketing strategies on the analysis of a large amount of information, and on the individual consumers that need to quickly compare the Pros and Cons of the products or services they want to buy. For this reason, the present research focused on the automatic identification and summarization of the benefits and the of drawbacks expressed by internet users in customer reviews. We tested our approach on a dataset of hotel reviews and we obtained satisfactory results. In future works we plan to face the limitations of our tool by enlarging our dataset on more domains and by enhancing our subjective and objective resources. In detail, we will add semantic annotation also to the Italian dictionary of Abstract nouns, that will supplement the Concrete nouns dictionary in the Feature Pruning stage. Furthermore, we will include other semantic relations, such as synonymy or antonymy, in our dictionaries. Because the Italian module of Nooj is not already provided with information of that sort, in this work we simply listed into a grammar node all the words related to a semantic concept (see Figure 3). Anyway, planning to extend the present work on other domains means working in this direction.

References

1. Pride, W., Ferrel, O.: Foundations of Marketing. Houghton Mifflin Company, Boston (2004)
2. Vollero, A.: E-Marketing e web communication. Verso la gestione della corporate reputation on-line. Giappichelli (2010)
3. Popescu, A.M., Etzioni, O.: Extracting product features and opinions from reviews. In: Natural language processing and text mining, pp. 9–28. Springer, London (2007)
4. Zhao, L., Li, C.: Ontology based opinion mining for movie reviews. In: Karagiannis, D., Jin, Z. (eds.) KSEM 2009. LNCS, vol. 5914, pp. 204–214. Springer, Heidelberg (2009)
5. Ghobadi, A., Rahgozar, M.: An Ontology based Semantic Extraction Approach for B2C eCommerce. The International Arab Journal of Information Technology 8(2), 163–170 (2011)

6. Holzinger, W., Krüpl, B., Herzog, M.: Using ontologies for extracting product features from web pages. In: Cruz, I., Decker, S., Allemang, D., Preist, C., Schwabe, D., Mika, P., Uschold, M., Aroyo, L.M. (eds.) ISWC 2006. LNCS, vol. 4273, pp. 286–299. Springer, Heidelberg (2006)
7. Somprasertsri, G., Lalitrojwong, P.: Mining Feature-Opinion in Online Customer Reviews for Opinion Summarization. J. UCS 16(6), 938–955 (2010)
8. Carenini, G., Ng, R.T., Zwart, E.: Extracting knowledge from evaluative text. In: Proceedings of the 3rd International Conference on Knowledge Capture, pp. 1–18. ACM (2005)
9. Hu, M., Liu, B.: Mining opinion features in customer reviews. In: AAAI, vol. 4, pp. 755–760 (2004)
10. Hu, M., Liu, B.: Opinion Feature Extraction Using Class Sequential Rules. In: AAAI Spring Symposium: Computational Approaches to Analyzing Weblogs, pp. 61–66 (2006)
11. Riloff, E., Patwardhan, S., Wiebe, J.: Feature subsumption for opinion analysis. In: Proceedings of the 2006 Conference on Empirical Methods in Natural Language Processing, pp. 440–448. Association for Computational Linguistics (2006)
12. Wiebe, J., Wilson, T., Bruce, R., Bell, M., Martin, M.: Learning subjective language. Computational Linguistics 30(3), 277–308 (2004)
13. Zhang, L., Liu, B., Lim, S.H., O'Brien-Strain, E.: Extracting and ranking product features in opinion documents. In: Proceedings of the 23rd International Conference on Computational Linguistics: Posters, pp. 1462–1470 (2010)
14. Xia, R., Zong, C.: Exploring the use of word relation features for sentiment classification. In: Proceedings of the 23rd International Conference on Computational Linguistics: Posters, pp. 1336–1344 (2010)
15. Khan, K., Baharudin, B.B., City, T.: Identifying Product Features from Customer Reviews using Lexical Concordance (2012)
16. Khan, K., Baharudin, B., Khan, A.: Identifying Product Features from Customer Reviews Using Hybrid Dependency Patterns (2012)
17. Zhang, L., Liu, B.: Identifying Noun Product Features that Imply Opinions. In: ACL (Short Papers), pp. 575–580 (2011)
18. Wei, C.P., Chen, Y.M., Yang, C.S., Yang, C.C.: Understanding what concerns consumers: a semantic approach to product feature extraction from consumer reviews. Information Systems and E-Business Management 8(2), 149–167 (2010)
19. Osgood, C.E.: The measurement of meaning, vol. 47. University of Illinois press (1957)
20. Silberztein, M.: NooJ manual (2003), http://www.nooj4nlp.net
21. Polanyi, L., Zaenen, A.: Contextual valence shifters. In: Computing attitude and affect in text: Theory and applications, pp. 1–10. Springer, Netherlands (2003)
22. Maisto, A., Pelosi, S., Guglielmo, D.: A Lexicon-Based Approach to Sentiment Analysis. In: International Nooj 2014 Conference, Book of Proceedings of the Italian Module for Nooj (2014)
23. Engstrm, C.: Topic dependence in sentiment classification. Unpublished MPhil Dissertation. University of Cambridge (2004)
24. Andreevskaia, A., Bergler, S.: When Specialists and Generalists Work Together: Overcoming Domain Dependence in Sentiment Tagging. In: ACL, pp. 290–298 (2008)

A Knowledge-Based Platform for Managing Innovative Software Projects

Miguel Ángel Rodríguez-García[1], Rafael Valencia-García[1],
Gema Alcaraz-Mármol[2], and César Carralero[3]

[1] Departamento de Informática y Sistemas,
Universidad de Murcia, Campus de Espinardo 30100 Murcia, Spain
miguelangel.rodriguez,valencia}@um.es
http://www.um.es
[2] Departamento de Lenguas Modernas,
Universidad Católica de Murcia, Murcia, Spain
galcaraz@ucam.edu
http://www.ucam.edu
[3] Quality Objects S.L.,
C\Santa Leonor 65, Edif C, 2 Izq. Madrid, Spain
ccarralero@qualityobjects.com
http://www.qualityobjects.com

Abstract. Innovation is one of the keys to success in the business world.
More concretely, open innovation is gaining momentum so different tools
for supporting the collaboration between experts and developers in this
field are needed. On the other hand, ontologies and semantic technologies provide a consistent and reliable means to represent and aggregate
knowledge from different sources. In this paper, an open innovation platform based on social networks and semantic web technologies to assist in
managing innovative software projects is proposed. The platform takes
advantage of semantic information that can be classified and annotated
by means of domain ontologies. The behaviour of the system has been
illustrated through a use case scenario in the software development domain.

Keywords: open innovation, ontologies, semantic annotation,
knowledge-based systems, knowledge management.

1 Introduction

Innovation means bringing new solutions to satisfy the needs of individuals and
society. In particular, the need for innovation is more relevant to the companies
that want to surpass their competitors. The innovation process in a company is
based on a set of processes and procedures used to ensure that the organization
makes all necessary tasks in order to achieve its objectives. This process can
be based on internal or external sources of knowledge depending on the model
of innovation used by the company. Internal Research and Development (R&D)

R. Meersman et al. (Eds.): OTM 2014 Workshops, LNCS 8842, pp. 309–318, 2014.

can be seen as a strategic asset or a barrier to competitive entry depending on the size of industry where the model is applied. In the case of large industries with significant resources and longterm research programs, internal R&D is developed, but in smaller or medium-sized enterprises it is necessary to work with highly prepared staff inside and outside the company [1]. Nowadays, companies know that taking advantage of external sources of technology into a company's innovation process increases the number of possible sources of innovation [2]. In most cases, the competitive advantage comes from the practice of leveraging the discoveries of other company needs not only their own R&D [3].

Open innovation is a paradigm that assumes that firms can and should use external ideas as well as internal ideas, and use purposive inflows and outflows of knowledge in order to accelerate internal innovation, and expand the markets for external use of innovation [1]. Open innovation assumes that internal ideas can also be taken to market through external channels, outside a firm's current business, to generate additional value. [2].

Although the era of open innovation has begun for many firms, there is no clear understanding of the mechanisms, inside and outside the organization, as well as when and how to fully profit from the concept [4]. In this line, the work proposed in this paper presents a social network as a platform to exploit both channels of knowledge.

On the other hand, semantic technologies provide a consistent and reliable basis to face the challenge of organizing, manipulating and visualizing data and knowledge. Consequently, the possibility of using knowledge-oriented query answering to exploit the benefits of semantics has become a top-class research challenge.

Ontologies are the paramount technology of the semantic web. An ontology can be defined as "a formal and explicit specification of a shared conceptualization" [5]. In this work, the Web Ontology Language (OWL), which is the W3C standard for representing ontologies in the Semantic Web, has been used to represent the concepts and features of the application domain. Knowledge in OWL ontologies is mainly formalized by using five kinds of components: classes, datatype properties, object properties, axioms and individuals.

This paper presents a social semantic web based on a platform to assist in managing and evaluation of innovative ideas of software projects. The rest of the paper is organized as follows. The components that take part in the platform and its overall architecture are described in Section 2. In Section 3, a use case scenario in the software development domain is shown. Finally, conclusions and future work are put forward in Section 4.

2   Platform Architecture

The main function of the system proposed here is to manage external cooperation in innovative software projects. On the one hand, the social network platform stores information of software companies, workers and collaborators such as the projects in which they have been involved, the proposals derived from innovative workers' ideas and their curricula. All this information is kept on three repositories: the relational database that supports the social network, the ontology repository which stores the semantics descriptions, and the annotation repository which contains the semantics annotations of these elements.

The architecture of the proposed knowledge-based platform is shown in Fig 1. The platform is composed of three main components: the social network, ontology repository and annotation repository. In a nutshell, the system works as follows: The company data and workers' data such as software projects, proposals and curricula are semantically described by means of ontologies and stored in the ontology repository. This information is also semantically annotated and indexed by means of the annotation repository. When a new user, organization, software proposal or project is inserted into the system, a semantic description is created and a semantic index is built. The semantic information is used by the system in the searching process to obtain profiles that are similar to others. For example, the system can obtain the projects, proposals and people that are similar to a specific innovative project based on the semantic similarity of the profiles.

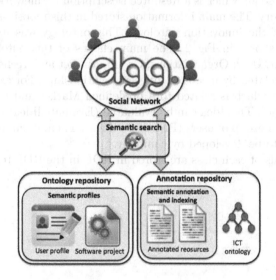

Fig. 1. System architecture

2.1   Social Network

Elgg is an award-winning open social networking engine that provides a robust framework in which several kinds of social environments can be built. The framework combines a number of social media tools such as: blogging, file upload and sharing, RSS feeds, social bookmarking and social networking for personal and group use.

The main objective of the social network component is to provide the user with an interface and other social networking services. It connects people who share interests and activities related to innovative software proposals and projects. The social network can be seen as a huge container of information where companies and workers store different types of information about previous software ideas and projects. This data is stored in two repositories: Elgg's relational database, which contains information related to the social network infrastructure such as users profiles, relationships and comments, among others; and the semantic repository, where this information is transformed in RDF triples according to the ontological model which is explained in detail in the next section. That is to say, the social network offers a facade that allows users to interact, providing them with an interface of the platform.

2.2   Ontology Repository

The main objective of this module is to store the ontologies used by the system so that each entity in the social network can be described. This module is implemented in Virtuoso [6], which is a Resource Description Framework (RDF)-based semantic repository. The main information stored in this repository corresponds to individuals of the innovation ontology. This ontology was implemented in OWL and it is shown in Fig 2. The main classes of this ontology are Idea, Proposal, Project, User, Organizations, Group, Market and Techonology. These classes are interrelated by means of different relationships. For example, a User proposes an Idea which is related to a predefined Market and implements different Technologies. This Idea can be evaluated (EvaluatedIdea) and selected to be developed by a group of users (PreselectedIdea). Then, it can be transformed into a Proposal to be developed by company.

The individuals of each class are stored in RDF in the RDF repository.

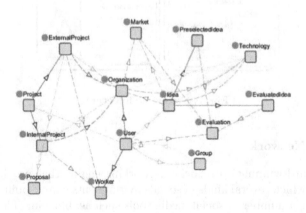

Fig. 2. An excerpt of the innovation ontology

2.3   Annotation and Indexing Module

This module is in charge of maintaining and creating the semantic annotations and indexes. The input received by this module corresponds to a specific domain ontology, an Information Communication Technology (ICT) ontology in our case, and the natural language descriptions and documents of each individual or semantic profile that are defined in the innovation ontology (i.e. Idea, Project, User, etc.). These natural language texts are then semantically annotated and indexed with the classes and instances of the domain ontology. In this case, the domain corresponds to information and communication technology (ICT). Therefore, an ontology describing this domain has been developed.

The first problem with defining this domain is related to the organization of the information in the interest domain, especially as regards its structure. Both problems were solved so that other information source could be reused to structure and organize the information domain. This information source is the Wikipedia website, which has been our main information provider. Wikipedia is one of the biggest information containers on the Internet. We have focused on the design of an extraction process to facilitate the recovering and organization of the information of the domain at issue.

As it has been stated before, this module is formed by two different stages. First, the semantic annotations are extracted from these natural language texts by using a set of natural language processing (NLP) tools, and they are in accordance with the domain ontologies. This process is based on the methodology presented in [7], which is divided into two main stages: (i) identification, and (ii) classification. During the identification phase, the most relevant linguistic expressions are identified by means of statistical approaches based on the syntactic structure of the text. Then, during the classification stage, the system attempts to determine whether each linguistic expression is an individual of a class within the domain ontology. The semantic representation module carries out these tasks by making use of the GATE framework.

Once the semantic annotation has been completed, the system retrieves all the annotated knowledge and attempts to create fully-filled annotations with these elements. This step is based on the work presented in [8]. The annotation of each semantic profile is stored in a database and is assigned a weight, which reflects how relevant the ontological entity is for the profile meaning. Weights are calculated by using the TF- IDF algorithm [9], which is shown in Eq. (1):

$$(tf - idf)_{i,p} = \frac{n_{i,p}}{\sum_k n_{k,p}} * \log \frac{|P|}{N_i} \tag{1}$$

where $n_{i,p}$ is the number of occurrences of the ontological entity i in the semantic profile p, $\sum_k n_{k,p}$ is the sum of the occurrences of all the ontological entities identified in the semantic profile p, $|P|$ is the set of all documents and N_i is the number of all documents annotated with i.

In this scenario, an index is calculated for each semantic profile based on the adaptation of the classical vector space model presented in [8]. Each semantic profile is represented as a vector in which each dimension corresponds to a separate ontological concept of the domain ontology. The value of the dimension of each ontological concept is calculated as follows (see Eq. (2)):

$$(v_1, v_2, ..., v_n)_p \quad where \quad v_i = \sum_{j=1}^{n} \frac{tf - idf_{j,p}}{e^{dist(i,j)}} \qquad (2)$$

where $dist(i,j)$ is the semantic distance between the concept i and concept j in the domain ontology. This distance is calculated by using the taxonomic (sub-class_of) relations of concepts in the domain ontology. Thus, the distance between a concept and itself is 0, the distance between a concept and its taxonomic parent or child is 1, and so on and so forth.

2.4 Semantic Profile Similarity Detection Module

It can occur that lots of ideas are proposed and some of them could be evaluated and eventually rejected because they are not viable. Besides, some of these ideas might be focused on the same topics so that they can be similar between them.

The aim of this module is to find semantic profiles which are similar to the predefined semantic profile. That is, this system obtains semantic profiles of Ideas, Projects, Users, etc which are similar to a selected profile. For example, the resources similar to a predefined idea can be obtained and ranked with this module. This process takes advantage of the semantic information and annotation retrieved by the system on the annotation process.

The entry that the module receives is the reference semantic profile. Then, the index of this profile is obtained. As it has been explained in the previous section, this index is represented by a vector. Then, this module uses the cosine similarity formula (see Eq 3) to obtain the similarity values between the vector of the reference profile q and each semantic profile sp.

$$sim(q, sp) = \cos \vartheta = \frac{q \bullet sp}{|q| \bullet |sp|} \qquad (3)$$

A ranking of the most relevant semantic profiles is defined by using the cosine similarity function represented in equation 3. The vector represents the vector calculated by equation 1 for each semantic profile in the system. The vector, on the other hand, is the index of the reference semantic profile. The ϑ symbol represents the angle that separates both vectors, and it describes the similitude grade between two vectors.

For example, Fig 3 shows a screenshot of the similar semantic profiles to the project entitled "Semantic analysis". As it can be seen, three different semantic profiles are obtained by this module. Each profile represents one individual in the ontology. For instance, "Retriever" is a project that is similar to the current one in 85%; "Semantic annotator" is an idea that is 70% similar to the current project. Finally, the system has detected that "Cesar Carralero" could be a good collaborator in the current project due to the fact that the similarity between these profiles is 70%.

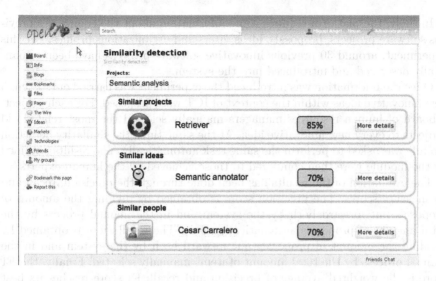

Fig. 3. Screenshot of the similarity detection functionality.

3   Use Case Scenario

Quality Objects Group is a holding of highly specialized consulting firms that was founded in Madrid. The company goal then was to become a high quality referential in technology services. It has extended its range of services (on-site/offshore) and its activity sectors (banking, health, aerospace, tourism, Civil Services, etc.). It has also strong reinvestment in R+D, and a development of proprietary products that increase the quality of the services and the customers' business.

Currently, Quality Objects Group is evaluating the platform presented in this paper. For this purpose an ICT ontology was developed and some details of this ontology are shown in table 1.

Table 1. Details of the ICT Ontology

	ICT Ontology
Classes	890
Datatype properties	20
Subclass_of relationships	2152
Classes with Multiple Inheritance	130
Max. Depth of Class Tree	6
Min. Depth of Class Tree	2
Avg. Depth of Class Tree	4
Max. Branching Factor of Class Tree	56,5
Min. Branching Factor of Class Tree	1
Avg. Branching Factor of Class	4

Initially, the platform requires some information about the company's previous software projects, proposals, ideas, users and organizations profiles. For this experiment, around 30 previous innovative software projects have been semantically described and introduced into the system.

Once the information was introduced the experiment was carried out. Then, 5 new innovative ideas within the context of ICT were proposed. For each project, a board of human resources managers manually selected the most related old projects to every new innovative idea. At the same time, the similarity detection module was asked to perform the same task automatically. The results obtained by the module were then compared to those achieved by the human experts.

The evaluation of the results has been done through the precision, recall and F1-measure scores. The precision score is obtained by dividing the amount of proposals put forward both by the system and in the manual process by the total amount of proposals automatically made. The recall score is obtained by dividing the amount of proposals put forward both by the system and in the manual process by the total amount of items manually selected. Finally, the F1 score is the weighted average of precision and recall; F1 score reaches its best value at 1 and the worst score at 0.

The innovative projects used in this experiment can be classified into two main categories: software engineering and network projects. Results are shown in Table 2.

Table 2. Precision, recall and F1 scores from the experiment.

Project type	Project	Projects suggested		
		Precision	Recall	F1
Software engineering(3)	1	0,83	1	0,91
	2	0,81	0,88	0,84
	3	0,86	0,92	0,89
Networks (2)	4	0,74	0,71	0,72
	5	0,8	0,9	0,85
Total avg		0,81	0,88	0,84

4 Discussion

Table 2 provides information about the performance of the results obtained for similar project suggestions in terms of precision, recall and F-measure. Results seem promising.

The difference in the precision values of the similar projects suggestion is significant. For example, project 4 obtains a low precision score (i.e., 74%). This is due to the fact that the company is short of experience in networks projects and there are no similar previous projects in the system. On the other hand, project 3 shows a very good precision score (i.e., 86%). This is because the company has been centred in the development of software engineering technologies and there is a broad background of previous projects in the ontology repository.

Regarding the recall score, project 4 shows the worst results, namely 71%, because a very low number of similar projects were obtained with the network projects. Again, the best results are found in the software engineering projects, due to the fact that this kind of projects are very specific and less ambiguous, and almost all of them were suggested. Finally, the method achieved the best results in the F-measure in project 1, obtaining a score of 91%.

The overall results for project suggestions seem promising with a precision score of 81%, a recall score of 88% and an F-measure score of 84%.

5   Conclusions

Nowadays, the achievement of sustainable competitive advantages is a must. Competitive advantage is mainly based on innovation. In fact, innovation is considered the key to success in present-day business. Innovation improves the quality of the outcome and decreases production costs, which at the same time leads to profit increase. The innovation process is based on innovative projects, which allow companies to fulfil their strategic and business goals. Therefore, it seems essential to achieve greater and more effective investment on innovation given the global marketplace that is becoming more and more crowded and competitive. Unfortunately, the need of sharing heterogeneous data among different departments and levels is a drawback for traditional management systems.

Ontologies and semantic technologies have proved to be highly effective for capturing, defining, sharing and reusing knowledge in a specific domain. Besides, the use of ontologies may help overcome the limitations of traditional methods in natural language processing. They are also relevant in the scope of some related methods such as recommendation [10], service discovery [11] and expert finding [12].

This study presents a semantically-enhanced platform for innovative project management. The main idea behind this new platform is to model innovation related data by means of ontologies. A more precise, improved open innovation management system has then been built by leveraging the formal underpinnings of ontologies and by applying semantic techniques and methods.

The approach presented here has a number of important benefits that result from adding semantics to an open innovation management system. They include:

1. The definition of a completely explicit information model. The use of ontologies serves as a reference for communication, both among people and computers, and it also helps to improve data quality and consistency.
2. Improved search capabilities, obtained by describing all the elements by semantic profiles in terms of a well- defined and formal domain model.
3. A more precise matcher between innovative projects and ideas, people and all the elements modelled in the platform, since the comparison between one and another is done at knowledge level.

As further work, we also plan to extend the scope of the application to cover the whole open innovation management lifecycle. The ultimate goal is to conduct an open innovation management in companies in an integrated and holistic manner. All the departments in the company should be involved in this process, which must be cyclical as far as the use and generation of knowledge are concerned. The entire lifecycle must therefore be considered throughout the whole process, from the initial brainstorming to the analysis of the results of the finished projects.

The main limitation of the proposed framework is that the "Annotation and indexing module" only works with unstructured, natural-language text. We plan to extend this module so as support for more structured content can be included (e.g. database tables).

Acknowledgments. This work has been supported by the Ministry of Industry, Energy and Tourism through project OPEN-IDEA (TSI- 020603-2012-219).

References

1. Chesbrough, H.W.: Open innovation: The new imperative for creating and profiting from technology. Harvard Business Press (2003)
2. Chesbrough, H.: Open innovation: a new paradigm for understanding industrial innovation. In: Open Innovation: Researching a New Paradigm, pp. 1–12. Oxford University Press, Oxford (2006)
3. Chesbrough, H., Crowther, A.K.: Beyond high tech: early adopters of open innovation in other industries. R&d Management 36(3), 229–236 (2006)
4. Enkel, E., Gassmann, O., Chesbrough, H.: Open r&d and open innovation: exploring the phenomenon. R&d Management 39(4), 311–316 (2009)
5. Studer, R., Benjamins, V.R., Fensel, D.: Knowledge engineering: principles and methods. Data & Knowledge Engineering 25(1), 161–197 (1998)
6. Blakeley, C.: Virtuoso rdf views-getting started guide. OpenLink Software (2007)
7. Rodríguez-García, M.Á., Valencia-García, R., García-Sánchez, F., Samper-Zapater, J.J.: Ontology-based annotation and retrieval of services in the cloud. Knowledge-Based Systems 56, 15–25 (2014)
8. Castells, P., Fernández, M., Vallet, D.: An adaptation of the vector-space model for ontology-based information retrieval. IEEE Trans. on Knowl. and Data Eng. 19(2), 261–272 (2007)
9. Salton, G., McGill, M.J.: Introduction to Modern Information Retrieval. McGraw-Hill, Inc., New York (1986)
10. Carrer-Neto, W., Hernández-Alcaraz, M.L., Valencia-García, R., Sánchez, F.G.: Social knowledge-based recommender system. application to the movies domain. Expert Syst. Appl. 39(12), 10990–11000 (2012)
11. García-Sánchez, F., Valencia-García, R., Martínez-Béjar, R., Fernández-Breis, J.T.: An ontology, intelligent agent-based framework for the provision of semantic web services. Expert Syst. Appl. 36(2), 3167–3187 (2009)
12. Lin, F., Butters, J., Sandkuhl, K., Ciravegna, F.: Context-based ontology matching: Concept and application cases. In: 2010 IEEE 10th International Conference on Computer and Information Technology (CIT), pp. 1292–1298. IEEE (2010)

ArThUR: A Tool for Markov Logic Network

Axel Bodart, Keyvin Evrard, James Ortiz, and Pierre-Yves Schobbens

Computer Science Faculty, University of Namur
{axbodart,kevrard}@student.fundp.ac.be, {jor,pys}@info.fundp.ac.be

Abstract. Logical approaches-and ontologies in particular-offer a well-adapted framework for representing knowledge present on the Semantic Web (SW). These ontologies are formulated in Web Ontology Language (OWL2), which are based on expressive Description Logics (DL). DL are a subset of First-Order Logic (FOL) that provides decidable reasoning. Based on DL, it is possible to rely on inference mechanisms to obtain new knowledge from axioms, rules and facts specified in the ontologies. However, these classical inference mechanisms do not deal with : uncertainty probabilities. Several works recently targeted those issues (i.e. Pronto, PR-OWL, BayesOWL, etc.), but none of them combines OWL2 with Markov Logic Networks (MLN) formalism. Several open source software packages for MLN are available (e.g. Alchemy, Tuffy, RockIt, etc.). In this paper, we present ArThUR, a Java framework for reasoning with probabilistic information in the SW. ArThUR incorporate three open source software packages for MLN, which is able to reason with uncertainty information, showing that it can be used in several real-world domains. We also show several experiments of our tool with different ontologies.

1 Introduction

In the last years, the Semantic Web (SW) [2] has acquired significant relevance in academic, industrial, military, health care and biological. SW is currently the major commitment of the W3C[1] and to offer the greatest evolution of the World Wide Web (Web). The main ideas behind the SW are : the implementation of cooperative agents and methods for processing the information in the Web, the uses of ontologies [7] for a precise definition of shared terms in the Web and using reasoning languages for automated inference from ontologies [2]. Ontologies are common vocabularies that define concepts and their relationships. The standard Web Ontology Language is OWL2 [14] from the W3C. OWL2 is an expressive Description Logic (DL) ($\mathcal{SROIQ(D)}$) [1] with an RDF syntax [9]. More generally, DL is a type of logic to describe concepts and relationships. It is based on First-Order Logic (FOL) with the idea to formalize SW. Moreover, DL allows the use of deterministic reasoner tools (i.e. Pellet[2], FaCT++ [3], TrOWL[4], etc.) and verifying

---

[1] http://wwww.W3C.org

[2] http://wwww.mindswap.org/pellet

[3] http://owl.cs.manchester.ac.uk/tools/fact/

[4] http://trowl.eu/

R. Meersman et al. (Eds.): OTM 2014 Workshops, LNCS 8842, pp. 319–328, 2014.

if statements are true or false. However, this DL is less effective in those areas where the information to be represented comes along with uncertainty. For example, how to represent the uncertain relations between bacteria and antibiotics in statements such as: "Mycobacterium Smegmatis is resistant to Rifampicin with the degree of certainty 90% and is not resistant with he degree of certainty 10%". Fortunately, DL was extended to deal with uncertainty, especially was extended the logic behind DL in order to be able work with the uncertainty representations and reasoners. Several formalisms and tools for dealing with the knowledge uncertainty SW have been successfully applied over the last years. Formalisms like : Bayesian Networks [8], Fuzzy Logic [11], Markov Logic Networks (MLN)[6]. Probabilistic Description Logic (PDL) like : P-$\mathcal{SHOIN}(\mathcal{D})$ [10], P-$\mathcal{SHIF}(\mathcal{D})$ [13]. Reasoner tools like : Pronto[5], Incerto[6], ContraBovemRufum [15] and Probabilistic OWL like PR-OWL[7], BayesOWL [5], OntoBayes [19].

Several open source software packages for MLN (reasoners MLN) are available in the Web like Alchemy[8], Tuffy[9], ProbCog[10], and Markov TheBeast[11], RockIt [12] but none of them combines their MLN formalism with OWL2. Furthermore, these implementations do not present a very friendly graphical user interface that would facilitate the creating, editing and making probabilistic inferences from any ontology. Also in some of them there is only command line interface.

In this paper is presented ArThUR, an implementation in Java that consists of a graphical user interface and which combines three reasoners MLN (Alchemy, Tuffy, Rockit). The aims of ArThUR are to ease the modeling, editing and translating from OWL2 ontologies to MLN files. Furthermore, ArThUR makes probabilistic inferences, comparison, research and statistical result analysis of the probabilistic rules present in the MLN files. Finally, it is also possible to edit and to persist these structures as a standard MLN file and OWL2 ontology.

Structure of the paper. The rest of the paper is organized as follows. In sections 2, we introduce the ontologies and SW. In section 3, we give a brief introduction to MLN, uncertainty in the SW. In section 4, we present some open source software packages for MLN. In section 5, we present the ArThUR architecture. In section 6, we present the experimental work done and its main results. Finally, in section 7, we conclude and outline future work.

2   Background

2.1   Semantic Web

The SW is a project of the evolution of our current Web (Web 2.0) initiated by the W3C. This initiative is also known under the names of : Linked Data, Linked

---

[5] http://weblog.clarkparsia.com/2007/09/27/introducing-pronto
[6] https://code.google.com/p/incerto/
[7] http://www.pr-owl.org/
[8] http://alchemy.cs.washington.edu/
[9] http://hazy.cs.wisc.edu/hazy/tuffy/
[10] http://ias.in.tum.de/research/probcog
[11] https://code.google.com/p/thebeast/
[12] https://code.google.com/p/rockit/

Open Data or Linking Open Data. The main aim of this movement is to ensure that the amount of data displayed on the Web is also available in a standard format, accessible and manipulable in an unified manner by all Web applications.

2.2 Ontologies and Inferences

The term ontology is strongly linked to the SW. Several definitions have been given, including [7] and [16]. The first gives a very abstract definition of ontologies though popular in the community : "An ontology is an explicit specification of a conceptualization." The second proposes the following: "An ontology defines the basic terms and relations comprising the vocabulary of a topic area as well as the rules for combining terms and relations to define extensions to the vocabulary". Ontologies are used to capture knowledge about some domain of interest.

Inference is the process to deriving new knowledge from existing facts. In the case of ontologies, it is practical to discover new triplets from known triplets by exploiting the structure of the ontology and the logical constraints specified. Inference highlights implicit facts that are otherwise hidden in complex models. These inference mechanisms can be used to check the quality of knowledge bases and to add implicit knowledge to the ontologies. Various reasoners support deterministic inference (e.g. Pellet, FaCT++, HermiT, etc).

3 Logic and Uncertainty

3.1 Uncertainty and Semantic Web

Uncertainty is a fundamental and inevitable property present in many domains, including the Medical Domain (MD). Uncertainty in MD is represented with probabilistic approaches (e.g. represent the uncertain relations between Breast Cancer (BRC) and European woman in statements such as "European women have 12% risk of developing BRC in their lifetime"), which are considered as the scientific norm for this purpose. The majority of probabilistic approaches are based on probabilistic formalisms, such as Bayesian Networks [8] and Markov Logic (ML) [6].

There are several approaches combining probabilistic information and SW. A first approach is providing an ontology model to classify the probabilistic information (such as PR-OWL). A second approach to extend the ontology with primitives to represent the probabilistic information. For example: Pronto which extends the traditional DL's by associating a probability value to the axioms. And finally OWL2, FOL and probabilistic graphical models are currently being combined.

3.2 Markov Logic Networks

ML is a same language as FOL that provides that capability, joining in the same representation probabilistic graphical models to represent the uncertainty, and

FOL to represent a set of constraints on possible worlds. The main idea behind ML is that, unlike FOL, a world that violates a formula is not invalid, but less probable. This is done by attaching weights to FOL formulas: the higher the weight, the bigger is the difference between a world that satisfies the formula and one that does not, other things been equal. These sets of weighted formulas are called a ML network (MLN). Below, we consider two relevant tasks for MLN : Weight Learning and Inference [3][18].

4   Markov Logic Reasoning

A Markov Logic Reasoner (MLR) is composed of a set of algorithms that allows (weight) Learning and Inference based on MLN. Learning leads to estimating the weight associated with each formula of a given MLN [3]. Inference find the most likely state of the world consistent with some evidence, and computing arbitrary marginal or conditional probabilities [18]. The main MLN currently available are:

1. **Alchemy** was designed for Linux platforms. Alchemy is not portable due to its Linux C/C++ implementation, but nevertheless is currently the MLR most complete and most used. It includes implementations for all the major existing algorithms for structure learning, generative weight learning, discriminative weight learning, and inference [12]. The advantage of Alchemy it has a large community. The disadvantages are : (1) The grounding[13] takes very long and even for medium sized models the execution time might be very large [12]. (2) Hard formulas in Alchemy are not guaranteed to hold in the final MAP (Maximun A-Posteriori Query[14]) state. This is due to the fact that Alchemy only sets very large weights for hard formulas which may be violated in the MAP state [12].
2. **Tuffy** is implemented in Java programming language. Contrary to Alchemy, Tuffy does not offering different implementations of algorithms for learning and inference, but it offers those their have been proven to be among the most efficient experimentally. The Tuffy system is faster in performance than the Alchemy. The main disadvantage of Tuffy is the handling of negative weights in formulas. Tuffy proposes a bottom-up approach in its algorithms and combining the main memory and the use of a database to optimize processes. Additionally, Tuffy proposes partitioning techniques allowing networks to implement a parallelism strategy which significantly improves performance.
3. **Markov TheBeast (MTB)** is an open-source Statistical Relational Learning software based on MLN. It is developed in Java, it does not have much documentation. In contrast to Alchemy, MTB uses a different MAP inference technique : Integer Linear Programming with Cutting Planes.
4. **ProbCog** is an open source software for Statistical Relational Learning that supports learning and inference for relational domains. ProbCog is built on

---

[13] A ground term of a formal system is a term that does not contain any free variables.
[14] Informally, the MAP can be used to obtain a point estimate of an unobserved quantity on the basis of empirical data.

basis of PyMLN[15], a toolbox and a software library for learning and reasoning in MLN. Most of the code of ProgCog is developed in Java, although PyMLN is developed in Python.

5. **RockIt** is more recent and is also developed in Java programming language. A disadvantage here is that by the fact that it is relatively new, it is not yet entirely stable and changes often. In addition, it is very difficult to find documentation about its implementation. RockIt also uses a database, enables the parallelism (and implements optional techniques to improve performance).

4.1 Comparison of Reasoners

We have used several criteria for guide our choice of MLN, which are:

1. Methodology : This criteria indicates the use of database by the reasoners.
2. Platforms : This criteria indicates operating systems on which reasoners can work. i.e: Windows, Linux and Mac.
3. Runtime : This criteria indicates the time taken to perform queries for the set of concepts in the ontologies by the reasoners.
4. MLN Tasks : This criteria indicates the use of inferences and learning tasks by the reasoners.
5. Availability : This criteria ensures that the reasoners are freely available as open source.
6. Jena Support : This criteria indicates whether the reasoners can be used with Jena API[16] or not.
7. Friendly Grammar : This criteria indicates whether the grammar of the reasoners facilitates the extension and implementation phases.

	Alchemy	Tuffy	RockIt	MTB	ProbCog
Methodology	-	+	+	-	-
Platforms	+	+	+	+	+
Runtime	-	+	+	-	-
MLN Tasks	+	+	-	+	+
Availability	+	+	+	+	+
Jena Support	+	+	+	+	+
Friendly Grammar	+	+	+	-	-

5 Development

5.1 Architecture

ArThUR is using the three MLR (Alchemy, Tuffy, Rockit). It supports translating a OWL2 ontology into a MLN file, running learning and inference processes over the ontologies and statistical analysis of the results obtained. ArThUR has been written in Java and more specifically in Java SE 1.6 edition, an object-oriented

---

[15] http://alchemy.cs.washington.edu/
[16] https://jena.apache.org/

language known to provide platform independence and to enable fast and efficient program development. Furthermore, support for the development of Graphical User Interface (GUI) as well as grammar parsers are available. The design and implementation of ArThUR took approximately 5 months, with about 25000 lines of code for the kernel and 3000 lines of code for the GUI implementation. The tool architecture consists of five components, see Figure 1.

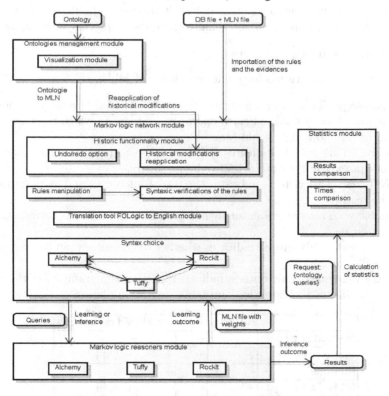

Fig. 1. The ArThUR architecture

1. **GUI Component:** In Figure 2, we can see the different options offered to the user. The user can load, save and visualize ontologies files. Furthermore, the user can translate ontologies files to MLN files, verify MLN rules and learn/infer from the MLN files using the three reasoners. The GUI prints results on screen or writes them into a file and allows the user to analyze the results and compare them with results achieved with other algorithms present in the reasoners.

2. **Input Files Component:** The input files are : a MLN file, an evidence file and a query file. The last one can be replaced allowing to user to choose what query predicates to use. Figure 2 shows how to load these three files and the possibility to select the query predicates through a choice box field.

3. **FOL Rules Component:** As the MLN file and the evidence files are being loaded, their terms (i.e. declarations, query, weighted formulas, rules (FOL)

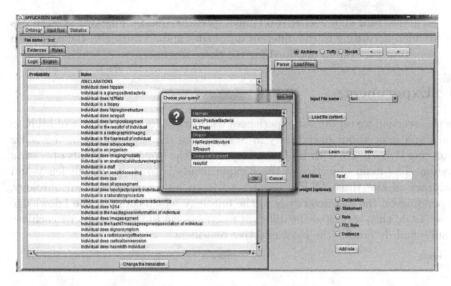

Fig. 2. User Interface of ArThUR

and evidences) are separated and organized in data structure in order to check the syntax in each term. Moreover, adding and removing terms are almost similar except that it necessary check that this terms does not already exist in the set of existing terms. Every change made through this features is persisted in the original file. This feature makes it easier for the user to include or remove terms in a MLN file. Furthermore, for the transformation of the FOL in Conjunctive Normal Form (CNF): (1) Eliminate conditional and bi-conditional of the logical formula. (2) Move negation operators inside of the logic formula. (3) Move the quantifies operators outside of the logical formula. (4) Apply skolemization. (5) Remove universal quantifiers operators. (6) AND to OR operators are distributed across the parentheses. An another processing step of this component is to translate FOL to natural language rules (English rules). We reuse our data structure to create transformation rules on the logic formula to english natural rules. The translation data is stored as java object and then stored in a file to ensure the persistence of these data.

4. **Markov Logic Component:** This is the component that supports inference and learning algorithms of the three reasoners. The weight learning consists in finding formula weights that maximize either the likelihood or pseudo-likelihood measure [3] for generative learning or either the conditional likelihood or max-margin measures [18] for discriminative learning. Inference consists in finding the marginal and conditional probabilities of a formula given an MLN, based on randomized and MC-SAT [17] algorithms.

5. **Statistical Component:** Finally, we developed a statistics component and comparison tools through an XML file, allowing us to share data persistence when closing the application and, secondly, giving us a system with a simple

structure that allows search and make specific requests. The XML structure is divided according to the different ontologies and according to the execution time and the results obtained for the three reasoners.

6 Experiments

In this section, we report out experiences with ArThUR in the context of MLN to learn and infer about uncertainty in SW. We ran the experiments on a 2.2GHz Intel core i7-2670 QM with 8 GO memory under the Windows 7 64 bits operating system. The main objective of these experiments is to show the efficiency and accuracy of the three MLR reasoners to learn and reason from an ontology, depending on the characteristics of the ontology which contains the knowledge base. To do this, we tested the different reasoners via ArThUR in order to achieve results and determine the most effective reasoners.

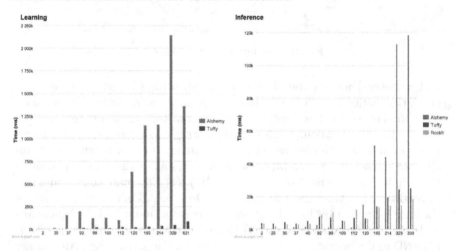

Fig. 3. Weight Learning Process   **Fig. 4.** Inference Process

Regarding MLR differences, we had to decide which algorithms to use for the different reasoners in the steps of learning and inference. For the Weight Learning Process, we have chosen the "Scaled Conjugate Gradient" algorithm for Alchemy because it appears that it is the most effective method in [18]. In Tuffy, we opted for the "Diagonal Newton" algorithm. The Newton method can converge to the minimum in a single step. To do this, it multiplies by the inverse gradient of the Hessian matrix [17]. In RockIt no weight learning had been implemented yet when we developed ArThUR. For the Inference Process, we have chosen the "Marginal inference" method and MC-SAT algorithm because it appears that it is the most effective method in [18]. The fundamental difference between the MC-SAT algorithm and other sampling algorithms is that MC-SAT provides a certain robustness. Hence, we have chosen this algorithm for both Tuffy and Alchemy. On the other hand, RockIt implements a Gibbs sampling algorithm. This is a method where at each iteration the algorithm selects any atom and varies its truth value. If after variation there is no strong constraints, cardinality constraints or existential constraints are violated then the probability of the atom is updated.

Once the methods has been selected, we used our tool to obtain the runtime of three MLR for learning and inference, and to get the results returned by these three reasoners. In this context, we have selected various ontologies on the internet and from the Orthogen Project [4] that conform to the OWL2 standard. The ontologies used from Orthogen Project range from 2 to 621 rules, from 50 to 531 declarations and from 40 to 383 evidence or individuals. Figures 3 and 4 below, show the runtime according to the number of rules, this factor alone does not establish a new information from which we would be able to make specific predictions about our ontologies.

Finally, after a series of tests, we have opted for a relationship between both number of rules and number of ground clauses. The reason for this choice is justified by the fact that the number of rules influences the grounding phase producing ground clauses while the ground clauses have an impact on the runtime of the inference (see Figure 5 and 6).

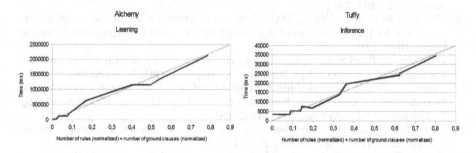

Fig. 5. Alchemy Learning   **Fig. 6.** Tuffy Inference

7   Conclusions

In this paper, we presented ArThUR, a tool to deal with uncertainty reasoning in SW using MLN. ArThUR presents a GUI for three reasoners : Alchemy, Tuffy and Rockit. We have shown how ArThUR can be used in practice to perform reasoning with ontologies and MLN files. The user can translate from ontologies files to MLN files, verify MLN rules and learn/infer the MLN files from the three reasoners. Moreover, we developed a statistics component and comparison tools through an XML file allowing us to share data persistence when closing the application. Secondly, we have a very fast system with a simple structure that allows search and specific queries. Moreover, from our experimental results, we conclude that the algorithms are sound, reliable and can successfully be applied to real-world domains. Finally, as future work, we want to obtain ontologies with enough facts, so that weight and rules can be learned with a high degree of confidence.

References

1. Baader, F., Calvanese, D., McGuinness, D.L., Nardi, D., Patel-Schneider, P.F.: The Description Logic Handbook: Theory, Implementation, and Applications. Cambridge University Press, New York (2003)
2. Berners-Lee, T., Hendler, J., Lassila, O.: The semantic web. Scientific American 284(5), 34–43 (2001)
3. Besag, J.: Statistical analysis of non-lattice data. Journal of the Royal Statistical Society. Series D (The Statistician) 24(3), 179–195 (1975)
4. DeNizza, D., Ortiz, J.J., Meurisse, H., Schobbens, P.-Y.: Orthogen: Système d'information intégré pour la traçabilité et la gestion multi-paramètres des infections orthopédiques. In: INFORSID, pp. 421–436 (2013)
5. Ding, Z., Peng, Y., Pan, R.: BayesOWL: Uncertainty Modeling in Semantic Web Ontologies. Soft Computing in Ontologies and Semantic Web, 3–29 (2006)
6. Domingos, P., Lowd, D., Kok, S., Poon, H., Richardson, M., Singla, P.: Just Add Weights: Markov Logic for the Semantic Web. In: Costa, P.C., D'Amato, C., Fanizzi, N., Laskey, K.B., Laskey, K.J., Lukasiewicz, T., Nickles, M., Pool, M. (eds.) URSW 2005-2007. LNCS (LNAI), vol. 5327, pp. 1–25. Springer, Heidelberg (2008)
7. Gruber, T.R.: A translation approach to portable ontology specifications. Knowl. Acquis. 5(2), 199–220 (1993)
8. Gu, T., Pung, H.K., Zhang, D.Q.: A bayesian approach for dealing with uncertain contexts. In: Proceedings of the Second International Conference on Pervasive Computing (2004)
9. Horrocks, I., Patel-Schneider, P.F., van Harmelen, F.: From shiq and rdf to owl: the making of a web ontology language. J. Web Sem. 1(1), 7–26 (2003)
10. Klinov, P., Parsia, B.: Probabilistic modeling and owl: A user oriented introduction to p-shiq(d). In: Dolbear, C., Ruttenberg, A., Sattler, U. (eds.) CEUR Workshop Proceedings. CEUR-WS.org, vol. 432 (2008)
11. Klir, G.J., Yuan, B.: Fuzzy Sets and Fuzzy Logic: Theory and Applications. Prentice-Hall, Inc., Upper Saddle River (1995)
12. Kok, S., Domingos, P.: Learning Markov Logic Network Structure via Hypergraph Lifting. In: Danyluk, A.P., Bottou, L., Littman, M.L. (eds.) ACM International Conference Proceeding Series, ICML, vol. 382, p. 64. ACM (2009)
13. Lukasiewicz, T.: Expressive probabilistic description logics. Artificial Intelligence 172(6-7), 852–883 (2008)
14. McGuinness, D.L., van Harmelen, F.: Owl web ontology language overview. Technical report (2004)
15. Näth, T.H., Möller, R.: Contrabovemrufum: A system for probabilistic lexicographic entailment. In: Baader, F., Lutz, C., Motik, B. (eds.) Description Logics, vol. 353 (2008)
16. Neches, R., Fikes, R., Finin, T., Gruber, T., Patil, R., Senator, T., Swartout, W.R.: Enabling technology for knowledge sharing. AI Mag. 12(3), 36–56 (1991)
17. Poon, H., Domingos, P.: Sound and efficient inference with probabilistic and deterministic dependencies. In: Proceedings of the 21st National Conference on Artificial Intelligence, AAAI 2006, vol. 1, pp. 458–463. AAAI Press (2006)
18. Singla, P., Domingos, P.: Discriminative training of markov logic networks. In: Proceedings of the 20th National Conference on Artificial Intelligence, AAAI 2005, vol. 2, pp. 868–873. AAAI Press (2005)
19. Yang, Y., Calmet, J.: Ontobayes: An ontology-driven uncertainty model. In: Proceedings of the International Conference on Intelligent Agents, Web Technologies and Internet Commerce (IAWTIC), Vienna, Austria (2005)

An Overview of Attributes Characterization
for Interoperability Assessment
from the Public Administration Perspective

José Marcelo A.P. Cestari[1], Eduardo de Freitas R. Loures[1], Eduardo A.P. Santos[1],
Yongxin Liao[1], Hervé Panetto[2], and Mario Lezoche[2]

[1] Pontifical Catholic University of Parana, Industrial and Systems Engineering, Curitiba, Brazil
{jose.cestari,eduardo.loures,
eduardo.portela,yongxin.liao}@pucpr.br
[2] Université de Lorraine, CRAN, UMR 7039, Vandoeuvre-lès-Nancy, France
{herve.panetto,mario.lezoche}@univ-lorraine.fr

Abstract. The government interoperability frameworks (GIFs) are mainly cen-
tered on technical perspective neglecting important actual issues in Public Administration (PA) as the performance of their services and process as well its
strategic, legal and politic positioning. This wide spectrum of organizational
knowledge demands specific interoperability assessment (IA) methods based on
a preliminary step of identifying and organizing adequate attributes that allow a
wider view on the PA domain regarding interoperability requirements. This paper proposes a knowledge discovering and extraction method from PA and IA
literature, presenting a rationality through a conceptual model in order to identify and organize attributes that will be used as input for an IA model. A preliminary set of attributes is presented, as well as a future approach of how to deal
with these attributes using AHP (Analytic Hierarchy Process) in order to evaluate them with experts through a specific structure suited to the IA process itself.

Keywords: Interoperability Assessment, Public Administration, Attributes Extraction, e-Government.

1 Introduction

Organizations are facing a competitive marketplace and they must develop partnerships and work in an integrated way with competitors and stakeholders. As one of the
important factor of this collaboration, interoperability [1, 2] is the ability of two or
more systems (or components) of: sharing specific information, using them with a
specific semantics and creating, with that information, a specific mission in a precise
context. Interoperability takes into account dimensions such as concerns, barriers,
degrees of maturity and assessment, and consists of more than technical aspects [3].
Interoperability assessment (IA) is the method that defines some formal metrics to
quantify and qualify the level of interoperability between heterogeneous systems from
one or more organizations [4]. With the increasing use of ICT (Information and

R. Meersman et al. (Eds.): OTM 2014 Workshops, LNCS 8842, pp. 329–338, 2014.
© Springer-Verlag Berlin Heidelberg 2014

Communication Technologies) in government institutions, the concept of eGovernment emerges in the late 1990s [5]. The term eGovernment, e-gov, eGov and similar are an abbreviation of "electronic government" and refers to the use of ICT to support the government business, providing or enhancing public services or managing internal government operations [6]. Assembling the concepts of interoperability and eGovernment, an eGovernment interoperability domain arises, in a broad sense, as the ability of constituencies (or public agencies) to work together [7].

The literature analysis, presented in [8], reveals that there are many works regarding interoperability models and government initiatives of eGov models and frameworks. Nevertheless, since 2000 it was not possible to identify specific models, frameworks or assessment procedures regarding the evaluation of government entities not related to (almost entirely) technical issues and also it was not found in the literature review papers describing the rules (rationale and procedures) regarding the knowledge discovering steps [9, 10, 11].

The desire to map the concerns and identify the barriers (other than the technical ones) is a recent interest in the literature [12]. This new approach, focused on semantics, opens an important issue regarding the proper collection of attributes related to interoperability of these other dimensions related to public administration (e.g. processes, services, governance, legal and political). Obtaining, identifying and organizing relevant knowledge are important steps to the IA considering also the models and frameworks established in Enterprise Interoperability Assessment (EIA) in the private industrial sector, as well as the work done in eGov.

An exploratory approach into the literature sources will allow the identification of important dimensions (concerns, barriers and attributes) for the evaluation of the ability to interoperate in the governmental entities. There is need of a specific rationale for this broader knowledge extraction of organizational behavior into the public domain. In fact, to characterize the qualification attributes and the IA in their different visions other than the technological, such attributes and guidelines should present the structure, the quality and the completeness of observation in the IA performed by a method that ensures these requirements.

It is important to contextualize that this paper is part of a wider research scope, represented in Figure 1 and more specifically related to the process A2 and A3. The IDEF0 diagram [13] identifies basic steps (which are contained in phases and may contain activities), proposing an attributes' and guidelines' structure collection and composition as well as the assessment method definition. The results of A0 and A1 processes can be summarized as (i) definition of a database of related papers, (ii) analysis regarding the world publication and authoring, helping the justification of the research and mapping the distribution of the subject, (iii) domain definition and (iv) identification of gaps regarding the existence models and related works. Based on the information gathered from A0 and A1, the next step (A2) relates to the identification of preliminary set of attributes and guidelines and in A3, in conjunction with expert assessment, a fact-oriented transformation (FOT) method is applied to evaluate and gather new (if any) attributes from other knowledge sources and types of databases. Those identified objects can be considered as a set of best practices, requirements or desired interoperability characteristics within public entities. The organization, methods and tools regarding the process A2 is exposed in Figure 2, which also provides an overview of the structure and main goals of this paper.

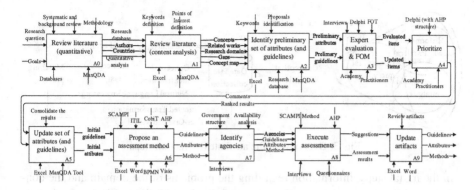

Fig. 1. Full research methodological steps

Considering all the presented aspects, this paper exposes the rationale for the extraction of attributes, as well as a set of preliminary attributes themselves in order to help the IA of public administration entities. Figure 2 shows a general structure of the components adopted as basis for the extraction process, taking into account that the solution space helps to provide information in order to solve issues related to the problem space.

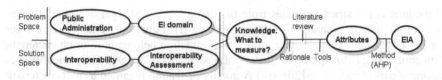

Fig. 2. Structure of the attributes extraction and its application for EIA

After that, a join of the aspects leads to reflections associated to measurement selection, culminating in the generation of a set of attributes and its use into the EIA applications and domain. In addition, a proposal of ranking mechanism (for the attributes) based on AHP [14] is presented as one of the next steps of the research.

2   Methodology

According to [15], knowledge is a justified belief that increases an entity's capacity for taking effective action. In [16] the authors defines knowledge as experience, facts, rules, assertions and concepts about their subject areas that are crucial to the business (customers, markets, processes, regulations). There are two basic dimensions of knowledge: tacit and explicit [15], which can be combined to an ontological dimension. In complement, knowledge management is a process of identifying, capturing and leveraging collective knowledge to help the organization compete [17]. Knowledge can be represented using different formal forms, among others, semantic nets, rules, ontologies, mind maps and conceptual maps. A general model of the information retrieval process is exposed in Figure 3, based in [18].

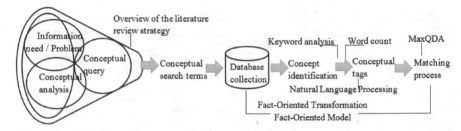

Fig. 3. Overview of the attributes extraction steps

In the initial steps, information regarding the problems of the domain and the concepts involved were processed with conceptual queries in order to filter and select an initial documents database with the execution of conceptual searches. In summary, considering the existence of a database collection, the steps to extract the attributes are: (i) concept identification; (ii) keyword analysis and word count as support mechanisms; (iii) tagging words to identify groups of knowledge and (iv) matching process to search for relations among the words found and root concepts of the research. These steps are described in the subsections bellow.

2.1   Concept Identification

As the goal is to extract attributes from the literature (knowledge) database, it is important to define and characterize attributes as in: (i) A quality or characteristic given to a person, group, or some other thing. An abstraction belonging to or characteristic of an entity [19]; (ii) A quality or feature of a person or thing, especially one that is an important part of its nature [20]; (iii) A quality or feature regarded as a characteristic or inherent part of someone or something [21] and (iv) Regarding class diagrams, an attribute represents a data definition for an instance of a classifier. An attribute describes a range of values for that data definition and may describe the structure and value of an instance of a class [22].

Although the grammar structure is a specific body of knowledge (and not the focus of this research), it is important to mention that attributes are nouns and/or adjectives that modify that noun (e.g. collaboration (noun), collaborationist (adjective)), and guidelines are suggestions to show how to behave and usually derives action from its statements [19]. Guidelines can contain (or suggests) attributes and they (guidelines) will be used (along with the attributes themselves) to assess the interoperability of the entities, with a similar approach exposed in [23]. Figure 4 illustrates the relation among important concepts for the research, which is useful in the process of attributes extraction and the idea is to expose the components that are connected (somehow) primarily with an attribute and secondly with a guideline. Considering the database of files regarding the domain (150 documents), a keyword analysis and counting was made as a first attempted to derive some attributes. The rationale adopted was that if a document deals with such important issues of the government interoperability aspects, there is a chance that qualification words (attributes) could be cited in the keywords of the paper.

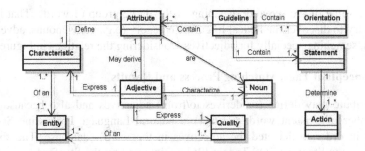

Fig. 4. Concept model of attributes

The keywords are not only "one word", but may be also a group of words separated by commas or other symbols. The MaxQDA software [24] was used to count (and organize) the keywords of the documents and the results are represented in Table 1.

Table 1. Quantitative overview of keywords

# of appearances	# of words	# of appearances	# of words
1	178	7	2
2	21	8	1
3	6	10	1
4	4	55	1
6	1	53	1

The highest appearance are the words "interoperability" (55 times) and "e-government" (53 times) and this was expected because of the rules adopted during the literature review (these two words were one of the most important composing the search strings) [8]. Nevertheless, as the idea is not have a sort of a "sample" approach, the quantity and distribution of the keywords are not as important as the meaning in terms of creating knowledge [15]. However, after the analysis of all keywords retrieved, it was detected that most of them are related to the paper itself (as expected) but in general ways. That is, the keywords tends to show generic aspects of the paper, containing words of global meanings, in order to introduce to the reader some "tags". Because of this, it was not possible to find words that could be used (directly or indirectly) to compose the preliminary set of attributes.

As the keyword analysis did not bring information about possible attributes, it was defined that the extraction of the attributes would follow a process based on a word counting and Natural Language processing analysis. According to [25], an average English word has from 4.5 to 7 characters and, using the MaxQDA software [24], the whole documents database were scanned searching for words of six characters length. In a first round, 44,111 words were found and, after a second round of execution (with the elimination of authors names, symbols, irrelevant words and words that appeared less than 10 times) a total of 21,644 words were selected. The quantitative analysis by itself does not solve the problem of finding attributes, so it was necessary investigate some of the semantic meaning of this large group of words. That is, as a next step, try to discover the lexical linguistic category (e.g., verbs, nouns, adverbs) of the words, searching specially for adjectives (considering the relations in Figure 4).

2.2   Conceptual Tags, Matching Process and Results

As an attribute may define (or derives to/from) adjectives and also because of the large number of existent words (21,644), a Natural Language Processing Software was used in order to detected the adjectives in the word's database. The software adopted was the Stanford POS Tagger [26], maintained by the Stanford Natural Language Processing Group and built based on the research of a log-linear part-of-speech taggers described in [27]. A Part-Of-Speech Tagger (POS Tagger) is a software that reads text in some language and assigns parts of speech to each word (and other token), such as noun, verb and adjective. The tool was also used in [18] within the natural language processing approach. The list of 21,644 words were processed with the Stanford POS Tagger and the results were 3,739 words tagged as adjectives.

At this point, considering that the set of words identified as adjectives could contain a subset of attributes, there is a need to search for a connection among each of the identified words with the concept words that represents the research subject domain (interoperability within public administrations/government). This process was done using a lexical matching functionality of MaxQDA tool and the results are the following preliminary list of attributes: adaptability, collaboration, commitment, communication (semantic), conflicts, cooperation, economical, efficiency, historical, integration, loyalty, politic, process, responsibility, senior management support, sociological, standardization.

2.3   Conceptualization Process (with Fact-Oriented Transformation)

Figure 5 presents an approach related to the process A3 (Figure 1), aimed to evaluate (expert view) and gather new information from other types of knowledge sources and databases (structured or semi-structured data) in order to corroborate and improve/refine the obtained set of attributes.. The first step is a reverse engineering method through which a model from the application or schema level can be derived (Step 1). Then, the resulted model is enriched through a step of Application Knowledge Injection (AKI) where the model is automatically compared and matched with existing domain and application ontology (Step 2). The model is corrected through a Knowledge Extraction and Mapping Validation in a harmonizing step (Step 3). In fact, the model is examined with the help of a domain expert or an end-user, who is a qualified person to describe the context of the peculiar domain and to put in evidence the contextual knowledge. The next step (Step 4) is a FOT through the application of a set of patterns rules for transforming the enriched conceptual model to a Fact-Oriented Model (FOM) with its finest-grained semantic atoms completely displayed [28]. The Step 5 represents a structural optimization through the application of the Formal Concept Analysis methodology. The output of the entire conceptualization process is a set of formal objects (attributes) inserted in an optimized structure derived from the data analysis and ready to be conceptually analyzed and tagged.

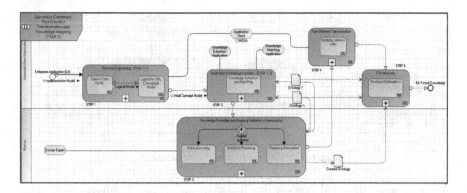

Fig. 5. Entire conceptualization process overview for concept identification

2.4   The Use of Attributes and Guidelines on an AHP Structure

The AHP method, proposed in [14], is one of the widely accepted and frequently used mathematic analysis method that supports multi-criteria decision-making. The priority assessment in AHP is based on mathematical analysis of pairwise comparisons defined on hierarchical tree structure, in which, the priority scales between each two related terms are relying on the judgments of domain experts. A significant number of research projects employing AHP method has been proposed in several domains [29], however, as highlighted in [30], little work has been done in specifying and formalizing the important concepts together with their relationships from the AHP method itself. In [30] the authors propose an ontological representation of AHP method to deal with the lack of a deep conceptual understanding on its objects (attributes and reasoning) as well as the lack of flexibility and reusability. This conceptual model (Figure 6) acts in this research as a reference model to facilitate the concept mapping between the domain ontology (obtained in previous knowledge discovering and extraction process) and the IA method.

The importance of having an AHP ontology (Figure 6) merged with a concept model of the attributes (Figure 4) is that, for EIA purposes, each attribute is considered a criterion. Such connection helps the prioritization and evaluation of attributes, made by practitioners and academy, by adopting the AHP technique as a tool to compare the criteria. In addition, during the assessment activities, as each criterion is being compared with others, it is possible to have an adherence degree related to the achievement of the attributes (and guidelines).

The proposed attributes will be firstly evaluated by domain experts and then validated in a selected organization. Figure 7 overviews the evaluation and validation scenario, as a zoom in process A4 (Figure 1). The preliminary attributes (and guidelines) are inputs to expert evaluation process in order to refine those objects. The validation process is divided in two modes: design and execution mode. In the design mode, a decision hierarchy is firstly created based on refined attributes and the AHP method.

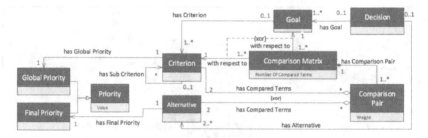

Fig. 6. Ontological representation of AHP

Then, an algorithm will process this hierarchy and produce corresponding questionnaires for criteria assessment and alternative assessment. In the execution mode, practitioners and experts related to the entities will be invited to answer these questionnaires. Finally, based on the assessment of criteria and the alternatives (with respect to each criterion), this validation process will generate the ranked results used as input for the A5 step (Figure 1).

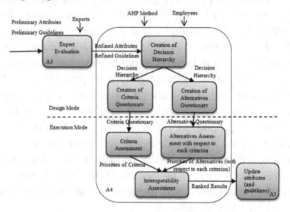

Fig. 7. Overview of the evaluation and validation scenario

Regarding the planning of the assessment and the assessment itself (Figure 1, A6 and A8), the AHP can provide a structure to assess two aspects of EI: potentiality and compatibility [31]. Potentiality can be analyzed as an internal characteristic that reflects the readiness (adherence to attributes) and preparation to interoperate with a possible future partner. Compatibility can also be analyzed regarding internal characteristics, but comparing them between two (or more) known public entities willing to interoperate. In this research, the compatibility approach intends to evaluate which entity, from a group of alternatives (Figure 8, GE B...Z) will better interoperate with a specified entity (Figure 8, GE A). A potential approach implies the ranking of the attributes in order to create ranges that are related to some maturity level. That is, according to the ranking of the group of attributes of an entity A, the entity is associated to a certain maturity level, with a potential degree for future interoperability actions (Figure 8, ML-1, ML-2 and ML-N).

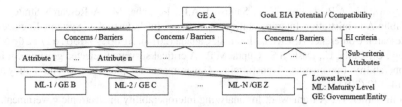

Fig. 8. Potential and compatibility EIA into AHP structure

3   Conclusions

The problem of obtaining, identifying and organizing relevant knowledge is an important issue to the IA in public administration. Considering the models and frameworks established in EIA (in private and public sector), it was detected a gap in the literature regarding the extraction of measurements attributes and criteria. This paper is part of the result of a wider research scope (Figure 1) and presented a rationale of an attributes' extraction from a literature database in order to help the definition and composition of guidelines regarding the IA of public entities. The presented rationale follow steps related to identification of concepts, word count and word analysis, resulting in a set of 17 preliminary attributes and a wide structured and formalized knowledge formal concepts set. The paper also presents an approach of how to adopt a decision-making technique (AHP) in order to organize the attributes (during a validation phase) and assess the interoperability (during an assessment phase).

References

1. IEEE Standard computer dictionary. A Compilation of IEEE Standard computer glossaries, IEEE Std 610, p. 114 (1991), doi:10.1109/IEEESTD.1991.106963
2. Carney, D., Fisher, D., Place, P.: Topics in Interoperability: System-of-Systems Evolution. Technical Note, CMU/SEI-2005-TN-002. Software Engineering Institute, Carnegie Mellon University, Pittsburgh, PA (2005), http://www.sei.cmu.edu/reports/05tn002.pdf
3. Pardo, T.A., Burke, G.B.: Improving Government Interoperability: A Capability Assessment Framework for Government Managers. Technical report. Center for Technology in Government, University at Albany, NY, USA (2008), http://goo.gl/20z27B (retrieved)
4. Yahia, E., Aubry, A., Panetto, H.: Formal measures for semantic interoperability assessment in cooperative enterprise information systems. Computers in Industry 63(5), 443–457 (2012), doi:10.1016/j.compind.2012.01.010
5. Camargo, A.R.: Cidade e informática, contatos e interações: explorando manifestações de urbanização virtual, Pesquisa CNPq Proc 301383 /2005-7. Escola de Engenharia de São Carlos, USP, São Carlos, SP (2009)
6. Novakouski, M., Lewis, G.: Interoperability in the e-Government Context. Technical Note, CMU/SEI-2011-TN-014, Carnegie Mellon University, Pittsburgh, PA (2012), http://www.sei.cmu.edu/reports/11tn014.pdf (retrieved)
7. UNDP (United Nations Development Programme). e-Government Interoperability: Overview (2007), http://goo.gl/bfK0ix

8. Cestari, J.M.A.P., Loures, E.R., Santos, E.A.P., Lezoche, M.: A Research Strategy for Public Administration Interoperability Assessment. In: Industrial & Systems Engineering Research Conference (ISERC), Montreal, Canada (2014), http://goo.gl/z26gDG

9. Ray, D., Gulla, U., Dash, S.S., Gupta, M.P.: A critical survey of selected government interoperability frameworks. Transforming Government: People, Process and Policy 5(2), 114–142 (2011)

10. Solli-Sather, H.: A framework for analyzing interoperability in electronic government. International Journal of Electronic Finance 5(1), 32–48 (2011)

11. Gottschalk, P.: Maturity levels for interoperability in digital government. Government Information Quarterly 26(1), 75–81 (2009)

12. Zutshi, A., Grilo, A., Jardim-Goncalves, R.: The business interoperability quotient measurement model. Computers in Industry 63(5), 389–404 (2012)

13. National Institute of Standards and Technology (NIST). Integration Definition for Function Modeling, IDEF0 (1993), http://www.idef.com/pdf/idef0.pdf

14. Saaty, R.W.: The analytic hierarchy process—what it is and how it is used. Mathematical Modelling 9(3–5), 161–176 (1987)

15. Nonaka, I.: A dynamic theory of organizational knowledge creation. Organization Science 5(1), 14–37 (1994)

16. Swan, J., Newell, S., Scarbrough, H., Hislop, D.: Knowledge management and innovation: networks and networking. Journal of Knowledge Management 3(4), 262–275 (1999)

17. Von Krogh, G.: Care in knowledge Creation. California Management Review 40(3), 133–153 (1998)

18. Keeling, J.: Development of Systematic Knowledge Management for Public Health: A Public Health Law Ontology. PhD Thesis, Graduate School of Arts and Sciences, Columbia University (2012)

19. Vocabulary Dictionary, http://www.vocabulary.com/

20. Cambridge Dictionaries Online, http://dictionary.cambridge.org/us

21. Oxford Dictionaries, http://www.oxforddictionaries.com/us

22. Object Management Group, http://www.uml.org/

23. Deschamps, F.: Proposal for the systematization of enterprise engineering contributions: guidelines for enterprise engineering initiatives. PhD Thesis, PUCPR, Curitiba (2013)

24. MaxQDA, http://www.maxqda.com/

25. Pierce, J.R.: An introduction to information theory: symbols, signals & noise by John Robinson Pierce, p. 336. Dover Publications, Subsequent (1980)

26. Stanford POS Tagger software, http://nlp.stanford.edu/software/tagger.shtml

27. Toutanova, K., Klein, D., Manning, C., Singer, Y.: Feature-Rich Part-of-Speech Tagging with a Cyclic Dependency Network. In: Proceedings of HLT-NAACL, pp. 252–259 (2003)

28. Lezoche, M., Panetto, H., Aubry, A.: Conceptualisation approach for cooperative information systems interoperability. In: ICEIS 2011 (2011)

29. Vaidya, O.S., Kumar, S.: Analytic hierarchy process: An overview of applications. European Journal of operational research 169(1), 1–29 (2006)

30. Liao, Y., Loures, E.R., Panetto, H., Canciglieri, O.: A Novel Approach for Ontological Representation of Analytic Hierarchy Process. Adv. Materials Research, Online (2014)

31. Guédria, W., Naudet, Y., Chen, D.: A maturity model assessing interoperability potential. In: Halpin, T., Nurcan, S., Krogstie, J., Soffer, P., Proper, E., Schmidt, R., Bider, I. (eds.) BPMDS 2011 and EMMSAD 2011. LNBIP, vol. 81, pp. 276–283. Springer, Heidelberg (2011)

Key Deficiencies of Semantic Business Process Search

Avi Wasser and Maya Lincoln

University of Haifa, Israel
awasser@haifa.ac.il, maya.lincoln@processgene.com

Abstract In recent years, researchers have become increasingly interested in developing frameworks and tools for searching business process model repositories. While research on searching structured repositories has been extensive, little attention was dedicated to searching business process content within unstructured repositories, such as the Web. We demonstrate why current search technologies are not useful for extracting process content from the Web, and explain the core reasons for the deficiency. We then express the requirements for a framework that could overcome the presented shortcomings.

Keywords: Business process search, Business process repositories, Natural language processing, semantic search, operational search.

1 Introduction

Business Process Models (BPMs) are considered an important mine of organizational knowledge, and therefore are a major source for searching and retrieving operational and enterprise related data [18].

Researchers have become increasingly interested in developing methods and tools for retrieving information from business process repositories [3,14,19]. While research on searching structured repositories has been extensive, little or no attention was dedicated to searching business process content within unstructured repositories, such as the Web. Such repositories are constantly becoming more extensive, and are accessible to a wide user population through search engines.

Two common methods for retrieving information from a repository are querying and searching. Querying is aimed at retrieving information using a structured query language. The significance of querying business processes has been acknowledged by BPMI[1] that launched a Business Process Query Language (BPQL) initiative. Searching, on the other hand, allows information retrieval using keywords or natural language and was shown to be an effective method for non-experts.

Research in the field of business process retrieval has mainly focused on *semantics* and *structural* similarity analysis techniques [3,15,4,11]. Using these frameworks one can retrieve process models that either contain semantically

---

[1] Business Process Management Initiative, http://www.bpmi.org/

R. Meersman et al. (Eds.): OTM 2014 Workshops, LNCS 8842, pp. 339–346, 2014.

related components (e.g. activity names with a specified keyword) or match a requested graph structure: e.g. that presents a sequence of activities. While these methods can be applied on structured process repositories, it is practically impossible to apply them on the unstructured Web.

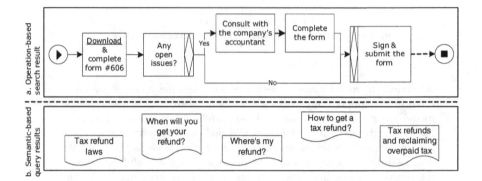

Fig. 1. An example of search results for "how to claim a tax refund"

In order to illustrate why semantic search is not adequate for process retrieval from unstructured repositories, we will present a motivating example, as follows. Consider an employee interested in finding out "how to claim a tax refund." An expected outcome of this retrieval request would be a *process model* that represents the order of activities that one should follow in order to achieve the required process goal, as illustrated in Fig 1a. The benefit of such a retrieval framework is that the result is ready for execution. Without any preliminary knowledge of the underlying repository structure, the user can receive a full-fledged process model.

The retrieval output is related to the search phrase in *operational* terms. For example, Fig 1a provides a segment that is *not* similar semantically to the search phrase text. Specifically, all three search phrase terms ("Claim", "Tax" and "Refund") are not represented by any of its activities. Such "how-to" questions are hard to fulfill using common query languages due to the complex logic that is embedded within such questions [4] and especially without specific knowledge on process structure and activity naming. Therefore, using querying techniques on the Web, would yield a list of data items (e.g. Web pages, or media items) with semantically similar titles, as illustrated in Fig 1b. Such outcome does not tell the user "how-to" fulfill the process goal in a structured and operational manner.

In this work we present the key deficiencies of semantic business process search. We demonstrate the current shortcomings using examples from top four search engines.

The rest of the paper is organized as follows: we present related work in Section 2, positioning our work with respect to previous research. In Section 3 we present the major shortcomings of current Web search engines in extracting process data. We discuss future research elaborations and conclude in Section 4.

2   Related Work

Related works include query and search techniques in BPM. Works such as [16,17,4,2,7] query business process repositories to extract process model (graph) segments. Such methods require prior knowledge of the structure of the process repository and the exact notation that is used to express it. Therefore, they are not adequate for search on the Web that should work well even without prior knowledge regarding the process repository.

Keyword search on general tree or graph data structures can also be applied to process repositories [10,8,9]. These methods allow users to find information without having to learn a complex query language or getting prior knowledge of the process structure. Therefore, this method is also applied by leading business process management (BPM) software vendors, such as ProcessGene[2], SAP[3], Oracle[4] and others. Some works extend the tree and graph keyword search methods to support a more intuitive interface for the user by enabling searches based on natural language [13,12]. According to [1], the straightforwardness of a natural language makes it the most desirable database query interface. The retrieved information in both keyword and natural language search methods is in the form of single process model components such as activities and roles that are semantically similar to the searched phrase. These techniques are merely relevant to process search on the Web, since in this case (a) users are seeking to receive a complete process; and (b) the expected process result is usually not related *semantically* to the search phrase, but rather *operationally*.

The work in [14] extends the above line of works. This work supports the retrieval of complete process segments by applying dynamic segmentation of the process repository. The search result is a compendium of data (a segment of a business process model) related to the operational meaning of the searched text. Nevertheless, as all other works, this method relies also on a process-structured database, and cannot work "as is" on an unstructured repository, such as the Web.

Another line of work focuses on automatic construction of process data ontologies. The work in [5] proposes a query-by-example approach that relies on ontological description of business processes, activities, and their relationships, which can automatically be built from the workflow models themselves. The work in [6] automatically extracts the semantics from searched conceptual models, without requiring manual meta-data annotation, while basing its method on a model-independent framework. The work in [14] automatically extracts and uses the operational layer (the "how-to") and the business rules encapsulated in a process repository. Such automatic ontology extraction techniques are important for analyzing data encapsulated in the Web. Nevertheless, the current research literature is based solely on process-flow structured repositories and not on unstructured repositories such as the Web.

---

[2] http://www.processgene.com
[3] http://www.sap.com
[4] http://www.oracle.com

3   Key Deficiencies of Semantic Business Process Search

Current Web searches are based on keyword queries and semantic similarity lookups. This makes data extraction relatively easy and simple for users. Nevertheless, and as demonstrated in Section 1, it is practically impossible to extract processes from the Web using current semantic search engine technology. This is an inherent material weakness that in our opinion presents a significant barrier for the evolution of Web usability.

The main search engines (e.g. Google[5], Microsoft Bing[6], Yahoo[7], Ask[8] and others) are still at experimental, initial phases of enabling Web process-searches. For example, recent R&D efforts of Google yield lists of "how to" instructions for very limited process sets. For instance, when searching in Google "how to issue an invoice," a set of related documents and media is retrieved, without any process-formatted results, as illustrated in Fig. 2. However, in some cases, we identified initial attempts to retrieve instruction-based results for certain "how to" queries. These results are presented before the standard Google search results, within a dedicated frame, in a list-format, which is a first step in aiming to retrieve and present process-flow formats. This presentation is still at a preliminary phase as Google requests users' feedback regarding the quality of these instruction lists. An example of such a list resulted from the search phrase: "How to take a screenshot from Windows" is presented in Fig. 3.

Besides these attempts to present somewhat process-driven results, we note that standard search results for "how-to" or "process-driven" queries are very limited, again due to the aforementioned material weakness of semantic search. We sampled the top 4 search engines (Google, Bing, Yahoo and Ask) with the following examples of process-search scenarios, as presented in Table 1. As demonstrated, current search technologies cannot provide adequate results. We included not only business process but also personal process queries as we believe that the size and amount of data presented in the Web will also extend the scope of process related searches beyond the domain of BPM.

Clearly, these results encompass a large, unstructured, set of data with a low level of usability:

- Results are not presented in standardized process notations - nor in basic flowchart formations. Therefore, practically, for the end-user, it is not possible to deduct an actual process from search results.
- It is not clear what the required steps are and what is the order of activities for achieving the process goal.
- It is also not possible to assess the quality and relevance of the suggested results from an operational viewpoint - as ranking is based on semantics and not on operational characteristics of a process.

---

[5] https://www.google.com
[6] http://www.bing.com
[7] https://www.yahoo.com
[8] http://www.ask.com

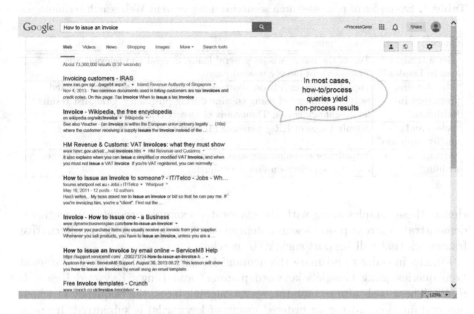

Fig. 2. An example of search results for "how to issue an invoice"

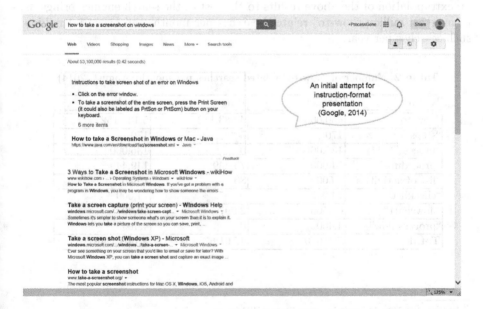

Fig. 3. An example of list-formatted search results for "how to take a screenshot on Windows"

Table 1. Examples of process-search scenarios using current Web search technologies

Query	Result Samples
"Get a student loan in London"	Top of the page: Ads on general loans. Several non relevant ads. Thousands of loosely related pages.
"Monitor first pregnancy in Baltimore"	Top of the page: Ads on abortion and monitor sales. highly ranked results- damages of using cocaine during pregnancy, Craig-list results on pregnancy issues. Thousands of loosely related pages.
"Select and qualify suppliers"	Mainly pages of HR / personnel recruitment companies.
"Arrange a wedding"	Tripadvisor recommendations on wedding locations, ads on churches and, explanations on flower bouquets.

Hence, these samples along with the elaborated example presented in section 1 demonstrate current process-search deficiencies and the need for an alternative framework that will support such Web searches.

Finally, in order to estimate the demand for such a solution we ran targeted Web queries using Google's keyword planner[9] and Bing's Keyword Research tool[10]. These tools aim to monitor, on an ongoing basis, the frequency in which any certain keyword (or an ordered group of keywords) is submitted. It turns out that "how-to" related keywords are searched over 5.5 million times every month by Google and Bing together, as demonstrated in Table 2. As of July 2014 Google and Bing hold over 73% of the search engine market[11]. Therefore, an extrapolation of the above results to the rest of the search engines brings us to over 7.6 million "how-to" related searches per month, and over 91.4 million such searches per year.

Table 2. Number of "how-to" related searches per month (August, 2014)

Keyword	Google	Bing	**Total**
"how to"	450,000	4,683,152	5,133,152
"steps for"	170	0	170
"process"	135,000	0	135,000
"procedure"	74,000	75,449	149,449
"list of activities"	1,600	80	1,680
"checklist"	74,000	0	74,000
"flowchart"	60,500	2,997	63,497
"process flow"	4,400	0	4,400
Total	799,670	4,761,678	**5,561,348**

---

[9] https://adwords.google.com/KeywordPlanner

[10] https://www.bing.com/webmaster/diagnostics/keyword/research

[11] According to Netmarketshare, http://www.netmarketshare.com/
search-engine-market-share.aspx?qprid=4&qpcustomd=0

Apparently, there is a relatively high demand for such queries, and despite this large target market there is no feasible solution for conducting these process-driven searches.

4 Conclusions

In this work we presented the key deficiencies of semantic business process search within the Web. The need for unstructured search capabilities exists not only for organizations, but also for a large audience of individuals that seek an accessible solution for "how to" queries. As future work, we propose to structure a framework that could overcome the shortcomings of existing search technologies within unstructured repositories. Such a framework should describe: (1) how to extract full-fledged process models out of unstructured repositories; (2) a process-based ranking and relaxation mechanisms. In addition, it will be required to provide an applicative case study and experiments to measure the efficiency of the proposed framework. It is hoped that by expanding search and query capabilities of processes within the Web, users will be able to extract operational knowledge more simply and efficiently.

References

1. Androutsopoulos, I., Ritchie, G.D., Thanisch, P.: Natural language interfaces to databases-an introduction. Natural Language Engineering 1(01), 29–81 (1995)
2. Awad, A.: BPMN-Q: A Language to Query Business Processes. In: EMISA, vol. 119, pp. 115–128 (2007)
3. Awad, A., Polyvyanyy, A., Weske, M.: Semantic querying of business process models. In: 12th International IEEE Enterprise Distributed Object Computing Conference, pp. 85–94. IEEE (2008)
4. Beeri, C., Eyal, A., Kamenkovich, S., Milo, T.: Querying business processes with BP-QL. Information Systems 33(6), 477–507 (2008)
5. Belhajjame, K., Brambilla, M.: Ontology-based description and discovery of business processes. Enterprise, Business-Process and Information Systems Modeling, 85–98 (2009)
6. Bozzon, A., Brambilla, M., Fraternali, P.: Searching repositories of web application models. In: Benatallah, B., Casati, F., Kappel, G., Rossi, G. (eds.) ICWE 2010. LNCS, vol. 6189, pp. 1–15. Springer, Heidelberg (2010)
7. Goderis, A., Li, P., Goble, C.: Workflow discovery: the problem, a case study from e-Science and a graph-based solution (2006)
8. Guo, L., Shao, F., Botev, C., Shanmugasundaram, J.: XRANK: Ranked keyword search over XML documents. In: Proceedings of the 2003 ACM SIGMOD International Conference on Management of Data, pp. 16–27. ACM (2003)
9. He, H., Wang, H., Yang, J., Yu, P.S.: BLINKS: ranked keyword searches on graphs. In: Proceedings of the 2007 ACM SIGMOD International Conference on Management of Data, pp. 305–316. ACM (2007)
10. Hristidis, V., Papakonstantinou, Y., Balmin, A.: Keyword proximity search on XML graphs (2003)

11. Karni, R., Wasser, A., Lincoln, M.: Content analysis of business processes. International Journal of E-Business Development (2014)
12. Katz, B., Lin, J., Quan, D.: Natural language annotations for the SemanticWeb. On the Move to Meaningful Internet Systems 2002: CoopIS, DOA, and ODBASE, 1317–1331 (2010)
13. Li, Y., Yang, H., Jagadish, H.V.: NaLIX: A generic natural language search environment for XML data. ACM Transactions on Database Systems (TODS) 32(4), 30 (2007)
14. Lincoln, M., Gal, A.: Searching business process repositories using operational similarity. On the Move to Meaningful Internet Systems: OTM, 2–19 (2011)
15. Markovic, I., Pereira, A.C., Stojanovic, N.: A framework for querying in business process modelling. In: Proceedings of the Multikonferenz Wirtschaftsinformatik (MKWI), Munchen, Germany (2008)
16. Momotko, M., Subieta, K.: Process query language: A way to make workflow processes more flexible. In: Benczúr, A.A., Demetrovics, J., Gottlob, G. (eds.) ADBIS 2004. LNCS, vol. 3255, pp. 306–321. Springer, Heidelberg (2004)
17. Shao, Q., Sun, P., Chen, Y.: WISE: a workflow information search engine. In: IEEE 25th International Conference on ICDE 2009, pp. 1491–1494. IEEE (2009)
18. Wasser, A., Lincoln, M., Karni, R.: Accelerated enterprise process modeling through a formalized functional typology. In: van der Aalst, W.M.P., Benatallah, B., Casati, F., Curbera, F. (eds.) BPM 2005. LNCS, vol. 3649, pp. 446–451. Springer, Heidelberg (2005)
19. Wasser, A., Lincoln, M., Karni, R.: Processgene querya tool for querying the content layer of business process models. In: Demo Session of the 4th International Conference on Business Process Management, p. 18 (2006)

Semantic Representation and Computation of Cloud-Based Customer Relationship Management Solutions

Ricardo Colomo-Palacios[1] and José María Álvarez-Rodríguez[2]

[1] Østfold University College, Faculty of Computer Sciences
B R A Veien 4, 1783 Halden, Norway
Ricardo.colomo-palacios@hiof.no
[2] Universidad Carlos III de Madrid, Computer Science Department
Av. Universidad 30, Leganés, 28911, Madrid, Spain
joalvare@inf.uc3m.es

Abstract. This paper introduces a RDF vocabulary to semantically represent and compute quantitative indexes with the aim of providing a context-aware system to manage Customer Relationship Management (CRM) quality indicators. This tool is based on CRM Index, tailor made index based on Service Measurement Index to measure cloud CRM solutions. Apart from the tool itself, in the paper the authors introduce categories and attributes defined for the CRM world along with specific metrics.

Keywords: Customer Relationship Management, Vendor Selection, Quantitative Composite Index.

1   Introduction

Companies make large investments on CRM software in order to achieve the maximum return from their customers through sales, marketing, and other related activities [1]. In this line, Gartner asseverates that CRM software revenue is forecast to reach $23.9 billion in 2014, with cloud revenue accounting for 49 percent. SaaS or cloud-based CRM deployments currently represent more than 40 percent of all CRM deployments, and look set to reach 50 percent during 2015 [2]. Thus, the market for CRM software is becoming stable and clearly segmented [1]. In general, almost all solutions present two kinds of deployments: On-premise and cloud-based. The decision to adopt cloud-based solutions requires a qualitative and quantitative comparison of software acquisition approaches that goes beyond the scope of this work. Literature reported several models to support decision process being the work of Bibi et al. [3] one of the most recent and accurate models.

However, and once decided to embrace a cloud model, a key issue is how organizations are able to choose the best cloud-based CRM solution that would suit their needs and constraints. Not in vain, selecting suitable CRM systems is a decision problem with economic, behavioral, technical and functional implications [4]. Given this importance literature has reported several works devoted to guide companies in

R. Meersman et al. (Eds.): OTM 2014 Workshops, LNCS 8842, pp. 347–357, 2014.

the selection process [4–6]. The purpose of this paper is to present an innovative tool to select the best cloud-based CRM system from a company's perspective. This approach will be based in three different pillars, semantic-based representation and computation of quantitative indexes, cloud intelligence, the Analytic Hierarchy Process (AHP) and an adapted version of the Service Measurement Index (SMI). Thus, authors firstly propose a semantic representation of a quantitative index with the aim of being able to validate and compute weighted indicators in an automatic way. Afterwards the indicators adapted from the SMI are defined under this formal model to finally assign weights to the different indicators by means of applying the AHP method and compute the index for the selected CRM vendors.

2   Literature Review

2.1   The Analytic Hierarchy Process (AHP)

AHP is a model developed by Saaty [7] as a single author and later expanded by Wind and Saaty [8] aimed to solve multi-criteria decision problems. AHP, which is a qualitative and quantitative method, is a useful approach for evaluating the alternatives of complex multiple criteria involving subjective judgment. AHP is an especially symmetric way that could transform complex problems into simple hierarchic structure [9]. AHP technique is nowadays very popular and has been applied in wide variety of areas including planning, selecting the best alternative, resource allocation and resolving conflicts [10]. Focusing on the topic of this paper, the process of evaluation and selection of the software solutions involves simultaneous consideration of multiple attributes to rank the available alternatives and select the best one [11]; therefore, software evaluation can be formulated as multiple criteria decision making problem [12]. As a consequence of this, AHP has been presented in several works on the topic. Maybe the most fertile area is ERP selection e.g. [13, 14]. Given the diversity of cloud service offerings, an important challenge for customers is to discover who are the "right" cloud providers that can satisfy their requirements [15]. AHP has been widely used in CRM assessments e.g. [1], [5], [16], [17], [18]. However and in spite of its popularity, to the best of authors' knowledge, this is the first attempt to combine AHP and SMI in a system to provide recommendations for CRM service providers in cloud settings. Moreover, this paper not only describes the list of criteria included in AHP, but also presents the underlying technological infrastructure to represent and compute a quantitative and hierarchical index comprising different indicators. To do so and due to the growing interest in the use of semantic-based technologies [19], the Resource Description Framework (RDF) is used as a common and shared data model to elevate the meaning of information resources. In this context both the structure of the index and the computation process are represented in RDF with the aim of boosting transparency, standardization, adaptability and extensibility, to name a few, providing a tool for taking the most of data and for easing policy-making processes such as CRM vendor selection.

2.2   Service Measurement Index (SMI)

The Cloud Service Measurement Index Consortium (CSMIC) proposed a framework based on common characteristics of cloud services. The Service Measurement Index (SMI) is a set of business-relevant Key Performance Indicators (KPIs) that provide a standardized method for measuring and comparing a business service regardless of whether that service is internally provided or sourced from an outside company [20]. The SMI is a hierarchical framework whose top level divides the measurement space into 7 categories: Accountability, Agility, Assurance, Financial, Performance, Security and Privacy and, finally, Usability. Each category is further refined by 3 or more attributes. At this moment, there are no standardized available metrics or methods to define KPIs and compare cloud providers, and the only work in this direction [15] is not part of the SMI outputs. Work in CSMIC is currently ongoing on the definition of the KPIs and measures related to several attributes [20]. As a result of its importance, SMI has been a backbone in several works devoted to measure diverse aspects in the cloud computing arena e.g. [21, 22]. In this work, authors present the framework for assessing CRM services in cloud environments based on a particularization of KPIs for CRM systems and a set of metrics for each measurable attribute.

3   Theoretical Modeling of a Quantitative Composite Index

3.1   Background Motivation and Concepts

Public and private bodies are continuously seeking for new analytical tools and methods to assess, rank and compare their performance based on distinct indicators and dimensions with the objective of making some decision or developing a new policy. In this context, the creation and use of quantitative indexes is a widely accepted practice that has been applied to domains such as Bibliometrics and academic performance and quality (the Impact Factor by Thomson-Reuters, the H-index or the Shanghai and Webometrics rankings), the Web impact (the Webindex by the Webfoundation) or cloud computing (the Global Cloud Index by Cisco, the CSC index, the VMWare Cloud Index, etc.) to name a few (apart from the traditional ones such as the gross domestic product). Nevertheless the sheer mass of data now available is raising a new dynamic and challenging environment in which traditional tools are facing major problems to deal with data-sources diversity, structural issues or complex processes of estimation. New paradigms and tools are required to take advantage of the existing data-based environment to design and estimate actions in this dynamic context and with the aim of providing new context-aware and added-value services that can help a deeper and broader understanding of the impact of a policy in a faster and more efficient way. As a consequence, common features and requirements can be extracted from the existing situation out: 1) Data sources. Data and information is continuously being generated as observations from social networks, public and private institutions, NGOs, services and applications, etc. creating a tangled environment of sources, formats and access protocols with a huge but restricted potential for exploitation. 2) Structure. Quantitative indexes are usually defined (a mathematical model) by experts to aggregate several indicators (in a hierarchical structure) in just one value to provide a measure of the impact or performance of some policy in a certain context. The structure of these indexes is obviously subjected to change over time to collect more information or adjust their composition and relationships. 3) Computation process. Observations are gathered from diverse data sources and aligned to the index structure, commonly indicators that are processed through various mathematical operators to generate a final index value. Nevertheless the computation process is not always described, so it cannot be easily replied for third-parties with other purposes. And 4) Documentation. New policy-making or quality management strategies go ahead of a simple and closed value and it is necessary to bring new ways of exploiting data and information.

On the other hand, one of the mainstreams in the Semantic Web area lies in the application of the Linked Data initiative in different domains with the aim of solving existing problems of integration and interoperability. In this context, the present work is therefore focused in applying semantic web vocabularies and datasets to model quantitative indexes from both structural and computational points of view in a "policy-making" context, more specifically in CRM vendor selection. In order to reach the major objective of building a re-usable Web of Data, the publication of information and data under a common data model (RDF) and formats with a specific formal query language (SPARQL) provide the required building blocks to turn the web of documents into a real database. In the particular case of statistical data, the RDF Data Cube [23], a W3C Working Draft document, is a shared effort to represent statistical data in RDF reusing parts (the cube model) of the Statistical Data and Metadata Exchange Vocabulary (SDMX), an ISO standard for exchanging and sharing statistical data and meta-data among organizations. The Data Cube vocabulary is a core foundation which supports extension vocabularies to enable publication of other aspects of statistical data flows or other multi-dimensional data sets. Previously, the Statistical Core Vocabulary [24] was the *de facto* standard to describe statistical information in the Web of Data. Some works are also emerging to mainly publish statistical data following the concepts of the Linked Data initiative such as [25], among others. Mainly semantics allows us to model logical restrictions on data and the computation process while linked data enables the description of indexes in terms of existing concepts and the publication of new data and information under a set of principles to boost their re-use and automatic processing through machine-readable formats and access protocols. This light semantic-based technology can partially address this challenging environment for supporting new quality-checking strategies. That is why two main concepts are introduced: 1) a high-level model on top of the RDF Data Cube Vocabulary, a shared effort to model statistical data in RDF reusing parts (the cube model) of the Statistical Data and Metadata Exchange Vocabulary (SDMX), to represent the structure and computation of quantitative indexes, and 2) a Java-SPARQL based processor to exploit the meta-information and compute the new index values.

Finally, as a motivating and on-going example, a quality manager wants to re-use quality indicators to model and compute a new index, "The Naive CRM Quality Index". This index uses the components "Maintainability" (c_1) and "Usability" (c_2) with the aim of comparing and selecting a CRM vendor. From these components two indicators have been respectively selected by experts: "Stability" (in_1) and "Understandability" (in_1). Following a top-down approach the index, i, is calculated through an ordered weighted averaging (OWA) operator using the formula: $\sum_1^n w_i c_i$, where w_i is the weight of the component c_i. On the other hand, both components only aggregates one indicator, the computation must also consider the observation status and values must be normalized using the *z-score* before computing intermediate and final values for each indicator, component and index. Furthermore, this index is supposed to change in the future adding new components or indicators, modifying the computation processes (weights) or the structure (new components, indicators and dimensions).

Table 1. Example of observations from "The Naive CRM Quality Index"

Description	CRM Vendor	Value	Status
Indicator			
Stability	C_1	0.5	Normal
Understandability	C_1	0.8	Normal
Stability	C_2	0.3	Normal
Understandability	C_2	0.7	Normal
Component			
Maintainability	C_1	0.5	Estimated
Usability	C_1	0.8	Estimated
Maintainability	C_2	0.3	Estimated
Usability	C_2	0.7	Estimated
Index			
The Naive CRM Quality Index	C_1	0.4*0.5+0.6*0.8 = 0.64	Estimated
The Naive CRM Quality Index	C_2	0.3*0.5+0.7*0.8 = 0.68	Estimated

3.2   Theoretical Modeling of a Quantitative Composite Index

Essentially a quantitative index is comprised of the aggregation of several components. In the same way, a component consists of an aggregation of indicators that keep concrete observations. From this initial definition some characteristics and assumptions can be found: 1) Although observations can be directly mapped to an index or a component, they are frequently computed applying a bottom-up approach from an indicator to a component and so on. 2) An observation is a real numerical value extracted from some agent under a precise context. Generally, observations only take one measure and are considered to be raw without any pre-processing. 3) Before aggregating observation values, components and indexes can estimate missing values to finally normalize them in order to get a quantitative value. According to the aforementioned characteristics and assumptions, an *observable* element (index, component or indicator) is a dataset of observations under a specific context (dimensions and/or meta-data) that can be directly gathered from external sources or computed by some kind of OWA operator.

Definition 1 (Observation o). It is a tuple$\{v, m, s\}$, where v is a numerical value for the measure m with a status s that belongs to only one dataset of observations O.

Definition 2 (Dataset q). It is a tuple$\{O, m, D, A, T\}$, where O is a set of observations for only one measure m that is described under a set of dimensions D and a set of annotations A. Additionally, some attributes can be defined in the set T for structure enrichment.

Definition 3 (Aggregated Dataset aq). It is an aggregation of n datasets q_i (identified by the set Q) whose set of observations O is derived by applying an OWA operator p to the observations O_{q_i}

As a necessary condition for the computation process, an aggregated dataset aq defined by means of the set of dimensions D_{aq} can be computed $iif\ \forall\ q_j \in Q: D_{aq} \subseteq D_{qj}$. Furthermore, the OWA operator p can only aggregate values belonging to the same measure m. As a consequence of the aforementioned definitions, some remarks must be outlined in order to restrict the understanding of a quantitative index (structure and computation): 1) The set of dimensions D, annotations A and attributes T for a given dataset Q is always the same with the aim of describing all observations under the same context. 2) An index i and a component c are aggregated datasets. Nevertheless this restriction is relaxed if observations can be directly mapped to these elements without any computation process. 3) An indicator in can be either a dataset or an aggregated dataset. 4) All elements in definitions must be uniquely identified. 5) An aggregated dataset is also a dataset.

3.3   Representation of a Quantitative Composite Index in RDF

Since the previous section has stated the key definitions to represent quantitative indexes by aggregation, a direct translation built on the top of the RDF Data Cube Vocabulary, SDMX and other semantic web vocabularies is presented in Table 2.

Table 2. Summary of mapping between the index definition and the RDF Data Cube Vocabulary

Concept	Vocabulary element	Comments
Observation o	qb:Observation	Instance of the class qb:Observation to collect values and their context
Numerical value v	xsd:double	Restriction to numerical values
Measure m	qb:MeasureProperty and sdmx-measure:obsValue	Restriction to one measure
Status s	sdmx-concept:obsStatus	Defined by the SDMX-RDF vocabulary
Dataset q	qb:dataset and qb:DataStructureDefinition	Metadata of the qb:Dataset
Dimension $d_i \in D$	qb:DimensionProperty	Context of observations
Annotation $a_i \in A$	owl:AnnotationProperty	Intensive use of Dublin Core
Attribute $at_i \in T$	qb:AttributeProperty	Link to existing datasets such as DBPedia
OWA operator p	SPARQL 1.1 aggregation operators	Other extensions depend on the RDF repository
Index, Component and Indicator	skos:Concept	SKOS taxonomy (logical structure)

Since the structure and the computation processes can be built on the top of existing RDF vocabulary, it is then possible to make a translation to a generic SPARQL query (includes the basic OWA operator). The first implementation of an interpreter[1] for this vocabulary is based on traditional language processor techniques such as the use of design patterns (e.g. Composite or Visitor) to separate the exploitation of meta-data from the interpretation. Thus the processor works and

---

[1] It has been merged in a joint effort with the Computex service:
http://computex.herokuapp.com/

provides the following functionalities (hereafter load and query an endpoint are completely equivalent due to data is separated from access and storage formats): 1) The concepts and relationships (ontology) of the vocabulary are loaded to have access to common definitions. 2) The structure of an index described with the aforementioned vocabulary is also loaded to create a kind of Abstract Syntax Tree (AST) containing the defined meta-data. 3) Once the meta-data structure is available in the AST, it can be managed through three AST walkers that performs: a) validation (structure and RDF Data Cube normalization), b) SPARQL queries creation, and c) documentation generation (optional). 4) In order to promote new observations to the different components and indexes, a set of raw observations is also loaded and a new AST walker generates new values, through SPARQL queries, in a bottom-up approach until reaching the upper-level (index).

4 Quality Model for CRM Cloud Solutions

Based on SMI hierarchical framework, in this work authors adopted categories and attributes to build the CRMIndex. In this section, seven categories and their attributes are explained with particularization to CRM cloud solutions. Definitions are taken from SMI [20] and adapted taking into account recent developments in literature in CRM and cloud services area e.g. [1, 15]. Once a definition for each indicator has been stated, relevant metrics and how to calculate all of them are presented in the next table. Commonly, the transition from a qualitative indicator to a quantitative measure is not a mere process of establishing a numerical value. That is why the following metrics, see Table 3, seek for overcoming this issue by providing objective and quantitative metrics in a good percentage of the indicators. In order to define a formula for each metric, the next strategies have been defined: 1) if the metric can be calculated by checking features of the CRM vendor, then use a percentage-based formula; 2) if there is not easy way or agreed formula to calculate a quantitative measure, then use a Likert scale between 1..10;the value 1 should be used in case of unknown or missing metric instead of 0 to avoid potential misunderstanding during the evaluation. And 3) in some cases, the metric can be evaluated as 1 if the indicator is found, and 0 otherwise.

Table 3. Summary of indicators and metrics

Indicator	Metric
Accountability	
Auditability	$\dfrac{number\ of\ auditable\ CRM\ components}{number\ of\ CRM\ components}$
Compliance	$\dfrac{number\ of\ auditable\ CRM\ components\ that\ have\ been\ certified}{number\ of\ auditable\ CRM\ components}$
Contracting experience	Likert Scale 1-10
Ease of doing business	Likert Scale 1-10
Governance	$\dfrac{number\ of\ console\ managed\ CRM\ components}{number\ of\ CRM\ components}$
Ownership	Likert Scale 1-10

Table 3. (*continued*)

Provider business stability	$social\ reputation * p_{change} = 1 - (\frac{num\ of\ non-renovated\ clients}{n}) * p_{change}$, where *num of non-renovated clients* is the number of users that have decided to change the service provider, n is the number of users and p_{change} is the probability of change after time t renovations
Provider Certifications	$\frac{number\ of\ certified\ CRM\ components}{number\ of\ CRM\ components}$
Provider Contract/SLA Verification	$\frac{number\ of\ SLA\ aggrements\ provided\ by\ the\ service}{number\ of\ SLA\ aggrements\ required\ by\ the\ customer}$
Provider Ethicality	Likert Scale 1-10
Provider Personnel	$\frac{number\ of\ personnel\ requirements\ provided\ by\ the\ service}{number\ of\ personne\ requirements\ required\ by\ the\ customer}$
Provider Supply Chain	$\frac{number\ of\ certified\ SLA\ aggrements\ provided\ by\ the\ service}{number\ of\ SLA\ aggrements\ provided\ by\ the\ service}$
Sustainability	Likert Scale 1-10
Agility	
Adaptability	$\frac{number\ of\ customized\ CRM\ components}{number\ of\ CRM\ components}$
Elasticity	$\frac{number\ of\ time\ adaptable\ CRM\ components}{number\ of\ CRM\ components}$
Extensibility	$\frac{number\ of\ extended\ CRM\ components}{number\ of\ CRM\ components}$
Flexibility	$\frac{number\ of\ all\ new\ features\ added\ to\ the\ service}{number\ of\ all\ available\ features}$
Portability	$\frac{number\ of\ CRM\ components\ with\ export\ capabilities}{number\ of\ CRM\ components}$
Scalability	$\frac{number\ of\ distributed\ and\ scalable\ CRM\ components}{number\ of\ CRM\ components}$
Assurance	
Availability	$\frac{total\ service\ time - (total\ time\ for\ which\ the\ service\ was\ not\ available)}{total\ service\ time}$
Maintainability	$\frac{total\ service\ time - (total\ time\ for\ which\ the\ service\ was\ in\ maintenance)}{total\ service\ time}$
Recoverability	$\frac{total\ service\ time - (total\ time\ for\ which\ the\ service\ was\ being\ repared)}{total\ service\ time}$, it can be also measured using the metrics MTTF (mean time between failures, defined as the predicted elapsed time between inherent failures of a system) and MTTR (mean time to recover the service, measured as the average time that a device will take to recover from any failure)
Reliability	$Reliability = probability\ of\ violation * p_{tmf} = 1 - (\frac{num\ failure}{n}) * p_{tmf}$, where *num failure* is the number of users that have experienced a failure, n is the number of users and p_{tmf} is the promised mean time to failure
Resiliency/Fault Tolerance	$\frac{number\ of\ non-essential\ features}{number\ of\ essential\ features}$

Table 3. (*continued*)

Service stability	
Serviceability	$T = (T_f + T_s)$, there T_f time to find a failure and T_s time to solve it.
Financial	
Billing Process	Likert Scale 1-10
Cost	Cost depends on two main attributes: acquisition and on-going. It is not a mere question to compare CRM vendors regarding the cost but a simple formula can be fit to different CRM providers. $$\frac{cost\ of\ features\ required\ by\ the\ customer}{cost\ of\ features\ provided\ by\ the\ service} +$$ $$\frac{cost\ of\ maintenance\ of\ the\ features\ required\ by\ the\ customer}{cost\ of\ maintenance\ of\ the\ features\ provided\ by\ the\ service}$$
Financial Agility	Likert Scale 1-10
Financial Structure	Likert Scale 1-10
Performance	
Accuracy	$$\frac{number\ of\ features\ provided\ by\ the\ service}{number\ of\ features\ required\ by\ the\ customer}$$
Functionality	$$\frac{number\ of\ non-essential\ features\ provided\ by\ the\ service}{number\ of\ features\ provided\ by\ the\ service}$$
Suitability	$$\frac{number\ of\ non-essential\ features\ provided\ by\ the\ service}{number\ of\ non-essential\ features\ required\ by\ the\ customer}$$ if only essential requirements are satisfied = 1 if all features are satisfied = 0 otherwise. $number\ of\ features$
Interoperability	$$\frac{number\ of\ platforms\ that\ can\ connect\ to\ the\ service}{number\ of\ platforms\ that\ the\ customer\ needs\ to\ connect}$$
Service Response Time	• Average time to perform an operation. Time for an operation divided by the average time of all operations available in the service. • Maximum time to perform an operation is the maximum promised response time by the cloud provider for the service. • Response Time Failure is given by the percentage of occasions when the response time was higher than the promised maximum response time. Therefore, it is given by $100 * (n'/n)$, where n' is the number of times when the service provider was not able to fulfill their promise.
Security & privacy	
Access Control & Privilege Management	$$\frac{number\ of\ secured\ CRM\ components}{number\ of\ contracted\ CRM\ components}$$
Data Geographic/Political	Likert Scale 1-10
Data Integrity	Likert Scale 1-10
Data Privacy & Data Loss	Likert Scale 1-10
Physical & Environmental Security	Likert Scale 1-10
Proactive Threat & Vulnerability Management	$$\frac{number\ of\ contracted\ CRM\ components}{number\ of\ CRM\ components\ that\ can\ be\ managed\ under\ potential\ threats}$$
Retention/Disposition	Likert Scale 1-10
Security Management	Likert Scale 1-10
Usability	
Accessibility	Likert Scale 1-10
Client Personnel	

Table 3. (*continued*)

Requirements	
Installability	
Learnability	
Operability	
Transparency	
Understandability	

5   Conclusions and Future Work

Cloud offerings enable both private and public institutions to take advantage of scale economies by migrating existing services to the cloud. Nevertheless and due to the tangled environment of cloud providers and information, the selection of a SaaS-based CRM vendors is becoming a major task in which a good number of indicators and data must be consider. In this new data-based realm, new techniques must be applied to provide an intelligent environment in which decisions can be made in a more timely and accurate fashion by the automatic and flexible processing of data and information. That is why the current situation of CRM vendor selection in the cloud has been introduced as a motivating and relevant scenario in which new techniques are required. A semantic-based definition of composite quantitative indexes and an agnostic processor have been depicted to represent the structure and the computation process of these indexes. Moreover, a quality model based on the exiting SMI framework has been customized to the context of cloud CRM selection by defining the CRMIndex. Thus, the two major outcomes of this paper rely on the definition of a semantic-based quantitative index and the application of the AHP method to make a rank of cloud CRM vendors. We firmly believe that the SMI framework represent a step towards the establishment of a quality framework for any kind of service and we have provided here a kind of semantic-based implementation that also addresses some challenges such as integration of different data sources, flexible creation and update of indexes, automatic generation of documentation, etc. In this sense, we consider that the expressivity of our vocabulary can be easily extended to be adapted in order contexts to deliver a real tool for cloud intelligence and more specifically for the creation of semantic-based composite quantitative indexes.

References

1. Lee, Y.-C., Tang, N.-H., Sugumaran, V.: Open Source CRM Software Selection using the Analytic Hierarchy Process. Inf. Syst. Manag. 31, 2–20 (2014)
2. Correia, J., Thompson, E., Dharmasthira, Y.: Market Trends: CRM Digital Initiatives Focus on Sales, Marketing, Support and E-Commerce. Gartner Inc. (2014)
3. Bibi, S., Katsaros, D., Bozanis, P.: Business Application Acquisition: On-Premise or SaaS-Based Solutions? IEEE Softw. 29, 86–93 (2012)
4. Friedrich, I., Kosch, L., Breitner, M.H.: A practical test of a process model for customer relationship management system selection with an automotive supplier. In: Proc. ECIS 2012 (2012)
5. Hsu, P.-F., Lan, K.-Y., Tsai, C.-W.: Selecting the Optimal Vendor of Customer Relationship Management System for Medical Tourism Industry Using Delphi and AHP. Int. J. Enterp. Inf. Syst. 9, 62–75 (2013)

6. Colomo-Palacios, R., Gómez-Berbís, J.M., García-Crespo, Á.: An integrated methodology for customer relationship management customization. JISTEM - J. Inf. Syst. Technol. Manag. 4, 287–300 (2007)
7. Saaty, T.L.: A scaling method for priorities in hierarchical structures. J. Math. Psychol. 15, 234–281 (1977)
8. Wind, Y., Saaty, T.L.: Marketing Applications of the Analytic Hierarchy Process. Manag. Sci. 26, 641–658 (1980)
9. Chen, M.K., Wang, S.-C.: The critical factors of success for information service industry in developing international market: Using analytic hierarchy process (AHP) approach. Expert Syst. Appl. 37, 694–704 (2010)
10. Subramanian, N., Ramanathan, R.: A review of applications of Analytic Hierarchy Process in operations management. Int. J. Prod. Econ. 138, 215–241 (2012)
11. Jadhav, A.S., Sonar, R.M.: Framework for evaluation and selection of the software packages: A hybrid knowledge based system approach. J. Syst. Softw. 84, 1394–1407 (2011)
12. Jadhav, A.S., Sonar, R.M.: Evaluating and selecting software packages: A review. Inf. Softw. Technol. 51, 555–563 (2009)
13. Kahraman, C., Beskese, A., Kaya, I.: Selection among ERP outsourcing alternatives using a fuzzy multi-criteria decision making methodology. Int. J. Prod. Res. 48, 547–566 (2010)
14. Karaarslan, N., Gundogar, E.: An application for modular capability-based ERP software selection using AHP method. Int. J. Adv. Manuf. Technol. 42, 1025–1033 (2009)
15. Garg, S.K., Versteeg, S., Buyya, R.: A framework for ranking of cloud computing services. Future Gener. Comput. Syst. 29, 1012–1023 (2013)
16. Kim, H.-S., Kim, Y.-G.: A CRM performance measurement framework: Its development process and application. Ind. Mark. Manag. 38, 477–489 (2009)
17. Colombo, E., Francalanci, C.: Selecting CRM packages based on architectural, functional, and cost requirements: Empirical validation of a hierarchical ranking model. Requir. Eng. 9, 186–203 (2004)
18. Öztayşi, B., Kaya, T., Kahraman, C.: Performance comparison based on customer relationship management using analytic network process. Expert Syst. Appl. 38, 9788–9798 (2011)
19. Käfer, T., Abdelrahman, A., Umbrich, J., O'Byrne, P., Hogan, A.: Observing Linked Data Dynamics. In: Cimiano, P., Corcho, O., Presutti, V., Hollink, L., Rudolph, S. (eds.) ESWC 2013. LNCS, vol. 7882, pp. 213–227. Springer, Heidelberg (2013)
20. CSMIC: Service Measurement Index Framework Version 2.0 (2014), http://csmic.org/wp-content/uploads/ 2014/01/SMI_Overview_140113.pdf
21. ur Rehman, Z., Hussain, O.K., Hussain, F.K.: Parallel Cloud Service Selection and Ranking Based on QoS History. Int. J. Parallel Program. 42, 820–852 (2014)
22. Kourtesis, D., Alvarez Rodríguez, J.M., Paraskakis, I.: Semantic-based QoS management in Cloud Systems: Current Status and Future Challenges. Future Gener. Comput. Syst. (2014)
23. Cyganiak, R., Reynolds, D.: The RDF Data Cube Vocabulary. W3C (2013)
24. Hausenblas, M., Halb, W., Raimond, Y., Feigenbaum, L., Ayers, D.: SCOVO: Using Statistics on the Web of Data. In: Aroyo, L., et al. (eds.) ESWC 2009. LNCS, vol. 5554, pp. 708–722. Springer, Heidelberg (2009)
25. Zapilko, B., Mathiak, B.: Defining and Executing Assessment Tests on Linked Data for Statistical Analysis. COLD (2011)

ISDE 2014 PC Co-Chairs Message

Information System in Distributed Environment (ISDE) is becoming a prominent standard in this globalization era due to advancement in information and communication technologies. In distributed environments, business units collaborate across time zones, organizational boundaries, work cultures and geographical distances, to an increasing diversification and growing complexity of cooperation among units. The advent of the Internet has supported Distributed Software Development (DSD) by introducing new concepts and opportunities, resulting in benefits such as scalability, flexibility, interdependence, reduced cost, resource pools, and usage tracking. DSD brings challenges to distributed software development activities due to geographic, cultural, linguistic, and temporal distance among project development teams. The number of organizations distributing their software development processes worldwide to attain increased profit and productivity as well as cost reduction and quality improvement is growing. Despite the fact that DSD is widely being used, the project managers and software professionals face many challenges due to increased complexity, cultural as well as various technological issues. Therefore, it is crucial to understand current research and practices with researchers and practitioners in these areas.

Following selected papers of ISDE 2014 international workshop in conjunction with OTM conferences present recent advances and novel proposals in this direction.

Juan Garbajosa, Agustin Yagüe, Eloy Gonzalez in their work on communication in agile global software development: an exploratory study reports an exploratory study on the impact of different communication elements, including tools, obtained both from monitoring some agile distributed projects, and from getting the perceptions of team members.

In collaborative brainstorming activity results and information systems by Claude Moulin, Kenji Sugawara, Yuki Kaeri, Shigeru Fujita, Marie-Hélène Abel presented the architectural design of the distributed application used for the resource channel using several tactile devices with different size that display the resources. Finally, it reports an experiment with two teams situated in Japan and France.

Liguo Yu, Alok Mishra, Deepti Mishra in their empirical study of the dynamics of GitHub repository and its impact on distributed software development reviewed different kinds of version control systems and study the dynamics of GitHub, i.e., the ability and scalability of GitHub to process different requests and provide different services to different GitHub projects and GitHub users.

Patterns of Software Modeling by Wolfgang Raschke, Massimiliano Zilli, Johannes Loinig, Reinhold Weiss, Christian Steger, Christian Kreiner provided an evolutionary view of software systems and models which helps to understand current problems and prospective solutions.

Jesus Vallecillos, Javier Criado, Luis Iribarne, Nicolas Padilla proposed an architecture for specification, storage, management and visualization of components, built from widgets complying with the W3C recommendation, for making web user interfaces.

Jukka Kääriäinen, Susanna Teppola, Matias Vierimaa, Antti Välimäki discussed significance of a systematic upgrade planning service in a distributed operational environment and presented the process description and related tools that have been composed based on an industrial case study in an automation company.

Privacy-aware agent-oriented architecture for distributed eHealth systems by Adel Taweel, Samhar Mahmoud, Arahman Tawil presented an approach for privacy-preserving agent-oriented architecture that enables organizations to work together overcoming sharing sensitive data and evaluates its use within a real-life project.

In the paper policy-based authorization framework in audit rule ontology for continuous process auditing in complex distributed systems, Numanul Subhani, and Robert Kent proposed a mechanism, materialized views, for frequently accessed authorized data in near real-time for distributed decision support systems.

A novel mechanism for dynamic optimization of intercloud services by Lohit Kapoor, Seema Bawa, Ankur Gupta proposed a dynamic service ranking and selection mechanism which allows users fine-grained control over service consumption, while maximizing service provider revenues.

Literature review of DSD and cultural issues have been discussed by Alok Mishra and Deepti Mishra. They reported although many studies have been performed in culture and distributed software development, still impact of culture in distributed software development in different dimensions and empirical comparative studies received less attention.

A distributed service-based system for homecare self-management by Adel Taweel, Lina Barakat, Simon Miles reported design of a distributed system that enables homecare in the context of management of self-feeding through balanced nutritional intake.

September 2014   Alok Mishra
                                                       Jürgen Münch
                                                       Deepti Mishra

A Distributed Service-Based System for Homecare Self-Management

Adel Taweel[1,2], Lina Barakat[1], and Simon Miles[1]

[1] King's College London, UK
{adel.taweel,lina.barakat,simon.miles}@kcl.ac.uk
[2] Birzeit University, WB
ataweel@birzeit.edu

Abstract. Aging is becoming a critical issue for Europe and many countries around the world. It is imposing significant burden on societies and their national services. Enabling longer home independent living is seen one of the most promising ways to overcome this issue. However, to achieve a number of challenges need to be overcome, especially those related to management of health and disease let alone other social and logistical barriers. One of these challenges is malnutrition, which is considered one of the root causes for the occurrence of other diseases. This paper presents the design of a distributed system that enables homecare in the context of management of self-feeding through balanced nutritional intake. The design employs a service-based system that incorporates a number of services including monitoring of activities, nutritional reasoning for assessing feeding habits, diet recommending for food planning, and marketplace invocation for automating food shopping to meet dietary requirements.

Keywords: Serviced-based design, SOA, eHealth, Homecare, distributed systems.

1 Introduction

The aging population, in many countries, is placing a huge demand on health and social services. These demands do not only include costs, but also logistical and capacity limitations. If left unaddressed, it will eventually affect the whole society not only in the quality of services they receive, but also in their ability to meet these demands. Enabling the elder population to live longer at home is seen one of the most promising solutions. Not only to reduce costs, but also to address other psychological and social factors [6]. One of the critical issues affecting elderlies' ability to live independently at home is malnutrition [2]. Studies have shown that in Europe more than 15% of the older population is affected by poor nutrition and malnutrition caused by the problems of ageing due to decrease in sensitivity, poor dental health, lack of transportation, physical difficulty, forgetfulness and other issues [1].

R. Meersman et al. (Eds.): OTM 2014 Workshops, LNCS 8842, pp. 361–366, 2014.

As part of the DIET4Elders project[1], this paper presents the design of a service-based solution for homecare self-management focusing on malnutrition. It enables older adults self-manage their nutritional intake by preventing unhealthy self-feeding habits, which recent studies report that more than 60% of cases in nursing homes [3], and more than 15% of those living at home [2] are affected by malnutrition. The solution uses a distributed service-based design that incorporates several services, including:

(i)   monitoring services aimed at detecting food intake and activities.
(ii)   data collection and reasoning services to help the nutritionists to establish the degree in which the older adults follow their prescribed diet and to dynamically re-plan it.
(iii) diet recommending services for planned long term diet plans that can be used and adjusted by dieticians.
(iv)   food generation services that can be used to generate longer-term diet interventions coupled with suitable meal and food plans.
(v)   marketplace services, that enable food providers to register their services and offerings.
(vi)   food shopping services that enable the dynamic selection, based on the prescribed diet, of suitable food service providers, potentially enabling automated shopping.
(vii) user feedback and reporting services, to assist older adults and their informal carers during daily self-feeding activities aimed at creating a continuous feedback and interaction loop not only to detect and prevent the instauration of malnutrition, but also other health issues.

The rest of the paper describes the system design and services that DIET4Elders intends to develop in close collaboration with its target older adults. Section 2 describes the overall design of the system and its services; section 3 presents a brief conclusion.

2   Overall Service-Based System Design

The overall system design is shown in Fig. 1. The design uses services to enable collecting and providing the related recommendations directly to the older adults in their home environment as well as to their dietician and informal carers. The design include a number of services to achieve a complete cycle of monitoring, analysis, through diet recommendation to food ordering services, these are described below.

Monitoring Services

These include a number of services. It relies on the home environment monitoring infrastructures, where wireless sensors are used to monitor and collect related diet

---

[1] Dynamic nutrItion bEhaviour awareness sysTem FOR the Elders
(www.diet4elders.eu)

data including food intake, activities, health data and so forth. For similar types of sensors (e.g. activity sensors), data monitoring services are created that collect the relevant data. A local communication infrastructure pushes the data to respective data monitoring services, which pushes data to the data collection service. This is enabled by the use of advanced sensors technologies to track and detect older adult's daily activities and the context in which these activities took place. The project is looking at using and/or where not available developing advanced wireless non-intrusive sensors that monitors the daily diet intake and physical activities aspects of older adults, including smart containers, smart fridges, accelerometers, health monitoring devices, positions sensors, RFIDs, smart tablets or phones etc.

Diet Collection and Analysis Services

A data collection service collects data from all monitoring services, which are further semantically categorised to enable both context and semantic analysis linked to temporal and longitudinal diet behaviour. Valid and effective diet advice is one key objective of the design. This is pinned by the need to build a dynamic mechanism not only closely linked to accurate monitoring technologies but also based on evidence-based diet knowledge. For such, the project is developing a computational representation of diet knowledge drawn from existing well-established diet evidence. It is drawing knowledge with standardised units and measurements to be able to computationally reason over such knowledge correlated to the specific knowledge collected about individual users, taking into account not only their level of health and chronic diseases that they suffer from, but also the context and culture variations. The need is to be able to reason over collected data to drive and identify self-feeding behavioural patterns that lead to malnutrition and create counter mechanisms to address them. This will require the development and employment of reasoning techniques including graph theory and prediction techniques to discover patterns from chain of activities abstracted to the diet and context of use. With direct input from nutritionists, it will also require the development of learning algorithms with continual feedback and human intervention to achieve more precise and accurate identification of unhealthy behaviour patterns.

Assessment, Feedback and Recommendation Services

Analysis services feed their results into these services. The system will employ a number of services that interconnect with the above technologies to circumvent unhealthy feeding behaviours and interconnect with the older adults directly so they are aware of where they could improve on their feeding habits. These will also provide intelligible and useful feedback to both carers and dieticians to monitor changing behaviours in feeding patterns. The key is to produce current and quantifiable information of value to the older adults as well as their dieticians. Given the amount of data collected over time, this becomes a complex data-mining issue, potentially requiring large computational resources required to produce meaningful information in a relatively short time for potentially large number of users. Thus the need is for a system design that employs a distributed infrastructure to enable such analysis. The intended outcome of these services is to produce a computational representation of these results that can be further used by the system and subsequent services, where decisions are drawn from. Given the sensitivity and impact of these recommendations on the older adult health, continual expert reviews of the validity of drawn results and discovered patterns are integrated within the services workflow.

Food and Meal Plan Generation Services

These services receive unhealthy behaviours and nutritional deficiencies information into a computational form from the assessment services. This information is then used by diet plan generation services, to draw actionable food intake meals and food plans that can overcome identified diet and nutritional deficiencies. These draw a longer-term individual plan, based on the older adult preferences, their health profile and their chronic illnesses. Dieticians are able to adjust these plans based on further discussion and feedback from the user. User feedback is critical to incorporate in the process for these meal plans uptake so they eventually result into effective outcomes [5]. These will require taking a number of various factors into consideration, including health, contextual and cultural variations.

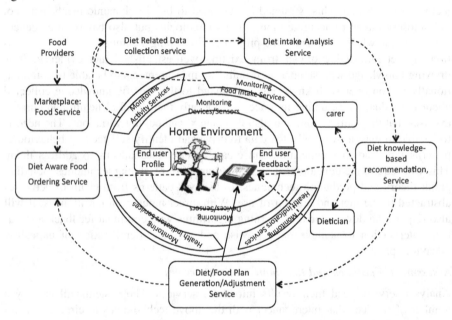

Fig. 1. Service-based Homecare Self-management

Market Place Services

There are a large number of potential food providers with different capabilities and offerings that already provide meal services to older adults, in both nursing homes or at home. However, these mostly employ a manual process and not all provide all types of meals. The system will develop a service-based mechanism with well-defined diet specific market place that allows food providers to register their services and food offerings. It will develop reliability-augmented service descriptions and mechanisms with clear quality indicators that not only enable users to have informed decisions about the food ordering but also enable the system to make informed judgement of suitable combination of food ordering with suitable levels of nutrition that meet the specific needs of the user. These will include developing mechanisms to capture and validate key quality indicators of food services, not only at the service level but also at nutritional and contextual levels.

Diet Aware Food Ordering

For complex diet requirements and/or user preferences, several food providers are potentially required to meet these requirements or preferences. The selection of the combination of food services, to satisfy potentially complex criteria of the older adult recommended diet or preferences, can thus be a non-trivial task. There are a large number of food delivery services available on the market offering various types of food, which makes finding optimal combination a NP-hard problem, which cannot be solved in reasonable time using conventional techniques. The system will model the problem as a combinatorial optimization problem and solve it using hybrid bio-inspired techniques that should combine the strength elements of different bio-inspired meta-heuristics.

3   Conclusions and Future Work

The paper presents a service-based distributed system design and architecture for homecare self-management. It describes briefly the design and the employed services that will be used by the project to enable self-management of a balanced nutritional intake based on monitoring daily activities, and self-feeding habits. The project builds its solution using a service-based design and employs a number of services to provide nutritional advice, interact with dieticians and carers, and enable food ordering through a reliability-augmented and well-specified marketplace. Although the solution is based on malnutrition management, but it presents a generic solution which can be used to enable effective management of demanding requirements of large data collection and analysis for homecare environments. Such system design need to meet potentially very large-scale requirements, especially as it is required to serve large number of older adults, geographically distributed at their homes, with varied and complex health needs.

The initial version of the design is already being developed part of the project with anticipated incremental planned evaluation and deployment of its components in selected older adults homes. Given the amount of potential data generated by monitoring services, other design considerations will look at the use of big data techniques for data management and analysis.

Acknowledgment. The authors would like to thank all colleagues from the DIET4Elders project who contributed to this work.

References

1. Elia, M.: Detection and management of under nutrition in the community. A report by the Malnutrition Advisory Group (A standing committee of the British Association for Parenteral and Enteral Nutrition), Maidenhead, BAPEN (2000)
2. Elia, M., Russell, C. (eds.): Combating malnutrition; Recommendations for Action. A report from the Advisory Group on Malnutrition, Redditch: BAPEN (2009)
3. Ahmed, T., Haboubi, N.: Assessment and management of nutrition in older people and its importance to health. Clin Interv Aging 5, 207–216 (2010)
4. Ljungqvist, O., Man, F.: Under nutrition: a major health problem in Europe. Nutr Hosp 24(3), 369–370 (2009)
5. Astell, A., Williams, L., Adlam, T., Hwang, F.: NANA: Novel assessment of nutrition and ageing. Gerontechnology 9(2), 95–96 (2010)
6. Volkert, D., Saeglitz, C., Gueldenzoph, H., Sieber, C.C., Stehle, P.: Undiagnosed malnutrition and nutrition-related problems in geriatric patients. J Nutr Health Aging 14(5), 387–392 (2010)

Incorporating Policy-Based Authorization Framework in Audit Rule Ontology for Continuous Process Auditing in Complex Distributed Systems

Numanul Subhani and Robert Kent

School of Computer Science, University of Windsor
401 Sunset Ave, Windsor, Ontario N9B 3P4
{hoque4,rkent}@uwindsor.ca
http://www.uwindsor.ca/cs

Abstract. Complex distributed information systems that run their activities in the form of processes require continuous auditing of a process that invokes the action(s) specified in the policies and rules in a continuous manner. A shared vocabulary, or common ontology, used to defined the processes, and the audit rule ontology for processes or modules are integrated to form a hybrid ontology that supports the acquisition and evolution of ontologies. A methodology to construct a Common Ontology and an audit rule ontology by coupling to an expert system for Continuous Process Auditing (CPA) has been introduced recently. In this paper, we present a policy-based authorization methodology incorporating Audit Rule Ontology for CPA within distributed audit rule ontology. We also propose the use of probabilistic risk determination and evaluation of risk level, along with access history heuristics that define the adaptable access control policies before making policy decisions.

Keywords: Policy-based Authorization, Continuous Process Auditing, Audit Rule Ontology, Authorization and Access Control, Semantic Web, Risk-Adaptive Access Control (RAdAC).

1 Introduction

Auditing encompasses a variety of methods used to measure and assess the compliance of a system to defined rules and policy guidelines. Auditing is just one facet of a more extensive set of processes, often rooted in accounting, intended to support assurance that the system is functioning as intended. Auditing is applied in many domains, such as government, business, education and health care, among others. Underscoring the breadth of auditing applications is the fact that most auditing is still performed by human agents, trained and experienced in many aspects of evidence gathering, interpretation of rules and guidelines, and clarifying of final reports in respect of limitations.

Increasingly, complex systems have grown beyond the capacities of human driven auditing to perform meaningful audits in a timely fashion that serves

R. Meersman et al. (Eds.): OTM 2014 Workshops, LNCS 8842, pp. 367–376, 2014.

stakeholders and oversight bodies. Such systems encompass networks of human agents and also highly automated software systems with semi-autonomous subsystems, all of which are assumed to be vulnerable to risk. Researchers have focused attention on automating significant parts of auditing, both as embedded components within systems working autonomously, and as decision support components serving human analysts.

One vital element throughout auditing concerns knowledge, namely, its acquisition, interpretation and uncertainty, or vagueness, in reasoning. Auditing practice dictates that meaningful definitions must be determined and documented; for the system components and processes to be audited, evaluation measures, rules and actions to be applied, and limitations or constraints must be expressed. Auditors must work with suitable knowledge expressed in natural language terms for human consumption, but also expressed in terms appropriate for application and reasoning through computational logic. In Continuous Process Auditing (CPA) methodology, an audit rule sheet is defined for each process or module. The matter of continuity of application in CPA ranges from continuous time-dependent modeling to discrete time steps of audit application adapted to application requirements through use of coarse-grained analysis of sub-systems, and estimation techniques based on limited rule sets. This consideration is used to determine the degree of conceptualization as knowledge, audit measures using sensors and reasoning through rules and inference.

Knowledge is an essential part of most Semantic Web applications and ontology, which is a formal description of concepts or classes in a domain of discourse [1], is an essential approach for structuring the knowledge. Extracting knowledge from text in a semi-automatic way and identifying effective procedures for achieving useful and reliable results are challenging research areas. In auditing applications, most rules are defined in the context of human understanding and language and can be used to support human cognitive reasoning and inference. Ontology-based reasoning has known shortcomings and limitations compared with rule-based reasoning [2]. To represent inferential knowledge, ontology alone is insufficient [3]; but, inferential rules are an essential part of the knowledge in an audit rule ontology for a process or module in CPA for real-time Decision Support systems [4]. Though chronological, topological, and other types of semantic relations already exist [5], within these methods only hierarchical concepts are extracted and reduced sets of semantic relations are in use.

Many systems, such as health care and government, are complex and heterogeneous in nature and their data sources are semantically heterogeneous. A common ontology approach is straightforward for dealing with homogeneous semantic data sources. Hybrid approaches and multiple ontologies to deal with the heterogeneity problem of ontologies have been discussed [6, 7]. Recently, we proposed a hybrid audit rule ontology approach that couples with an expert system to infer new relations from the existing concepts [8]. In autonomous pervasive distributed systems (e.g. hospital, nuclear power plant, manufacturing), accessing authorized data in real-time and enforcing data security as highly encrypted-sensitive data are transported from one layer to another in various geographic locations are essential issues to handle before CPA is deployed.

Determination of security risk and evaluation of risk level are critical issues in evolving complex distributed systems. Demand for generating adaptable access control policies that use previous knowledge of access history and acceptable risk level is on the rise, especially in cloud-based distributed systems. The objective of this paper is to present an authorization and access control mechanism for audit rules along with a risk-adaptive policy based authorization framework for Continuous Process Auditing. The rest of the paper is organized as follows. Audit rule ontology and its hybrid layered construction approach are briefly discussed in section 2. A general discussion of the authorization and access control of continuous process auditing in the context of audit rule ontology is provided in section 3. Our proposed Policy-based authorization framework incorporating with audit rule ontology for any autonomous pervasive distributed systems is presented and illustrated using an use-case scenario in section 4. Finally, conclusion and future research directions are drawn in section 5.

2 Audit Rules and Ontologies

Following Gruber, an ontology is an explicit specification of conceptualization [1], that can serve as an effective and powerful tool to capture, store and work with domain knowledge in knowledge-based information systems. In terms of knowledge representation, there are several types of ontology, including high-level, generic, domain and application. Domain ontologies are intended to specify conceptualization of particular real-world domains and processes, such as finance or industries involved in the production or delivery of goods and services. In this section we describe the ontology aspects relevant to processes, then audit rules and finally hybrid approaches.

2.1 Process Ontology (PO)

All activities in a process are linked as sequential steps, either defined by higher business modelers or discovered by various established methodologies, such as workflow mining from labeled and unlabeled event logs, stochastic workflow analysis or rule-based approaches. There are two approaches to the study of any system and its behavior: the micro system (μ), which studies the algorithms, sensors for collecting data, and atomic devices; and the macro system (M), which studies and models large systems composed of large numbers of algorithms, devices and connections [8]. Process Ontologies (PO) are constructed for each process with their defined concepts and databases that might be either homogeneous or heterogeneous in nature, and an expert system for PO mappings is coupled to construct a hybrid layered ontology for process audit rules.

2.2 Audit Rules and Audit Rule Ontology of a Process (AROP)

As a first step, audit rules are defined for an activity or component within the scope of human-performed auditing. Audit rules are based on both the hierarchical structure of an organization and the enforced business controls. The same audit rules discernment and definition approach can be applied and implemented in any Continuous Process Auditing system where a process has to traverse through various components, and by applying audit rules sequentially through the traversal. An Audit Rule Ontology for a Process (AROP) may be used to detect exceptions to the audit rules in a process during CPA. Semantic rule-based reasoning can facilitate construction of AROP in a semi-automatic way. AROPs would be used as second layer under common ontology in a hybrid layered ontology model. We assume that human approval of all audit rules is enforced; autonomous automated approval through artificial intelligence is not considered in this discussion.

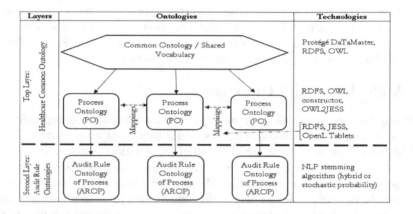

Fig. 1. Conceptual Model of Hybrid Audit Rule Ontology

2.3   Ontology Design: A Hybrid Layered Model

Domain ontologies may be divided into linguistic and conceptual ontologies. According to Gruber [1], Conceptual Ontologies (CO) represent the domain objects, distinguishing between the primitive concepts and the defined concepts, whereas Linguistic Ontologies (LO) define words or contextual usages of words. The Process Ontology (PO) contains only the defined concepts and the Mapping Ontology (MO) contains both the defined and the underlying primitive concepts. The observation in [9] led to identifying some relationships between POs, MOs and LOs. Mappings between POs may be defined in terms of equivalence operators of some MO. The various meanings of words in MO references may be defined by LOs and this reference would provide a basis for formal, and exact or uncertain reasoning, and automatic translation of context-specific terms.

In our proposed single common ontology approach to domain ontology construction each PO is attached to a database that might be heterogeneous in nature with other databases. Each PO describes the semantics of data sources individually. Inter-PO mapping is realized by the MO, which is defined with primitive concepts. The simplicity and flexibility permitting addition of new sources (like new POs) with little or no need of modification, is the main advantage of this mechanism. To integrate several POs addressing the same domain, this mechanism exploits the MO's capability to define equivalent and similar concepts.

As detailed by Wache [6], one develops the Common Ontology using multiple POs in the top-most layer, then Audit Rule Ontologies of Processes would be stemmed as a second layer under the top-most layer to form a Hybrid Layered Ontology. Fig. 1 visualizes the conceptual model of both the layers alongside with the technologies to be used to integrate and develop the entire operable Audit Rule Ontology system. More abstract description of construction, development and operational mechanism are discussed in [8].

3   Authorization and Access Control of Continuous Process Auditing

A Continuous Process traverses through multiple modules or micro processes [8] and it requires seamless access control to all data sources in a complex distributed system for assessing audit rules. Different stakeholders, actors and networking modules that are part of a process need various levels of authorization policies for access control. In distributed environments, it is daunting challenging task to provide authorization and access control and many different mechanisms have been investigated. Most distributed systems employ numerous policies to provide authorization for access control. Policy based authorization mechanism is being investigated [10–12] and the policy conflict resolution problem has yet to be addressed while eliminating real-time performance bottlenecks.

Organizations are constantly evolving. Thus, the authorization policies that guide them must also be adaptable and extend to a variety of risk factors. In audit rule ontology, a CPA requires all the authorization policies to access control of all data sources for each module, or micro process, before assessing the audit rules. Assessing audit rules that deal with a variety of audit risks is one of the major access control requirements as well within AROP. Since common ontology lies on top of all ontologies (Fig. 1), its audit rules require the access control and authorization policies to all data sources of common ontology; the same is true for the all other ontologies in 2nd and 3rd layers of ontologies as well.

To gain the access control and authorization policies of all data sources in different layers of ontologies, we proposed a policy-based authorization framework incorporating with AROP and we also devised a modified Risk-Adaptive Access Control (RAdAC) model [13] to enforce adaptable and risk-aware access control in any complex distributed system, particularly in real-time.

4   Policy-Based Authorization Framework Incorporating with Audit Rule Ontology

In Section 2.3, we proposed the hybrid ontology for Audit Rule Ontology for Process. A Process traverses through Common Ontology first, then Process

Ontology before reaching to AROP. An Audit Rule Ontology of Process (AROP) is constructed with audit rules obtained from two layers of ontologies i.e. Common Ontology and Process Ontology (Fig. 1). Process ontologies are mapped in-between by Mapping Ontology. Authorization Policies are also deployed and enforced along with the ontologies in their nodes. Polices must be defined incorporating with the ontological predicates. Common authorization policies that have to applied/enforced for all the branches of ontologies must be deployed and enforced in Common Ontology and same way process specific authorization polices must be deployed and enforced in Process Ontology. After getting authorization from CO and PO, Audit Rule Authorization Polices (ARAP) are also enforced in AROP. Before making decision and providing access to the access control for data access layer, ARAP must adjust or adapt to the security risk (automatically or semi-automatically) to resources associated with that process and audit rule. Below we have described the framework of RAdAC using Audit Rule Ontology for Process.

4.1 Audit Rule Authorization Policy (ARAP)

Audit Rule Authorization Policies define the process goals of the system and event triggered reactions from the policies in order to deal with them. Events are produced, or may be produced some time in future, by receiving a message from an ontology object within the system. There are currently two basic policy types defined: Obligation Policies and Authorization Polices. Obligation Polices specify the actions that must be performed by CO and PO within the system when certain events occur and provide the ability to respond to changing circumstances. Authorization Polices are essentially access control policies, to allow or deny message passing between objects (ie. resources and services).

4.2 Risk Determination and Evaluation

Probabilistic determination of the security risk associated with granting the requested access is made based on examining several external factors. The level of risk is calculated from several areas such as the risk associated with the users, protection capabilities and robustness of system components, the operating threat level of the environment and access history. We only define the user (as an entity that is requesting access) and connection (as any communication channel on the users device) to capture the security risk. In future, we plan to consider the risk of device, associated components, operational matter, service provider's trustworthiness and the risk level assurance. This process provides quantitative indication of the level of risk and the risk evaluation on risk associated with each of these components as well as heuristics described below.

4.3 Heuristics of Access History and Acceptable Risk Level

Knowledge of the past access control decisions help to fine-tune the access control policy to improve the rate of positive access control decisions and can be used to develop better algorithms for determining risk. Policy must specify the degree to which heuristics should be considered in each access decision, as well as how each decision should be incorporated into the learning process. The policy will have to specify an acceptable risk level for each area, or a risk range. We consider access history and acceptable risk level to capture the characteristics of heuristics. It updates the object access history repository with acceptable risk level in the access request and the access control decision, then it provides access for making future access decisions.

4.4 Adaptable Access Control Policies

This specifies the rules for access control for various classes of information objects under different conditions. The purpose of adaptable access control policies is defined to capture an audit rule's need to access an object. User and connection are defined to capture the security risk. Access history and acceptable risk level are defined to provide feedback to the access decision process and to capture the access decisions. Since our main purpose is to access for audit rule, we did not consider including overriding process where an allowed authority can override an access decision made by the system under specific conditions.

4.5 Policy Decision and Post Processing

A Policy Decision sequence is defined by: (a) ARAP defined by specifying the heuristics and acceptable level degree of risk, (b) determining security risk as a quantifiable amount then evaluating security risk with heuristics knowledge of access control decision and acceptable risk level, (c) capturing the access control decision and acceptable risk level to update the object access history repository then providing access for making future access decisions. This heuristics step gives feedback to the "risk determination and evaluation" and to define the "adaptable access control polices" steps as well, and lastly, (d) decision making and post decision processing. Complete policy decision sequence flowchart is presented in Fig 2.

Post decision processing, among other tasks, is aimed at supporting the need for access control to filter out the authorized data from the data access layer based on the access decision. Various tools are available to filter out data from the data access layer; we are considering XACML to do this job in the following two ways: (a) filtering authorized data returned from data sources, and (b) modifying input parameters according to the authorization before retrieving the data from data sources. In typical complex distributed systems, there are a large number of data sets to filter out. We adopt the approach of modifying the input parameter, and are investigating if this is the preferred approach. Associated with this matter is how to manage efficiently frequently accessed authorization data for making decision in near real-time.

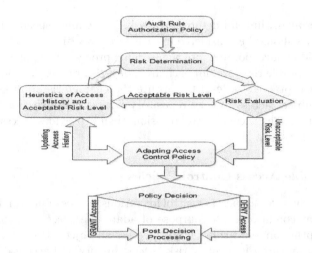

Fig. 2. Conceptual Model of Audit Rule Ontology based Risk-Adaptive Access Control Framework

4.6   Use-Case Scenario for an Audit Rule Authorization Policy

An example of Risk-Adaptive Access Control Framework (RAdAC) is illustrated in the following as sequential steps from audit rule authorization policy towards granting or denying access to services aor resources for a facility management system. In this scenario, Alice is a junior employee working in the IT department of a firm, within a team led by John, who has placed Alice under the supervision of Mark, a senior member of Johns team. To aid in identifying mistakes made due to unauthorized access, a continuous audit system should be capable of capturing and analyzing non-compliance with established policies, especially in cases where such policies may apply only after deriving a reasonable and consistent inference.

1. *Authorization Policy:* An audit rule authorization policy that defines the goal of approving contract worker overtime might be stated as: Allow contract worker to work overtime maximum of 6 hours. A contract worker overtime process definition (including working condition, payment method, overtime rate, work shift schedule, worker specific contract terms, etc.) should be clearly defined in the process ontology of a contract worker overtime module. This authorization policy governs the access control of providing and using services, and using resources by contract workers. As an example, Alice, a contract worker, is hired as an electrician to work only in morning shift under Marks supervision. Should Alice be given access to work overtime in the server room in midnight shift without any supervision?

2. *Risk Determination and Evaluation:* Determining the risks associated with granting Alice the requested access is made probabilistically by examining several external factors such as Alices security clearance level, the operating threat level of environment, access history and so on. As mentioned earlier, we consider only a user as an entity and a connection as a

communication channel on the user device to calculate the level of risk. Each component (for Alice only entity and connection) relating to granting of requested access is equipped with appropriate tools or devices to calculate the level of risk. Acceptable Threshold level of risk is determined by the authorization policy from audit rule ontology. For instance, if the entity risk level is 4 and connection risk level is 8, and for Alice, acceptable entity risk threshold level is 3-5 and connection threshold level is 4-7, authorization to access should not be granted.

3. *Heuristics of Access History:* Since Alices connection risk level is not within the threshold level, the audit system needs to adapt an access control policy for Alice by using heuristics of her access history along with acceptable risk level. By examining the access history, Alice was given access 5 times to the server room manually by her supervisor Mark with connection risk level 8, three times under his own supervision in the morning shift and two times under supervision of team leader John, who is Marks supervisor, in the midnight shift. After analyzing the access history and acceptable risk level for Alice, heuristics pointed out two facts: (a) all 5 times Alice was given access to the server room under an employee supervision (assume both Mark and John have security clearance level 3, and John is superior to Mark) that has required security clearance 3, and (b) this time Alice is requesting access without supervision

4. *Adapting an Access Control Policy:* Based on the heuristics, facts and level of risk associated to granting the requested access, an access control policy must be adapted that Alice can be given the requested access under supervision by an employee with level 3 security clearance.

5. *Decision Making:* Since Alice was always supervised by an employee with level 3 security clearance and she is now seeking access without supervision, then she should NOT be given access to the server room.

Although Alice was given access to the server room several times earlier with supervision, the security risk associated with entity, connection, and the knowledge of the past access control decisions aided the RAdAC system to adapt an access control policy for similar kind of events without any intervention from human administrators.

5   Conclusion and Future Work

We have presented a conceptual policy-based authorization framework incorporating audit rule ontology. This framework adapts the modified version of Risk-Adaptive Access Control (RAdAC) with the security risk components of users and connections between devices. We believe that policy-based authorization framework with modified RAdAC in Audit Rule Ontology for Process (AROP) addresses real world scenarios where risk in an important factor in Continuous Process Auditing and making access control decisions.

In future, we will include more security risk components such as the risk of device, associated device components, operations, service provider trustworthiness and risk level assurance. We plan to use the heuristics of user security history, and service provider's risk level of asserted algorithmic and authentication strength as well. A resolution mechanism for policy conflict will be addressed as well in future extensions of this framework.

Acknowledgment. We acknowledge support from the Canadian Institutes for Health Research (CIHR).

References

1. Gruber, T.: A translation approach to portable ontology specifications. Knowledge Acquisition 5(2), 199–220 (1993)
2. Horrocks, I.: Daml+oil: A description logic for the semantic web. IEEE Data Enggineering 25(1), 4–9 (2002)
3. Harmelen, F., Fensel, D.: Practical knowledge representation for the web. In: Proc. 16th Int'l Joint Conf. Artificial Intelligence (1999)
4. Baksa, R., Turoff, M.: Continuous auditing as a foundation for real time decision support - implementation challenges and successes. Annals of Information Systems Supporting Real Time Decision-Making 13, 237–252 (2011)
5. Valencia-Garcia, R., et al.: An incremental approach for discovering medical knowledge from texts. Expert Systems with Applications 26(3), 291–299 (2004)
6. Wache, H., et al.: Ontology-based integration of information - a survey of existing approaches. In: Proceedings - IJCAI Workshop, pp. 108–117 (2001)
7. Klein, M.: Combining and relating ontologies: an analysis of problems and solutions. In: Proceedings - IJCAI Workshop, pp. 53–62 (2001)
8. Subhani, N., Kent, R.: Novel design approach to build audit rule ontology for healthcare decision support systems. In: International Conference on E-Learning, E-Business, Enterprise Information Systems, and E-Government, pp. 133–138 (2014)
9. Jean, S., Pierra, G., Ait Ameur, Y.: A domain ontologies: A database-oriented analysis. In: Jean, S., Pierra, G., Ait-Ameur, Y. (eds.) WEBIST 2005/2006. LNBIP, vol. 1, pp. 238–254. Springer, Heidelberg (2007)
10. Twidle, K., Dulay, N., Lupu, E., Sloman, M.: Ponder2: A policy system for autonomuous pervasive environments. In: International Conference on Autonomic and Autonomous Systems, pp. 330–335 (2009)
11. Singh, S., Singh, K., Kaur, H.: Design and evaluation of policy based authorization model for large scale distributed systems. IJCSNS International Journal of Computer Science and Network Security 9(11), 49–55 (2009)
12. Cao, J., Chen, J., Zhao, H., Li, M.: A policy-based authorization model for workflow-enabled dynamic process management. Journal of Network and Computer Applications 32(2), 412–422 (2009)
13. Kandala, S., Sandhu, R., Bhamidipati, V.: An attribute based framework for risk-adaptive access control models. In: Availability, Reliability and Security (ARES), pp. 236–241 (2011)

A Novel Mechanism for Dynamic Optimization
of Intercloud Services

Lohit Kapoor[1], Seema Bawa[1], and Ankur Gupta[2]

[1] Thapar University, Patiala, India
{lohit.kapoor,seema}@thapar.edu,
[2] Model Institute of Engineering and Technology, Jammu, India
ankurgupta@mietjammu.in

Abstract. Managing services in an intercloud environment is challenging since it requires large scale orchestration between users, service providers and heterogeneous cloud service providers. Each stakeholder in the intercloud services ecosystem needs to optimize their cost to performance ratio which is not trivial. This research paper proposes a dynamic service ranking and selection mechanism which allows users fine-grained control over service consumption, while maximizing service provider revenues. The mechanism is based on service performance analytics and provides seamless orchestration between all stakeholders. Initial experimental results establish the viability of the proposed mechanism.

Keywords: Intercloud, Service orchestration in Intercloud, Service ranking and selection.

1 Introduction

Services management in an intercloud environment encompasses the deployment, configuration, provisioning, operation and portability of cloud resources across different Cloud Service Providers (CSPs). The intercloud provides a strong motivation for the deployment of large-scale services which need to cater to diverse geographical locations of their users besides optimizing latency and cost while ensuring quality-of-service and complying with service-level agreements. Thus, a mechanism which allows users customized and seamless access to services in an intercloud scenario is required. A major concern for any inter-cloud services management framework is the orchestration of services across CSPs and allowing end-users fine-grained control over how they select and consume services without knowing the deployment and location details [1]. The intercloud has emerged as a logical evolution of the cloud computing paradigm allowing for the creation of a community of CSPs to offer greater value-add to the end consumer while facilitating enhanced elasticity, ensuring QoS even at peak loads, service/data portability and migration and collaborative services for mutual benefits. For small and medium CSPs this model is fairly intuitive from a resource sharing perspective [2]. For Large CSPs the intercloud offers them the possibility of offering services in the geographical

R. Meersman et al. (Eds.): OTM 2014 Workshops, LNCS 8842, pp. 377–388, 2014.

proximity of their customers and improving responsiveness. The intercloud also alleviates the issue of data/vendor lock-in [5]. In any case end-users want flexibility to shift from one cloud to another or from one service to another, due to various reasons like performance degradation, high cost, legal issues etc. Infrastructure as a Service (IaaS) provides the user much greater control, but in Platform as a Service (PaaS) and Software as a Service (SaaS) the consumers do not have much control of their data because of proprietary APIs. Service portability can solve these issues [1] [3], but a large numbers of CSPs makes it difficult for service providers and end users to decide which CSP will be a best-fit for their requirements. Cloud brokers have emerged as the de facto intermediaries between service providers, users and the CSPs [4]. This research paper proposes a comprehensive Unified Services Management Framework (USMF) for the intercloud environment. We propose the "Services Cloud (SC)" framework, a distributed trusted third party framework which encompasses brokering services, service performance management and provides a service ranking and. selection mechanism for end-users. The Services Cloud is in parts inspired by the mobile number portability technique employed by the telecommunications industry allowing cell phone customers to move seamlessly between different telecom service providers without changing their cell number [6]. Only the call routing logic needs to be changed to facilitate mobile number portability. The SC receives user's request, provides a customized ranking of various available services (across CSPs) and allocates the service based on user selection. Further, in the case the user finds the services not meeting their expectations, it can select a different service instance on the intercloud. Moreover, a service provider can also initiate a migration of a service instance to some other CSP to better meet its SLAs with the end users. The aim of the proposed framework is to enable the users to consume customized services as per their choice in the intercloud ecosystem and present them a variety of services options which best meet their requirements.

The main contributions of this paper are:

- Proposes a comprehensive Unified Services Management Framework for an intercloud environment.
- Presents a service ranking mechanism in an intercloud based on detailed performance monitoring and historical analysis.
- Presents a fine-grained control mechanism to the end users for optimal service selection based on different parameters.

Presents model of automated service scaling and deployment for service providers in an intercloud based on dynamic service consumption patterns.

2   Background and Related Work

Intercloud service management is challenging yet essential in deploying the next-generation of large-scale global services which span multiple Cloud Service Providers (CSPs). Many of current vendors provide solutions to manage services across multiple clouds. TM forum (TMF) [7] presents a unified service delivery management model which focuses on deployment of federated services. As per Forrester Research's, Cisco commissioned research on Global Managed Services Opportunity

(2009) the demand for managed "on-demand" services is identified as a key shift in user preferences [8]. Therefore the necessary intercloud infrastructure and middleware required to support service orchestration across CSPs needs to be in place to realize this market requirement. Research in intercloud services management is in nascent stage. Existing literature in the field addresses some challenges of deploying and managing services in an intercloud environment, but the big picture seems missing.

Several brokers exist in literature which can operate across CSPs and focus on specific issues such as interoperability, performance monitoring of virtual machines, data migration and orchestration. RightScale [9] is a real world cloud broker around a middleware which is adaptable and automated. It analyzes past events for better cloud control, administration, and life-cycle management of applications across multiple clouds. It relies on monitoring the performance parameters of instances of different clouds (in terms of virtual machine performance) but is service agnostic. Service performance can vary significantly in different production environments, but RightScale does not provide any mechanism to monitor the performance of different services across CSPs. Thus, optimal service selection remains a challenge. Authors in [10] propose a "cloud coordinator" between multiple clouds which allows customers to dynamically scale their services for optimal performance. Authors in [11] present a ranking mechanism of different services in order to provide a comparative view to users to choose a particular service over another under different use-cases. In this work authors proposes SMICloud Broker which performs service discovery and ranking on different Key Performance Indicators (KPIs). However this mechanism does not provide any autonomic technique to redirect the users request in the case of flash-crowd scenario, fault incidence etc. to ensure minimal SLA violations and revenue loss to the service provider.

Thus, most of the current cloud brokering mechanisms provide scheduling or routing of service requests based on monitoring the virtual machines on which the services are deployed. In most of the cases customers can select, monitor and migrate these virtual instances across CSPs without having a comprehensive service-view of the intercloud. The service-view of the intercloud is important to a) optimize service deployment and management for the service provider (auto-scaling, replication, migration) b) optimize service selection for the end-user (cost, response-time, QoS-compliance).

This research paper provides details of the framework to meet the above requirements and proposes a Services Cloud (SC) with a services broker which manages service orchestration and consumption across different CSPs in a seamless manner.

3 System Model

In this section the detailed system model of the proposed Services Cloud (SC) is discussed. A Cloud Service Provider (CSP) may encompass multiple data-centers at different geographical locations. Data-Centers belonging to a CSP are managed by a central broker which distributes the resource requests within the CSP. Each CSP participates in a federation of CSPs i.e. the intercloud. The proposed Services Cloud

(SC) consists of compute resources contributed by each CSP participating in the intercloud and has its own master broker for scheduling services across CSPs. Thus the SC broker talks to individual CSP brokers for scheduling services across the intercloud. Each service may consist of a number of instances which can be deployed anywhere in the intercloud.

Further, the SC employs caching for maintaining references to the most frequently-used services and the frequently-accessed data sets to speed up the service lookup time and minimize the service response time. The proposed Services Cloud (SC) architecture for the intercloud environment is depicted in Figure 1. At a broad level the architecture consists of four entities: a) Services Cloud b) Cloud Service Providers c) Service Providers and d) Service Consumers The SC is not monolithic, but composed of several sub-components. Prominent among these are the user-management module, services performance monitoring module, services deployment and management module and the scheduler module (for routing end-user requests to appropriate/selected service).

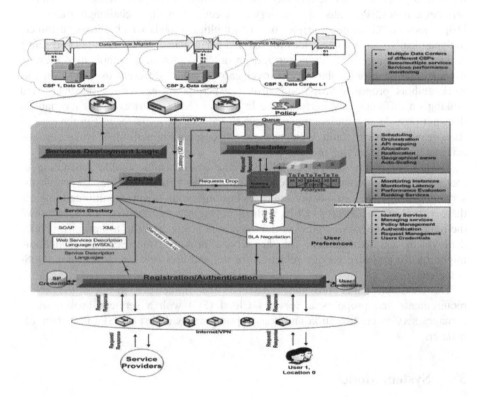

Fig. 1. Schematic of intercloud service management system

4   Major Operations

A) Service Registration: Service Providers (SPs) need to register their service offerings with the Services Cloud (SC) through a well-defined interface. A service registration request contains complete service description including generic information, service components, related files and dependencies which facilitate automated service deployment. Upon successful registration services are reflected in the central service directory maintained by the SC.

B) Service Deployment: The process of service deployment is based on the resource requirements and constraints of a particular service. For instance a specific platform may be a dependency for service deployment. Also, the physical resources (number and desired configuration of virtual machines), their location and cost ($ per hour per virtual machine) can be important constraints for the SP. In that case the SC deploys the service at the CSP which best meets the requirements of the SP.

C) Service Monitoring: Once a service is deployed by the SC, the service monitoring module starts real-time monitoring of the service. It obtains the service handle from the service directory and keeps sending heartbeat messages to the deployed service instance after a pre-defined interval for checking uptime, availability and response times. Thus, a strong basis for service ranking and selection and further optimization is created by the service monitoring module in the SC.

D) User Registration: User registration involves account creation and generation of authentication credentials. The user management module maintains a profile for each user with services consumed, feedback/rating and billing information included.

E) Service Ranking and Selection (SRS): Since detailed performance profiles of each service instance are created by the service performance monitoring module it is straightforward for the SC to rank comparable services (belonging to the same category). This is done through a weighted formula based on different parameters such as latency, reliability, availability and user rating while remaining within the overall cost constraints specified by the consumer.

F) Service Consumption and Management: All the preceding operations contribute to major real-time optimizations during service consumption phase. If the SC detects that the service request queue has reached its threshold (can be determined by observing past correlation between service queue length and response time) then the SC can perform auto-scaling including duplication of service instance.

G) Accounting: Finally, after the services have been consumed, requests processed and violations noted, the accounting process is applied to compute the dues of the end-users. Similarly, the dues of the SP towards the CSP are also computed and the settlements processed.

5   Performance Metrics

Service Measurement Index (SMI) [12] is a set of business-relevant Key Performance Indicators (KPI's) that provide a standardized method for measuring and comparing a business service regardless of whether that service is internally provided or sourced from an outside company. SMI enables individual preferences to be the basis for what defines a good service. We have identified five parameters as shown in Table 1 from SMI as a basis for defining service quality *(p) for the proposed framework.*

Table 1. Identified Parameters

Service Quality Parameters	Standard Weight-age
Network Latency (ϕ_1)	0.20 (wt$_1$)
Processing Time (ϕ_2)	0.20 (wt$_2$)
Reliability (ϕ_3)	0.20 (wt$_3$)
Reputation (ϕ_4)	0.20 (*wt$_4$*)
Availability(ϕ_5)	0.20 (wt$_5$)

Based on their contribution, a weight age is given to all the Service Quality factors and as a final point aggregated to compute ranking score (R) of a service is given by:

$$R = {}^{n}\sum_{i=1} wt_n \, \phi_n \leq 1$$

After computing the rank a service list is presented to the user and final negotiation process is initiated as shown in algorithm below (Figure 2)

	Algorithm: Service Ranking and Selection
1:	// Collecting users' preferences and discovering service
2:	for each user
3:	getCustomWeights(userweights)
4:	getCostConstraints(cost)
5:	getServiceCategory(category)
6:	services = ServicesDirectory.lookup(category)
7:	// Computing rank and negotiating SLAs
8:	for each service in services[i]
9:	topServices=computeRank(services[i], userweight)
10:	user.showRank(topServices)
11:	user.recordSelection(service)
12:	service.negotiateSLAvalues(SLAvalues,cost)
13:	end for
14:	end for

Fig. 2. The algorithm for selection and ranking of services

The deployment scenario of multiple instances of same service at different location is reffered as "Multiple Instances Multiple Locations (MIML)". The Ranking scores (R) for each distributed replicated services deployed at different data centers located in different physical locations of 1 or more

CSPs instance are calculated periodically by the service performance monitoring module which maintains hourly, daily, monthly, quarterly, semi-annual and annual averages of various performance parameters discussed above. Within the Services Cloud the standard weights for the five service quality parameters are fixed equally at 0.20, although individual service consumers can define their own weights to derive their customized service rankings as per their needs.

6   Experimental Setup, Simulations and Results

To validate the proposed framework we have developed a custom simulator which works on real-world data as its base input. For the purposes of collecting real-world data pertaining to various deployed services, we consider three popular CSPs - Amazon EC2 [13], Windows Azure [14], and GoGrid [15]. The test environment had a total of 3 CSPs, 6 data centers at 6 different physical locations and 10 service instances deployed at various CSPs locations. We further consider only one type of virtual machine instance in different CSPs since in [16] authors have concluded that both medium and large vm instances gets overloaded with the similar level of concurrent requests.

Therefore in order to save experimental cost without compromising on service performance measurements we use instances shown in Table 2 for service deployment.

Table 2. Virtual Machine configuration

OS	CPU	Cores	Memory(MB)
Linux/ubuntu	AMD Opteron 2 GHz	1	1024
Windows Server 2012	Intel Xeon E52670	1	1024

We replace actual CSP names with "CSP_1, CSP_2 and CSP_3" and replace actual data-center locations with generic locations "L_1, L_2, L_3, L_4, L_5 and L_6". Our experimental workload comprises an application based on Photo Storage which is implemented on each CSPs datacenter location. Using this test setup we measure for each service instance its latency, processing time, availability and reliability.

For measurement purposes we use HTTP HEAD Requests using curl for latency measurements instead of ICMP ping command because MS Azure has barred incoming/outgoing ping requests [17]. We take measurements in every 5 minute interval and compute averages for each parameter every 1 hour. Intuitively network latency is dependent on the intercloud environment can lead to counter-intuitive results.

The results obtained in the test setup are shown in Figure 3 which concurs with those obtained in [18]. It can be seen that the average percentage variation for one location is up to 18% i.e. latency varies significantly over 24 hours for the same location which implies that any QoS-complaint service deployment scheme requires factor these latency variations to effectively meet defined SLAs.

Further we use Manage Engine's Application Manager [19] to measure service performance in a virtualized environment. We also used httperf [20] as our benchmark to generate the workload for different service instances. Since our service is web-based, therefore detailed information on the number of connections, rate of connections, request size, request rate, reply time/size and rate etc. is required.

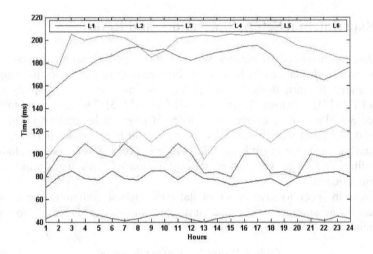

Fig. 3. Observed latency for different service instances over a 24 hour period

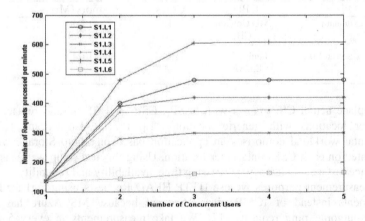

Fig. 4. Number of Requests processed/minute by different service instances in MIML deployment scenario

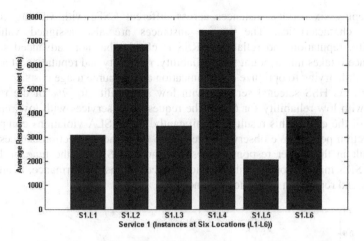

Fig. 5. Average Response Times for different service instances in MIML deployment scenario

We perform our benchmark tests on each deployed service instance in our test environment. We measure the variations in the number of requests processed per minute and average response time for different service instances under Multiple Instances deployed in Multiple Locations (MIML) scenario. The results which are depicted in Figure 4 and Figure 5 respectively shows the number of requests processed per minute is dependent on the latency between the user and location of the service and the variations of up to 60% are observed.

Here the location of the user remains the same. Similarly the variations up to 375% were observed in response time for various service instances. In the real world varied users locations can result in greater variations in service instances performance. We use the photo-storage service to look-up and download a 5KB file in all these tests.

Further service selection can be based on:

a) Cost based service selection (CSS): In this type of selection policy scheduler looks out for the cheapest service offer (in case of similar competing services). It selects the least cost service and allocates it to the user. This kind of service selection is best fit for the users who are not performance oriented and want to pay less. Here the probability of response-time based SLA- violations is very high.

b) Work load based service selection (WSS): It monitors the work load on each service deployed in datacenter and find out the least loaded service with less service requests pending. This type of policy is optimal when performance is paramount but very prone to cost based- SLA violations.

c) Hybrid service selection (HSS): This policy takes care of both cost and workload of a service. It uses cost as an upper bound and finds out the least loaded service.

We have compared the performance of the HSS policy with our Service Ranking and Selection (SRS) policy on several parameters. We use the MIML deployment strategy for both the SRS and HSS and observe the overall response time and SLA violations.

We deploy six service instances across different CSPs with varying cost and workload characteristics. The service instances are also assigned values for availability, reputation and reliability. RSS is clearly the more advanced selection policy since it takes into account the availability, reliability and reputation of a service instance while trying to optimize communication and resource usage costs.

In our tests HSS selected services with low availability for 7% of the requests, services with low reliability for 6% of the requests and services with low reputation for 10% of the cases. This result in significantly higher SLA violations compared to SRS selection policy. We observe in the Figure 6 that poor selection choices by the HSS result in the higher response times compared to SRS to the tune of 17% on average. SRS makes more credible choices based on past performance, availability, reliability and reputation of service instances.

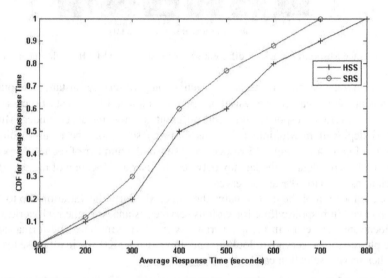

Fig. 6. CDF for average response time for HSS and SRS service selection policies

Table 3. (a):Optimization achieved by HSS and SRS over CSS service selection policy

Parameters	HSS	SRS
SLA-violations optimization	31 %	58%
Cost optimization	9%	22 %

Table 3(b):Optimization achieved by HSS and SRS over WSS service selection policy

Parameters	HSS	SRS
SLA-violations Optimization	22 %	47%
Cost optimization	19 %	34 %

Again in Table 3(a) and Table 3(b) we compare HSS and SRS on cost optimization achieved and SLA violations observed with CSS and WSS selection policies as the base. SRS outperforms HSS due to: a) qualitatively better service selection b) geographically-aware auto-scaling and c) caching of frequently used service handles and responses.

7   Conclusion and Future Work

This paper proposes a Unified Services Management Framework for an intercloud environment which facilitates a) optimal service deployment and geographically-aware auto-scaling and b) optimal service selection and consumption by the end-user in a seamless manner. We evaluated the effectiveness of the proposed framework using a custom simulator based on real world service performance measurements across different CSPs. The results indicate that from a service provider perspective achieving high performance at reasonable cost is dependent on the service deployment scheme. Future work shall involve more real-world testing for different service types and categories, service deployment scenarios and varying user requirements over sustained periods to create formal benchmarks for intercloud services.

References

1. Petcu, D., Macariu, G., Panica, S., Crăciun, C.: Portable Cloud applications—From theory to practice. Future Generation Computer Systems 29, 1417–1430 (2013)
2. Gupta, A., Kapoor, L., Wattal, M.: C2C (Cloud-to-cloud): An ecosystem of cloud service providers for dynamic resource provisioning. In: Abraham, A., Lloret Mauri, J., Buford, J.F., Suzuki, J., Thampi, S.M. (eds.) ACC 2011, Part I. CCIS, vol. 190, pp. 501–510. Springer, Heidelberg (2011)
3. Chandra, K.: The AppScale Cloud Platform: Enabling Portable, Scalable Web Application deployment. Internet Computing 17(2), 72–75 (2013)
4. Cloud computing brokers: a resource guide (December 2013),
   http://www.datacenterknowledge.com/archives/2010/01/22/cloudcomputingbrokers-a-resource-guide/
5. Kapoor, L., Bawa, S., Gupta, A.: Hierarchical Chord based Resource Discovery in Intercloud Environment. In: UCC 2013, pp. 464–469. ACM (2013)
6. http://www.portabil.pt/fileadmin/systor/NP_WhitePaper.pdf
7. https://www.tmforum.org/InterCloudService/8480/home.html (accessed 5, December 2013)
8. http://www.sbtpartners.com/_etc/managed_services_paradigm.pdf (accessed 1, November 2013)
9. RightScale home page, http://www.rightscale.com/ (accessed 10, December 2013)
10. Calheiros, R.N., Toosi, A.N., Vecchiola, C., Buyya, R.: A coordinator for scaling elastic applications across multiple clouds. Future Generation Computer Systems 28, 1350–1362 (2012)

11. Garg, S.K., Versteegb, S., Buyya, R.: A framework for ranking of cloud computing services. Future Generation Computer Systems 29(4), 1012–1023 (2013)
12. http://www.cloudcommons.com/about-smi (accessed 1, November 2013)
13. Amazon EC2 home page, http://aws.amazon.com/ec2/
14. Gogrid home page, http://www.gogrid.com/
15. http://www.windowsazure.com/en-us/
16. L-Sumarro, J.L., Moreno, R., Montero, R.S., Llorente, I.M.: Scheduling strategies for optimal service deployment across multiple clouds. Future Generation Computer System 29, 1431–1441 (2013)
17. Outbound Ping on Azure VM,
    http://social.msdn.microsoft.com/Forums/windowsazure/
    en-US/e9e53e84-a978-46f5-a657-f31da7e4bbe1/icmp-outbound-
    ping-on-azure-vm?forum=WAVirtualMachinesforWindows
18. Whu, Z., Madhyastha, H.V.: Understanding latency benefits of multi-cloud Web-services deployments. ACM SIGCOMM Computer Communication Review 43(2), 13–20 (2013)
19. http://www.manageengine.com/products/applications_manager/
20. http://www.hpl.hp.com/research/linux/httperf/

The Upgrade Planning Process in a Global Operational Environment

Jukka Kääriäinen[1], Susanna Teppola[1], Matias Vierimaa[1], and Antti Välimäki[2]

[1] VTT, Oulu, Finland
{jukka.kaariainen,susanna.teppola,matias.vierimaa}@vtt.fi
[2] Metso Automation Inc., Tampere, Finland
antti.valimaki@metso.com

Abstract. Industrial automation systems are multi-technological systems that contain in-house developed and COTS hardware and software sub-systems. Automation systems can be used to control various industrial processes ranging from water management to pulp and paper production. These systems are used for a long time and are upgraded in order to keep the system up-to-date. Typically, automation system providers serve their customers worldwide, meaning that the service operations are spread geographically over several continents. Furthermore, the service organisation needs to cooperate internally with R&D and externally with customers and COTS providers so as to gain a necessary understanding of which upgrades are urgent and which can be done later. This paper discusses the importance of a systematic upgrade planning service in a distributed operational environment and presents as well as demonstrates the process description and related tools that have been composed based on an industrial case study in an automation company.

Keywords: Automation system, Upgrade, Lifecycle, Transparency.

1 Introduction

Industrial automation systems are used in various industrial segments, such as power generation, water management and pulp and paper [1]. The systems comprise HW and SW sub-systems that are in-house developed or COTS (Commercial off-the-shelf) components. Since these systems have a long lifetime, the automation system providers offer different kinds of life cycle services for their customers in order to keep their automation systems running smoothly. One key service is called an "upgrade service". An upgrade service is used to keep the customer's automation system up-to-date by upgrading it based on a jointly (customer – provider) agreed plan.

This paper discusses an important part of the upgrade service – upgrade planning. Systematic upgrade planning is crucial so as to avoid upgrade implementation problems that may result from an insufficient understanding of the customer's automation system. It is important to identify the configuration of the customer's automation system and to understand its upgrade needs so as to be able to negotiate with the customer about the scale and price of the upgrade. Since the operational environment is

R. Meersman et al. (Eds.): OTM 2014 Workshops, LNCS 8842, pp. 389–398, 2014.
© Springer-Verlag Berlin Heidelberg 2014

global, the process and information systems should enable operation in a geographically distributed environment in cooperation with service, customers, R&D and COTS providers.

This paper presents the second iteration of the research aimed at a better understanding system upgrades in the case study company's service sales team, and at enhancing the solutions for handling upgrade identification and analysis in the case study company. The paper introduces the upgrade planning process and related tools as well as demonstrating their usage in a real-life industrial scenario. The first iteration of the research has been presented in [2].

The paper is organized as follows: Section 2 presents the background to industrial automation systems and their upgrade challenges. The research process is discussed briefly in Section 3. Section 4 presents an upgrade planning process description. Section 5 introduces a demonstration that discusses the applicability of the solution in real-life case. Section 6 draws the conclusions.

2   Background

Industrial automation systems control industrial processes in various industrial segments. They are used in pulp and paper, water management, power generation, chemical industry, for instance [1]. In some cases, these systems need to meet the requirements of safety-criticality. Automation system vendors are also using COTS components in their systems, for instance, third-party operating systems (e.g. Windows). Basically, factors that drive the upgrades for automation systems are the technical deterioration of the system and changes to the system requirements [3]. Automation system providers offer their automation systems and industrial services in order to keep customer's processes running smoothly (see Fig 1). In literature, e.g. Poulsen [3] presents an approach for the organisation and planning of upgrades and replacements.

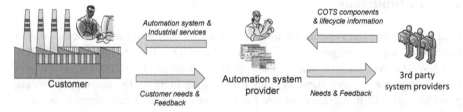

Fig. 1. Customers, automation system providers and third party system providers

Today services are forming an important part of the manufacturers' offering. The shift from products to services has been taking place in the software product industry from 1990 onwards [4]. The importance of service business for manufacturers was also understood at approximately the same time. It was noticed that substantial revenue can be generated from an installed base of products with a long life cycle [5, 6]. The slow economic growth during recent years has boosted the development of product-related services even more – services have brought increasing revenue for the manufacturing companies in place of traditional product sales [7, 8]. The importance of service business has been understood for a while, but more systematic and integrated product and service development processes are needed [9]. During recent years the focus has shifted towards understanding the customer's needs and early validation of the success of developed services [10].

Delivering the right services in a cost-effective manner requires a good understanding of the customer installed systems, as well as, the context and business environment in which the customer is working. Customer's automation system may undergo many upgrades which need to be followed. This requires automation, as manual analysis is typically very time consuming and error-prone. One example of this kind of automated approach is from Jetley et al. [11], where code comparison between program versions can be computed and differences visualised for maintainers in a way that significant improvements can be achieved in time used for this type of analysis. Keeping the development costs down requires automation in procedures, reusable, flexible architecture solutions, which enable cost-effective services during the system lifecycle. All this means that the different functions, customer service, service and product design must go hand in hand, so that they can take into account each other's different needs and constraints. This requires strong co-operation, common processes and transparency to fulfil cross-operative functions within an organisation, but also outside the organisation, to the customer interface. When planning product upgradeability, safety-critical companies in particular need to consider several alternate scenarios that may require upgrades, such as business/market changes, safety-critical standard development and technology evolution. Different scenarios form a set of possible future roadmaps that need to be prepared for in the upgrade planning process.

3   Research Process

This work was carried out within the international research projects Varies (Variability in Safety-Critical Embedded Systems) [12] and Promes (Process Models for Engineering of Embedded Systems) [13]. The case company operates in the automation systems industry. The company offers automation and information management application networks and systems, intelligent field control solutions, and support and maintenance services. The case focuses on the automation system product sector and includes the upgrade service. Typically, the customer-specific, tailored installation of the system is based on a generic product platform, and a new version of this product platform is released annually. Automation system vendors are also using COTS components in their systems, for instance, third-party operating systems (e.g. Windows). Therefore, automation systems are dependent on, for instance, the technology roadmaps of operating system providers. The (generic) main sub-systems in an automation system include: Control Room, Engineering Tools, Information Management and Process Controllers.

Engineering tools are used to configure the automation system so as to fit the customer's context. This includes, for instance, the development of process applications and related views. Automation systems have a long life and they need to be maintained and updated, if necessary. Therefore, the case company offers upgrade services to keep the customers' automation systems up-to-date. Each update will be analysed individually so as to find the optimal solution for the customer based on the customer's business needs. Service operation is highly distributed since the case company has over 100 sales and customer service units in 38 countries serving customers representing various industrial segments in Europe, Asia, America, Africa and Australia.

Because of the demands of customer-specific tailoring, there are many customer-specific configurations (i.e. the customer-specific variants of an automation system) in the field containing sub-systems from different platform releases (versions). Therefore, the service organisation (the system provider) needs to track each customer configuration of an automation system and detect what upgrades are possible for each customer.

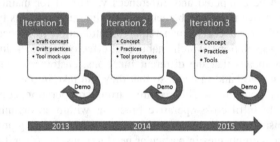

Fig. 2. Iterative plan for the development of concept, practices and tools in collaboration with a case study company [2]

This research is part of broader research project aiming at a better understanding of system upgrades in the case study company's service sales team, and at enhancing the solutions for handling upgrade identification and analysis in the case study company. Furthermore, the research highlights the importance of common processes and activities as well as the transparency of related data to make upgrade planning activities effectively and systematically. The research will be done in three iterations. The results of the first iteration have been reported in [2]. The aim of the paper is to present the results of the second research iteration (Fig. 2). During this iteration we defined and described an upgrade planning process and demonstrated its usage in a real-life industrial scenario. The original plan was to implement separate tools for installed base management and lifecycle plans. However, lifecycle plans are currently generated as reports as part of the InstalledBase tool (no separate Life Cycle Planner tool (see [2] for background)).

We have applied the meta-model defined by Charalampidou et al. [14] in the Promes project as a frame for upgrade planning process description. The process description and demonstration presented in this paper are based on the longitudinal case study data that was collected using interviews, workshops and meetings with case company representatives during the autumn of 2012 and spring of 2014. Between autumn 2013 and spring 2014 in cooperation with the case company we defined and documented a demonstration that validated the process and tools against a real-life industrial upgrade planning scenario.

4   Upgrade Planning Process

This section presents a process description for upgrade planning. The description is presented in Fig. 3. The Product Life Cycle process contains all industrial service processes. The product life cycle process is divided into phases. Each phase represents one service (e.g. Upgrade Service is one phase). Phases are divided into activities that represent collections of tasks that will be carried out by the workers (e.g. Service Manager). One worker has the responsibility (author) for the activity, and other workers work as contributors. Activities create and use artefacts that will be retrieved from or stored in tools (information systems).

The upgrade service process is divided into six activities. The first four form the Upgrade Planning process. The last two represent subsequent steps, as the implementation of upgrade and follow up. The process contains a sequence of activities to keep the presentation simple, even though in real-life parallelism and loops/iterations are also possible. For instance, new customer needs may emerge during price negotiations that will be investigated in a new upgrade planning iteration. The Global Installed-Base tool is ready and has been piloted. The case company has a customer extranet tool, but it will be replaced with new tool in the near future.

The process starts with the identification of upgrade needs. The input for an upgrade need may come from various sources, for instance, directly from customer, from a service engineer working on-site at the customer's premises, from component end-of-life notification, etc. The service manager is responsible for collecting and documenting upgrade needs originating from internal or external sources.

The service manager is responsible for carrying out "Identify installed system" activity. In this activity, the customer's automation system configuration information (i.e. customer-specific installed report) is retrieved from the InstalledBase tool. The information is updated based on information collected automatically from the automation system (automatically via a network connection with the customer's automation system ("tell me your configuration")) and manually by a site visit, if needed. The updated information is stored in the InstalledBase tool. The InstalledBase tool is a globally used database that is used by service managers and service staff worldwide. Information transparency is crucial. Accurate and timely configuration information is needed to minimize errors and to speed up time-to-service in the upgrade planning process since the existing configuration is needed as a baseline for upgrade analysis.

In the "Analyse the system / compose LC (life cycle) plan" activity service manager is responsible for analysing the instant and future upgrade needs for the customer's automation system. The InstalledBase tool contains life cycle plan functionality. This means that the tool contains some life cycle rules related to the automation systems. Life cycle rules are composed by a product manager who works in service interface. These rules originate from internal and external sources. External information is collected from third-party system providers (COTS providers). This information comes, for instance, from operating system providers (a roadmap that shows how long operating system versions will be supported). Internal life cycle information originates from R&D (product creation and technology research functions). Internal life cycle information defines in-house developed automation system components and their support policy). Furthermore, lifecycle information about system dependencies is also important (compatibility information). Dependency information shows the dependencies between sub-systems and components so as to detect how changes in one sub-system may escalate to other sub-systems in a customer's configuration. Finally, rules are also affected by a company's overall life cycle policy (i.e. the policy on how long (and how) the company decides to support the systems). Not all rules are implemented into the InstalledBase tool since some rules need to be applied manually depending on the case. However, the InstalledBase tool contains a common lifecycle frame for global service team to systematise upgrade planning. The service manager generates a life cycle report from the InstalledBase tool and starts to modify it based on negotiations with the customer.

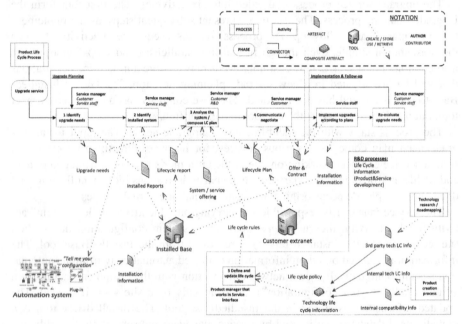

Fig. 3. Upgrade planning process description

In the "Negotiations" activity the service manager modifies life cycle plan based on the maintenance budgets and downtime schedules of the customer. The final life cycle plan presents the life cycle of each part of the system, illustrating for a single customer what needs to be upgraded and when, and at what point in time a bigger migration might be needed. The plan supports the customer in preparing themselves for the updates, for instance by predicting costs, schedules for downtimes, rationale for management, etc. For the service team, this provides an understanding of upgrade needs from which they can propose and justify updates for a customer in a timely manner that maintains the customer's automation system in good condition. The global customer extranet database is used as a medium when communicating with the customer. Based on the negotiations and offer, the upgrade implementation starts according to contract. Furthermore, the service manager is responsible for periodically re-evaluating the upgrade needs.

5   Demonstration

The case company arranged a demonstration where the process and tools were applied in order to understand their operation in a real-life case containing real-life data. The demonstration was based on a scenario that was defined as a user story. In the demonstration we used an easy-to-understand scenario that is based on the fact that security updates for Windows XP will stop in the spring of 2014.

Table 1. User story for a demonstration

User Story – Installed Base and Life Cycle report : "As a service manager, I want to study the situation of a customer concerning Windows XP and produce a life cycle plan so that I can quote and plan upgrades to my customer"		Process activity
Starting point	Windows XP security updates stop in 2014.	Identify upgrade needs
Step 1	I start by selecting the customer from the customer search engine.	Identify installed system
Step 2	A customer-specific report list is generated.	
Step 3	I select an Installed Base report from the report list.	
Step 4	The Installed Base report is generated and I can analyse the situation of the customer concerning Windows XP.	
Step 5	I select Life Cycle Report from the report list.	Analyse the system / compose LC plan
Step 6	A life cycle report for the next ten years is generated based on life cycle information in the InstalledBase tool.	
Step 7	I start to edit the final life cycle report for the customer based on schedule and budget information received from the customer.	Communicate / negotiate
Step 8	I store the Life Cycle plan and related material to the Customer Extranet tool and continue negotiations with the customer.	

The starting point for the scenario is that the service manager needs to know whether a customer has an automation system that contains Windows XP installations (security updates stop in 2014). Service manager starts the InstalledBase tool and selects a customer using the customer search tool. From the customer-specific reports list, the service manager selects "Installed Base Report" (Fig. 4).

This opens a view in which the customer's installed automation system (part of the Control Room sub-system) is presented at a node level (Fig. 4). For each node, the report shows e.g. the platform release (i.e. collection) and used operating system. Fig. 4 shows that customer-specific configuration may contain components from different platform releases that result from earlier partial upgrades. This report is collected automatically from the customer's automation system via a network connection and is updated manually, if necessary, based on, for instance, a site visit. The service manager checks whether the customer is still using Windows XP.

Fig. 4. InstalledBase report

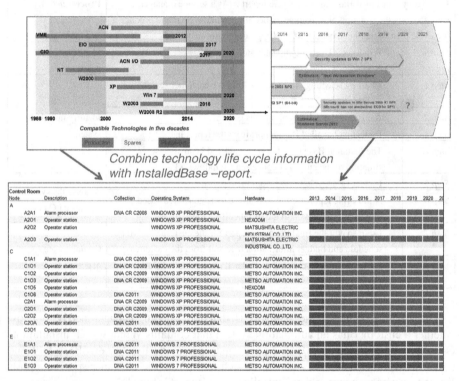

Combine technology life cycle information
with InstalledBase –report.

Fig. 5. Lifecycle –report is generated based on life cycle information and the InstalledBase report

The service manager continues their analysis by selecting "Lifecycle Report" from the customer specific reports list (see Fig. 4). The InstalledBase tool generates a lifecycle report for a customer (Fig. 5). The report is generated by combining data from the lifecycle policy, InstalledBase report and technology lifecycle rules that originate from internal and external (e.g. [15]) life cycle decisions as well as from automation system compatibility information (dependencies between sub-systems).

The report indicates that nodes A and C contain stations with Win XP installations and node E stations already have Windows 7. Furthermore, the report indicates that stations with XP need to be upgraded instantly (OS, SW and HW). Stations with Win 7 are supported until the spring of 2020 and, therefore, they need to be upgraded before that. The service manager exports the report to Excel and discusses with R&D whether there are lifecycle issues that have remained open. The service manager discusses with the customer their budget and downtime schedules that impose important constraints on the planning work. The service manager starts to update Lifecycle Report based on their discussions. The report is stored in the Customer Extranet tool that works as a collaborative medium between a case company and a customer.

6   Conclusions

This paper discusses the importance of systematic upgrade planning in a distributed operational environment, and presents as well as demonstrates the process description and related tools that have been composed based on an industrial case study in an automation company. Common process and activities as well as transparency of related data are important enablers for the company to conduct upgrade planning activities effectively and systematically. The research is part of broader research project aiming at a better understanding of system upgrades in the case study company's service sales team and at enhancing the solutions for handling upgrade identification and analysis in the case study company. This creates the basis for a company to provide life cycle services for customers in a cost-effective manner. This paper presents the second iteration of research. Iterative research, practical solution development and demonstration gradually accumulate and validate the whole solution.

The demonstration has showed that the process and tools were able to support the upgrade planning function. Information systems systematize work and enable operation in a global service environment in cooperation with different stakeholders. If compared with the approach presented in [3], it can be noted that our approach emphasises more the usage of IT systems during the upgrade process. However, the basic phases are somewhat similar starting from the identification of needs through clarification of installed system and analysing the upgrade effects.

Companies and research institutes will benefit from this research since it describes the concept of upgrade planning that helps them to understand the complexity of the phenomenon in industrial companies. Furthermore, the concept helps to identify the kinds of IT systems and the processes that are needed to tackle the problem of upgrade planning in global operational environment.

The next research step (iteration 3) will be the full deployment of the process and tools in the company. The next demonstration will provide us with feedback from real-users on the solution in a global environment. In the Varies-project [12], several research studies have been conducted in order to understand what drives variability i.e. to understand the reasons behind variability decisions. From an upgrade planning process perspective, understanding the main drivers for future upgrade needs and prioritising the drivers would help companies in understanding their most urgent needs.

Acknowledgements. This research has been done in ITEA2 project named Promes [11] and Artemis project named Varies [10]. This research is funded by Tekes, Artemis joint undertaking, Metso and VTT. The authors would like to thank all contributors for their assistance and cooperation.

References

1. Koziolek, H., Weiss, R., Durdik, Z., Stammel, J., Krogmann, K.: Towards Software Sustainability Guidelines for Long-living Industrial Systems. In: Proceedings of Software Engineering 2011. 3rd Workshop. Long-living Software Systems (L2S2), pp. 47–58 (2011)
2. Kääriäinen, J., Teppola, S., Välimäki, A.: Building a concept solution for upgrade planning in the automation industry. In: Demey, Y.T., Panetto, H. (eds.) OTM 2013 Workshops 2013. LNCS, vol. 8186, pp. 312–321. Springer, Heidelberg (2013)
3. Poulsen, L.: Life-cycle and long-term migration planning. InTech Magazine (a publication of the international society of automation), 12–17 (January/February 2014)
4. Cusumano, M.A.: The Chaning Software Business: Moving from Products to Services. Published by the IEEE Computer Society, 0018-9162/08, 20–27 (January 2008)
5. Knecht, T., Leszinski, R., Weber, F.: Making profits after the sale. The McKinsey Quarterly 4 (1993)
6. Potts, G.W.: Exploiting your product's service life cycle. Harward Business Review 66(5), 32–35 (1988)
7. Borchers, H.W., Karandikar, H.: A Data Warehouse approach for Estimating and Characterizing the Installed Base of Industrial Products. In: IEEE International Conference on Service Systems and Service Management, vol. 1, pp. 53–59 (2006)
8. Oliva, R., Kallenberg, R.: Managing the transition from products to services. International Journal of Service Industry Management 14(2), 160–172 (2003)
9. Hanski, J., Kunttu, S., Räikkönen, M., Reunanen, M.: Development of knowledge-intensive product-service systems. Outcomes from the MaintenanceKIBS project. VTT, Espoo. VTT Technology 21 (2012)
10. Bano, M., Zowghi, D.: User involvement in software development and system success: a systematic literature review. In: Proceedings of the 17th International Conference on Evaluation and Assessment in Software Engineering, Australia, Sydney, pp. 125–130. ACM, New York (2013)
11. Jetley, R., Rath, A., Kumar, D., Prasad, V., Ramaswamy, S.: An Approach for Comparison of IEC 61131-3 Graphical Programs. In: IEEE 18th Conference on Emerging Technologies & Factory Automation (ETFA) (2013)
12. Varies -project web-site (Variabilit in Safety-Critical Embedded Systems), http://www.varies.eu/ (accessed June 6, 2013)
13. Promes -project web-site: (Process Models for Engineering of Embedded Systems), https://itea3.org/project/promes.html (accessed 6th June)
14. Charalampidou, S., Ampatzoglou, A., Avgeriou, P.: A process framework for embedded systems engineering. Accepted to Euromicro Conference series on Software Engineering and Advanced Applications (SEAA 2014), Verona, Italy, August 27-29. IEEE Computer Society (2014)
15. Windows lifecycle fact sheet, Last updated (April 2014), http://windows.microsoft.com/en-us/windows/lifecycle (accessed June 6, 2014)

Collaborative Brainstorming Activity Results and Information Systems

Claude Moulin[1], Kenji Sugawara[2], Yuki Kaeri[2],
Shigeru Fujita[3], and Marie-Hélène Abel[1]

[1] Heudiasyc, JR Unit - CNRS 7253, Université de Technologie de Compiègne
Centre de Recherche de Royallieu, 60205 COMPIEGNE Cedex, France
{claude.moulin,marie-helene.abel}@utc.fr
[2] Faculty of Information and Network Science, Chiba Institute of Technology, Japan
suga@net.it-chiba.ac.jp
[3] Faculty of Information and Computer Science, Chiba Institute of Technology, Japan
fujita@cs.it-chiba.ac.jp

Abstract. The motivation of our research is the design and the implementation of tools supporting brainstorming activities of teams and mainly distant teams which have to collaborate. During parallel sessions, each team interacts with a large multi-touch device, produces and manipulates virtual post-it notes displayed and synchronized on both surfaces.

Starting from an experimental point of view, the paper presents different tools that we consider mandatory for supporting these activities: a resource channel for displaying and synchronizing the resources on each device, a TV channel for allowing the oral and visual communication between teams and an informationg system for storing and retrieving the resources related to activities. The paper also mentions the architectural design of the distributed application used for the resource channel. It involves several tactile devices with different sizes that display the resources. Finally, the paper describes an experiment where two teams situated in Japan and in France used these tools.

Keywords: Brainstorming activity, Multi-touch device, Synchronous collaboration, Semantic Information System.

1 Introduction

In our experiment scenario, two remote teams (a Japanese one and a French one) have to design a Web site useful for French visitors who have to discover Japan and also some Japanese cultural aspects. They have to organize several meetings where they can discuss, produce ideas, agree on some results written on notes and categorized into clusters.

More generally, at the very begining of a project, teams have to design a new product and define new concepts during several meetings. They collaborate during brainstorming activities where the main ideas, problems and solutions emerge from discussions between participants. The results of these activities are capitalized and some reporting can be made from that.

R. Meersman et al. (Eds.): OTM 2014 Workshops, LNCS 8842, pp. 399–407, 2014.

These activities are usually conducted in traditional meeting rooms with pen and paper media. Results are generally written on post-it notes and then significant efforts are necessary to render these hand written notes into a digitally exploitable format.

Previous attempts of computer-supported solutions did not encounter a huge success, because they introduced additional instruments that prevent the natural collaboration between participants.

Technologies such as interactive tabletops, interactive whiteboards and hand-held devices (tablets and smartphones) are now widely diffused. Large devices look like physical configurations of traditional pen-and-paper environments and they could evidently be used to display virtual post-it notes. Inputs based on multi-touch gestures reproduce usual input and the collaboration between co-located groups of users is influenced and augmented.

In this paper we first describe the types of brainstorming we consider for our research (Section 2). Then, Section 3 we present the resource channel, i.e. the suite of applications runing on interactive devices (table, whiteboard and tablet). Then Section 4, we present the tools useful for oral and visual communication between teams. In Section 5 we describe the model of information that we use to store the brainstorming results. In Section 6, we relate an experiment that have been conducted both at the University of Compiègne (UTC, France) and at the Chiba Institute of Technology (CIT, Japan).

Our research can also be considered from an ecosystem point of view. We consider that people communicating about well identified subjects, creating and sharing different kinds of resources, and commenting different contributions, participate to the same ecosystem [8,2]. We also study how the use of large collaborative devices can help and support members [1] to produce new resources.

2   Collaborative Activities

In this section we focus on collaborative activities and their tangible results in the context of co-located meetings. Generally speaking, collaborative activities are activities produced by one individual for the benefit of other people. For example, people insert in a common repository a new document, annotate a document [3] or a fragment of a document produced by others.

We call brainstorming sessions, the type of meetings where people can progressively agree on some definitions and on some decisions. Discussions and argumentations may require the study of external resources. However, results achieved by teams have to be capitalized in some way [7]. We propose that these results take the form of notes (a shortcut for virtual post-it notes) grouped by clusters.

Brainstorming sessions are always sessions where the activities are synchronous. We call co-located brainstorming sessions, the meetings where participants are situated in the same room. At least one surface is designed to be the common support where all the participants can see the resulting notes. Notes can be created directly on this surface or can be created on other devices like tablet pc. However, a note interesting a group must always be visible on the common surface and should be transfered from individual devices.

We consider that people manipulating virtual post-it notes displayed on a large interactive surface benefit of a good digital support for their activities [6] and bring real advantages (capitalization, reuse, interoperability with other applications, etc.). We claim that digital devices allowing data storing and enhancing the exchanges between participants are a necessary support for teams involved in brainstorming sessions[11,10]. Without this, two many efforts have to be deployed in order to register what have been written on different sheets of papers.

We call remote brainstorming sessions, sessions where several co-located teams (at least two) participate to the same brainstorming activities. Their actions must be supported by specific software applications [9]. For example, two instances of the same application run on peer systems located in two distants rooms. Teams involved in these sessions interact with the same type of graphical user interface communicating in real time and synchronized, i.e. all the actions on one common surface are reproduced on the common remote surface. A lock system must be installed to prevent concurrent actions on the same element already selected elsewere. A graphical indication must be added during an action in order to make people understand that somebody else in the remote team has already selected an element.

In our system we don't have implemented the possibility of annotating something. However it is interesting to consider collaborative annotations. This takes place when an annotation itself is shared between individuals who have access to the annotated resource and has an impact on individuals who view it. An annotation is like a note but concerning another resource and anchored on it. For example, it is possible to add an annotation explaining why some notes have been grouped in the same cluster. In our system people could create notes for this purpose, and group them into a specific cluster.

3   Resource Channel

We have developed a suite of applications for supporting brainstorming activities. The most important one must be run on a large tactile device, either an interactive table or a whiteboard. The interaction between people is not exactly the same. A table has an horizontal display and people are standing around the table. A board (see Figure 1)[1] has a vertical display and generally people are sitting looking at the board. However, their dimension and their multi-touch characteristics allow the interaction of several people. The suite of applications consists in several modules running on different devices: a server, an interactive board or table and tablet pcs. When two distant meetings occur at the same time, two suites of applications run simultaneously in the different locations.

---

[1] The languages used during the experiment is out of the scope of the paper. We can precise that exchanges between people were in English. Technologically, the notes can be written in three different languages, English, Japanese and French. Each team can add elements in its own language. A note can be displayed in each of these languages.

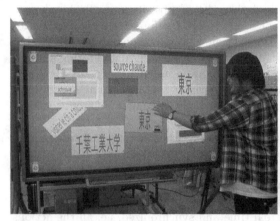

Fig. 1. The left figure shows the meeting moderator moving a note written in Japanese characters on a large interactive surface. The note is locked. A padlock appears on the note and on the remote corresponding note to indicate that somebody interacts with this element. The right figure shows a tablet pc where people can write Japanese characters. The notes are then sent to the board.

Each module is independant and contains at least one agent responsible of the necessary communication between modules. So the suite of applications is built around a multi-agent system [5].

On the server are running the agents responsible of the logistics and are belonging to the core of the agent platform. They maintain the white and yellow pages of the multi-agent system and know everything about the location of the different agents and the services they deliver. They are in charge of the distribution of messages between agents. A specific federator agent is responsible of the communication with remote equivalent agent systems. It owns a list of station address that it could reach and so is able to discover other platforms and transfer messages representing the actions of people on the interactive device.

Several agents run on the stations linked to the interactive surfaces, together with the applications. The meeting agent recognizes and allows actions of the users. It delivers messages about actions of the users to the logistic agent that propagates them to the external platforms. The persistence agents keep locally the content and the localisation (position, size, orientation) of the post-it notes and clusters displayed on the large surfaces. They saves the brainstorming content after each user's action. Another agent is responsible of the communication with the Information System for storing and indexing the brainstorming results. The main actions of users consist in creating notes and clusters, moving elements, inserting notes into clusters and deleting elements.

On tablet pcs the application allows users to prepare collaborative sessions, creating notes and clusters. It contains a personal agent that can enter the multi-agent system. Once connected, its main role is to send post-it notes written on tablet pcs, to the corresponding meeting agent. The system is scalable and may accept several personal agents, i.e. one for each participant. This way of creating a note has two advantages. It is an alternative way of adding post-it notes during a meeting in a more confortable way and it is the only way to write strings belonging to some languages, like the Japanese language, because the virtual keybord of the tablet is adapted to the local language. On tabletops, only some virtual keybords are developped in the main application, which limits the available languages.

However, adding new elements from tablet pcs to the main surface could generate some perturbation, if they were automatically visible on the main device (they would also appear on synchronized stations). To avoid this, the meeting agent stores the incoming notes in a mail box that can be open by users, but only at the most adequate instant. During a discussion, participants can add the mail box elements to the display.

In the resource channel, data can move from one site to another one and from tablet pc to the main surface. More exactly, copies of data move from one place to another one. Nothing disappears.

4   Video Channel

During remote brainstorming sessions, members of one team have to communicate with members of other teams. Video transmissions have to be installed for allowing exchanges in both directions between remote teams. People must be able to communicate and discuss about the shared ideas written on post-it notes with all the participants, local and distant, in the same way as if everybody was in the same room. People can see what happens in the remote room only thanks to the video channel. It is interesting to consider several cameras in order to capture people themselves but also some other particular points of view and to show important elements happening in the remote room. It is important to capture the remote atmosphere. Moving from times to times the cameras may be interesting according to local events. The main surfaces are synchronized, however it is interesting to show the display to the other team, above all if the surfaces are not the same. From a technical point of view, video streams of the same room are mixed into a unique one and broadcast for the other team.

Recording video transmissions is also very imortant for a future exploitation. The sender of the stream is responsible for this. Videos can then be exchanged by mail if necessary. Sometimes important things are said and not necessarily transfered to a note or a cluster. People can add later a missing or forgotten information.

5   Semantic Information System

An information system is also necessary for storing data related to brainstorming activities. We have choosen the MemoraE Information System [4]. We show how its semantic model is coherent with our needs. An excerpt of this model is shown

404   C. Moulin et al.

Figure 5. The model is very rich but we only present the concepts related to our needs.

Our application only creates notes and clusters of notes. These types respectively inherit of `SimpleResource` and `CompositeResource`. The main type of `SimpleResource` is `Document`. It encapsulates resources like PDF documents, archives or textual documents but it is useless to have specification for any kind of documents. In the model, any `Note` has a body which is a `Resource` because the model allows a note being an image or anything else. In our case a note body is an anonymous textual document. Anonymous means that this document can only be reached by the corresponding note. In the same way the body of a `NoteCluster` is a textual document. A `NoteCluster` is `composedOf` of `Note` and `NoteCluster`.

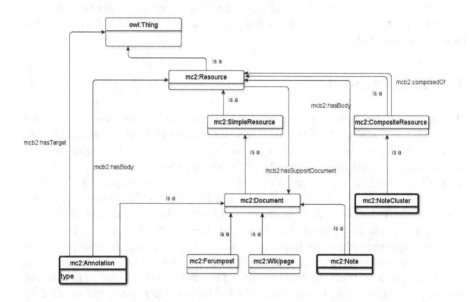

Fig. 2. Excerpt of the model describing the resources in the MemoraE Information System. The mc2 prefix denote the model. Only Annotation, note, cluster and their super types are shown.

Any resource has to be displayed by one or more applications. For example, a resource can be displayed by a web application and an application running on a tablet pc. Often they are created with one device and have be displayed by different devices. As we are using interactive table top and whiteboard, it is necessary to store with a `Note` and a `NoteCluster`, other data added by the applications running on these devices like colors or data useful to locate the resources. These data are very dependent on the applications and are quite impossible to describe in the model. Each time we create a new application we do not have to modify the model. In order to reach this purpose, the model allows each resource to get one or more documents that contain these data. The relationship `mcb2:hasSupportDocument` whose domain and range are `Resource` and `Document` generally associates a textual document to a resource, formatted with a JSON[2] structure.

The videos taken during brainstorming sessions are also documents that have to be stored in the information system and linked in some way to the data (`Note` and `NoteCluster`) produced during sessions. They can be stored under the `Document` type. The `Event` concept not visible Figure 5, allows to describe a brainstorming session as an `Event` and to link it to the resources concerning it. In particular, all the notes and clusters produced during a session are encapsulated inside a unique super cluster attached to the session event. The MemoraE model gives the opportunity to find notes as any other documents but also from the event they were created in.

6   Experiment and Discussion

In this section, we describe the experiment conducted simultaneously at the University of Compiègne (UTC) in France, and at the Chiba Institute of Technology (CIT) in Japan. Two teams, one at the UTC and one at the CIT decided to collaborate on the preliminary design of a website for French travelers in Japan.

Both teams are involved in a remote brainstorming session and use the application described above. they have to create and classify ideas about this project. Ideas are written on notes, grouped in clusters and displayed on an interactive device. The actions of one team are transmitted in real time to the devices of the other team. Figure 6 shows the different channels during the experiment.

At the UTC, people were working around an interactive table. They could move, change the size of virtual post-it notes displayed on the table. They could also group post-it notes inside clusters. A single camera directed on the table transmitted the scene showing people acting on table. People in the CIT could see and hear them from this stream.

People at the UTC received the video stream from the CIT with a computer linked to a large screen. They could see people and activities in Japan thanks to the integration of three camera streams. They could see the device were post-it notes were displayed and the session monitor, people sit and participating to the sessions and a particular device. Sometimes the orientation of cameras were changed according to the discussions. They could see how the results of their actions on the table were repeated in real time on the Japanese device. There was no real mediator as everybody could interact directly with the commmon surface.

At the CIT, scenes were displayed on an interactive whiteboard but allowing only one interaction point. A priori moving was possible ; zooming, turning not. However, we have designed specific zones around the edges of post-it notes representation that make these actions also possible on one-touch surfaces. One person, as a mediator, was standing up near the whitebord moving and grouping

---

[2] JSON site: —http://www.json.org/

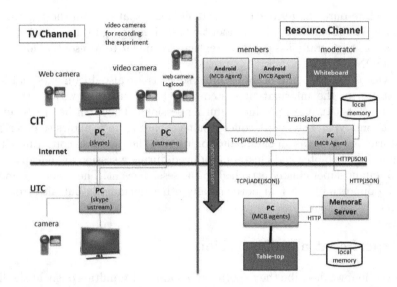

Fig. 3. Video and Resource channels are represented vertically. CIT and UTC organizations are represented horizontally.

elements according to the discussions with other team members (see Figure 1). In these circumstances, it is not easy and even undesirable for this person to write the content of a note. That means: open a virtual keyboard, type on keys, and so on. Other participants had tablet pcs and, thanks to the specific application running on them, could create notes and send them to the whiteboard.

The common session lasted more than two hours without any communication problems between sites. The resource channel was faster than the TV channel. Our experiment and our contacts with Japanese colleagues have also a multi-cultural approach. Indeed, we considered notes also for a conceptual approach. Discussions were useful in order to explicit some concepts and notes have been written after that. We are satisfied from two points of view: technically, everything was ok and the experiment did not suffer of network problems and methodologically, an interesting number of productions have been made.

7   Conclusion

In this paper we have presented the three dimensions of remote brainstorming activities: the resource dimension, the audio-visual dimension and the data persistence dimension. We have proposed the suite of applications we have developped for the first one, the use of recent standard cameras for the second one and a specific information system for the last one. We have tried to put in evidence the main characteristics that any system should have to fulfil our objectives.

Our system is part of an on-going research and we are currently investigating complementary aspects. The first thing is to find alternative ways for creating resources. First, we study how to integrate a vocal interpretation system that does not disturb the participants during collaborative activities. The multi-agent infrastructure allows easily to do it, however usability issues have not still found a solution. The second approach consists in moving the video channel closer to the resource channel.

References

1. Boyd, D., Ellison, N.: Social network sites: Definition, history, and scholarship. Journal of Computer-Mediated Communication 13(1), 210–230 (2008)
2. Bray, D.: Knowledge ecosystems: A theoretical lens for organizations confronting hyperturbulent environments. In: McMaster, T., Wastell, D., Ferneley, E., DeGross, J.I. (eds.) Organizational Dynamics of Technology-Based Innovation: Diversifying the Research Agenda. IFIP AICT, vol. 235, pp. 457–462. Springer, Heidelberg (2007)
3. Brézillon, P.: Explaining for sharing context in communities. In: International Conference on Computer Supported Cooperative Work in Design, CSCWD 2011, Lausanne, Switzerland, pp. 819–826 (June 2011)
4. Deparis, E., Abel, M.H., Lortal, G., Mattioli, J.: Designing a system to capitalize both social and documentary resources. In: Proceedings of the 17th IEEE International Conference on Computer Supported Cooperative Work in Design, Canada, pp. 581–586 (June 2013)
5. Jones, A., Kendira, A., Gidel, T., Moulin, C., Lenne, D., Barthès, J.P.: Personal assistant agents and multi-agent middleware for cscw. In: 16th IEEE International Conference on Computer Supported Cooperative Work in Design (CSCWD), Wuhan, China (2012)
6. Moulin, C., Jones, A., Barthès, J.-P., Lenne, D.: Preliminary design on multi-touch surfaces managed by multi-agent systems. International Journal of Energy, Information and Communications 2(4), 195–210 (2011)
7. Piorkowski, B.A., Evans, R.D., Gao, J.X.: Development of a face-to-face meeting capture and indexing process. In: CSCWD 2011, 15th International Conference on Computer Supported Cooperative Work in Design, Lausanne, Switzerland, pp. 4–8 (June 2011)
8. Rajagopalan, R., Sarkar, R.: A digital ecosystem approach to using ict for sustainable development in communities. In: Second IEEE International Conference on Digital Ecosystem and Technologies, pp. 413–418 (2008)
9. Sugawara, K., Manabe, Y., Moulin, C., Barthès, J.P.: Design assistant agents for supporting requirement specification definition in a distributed design team. In: 15th Int. Conference on Computer-Supported Cooperative Work in Design (CSCWD), June 8-11, pp. 329–334. IEEE, Lausanne (2011)
10. Wallace, J.R., Scott, S.D., MacGregor, C.G.: Collaborative sensemaking on a digital tabletop and personal tablets: prioritization, comparisons, and tableaux. In: CHI 2013, SIGCHI Conference on Human Factors in Computing Systems, New York, USA, pp. 3345–3354 (2013)
11. Wigdor, D., Fletcher, J., Morrison, G.: Designing user interfaces for multi-touch and gesture devices. In: CHI 2009 Extended Abstracts on Human Factors in Computing Systems, pp. 2755–2758 (2009)

Communication in Agile Global Software Development: An Exploratory Study

Juan Garbajosa[1], Agustin Yagüe[1], and Eloy Gonzalez[2]

[1] Technical University of Madrid (UPM), CITSEM,
E.T.S.I Sistemas Informáticos, Madrid, Spain
jgs@eui.upm.es, agustin.yague@upm.es
[2] Indra Software Labs, Madrid, Spain
egonzalezort@indra.es

Abstract. Agile Global Software Development is gaining relevance and importance. While communication is key for exchanging information between team members, multi-site software development introduces additional obstacles and delays. This paper reports an exploratory study on the impact of infrastructure on communication. Although this topic has been a subject of interest many issues remain unaddressed. In this paper we address both team member communication and the combination of project and product development. One of the main conclusions is that communication can be improved if tool infrastructure combine different levels of information (i.e. team members, project status and product status). The use of simple tools, such as Vsee in SmartBoards is useful for reducing distance between sites. Dependency on bandwidth is not a new issue but is still relevant.

Keywords: Global Distributed Software Development, Agile, Exploratory research, Tools, Technologies, Infrastructure.

1 Introduction

Global software development (GSD) is gaining relevance and importance. [1] As communication is key for exchanging information between team members, multi-site software development introduces additional obstacles and delays [2]. None of these obstacles are new, with a number of them having been reported in 2003 [10]; however, recent publications and reviews show that they are still serious concerns [2,28]. Communication is even more critical in the case of Agile Global Software Development (AGSD) in which communication plays a primary role: "Business people and developers must work together daily throughout the project"[4]. Communication problems in AGSD have also been broadly addressed [13,1,28], and these have shown that distributed teams strongly depend on tools for communication and, on agile teams to a larger extent [1,16,28]. Though the tool technology to support efficient communication in AGSD has been addressed, it is still an open issue [1,2,16,28].

---

[1] Work partially sponsored by MICINN, Spain. Ref IPT-430000-2010-38.

R. Meersman et al. (Eds.): OTM 2014 Workshops, LNCS 8842, pp. 408–417, 2014.
© Springer-Verlag Berlin Heidelberg 2014

This paper reports an exploratory study on the impact of different communication elements, including tools, obtained both from monitoring and the perceptions of team members in three industrial distributed projects. Observations were obtained from three perspectives: communication among team members, communication of the development process status, and communication of the product progress status.

The rest of this paper is structured as follows. Section 2 presents a short background about communication and supportive tools in AGSD. Section 3 describes the research methodology. Section 4 presents the findings on the impact of different practices and tools. Finally, Section 5 summarizes the main conclusions obtained from this research.

2 Background

Communication is the core function of cooperation to exchange information between team members [1]. When development is distributed, dispersed members tend to feel a lack of access to all the information, while on-site members have access [14]. Korkala and Maurer later reported a "lack of involvement, lack of shared understanding, outdated information, restricted access to information and finally scattered information" [16]. Cultural differences also matter [1].

Communication has been classified as spontaneous or informal versus formal, or synchronous versus asynchronous [1]. Communication has also been classified according to whether it is performed face-to-face or using technology (e.g. electronic media, or telephone). Tools and technology have been regarded as an effective support for communication in distributed teams. Sinha et al. reported on the great dependency that geographically distributed teams have to (communication) tools[29]. However, Johnston et al. highlighted that Information and Communication Technologies (ICT) restricts communication because it is less rich than face-to-face communication [14]. Centralized infrastructures can be useful in AGSD frameworks to share information as a way to facilitate team communication [15].

To overcome the identified challenges, Herbsleb stated that GSD should combine different communication media, such as telephone, teleconferences, email or instant messaging [10]. Niinimaki et al. [22] reviewed how communication problems had been addressed in global organizations using different media and systems, and studies on the impact of media selection [7,11,15,22,25] on AGSD have been performed. The impact of cloud infrastructures in agile distributed teams has also been reported [24].

Studies published recently show that current tool support for communication in AGSD is far from satisfactory[1,16,2]. Therefore, more information is required to understand the root causes of the reported problems.

3   Research Methodology

3.1   Research Environment

This research was performed in Smart Software Factories (SSF), an experimental research facility[19]. SSF is a software engineering research and education laboratory located initially at the University of Helsinki (UH), then at the Technical University of Madrid (UPM) and Indra Software Labs (ISL), a subsidiary of Indra, a global engineering company.[2]

Each SSF was equipped with video cameras to provide a general view of the room, ambient microphonesand a Smart Board 685i, which is an electronic whiteboard to support inter-site interaction. Each computer had a camera and a microphone. *Software development and management infrastructure* was centralized and consisting of Redmine, Hudson, Sonar, and SVN tools and plugins.[3] All the SSF laboratories had basically the same infrastructure in terms of computers, video, audio and recording equipment.

3.2   Research Design

This research was designed following the guidelines proposed by Runeson and Höst for conducting case studies [26] and comprised five main steps: study design, preparation for data collection, collecting evidence, data analysis and reporting. In the *study design*, we used an *exploratory and qualitative* research method following Cresswells recommendations and suggestions [6] due to the nature of the research topic and the research objectives. The research question was: "How does communication infrastructure impact information sharing in Agile Global Software Development?" This research question addressed the lack of communication perceived by dispersed members. Observations were obtained from three *perspectives*: team member communication, communication of the development process and communication of the product status. Data were collected and classified, following Lethbridge et al's. [18] approach, into direct, indirect and third degree and according to a number of measures that were defined. The objective of the measures was analyse the impact of SSF infrastructure on communication, and to identify the advantages, disadvantages and challenges. To perform the exploration, four projects of different nature were selected. These projects are described in section 4.1 and they were real distributed agile projects *owned* by the industrial partner ISL.

In the next step, *preparation for data collection*, the procedures and protocols for data collection were defined. Classification surveys and focus groups [6,26] were used for direct data collection; indirect data were collected from measures obtained from raw data produced by the software development and management infrastructure; and third degree data consisted of studying the project outputs

---

[2] UH - http://www.helsinki.fi/university/,
   UPM - http://www.upm.es/internacional, ISL -http://www.indracompany.com/en
[3] http://www.redmine.org/, http://hudson-ci.org, http://www.sonarqube.org/,
   https://subversion.apache.org/

and generated documentation (including meeting minutes). Surveys were defined following the guidelines provided in [8,26] and were structured into six sections to cover the three perspectives mentioned above. Survey questions, identified from the literature, related to software measurement in agile processes [9,28]. Interviews were conducted through focus group following the guidelines provided by Krueger and Casey's [17]. Briefly, focus groups were questioned about personal perceptions of the impact of communication tools. For indirect data collection, raw data measures were obtained by reviewing the literature on ASD and AGSD. A set of 41 measures were identified, by considering the research question, the three monitoring perspectives (team communication, development process status and product status) and the reported measures found in the literature. This method is similar to how GQM [3] is applied. Each measure was documented specifying its nature, description, value range, usefulness and how and when it should be collected.

Third-degree data were obtained by researchers studying outputs produced by the project while the project was running; this process extracted measures that could not be obtained directly such as those obtained from sessions that were recorded, such as the duration or the number of participants of each meeting.

Table 1. Team and software size of the projects explored

Project name	Language	Factories	Team size	Size
Optimeter I	Java	UPM and ISL	9	6589 LOC
Optimeter II	Java	UPM, ISL and UH	21	9652 LOC
Research4us	PHP	UPM and ISL	10	56139 LOC
Habeo Ideam	PHP	UPM and ISL	15	37034 LOC

Collecting evidence was the third step. The projects used to get evidence are described in Section 4.1. At least two SSF teams participated in each project. Following the classification provided in [26], observations were performed by external observers with a low interaction with the development team. Meetings were recorded for both audio and video and later transcribed. Codes were defined using an open code method [17], and each statement was coded and classified separately by two researchers. Confidentiality and anonymity agreements were signed by researchers and team members. Focus groups were used to collect data following the guidelines provided by Krueger and Casey's [17].

Two observation and analysis levels were implemented: one at an iteration level so that every two weeks, measures were collected and analysed, and results reported; the second at the end of the project. Software development and management infrastructure were used to collect the indirect evidence. Direct evidence was collected from surveys[4], focus groups. Occasionally, third degree evidence from video observations.

The data were analysed following quantitative and qualitative methods depending on their nature, but seeking qualitative outputs. Some of these measures

---

[4] Electronic surveys were created at https://www.surveymonkey.com/

were non-subjective (e. g. meeting duration), and some subjective (e. g. meeting satisfaction). Data analysis was performed following the guidelines suggested by [26], and by Fink et al. [8] for all the subjective measures. Finally, reports were produced to communicate the findings of the research.

Validity has been approached following [31]. Construct validity was achieved using several multiple data sources, documenting the research process, searching a of chain evidence, discussing conclusions and introducing triangulation where it was required. Several projects were performed with different teams, so that many of the effects could be verified. Concerning external validity, the limitation of having the same context applies. It should noticed that according to[23] interpretive case studies do not seek generalizability.

4   Measures and Results Obtained

This section briefly describes the projects that were used for exploration, then a subset of measures are presented and, finally, the most relevant findings are enumerated and justified.

4.1   Project Decriptions

Four projects were used to obtain evidence. The column *"Factories"* in Table1 shows the acronym of the SSF participating in each project. The duration of each project was seven weeks with two-week iterations; all projects were managed with Scrum [27]. Engineers participating in these development projects had at least two years of software development experience. Senior engineers performed Scrum master and product owner roles. Table 1 shows the indicators of the projects. The *first and second project, Optimeter I and II*, were traversal activities to two European ITEA2 projects: IMPONET[5] (127 man years) and NEMO&CODED[6] (112 man years), and a third Spanish project called ENERGOS[7] (budget 24.3 million euros); these three projects focused on supporting power *smart grids*. Both Optimeters benchmarked massive data distributed processing and storage using Apache Hadoop, NoSQL databases to build a system to optimize searching and management of massive data in the Smart Grid domain. The Optimeter II project involved three sites with different time zones (one hour difference) and, teams with different cultures. The third project was Research4us. This was a customized wiki system based on Dokuwiki[8] to add specific functionalities for researchers and was a typical PHP project with MySQL running on an Apache 2 server. Finally, Habeo Ideam, the *fourth project*, consisted of implementing PHP extensions to a Joomla Content Management System (CMS)[9] to manage innovative ideas.

---

[5] IMPONET Intelligent Monitoring of Power NETworks
   http://www.itea2.org/project/index/view?project=10032.
[6] NEMO NEtworked MOnitoring & COntrol, Diagnostic for Electrical Distribution
   http://www.itea2.org/project/index/view?project=1131.
[7] http://innovationenergy.org/energos/
[8] https://www.dokuwiki.org/dokuwiki
[9] http://www.joomla.org/

4.2   Measures

Table 2 shows a subset of the measures collected, classified by type (direct, indirect and third degree) and perspective (communication among team members, and related to process and, product status). Columns two to four represent the dimensions covered by this research. Rows are grouped by the method applied to collect data. The name of the measure and the where it was collected is in each cell.

Table 2. Subset of measures collected in the four projects. *Nof* stands for number of, *comm* communication, *mech* mechanisms, *prj* project, *itr* iteration, *sat* satisfaction, *meet* meeting, *ret* retrospective, *part* part, *rate* use rate, *usefl* usefulness, *art* artefact.

Perspective / Type	Team communication	Development Process status communication	Product status communication
Direct	Meet sat level (Prj) Comm channels rate(Prj) comm channels usefl(Prj)	Comm mech sat (Prj) comm mech rate(Prj) comm mech usefl(Prj)	Comm mech rate(Prj) comm mech usefl(Prj)
Indirect		Nof art created (Itr) Nof Wiki inputs (Prj) Nof News (Prj) Nof documents (Project)	Nof SVN revisions (Prj) Nof builds (Prj)
Third degree	Nof meetings: daily, sprint planning, sprint reviews, retrosp.(Itr) (each) meet time length(Itr) (each) meet part (Itr)		

Team Communication Perspective. This perspective focused on the analysis of the impact of SSF infrastructures to support communication among team members within the scope of AGSD. Two types of measures were collected: direct and third degree. Direct measures were collected by using the surveys built to capture perceptions of the team about the usefulness of tools, the rate of use and meeting satisfaction. The objective of these measures was to understand how each media type impacted the communication of teams. Third degree measures were collected by researchers after analysing the information recorded and stored during the project. Measures included attendees, time duration or meeting frequencies. Video-conferencing systems, white boards, meeting rooms, emails and instant messaging systems were some of the communication media analysed. The literature used to identify measures was e.g. [16,25,11].

Development Process Perspective Status. This perspective focused on the analysis of the impact of SSF infrastructures available to support the communication of the development process status to the team. Two types of measures were collected: direct and indirect. Surveys were used to collect direct measures to get perceptions about the usefulness of software development and management infrastructure. Indirect measures were extracted from the software development and management infrastructure to get evidence of the amount of shared information in the project and the use of tools. Several references were used to identify project measurement status [30,9]

Product Perspective Status. This perspective focused on the analysis of the impact of SSF infrastructures to communicate the status of the project by using software product status indicators, mainly quality characteristics. Two types of measures were collected: direct and indirect. Direct measures were obtained from surveys focussed on how the product status and evolution of the product was shared. Indirect measures, extracted from the software development and management infrastructure, provided quantitative evidence about the status and quality of the product. McCall's model [20], Boehm's [5] and international standards as ISO 25000 [12] were used for product measurement.

4.3   Findings

1. Tools to support bi-directional face-to-face and one-to-many communication are critical to facilitate team building in the case of GSD. Tools such as VSee and Skype with open sessions while teams were working helped teams to see and talk to each other as if they were in the same room. In this case Vsee or Skype ran on the Smartboard. This finding is not fully in agreement with that of Niinimaki et al. [22]. Even with a language barrier, having a viewable team member helped. Face-to-face communication tools were the most recognised media for team members to support team communication and to increase the feeling of working as a team. This fact was highlighted by one of the participants in one focus group: *"... if there's a problem, you ask someone and they answer right away. Also for sharing files or sharing the screen. - Hey, something's not working here - and everyone would look into it, or we'd try to find solutions among us for some of the things that caused problems."*. Another participant said: *"But also the usefulness of this kind of infrastructure is clear in terms of communication and visibility. It seemed that we were far away from each other, but with these tools that distance decreased."*. Sinha [29] suggested that developers should be able to initiate conversations easily and one-to-many communication tools support this facility.

2. The use of centralized repositories enabled knowledge sharing in GSD. The use of tools like SVN, and Redmine helped teams share information as if the team were co-located. The usefulness of the complete infrastructure was summarized by one of the participants in a focus group: *"We're looking at each of the tools separately, but what we had was a single system of infrastructures and all of them together helped us. In other words, we had, like, a lot of alarms Sonar, Hudson... - So you'd arrive and see if the day looked bright or not, and in fact... The problem was when all of the alarms went off, that was the problem."*

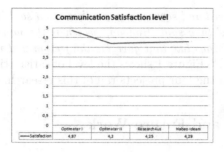

Fig. 1. Communication satisfaction level perceived in analysed projects

3. The use of smartboards or large screens and cameras, running for instance VSee, enhanced the feeling of being a co-located team. A smartboard was an open window to the other sites. This combined with cameras was considered as important as software development and management infrastructure to share information about the status of the project. The availability of this infrastructure was highlighted during one of the focus groups: *"Multiconference communication. It wasn't one-to-one, but rather five, six, seven on screen and all working and seeing each other's face, seeing each other's screen. Even, by clicking on a camera - not only one person, but clicking different people's cameras - you could really see those people working"*. This could be a solution to some of the challenges identified by Sinha et al.[29] and at the same time mitigates the problems related to customer interaction.

4. There is a huge dependency on bandwidth. Having VSee with a high frame rate (25 frames per second) open the whole time, requires a high bandwidth rate. Therefore, with respect to limitations in the bandwidth some constraints must be applied, such as to reduce the frame rate or to limit the number of simultaneously opened connections. This issue was also noted by team members during the focus groups. One developer mentioned: *"... weve had some problems with the audio and video, though its also true that there have been various changes in the material used ..."* and another developer commented: *"On the one hand, there's the network communication between rooms, because there have been problems when it came to using servers, or installing some of the tools that needed to communicate between various servers and couldn't do so because the communication wasn't good. "* This issue has previously been cited [16].

5. In the case of shared rooms for different projects, the infrastructure could be affected by noise or some other projects could be disturbed by this face-to-face connection with the remote site.

6. Infrastructure as understood in this study, i.e. combining media, and project and process status sharing, provides visibility on the whole project, facilitating the integration of communication media, in accordance with [21]. This integration is always complex. In any case, these infrastructures enhanced the communication and allowed teams feel like they were working together. In one of the focus groups, one of the participants noted: *"Someone in one*

of the rooms sneezed and someone in another room said 'Hadoop.' Instead of saying 'Bless you' they said 'Hadoop,' which is the name of the technology we were using. Things like that gave me the feeling that we were all working in the same room. ". Figure 1 shows the level of satisfaction with the overall communication in the four projects ran of this research.

5   Conclusions and Future Work

This paper has summarized an exploratory research study on communication in AGSD. The main focus was how infrastructure can impact communication. One of the main conclusions is that communication can be improved as long as tools combine different levels of information (i.e. team members, project status and product status). The use of simple tools like Vsee in SmartBoards, proved much more useful than in team members computers. However, dependency on the bandwidth is clear; however, this is not a new issue. Future research will be focused on exploring the relations between the different levels of information, and the influence of cultural factors.

References

1. Alzoubi, Y.I., Gill, A.Q.: Agile global software development communication challenges: A systematic review. In: Siau, K., Li, Q., Guo, X. (eds.) PACIS 2014 (2014)
2. Babar, M.A., Lescher, C.: Editorial: Global software engineering: Identifying challenges is important and providing solutions is even better. Inf. Softw. Technol. 56(1), 1–5 (2014)
3. Basili, V.R.: Software modeling and measurement: The goal/question/metric paradigm. Tech. rep., U. of Maryland at College Park, MD, USA (1992)
4. Beck, K., Beedle, M., van Bennekum, A., Cockburn, A., Cunningham, W., Fowler, M., Grenning, J., Highsmith, J., Hunt, A., Jeffries, R., Kern, J., Marick, B., Martin, R.C., Mellor, S., Schwaber, K., Sutherland, J., Thomas, D.: Manifesto for agile software development (2001), http://www.agilemanifesto.org/
5. Boehm, B.W.: Characteristics of Software Quality, 1st edn., vol. 1. North-Holland Publishing Company (June 1978)
6. Creswell, J.: Research Design: Qualitative, Quantitative, and Mixed Methods Approaches. SAGE (2014)
7. Fernando, B.A.J., Hall, T., Fitzpatrick, A.: The impact of media selection on stakeholder communication in agile global software development: A preliminary industrial case study. In: SIGMIS-CPR 2011, pp. 131–139. ACM, NY (2011)
8. Fink, A.: How To Conduct Surveys: A Step-by-Step Guide. Sage (2012)
9. Hartmann, D., Dymond, R.: Appropriate agile measurement: Using metrics and diagnostics to deliver business value. In: Proc. of AGILE 2006, pp. 126–134. IEEE CS, Washington, DC (2006)
10. Herbsleb, J., Mockus, A.: An empirical study of speed and communication in globally distributed software development. IEEE TSE 29(6), 481–494 (2003)
11. Hummel, M., Rosenkranz, C., Holten, R.: The role of communication in agile systems development. Business and Inf. Sys. Eng. 5(5), 343–355 (2013)

12. ISO/IEC25000: Systems and software engineering – systems and software quality requirements and evaluation (square). Tech. rep., "ISO" (2014)
13. Jalali, S., Wohlin, C.: Global software engineering and agile practices: a systematic review. Journal of Software: Evolution and Process 24(6), 643–659 (2012)
14. Johnston, K., Rosin, K.: Global virtual teams: How to manage them. In: CAMAN 2011, pp. 1–4 (May 2011)
15. Kääriäinen, J., Eskeli, J., Teppola, S., Välimäki, A., Tuuttila, P., Piippola, M.: Extending global tool integration environment towards lifecycle management. In: Meersman, R., Herrero, P., Dillon, T. (eds.) OTM 2009 Workshops. LNCS, vol. 5872, pp. 238–247. Springer, Heidelberg (2009)
16. Korkala, M., Maurer, F.: Waste identification as the means for improving communication in globally distributed agile software development. Journal of Systems and Software 95, 122–140 (2014)
17. Krueger, R., Casey, M.: Focus groups: a practical guide for applied research. Sage (2009)
18. Lethbridge, T.C., Sim, S.E., Singer, J.: Studying software engineers: Data collection techniques for software field studies. Emp. Softw. Eng. 10(3), 311–341 (2005)
19. Martin, J., Yague, A., Gonzalez, E., Garbajosa, J.: Making software factory truly global: the smart software factory project. Software Factory Magazine (2010)
20. McCall, J.: Factors in Software Quality: Preliminary Handbook on Software Quality for an Acquisiton Manager, vol. 1-3. General Electric (November 1977)
21. Mishra, A., Münch, J., Mishra, D.: Distributed development of information systems. Journal of Universal Computer Science 18(19), 2599–2601 (2012)
22. Niinimaki, T., Piri, A., Lassenius, C.: Factors affecting audio and text-based communication media choice in global software development projects. In: ICGSE 2009, pp. 153–162 (July 2009)
23. Orlikowski, W.J., Baroudi, J.J.: Studying information technology in organizations: Research approaches and assumptions. Inf. Sys. Res. 2(1), 1–28 (1991)
24. Oza, N., Münch, J., Garbajosa, J., Yague, A., Gonzalez Ortega, E.: Identifying potential risks and benefits of using cloud in distributed software development. In: Heidrich, J., Oivo, M., Jedlitschka, A., Baldassarre, M.T. (eds.) PROFES 2013. LNCS, vol. 7983, pp. 229–239. Springer, Heidelberg (2013)
25. Persson, J.S., Mathiassen, L., Aaen, I.: Agile distributed software development: enacting control through media and context. Inf. Sys. J. 22(6), 411–433 (2012)
26. Runeson, P., Höst, M.: Guidelines for conducting and reporting case study research in software engineering. John Wiley Sons (2012)
27. Schwaber, K.: Agile Project Management With Scrum. Microsoft Press, Redmond (2004)
28. da Silva, F., Costa, C., Francanda, A., Prikladinicki, R.: Challenges and solutions in distributed software development project management: A systematic literature review. In: ICGSE 2010, pp. 87–96 (August 2010)
29. Sinha, V., Sengupta, B., Chandra, S.: Enabling collaboration in distributed requirements management. IEEE Software 23(5), 52–61 (2006)
30. Unterkalmsteiner, M., Gorschek, T., Islam, A., Cheng, C., Permadi, R., Feldt, R.: Evaluation and measurement of software process improvement - a systematic literature review. IEEE Transactions on Software Engineering PP(99), 1 (2011)
31. Yin, R.K.: Case study research: Design and methods. Sage Publications (2003)

Privacy-Aware Agent-Oriented Architecture
for Distributed eHealth Systems

Adel Taweel[1,2], Samhar Mahmoud[1], and A. Rahman Tawil[3]

[1] King's College London, UK
adel.taweel@kcl.ac.uk
[2] Birzeit University, WB
ataweel@birzeit.edu
[3] University of East London, UK
a.r.tawil@uel.ac.uk

Abstract. Distributed Integrated ehealth systems are becoming a key need for achieving improved healthcare, in which healthcare processes across organisations must work in tandem to achieve this goal. However, at its core, enabling data-sharing safely while maintaining privacy and confidentiality is a critical requirement. The wide spread of electronic health record systems to manage health data and healthcare processes may provide the needed infrastructure to facilitate data-sharing. However, most of these systems are often designed to work within localised settings and rarely across organisations. In a health service, organisations and individuals are autonomous and often obey different data governance policies and would require different levels of data-sharing needs, depending on their roles and goals within the service. This would make agent-oriented architecture a strong candidate to enable privacy-aware seamless data-sharing between participating organisations. The paper presents an approach for privacy-preserving agent-oriented architecture that enables organisations to work together overcoming sharing sensitive data and evaluates its use within a real-life project.

Keywords: eHealth, Agent Architectures, privacy, security, System of Systems.

1 Introduction

The benefits of technology supported integrated health is increasingly recognised as one of the key needs of a modern health service. It is crucial not only to reduce costs, improve healthcare and patient safety but also due to the increase expectation of patients to receiving care at points of care irrespective of location or time [15][16]. However, to achieve they require health organisations to share and exchange clinical-sensitive information within a robust privacy-preserving environment. Organisations, within a single health service let alone across different ones, often operate autonomously governed by their individual data governance policies. The widespread of the use of electronic health record systems, in health organisations, and recent advances in networking and information systems provide the needed infrastructure to enable such paradigm [15][16]. However, transferring highly-sensitive data is not without

R. Meersman et al. (Eds.): OTM 2014 Workshops, LNCS 8842, pp. 418–427, 2014.

risks and poses several security concerns [1][9][10][11] especially when different orgnisations require sharing such data to achieve their function, in which demands for different levels of data-sharing needs vary, and where privacy preservation and control of usage is required [2][3][6][7].

On the other hand, multi-agent systems provide potential solutions to address some of these issues. In their intrinsic design, they have shown to meet needs in several applications including high-speed, mission-critical, content-rich, distributed information systems where mutual interdependencies, dynamic environments, uncertainty, and sophisticated control play a notable role [5][12][13][19]. eHealth applications can utilize these intrinsic characteristics of multi-agent systems given the notable features that these applications expose. They are often composed of autonomous (complex) systems, realised by heterogeneous components and legacy systems; designed to dynamically manage distributed data and resources within inherent regulatory frameworks, and built with regulated interactions for collaboration [17][18]. The key requirement however here is to provide an approach to enable sharing of data between different organisations and/or institutions while preserving the privacy of patients and users of the systems, and only allow access at the right points of access by the right people in the system. This would require providing adequate data processing security aligning with privacy legislation. Several approaches have been proposed, which often focus on control [3][6][7] and/or enforcement mechanisms [2][4][8]. These approaches, often however take heavy-handed approach with management of policy configurations, verification and validation steps that may make them unnecessarily expensive and potentially not scalable for some applications.

This paper proposes a different approach to enable data-sharing while preserving the privacy and confidentiality of data between participating organisations. It considers a particular application, in which different types of organisations have different goals and actors carry out different roles, yet they are required to collaborate and share information to meet the system requirements. It proposes an agent-oriented architecture that uses one-directional hashing for the sharing of sensitive data, where agents integrate with information systems (e.g. EHRs) and handles data transfers and the levels of encryption of data where only destination organisations can re-identify. This architecture is evaluated in the context of a real-life project environment, which demonstrates such architecture can meet the system set goals.

Section 2 describes the case study of a distributed ehealth system and summarizes its main attribute and challenges as an ehealth system and its particular requirements for privacy and confidentiality; Section 3 describes the privacy-aware architecture, its components and usage through a scenario; section 4 describes the evaluation and lesson learned from deploying the architecture in a real-life environment; finally, Section 5 presents some conclusions and future work.

2   Case Study

One of the major obstacles in clinical research is finding enough eligible participants to recruit in clinical trials [13][14][15]. Eligible participants can potentially be found automatically, but not without accessing their clinical information. Patients' clinical data, however, is stored into EHRs, located in their local clinics, which are only accessible by their own clinicians. In the UK, healthcare organisations are autonomously isolated and function within a separate framework from that of clinical academic or clinical research institutions, which makes accessing patient information by clinical researchers extremely difficult and not without going through an enormous governance and regulatory process. The IDEA project aims to locate, identify and invite patient to participate in trials. However, to do so, it requires enabling data sharing between these different types of organisations, potentially on a large scale.

Fig. 1 illustrates the overall conceptual architecture of IDEA. It notifies practitioners in real-time whenever an eligible patient is in consultation. When a patient visits a practice, IDEA compares their details against a registry of actively recruiting trials; if the patient is found eligible for one or more, the practitioner is prompted to help recruit the patient if they are interested. The IDEA project is described in more details here [13] [5].

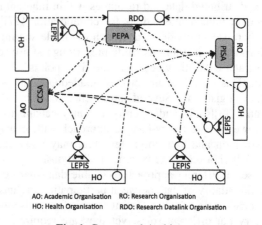

AO: Academic Organisation   RO: Research Organisation
HO: Health Organisation   RDO: Research Datalink Organisation

Fig. 1. Conceptual Architecture

However, to enable a more open system in which these organisations can share different levels of data, a flexible agent-oriented architecture was developed. As shown in Fig. 1 there are four types of organisation in this case study:

- *Healthcare Organisations* (HO): *HO* organisations have and must follow strict clinical and governance regulations concerning the privacy and security of their patients. Each adhere to national regulations but also implements their own set of data access policies. These organisations, in our case study, are represented by the General Practice clinics, which each has a pool of patients that only a designated set of local staff can access their data.

- *Research Datalink organisations* (RDO): *RDOs* represent a trusted third party organisations that also have access to a pseudnomyised (i.e. have access to clinical structured data but no access to personal identifiable information). *RDOs* are often national organisations created to enable clinical research through ethically controlled access to clinical data by clinical researchers.

- *(Clinical) Research Organisations* (RO): *ROs* represent research institutes or clinical researchers who run clinical trials. They do not have access to clinical data but require identifying eligible participants for their trials. Only once participants agree to participate in a respective trial, they may obtain their clinical.

-Academic Organisations (AO): *AOs* are organisations that undertake clinical or technical research within academic settings. They do not have nor allowed access to clinical data.

The case study presents several challenges that need to be addressed to achieve its objectives; some of the relevant challenges are identified below to gain a better understanding of how the architecture may need to meet the privacy objectives of the system.

Privacy. The architecture must provide organisations with mechanisms to safely share data meeting governance and regularity requirements, especially *HOs, RDOs* and *ROs* while ensuring only 'right' organisations can access and re-identify patients. For example, *HOs* can only access their own patients' data, *RDOs* can only access their own data and *ROs* can only access consented participants data and so forth.

System interactions. To be able to recruit eligible patients, it is necessary for researchers, practitioners, patients, databases and practices to interact. This means that several independent institutions, which are completely autonomous and have their own independent goals, must cooperate to achieve a common objective. However, the integration of multiple heterogeneous and autonomous systems can be a complicated and resource-consuming task. There are several issues to address here, including interoperability, distributed data etc., which are beyond the scope of this paper. The focus here is on privacy-preserving between organisations, which is key for the function of the system. The developed privacy-preserving mechanism, however, should not constraint these critical interactions in meeting the system function.

Scalability and performance. To maximise chances of finding more eligible participants, the system must be able to get the information from as many practices as possible (more than 10K GP practices in the UK) and manage a huge number of clinical trials requirements. However, due to the number of potential active trials (potentially several hundreds) with the size of each trial description and eligibility criteria makes it impossible for GPs to know all active trials to assess patient eligibility during, the often short, consultation period.

3   Privacy-Aware Architecture

This section details the design and components of the architecture. Fig. 2 depicts the main structure of the architecture mainly illustrating the components that handles privacy-perserving mechanism. The architecture adopts a decentralised approach, where a decision of access is decided at the point of access and controlled by individual organisations. Since each organisation is assumed autonomous, each employs an agent that defines its roles, goals, and policies. These determine the behaviour of agents when sending or receiving data. Each agent has the full authority to determine its action with respect to data. When data originates from another organisation, the source-organisation sends data in a data-bucket (DB), which includes four elements:

DB=<PE, DE, OIK, LoE>
-*Protocol_Element* (PE): defines the characteristics of eligible participants (often named eligibility criteria), which include a Protocal_Id_Key (PIK);

-*Data_Element* set (DE): include specific data of potentially eligible patients, which contains fields of data and Data_Id_Key (DIK) that defines a set of keys of the Data_Element IDs, which specifies the Id of each element in the data set;

   -*Organisation_Id_Key* (OIK): key of ID of the organisation where the data originated;

   -*Level_of_Encryption* (LoE): specifies how many times the data has been encrypted;

DE (including DIK), PIK, OIK are encrypted, however PE (eligibility criteria) and LoE are not. These are encrypted using a standard one-direction hashing algorithm (e.g. MD5). As mentioned above with for the four types of organisations, four types of agents are created to represent each function and role. Although these are generic types, individual agent mirror individual organisations, and thus their exact behaviour depends on the policies and exact role of each organisation. As mentioned above, *HOs* have identified version of the data of their patients, whereas *ROs* do not have access to data, only except after a participant has consent and provided their data. *AOs* do not and should not have access to data. *RDOs* may have patient clinical data but not necessarily personal information. The function and role of each these agents are described below in more details.

PISA: *Protocol Information Service Agent* is a software agent that represents a *RO*. It represents a *Protocol Manager Role*, which defines and creates protocol eligibility criteria and defines the protocol characteristics. It includes the *Researcher Role*, which is responsible for defining the specific features of each trial under its jurisdiction. Researchers are also responsible for ensuring consistency of their protocol, determine which type of trial this protocol belongs to (see below) and activating the trial in CCSA (see below). They are not allowed to directly contact patients unless they have agreed and consented to participate in one of their own clinical trials. For obvious reasons, each researcher should be part of a specific research institution and follow its specific restrictions. There are two types of trial protocols: *T1*: trials that define participants characteristics only (e.g. age>40 & gender=male etc.), and *T2*: trials that specifies complex characteristics which require pre-specifying potentially eligible patients and their authorised clinicians. The latter (i.e. *T2*) requires further epidemiological pre-processing to identify potential participants that meet particular risk assessment. For the former (i.e. *T1*), *ROs* (*Protocol Manager*) can create these, however for the latter (i.e. *T2*), *ROs* require to pre-consult with RDOs (PEPA) to create these trials before they are sent to the CCSA.

PEPA: *Potential Eligible Patient Agent* is a software agent that represents the *RDO Manager Role*, which is responsible for updating and controlling access to the *RDO* database. It offers a service to pre-compute potential eligible patients for individual trials that have complex search criteria (*CreateEligibleList* service). The role also offers a service to identify whether a GP (and their own practice) is authorized to perform recruitment for each trial (*AuthorizedGP* service), while adhering to local and good clinical practice regulations. This agent (*PEPA*) provides *ROs* with a list of potentially eligible patients, their practices and authorised GPs. However, since *ROs* are not allowed to have access to this data (yet), data is encrypted as part of the *DE* data-bucket. Since this encryption is irreversible, only *HOs* that have respective patient data are able to re-identify it. When an *HO* receives this data, using *DIK*, they can match it to their local data and re-identify the patient using a simple encrypt-search algorithm (see below). *PEPA*, for some cases, could choose to double-encrypt the *DE*, depending on their policy, if so, the agent then increments *LoE*, so other receiving agents can determine the number of encryptions they need to perform in their matching algorithm.

CCSA: *Central Control Service Agent*, represents *AOs*. *AOs* provide the patient recruitment service along with their network of recruiting agents (*LEPIS*) that are connected to respective *HOs*. It represents the *CCSA Manager Role*, a software application responsible for controlling the *CCSA* database, which stores data about active clinical trials. It offers three services to the other members of the system: (i) a *Register New or update existing Trial* service that allows researchers *(PISA)* to register new clinical trials in *CCSA*; which also verifies that trials follows the specified standards and regulations; (ii) an *Update LEPIS Status* service that ensures consistency with *LEPIS* agents to optimize *LEPIS* updates; and (iii) a *Patients Response* service that, in communication with *LEPIS* Agents, records the response of each consulted patient (and/or their GP) (whether they have agreed or refused to participate in a trial). Since *AOs* are not allowed to have access to clinical data, thus *CCSA* stores databuckets (*DB*), as received, encrypted.

LEPIS: *Local Eligible Patient Identification Service* agents represents *HOs* within this role of recruitment. It defines the *LEPIS Manager Role* as a software application that resides in each practice and investigates the eligibility of patients. *LEPIS* agent plays this role for each practitioner in each GP practice participating in the recruitment system. *LEPIS* agents continually communicate with the *CCSA* to acquire information about trials related to the type of patients and speciality of GPs and practices and other updates on each trial status. They also provide the GP with a simple GUI interface to notify them of a patient's eligibility. As *LEPIS* agents communicate with GPs through their GUI interface, they collect information about patient and GP responses. However, since *LEPIS* obtains the data encrypted from CCSA, it is kept encrypted in it local data store. To match the eligibility of patients for *T2* type trials, it uses a simple encrypt-search algorithm, in which when a patient is in consultation with a GP, their *DIK* is only encrypted to match with *LEPIS*'s stored encrypted key. If it matches, the rest of the criteria are matched against the patient record to identify eligibility. Since *LEPIS* represents *HOs*, it is authorised by its role to access the data, but no identifiable data is transferred by *LEPIS* outside the *HO* to other agents. *LEPIS* only communicates patients/GP responses back to *CCSA* using their encrypted *DIKs*. If the patient agreed to participate in a trial, *LEPIS* identifies and communicate *PIK* back to the respective *RO (PISA)*, which consequently can invoke the appropriate case report form to complete the recruitment of the patient into that trial. In this case, to preserve privacy *LEPIS*, sends the encrypted *DB* to *PISA*. Depending on the *LoE*, *PISA* could easily re-identify *PIK* using a simple encrypt-search algorithm.

SEC: *Search-Encrypt Component* is a software application that includes a search-encrypt algorithm. The algorithm uses a sequential search mechanism to locate *DIK* with the local database, encrypt and provide to the agent to match it the encrypted *DIK* in the data-bucket. It's not always used by respective agent, or by all agents, depending on its functionality and role. *CCSA*, for example does not invoke this component, since it has no access to the source data and its role does not require it to re-identify users.

NCC: *Node Connector Component* is a software application that allows agents to connect to local software in each organisation. Its detailed description is beyond the scope of the paper and covered in more details elsewhere [14][15], but its main function is to overcome interoperability issues with local systems including databases. This has been mainly designed to provide uninform programmable interface to communicate with agents, thus providing transparency over local software or databases.

Within the architecture, each organisation respective agent can push or send that information, on request, to other agents, or act based on their workflow for respective actions. Receiving agents once they receive the data bucket, depending on their role, they decide whether to store it as is or need to do further processing on it. For agents that require further processing, since the data is irreversible, they can use *SEC* to allow them find to whom patient/user this data belongs. Once found, they can do further processing based on their role.

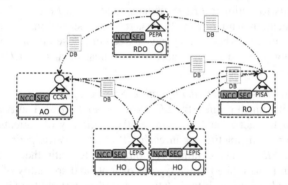

Fig. 2. Agent-oriented Architecture: agents, services and organisations

4   Evaluation and Lessons Learned

This section describes the evaluation of the architecture and lessons learned. The architecture was employed in the IDEA project, described in section 2 above. The architecture was realised using service oriented web services with well-defined interfaces, given its well-established standards. The services were deployed to enable four different types of organisations to achieve patient recruitment into clinical trials. The main challenge was to overcome the regulatory and their consequent networking barriers. It requires that involved organisations obey their individual regulatory constraints, where only allowed staff in respective organisation accesses safely their patient data, while staff in other organisations must not. The *AOs* and *ROs* are the two organisations that do not and are not allowed to have access to clinical data, yet they want to use the data to find, identify and recruit patients. *RDOs* have often access to the data aggregated from participating *HOs* but only pseudonymised. The case study's *RDO* aggregate clinical data from 640 primary care clinics (*HOs*) on a monthly, and from some on a daily, basis keeping data periodically updated. In the IDEA project 60 *HOs* participated in which *LEPIS* agents were installed on 134 GP machines within these clinics. These GP clinics are geographically distributed across the UK and possess limited Internet connectivity.   Three key elements were evaluated in these settings: agents, the privacy-preservation and functionality in meeting the objective of the study. The main objective and functionality of the architecture is to share data between these organisations to enable recruiting patients while preserving their privacy at all time and only organisations that already have patients data are only able to identify them. These three elements are reflected upon below:

Functionality: the architecture was able to successfully recruit patients from the participating *HOs* while protecting patient privacy. Three clinical trials were deployed in the system, and all recruited successfully meeting their targets – a more details on recruitment is reported elsewhere [12].

Privacy-preservation: as described in the scenario above, data-origin-organisations when releasing patients in the architecture, data is encrypted using a simple but effective irreversible hash encryption algorithm. The well-known MD5 algorithm was used to encrypt the data. To ensure that the encrypted data matching algorithm works, the same version is used in all agents and organisations. As per the follow described above, while *RDO* and *HOs* have access to clinical data, only *RDO* (and in cases *ROs*) was originating encrypting data and *HOs* were only performing data matching to re-identify their own patients. That meant, with any data request, *AOs* and *ROs* would only have access to encrypted data within the platform, which is not identifiable. For *RDO* and *HOs*, to identify if they have access to the encrypted data, they use a search-encrypt algorithm, named as *SEC* above. This algorithm used by *SEC*, to match *DIKs*. Since it does not have access to actual local keys it performs a linear search on the local database, where it sequentially encrypts each local Data ID and then matches to the encrypted *DIK* in the data-bucket. In the participating *HOs*, sizes of their patient pool is between 5k-10k patients, which the sequential execution of the *SEC* algorithm did not show as a bottleneck or slowed the performance., however, we recognise this may prove inefficient for large databases. In the case study above, since patients are only invited for recruitment while in consultation, this was not an issue, since only that patient is used for matching by the *SEC* algorithm.

Roles and Agents: as mentioned above four types of agents were developed in the architecture: *LEPIS* (for *HOs*), *PISA* (for *ROs*), *PEPA* (for *RDO*) and *CCSA* (for *AOs*). One instance of each of the latter three agents were deployed in respective organisations, while 134 *LEPIS* agents were deployed in participating *HOs*. Although these agents fall within four types, nevertheless the exact behaviour of individual agents and the decisions they make regarding their role and data processing depends on the local policy configuration of individual organisations and their own workflow configuration that specifies their communication with other agents. Four types were deemed sufficient for the purpose of the IDEA project, but the architecture allows expanding and adding other types. The most complex of these agents was *LEPIS*, given the amount of decisions and interactions it has to perform with local GPs. *PISA* and *PEPA* have some complexity but since interactions were limited to only limited users, their GUI design was minimal. As the IDEA project is being scaled up, the design of these agents is being revised.

A number of key lessons have been learnt from the deployment of this architecture, these include:

Scalability: no scalability issue was observed. However, although there are more than 134 agents deployed in the system to test scalability of the system, scalability may pose a challenge when the size substantially increases. The amount of communication between *LEPIS* agents and *CCSA* is limited to three times a day, but given the potential scale, *CCSA* may prove to be a bottleneck. To overcome, *LEPIS* agents have been designed to communicate with each other, within a common domain or clinic. Scalability of this designed has been tested and detailed somewhere else [20], which was found to achieve greater efficiency opposed to the initial workflow design.

Security barriers: in the medical domain, in *HOs*, network security is critical but it can be cumbersome. Often, these domains are tightly network secured with stringent firewalls in place. However, these often only allow communication to be initiated from within the domain. Thus this posed some challenge deploying the platform to enable system agents to communicate at will. To facilitate the process, agents have been designed to initiate outgoing communications with other agents, according to a configurable communication flow that defines each agent communication pattern.

SEC algorithm: because the SEC algorithm uses sequential search mechanism to match and re-identify local participants, this may pose another scalability challenge. Although in the current set-up, the data size is limited and thus this was not an issue, future designs may need to consider other mechanisms to improve efficiency for larger size data.

5   Conclusions and Future Work

The paper presents a simple yet effective privacy-ware agent-oriented architecture that enables data sharing between organisations while preserving privacy. The architecture employed the use of role-driven agents that each represented the goals and policies of each organisation, with enabled communication to meet their specific functionality. The agents were designed with privacy-awareness so that their behaviour is controlled within their local settings, including governance and communication policies, taking decisions in regards of how to process and handle data. The architecture was evaluated within a real-life ehealth project and has been shown to maintain privacy of patients, while enabling data sharing which was employed for the identification of eligible patients for clinical trials in real-time. The results obtained show that the architecture has successfully met the sought functionality of the system to recruit patient for three trials, while enable safe sharing of data.

The evaluation has also shown a number of lessons learned from the deployment of the architecture, and potential future development to address these lessons. In particular, lessons related to ehealth environments and their potential scalability needs, posing a potential limitation of the approach.

Acknowledgment. The author would like to thank all colleagues from the IDEA project who contributed to this work, through discussions or providing insights.

References

1. Leon, M., Hipolito, J., Garcia, J.: A Security and Privacy Survey for WSN in e-Health Applications. In: Electronics, Robotics and Automotive Mechanics Conference, CERMA 2009, pp. 125–130 (2009)
2. Rath, A.T., Colin, J.: Towards purpose enforcement model for privacy-aware usage control policy in distributed healthcare. IJSN 8(2), 94–105 (2013)
3. Rath, A.T., Colin, J.: Modeling and expressing purpose validation policy for privacy-aware usage control in distributed environment. In: ICUIMC 2014, vol. 14 (2013)

4. Dong, N., Jonker, H., Pang, J.: Challenges in eHealth: From Enabling to Enforcing Privacy. In: Liu, Z., Wassyng, A. (eds.) FHIES 2011. LNCS, vol. 7151, pp. 195–206. Springer, Heidelberg (2012)

5. Bergenti, F., Poggi, A.: Multi-agent systems for e-health: recent projects and initiatives. In: 10th Int. Workshop on Objects and Agents (2009)

6. Solanas, A., Martínez-Ballesté, A., Pérez-Martínez, P.A., Pena, A., Ramos, J.: m-Carer: Privacy-Aware Monitoring for People with Mild Cognitive Impairment and Dementia. IEEE Journal on Selected Areas in Communications 31(9-Suppl), 19–27 (2013)

7. Armellin, G., Betti, D., Casati, F., Chiasera, A., Martinez, G., Stevovic, J.: Privacy preserving event driven integration for interoperating social and health systems. In: Jonker, W., Petković, M. (eds.) SDM 2010. LNCS, vol. 6358, pp. 54–69. Springer, Heidelberg (2010)

8. De Coi, J., Delaunay, G., Albino, A., Muhlenbach, F., Maret, P.: The Comprehensive Health Information System: a Platform for Privacy-Aware and Social Health Monitoring. In: IADIS e-Health 2012, Lisbon, Portugal (2012)

9. Appari, A., Johnson, M.E.: Information security and privacy in healthcare: Current state of research. Int. J. Internet Enterprise Manage 6(4), 279–314 (2010)

10. Karygiannis, A., Antonakakis, E.: Security and privacy issues in agent-based location-aware mobile commerce. Saf. Sec. Multi-agent Syst., 308–329 (2011)

11. Rashvand, H.F., Salah, K., Calero, J.M.A., Harn, L.: Distributed security for multi-agent systems - review and applications. IET Inf. Secur. 4(4), 188–201 (2010)

12. Mahmoud, S., Tyson, G., Miles, S., Taweel, A., Vanstaa, T.: M Luck, B. Delaney. Multi-agent system for recruiting patients for clinical trials. In: Proc. AAMAS 2014, Proceedings of the 2014 International Conference on Autonomous Agents and Multi-agent Systems (2014)

13. Tyson, G., Taweel, A., Miles, S., Luck, M., Staa, T.V., Delaney, B.: An agent- based approach to real-time patient identification for clinical trials. In: Proc. 4th Intl. Conference on eHealth 2011 (2011)

14. Tyson, G., Taweel, A., Zschaler, S., Staa, T.V., Delaney, B.: A model-driven approach to interoperability and integration in systems of systems. In: Modelling Foundations and Applications: MBSDI (2011)

15. Taweel, A., Delaney, B., Speedie, S.: Towards achieving semantic interoperability in ehealth services. In: Watfa, M. (ed.) E-Healthcare Systems and Wireless Communications: Current and Future Challenges, pp. 388–401. IGI (2012)

16. Taweel, A., Speedie, S., Tyson, G., Tawil, A.R., Peterson, K., Delaney, B.: Service and model-driven dynamic integration of health data. In: Proceedings of the first international workshop on Managing interoperability and complexity in health systems, MIXHS 2011, pp. 11–17. ACM (2011)

17. De Loach, S.A.: Developing a multiagent conference management system using the o-mase process framework. In: Proc. Int. Conf. on Agent-oriented Software Engineering VIII, pp. 168–181 (2008)

18. Gonzalez-Velez, H., Mier, M., Julia-Sape, M., Arvanitis, T., Garcia-Gomez, M.R.J., Lewis, P., Dasmahapatra, S., Dupplaw, D., Peet, A., Arus, C., Celda, B., Huel, S.V., Lluch-Ariet, M.: Healthagents: distributed multi-agent brain tumor diagnosis and prognosis. Applied Intelligence 30 (2009)

19. Vecht, B., Dignum, F., Meyer, J.-J., Dignum, M.: Handbook of research on multi- agent systems: Semantics and dynamics of organizational models. In: Autonomous Agents Adopting Organizational Rules. IGI Global, pp. 314–333. IGI (2009)

20. Feyisetan, S., Tyson, G., Taweel, A., Vargas-Vera, M., Staa, T., Delaney, B.: ePCRN-IDEA2: An Agent-Based System for Large-Scale Clinical Trial Recruitment. In: Proc. AAMAS Workshop on Agents Applied in Health Care (A2HC), Spain, (2012)

Patterns of Software Modeling

Wolfgang Raschke[1], Massimiliano Zilli[1], Johannes Loinig[2], Reinhold Weiss[1],
Christian Steger[1], and Christian Kreiner[1]

[1] Institute for Technical Informatics
Graz University of Technology, Graz, Austria
{wolfgang.raschke,massimiliano.zilli,rweiss,steger,
christian.kreiner}@tugraz.at
[2] NXP Semiconductors Austria GmbH, Gratkorn, Austria
johannes.loinig@nxp.com

Abstract. Software systems start small and grow in complexity and
size. The larger a software system is, the more it is distributed over organizational and geographical confines. Thus, the modeling of software
systems is necessary at a certain level of complexity because it can be
used for communication, documentation, configuration and certification
purposes. We came to the conclusion that several patterns of software
modeling exist. The existence of such patterns is dependent on the history and the evolution of the system under consideration. We will show
that a software system in its lifecycle has to face several crises. Such a
crisis is a watershed in the application of new patterns. We provide an
evolutionary view of software systems and models which helps understanding of current problems and prospective solutions.

Keywords: Model-Based Software Development, Collaborative Software
Development, Application Lifecycle Management, Software Process
Improvement.

1   Introduction

Typically, software systems are always increasing in complexity. This impacts development teams, inter-organizational software development, and geographical
distribution. The distribution of the development process complicates communication and sharing of knowledge. Software modeling is a successful approach
to mitigate these issues. However, there are currently a plethora of different
approaches with regards to the modeling of software, requirements and specifications, such as requirements engineering, domain-specific modeling (DSM),
software product lines (SPL), agile requirements engineering and application lifecycle management (ALM). It is hard to select an appropriate approach, because
the success of it heavily depends on the context of the organizational situation.
Thus, we provide a conceptual framework that helps to characterize the different
approaches. This framework aims to facilitate the selection of a suitable software
modeling method. We define several modeling patterns which we name and explain. Such a pattern is an abstraction and is kept simple in order to make a

R. Meersman et al. (Eds.): OTM 2014 Workshops, LNCS 8842, pp. 428–437, 2014.
© Springer-Verlag Berlin Heidelberg 2014

clear difference between the basic characteristics of today's software modeling approaches. We outline the observation that during the lifecycle of software, the dynamics cause a change in its context. Within the new context, solutions often turn into problems. This effect results in a time of change and turmoil, a so-called *revolution* phase. We introduce the concept of Greiner [1] which regards the learning and development of systems as a sequence of evolutions which are interrupted by revolutions. Regarding this viewpoint, we derive an explanation and categorization of software modeling patterns. We show that the emergence of software modeling trends follow a generic pattern.

2 Conceptual Background

Usually, we apply known solutions to problems. If a solution has succeeded many times in the past, we are tempted to see this as a universal solution. Unfortunately, this attitude overlooks the fact that solutions always work in a specific situation, the so-called *context*. Fig. 1 shows the concept of a pattern: the problem is located in the context-free *problem space*. The solution is part of the *solution space* and it is constrained by the context. In the traditional view of a design pattern, the context is fixed and does not alter [2,3].

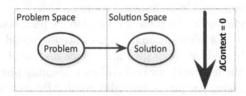

Fig. 1. Problem and solution in a fixed context

Dynamics arise when the context changes. Fig. 2 demonstrates that solutions turn into problems within the new context. The new problem has to be solved again in a constrained environment. This process may perpetuate for several iterations. These kinds of dynamics can be observed very often [4]. We use it as a reference for the development of modeling archetypes. For example, regarding transportation the dynamics are as follows: The petrol powered vehicle has been the solution to the problem of transportation over long distances. This solution has changed its environment because of pollution and the decreasing amount of petrol ultimately available. These new problems may one day be addressed by the electrical vehicle. This new solution will then itself cause new problems.

Greiner [1] describes a model where evolutionary development is interrupted by revolutions. These revolutions are caused by the changing context of size and time. The solutions no longer work within the altered context. Moreover, they are then the cause of the new issues. He describes five phases of organizational development, their crises and the ensuing solutions. Although the phases of Greiner's model are different to the archetypes we state here, they have served as inspiration.

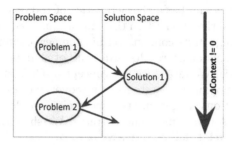

Fig. 2. The dynamics of problems and solutions in a changing context

3 Software Modeling Patterns

We gathered experiences from the development of two industrial RMS. More-over, in order to build up a catalog of patterns we interviewed experts from the following domains: automotive software, logistics software, secure software and financial software. Each of the patterns occurred in at least one of the software projects that was studied. The sample is broad and representative enough to formulate basic patterns within a changing context.

In Fig. 3 the continuous lines represent evolutionary phases with no change of the modeling pattern. These evolutionary phases are disrupted by revolutionary phases which are indicated by the dashed lines. Such a phase denotes the change from one pattern to the next and always involves a learning phase. This learning phase includes recognizing the problems and searching for new solutions. It takes some time to pass through this phase and proceed further.

In Fig. 3 it can be seen that the two influencing factors (the context) here are *complexity* and *time*. Complexity increases with size and mainly influences the style of modeling. The second factor is time: it is needed to adapt to new circumstances. Thus, it is mainly an influencing factor during a time of crisis. Then, neither size nor complexity grow rapidly. In the following we describe the patterns in more detail.

The patterns are structured as follows: The first patterns begins with a starting point which describes the situation at the beginning of a small software system. The problem section is part of each pattern: it depicts the established working practices. After the solution, we provide the context section. The context describes the environment and the situation. The solution must work within the context. If the context changes, the solution turns into a problem, as a consequence. The consequences of a pattern characterize the problem of the following pattern.

3.1 Backward Engineering (BE)

Starting Point. Initially, the software is small and only a few developers work on it. There is no clear division of functionality between people, so each

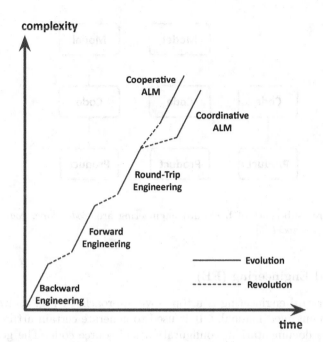

Fig. 3. The development of software modeling patterns within the context of complexity and time

developer works on the whole system. Thus, it can be assumed, that everyone has knowledge of the complete system. Hence, there is no need for explicit modeling of the software.

Solution. The first pattern is outlined in Fig. 4. The sub-types *code-alone*, *code-parallels-model* and *code-to-model* are similar. We do not see a major difference in the three depicted types regarding the effect on the development process. Thus, they are collected within one single pattern. In *code-alone*, code is written and compiled to a finished product. This is the simplest model that can exist. Very soon, a mental model emerges which parallels the code development (*code-parallels-model*). This model can be written documentation or a domain vocabulary. The main point is that it is not explicitly derived from the code. It emerges on an *ad hoc* basis. The next step is *code-to-model*: to derive the model from the source code. Such a model may be documentation. It can be generated automatically via document generators. This method can be refined to a certain degree. It is simple and can applied without a high overhead, even in small software projects.

Context Change and Consequences. Successful software systems tend to grow in complexity and size. Thus, the number of software developers also grows. At a certain point, the whole system can no longer be understood by each developer. Communication becomes more difficult because of the increasing number of developers.

432   W. Raschke et al.

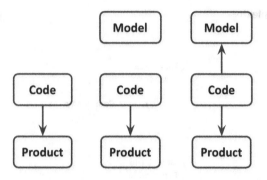

Fig. 4. The three sub-types of backward engineering are: *code-alone, code-parallels-model* and *code-to-model* [5]

3.2 Forward Engineering (FE)

Solution. Forward engineering is a top-down approach. In Fig. 5, *Model A* is created and maintained manually. It is used to generate certain artifacts, such as parts of the documentation, configuration and source code. The generation of redundant code is efficient and works well with an explicit model. Moreover, documentation artifacts are generated which go beyond the functionality of a general-purpose document generator. The architecture is crafted in the model and the source code artifacts (header files, class skeletons) are generated. So, the generated architecture is consistent with the model. UML[1] is a prominent example for such an approach. However, there is still a very high manual effort in maintaining these models.

In Fig. 5 it can also be seen that *Model B* is created from the source code. This is not a contradiction to the concept of FE because each arrow only points in one direction. Thus, no synchronization is provided.

Context Change and Consequences. The forward engineering principle works adequately for software of small and middle complexity with a relatively low system dynamic. In this context, this method works perfectly. Such a model grows with the complexity and the size of the software. It requires increasingly more effort to maintain this model and at one point there are several thousand changing information items. It is then hard to keep the model consistent with the fast changing software. There are no synchronization methods available. Thus, concurrent work on the models is virtually impossible. All these ingredients form a bottleneck, so that the model is not able to follow the source code. At this point it is likely that maintenance of the model is stopped.

---

[1] www.uml.org/

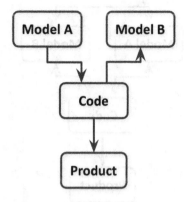

Fig. 5. In forward engineering the information flow is either from model to code or from code to model

3.3   Round-Trip-Engineering (RTE)

Solution. Round-trip engineering incorporates forward engineering, backward engineering and the synchronization of both. Fig. 6 shows that the information flow between model and code goes in both directions. So, the high amount of manual work required for synchronization can be leveraged by recovering the model from the code. Changes in the code can be synchronized with the model. Moreover, it can be seen in Fig. 6 that synchronization between models is also possible. Hence, these approaches need advanced synchronization mechanisms, such as *model-to-model*, *text-to-model* and *model-to-text* transformations. For the synchronization of different versions of such a model, two techniques are needed: *merge* and *diff*. If all these algorithms are supported, most of the artifacts can be synchronized automatically. Still, such a synchronization has to be controlled by responsible roles.

Context Change and Consequences. Round-trip engineering is still, at the moment, a high-end solution and expensive to establish. Thus, it can be expected that it is present only in medium and large software. The bottleneck of the previous pattern is now resolved. In any case, the level of information flow escalates. There are now several versions of the software and the model. It becomes increasingly difficult to coordinate these different versions. Anyone can integrate results with the model. As a consequence, the introduction of flaws is more likely. Moreover, there are no clear responsibilities and access rights.

First, the size of the software leads to the effect that the domain experts (who are rare) are more involved in the specification of the system. Programming activities can be outsourced more easily. As a consequence the software may be constructed by several software suppliers. Such a *software ecosystem* [6,7] exists for example in the automotive industry. There, tier 1 and tier 2 suppliers work together with the car manufacturer. However, such a software ecosystem

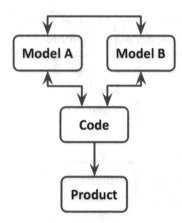

Fig. 6. Round-trip engineering enables synchronization between models and between model and code

comes with many risks and uncertainties because the software development can no longer be controlled as a whole [8].

As we can see, the crisis stems from two reasons: first, the increased information flow that is caused by the high number of different versions (synchronization). Second, the uncertainty and risks within a software ecosystem remains a problem. Both issues are addressed in the following patterns: *Coordinative Application Lifecycle Management* and *Cooperative Application Lifecycle Management.*

3.4   Coordinative Application Lifecycle Management

Solution. Until now, the evolution of model-based systems only incorporated structural models. Fig. 7 shows a workflow engine controlling information flow as an addition to RTE. The next logical step is such a workflow (process) integration with models. This means, that all steps within a process shall be controlled, documented and delegated to the appropriate roles. Thus, artifacts within a model have states (started, analyzed, finished) and roles (accountability, responsibility, access rights). Examples for such workflow management systems are: support of reviews, project plans, allocation of roles to tasks and the like. For certification issues, all these processes have to be documented. We expect tool chains with a tight integration of test results, bug reports, bug resolving, reviews, project plans and so on. Thus, a seamless documentation to provide evidence for process maturity (e.g. SPICE [9], CMMI [10] and dependability (e.g. security [11], safety [12]) is possible from such a model. This phase puts emphasis on coordination which is, generally speaking, the formal performing of actions.

Context and Consequences. It is very difficult to ascertain a higher level of process maturity. There is a high cost overhead for establishing these processes. This high cost overhead makes it difficult for smaller companies to exist within

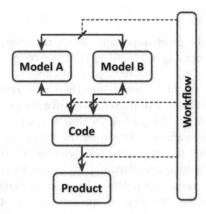

Fig. 7. In coordinative ALM the information flow is coordinated by an integrated workflow management

such a supply chain. This issue can be mitigated through highly integrated tool chains and outsourcing of process knowledge. So, developers can concentrate on domain expertise. We expect a high degree of dependency of these firms in the supply chain on external consulting and tool providers. At the moment, the software industry comes up with so-called ALM tools. They extend traditional requirements engineering with a process integration.

3.5   Cooperative Application Lifecycle Management

Solution. In Cooperative ALM, communication needs to be bound to artifacts within a software model. Such artifacts can be: activity-based (tasks, change requests) or structural (architecture, requirements). Moreover, synchronous and asynchronous communication mechanisms need to be implemented. Respective tools enable a notification based on the state of the artifacts. For instance, the completion of a task is an event which triggers a notification message. High-end RMS integrate these mechanisms. Prominent examples are: Attlassian JIRA[2] and CollabNet TeamForge[3].

Context and Consequences. Cooperative ALM seems to parallel the Coordinative ALM. The objective of Coordinative ALM is to provide evidence for trust through formal processes. Whereas, the goal of Cooperative ALM is to foster and enable the sharing of information. Unfortunately, this cannot be done efficiently via formal channels. So, the principle is based on collaboration instead of coordination. A corresponding trend in software engineering is agile working. Information interchange has become more difficult because the development sites are scattered over distinct places throughout the world. Sophisticated tools facilitate and foster the sharing of information.

---

[2] www.atlassian.com/JIRA
[3] http://www.collab.net/products/teamforge

4 Conclusion

We listed a catalog of the most important issues regarding software modeling. We complemented the catalog with issues that we collected during industrial software projects. Moreover, we strove to present these issues in relation to each other. Additionally, we sought to investigate their relationship with the respective situation. Thus, we stated five patterns of software modeling which exist in today's industrial software development. In addition, we stated the typical context of each pattern. We examined the sequential development from one pattern to the next. It is important to understand the dynamics of this development: long periods of steady development are disrupted by crises which are a watershed in the application of a new modeling pattern. In order to make our developmental model as generic as possible, we omitted unnecessary details and abstracted it to only five basic patterns. Certainly in a real software project, the development will never exactly follow our model. Nevertheless, some issues are still symptomatic. Knowledge of these symptomatic issues helps to characterize the actual problems and design new solutions with the contextual setting in mind.

Acknowledgment. Project partners are NXP Semiconductors Austria GmbH and TU Graz. The project is funded by the Austrian Federal Ministry for Transport, Innovation, and Technology under the FIT-IT contract FFG 832171. The authors would like to thank pure systems GmbH for support.

References

1. Greiner, L.: Evolution and revolution as organizations grow. Harvard Business Review (January 1997)
2. Alexander, C., Ishikawa, S., Jacobsen, M., Fiksdahl-King, I., Angel, S.: A Pattern Language: Towns, Buildings, Construction. Oxford University Press (August 1977)
3. Gamma, E., Helm, R., Johnson, R., Vlissides, J.: Design Patterns. Pearson Education (October 1994)
4. Watzlawick, P., Weakl, J.H., Weakland, J.H., Fisch, R.: Change: Principles of Problem Formation and Problem Resolution. W.W. Norton (1973)
5. Kelly, S., Tolvanen, J.P.: Domain-Specific Modeling: Enabling Full Code Generation. Wiley (2008)
6. Messerschmitt, D.G., Szyperski, C.: Software Ecosystem. MIT Press (2002)
7. Manikas, K., Hansen, K.M.: Software ecosystems – A systematic literature review. Journal of Systems and Software 86(5), 1294–1306 (2013)
8. McGregor, J.D.: A method for analyzing software product line ecosystems. In: Proceedings of the Fourth European Conference on Software Architecture, pp. 73–80 (2010)
9. Messnarz, R., Ross, H.L., Habel, S., König, F., Koundoussi, A., Unterrreitmayer, J., Ekert, D.: Integrated Automotive SPICE and safety assessments. Software Process: Improvement and Practice 14(5), 279–288 (2009)

10. Chrissis, M.B., Konrad, M., Shrum, S.: CMMI Guidlines for Process Integration and Product Improvement. Addison-Wesley Longman Publishing Co., Inc. (2003)
11. Common Criteria. Common Criteria for Information Technology Security Evaluation - Part 1-3. Version 3.1 Revision 3 Final (July 2009)
12. International Organization for Standardization. ISO/DIS 26262 road vehicles Functional Safety, Part 1-10

Dynamic Mashup Interfaces for Information Systems Using Widgets-as-a-Service

Jesús Vallecillos, Javier Criado, Luis Iribarne, and Nicolás Padilla

Applied Computing Group, University of Almería, Spain
{jesus.vallecillos,javi.criado,luis.iribarne,npadilla}@ual.es

Abstract. Web Information Systems intend to adapt to the users' preferences as new data available on the network. In this regard, the composition and reuse of services which are involved in a web application is an interesting research topic, since these techniques pursue the dynamic construction of applications that can be adapted at design or run time. As for the visualization of these applications, web user interfaces play a key role, serving as a connection point between users and the rest of the system. This article proposes an architecture for specification, storage, management and visualization of components, built from widgets complying with the W3C recommendation, for making web user interfaces. We follow a service-based approach for the interface deployment and communication management, introducing the concept of Widgets-as-a-Service (WaaS). To illustrate this proposal, an example of widget-based Web Information System is shown.

Keywords: GUI, mashup, Widget-as-a-Service, components.

1 Introduction

Web Information Systems are largely dependent on web platform, which is a dynamic and constantly changing domain, that also relies on web services that provide the required data. In this regard, web services are, increasingly, elements that need to be changed and updated in order to be adapted to the new available information and also to the user profiles. Web interfaces do not get out of this necessity and also require the service they offer as an interface to be dynamic and adaptive to the user. With this aim, new projects and proposals have come up in the last few years to build customized web interfaces through the configuration of widgets that the user wants to visualize [8]. For these applications, the user has one or more graphical interfaces available that he/she can configure to create some kind of dashboards. These interfaces are built according to graphical components of high or medium granularity (that is, they are not simple buttons or text fields) that group together some functionalities related to each other and give rise to *mashup* applications based on widgets [3]. Some of the most interesting and currently supported projects are Netvibes (http://www.netvibes.com), MyYahoo (https://my.yahoo.com) or Ducksboard (https://ducksboard.com).

R. Meersman et al. (Eds.): OTM 2014 Workshops, LNCS 8842, pp. 438–447, 2014.
© Springer-Verlag Berlin Heidelberg 2014

Our research work is focused on dynamic management of component-based graphical user interfaces (GUIs). From our perspective, the representation of this type of interfaces can be "abstracted" in order to create a definition through fragments or pieces analogously to a *bottom-up* approach within the *Component-based Software Engineering* (CBSE). At subsequent steps, we can manipulate this abstract representation to adapt it to the changes according to the user's preferences or any other changes derived or not from the interaction and then make again the graphical interface shown to the user (see Figure 1). This mechanism allows us to work with simplified models of interfaces and later obtain new widgets to be shown as a service dynamically embedded into the GUI (which have been named *Widgets-as-a-Service*, WaaS). This research uses web technologies to facilitate exchange and sharing of information, and also to allow users to cooperate and integrate data.

On the other hand, the components in most widgets-based GUI proposals are isolated from each other, that is, there is no relationship or communication between them. Those proposals that do not deal with isolated components have the difficulty of communication, especially in the web domain, as the communication between some elements may cause some security problems that must be taken into account and solved at design time when programming widgets and application [4]. In this sense, our approach certainly allows relationships and communication between widgets and it suggests an indirect communication mechanism by means of a service that mediates between their components.

As an application scenario for the web domain, this article focuses on widget-based web user interfaces that are being developed for the Environmental Information Network of Andalusia (REDIAM) as a transfer of the research results within the framework of ENIA project (http://acg.ual.es/enia), a project

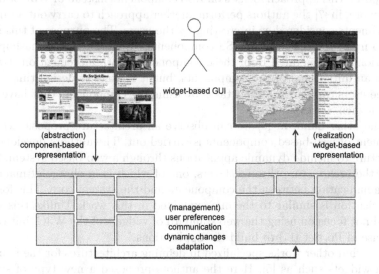

Fig. 1. Our view of widget-based GUI

of excellence funded by Junta de Andalucía (ref. TIC-6114). This project deals with geographic information and users should have a GUI that enables them to access to the multiple services available. For this, each user has access to a graphical interface that allows him/her to manage different widgets that offer certain services such as loading layers of geographic information on a map from OGC services (http://www.opengeospatial.org) provided by REDIAM. We also consider these widgets as services to which users can access.

The rest of the paper is organized as follows. Section 2 revises some related work. Section 3 describes the structure of the WaaS model for GUI, in which we analyze the various layers of the architecture developed and the data model to define the components. Section 4 shows a case study. Finally, Section 5 presents the conclusions and future work.

2   Related Work

Next we are going to revise some works focused on the development of *mashup* web applications, architecture systems that manage user interfaces built from components and also some works that study how to establish the communication between components.

In [1], the authors show a system that holds fast and intuitive development of mashup construction. This system is based on a mechanism of autocompletion of graphical user interfaces. The authors propose a method to link the components with each other in order to help the users to complete their workspace in the web application. These links help users to decide which components describe their application. Then, the user selects the components that are going to be loaded into the user interface when the application is deployed. In contrast to our proposal, this approach focuses on RSS components instead of W3C widgets. Furthermore, in [7] the authors perform another approach to carry out a ranking of components considered as interesting by the users. The purpose of this ranking is to make the selection of RSS components easier. Then, the mashup web applications are generated from these components. Both aforementioned works perform an initial load of the components, but it is done at design time. After that, the users can perform their tasks by using the components that have been loaded in their workspace.

On the other hand, in [6] we can observe an architecture proposal where a deployment of web-based components is carried out. The authors developed an architecture to include dynamic applications through a web-based system. They studied the architecture through layers, one of which is in charge of managing the communication between the components and the system core. This form of communication is similar to the one explained in this work. Unlike this work, they did not focus on using the web standard of widgets of the W3C, but rather on the use of Portlet [11] to build the applications.

We can find other works specialized in defining architectures for the management of widgets such as [5]. Here the authors proposed a new type of system for widget-based digital television platforms. They focused on widgets that are built with web technology rather than widgets that follow the web standard of the W3C. Unlike the means of communication described here, based on a JavaScript server, the authors used a mode of communication via AJAX to obtain the information stored in XML in a server. Another platform where we can use widget-based architectures is mobile applications. In [12] the authors defined an architecture made up of a widget component container that manages the interaction and a software platform that manages its dynamic life cycle. These widgets operated by the architecture are specific for the mobile platform which we are working with.

There exist other works like [13] which make adaptations of the code of the graphical user interface according to the user's preferences. The authors made the GUI more dynamic by developing it according to widget components. Unlike the widget components based on the web standard of the W3C used in this proposal, they implemented these components by making use of Java Swing. Moreover, they defined seven types of roles in order to improve the adaptation and reloading of widgets. Depending on the type of role, there are widgets considered as preferential to make their adaption.

3   WaaS-Based Architecture

In order to offer Widgets-as-a-Service (WaaS), we needed to develop an architectural system to support it. Furthermore, to isolate the proposal from the domain and to be able to manage component-based applications for different platforms, we built the system according to a three-layer architecture. Let us see some features of the layers of this architecture as well as the used data model.

3.1   Architecture Layers

The **client layer** is the upper layer of the architecture (see Figure 2). In our case, the client uses the services that the architecture deploys, coming from the "platform dependent" layer. In our example domain, the client is a web application, which means that this application has been developed under this technology and it must be accessed through a browser. Such application is built on the basis of components that, as it is web technology, have been implemented through widgets. The widgets in which the application has been developed, follow the recommendation of widget of the W3C. Moreover, the application is supported on the services that the architecture deploys to obtain the functionality it requires. By means of these services of the system architecture, the component-based web application can be initialized, receive support for the communication between components and give support to the components that form the application.

The **platform dependent layer** constitutes the intermediate layer of the system architecture. This layer deals with providing the client with the required services and interacting with the independent part of the platform (the bottom level), thus getting some services from it and providing it with others. Regarding the first services, (Figure 2-(a)) this layer gets the code necessary to create the start-up web application and consults the path to be followed by the information to communicate the components with each other. We achieved this by using web services implemented in the independent part of the platform (Figure 2-(b)). On the other hand, this layer provides the independent part of the platform with some information about the components it manages, such as the direction of the widgets instances which it will use to create the code defined by the web application. In these layers, we can find not only the web client that carries out the functions of the graphical user interface with the system, but also those servers that have been specifically developed to use our proposal within the domain of component-based web user interfaces (Figure 2-(c)).

On the other hand, the components managed by our architecture are black-box components, in which their behavior is hidden and the component is represented by a specification template. This specification describes both the functional part and the extra-functional part (as well as some additional information) of components and this is the only way through which the system can make use of them. Therefore, the only components managed by our system are those defined and built according to this specification, which have also been registered for use. In order our component specification to be valid for any type of components of third parties, we have extended the specification based on COTS (Commercial Off-The-Shelf) components [10]. Our components are called COTS-gets [9], this name comes from COTS and gadgets, being understood a gadget as a software artifact that encapsulates a certain functionality. For further details about the structure and content of the component specification used, please see http://acg.ual.es/definitions/component.xsd.

Furthermore, we developed the architecture of our system by using a **platform independent layer**. This layer has a server providing the system services that are valid for all platforms (Figure 2-(d)). For this, its functionalities are based only on the description of components and their relationships, regardless of the platform where they will be deployed. It is true that, at the deployment level, there are certain characteristics of each platform that should be taken into

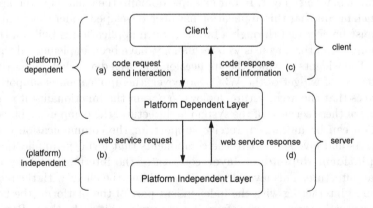

Fig. 2. WaaS-based Architecture Layers

account. For instance, the initialization of a web user interface architecture may be different from any other component-based architecture implemented in Java; or the invocation of methods between components, as part of a communication task, might be different as well. However, there is a common area, an abstract view of such behaviors that can independently be extracted and implemented from the platform. As regards the above examples, we referred to "component architecture initialization" or "communication management", respectively.

Therefore, the services offered in this layer are the same for all platforms, hiding the distinction between different platforms and allowing our proposal to be modular and scalable, and be able to gradually add new functionalities for new platforms supported by the system. As this server has the core of the proposal for the management of component-based architectures, it has been named as *COScore* (COTSget-based architecture Operating Support).

3.2 Component Data Model

Although this article is based on dynamic deployment of widgets in web user interfaces, our ultimate goal is that the system can be able to manage component-based architectures for different platforms. Moreover, another objective is that the components managed by the system should not be just those predefined by the proposal developers but some external developers and third-parties can also take part in the extension and update of repositories. For both reasons, we developed a three-level data model as shown in Figure 3 (described as follows).

The ECR (**External Component Repositories**) level corresponds to the external repositories of components, that is, the repositories of third-parties. These components are stored in their place of origin. This level is dependent on the platform because the components that it stores are specific for the mechanism they are assigned to. The ECR set is formed by each of the external repositories (ER) to be taken into account, that is, $ECR = \{ER_1, ER_2, \dots, ER_n\}$.

The next level MCR (**Managed Component Repositories**) has a set of repositories of components managed by the system. This level stores the components that meet the structure and the construction guidelines established. It is also dependent on the platform since it is formed by modified versions of the ECR components so that they can be managed by our system and by a set of components developed for the system (MR_0). Therefore, $MCR = \{MR_0, MR_1, MR_2, \dots, MR_n\}$, being MR_i $(i > 0)$ a subset of ER_i for which the components have been embedded with the information and behavior required. At the same time, each MR repository is formed by a set of components (C) and a set of components instances (CI) created and associated to such components. Each instance is created with a piece of information related to the user or client for whom the component was instantiated. This information contains, among other data, the instance identifier, the associated user and the component state. With this information, the system will be able to provide each user with the corresponding set of instances in the proper state.

Finally, the CS (**Component Specifications**) level stores component specifications. These specifications are referenced from the models that the

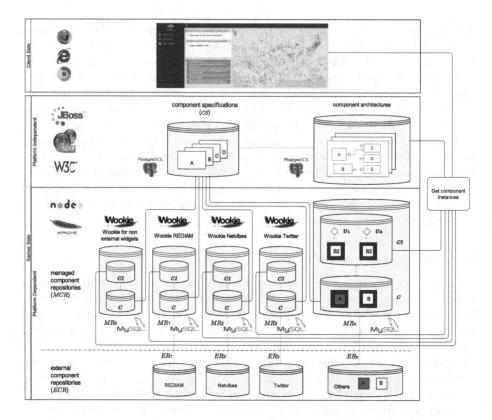

Fig. 3. Component Data Model for widget-based web user interfaces

component architectures describe so as to indicate which component should be chosen for its construction. When a developer registers one component in the system, he/she must register not only the component in the corresponding MR repository but its specification, too. That is the only way through which the system can take into account this component for future architecture construction and so that it can be embedded into a resulting component-based application. These specifications are managed by the platform independent server.

Our proposal is oriented to the deployment of services in the cloud. Therefore, this data model seems to be suitable for the use of cloud technologies, being able to transfer each layer to different servers or even deploy each repository in different servers. In this way, the components, the instances and even the specifications will be considered from the point of view of "resource-as-a-service" (RaaS). In this scenario, the level that is dependent on the platform corresponds to the domain of web applications and consequently the repositories managed by the system (MCR) store widgets. These widgets either have been specifically developed for the system (MR_0) or built from external repositories (ECR). In the second case, two different situations may occur: (a) that the external repositories store widgets, in which case we should create a *wrapper* upon the existing widget that can perform operations on it in order to be managed by our system; (b) or that the external repositories store a service that is not a widget, in which case we need to create a widget that uses the service concerned.

Figure 3 shows how the system can manage external widgets created from services of REDIAM (http://www.juntadeandalucia.es/medioambiente/site/rediam), Netvibes or Twitter (https://twitter.com/settings/widgets). In this way, the system has all the elements available to be able to manage the widgets as a service (Widgets-as-a-Service) and dynamically build the web GUIs.

4   Case Study

In this section, we present a case study in order to test the behavior and applicability of the work. This example scenario describes a web user interface that is dynamically constructed from components by applying the proposed architecture layers. The case study has been developed within a project of excellence funded by Junta de Andalucía (ref. TIC-6114), which deals with geographic information. For this purpose, we have built a web application which allows us to load visual layers with geographic information. These layers offer data obtained from an example set of OGC services provided by the REDIAM.

In this case, the OGC services and the rest of operations related to the management of geographic information, are encapsulated into widgets and therefore they are treated as Widget-as-a-Service (WaaS). By deploying these services, the application allows users to view and query geographic information about the soil under study within the project (see Figure 4). The application is made up of three widgets: a map that displays the visualization area and wherein the geographic information is loaded (Map); another widget that allows us to select which layers of geographic information will be loaded on the map (Options); and a legend

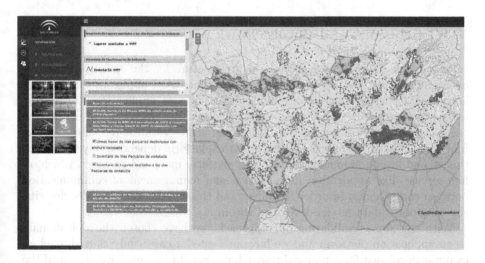

Fig. 4. Widget-based Web User Interface

where information about the layers loaded on the map is shown (Legend). This application is available at the address http://acg.ual.es/enia/uiexample.

Starting from this scenario, the web application behavior is defined as follows. When a user interacts with the system and accesses to the web address, the application is loaded into the browser. The web page that is accessed does not contain the code for the widgets statically, but the code is constructed dynamically and at run time. To execute this dynamic construction process, JavaScript (Node.js) server performs the role of mediator between the application and the COScore of the architecture. Then, the platform independent server decides which components are going to be loaded and returns the HTML code to Node.js. This code must be embedded in the web application, which contains the components that define the web user interface. Next, this code is sent to the web application, and the client is in charge of inserting the three widgets.

In the following steps, the user interacts with the widgets, and this interaction may involve either exchanging information between these components or notifying the system. In this communication process, the Node.js acts again as a mediator. This server receives the client interactions and invokes the web service of the platform independent layer that is in charge of solving the communication process. Then, within this service, the COScore server resolves the message content and the target widgets and sends the response to the JavaScript server. Finally, the Node.js server sends the message to the corresponding widgets of the user interface. As an example of communication, let us suppose that the user selects a layer in the Options widget. This interaction is sent from the widget to Node.js and the message contains information about the source and the selected layer. Then, Node.js invokes the web service of COScore obtaining as a response that this message must be routed to the Map and Legend widgets. Consequently, the first widget displays the layer into the map, and the second one adds some information about the selected layer to its content.

5   Conclusions and Future Work

In this article we present a three-layer architecture for the specification, storage, management and deployment of component-based applications. Our aim is to abstract the definition and manipulation of such applications to describe behaviors that can be valid in multiple platforms. Within this architecture, the client layer deploys the applications or communicates with the rest of the system functionalities through services offered by the platform dependent layer. In turn, this second layer communicates with the platform independent layer, which offers services like application initialization and management of communication between components. In order to understand this architecture, we also describe the component data model developed within it.

With the aim of validating our approach, we have chosen the web domain as an application platform and we have presented a case study that showed an example developed for a regional research project. In this way, we described the use of widgets as a service (Widget-as-a-Service, WaaS) to dynamically build component-based GUIs. As future work, we would like to increase the number of application scenarios and validate the proposed architecture in other platforms through practical examples,. We also aim to improve the user's experience when managing widget-based graphical user interfaces [2].

Acknowledgments. This work was funded by the EU ERDF and the Spanish Ministry of Economy and Competitiveness (MINECO) under Project TIN2013-41576-R, and the Spanish Ministry of Education, Culture and Sport (MECD) under a FPU grant (AP2010-3259), and the Andalusian Regional Government (Spain) under Project P10-TIC-6114.

References

1. Abiteboul, S., Greenshpan, O., Milo, T., Polyzotis, N.: Matchup: Autocompletion for mashups. In: IEEE 25th International Conference on Data Engineering, ICDE 2009, pp. 1479–1482. IEEE (2009)
2. Cechanowicz, J., Gutwin, C.: Augmented Interactions: A Framework for Adding Expressive Power to GUI Widgets. In: Gross, T., Gulliksen, J., Kotzé, P., Oestreicher, L., Palanque, P., Prates, R.O., Winckler, M. (eds.) INTERACT 2009. LNCS, vol. 5726, pp. 878–891. Springer, Heidelberg (2009)
3. Daniel, F., Matera, M., Yu, J., Benatallah, B., Saint-Paul, R., Casati, F.: Understanding UI Integration: A survey of problems, technologies, and opportunities. IEEE Internet Computing 11(3), 59–66 (2007)
4. De Keukelaere, F., Bhola, S., Steiner, M., Chari, S., Yoshihama, S.: SMash: secure component model for cross-domain mashups on unmodified browsers. In: 17th WWWW, pp. 535–544. ACM (2008)
5. Fan, K., Tang, S., Liu, Y., Zhang, S., Wang, Y., Xu, Z.: A System Architecture of Widget-Based Digital TV Interactive Platform. In: ICGEC, pp. 360–363. IEEE (2012)
6. Gmelch, O., Pernul, G.: A Generic Architecture for User-Centric Portlet Integration. In: 14th CEC, pp. 70–77. IEEE (2012)
7. Hassan, O., Al-Rousan, T., Taleb, A., Maaita, A.: An efficient and scalable ranking technique for mashups involving RSS data sources. Journal of Network and Computer Applications, pp, 179–190 (2013)
8. Hoyer, V., Fischer, M.: Market overview of enterprise mashup tools. In: Bouguettaya, A., Krueger, I., Margaria, T. (eds.) ICSOC 2008. LNCS, vol. 5364, pp. 708–721. Springer, Heidelberg (2008)
9. Iribarne, L., Criado, J., Padilla, N.: Using COTS-widgets architectures for describing user interfaces of web-based information systems. International Journal of Knowledge Society Research (IJKSR) 2(3), 61–72 (2011)
10. Iribarne, L., Troya, J.M., Vallecillo, A.: A trading service for COTS components. The Computer Journal 47(3), 342–357 (2004)
11. Law, E., Müller, D., Nguyen-Ngoc, A.: Differentiating and Defining Portlets and Widgets: A survey approach. In: MUPPLE 2009, pp. 123–131 (2009)
12. Pierre, D., Marc, D., Philippe, R.: Ubiquitous Widgets: Designing Interactions Architecture for Adaptive Mobile Applications. In: DCOSS 2013, pp. 331–336 (2013)
13. Shirogane, J., Iwata, H., Fukaya, K., Fukazawa, Y.: GUI Change Method according to Roles of Widgets and Change Patterns. IEICE Transactions on Information and Systems 91(4), 907–920 (2008)

Cultural Issues in Distributed Software Development: A Review

Alok Mishra[1] and Deepti Mishra[2]

[1] Department of Software Engineering, Atilim University, Incek, Ankara
[2] Department of Computer Engineering, Atilim University, Incek, Ankara
{alok,deepti}@atilim.edu.tr

Abstract. Cultural impact is significant in global or distributed software development. Due to cultural differences, co-ordination and collaboration problems have been reported in case studies and this also leads to low quality deliverables and high turnover in software industry. This paper presents a literature review of distributed software development (DSD) or global software development (GSD) and cultural issues. The main focus is to highlight the current research, observations, as well as practice directions in these areas. Many studies have been performed in culture and global software development, still impact of culture in distributed software development in different dimensions received less attention among researchers.

Keywords: Distributed Software Development, Culture, Global Software Development.

1 Introduction

Software development is a human centric and socio-technical activity. Complex interaction of values, attitudes, behavioral norms, beliefs, communication approaches by members of a project with vastly different values may give rise to misunderstanding and misinterpretation of intent that may result in conflict, mistrust, and underutilization of talents [1].

Globalization does not imply homogenity of cultures [2]. Given the nature of globalization, organizations need to develop high cross-cultural understanding, intercultural communication skills and intercultural management competencies. Management of global organizations that can take account of the cultural context of their endeavours experiences better success [3].

Global Software Development (GSD) is an approach in which software development is performed in spite of cultural, temporal and geographical boundaries [4]. Globalization of software projects has increased demographic and cultural diversity obstructing smooth team functioning [5]. Culture is termed as the centrifugal issue in global software development [6] and cultural diversity is often mentioned as a barrier within distributed teams [7].

R. Meersman et al. (Eds.): OTM 2014 Workshops, LNCS 8842, pp. 448–456, 2014.
© Springer-Verlag Berlin Heidelberg 2014

Project managers must recognize and understand the cultural needs of the global software team as culture may differ accordingly in terms of organizational, geographical, national, religion, gender and power distance [8]. Some organizations consider that their corporate socializing process is adequate to address the cultural issues which arise when managing a DSD team [9], however, where there are major differences between corporate and national culture norms, this socialization is generally not sufficient [10].

Socio-cultural factors can affect global teams and increase risks [11, 12]. Globally distributed global team projects carry additional exposure to risks which are associated with managing a culturally diverse global team [13]. Managing a global team has an additional risk if there is a lack of information among local team members concerning the culture of remote staff as identified by some eastern culture's revering of hierarchy [6, 13]. For instance, some cultures do not promote individual responsibility and accountability and some cultures accept most suggestions without much discussion [13]. In these situations, individual team members are often required to communicate and work with people whom they do not know and whose cultures they may not understand [14]. In some cultures where often the objective is to avoid conflict at all costs; to disagree may be considered impolite [13]. In some far eastern cultures requests and instructions are accepted without question if they come from a senior person [15]. Without implementing formal reporting structures, there is risk that the remote team may not report correctly, due to cultural differences and misunderstandings [9].

The paper is organized as follows. The next section presents some background information related with culture in GSD/DSD areas. Section 3 describes major studies describing the importance of cultural issues in DSD. Finally, section 4 concludes with observations and suggestions in this area.

2   Background on Culture and DSD

Culture has visible and invisible attributes [16] and is the learned values and behaviors shared by a group of people and play a vital role in how a person performs his or her work based on individual patterns of thinking, feeling, and acting. Hofstede's cultural dimensions [17], E.T. Hall's cultural factors [18, 19], Alfons Trompenaars and Charles Hampden-Turner [20] are some important cultural theories which help professionals to understand culture in different ways. Hofstede's cultural dimensions [17] help managers to identify individual and group behaviors in different countries while Trompenaars and Charles Hampden-Turner [20] have a contradicting approach towards Hofstede's cultural dimensions where they view culture as process and propose that 'culture is the way in which a group of people solve problems and reconcile dilemmas'.

One significant issue with international teams is the impact of culture from different perspectives of national, organizational and professional [21]. It has been observed that culture has got attention of SE community for some time [22] and most of the work is related with Hofstede's [17] work on dimensions of national cultures.

Recognition of the importance and impact of cultural differences between remote colleagues play a key role in the successful operation of virtual software teams [6, 13, 23, 24].

Deshpande et al. [25] carried out research in contribution of culture in global software development and explained how project managers are handling and adopting different techniques with demands of cultural differences in a geographically distributed software development environment. Casey [26] identified the implications of misunderstanding due to cultural differences between Irish and Malaysian distributed software development teams which resulted in serious implications for the success of the projects concerned. He concluded that cultural differences should be leveraged and not exploited for short term gain at long term cost keeping in view that cultural distance is very important factor for successful implementation of a globally distributed software development strategy. Shah et al. [27] study also observed that cultural differences influence the perception of productivity for the client and vendor teams and create unproductive-productivity experiences among vendor teams. Casey reports on the "always say yes" behavior of some cultures [28]. Winkler et al. [29] discussed regarding rigid hierarchies in Indian organizations that result from the power distance in the Indian culture.

According to Abufardeh and Magel [30], most of the attention has turned towards understanding the impact of culture on the global software development process and little research addresses the impact of the cultural and linguistic aspects of global software globally developed. There is a need for more research to address the impact of cultural and linguistic aspects of global software globally developed.

3   Major Studies in Cultural Issues in DSD

Cultural diversity seems to be significant issue in GSD and research carried out to date has raised concerns over how to manage cultural differences in GSD [25]. As every person has a different context, this may lead to misunderstandings. Understanding the impact of culture on the GSD enable multinational development teams to communicate and operate successfully and multilingual and multicultural aspects are very critical to the success of GSD [30]. Major relevant studies displaying various challenges due to cultural diversity in GSD are shown in table 1.

Table 1. Major relevant papers in various challenges due to culture in GSD/DSD

Challenges due to Cultural diversity in GSD	Major Relevant Studies
Communication, Coordination & Collaboration	[9, 30, 33, 34, 35, 36, 37, 38]
Requirements Engineering	[22, 34, 45, 48, 49, 50, 51]
Knowledge Transfer/Management	[21, 34, 48, 51, 53, 54, 55, 56]

3.1 Communication, Coordination and Collaboration Challenges due to Cultural Differences

Damian et al. [31] reported that communication and coordination in GSD/DSD become more complex, because traditional face-to-face meetings are not the rule in distributed projects. Team members from different countries interact by using their cultural knowledge and communication styles [32]. Hsieh [22] argued that different cultures often have drastically different values, beliefs, and approaches to communication and problem solving. In the context of a GSD, these differences may lead to miscommunication.

Language barriers are one outcome of cultural differences as due to lack of cultural understanding, it influences in understanding communication and this lead to conflicting approaches for problem solving [33, 34]. Monasor et al. [35] provided a list of cultural and linguistic problems. Cultural tolerance and compassion between the project leader and the team prove to be a basic condition for the communicative openness required [36]. Linguistic distance limits the ability for coherent communication to take place [37] and can impact on the development of trust among teams [38]. Thus, managing virtual teams whose members are geographically and linguistically disperesed is seen as a daunting task [39] due to numerous constraints involved [40]. Abufardeh and Magel [30] recommended that multilingual and multicultural aspects are very critical to success of global software as these aspects affect directly the quality of the software, as well as GSD itself.

The operation of virtual teams requires a level of cooperation and coordination that cannot ignore the impact cultural distance plays and the barriers and misundestandings it can create [41, 42]. Coordination in large distributed software development projects is greatly affected by human and behavioural factors, relying on developers having a shared understanding since developers from different cultures have disparate problem-solving and communication processes [22]. Cultural compatibility is one of an important factor in determining the success of collaboration in international software development teams [26].

Richardson et al. [9] mentioned in their case study of one DSD project that cultural differences came to a head and team relationships and trust broke down, also instead of cooperating, team members actively sought to undermine and hinder each other which created problem in communication and cooperation. They further argued in another case study that cultural differences were misunderstood and helped to reinforce mistrust and fear. The reason was that remote colleagues were slow to communicate, using distance strategically to minimize information flow, which further impede the development of cooperation and very little knowledge transfer took place and eventually the projects failed.

3.2 Requirements Problems due to Cultural Diversity

One of the biggest challenges of global or distributed software development is to communicate the requirements correctly within the geographically distributed development team while distributed projects have an additional burden of language, team-building challenges and cultural barriers [43]. The risk of miscommunicated requirements becomes smaller if an organization has a living inquiry culture [43]. Developing a shared mental model in teams is not an easy task [44]. In globally distributed projects, the challenge is even more pronounced because geographical, temporal, organizational, and cultural boundaries make it difficult for the requirements engineers and developers to foster a consistent understanding of the system requirements along with common orientation to issues such as development methodology, schedules, and goals [45]. According to Hsieh [22], one factor that potentially has a significant impact on the development of a shared mental model in the distributed team is cultural diversity.

Understanding of requirements specification is a major challenge in DSD projects specifically during knowledge transfer from provider to receivers [34]. Knowledge management facilitates in requirements organization which is foundation of quality. Ensuring quality issues in GSD/DSD projects is a significant issue [46, 47]. Oshri et al. [48] also supported that challenge in DSD is to transfer knowledge about customer requirements from onsite to offshore team. Developers from different cultures may also have disparate interpretations of requirements [49] and ways to perform requirements engineering. Wiener and Stephan [50] also supported that in DSD, misunderstandings in requirements easily arise and it is required that sufficient understanding of specifications is reached on the vendor side before technical specification of the system begins. According to Salger et al. [51], customer reviews of requirements specification might be weak in DSD and team have difficulty in evaluating whether a SRS (Software Requirements Specifications) is correct.

3.3   Knowledge Management with Cultural Diversity

The knowledge-intensive nature of global software development efforts poses interesting challenges for organizations [52]. The existence of social ties has been shown to improve knowledge transfer and communication in general [53]. In an intercultural situation, the concepts of collective knowledge and mind as well as their manifestations in interrelations of practices, are complicated. Research in cultural studies suggests that intercultural factors may have a significant impact on how group knowing and mind are developed [22]. Building a common culture in DSD is a big challenge in knowledge transfer [54]. Dibbern et al. [55] found that there were extra costs involved in knowledge transfer due to cultural distances as offshore team required enhanced support during knowledge transfer due to their different learning approaches and strict following to specific documentation standards.

According to Boden et al. [21], the impact of culture on knowledge management in international teams is an important topic which is still not well understood. They further that argued the influences of national culture and site-specific organizational culture are subtle and not easy to separate from other factors. Based on their experiences, it has been recommended that in order to achieve an accurate understanding of knowledge sharing practices in globally distributed software development, these need to be studied in context, longitudinally, and from both the onshore and offshore perspectives. Boden et al. [21] further argued there are few studies [22, 25, 26, 35, 56] dealing with the issue of culture in regard to knowledge sharing work parctices in global software development. For researchers, it is also important to think of what kind of knowledge management activities an organization should engage in should be determined by how the organizations develop GSD [57].

4   Conclusions

The basis of this short paper is to present a snapshot on culture and GSD/DSD research. Cultural diversity is difficult and complex issue but it is an imminent aspect of GSD. There are very few empirical studies on comparative discussion of different countries' culture and GSD/DSD. Manager and senior management should take into account the existing cultural diversity between different distributed software development sites and formulate concrete strategies to handle potential impact of cultural differences on distributed software development. Researchers have also recommended the requirement for the provision of cultural training in related software development locations and suggested that if cultural differences are not taken into consideration, it can have serious implications for the successful implementation of a GSD strategy in such kind of organization.

References

1. Ozawa, H., Zhang, L.: Adapting Agile Methodology to Overcome Social Differences in Project Members. In: Agile Conference (AGILE), pp. 82–87 (2013)
2. Walsham, G.: Making a world of difference: It in a global context. Wiley, Chichester (2001)
3. Siakas, K.V., Balstrup, B.: Software outsourcing quality achieved by global virtual collaboration. Softw. Process: Improve. Pract. 11, 319–328 (2006), doi:10.1002/spip.275
4. Paasivaara, M., Durasiewicz, S., Lassenius, C.: Distributed Agile Development: Using Scrum in a Large Project. In: IEEE International Conference on Global Software Engineering, ICGSE 2008, August 17-20, pp. 87–95 (2008)
5. Beise, C.M.: IT project management and virtual teams. In: Proceedings of the 2004 SIGMIS Conference on Computer Personnel research: Careers, Culture, and Ethics in a Networked Environment (SIGMIS CPR 2004), pp. 129–133. ACM, New York (2004)
6. Carmel, E.: Global Software Teams: Collaborating Across Borders and Time Zones. Prentice Hall PTR, Upper Saddle River (1999)
7. Baugher, D., Varanelli, A., Weisbord, E.: Gender And Culture Diversity Occurring In Sellformed Work Groups. Journal of Managerial Issues 12(4), 391–407 (2000)
8. Casey, V., Deshpande, S., Richardson, I.: Outsourcing Software Development The Remote Project Manager's Perspective. In: Second Information Systems Workshop on Global Sourcing, Services, Knowledge and Innovation, Vald'Isére, France (2008)
9. Richardson, I., Casey, V., Mccaffery, F., Burton, J., Beecham, S.: A Process Framework for Global Software Engineering Teams. Inf. Softw. Technol. 54(11), 1175–1191 (2012)
10. Casey, V., Richardson, I.: Uncovering the reality within virtual software teams. In: First International Workshop on Global Software Development for the Practitioner, ICSE 2006, China, vol. 2006. ACM Press, Shanghai (2006)

11. Nurmi, N., Bosch-Sijtsema, P., Sivunen, A., Fruchter, R.: Who shouts louder?: exerting power across distance and culture. In: Proceedings of the 2009 International Workshop on Intercultural Collaboration. ACM, Palo Alto (2009)

12. Persson, J.S., Mathiassen, L., Boeg, J., Madsen, T.S., Steinson, F.: Managing risks in distributed software projects: an integrative framework. IEEE Transactions on Engineering Management 56(3), 508–532 (2009)

13. Karolak, D.W.: Global Software Development: Managing Virtual Teams and Environments. IEEE Computer Society Press, Los Alamitos (1999)

14. Jablokow, K., Myers, M.: Managing cognitive and cultural diversity in global IT teams. In: 5th IEEE International Conference on Global Software Engineering (ICGSE) (2010)

15. Casey, V.: Imparting the importance of culture to global software development. ACM Inroads, Special Issue on Global Intercultural Collaboration 1(3), 51–57 (2010)

16. MacGregor, E., Hsieh, Y., Kruchten, P.: The impact of intercultural factors on global software development. In: Canadian Conference on Electrical and Computer Engineering 2005, pp. 920–926 (2005)

17. Hofstede, G.: Culture's Consequences, Comparing Values, Behaviors, Institutions, and Organizations Across Nations. Sage Publications, Thousand Oaks (2001)

18. Hall, E.: Beyond culture, 2nd edn. Anchor Book (1997) (originally published in 1977)

19. Hall, E.: The hidden dimension, 2nd edn. Anchor Books (1990) (originally published in 1966)

20. Hampden-Turner, C., Trompenaars, F.: Response to Geert Hofstede. International Journal of Intercultural Relations 21(1), 149–159 (1997)

21. Boden, A., Avram, G., Bannon, L., Wulf, V.: Knowledge sharing practices and the impact of cultural factors: reflections on two case studies of offshoring in SME. J. Softw. Evol. and Proc. 24, 139–152 (2012)

22. Hsieh, Y.: Culture and shared understanding in distributed requirements engineering. In: Proceedings IEEE International Conference on Global Software Engineering, pp. 101–108. IEEE Computer Society Press, Silver Spring MD (2006)

23. Rutkowski, A.F., Vogel, D.R., Van Genuchten, M., Bemelmans, T.M.A., Favier, M.: Ecollaboration:The Reality of Virtuality. IEEE Transactions on Professional Communication 45(4), 219–230 (2002)

24. Casey, V., Richardson, I.: Practical Experience of Virtual Team Software Development. In: Euro SPI 2004 European Software Process Improvement, Trondheim, Norway (2004)

25. Deshpande, S., Richardson, I., Casey, V., Beecham, S.: Culture in Global Software Development - A Weakness or Strength? In: Proceedings of the 2010 5th IEEE International Conference on Global Software Engineering (ICGSE 2010), pp. 67–76. IEEE Computer Society, Washington, DC (2010)

26. Casey, V.: Leveraging or exploiting cultural difference? In: Fourth IEEE International Conference on Global Software Engineering, ICGSE 2009, pp. 8–17 (2009)

27. Shah, H., Harrold, M.J., Sinha, S.: Global software testing under deadline pressure: Vendor-side experiences. Inf. Softw. Technol. 56(1), 6–19 (2014)

28. Casey, V.: Software Testing and Global Industry: Future Paradigms. Cambridge Scholars Publishing, United Kingdom (2009)

29. Winkler, J., Dibbern, J., Heinzel, A.: The impact of cultural differences on outsourced offshoring. Information System Frontiers 10(2008), 243–258 (2008)

30. Abufardeh, S., Magel, K.: The impact of global software cultural and linguistic aspects on Global Software Development process (GSD): Issues and challenges. In: 2010 4th International Conference on New Trends in Information Science and Service Science (NISS), pp. 133–138 (2010)

31. Damian, D., Hadwin, A., Al-Ani, B.: Instructional design and assessment strategies for teaching global software development: a framework. In: Proceedings of the 28th International Conference on Software Engineering, pp. 685–690. ACM, Shanghai (2006)
32. Endrass, B., André, E., Huang, L., Gratch, J.: A data-driven approach to model culture-specific communication management styles for virtual agents. In: Proceedings of the 9th International Conference on Autonomous Agents and Multiagent Systems, Toronto, Canada. International Foundation for Autonomous Agents and Multiagent Systems, pp. 99–108 (2010)
33. Noll, J., Beecham, S., Richardson, I.: Global software development and collaboration: barriers and solutions. ACM SIGCSE Bulletin – Special Section on Global Intercultural Collaboration (September 2010)
34. Nidhra, S., Yanamadala, M., Afzal, W., Torkar, R.: Knowledge transfer challenges and mitigation strategies in global software development – A systematic literature review and industrial validation. International Journal of Information Management 33(2), 333–355 (2013)
35. Monasor, M.J., Vizcaíno, A., Piattini, M.: Cultural and linguistic problems in GSD: a simulator to train engineers in these issues. J. Softw. Evol. and Proc. 24, 707–717 (2012)
36. Boutellier, R., Gassmann, O., Macho, H., Roux, M.: Management of dispersed product development teams: the role of information technologies. R&D Management 28, 13–25 (1998)
37. Jensen, M., Menon, S., Mangset, L.E., Dalberg, V.: Managing Offshore Outsourcing of Knowledge-intensive Projects – A People Centric Approach. International Conference on Global Software Engineering (ICGSE 2007), Munich (2007)
38. Pauleen, D.J., Yoong, P.: Relationship building and the use of ICT in boundary-crossing virtual teams: A facilitator's perspective. Journal of Information Technology 16(4), 205–220 (2001)
39. Ebert, C., De Neve, P.: Surviving global software development. IEEE Software 18(2), 62–69 (2001)
40. Chudoba, K.M., Wynn, E., Lu, M., Watson-Manheim, M.B.: How virtual are we? Measuring virtuality in a global organization. Information Systems Journal 15(4), 279–306 (2005)
41. Herbsleb, J.D., Moitra, D.: Global Software Development. IEEE Software 18(2), 16–20 (2001)
42. Herbsleb, J.D., Mockus, A., Finholt, T.A., Ginter, V.: Distance, Dependencies and Delay in Global Collaboration. In: Proceedings of the 2000 ACM Conference on Computer Supported Cooperative Work 2000. ACM Press, Philadelphia (2000)
43. Mikulovic, V., Heiss, M., Herbsleb, J.D.: Practices and Supporting Structures for Mature Inquiry Culture in Distributed Software Development Projects. In: International Conference on Global Software Engineering, ICGSE 2006, vol. 246, pp. 245–246 (2006)
44. Levesque, L.L., Wilson, J.M., Wholey, D.R.: Cognitive Divergence and Shared Mental Models in Software Development Project Teams. Journal of Organizational Behavior 22, 135–144 (2001)
45. Orlikowski, W.J.: Knowing in Practice: Enacting a Collective Capability in Distributed Organizing. Organization Science 13, 249–273 (2002)
46. Mishra, D., Mishra, A.: A Global Software Inspection Process For Distributed Software Development. Journal of Universal Computer Science 18(19), 2731–2746 (2012)
47. Mishra, D., Mishra, A.: A software inspection process for globally distributed teams. In: Meersman, R., Dillon, T., Herrero, P. (eds.) OTM 2010. LNCS, vol. 6428, pp. 289–296. Springer, Heidelberg (2010)

48. Oshri, I., Van Fenema, P., Kotlarsky, J.: Knowledge transfer in globally distributed teams: the role of transactive memory. Information Systems Journal 18, 593–616 (2008)
49. Thanasankit, T., Corbitt, B.: Thai Culture and Communication of Decision Making Processes in Requirements Engineering. Proceedings of Cultural Attitudes towards Technology and Communication, 217–242 (2000)
50. Wiener, M., Stephan, R.: Reverse Presentations - A Client-Driven Method for Requirements Engineering in Offshore Software Development. Business & Information Systems Engineering 2(3), 141–153 (2010)
51. Salger, F., Sauer, S., Engels, G., Baumann, A.: Knowledge transfer in global software development—Leveraging ontologies, tools and assessments. In: Proceedings of the 5th IEEE International Conference on Global Software Engineering (ICGSE 2010), pp. 336–341. IEEE Computer Society (2010)
52. Mishra, D., Mishra, A.: Distributed Information System Development: Review of Some Management Issues. In: Meersman, R., Herrero, P., Dillon, T. (eds.) OTM 2009 Workshops. LNCS, vol. 5872, pp. 282–291. Springer, Heidelberg (2009)
53. Kotlarsky, J., Oshri, I.: Social ties, knowledge sharing and successful collaboration in globally distributed system development projects. Eur. J. Inf. Syst. 14(1), 37–48 (2005)
54. Chen, J., Sun, P.Y.T., McQueen, R.J.: The impact of national cultures on structured knowledge transfer. Journal of Knowledge Management 14(2), 228–242 (2010)
55. Dibbern, J., Winkler, J., Heinzl, A.: Explaining Variations in Client Extra Costs between Software Projects Offshored to India. MIS Quarterly 32(2), 333–366 (2008)
56. Desouza, K.C., Awazu, Y., Baloh, P.: Managing knowledge in global software development efforts: Issues and practices. IEEE Software 23, 30–37 (2006)
57. Mishra, D., Mishra, A.: Research Trends in Management Issues of Global Software Development: Evaluating the Past to Envision the Future. Journal of Global Information Technology Management 14(4), 48–69 (2011)

An Empirical Study of the Dynamics of GitHub Repository and Its Impact on Distributed Software Development

Liguo Yu[1], Alok Mishra[2], and Deepti Mishra[2]

[1] Computer Science and Informatics, Indiana University South Bend, South Bend, IN, USA
ligyu@iusb.edu
[2] Department of Computer & Software Engineering, Atilim University, Incek, Ankara, Turkey
{alok,deepti}@atilim.edu.tr

Abstract. GitHub is a distributed code repository and project hosting web site. It is becoming one of the most popular web-based services to host both open-source projects and closed-source projects. In this paper, we review different kinds of version control systems and study the dynamics of GitHub, i.e., the ability and scalability of GitHub to process different requests and provide different services to different GitHub projects and GitHub users. Our study shows that GitHub could handle hundreds of thousands of requests a day for all the projects and thousands of requests for one project. This capability of GitHub makes it suitable for supporting distributed software development.

Keywords: distributed software development, distributed version control system, Git, GitHub, web-based code storage, empirical study.

1 Introduction

Distributed software development is becoming an increasingly major trend for software industry. This can be seen in both open-source communities and for-profit software companies. On one side, most open-source projects are web based. Participants all around the world can make contributions to the project. Therefore, these projects are largely following the scheme of distributed development. Such examples include Linux kernel [1], Apache http server [2], and R [3]. On the other side, many software companies have oversea research and development sites. Accordingly, many of their products are developed globally. For example, Microsoft has research labs in Redmond (WA), Cambridge (UK), Beijing (China), Mountain View (CA), Munich (Germany), Bangalore (India), Santa Barbara (US), Cairo (Egypt), Cambridge (MA), New York City (NY), and Herzelia (Israel) [4]. Microsoft's products, such as Windows 7 are the result of globalized software development efforts [5].

Software version control and configuration management are important tasks in software development process. Version control and configuration management are even more complicated in a distributed development environment, because under this development scheme, an artifact could be forked and changed by many developers

R. Meersman et al. (Eds.): OTM 2014 Workshops, LNCS 8842, pp. 457–466, 2014.
© Springer-Verlag Berlin Heidelberg 2014

anytime and anywhere around the world. Without an appropriate version control system, it will be hard to manage so many different versions and so many different changes performed by so many different programmers from so many different locations.

GitHub, a web-based distributed revision control and source code management system, is launched in 2008. It is based on Git technology to manage versions of source code for distributed clients. According to GitHub.com [6], currently GitHub hosts 14 million repositories, which is the largest in the world.

In this paper, we discuss the features of GitHub and study its dynamic behavior. We analyze how GitHub and its similar technology could affect distributed software development. The data used in this paper is retrieved through GitHub Repository Statistics API.

The remaining of this paper is organized as follows. In Section 2, we briefly review the history of version control systems and code host hosting systems. In Section 3, we describe GitHub. In Section 4, we present our empirical study on the dynamics of GitHub and analyze the impact of GitHub on software industry, especially distributed software development. Our conclusions are in Section 5.

2   Review of Version Control Systems and Code Hosting Services

Version control or revision control is an important management activity in software development process. It helps programmers to manage changes to source code, documents, testing cases, or any other artifacts. Without version control system, the entire software development will be chaotic, which means unmanageable and unpredictable. Therefore, version control systems are clearly needed for modern software development that faces the increasing complexity of software process.

Whenever we talk about the evolution of version control system, we have to mention three milestones in its history: CVS, Subversion, and Git.

CVS [7] stands for Concurrent Versioning System, which is a client-server based system. This means on CVS, the server stores different versions of the source code and the client can check out an existing version and check in with a new version. CVS was first released in 1990 and the latest release was in 2008. While it might still be used widely, it is no longer under active development. Although CVS is no longer popular, its basic idea of version control is the foundation of many other advanced version control systems.

Subversion [8] has been the largest version control system used world-wide. For example, Apache, Ruby, Python, and many other open source projects use Subversion to manage their source code. The first version of Subversion was released in 2000 and it is currently part of the Apache project and under active development and maintenance. Similar to CVS, Subversion also has a client-server structure. However, it also has many advantages, such as supporting of binary file format and atomic commit. Subversion is good for any traditional centralized software development. However, its client server is structure is not scalable to support the increasing demand of distributed software development.

Git [9] is a distributed version control and code management system. It was first released in 2005 for Linux kernel development. The most important feature of Git is that it supports distributed development. Because there is no necessary to have a centralized code base and different clients could hold different parts of the code, Git supports rapid branching and merging, as often seen in distributed development. Now, Git has become the most widely used version control system in software industry [10].

Code hosting refers to storing source code in a web-based repository so that the clients can access it anywhere and anytime. Examples of code hosting include Google Code [11] and SourceForge [12], where SourceForge had been the largest web-based code repository based on both the number of users it had and the number of projects its hosted. However, most code hosting services, including Google Code and Source-Forge are designed majorly for code hosting; they are not good at supporting version control and configuration management. Most developers consider them as network drives instead of development tools, because they just could not easily provide the necessary services of a version control tools, such as branching and merging.

3   GitHub

GitHub is both a web-based version control system and a web-based code repository. On one side, GitHub implements the concept of Git technology, so it is a distributed version control system. This means GitHub supports distributed software development through regular web access, which makes it more popular than other competitors, such Mercurial [13]. On the other side, GitHub is a code repository, and because it supports development activities such as frequent branching and merging, it is not just a code repository targeting end users. Instead it is a dynamic repository for distributed developers. That is why GitHub has surpassed SourceForge and Google Code and become the largest web-based code repository for both open-source projects and commercial projects. Table 1 lists the 10 most popular code-hosting web sites [14].

Table 1. Top 10 popular code-hosting web sites [14]

Name	Number of Users	Number of Projects
GitHub	5,200,000	10,900,000
SourceForge	3,400,000+	324,000
Google Code	Unknown	250,000+
Bitbucket	1,000,000	93,661
Assembla	800,000+	60,000+
CodePlex	151,782	36,472
Gitorious	Unknown	33,750
Launchpad	2,145,028	32,699
BerliOS	52,811	4,863
GNU Savannah	57,591	3,487

To summarize, GitHub can be viewed as combining and utilizing two successful technologies, distributed version control and web-based hosting and it has done better than its predecessors, such as Subversion and SourceForge [15]. Figure 1 illustrates the emergence of GitHub as the evolution of version control systems and code-hosting systems. Since GitHub seems to be the most popular and robust repository as well as it has the data interface the authors selected it for this empirical study.

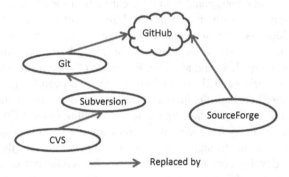

Fig. 1. The emergence of GitHub

4   Empirical Study

To understand the capability of GitHub, we study the events happened in GitHub by day, month, and on the most active projects. Again, we want to mention that the data used in this study was retrieved from data was retrieved from GitHub Repository Statistics API.

4.1   Events in a Day

As a version control system, GitHub needs to process various requests from users. These events could be a PushEvent that pushes the local changes up to the server repository, or it could be a CreateEvent that creates a new artifact in the server. Table 2 shows the total events happened to GitHub in September 10, 2013, which is a regular workday and picked by the authors randomly. It can be seen that these events are common version control operations. It should also be noted that these events are related to all the projects hosted in GitHub and the requests could be submitted by any user.

We can see that in a regular workday, GitHub needs to process over two hundred fifty thousands of requests. With the growing number of projects and growing number of users, the number of requests processed by GitHub is expected to double or triple in the next several years. To meet the increasing demand from more and more users, GitHub has refined its structure to reduce the response time [15]. For example, three protocols are used by GitHub clients to connect to the servers: HTTP for web browsing; SSH for cloning, pulling from, or pushing in a private repository; Git for cloning, pulling from, or pushing in a public repository [16]. The reason that three different protocols are used is that they have different response times. For example, SSH requests are relative slow to process; they are used only if necessary.

Table 2. Total events happened to GitHub in September 10, 2013

Event Type	Number of Events
PushEvent	127,150
CreateEvent	32,650
IssueCommentEvent	22,603
WatchEvent	21,762
IssuesEvent	12,904
PullRequestEvent	10,313
ForkEvent	9,563
FollowEvent	5,259
GollumEvent	4,131
GistEvent	3,507
PullRequestReviewCommentEvent	2,736
DeleteEvent	2,682
CommitCommentEvent	2,366
MemberEvent	1,340
ReleaseEvent	453
PublicEvent	214
Total	**259,633**

PushEvent and CreateEvent are two most popular events. As can be seen from Table 2, there are 127,150 PushEvents and 32,650 CreateEvents in September 10, 2013. Table 3 shows the top 10 projects (repositories) with the most number of PushEvents. Table 4 shows the top 10 projects (repositories) with the most number of CreateEvents.

Table 3. Top 10 repositories with the most number of PushEvents on September 10, 2013

Repository Name	Repository Language	Number of Pushes
mirror	null	1425
omgzorz	null	1327
boost	Shell	967
dotfiles	VimL	506
dotfiles	Shell	383
irc-logs	Shell	341
bind	C++	271
sample_app	Ruby	236
gaia	JavaScript	235
unordered	C++	234

From Table 3 and Table 4 we can see that any workday could be a really busy day for GitHub. Consider one repository, *spark* in Table 4, it has over two thousands requests in a day. These requests are unlikely came from a single user. They must come from many users. Therefore, we can see that GitHub is capable of supporting distributed version control with massive requests.

Table 4. Top 10 repositories with the most number of CreateEvents on September 10, 2013

Repository Name	Repository Language	Number of Creates
spark	Scala	2495
hive	Java	932
shark	Scala	757
test	null	243
PullRequestTest	null	147
gospel-library	null	121
liferay-portal	Java	87
demo_app	null	83
Test	null	81
Hello-World	null	68

4.2   The Growing Trend of GitHub

To see the growing dynamics of GitHub, we study the growing number of PushEvents and CreateEvents by month (from September 2012 to August 2013), which are shown in Figure 2 and Figure 3, respectively. In one year period, the number of PushEvents increased about 33% and the number of CreateEvents increased about 29%. With the double digit percentage of growing rate, we can expect GitHub to handle more and more events in the next several years.

Software development activities are correlated, which means if there are more events of one activity, there could be more events of other activities. To see this effect on GitHub, we study the correlation between number of PushEvents and number of CreateEvents monthly in GitHub. Table 5 shows the results of Pearson test, Spearman's rank test, and Kendall's tau-b test. All three tests demonstrate that the number of PushEvents and the number of CreateEvents are strongly correlated at or above the 0.001 significance level. This tells us that GitHub should be designed and configured to process the sudden surge of all different requests, because these events are likely to happen in the same period.

Table 5. The correlation between monthly number of PushEvents and monthly number of CreateEvents (September 2012 to August 2013)

Test Name	Correlation Coefficient	Significance
Pearson	0.967	<0.001
Spearman	0.916	<0.001
Kendall's tau-b	0.758	0.001
Dataset: 10 Test of significance: two-tailed		

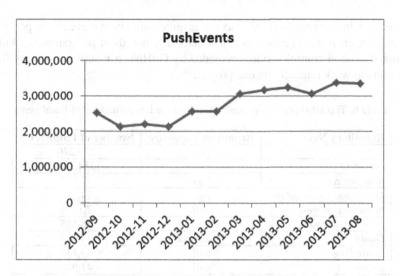

Fig. 2. The growing trend of PushEvents in GitHub by month

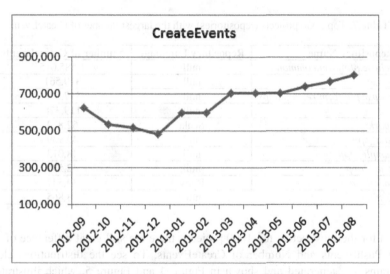

Fig. 3. The growing trend of CreatesEvents in GitHub by month

4.3 The Most Active Projects

Table 6 shows the top 10 projects that have the largest number of PushEvents during the period of April 2012 to September 2013. Table 7 shows the top 10 projects that have the largest number of CreateEvents during the period of April 2012 to September 2013. We can see that in about 18 months, there could be near three hundred thousand PushEvents in one project (repository), and there could be over one million

CreateEvents in one project (repository). It is quite unlikely that events are performed by a single user. It must be the work of dozens or hundreds of programmers. Without distributed version control services provided by GitHub, it would not be easy for so many users to work remotely on one project.

Table 6. Top 1000 projects (repositories) with the largest number of PushEvents

Repository Name	Repository Language	Number of PushEvents
websites	Perl	289,276
euro2012	null	154,224
llvm-project	C++	77,182
llvm-project-submodule	null	74,587
bcom-homepage-archive	null	7,1795
yhadoop-common	Java	46,543
Guido	JavaScript	44,963
ci-tracking	null	43,136
mirror	null	41,926
mozilla-central	C++	38,517

Table 7. Top 1000 projects (repositories) with the largest number of CreateEvents

Repository Name	Repository Language	Number of CreateEvents
eclipse.platform.common	null	1,585,015
try_git	null	319,561
eclipse.platform.releng.maps	null	317,508
test	null	119,328
spark	Scala	62,832
first_app	null	49,939
sample_app	null	48,013
demo_app	null	42,581
sample_app	Ruby	39,547
dotfiles	null	33,865

Even for the most active top 1000 projects, there are still great difference of number of PushEvents and Number of CreateEvents. To see the distributions clearly, histograms are generated and shown in Figure 4 and Figure 5, which illustrate the distributions of top 1000 to top 11 projects with the largest number of PushEvents and CreateEvents, respectively. From Figure 4 and Figure 5, we can see that number of events happened to different projects is uneven: most projects have small number of events and a few projects have large number of events. This challenging feature of project hosting requires GitHub to be scalable enough to handle request from projects that are least active and projects that are most active in an efficient way. In other words, GitHub must be flexible enough to handle different loads of requests from different projects submitted by different users in any locations.

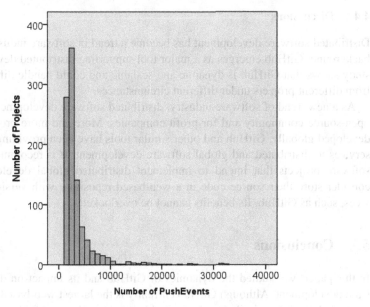

Fig. 4. The distribution of number of projects with respect to number of PushEvents in 18 months

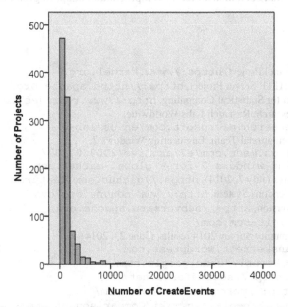

Fig. 5. The distribution of number of projects with respect to number of CreateEvents in 18 months

4.4   Discussions

Distributed software development has become a trend in software industry. Under this background, GitHub emerges as a major tool supporting distributed development. Our study shows that GitHub is dynamic and scalable and could handle different requests from different projects under different circumstances.

As a new trend of software industry, distributed software development attracts both open-source community and for-profit companies. More and more projects are being developed globally. GitHub and other similar tools have been providing the backbone services to distributed and global software development. It is recommended that any software projects that intend to implement distributed global development should consider store their source code in a web-based repository with version control services, such as GitHub. Its benefits cannot be overlooked.

5   Conclusions

In this paper, we studied the dynamics of GitHub and its impact on distributed software development. Although GitHub currently is the largest web-based code repository, we believe other similar products could emerge in the near future. In any sense, a web-based version control tool is surely needed for any open-source projects or commercial projects that seek distributed development and adapt to globalization.

References

1. The Linux Kernel Project, https://www.kernel.org/
2. The Apache HTTP Server Project, https://httpd.apache.org/
3. The R Project for Statistical Computing, http://www.r-project.org/
4. Microsoft Research: Research Labs Worldwide,
   http://research.microsoft.com/en-us/labs/
5. Windows International Team. Engineering Windows 7,
   http://blogs.msdn.com/e7/archive/2009/07/07/
   engineering-windows-7-for-a-global-market.aspx
6. GitHub features (July 7, 2014), https://github.com/features
7. Concurrent Versions System, http://www.nongnu.org/cvs/
8. Apache Subversion, http://subversion.apache.org/
9. Git, http://git-scm.com/
10. Eclipse Community Survey 2014 results, (June 23, 2014)
    http://Ianskerrett.wordpress.com
11. Google Code, https://code.google.com/
12. SourceForge, http://sourceforge.net/
13. Mercurial, http://mercurial.selenic.com/
14. http://en.wikipedia.org/wiki/Comparison_of_open-
    source_software_hosting_facilities
15. Finley, K.: GitHub has surpassed SourceForge and Google Code in popularity,
    http://readwrite.com/2011/06/02/github-has-passed-
    sourceforge
16. https://github.com/blog/530-how-we-made-github-fast

Meta4eS 2014 PC Co-Chairs Message

The future eSociety, addressed with our workshop, is an e-inclusive society based on the extensive use of digital technologies at all levels of interaction between its members. It is a society that evolves based on knowledge and that empowers individuals by creating virtual communities that benefit from social inclusion, access to information, enhanced interaction, participation and freedom of expression, among other.

In this context, the role of the ICT in the way people and organizations exchange information and interact in the social cyberspace is crucial. Large amounts of structured data are being published and shared on the Web and a growing number of services and applications emerge from it. The applications must be designed in such a way to help people use their knowledge at best and generate new knowledge in return, while keeping intact their privacy and confidentiality. A current popular initiative adopted by a growing number of actors from transversal domains (e.g. governments, city municipalities, etc.) encourage publishing structured data (e.g. RDF) on the Web of Data. Managing such data in order to produce services and applications for end-user consumption is presently a big challenge. The final goal is to lower the barrier between end-users and information and communication technologies via a number of techniques stemming from the fields of semantic knowledge processing, multilingual information, information visualization, privacy and trust, etc.

To discuss, demonstrate and share best practices, ideas and results, the 3rd International IFIP Workshop on Methods, Evaluation, Tools and Applications for the Creation and Consumption of Structured Data for the e-Society (Meta4eS 2014), an event supported by IFIP TC 12 WG 12.7, with a special focus on Energy and Sustainability, brings together researchers, professionals and experts interested to present original research results in this area.

We are happy to announce that, for its third edition, the workshop raised interest and good participation in the research community. After a thorough review process, with each submission refereed by at least three members of the workshop Program Committee, we accepted 4 full papers and 2 poster and demo abstracts covering topics such as ontology engineering, service choreographies, smart knowledge processing and extraction, knowledge management, social semantics, services, and applied to the fields of electrical appliances, e-Health, semantic profiling, digital advertising, sentiment analysis and organizational culture and innovation.

We thank the Program Committee members for their time and effort in ensuring the quality during the review process, as well as all the authors and the workshop attendees for the original ideas and the inspiring discussions.

We also thank the OTM 2014 Organizing Committee members for their continuous support. We are confident that Meta4eS will bring an important contribution towards the future eSociety.

September 2014

Ioana Ciuciu

Anna Fensel

Customizing Semantic Profiling
for Digital Advertising

Anett Hoppe, Ana Roxin, and Christophe Nicolle

CheckSem Research Group, Laboratoire Electronique, Informatique et Images,
Université de Bourgogne, Dijon, France
{first name.last name}@checksem.fr
www.checksem.com

Abstract. Personalization is the new magic buzzword of application
development. To make the complexity of today's application functionalities and information spaces "digestible", customization has become the
new go-to technique. But while those technologies aim to ease the consumption of media for their users, they suffer from the same problematic:
in the age of Big Data, applications have to cope with a conundrum of
heterogeneous information sources that have to be perceived, processed
and interpreted. Researchers tend to aim for a maximum degree of integration to create the perfect, all-embracing personalization. The results
are wide-range, but overly complex systems that suffer from issues in
performance and scalability. Starting from our own, similar experience,
we argue for a *personalization of personalization* - a clear-cut customization of profiling by limiting the information maintained in the system to
those elements that are crucially relevant for the target task. We demonstrate the concern based on an application developed in our laboratory:
a system that profiles web users based on their browsing history, with
the goal of personalizing digital advertisements.

Keywords: user profiling, semantic technologies, customization.

1 Introduction

The recent history of information science has been predominated by the emergence of "Big Data", summing up efforts to store, handle and analyse data
amounts that exceed experience in several attributes. The criteria that have
been adopted by the IEEE amongst others, are the following five [1]:

1. **Volume:** massive amounts of data have to be treated,
2. **Velocity:** those data arrive in high speed,
3. **Variety:** data types and formats are heterogeneous,
4. **Veracity:** data are not always sound and have to be verified,
5. **Value:** they have an inherent value that can be discovered by the application.

The sources may be scientific materiel and publications, or simply all the contents that emerge and falter on the Web. Whatever the origin of the information

R. Meersman et al. (Eds.): OTM 2014 Workshops, LNCS 8842, pp. 469–478, 2014.
© Springer-Verlag Berlin Heidelberg 2014

– algorithms that efficiently and reliably bring them to use are sparse. In an industrial context, mathematical models stemming from statistics and computational learning stay the most-applied techniques as they are known for the above criteria. However, it is known that those straight-forward methods suffer from limitations based on the underlying data structures and individual biases (see Section 2 for details).

Efforts to determine the *semantic* meaning of a phrase, and to determine the real-world concepts contained are not new. Semantic disambiguation, for example, has been mentioned already in the 1970s (e.g. [2]). Anyhow, for reasons of efficiency, the techniques developed since then have not yet found entry to Big Data analysis. Sophisticated methods for term distinction, syntactic analysis and the like seem out of place in a domain that still fights to cope with the data masses available.

Contrasting this intuitive rejection of semantic techniques, we propose to explore the applicability of semantic technology in a Big Data environment and, to handle performance-related issues with strong customisation to the targeted domain. In the case of the system presented in this article, we develop an application for user profiling from implicit information. We have been working with experts from digital advertising to identify attributes and concepts that are crucial for the prediction of a consumer's future behaviour. On the one hand, the application of semantic technologies allows to maintain a richer image of each user within the system – by extending the keyword-based representation to an ontology structure that relates real-world concepts with their semantic relationships. On the other hand, the limitation to entities that are crucial for consumer segmentation, allows light-weight, rapid processing.

The base of the profiling process is the implicit browsing information that is available to each online publisher: user IDs, paired with the contents requested and a user agent. Based on this information, the goal is to profile the user's engagement with certain contents and to predict the likeliness for him to react on a certain advertisement content, considering context information as the used device, the time of the day etc. All data modelling has been included in a customised domain ontology (further described in Section 3), that is integrated in a flexible system that extracts the raw user information from a structured file, retrieves the web contents in question and relates them to the content-related concepts within the ontology to allow on-the-fly-segmentation of user activity.

The proposition to use ontologies as a more expressive base structure to organize information is not new, neither is its application on user profiling. So far, however, the usage of semantic technology in the area of Big Data has been avoided. As [3] stated, the common sense opinion is that, whenever an abundance of data available, statistical methods will overpower all "more sophisticated" semantic approaches, in efficiency and performance. Without negating this point of view, we want to demonstrate that a system that targets a limited domain and focusses all analyses to that particular scope may compete with a similar, machine learning-based design. In this case, the information provided by ontological inference is richer, as modern reasoners allow to trace the origin of the perceived deductions. This explanatory component provides valuable insights into the knowledge base – that come in handy when communicating with customers or to handle noisy, erroneous data.

2 Related Work

It exceeds the scope of this work to give a full introduction user profiling. Therefore, we will limit our consideration to two important building blocks: On the one hand, the state of the art of methods in the target domain, digital advertising. On the other hand, the development of ontology-based profiling and its current state.

2.1 Profiling in Digital Advertising

The development of digital advertising in France has been dominated by actors originating from the Machine Learning (ML) domain. As M. Sabah discusses in a blog entry for the Rubicon Project, the domain "provides an excellent opportunity to apply ML" (Rubicon specializes in all processes related to automated buying and selling of advertising)[1]. He justifies this vision with two mayor keylocks: the richness of the data involved, as well as the challenges related to its predictive analysis and forecasting. Of course, the scope of the company comprises more than just user profiling, however, the expressed point of view reflects a general perspective. That is the data masses are vast and seem too abundant to apply overly sophisticated methodology (as for example semantic analysis). Hence, actors refer to reliable and knowingly efficient ways to process the data at hand. In consequence, the list of applied techniques features those that have been proven robust for extreme data amounts, notably neural networks, support vector machines (SVM) [4], and regression trees [5].

All above mentioned methods are widely based on a keyword-based representation. The analysed resources are thus summarised by extracting the set of their pertinent keywords. However, the combination of keywords with a vector-based distance computation comes with limitations that have been described in e.g. [6]. A mayor bias therein is the assumption that the relationship between a concept and its identifying term is bijective – meaning that for each concept, there is one single term that describes it; and each single term can be used for only one real-world entity. However, the reality of natural language is much richer and, in consequence, messier. Hence, the systems developed on this presumption are prone to errors when encountering synonymous or homonymous terms.

2.2 Ontology-Based Profiling

There have already been propositions that integrate semantic technology into user profiling. They vary in their degree of ontology integration and the choice of background knowledge repositories.

---

[1] http://www.rubiconproject.com/uncategorized/
   machine-learning-at-the-rubicon-project/

The development lead off with the construction of semantic networks to replace keyword sets. Starting from a base of fixed key-terms, semantic relations between terms were estimated based on co-occurrence in the document base and, new terms added if a relationship was judged likely [7]. The main focus was to tackle the problem of homonymy, terms in natural language that are written the same, but refer to different semantic concepts depending on their context of usage [8]. However, even the elaborate algorithms based on semantic networks did not solve the issue [9], at least not without adopting external knowledge sources. In the named approach, WordNet [10], a base of lexical knowledge of English language, has been used to create links to semantically defined entities.

As a result, more and more researchers explore the usefulness of ontologies for profiling purposes, e.g. [8, 11]. The integration points vary from the usage of ontologies as a background knowledge repository to the usage of ontology-structures user profiles. Numerous approaches use structured open linked data [12] as domain knowledge. A lot of them refer to WordNet[2] (e.g. [13,14]), DBPedia[3] (in [15]) or the Open Directory Project (ODP)[4] (in [16]). Those resources differ in the degree of structure that they induce to the contained concepts – WordNet's relational structure was obtained by manually grouping terms into "synset", words that bear a synonymous relationship; the ODP is a community-driven project to classify web content into a given set of categories. There are several works that refer to the ODP as an ontology. However, even though ODP allows the introduction of more than taxonomic relationships, those are not widely used. Thus, the actual ODP structure can be at most considered a light-weight ontology [17].

In turn, there are two recent approaches that make use of full-fledged ontologies for reference: [8] proposed a profiling system that relies on the Yago ontology [18]. [11] assume a non-further specified domain ontology as a base for their abstract system.

Finally, the chosen knowledge structure may be used in different ways. First techniques aimed to maintain the keyword-based representation, but use the ontologies to improve the keyword sets. The analysis of the keyword space and the context of usage allows some disambiguation. Furthermore, "synsets" or semantic relations can be used to extend the keywords space by synonymous or closely related terms [19]. [20] uses them to group semantically close terms to clusters and reduce the feature space for better performance.

Recent propositions advance the usage of the background knowledge by using an ontological structure for the profile itself. This enables them to not only extract additional concepts from the knowledge resource, but also use the relationships to enhance the user model. [8] extract parts of the Yago ontology related to the user's documents, based on the Spreading Activation algorithm [21].

From the above approaches, especially the most recent ones [8, 11] show similarities to ours. They both rely on keyword-based representations for the

---

[2] http://wordnet.princeton.edu/
[3] http://www.dbpedia.org
[4] http://www.dmoz.org/

characterisation of the resources of the users, that when included to the user profile, are enriched with semantics.

Even though especially [22] provides a detailed evaluation of the system, none of them has been tested in an industrial environment. Furthermore, none of the systems has been tested in conditions as extreme as a Big Data environment. Our goal is to come up with a system design that integrates semantic analyses in the profile construction, but focuses on a limited application domain to control losses in efficiency. The adaptation to the industrial context has to be deeply ingrained into the system by a customised domain ontology. We thus opt for a modular design to enable the transfer to alternative applications by simple exchange of the specialised components.

3   The Ontology

Former publications already presented first versions of our profiling ontology [23–25]. These first user models adopted the paradigm of full coverage and aimed to integrate all available information to the user profile. First benchmarks, realised based on the triple store *Stardog*[5] led to promising results, providing an analysis result within a few milliseconds. However, when matching the information within the user profiles with the facts that were actually relevant with the subsequent analysis of consumer behaviour, important deviations became visible:

The profiling process relies on a categorisation of the user's viewed contents to a set of topic classes. Coming from a research background, we opted for a generalised categorisation scheme such as the ODP directory [16]. The ODP project was conceived for the classification of web contents – and thus seems highly adequate for the contents that appear in browsing logs. Furthermore, it is an open standard that is widely used in research, allowing comparison of our approach with systems of similar scope.

However, when revisiting the set of ODP categories – e.g. "Arts", "Games", "Society" – with domain experts, we found that their scope differs importantly from the priorities of the advertising domain. In fact, the experts proposed a taxonomy of their own, featuring less general terms but a specialised vocabulary that is more focussed on consumer behaviour: "Children", "Luxury" or "Do it yourself". Considering the data-intensive application context of the profiling system, it is not desirable to introduce unnecessary noise to the knowledge base. Indeed, as already stated, it will act in a context of Big Data: User navigation traces are submitted in real-time, each time a user requests a resource from the content server, the corresponding data point directly enters the profiling system. The latter has to extract the necessary information and to create the appropriate instances and relationships in the ontology. New data instances arrive in the rapid speed and refer to the heterogeneous resources innate to web applications, all of which have to be rapidly integrated to the knowledge base.

The limitation of the categorisation module to the categories modelled based on the experience of domain experts, promises to reduce the contents of the

---

[5] http://stardog.com/

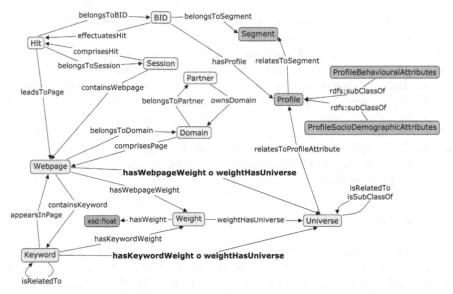

Fig. 1. Schematic view: Upper-level concepts of the ontology

knowledge base of the profiling system. For the target application, it is not forcedly necessary to be able to categorize every web content but to capture those features that are relevant to the analysis. However, a (partial) mapping between the two categorisation schemes is possible and can be effectuated to allow comparative evaluation with other experimental approaches.

Furthermore, the ontology design is kept modular. While the practical application within the advertising domain will use the expert-conceived categorisation scheme, it is easily possible to exchange the module for a more standardised scheme to enable evaluation.

Figure 1 shows the upper-level concepts of the customized domain ontology in a schematic view. The basic entities of the user profile, for instance, consist of attributes that are widely adopted in profiling applications, e.g. the user's age or gender. Others, as for example the chosen core concepts for the qualification of the web contents are customised for the eCommerce.

These customised concepts are grouped below a shared super-concept in thematic modules. The distinction of specialised and generic components enables to replace the application-specific element when transferring the data structure to an alternative domain.

User ID. The center of the profiling ontology is, of course, the user, qualified by an identification string. As an adaptation to the domain terminology, this string is called "BID", as an abbreviation for 'browser identification'. The BID-concept constitutes the center piece and connection point for all user-related information, be it the modellisation of her past navigations or high-level segment affiliations. It can be seen as the most generic constituent as most profiling systems include some kind of user identification.

Webpage. Web resources are the main source of semantic information. The respective concept is thus the second anchor point within the ontology. It is identified by a string that contains its URL and may be connected to further information concerning its domain and owning publisher. The information is relevant as a certain base domain might impose a bias on the topics covered within. The term "politics" appearing in a low-level domain, for instance, gives a strong hint on the topics covered in the child pages. Similarly, a certain partner might be connected to a limited set of thematics or preferred user segments.

Navigation History. The navigation history as depicted in the server logs contains the user ID, the page visited, time stamps, basic information about the used device and, at times, if that particular browsing activity represents a successful advertising conversion (meaning, that the page was reached by clicking of a displayed ad).

The entities related to this part of the user profile are "Hit" and "Session". The "Hit" groups all information captured for one single user event – the visited web page, time stamp and user agent. Those data are modelled using OWL datatype properties, including a boolean variable that captures if the user activity is a reaction on a displayed advertising.

The "Session" concept groups several clicks based on a time concept. For the moment, this groups all hits that have been effectuated in less than thirty minutes' distance. The temporal clustering is a technique applied by experts to constitute larger unities of analysis. However, a grouping based on other contextual information, such as the used device (e.g. Desktop PC, mobile phone etc.) might be an interesting lead for future evaluation.

Web Content Information. Each web page is related to summary concepts according to the results of the semantic analysis. This involves the key concepts that describe the documents content and, based on them, an affiliation to topic categories that qualify the page on a higher level. To simplify the work with the experts, those entities are, at the time, named according to the terminology that we encountered in the domain, "Keyword" and "Universe" respectively. Therein, the instances of "Keyword" capture the found key concepts. Please note that the system handles semantically qualified *key concepts*, not plain keywords. The term "Universe" refers to a customised topic category. The ensemble of universes constitutes a hierarchy of first-level topic concepts such as "Foods and Drinks" and "Kids". Subordinated are second-level subdivisions such as "Baby food" and "Diapers".

The categorization scheme is the module that is most influenced by the specialisation to digital advertising. It includes, for instance, such a fine-grained topic category as "Diapers" that has shown pertinent for consumer prediction. The same applies for first-level categories such as "Luxury" or "Hazardous Games" that, from a general point of view do not seem of such importance. They are, however, judged important factors for customer segmentation by domain experts.

We make this highly specific categorization scheme interoperable by relating the core concepts with their counterparts in existing semantic repositories such as DBPedia. This serves unique identification on the one hand; on the other hand it enables to take advantage of existing relational information. Furthermore, all categories are sub-classes of one central concept "Universe". The whole categorization module can thus be exchanged by an alternative scheme – be it adapted to another application domain or a general classification standard.

User Profile and Segments. The actual qualification of the user happens in two modules that distinguish two levels of abstraction – the generic user profile and the application-specific segmentation into customer groups.

The "Profile" class groups sub-classes that capture basic user properties deductible from browsing habits. This includes socio-demographic attributes, such as age and gender, and behavioural attributes as e.g. main activity periods during the day. Some of these criteria are generic to profiling, for instance the socio-demographic information. The behavioural elements however, mirror clearly the commercial focus of the application.

So do the user segments that have been exemplified. Indeed, this part of the user profile will be highly variable, based on current campaigns and clients. The sub-classes of "Segment" contain complex user clusters obtained by combination of features of the lower-level profile. In a simple example, a segment called "sporty mom" was introduced for a campaign that targeted female individuals that lived in a household with kids that showed an interest in sports-related publications. The goal was to find users that would be susceptible for a certain sports wear commercial.

3.1   Practical Experience

The totality of the developed application has been tested exemplarily on a set of navigation logs and an ensemble of segments provided by domain experts. During the demonstration, we had the opportunity to confront the advertising experts to graphical interfaces that have been developed to enable the intuitive design of new segments based on the entities in the ontology. This first test gave promising results and, more importantly, prompts concerning the necessary extensions of the prototypes and the underlying rule bases.

4   Conclusion

Today's data analysis community often focusses on integrating the maximum amount of information possible, based on the widespread belief that the quality of results will improve if just enough empirical evidence thrown at it. While this perspective may have its validity in some cases, we argue that the growing computing power may be better invested alternatively. Instead of using it to crunch more numbers in less time, we propose to adopt more sophisticated analysis approaches, while focussing on the portion of the data that is deemed relevant for the final target result.

We exemplify this view point based on an application developed in our laboratory, a profiling system based on users' web navigation that aims to predict future consumer decisions. Instead of embracing a general categorisation scheme like the ODP directory (as done in other similar research systems (e.g [16]), we apply a highly customized set of classes to summarize the interests expressed in the navigation logs. The summary of the web resources and the subsequent user profile are in consequence highly customised to the advertising domain.

The next project stages aim for important extensions of the ontology and general improvements of the surrounding analysis system:

a) Rule base: Extend the rule base for segment creation to enable more expressive design and extensive testing.
b) Relational Structure: So far, only basic relationships have been modelled among universes and keywords. An extension using external repositories promises the possibility of more interesting inferences.
c) Same applies for the relations among raw input values and the higher-level profile concepts, they have to be extended to allow the domain experts further expressiveness for segment creation.

References

1. Chui, M., Brown, B., Bughin, J., Dobbs, R., Roxburgh, C., Manyika, A.H.B.J.: Big data: The next frontier for innovation, competition, and productivity. McKinsey Global Institute, Tech. Rep (2011)
2. Hayes, P.J.: A process to implement some word-sense disambiguations (1976)
3. Halevy, A., Norvig, P., Pereira, F.: The unreasonable effectiveness of data. IEEE Intelligent Systems 24(2), 8–12 (2009)
4. eXelate, Employing adaptive audience intelligence, eXelate, Tech. Rep (2012), http://exelate.com/insights/white-papers/employing-adaptive-audience-intelligence-2/
5. Vogel, D.S., Asparouhov, O., Scheffer, T.: Scalable look-ahead linear regression trees. In: Proceedings of the 13th ACM SIGKDD International Conference on Knowledge Discovery and Data Mining, KDD 2007, pp. 757–764. ACM, New York (2007), http://doi.acm.org/10.1145/1281192.1281273
6. Ranwez, S., Duthil, B., Sy, M.F., Montmain, J., Augereau, P., Ranwez, V.: How ontology based information retrieval systems may benefit from lexical text analysis. In: New Trends of Research in Ontologies and Lexical Resources, pp. 209–231. Springer (2013)
7. Gentili, G., Micarelli, A., Sciarrone, F.: Infoweb: An adaptive information filtering system for the cultural heritage domain. Applied Artificial Intelligence 17(8-9), 715–744 (2003)
8. Calegari, S., Pasi, G.: Definition of user profiles based on the yago ontology. In: IIR (2011)
9. Magnini, B., Strapparava, C.: Improving user modelling with content-based techniques. In: Bauer, M., Gmytrasiewicz, P.J., Vassileva, J. (eds.) UM 2001. LNCS (LNAI), vol. 2109, p. 74. Springer, Heidelberg (2001)
10. Miller, G.A.: Wordnet: a lexical database for english. Communications of the ACM 38(11), 39–41 (1995)
11. Su, Z., Yan, J., Ling, H., Chen, H.: Research on personalized recommendation algorithm based on ontological user interest model. Journal of Computational Information Systems 8(1), 169–181 (2012)

12. Bizer, C., Heath, T., Berners-Lee, T.: Linked data-the story so far. International Journal on Semantic web and Information Systems 5(3), 1–22 (2009)
13. Agirre, E., Rigau, G.: Word sense disambiguation using conceptual density. In: Proceedings of the 16th conference on Computational linguistics, vol. 1, pp. 16–22 (1996)
14. Banerjee, S., Pedersen, T.: An adapted lesk algorithm for word sense disambiguation using wordNet. In: Gelbukh, A. (ed.) CICLing 2002. LNCS, vol. 2276, p. 136. Springer, Heidelberg (2002)
15. Demartini, G., Firan, C.S., Iofciu, T.: L3S at INEX 2007: Query expansion for entity ranking using a highly accurate ontology. In: Fuhr, N., Kamps, J., Lalmas, M., Trotman, A. (eds.) INEX 2007. LNCS, vol. 4862, pp. 252–263. Springer, Heidelberg (2008)
16. Gabrilovich, E., Markovitch, S.: Feature generation for text categorization using world knowledge. In: IJCAI, vol. 5, pp. 1048–1053 (2005)
17. Mizoguchi, R.: Part 3: Advanced course of ontological engineering. New Generation Computing 22(2), 193–220 (2004)
18. Suchanek, F.M., Kasneci, G., Weikum, G.: Yago: a core of semantic knowledge. In: Proceedings of the 16th International Conference on World Wide Web, pp. 697–706 (2007)
19. Bhogal, J., Macfarlane, A., Smith, P.: A review of ontology based query expansion. Information Processing & Management 43(4), 866–886 (2007)
20. Chua, S., Kulathuramaiyer, N.: Semantic feature selection using wordnet. In: Proceedings of the 2004 IEEE/WIC/ACM International Conference on Web Intelligence, pp. 166–172. IEEE Computer Society (2004)
21. Katifori, A., Vassilakis, C., Dix, A.: Ontologies and the brain: Using spreading activation through ontologies to support personal interaction. Cognitive Systems Research 11(1), 25–41 (2010)
22. Calegari, S., Pasi, G.: Personal ontologies: Generation of user profiles based on the {YAGO} ontology. Information Processing & Management 49(3), 640–658 (2013), personalization and Recommendation in Information Access, http://www.sciencedirect.com/science/article/pii/S0306457312001070
23. Hoppe, A., Nicolle, C., Roxin, A.: Automatic ontology-based user profile learning from heterogeneous web resources in a big data context. Proceedings of the VLDB Endowment 6(12), 1428–1433 (2013)
24. Hoppe, A., Roxin, A., Nicolle, C.C., et al.: Dynamic, behavior-based user profiling for the e-society-using semantic web technologies in a big data context. In: OTM 2013 Workshops (2013)
25. Hoppe, A., Roxin, A., Nicolle, C.: Dynamic semantic user profiling from implicit web navigation data. In: IE2014 Conference Proceedings (July 2014)

Traversing the Linking Open Data Cloud
to Create News from Tweets

Francisco Berrizbeita and Maria-Esther Vidal

Universidad Simón Bolívar, Caracas, Venezuela
{fberrizbeita,mvidal}@ldc.usb.ve

Abstract. We propose a two-fold approach that is able to both consume and exploit semantics encoded in the Linking Open Data (LOD) cloud, and create news that document events reported in micro-blogging posts that correspond to *documentary* tweets. A documentary tweet is similar to a newspaper headline and reports an incident or event. Knowledge extracted from documentary tweets are used to develop a story line which will be augmented with RDF facts consumed from the LOD cloud. The resulting news content is represented in RDF using the *rNews Ontology*, facilitating news generation and retrieval. We study effectiveness of our approach with respect to a gold standard of manually tagged tweets. Initial experimental results suggest that our techniques are able to generate content that reflects up to 76.38% of the manually tagged terms.

1 Introduction

Information access can be limited in situations where traditional media outlets are unable to cover events due to geographical limitations or censorship, e.g., civil unrests, or natural disasters. In these situations, citizen journalism replaces or complements traditional media in the documentation of such events. Micro-blogging services such as Twitter, have become effective in these scenarios because their mobile nature and multimedia capabilities. *Documentary* tweets or micro-blogging posts that report events, are commonly the only available information. A *documentary* tweet is a short message written with the intention to let other people know about a specific situation. It is well written: no abbreviations, correctly spelled, grammatically correct, and communicate a complete idea, similar to a *newspaper headline*. It should not express the authors opinion, but a concise description of the event. Figure 1 illustrates a documentary tweet.

Tweets are for human consumption and are composed of a small number of words that attempt to concisely describe an event. Developing both a story line and news content from short messages may require hours of specialized journalists. We aim towards the construction of an event repository that can be queried for history reconstruction. We propose an approach tailored for tweets reporting events, i.e., *documentary* tweets; tweets expressing opinions or status updates are out of the scope of the paper.

Photo: President Barack Obama talks with German Chancellor Angela Merkel and Mexican President... bit.ly/1sXvYtW

Fig. 1. A Documentary Tweet reports an event or incident

R. Meersman et al. (Eds.): OTM 2014 Workshops, LNCS 8842, pp. 479–488, 2014.
© Springer-Verlag Berlin Heidelberg 2014

Different approaches rely on ontologies for extracting knowledge from micro-blogging posts [2,3,6,8], while others implement machine learning techniques to detect sentiment analysis and opinion mining [1,5]. However, they mainly rely on information extraction techniques and knowledge encoded in the LOD cloud is not exploited to enhance the quality of the extracted knowledge. Recently, Muñoz et al. [4] developed a framework for mining relationships between entities in Wikipedia tables. The proposed approach guides the discovery process with knowledge extracted from DBpedia and improves the quality of the prediction with supervised machine learning classifier. The approach by Muñoz et al. [4] clearly shows the benefits of consuming Linked Data for mining semi-structure data; but, it is not clear the impact that this knowledge base can have in unstructured micro-blogging posts.

In this paper, we address the problem of developing news contents from documentary tweets, and propose a technique that relies on Linked Data and the rNews Ontology[1] to develop a story line and the content of the news from the tweet. We propose a two-fold approach that looks up DBpedia and related Linked Data sources to generate a news article from the concepts that are present in a documentary tweet; the algorithm named Tweet2News, implements our proposed approach. In the first phase, Tweet2News relies on WordNet[2] to automatically identify relevant terms in a documentary tweet. Then, these terms are used to search on Wikipedia and the LOD cloud. Retrieved LOD resources and relationships are used to populate the rNews ontology until a certain level of information has been collected; a metric is used to measure the amount of information that is gained during each look-up of the LOD datasets.

Our initial test was performed over a sample of media enhanced documentary tweets, and our initial results suggest that our method is able to automatically detect and exploit 76.36% of the expected semantic entities. For the evaluation, we gathered a dataset of 90 documentary tweets related to three topics: The riots in Brazil during the 2014 World Cup, Barack Obama, and Venezuela. The collected documentary tweets were manually tagged by two different people: a computer science master student and a journalist; discrepancies were resolved by a third person, a senior computer scientist. Manually detected tags correspond to our gold standard.

To summarize the contributions of this paper are the following: *i*) we propose a method to detect relevant terms from a micro-blogging post using WordNet and the Open Wikipedia API; *ii*) a metric for measuring the information gain obtained as the result of dereferencing resources in the documentary tweet story line; *iii*) the Tweet2News algorithm able to exploit knowledge encoded in the LOD cloud to develop the story line and content of a news from a documentary tweet; and *iv*) an experimental study to evaluate the efficiency of the Tweet2News algorithm on a set of 90 documentary tweets of three different topics.

This paper is organized as follows: Section 2 shows a motivating example of our problem, related works are described in Section 3. In Section 4, we explain in greater detail our approach. Experimental results are reported in Section 5. Section 6 concludes and outline our future works.

---

[1] http://dev.iptc.org/files/rNews/rnews_1.0_draft1.owl

[2] http://wordnet.princeton.edu/

2   Motivating Example: A Tweet Is Not a Document

Citizen journalism has become a very common practice with the arrival of smartphones and micro-blogging services such as Twitter. Due to the multimedia capacities of the devices and the mobile nature of social networks, people all over the world are documenting and publishing all sort events on the Web in real time. This type of journalism has particular importance in situations where the traditional media cannot cover events because government or self-imposed censorship, e.g., natural disasters, or civil protests.

Self-life of documentary tweets, as the one in Figure 2, is usually short. They may become inaccessible through the Twitter API after a period of time because of limitations of the blogging service, or even if they become available (e.g., via a data reseller like Topsy,[3] Data Sift,[4] or Gnip[5]) will be nothing more than a collection of status updates with no explicit relationship between them and their semantics. Nevertheless, the information of those short messages can be very valuable for documentary storytelling, being in many cases, the only source of information. In the example shown in Figure 2, we can observe a short description of an event, i.e., a blackout that occurred in Venezuela, caused the subway system to stop, traffic jams, and interrupted a presidential broadcast. Each of these terms: Venezuela, blackout, subway, traffic jam, and presidential broadcast are concepts in WordNet that are described in Wikipedia.

Venezuela blackout stops subway, causes traffic jams - and interrupts presidential broadcast tdy.sg/1nRsswE

Fig. 2. Documentary Tweet with Short Self-life

To the best of our knowledge, no existing tool is trying to create news articles directly from tweets and make the news accessible as an RDF document. Most efforts concentrate in analyzing user behavior such as engagement, influence and reach of specific tweets, e.g., social network management tools designed for marketers and community managers. These tools provide a way to analyze specific user accounts, searches, and hashtags. The main objective of these tools is to provide information for brands to expand their clients, and not for exploiting semantics from the tweet of a given incident or event to create a story line.

It is also a common practice nowadays to embed tweets in news articles, since celebrities and politicians often make announcement using the social network. Also in reporting events such as the one in the example, news blogs and media outlets often complement their news with a sample of tweets. This manually curated process does link tweets to a news article, but it is not semantically annotated and does not cover all the crowd generated content.

We propose a Linked Data based framework able to consume data from the LOD cloud and create news from micro-blogging posts. The news creator relies on a micro-blogging post to define the story line of the news. Retrieved Linked Data is integrated and described in terms of the rNews Ontology and used to expand the story line and generate the content of the news. Once we find the appropriate Wikipedia page for

---

[3] http://topsy.com
[4] http://datasift.com
[5] http://gnip.com

each term, it is possible to map directly to DBpedia using the *foaf:isPrimaryTopicOf* predicate. We use the retrieved information to populate the ontology and if necessary, it is possible to navigate the LOD cloud using the links associated with *owl:sameAs* predicate. Furthermore, information about the author is available in the Twitter API: name, screen name, biography, and picture. After the process in completed, we will finalize a semantically annotated news article where the title is the tweet itself while the author information is taken from the Twitter account; the body of the article is obtained from the LOD cloud together with the concepts relations, and the related media is also obtained from the tweet. This news article can now be stored in a RDF file, and it will become available via a SPARQL endpoint creating a stable, searchable, and semantically annotated document that can be used in the future by journalists.

3   Related Work

Information extraction approaches from Twitter and other micro-blogging platforms have been developed during the last years. Laniado et al. [3] propose a set of metrics to detect the semantic value of hashtags, and measure how much they correspond to entities in the real-world. Shinavier et al. [2] provide a grammar-based framework to write and translate tweets into RDF. A set of controlled vocabularies is provided while users have to create the appropriate URIs to identify and dereference resources. Ritter[6] exploits natural language processing and information extraction techniques to extract machine readable information over a corpora of tweets. Additionally, the Word-Net taxonomy is used to augment sentences and commonsense knowledge from large Web documents; they generated a knowledge base [8]. Although these approaches are able to detect semantics encoded in a tweet or a document, none of them exploits the LOD cloud for information extraction or for enriching a story line.

Pak et al. [5] implement machine learning-based approaches for sentiment analysis and opinion mining; documents are classified into positive, negative, and neutral. Abhimanyu et el. [1] model user opinions based of the opinions of their neighbors in the social network. Even though these approaches are able to describe a tweet according to the user sentiment, they do not exploit existing knowledge bases as the LOD cloud, to enhance the quality of the prediction. Finally, Muñoz et al. [4] develop a three-fold framework for: *i*) extracting the mining of Wikipedia tables by exploiting knwoledge from the DBpedia knowledge-base; *ii*) mining Wikipedia to enhance Linked Data; and *iii*) providing a SPARQL based querying infrastructure for Wikipedia tables. To address these challenges, Muñoz et al. [4] rely on entity resolution and Linked Data consumption strategies for information extraction; additionally, different machine-learning based classifiers are used to determine false RDF triples and increase accuracy of the prediction. Similarly, we use Wikipedia and DBpedia as *anchors* to search on the LOD cloud. Furthermore, our Tweet2News algorithm exploits knowledge encoded in WordNet to determine the entities in a tweet that will comprise the story line; relevant entities are used to search on Wikipedia and DBpedia, and to traverse the LOD cloud datasets. The Tweet2News algorithm stops the traversal when enough information has been gained. The rNews ontology is used to represent facts as *who, what, where, when*, and *why* that compose the news, and a metric that measures the amount of information represented in an instance of the ontology is used to decide the traversal stop condition. Currently, we do not perform any supervised learning approach, but in the future, we plan to train a classifier to improve the precision of our techniques.

4 Our Approach

The main objective is to obtain the semantically meaningful concepts expressed in the micropost from the LOD cloud, and then create a document that extends the original text with the retrieved concepts. If we succeed in this task, we will end up with a news article where the questions: *who, what, where, when,* and *why* are going to be derived from the micropost and extended with the LOD cloud. Figure 3 illustrates the overall process of news creation. As a proof-of-concept, we decided to focus on Twitter as the only microblog input and DBpedia as our first source of semantically annotated information. We navigate the LOD cloud by dereferencing URIs in the *owl:sameAs* links of datasets reachable from DBpedia until enough information has been collected.

4.1 Information Gathering and Text Preparation

The first task consists in gathering the posted information by a user of the social network; we collect not only the published text, but also the media when available and the author information. We obtain these information using the public API provided by Twitter; the only input the system needs is the tweet's ID. After the text is retrieved, it must be denoised before any further processing. All the stop words are removed as well as links and Twitter specific words such as, RT (Retweet) or FF (Follow Friday). The hashtag character (#) is removed leaving the remaining word.

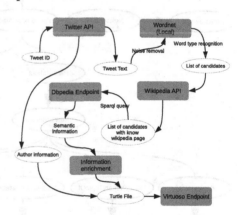

Fig. 3. Overall view of the Proposed News Creator Method

4.2 Selecting Relevant Entities for a Tweet

Before querying the DBpedia SPARQL endpoint, we first run a local analysis based on the WordNet database. Each word is analyzed and a matrix of acceptations for the words is created. Following a set rules, we create a list of possible 2-words and 1-word candidates that may be relevant concepts, places, or persons. By doing this, we expect to reduce the queries to be performed against the DBpedia SPARQL endpoint. Since the Wikipedia and the DBpedia are tightly related, we decided to query first the Wikipedia page using the API to obtain the Wikipedia page URLs of the selected relevant entities. We finalize this process with a list of candidates associated with their corresponding Wikipedia pages. For example, we obtain the list of entities with known Wikipedia pages shown in Table 1 for the documentary tweet shown in Figure 2.

4.3   Semantically Annotated Information Retrieval from the LOD Cloud

Next, DBpedia is used to extract information related to the relevant entities discovered previously. Once the information is recovered, this is merged with the author information retrieved from Twitter; all this comprises the story line. We used the rNews Ontology (International Press Telecomunication Counsil, 2011) as shown in Figure 4, to represent the story line. The corresponding RDF document is published and accessible through a SPARQL endpoint.

Table 1. Relevant Entities and their Wikipedia Page

Candidate	Wikipedia Page
traffic jams	<http://en.wikipedia.org/wiki/Traffic_congestion>
venezuela	<http://en.wikipedia.org/wiki/Venezuela>
blackout	<http://en.wikipedia.org/wiki/Blackout>
subway	<http://en.wikipedia.org/wiki/Subway>
interrupts	<http://en.wikipedia.org/wiki/Interrupt>
broadcast	<http://en.wikipedia.org/wiki/Broadcast>

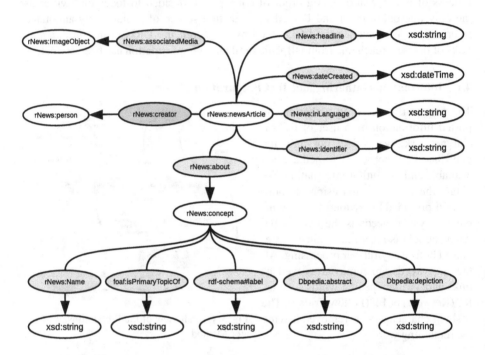

Fig. 4. Subset of the rNews Ontology used by the Tweet2News Algorithm

It is possible to expand the information beyond the scope of DBpedia by dereferencing inter- *owl:sameAs* links to other Linked Data datasets. This method provides a way to navigate the LOD cloud in order to include additional information to the concept that we want to explode. The proposed algorithm, outlined in the Tweet2News Algorithm 1 iteratively traverses the LOD cloud and dereference URIs until no new information is found. Thus, Tweet2News stops whenever one of the following conditions holds: *i*) the ontology is completely filled; *ii*) all the cross domains URIs have been dereferenced; or *iii*) no new information is gained by dereferencing during LOD lookups.

Information gain is calculated as the difference between the entropy of the ontology before dereferencing a URI and after, i.e., given two instances of the ontology o_i and

Input: A tweet T, a threshold Th of information gained
Output: An Instance O of the rNews Ontology describing content of T
1: C = getCadidates(T)
2: WKE = getWikipediaKnownEntities(C)
3: **for all** $wikitem$ in WKE **do**
4:     $DBPEntities$ = getEntities($wikiterm$)
5:     $SameAsURIs$ = getSameAsCrossDomainsURIs($SameAsURIs$, $DBPEntities$)
6:     O = fillOntology(O,$DBPEntities$)
7:     $informationGain$ = 1.0
8:     **while** NOT isOntologyComplete(O) **and** NOT allVisited($SameAsURIs$) **and** $informationGain$ >Th **do**
9:       $informationGain$ = 0.0
10:       $InnerSameAsURIs$ = array();
11:       **for all** URI in $SameAsURIs$ **do**
12:         markAsVisitedURI($SameAsURIs$,URI)
13:         $Entities$ = getEntities(URI)
14:         $URIInfomationGain$ = CalculateInformationGain(O,$Entities$)
15:         **if** $URIInfomationGain$ >Th **then**
16:           O = fillOntology(O,$Entities$)
17:           append($InnerSameAsURIs$,getSameAsCrossDomainsURIs($SameAsURIs$, $Entities$))
18:         **end if**
19:         $informationGain$ = $informationGain$ + $URIInfomationGain$
20:       **end for**
21:       append($SameAsURIs$,$InnerSameAsURIs$)
22:     **end while**
23: **end for**
24: **return** O

Algorithm 1. Tweet2News: The News Content Generator Algorithm

o_j such as o_j is subsequent to o_i, $H(o_j) - H(o_i)$ corresponds to the information gain. Suppose the threshold is 0.0 and the difference equals to 0.0, then the process does not provide any additional information, i.e., the ontology's entropy remains the same after this iteration. Next, we provide an example to illustrate in the behavior of our algorithm.

Suppose after the initial DBpedia information extraction, we ended up with 80% of our ontology filled for that particular concept, for simplicity, assume the ontology expected 10 entities and DBpedia provided only eight of those concepts. The entropy H of this initial set is calculated as follows:

$$H(x) = -[(8/10) * log(8/10) + (2/10) * log(2/10)] = 0.71 \qquad (1)$$

where, the first term of the sum corresponds to the found items while the second amount represents the concepts that are not still filled up in the ontology, i.e., the missed values. There are three different output after dereferencing the resources:

- No additional information is found and the entropy difference is 0.0.
- Expected information is found reducing the entropy. For example, assume the process found a new entity:

$$H(x') = -[(9/10) * log(9/10) + (1/10) * log(1/10)] = 0.46 \qquad (2)$$

In this case the information gain will be (0.71) - (0.46) = 0.25 >0.0.

- Unexpected information is found. For example, the process found four new entities that were not expected in the initial set.

$$H(x') = -[(12/14) * log12/14) + (2/14) * log(2/14)] = 0.59 \qquad (3)$$

Information gain in this case will be (0.71) - (0.59) = 0.22 >0.0.

The process ends when the information gained reaches a threshold Th. The news content corresponds to the knowledge represented in the instance of the rNews ontology.

5 Experimental Study

We empirically study the efficiency of our proposed approach. Below, we describe the experimental settings.

Dataset: We selected and manually tagged 90 documentary tweets on three subjects: The Brazilian riot during the 2014 World Cup, Barack Obama, and Venezuela; this set of tweets is available at github.com[6]. The process of collecting the micro-posts consisted on using the Twitter API and collecting the first 30 messages with an associated picture for each of the three topics, the tweets were collected on the 20th June, 2014. After the sample was obtained, we proceeded to manually tag each tweet. This tagging process was conducted twice by different persons (a computer science student and a journalist) to minimize the human errors, when discrepancies presented a third person (a senior computer scientist) checked again to resolve the problem; this set of terms corresponds to our gold standard. After the sample was manually tagged, we ran the Tweet2News algorithm implementation (1-hop with a threshold of 0.0) for each tweet and saved the results.

Metrics: we measure the precision, recall, and the error of the automatically found semantic entities. Precision and recall are measured as in the Information Retrieval context[7], and the error by the percentage of wrongly annotated entities. It is important to notice that sometimes Tweet2News can exploit candidates that have no relevant information but are not wrong, these cases will not be counted as errors or as correctly found. For example, we obtained the entity *broadcast* from the tweet in Figure 2, it is not wrong, but it would be better to obtain the concept *Presidential Broadcast* instead. In this case, the entity recognized by Tweet2News will not be classified either as right or wrong in the experiment.

Implementation: Tweet2News was implemented using PHP (Version 5.3.28) running on a Apache (Version 2.4) server in a laptop computer (Intel Core I5, 4Gb RAM, 500Gb HD). Data repositories and URIs were consumed using Curl, all the APIs (Twitter, Wikipedia, and DBpedia) returned the information in JSON format.

The goal of the experiment is to evaluate the impact of the proposed techniques on documentary tweets associated with a photo or video. We hypothesize that because media-related tweets have a documentary purpose, then Tweet2News will be able to exhibit a high precision and recall with respect to the baseline. The results are reported in Figure 5. We expected to find 415 terms for all tweets and found 433, of those 317 were an exact match to what was tagged during the manual tagging process. 63 of the terms resulted in information that is not wrong, but it adds no real value, while 53 terms were wrong concepts. We calculated the precision and recall from this output as follows: *i*) Precision = (317/433)=0.7321, and *ii*) Recall = (317/415) = 0.7638.

---

[6] https://github.com/fberrizbeitia/tweet2News

[7] In the Information Retrieval context, precision is defined as the fraction of retrieved documents that are relevant to the findings, while recall corresponds to the fraction of the documents that are relevant to the query and are successfully retrieved.

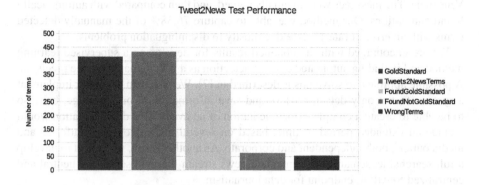

Fig. 5. Terms Frequency of the 90 Documentary Tweets. GoldStandard: 415 Terms; Tweets2NewsTerms: Number of Terms found by the Tweets2News algorithm; FoundGoldStandard: Number of Terms in the Gold Standard Found by Tweets2News; FoundNotGoldStandard: Good Terms found by Tweets2News but that did not belong to the Gold Standard; WrongTerms: Wrong Terms found by Tweets2News that were not in the Gold Standard

5.1 Discussion and Lessons Learned

We focused on a set of documentary tweets because their structure facilitates the extraction and discovery of the questions: *who, what, where, when,* and *why.* Our automated entity detection and annotation method needs correctly spelled words that express semantic concepts related to the subject of the tweet. Tweet2News is not able, and does not intent to perform well on poorly written tweets. Additionally, Tweet2News does not exhibit good performance in tweets that do not document an event. Thus, we selected topics and media enhanced posts that have a good chance of being documentary tweets, i.e., tweets that report an event or incident related to these topics.

Based on the observed results, it might be required to train a classifier to better detect documentary tweets. As shown in the approach by Pak et al [5], a Naïve Bayes classifier can be developed to do this task. The wrongly detected terms are mostly due to disambiguation problems in the entity detection procedure: the candidate ended up with a wrong Wikipedia page. It is possible to overcome this issue by taking into account the overall context of the message; a possible solution to this problem is proposed by Villar et al. [7]. The wrongly detected terms can be categorized in two sets: terms that do not have a Wikipedia page, and terms that point to a disambiguation Wikipedia page.

6   Conclusion and Future Work

We proposed a method to automatically create a news article from a documentary tweet using the LOD cloud. We developed the Tweet2News algorithm which receives a tweet ID as input and generates semantically annotated news article based on a subset of the rNews Ontology. To test our approach, we collected a group of 90 documentary tweets on three subjects: the Brazilian riots during the 2014 World Cup, Barack Obama, and

Venezuela. The messages were manually tagged, and then compared with automatically found annotations. Our method was able to capture 76.38% of the manually detected terms with an error of rate 12.24% due mostly to disambiguation problems.

We are encouraged with the obtained results for developing a supervised learning method and including automated context detection as a way to maximize the precision. A possible approach to solve this is described in [7]. We also plan to further implement a system, to not only detect, retrieve and save information of one message, but also to be able to create a complete documentation of an event. This documentation would include an extended period of time, based on several micro blogging platforms and media outlets, both independent and corporate. As another result, we expect to develop a full searchable, semantically annotated news stream that will serve as a neutral and centralized SPARQL endpoint for data journalism.

References

1. Das, N., Gollapudi, S., Munagala, K.: Modeling opinion dynamics in social networks. In: WSDM 2014 (2014)
2. Joshua, S.: Realtime. In: WWW 2010 (2010)
3. Laniado, D., Mika, P.: Making sense of twitter. In: Patel-Schneider, P.F., Pan, Y., Hitzler, P., Mika, P., Zhang, L., Pan, J.Z., Horrocks, I., Glimm, B. (eds.) ISWC 2010, Part I. LNCS, vol. 6496, pp. 470–485. Springer, Heidelberg (2010)
4. Muoz, E., Hogan, A., Mileo, A.: Using linked data to mine rdf from wikipedias tables. In: WSDM 2014 (2014)
5. Pak, A., Paroubek, P.: Twitter as a corpus for sentiment analysis and opinion mining. In: Seventh International Conference on Language Resources and Evaluation (2010)
6. Ritter, A.: Extracting Knowledge from Twitter and The Web. PhD thesis, University of Washington (2012)
7. Rodrguez, E.V., Ana, A.G., Torre Bastida, I., Rodrguez, M.G.: Using linked open data sources for entity disambiguation. In: CLEF Iniciative (2012)
8. Tandon, N., de Melo, G., Suchanek, F., Weikum, G.: Webchild: Harvesting and organizing commonsense knowledge from the web. In: WSDM 2014 (2014)

Semantic Annotation of Service Choreographies

Vinh Thinh Luu and Ioana Ciuciu

Université Joseph Fourier, Grenoble, France
Vinh-Thinh.Luu@e.ujf-grenoble.fr,
Ioana-Georgiana.Ciuciu@imag.fr

Abstract. In a previous paper, we discussed a methodology for the extension of the service choreography model based on ontologies. The main purpose was to extract syntactically and semantically correct recommendations (model annotations) for the process modeler in view of model analysis and improvement. This paper presents ongoing work with a focus on the ontology used for recommendation retrieval and the way the semantic recommender captures and analyses the modeler's intentions. We discuss similarity computation (which is at the basis of semantic model annotation) at several levels and illustrate it with examples.

Keywords: semantic annotation, ontology, service choreography, business process, similarity measure, recommender system.

1   Context and Motivation

In a previous study [1] we introduced a methodology for service choreography improvement based on ontologies. Service choreographies provide a global view that helps better understand, build, analyze and optimize inter-organizational processes involving services. In our approach, annotations are attached to the service choreography models in order to analyze and improve them. However, the annotation is not a straightforward task for the human process modeler (i.e, the user). It contains a high level of details and a vocabulary that is not always accessible to the process modeler. Therefore, we make use of ontologies and ontology-based similarity metrics implemented in a recommender system in order to capture the user design intent and recommend the customized and relevant annotations for the model.

This paper presents ongoing work focusing on the ontological model corresponding to a choreography model introduced in the above-mentioned approach, the vocabularies, and the similarity metrics at three levels - string, lexical and graph – with an illustration of the recommendations extraction. The focus of the paper is not the service choreography model itself, but the attached semantic annotation model.

The rest of the paper is organized as follows: section 2 briefly presents our ontological approach to service choreographies and the role the ontologies play. Section 3 presents the underlying ontology, the similarity algorithms used and the recommendation syntax. Section 4 illustrates the annotation extraction based on the previously presented concepts and approach. Section 5 concludes the paper.

R. Meersman et al. (Eds.): OTM 2014 Workshops, LNCS 8842, pp. 489–493, 2014.

2   Ontologies and Service Choreographies

Service choreography provides a description of the coordinated interactions between two or more distributed parties [2] involving services. An overview of the different choreography languages is given in [3].

In our choreography model, interest points have been defined in order to be able to analyze and improve the choreography. Interest points are attached to choreography element(s); their role is to guide the extraction of information concerning execution properties and model-specific properties. In our study, these interest points are called recommendations. They are modeled using a recommendation ontology that is used to extract information and to properly annotate (part of) a choreography model.

More precisely, ontologies are used to conceptualize the recommendation annotations attached to a choreography element. Ontology is a formal way to represent a common, explicit and agreed-upon conceptualization of a business domain in view of interoperability [4]. Since choreography models have a collaborative nature, semantic interoperability needs follow, in order to ensure the meaningful communication between parties. Ontologies are used in this study in order to ensure semantic interoperability of service choreographies, and more precisely to help the implemented recommender system to compute similarities and extract information in order to be able to derive correct recommendations. More details on the approach for coupling the choreography models with ontologies can be found in [1].

3   Ontology, Recommendations, Similarity Metrics

Ontology. The recommendation ontology is made-up of fact types; an application-specific example of binary fact types expressed in natural language, for the sake of clarity of the business rules (the DOGMA formalism [5]), is depicted in Table 1. Note that the business semantics formalism (DOGMA) can be translated into machine-readable formalisms, such as RDF(S) and OWL [6]. A knowledge base (KB) of facts is associated, populated from correctly derived recommendations.

Table 1. Example of binary fact types (partially) modeling the choreography metrics

Concept 1	Role	Co-role	Concept 2
Metric	is	is a	Number
Metric	is	is a	Percentage
Metric	is	is a	Mean

Recommendation. A graphical representation of the conceptualization of a recommendation is depicted in Fig. 1. A recommendation annotation recommends a criterion. It has a recommendation term and one or more metrics associated. It is defined for a choreography element.

The syntax of a recommendation annotation is specified by a term followed by a list of parameter-value pairs: `@RecommendationTerm[parameter=value]`. A parameter can be a criterion, a choreography element and one or more metrics representing numerical information on the recommendation.

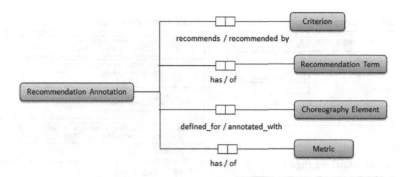

Fig. 1. Graphical representation of the conceptualization of a recommendation annotation

Similarity Metrics. Recommendation retrieval is based on similarity scores computed by various similarity algorithms and strategies of the ODMF framework [7]. As will be illustrated in the next section, the user input is processed and a similarity score with respect to annotations stored in the knowledge base is computed. Based on this score and on a threshold indicated by the user, appropriate recommendations are retrieved and presented to the user.

Given an ontology, the similarity algorithms and strategies perform the following: (i) map data into semantic networks; (ii) perform literal (string) computation, such as fuzzy similarity of literals; (iii) perform lexical computation, such as synonymous similarity and similarity based on user dictionaries; (iv) perform semantic computation, such as path recognition, path strength in scores, composite semantic similarity of semantic networks.

One of the matching strategies used, C-FOAM [7], is composed of two modules: 1) the *interpreter*; and 2) the *comparator*. The *interpreter* uses the lexical dictionary and the domain ontology to interpret the input term. Given a term that denotes a concept in the domain ontology, the interpreter returns the corresponding concept defined in the ontology. The *comparator* then uses any combination of the different ODMF graph algorithms in order to compute the path recognition between two concepts. The functions of these modules are exemplified in the following section.

4   Annotation Extraction

The use case scenario for annotation extraction using the recommender system presented in [1] consists of four steps: (1) the user provides input to the system, according to his/her design intentions; (2) the data matching engine runs various matching algorithms, depending on the user input; based on the similarity scores, the system retrieves a set of annotations; (3) the user is presented with the annotation suggestions; (4) the user selects the appropriate annotation from the set of suggested annotations and specifies values for the parameters (this can also include a retrieval step, using the same process). The simplified process is illustrated in Fig. 2.

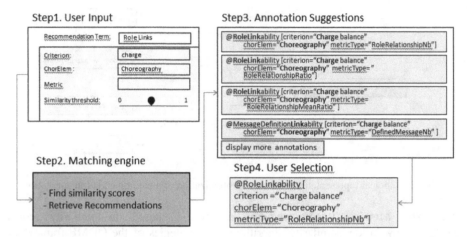

Fig. 2. Scenario for annotation extraction

Note that the matching engine makes use of the RDF(S) and OWL schemas, as well as of the instantiated triples in the knowledge base. Moreover, in order to allow organization-specific vocabularies, we align the multi-domain terminology with the ontology, as shown in Table 2. Such alignments will allow domain-independent querying of the triples.

String Matching. ODMF-specific and SecondString[1] matching algorithms are used to compute the similarity of two objects belonging to the same super-ordinate concept, based on the string similarity of their description. We focus on fuzzy string matching (e.g., JaroWinklerTFIDF) that allow to compensate for the user typing errors, thus increasing the user-friendliness of the system. Therefore, when the user types in, for example, "Chorography", the algorithm will be able to correct it finding the correct term "Choreography".

Lexical Matching. These algorithms compute the similarity of two objects belonging to the same super-ordinate concept, based on the semantic similarity of their descriptions. The objects descriptions should be terminologically annotated. The set of terms used to annotate an object description can be compared to a second set of terms annotating another object description in order to find their similarity, using the Jaccard similarity coefficient: $Jaccard(Set1, Set2) = |Set1 \cap Set2|/|Set1 \cup Set2|$.

For example, the security annotation description "RoleLinkability" could be annotated with the terms 'role' and 'linkability'.

Linguistic information is used in order to perform the matching. Two techniques are used: i) tokenization and lemmatization; and ii) an ontologically structured terminological database, based on WordNet[2] or user-defined dictionaries (see Table 2). Introperability is ensured through alignment (mapping) between user dictionaries and ontology. Suppose two organizations use different terms for "RoleLinkability": "role connection" and "role binding". They will be able to collaborate thanks to the agreed-upon ontological concept and the existing mapping.

---

[1] http://secondstring.sourceforge.net/
[2] http://wordnet.princeton.edu/

Table 2. Lexical synonyms, organization-specific terminology

Synonyms	Ontology Concept
"role connection", "role binding"	"RoleLinkability"
"job", "task"	"Role"

Graph Matching. Is used to compute the similarity between two objects representing two sub-graphs of the same semantic graph (ontology). Concepts are represented as vertices and semantic relations between concepts are represented as bi-directed arcs (i.e., the role and co-role in a binary fact type). This technique requires a domain ontology and an application ontology. A preprocessing step of data mapping is also necessary, from the user vocabulary to the domain ontology. The similarity score can be used also for identifying related objects, given an initial object, as it is the case in this paper. Matching at graph level in this study is work in progress.

5 Conclusion and Future Work

The paper presents the semantic concepts and techniques at the basis of an approach for coupling service choreographies with domain knowledge (ontology). We presume this to be extremely helpful as it opens the path towards interoperability in the context of service choreography and BPMN communities, reinforcing knowledge sharing between organizations with heterogeneous backgrounds. Moreover, it gives place to an opening towards the Semantic Web and the possibility to extend the model with other existing models. In this paper we focused on knowledge extraction through reasoning at different levels aiming to ease the human process modeler efforts.

Ongoing work exploits the graph-based matching for annotation retrieval and enrichment with new similarity metrics. Future work includes usability testing of the recommender system and the evaluation of the matching strategies, also with respect to the presumed advantages for service choreography model improvement.

References

1. Cortes-Cornax, M., Ciuciu, I., Dupuy-Chessa, S., Rieu, D., Front, A.: Towards the integration of ontologies with service choreographies. In: Demey, Y.T., Panetto, H. (eds.) OTM 2013 Workshops 2013. LNCS, vol. 8186, pp. 343–352. Springer, Heidelberg (2013)
2. Peltz, C.: WS orchestration and choreography. Computer 36(10), 46–52 (2003)
3. Decker, G., Kopp, O., Leymann, F., Weske, M.: BPEL4Chor: Extending BPEL for Modeling Choreographies. In: IEEE Int. Conf. on Web Services, pp. 296–303 (2007)
4. Gruber, T.R.: Toward Principles for the Design of Ontologies used for Knowledge Sharing. Formal Ontology in Conceptual Analysis and Knowledge Representation (1993)
5. Spyns, P., Tang, Y., Meersman, R.: An ontology engineering methodology for DOGMA. Applied Ontology 3(1-2), 13–39 (2008)
6. Debruyne, C., Tran, T.K., Meersman, R.: Grounding Ontologies with Social Processes and Natural Language. Journal on Data Semantics (2013)
7. Tang, Y., Meersman, R., Ciuciu, I.G., Leenarts, E., Pudney, K.: Towards Evaluating Ontology Based Data Matching Strategies. In: Proceedings of RCIS 2010, Nice (2010)

Selecting Ontologies and Publishing Data of Electrical Appliances: A Refrigerator Example

Anna Fensel, Fabian Gasser, Christian Mayr, Lukas Ott, and Christina Sarigianni

University of Innsbruck, STI Innsbruck
Technikerstr. 21a, 6020 Innsbruck, Austria
Anna.Fensel@sti2.at,
{Fabian.Gasser,Christian.J.Mayr,
Lukas.Ott,Christina.Sarigianni}@student.uibk.ac.at

Abstract. Application scenarios for the data generated from the Internet of Things are on the rise. For example, given the appliances' energy consumption data, energy measurement tools now make it possible to save energy whilst efficiently controlling the consumption of different household devices. Yet, when the precise structured data describing appliance models is missing, it is difficult for such application scenarios to be realized. The developed OpenFridge ontology defines a basic vocabulary for the domain of measuring a refrigerator's energy consumption, showing that the needed ontology schemata are already in place, but need to be identified and skillfully applied. Further, the ontology has been populated from the Web using data scraping, and the created dataset semantically describing the specifics of 1032 refrigerator models with 18665 triples, make these valuable assets for the development of further applications.

Keywords: Energy Efficiency, Semantics, Linked Open Data, Digital Preservation.

1 Introduction

In the European Union, the cost of energy has been rising from one year to the next [11]. From 2010 to 2011, there was a 6.3% rise in household electricity prices. In the previous year, the prices had already risen by 5.7% according to the European Union statistics office. The average price per 100 kWh in the 2nd half of 2011 in Austria was 19.7 Euro [3]. A survey on energy consumption shows that around 73% of the total annual electricity is used in buildings, equally divided into residential and commercial ones. The refrigerator and the alarm clock are devices that are active the whole day. Thus, replacing an old refrigerator with a new one that has less energy consumption, can lead to an enormous reduction in energy costs [1].

The European Commission has released a delegated regulation with regards to the energy labeling of household refrigeration appliances. This should help consumers, for example, to make a decision based on energy saving standards when replacing an old refrigerator with a new one. The energy efficiency index (EEI)

R. Meersman et al. (Eds.): OTM 2014 Workshops, LNCS 8842, pp. 494–503, 2014.
© Springer-Verlag Berlin Heidelberg 2014

categorizes refrigerating appliances from A+++ for very good to G for very bad. The EEI is defined by this regulation and shows an indication of the annual power consumption of the device relative to reference consumption. It denotes that an A+++ appliance saves a minimum of 78% of energy of the reference appliance [11]. The complementary standard for energy efficiency is called Energy Star.

Based on the above mentioned motivation, this paper focuses on an ontology that contains information about the devices, i.e., refrigerators, as well as basic information about the consumers and their households, and the collection of the data on the specific characteristics of refrigerators.

An ontology is a perfect mechanism to share a common understanding about the domain of energy consumption of refrigerators. It also enables the reuse of this domain knowledge and can be one of the tools and applications that can be used to support different stakeholders, such as customers, electric power companies, refrigerator manufacturers, etc. [12].

This paper is structured as follows. In Section 2, we describe the background of the paper. In Section 3, we discuss construction of the OpenFridge ontology. Section 4 discusses the data scraping for population of this ontology. In Section 5, we present the results. Finally, Section 6 concludes and summarizes our paper.

2   Background

As the vision of the Internet of Things[1] moves towards mainstream reality, several new challenges need to be addressed for better adaptation and interconnectivity of such systems. The reality is that data is growing every day. The challenge is dealing with this so called "Big Data". Nowadays, ontology technologies can solve problems in many areas. Each domain has its own thesaurus of words. There are many ways to represent data and semantic technologies can solve the interaction between different domains.

The first step of representing this reality is the creation of a model. Out of this model, a data representation can be derived, for example, with the Unified Modeling Language (UML). UML is not able to represent the semantics of a model. Therefore, the use of an ontology is adding more value. It is also due to the fact that when using ontologies, reasoning is made possible. A lack of model elements and inconsistent classes can be detected during the development of a model when semantic technologies are used. To represent this reality with a model, a Meta Model which gives the classes and properties of meta information should first be created. Out of this meta model, a meta model ontology can be mapped to create a basis for the reasoning engine. After the actual model is created this can also be mapped to the domain ontology. These relationships are described in the paper by Saeki and Kaiya [10].

As mentioned in the introduction, energy efficiency is necessary to reduce energy costs and greenhouse emissions. The first step in reducing energy usage is to gather information. That means understanding where energy is used. Thereafter, the information is converted and summarized. The information is then set into a context. The

---

[1] Wikipedia: Internet of Things:
http://en.wikipedia.org/wiki/Internet_of_Things

context is the basis for building an ontology of the context and setting up the rules for the context. An ontology with the sources of energy requirements is then created. Additionally, this ontology is enhanced with rules to define what is and what is not a cause. The next step in building an energy management system is to set up a control ontology with rules that enable the simulation. The simulation then enables the comparison of different ways of using energy to find one that is the most efficient [6].

The integration with a context aware system and a home appliance control system is an approach which is again based on semantic technologies. An initial, practical approach is demonstrated in the paper of Rosselló-Busquet and Soler [9]. The system in this paper is called Home Energy Management System (HEMS). The core idea is that ontology based rules are available on the web. Therefore, every home system can get access to the rules using the ontology as a web-service to automate the energy management at home.

The SESAME and SESAME-S projects [4],[12], have (as a core element), home automation in order to save energy at home and use the semantic smart metering of energy consumption data at home. Therefore, the home environment is divided into home automation services and home energy services. The energy service has two components, the utility energy service and the metering service. A semantic smart home system for energy efficiency that could be shown with a prototype has been created [13]. The system has sensors which are actuators connected to a controller. The controller sends the data with a router to a local PC or via a secured connection to a remote PC. The whole system is also based on several ontologies like the SESAME Automation Ontology, the SESAME Meter Data Ontology and the SESAME Pricing Ontology [14], and has been successfully deployed in two real-life buildings[2].

Exactly as in the smart metering of devices, the OpenFridge project[3] is set to measure the energy consumption of refrigerators [12]. The goal of the Open Fridge project is to provide a tool to measure energy consumption and to enable the user to compare the data with other users of the same refrigerator. Here, the ontology could work as a blueprint for other devices in the home environment, and enable the users to measure energy consumption of their own appliances and compare their performance with the similarly used appliances of the exactly the same brand and model. It is therefore the first step to higher energy awareness in the household, and a prerequisite to take an energy efficient action e.g. repair or replace a fridge after identifying its insufficient performance. Consequently, for having a comparison base, the data of the refrigerator producers must be procured.

3   Selection of Ontologies

This Section describes the requirements for the OpenFridge ontology modelling and the ontology construction itself.

---

[2] Smart Building Ontology SESAME-S:
   http://datahub.io/dataset/smartbuilding-sesames
[3] OpenFridge: http://openfridge.net

3.1   Requirements

This section examines the preconditions that are needed for building knowledge in the domain of household devices, especially for refrigerators, here referred to in their shortened, informal form as 'fridges'. The tools and devices for collecting the data on the energy consumption have specifications that have to be considered. More information about fridges in general is needed. Companies offer measurement tools (hardware and software) for collecting data on devices in the household. The product "Circle" by the firm Plugwise[4] is a measurement hardware tool that is placed between the power socket and the electrical device. The specifications on the website show that the measurement accuracy is ± 0.5 W.The Circles can be combined in groups, such that they are located in different rooms. In combination with the Plugwise software "Source" which monitors the collecting tools, it is possible to visualize the collected data for a period of time.

Fridges consume electricity the whole day, it is therefore important to have their specifications in mind. The website of "Kühlschrank Test"[5] provides some information on fridges and their manufacturers. Main manufacturers in Germany are Siemens and Bosch, Liebherr, Electrolux, and Whirlpool. A refrigerator can be generally categorized as standalone or build-in. Specifications of fridges contain this, as well as additional information such as dimension, capacity, energy efficiency, energy consumption per year, etc.

The assumption for building an ontology is that it is used in a system that uses a computing layer that accesses the triples stored in an external ontology data storage. The following competency questions should be answered by questioning the knowledge base defined by the ontology:

- How efficient is my fridge compared with others?
- Do I need a replacement for my old fridge?
- What are comparable refrigerator alternatives for my household size?
- How much energy was wasted by opening the door?
- How long are the intervals for cooling?

The information of the ontology should extend the data which is needed for visualization according to the above list. Information about household, user, and fridge itself can provide information on a higher, abstract level.

3.2   Ontology Construction

The domain of the ontology is a combination of the devices that consume energy in the household and the devices that measure the consumed energy. Further, the household and the user of the measuring tools are also included in the domain.

The ontology can be used as a common basis for measuring various services such as monitoring a fridge's energy consumption, performance or deterioration. According to the project specifications, an application should use the Open Fridge ontology in addition to integrating the above mentioned Plugwise technologies. Users of that

---

[4] Plugwise: http://www.plugwise.com
[5] Kühlschrank Test: http://www.kühlschrank-test.org

application can insert data about the fridge (type, age, etc.), and about the household (size, city and country).

After a period of time in which the energy consumption is measured, the user is informed to annotate the measurements. Annotations can contain information about the cooling level, the temperature, filling level of the fridge, how often the doors are opened, and actions that cause an increased consumption.

It is common to refine and extend existing ontology sources and adopt it to the particular domain and task [8]. A web search resulted in an existing ontology about fridges and freezers[6]. The namespace for another important ontology is http://purl.oclc.org/NET/ssnx/ssn that describes sensors and observations, and related concepts. The SSN ontology has been developed by the W3C Semantic Sensor Networks Incubator Group (SSN-XC)[7]. Further relevant ontologies can be located via search e.g. on the Linked Open Vocabularies (LOV) portal[8], and include e.g. Fridge and Freezer Vocabulary Language Reference: http://purl.org/opdm/refrigerator#. Our resulting ontology is also presented on the LOV portal, along with the links to the vocabularies which were selected for use within it.

The overall ontology has been constructed manually. The important terms for the Open Fridge ontology were found by going through different papers on measuring ontologies e.g. by Compton et al. [7]. Some terms came out of different refrigerator specifications that are online and available on manufacturer websites. The following terms are the main terms in the domain of measuring: energy sensing device with its unique identification number, power, sensor output, observation or measuring, observe/measure, start time, and end time. Terms for statistical data about the fridge, user of the system, and the household are the following: fridge, user, household, address, own fridge, annual energy consumption, energy ratings, etc.

In the Open Fridge ontology some main classes have been derived out of the above mentioned SSN ontology. The main classes are shown in Figure 1. The class power, for example, extends the SSN-class MeasurementProperty as an observed property. The class EnergySensingDevice extends the SSN-class SensingDevice as a special class observing the power property. The EnergyObservation class represents the central class of the ontology which connects to many other classes. The classes Fridge, SensorOutput, and SpatioTepoalRegion make the measurement part of the ontology complete.

The main classes, as provided in Figure 1, for the usage of the system and some household statistics, are stored in the classes OpenFridgeUser and OpenFridgeHousehold. Both are connected to another important class: PostalAddress. When integrating the ontologies, many more classes come into the Open Fridge ontology. These classes are mostly super classes of the self-created energy classes.

Most relations about the measurement and observation domain are already defined in the SSN ontology. They are denoted in Figure 1 with the namespace "ssn:", for example, observedBy, observedProperty, startTime, endTime, and observationResult.

---

[6] This ontology is located on: `http://purl.org/opdm/refrigerator` and was developed by a group of authors.

[7] W3C SSN Incubator Group:
`http://www.w3.org/2005/Incubator/ssn/wiki/Main_Page`

[8] Linked Open Vocabularies (LOV): `http://lov.okfn.org/dataset/lov/`

Those relations are attached to the most common classes in the SSN ontology. For any energy observation the relation towards the observed object is essential which is displayed in the notation featureOfInterest. The relation hasHousehold combines the OpenFridgeUser with the OpenFridgeHousehold class. Both have a relationship with the PostalAddress. Figure 1 also shows the relation from OpenFridgeUser to the Fridge class.

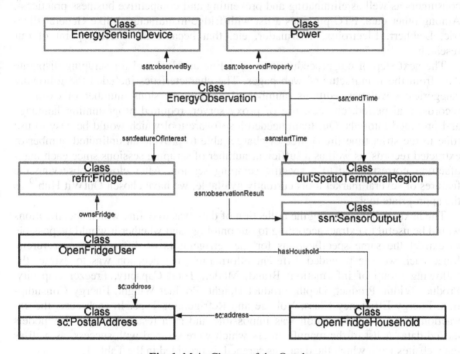

Fig. 1. Main Classes of the Ontology

The last remaining terms denote the attributes of the different classes. For example, the energy sensing device must have a unique identification number which is an attribute of the correspondent class. The fridge ontology provides all important attributes for describing a fridge, such as annual energy consumption, energy rating, type of the fridge, name, some descriptions etc. Additional attributes which describe the two classes OpenFridgeUser and OpenFridgeHousehold are for example the name of the user, number of persons living in the household, etc.

The previously mentioned properties are refined in this step. Restrictions on the cardinality, domain, and range of properties are defined. For example, the property hasHousehold that combines the shown two classes, takes the same classes respectively as domain and as range.

4   Data Scraping

A significant challenge was encountered during the completion of this project regarding the collection of data. Thus, to collect the needed information and define what could be useful for the project, in-depth research was conducted and different tools were utilized. In order to realize the challenges of this procedure, it is recommended to analyze it step by step.

The implementation of the data collection procedure started by searching for globally recognizable fridge manufacturers. For that purpose, the Federal Trade Commission (FTC) website provided us with valuable information. The FTC is an independent agency of the United States government with the mission of protecting consumers as well as eliminating and preventing anti-competitive business practices[9]. Among other data, FTC provides a list with fridge manufacturers like General Electric, Liebherr, Electrolux, Thermador, etc. that became the starting point of our research.

The next step of our procedure was to define an ideal tool for scraping disparate data from the manufacturers' web pages. The characteristics included the following categories: developer, editions, number of scraping sessions, number of extracted records, trial period, charges, use of proxy server, required programming language and provided tutorials. Our team needed a software tool which would be easy to use (due to the strict time limit), free of charge, able to provide an unlimited number of extracted records, as well as a sufficient number of scraping sessions since each manufacturer corresponded to a specific scraping session. After closely observing the features of several market tools currently available, we have chosen OutWit Hub[10] as the appropriate tool.

The next challenge during the collection of data was to define which specifications would be useful to extract according to our ontology and whether it would be possible to extract the same specifications for the refrigerators of different manufacturers. Since each website provided different information, the decision was to extract the following group of information: Brand, Model, Total Capacity, Freezer Capacity, Product Width, Product, Depth, Product Height, Product Weight, Energy Consumption, Energy Efficiency Class, Voltage and Refrigerator Type. In each case, the extraction of all the information was impossible and as a result, some of the models lacked data. A list of the manufacturers which were scraped with success, as well as the websites from which the data was scraped, is provided in the Table 1.

As described above, we have extracted data from different websites with very heterogeneous formats. Therefore, the next step in bringing the extracted data into the ontology was to import them into a tool and restructure them without removing and losing relevant information. Afterwards, we needed to bring them into an RDF/XML format that we could open with the Protégé ontology editor. Finally the code had to be adopted with the right location identifier where the ontologies are stored.

5   Results

The resulting ontology and the datasets have been published online in a publicly available URI[11] and repository[12] with a SPARQL endpoint. The namespace

---

[9] Wikipedia: Federal trade commission: http://en.wikipedia.org/w/
index.php?title=Federal_Trade_Commission&oldid=579273373
[10] OutWit: http://www.outwit.com
[11] OpenFridge ontology: http://owlrep.eu01.aws.af.cm/fridge
[12] OpenFridge data repository can be found online e.g. via the website www.openfridge.net

http://www.openfridge.net/2013/11/data# has been adapted to the datasets, where the data can be queried over a repository. The data repository contains descriptions of more than 1000 refrigerator models: currently 1032 various models, employing 18665 triples.

By applying the data scraping (see Section 4) for the 17 brands we created 42 documents with the XML/RDF type. A list of all brands with their relevant characteristics can be found in Table 2. As each fridge has to be identified with its brand and model name, these two elements are included in each table and file. Moreover, the sizes for depth, height and width for most of the brands were extractable (15 - 17 times), which is important information when people want to replace their old fridge with a new one. Furthermore, the capacity of the units (15 times) is an important criteria and is therefore almost contained as well. Similarly important is the freezer capacity, but this was only available 10 times. Energy consumption and energy efficiency rating information was lacking for all brands and as a result, could only be provided for 6 and 4 brands respectively. We were also able to add the information about the design/refrigerator type separately on six occasions.

Table 1. Refrigerator Manufacturers' Sources

	Website
Amana	http://www.amana.com/#refrigerators
Blomberg	http://www.blombergappliances.us/urun_liste.aspx?kat=1498&lang=en-US
Danby	http://www.danby.com/en/CA/our_products/refrigeration
Electrolux	http://www.electrolux.at/Products/Kuehlen/
Fisher&Paykel	http://www.fisherpaykel.com/nz/kitchen/fridges-freezers/fridges/
General Electric	http://www.geappliances.com/appliances/refrigerators.htm?omni_key=ge.com_refrigerator
Kenmore Appliances	http://www.kenmore.com/kitchen-refrigerators-freezers/b-1040176?&/Refrigerators&adCell=WH
KitchenAid	http://www.kitchenaid.com/shop/major-appliances-1/refrigerators-2/refrigerators-3/102020048/
Liebherr	http://www.liebherr.com/HG/en-GB/region-AT/products_hg.wfw/id-650083-0
Maytag Corporation	http://www.maytag.com/Kitchen-1/Kitchen_Refrigeration-2/102120030/
Miele	http://www.miele.co.uk/fridge-freezers/
Robert Bosch GmbH	http://www.bosch-home.co.uk/our-products/fridges-and-freezers.html
Samsung	http://www.samsung.com/us/appliances/refrigerators
Summit Appliances	http://summitappliance.com/refrigeration
Thermador Corporation	http://www.thermador.com/refrigeration
Whirlpool Corporation	http://www.whirlpool.com/Kitchen-1/Kitchen_Refrigeration_Refrigerators-3/102110023+102110368/
White Westinghouse	http://www.white-westinghouse-intl.com/section_Listing.asp?prod=RFR

Table 2. Refrigerator Brands Table

Brand	Model	Energy Efficiency Class	Energy Consumption	Voltage	Total Capacity	Product Width	Product Height	Product Depth	Product Weight	Freezer Capacity	Refrigerator Type
Amana	+	+	-	-	-	+	+	+	+	-	+	+
Blomberg	+	+	-	-	-	+	+	+	+	+	+	-
Danby	+	+	-	-	-	+	+	+	+	+	-	-
Electrolux	+	+	-	+	+	+	+	+	+	-	-	-
Fisher&Paykel	+	+	-	+	-	+	-	+	+	-	+	-
General Electric	+	+	-	-	+	+	+	+	+	+	+	-
Kenmore Appliances	+	+	-	-	-	+	+	+	+	-	+	+
KitchenAid	+	+	-	-	-	+	+	+	+	-	+	+
Liebherr	+	+	+	+	-	-	+	+	+	-	-	+
Maytag Corporation	+	+	-	-	-	+	+	+	+	-	+	+
Miele	+	+	+	+	+	-	+	+	+	+	+	-
Robert Bosch GmbH	+	+	+	+	+	+	+	+	-	+	-	-
Samsung	+	+	-	-	-	+	+	+	+	-	+	-
Summit Appliances	+	+	-	+	+	+	+	+	+	+	-	-
Thermador Corporation	+	+	-	-	-	+	+	+	+	+	-	-
Whirlpool Corporation	+	+	-	-	-	+	-	+	+	-	+	+
White Westinghouse	+	+	+	-	+	+	+	+	+	-	-	-

6   Conclusion

In this paper, the motivation for building an ontology for storing energy consumption data was shown. As energy prices will inevitably increase in the future, awareness of energy use must be built. The developed Open Fridge ontology provides all necessary classes and properties for dealing with the measurement data of systems, such as the Plugwise measurement tools. The main structure of the ontology is defined by integrated, freely available ontologies. The instances have been acquired from the real life resources of the Web, and were used to test the ontology by querying SPARQL on them. The ontology was developed in such a manner where an extension of it is possible. Therefore, for future work, an extension for measuring other household appliances should be easily achievable. The data acquisition also becomes simpler with the available tool support, however, to be usable as foreseen in the project, the dataset generated as descried still needs to be extended with further input from additional resources or users. The latter can be achieved for example applying crowdsourcing techniques on the OpenFridge portal, where the community would be providing and cross-validating the missing information about brands and models' features.

Acknowledgments. This work has been partially funded by the project OpenFridge supported by the Austrian Research Promotion Agency (FFG) within the program "Future ICT", as well as an EU-funded project PRELIDA: Preserving Linked Data. The authors gratefully acknowledge the contributions of our project partners, especially of FTW Telecommunications Research Center Vienna and Semantic Web Company, and thank Amy Strub for proofreading.

References

1. Bonino, D., Corno, F., De Russis, L.: Home Energy Consumption Feedback A User Survey. Energy and Buildings (2011)
2. Brandon, G., Lewis, A.: Reducing Household Energy Consumption: A Qualitative and Quantitative Field Study. Journal of Environmental Psychology 19, 75–85 (1999)
3. Eurostat Press Office,
   http://epp.eurostat.ec.europa.eu/cache/ITY_PUBLIC/8-25052012-AP/EN/8-25052012-AP-EN.PDF
4. Fensel, A., Tomic, S.: SESAME: Semantic Smart Metering – Enablers for Energy Efficiency. In: Proceedings of the Poster and Demonstration Track at the 2nd Future Internet Symposium (FIS 2009), Berlin, Germany (2009)
5. Fensel, A., Tomic, S., Kumar, V., Stefanovic, M., Aleshin, S., Novikov, D.: SESAME-S: Semantic Smart Home System for Energy Efficiency. Informatik-Spektrum 36(1), 46–57 (2012)
6. Han, J., Jeong, Y.K., Lee, I.: Efficient building energy management system based on ontology, inference rules, and simulation. In: Proceedings of the 2011 International Conference on Intelligent Building and Management, Singapore, vol. 5 (2011)
7. Compton, M., Henson, C.A., Neuhaus, H., Lefort, L., Sheth, A.P.: A Survey of the Semantic Specification of Sensors. In: SSN, pp. 17–32 (2009)
8. Noy, N.F., McGuinness, D.L.: Ontology Development 101: A Guide to Creating Your First Ontology. Stanford Knowledge Systems Laboratory Technical Report KSL-01-05 and Stanford Medical Informatics Technical Report SMI-2001-0880 (2001)
9. Rosselló-Busquet, A., Soler, J.: A novel web service based home energy management system. In: The Third International Conference on Advances in Future Internet, AFIN 2011, pp. 126–131 (2011)
10. Saeki, M., Kaiya, H.: On relationships among models, meta models and ontologies. In: Proceedings of the 6th OOPSLA Workshop on Domain-Specific Modeling, DSM 2006 (2006)
11. The European Commission,
    http://eurlex.europa.eu/LexUriServ/LexUriServ.do?uri=OJ:L:2010:314:0017:0046:EN:PDF
12. Tomic, S., Fensel, A.: A Platform for Data Economy for Energy Efficiency Data. In: Proceedings of BigData 2013: Data Economy in the Big Data Era, Silicon Valley, CA, USA (2013)
13. Tomic, S., Fensel, A., Pellegrini, T.: SESAME demonstrator: ontologies, services and policies for energy efficiency. In: Proceedings of the 6th International Conference on Semantic Systems, ACM (2010)
14. Tomic, S., Fensel, A., Schwanzer, M., Kojic Veljovic, M., Stefanovic, M.: Semantics for Energy Efficiency in Smart Home Environments. In: Sugumaran, V., Gulla, J.A. (eds.) Applied Semantic Technologies: Using Semantics in Intelligent Information Processing, pp. 429–454. Taylor and Francis (August 2011)

Non-intrusive Tongue Tracking and Its Applicability in Post-stroke Rehabilitation

Dan Mircea Suciu, Bogdan Andrei Pop, Rares Urdea, and Bogdan Mursa

Babes-Bolyai University, Cluj-Napoca, Romania
tzutzu@cs.ubbcluj.ro, {pbie1302,urie1493,mbie1438}@scs.ubbcluj.ro

Abstract. sMilestone is a medical software solution which achieves the goal of helping people who have lost their ability to speak as a result of neurological injuries such as strokes or brain tumors. It aids patients in the recovery process, improving the speed at which they recover while also alleviating the psychological implications associated with such a condition. All this is achieved by using a device called Kinect for capturing facial muscle and tongue movement. These captured movements are then used as input for games and activities that make use of occupational therapy and hasten the recovery process. This paper goes through the details of how the tongue movement tracking algorithm was developed in order to be used in speech recovery sessions.

1 Introduction

According to the World Health Organization, a stroke happens every two seconds. Consequently roughly 15 milion people, worldwide, suffer from strokes every year [12].

Out of the 10 million survivors, nearly a quarter are faced with speech impairment, yearly. Speech impairment is characterized by the difficulty encountered in the articulation of words. Examples include stuttering or problems producing particular sounds.

Speech and language therapists (SLTs) play a vital role at all stages along the care pathway. According to Royal College of Speech and Language Therapists, it is recommended that there should be at least one full time equivalent speech and language therapist per ten beds in every stroke unit [8]. Any assitant tools which could help SLTs during their rehabilitation activities could decrease the rehabilitation period and, at the same time, would allow an SLT to assist more than ten patients daily.

The field of computer assisted recovery has seen a huge growth lately, with a lot of time and effort being invested in research. The most important ones are those focused on non-intrusive methods of assisting recovery [2], [4], [6], [7], [9], [10], [13]. In an effort to keep up with medical issues, computer recovery software has come a long way. There are many solutions aimed at motor skill recovery, but only a few deal with speech recovery, and most of them are intrusive.

Our solution, sMilestone, is an application that makes use of Microsoft's device, Kinect, in order to capture facial muscle and tongue movement using a

R. Meersman et al. (Eds.): OTM 2014 Workshops, LNCS 8842, pp. 504–513, 2014.

non-intrusive method. Its aim was to help patients that suffered from any kind of neurological accidents or conditions, which lost control over their mouth and tongue muscles. It was tailored to offer a series of interactive and encouraging exercises, activities and games for the patient to practice in a positive environment. The application was made to not only help patients, but doctors as well, allowing them to attend to multiple patients while being able to keep track of their progress and being reassured that all of them exercise properly.

This paper will go into more details regarding how the tongue movements are tracked by sMilestone and regarding the main challenges we had to overcome during the implementation process.

In the next section the Kinect device is presented, as it is the main device that allows for the capture of the data of interest. The section covers aspects such as Kinect technical specifications and what data it can collect.

The third section follows the planning phase of the sMilestone project and describes in details the implementation of the tongue detection module by using the Kinect details. It also shows the difficulties we encountered while trying to come up with the solution, and the answers that managed to overcome those difficulties.

The last section contains some conclusions and future prospects.

2 Kinect Device

Kinect is a motion sensing device, developed by Microsoft, which enables hands-free control by tracking and interpreting users body movement in three dimension using an infrared projector and RGB camera [5]. At the moment there are two versions of the device, Kinect 1.0 and Kinect 2.0. For the present paper, we will focus on the Kinect 1.0 version.

Although the Kinect was developed as a gaming tool, it has a considerable potential in the realm of stroke therapy. The joint-tracking capability could enhance therapeutic diagnostics considerably. Doctors could use software developed with the Kinect to assess the performance of their patients and to track their improvement [4].

The Kinect could also be a useful tool for at-home therapy. Therapy at home is more flexible and convenient for the patient and allows for more frequent repetition of exercises. In order to stimulate neural reactivation in regions of the brain that control movement, exercises must be repeated many times every day [3]

2.1 Kinect 1.0 Hardware

The Kinect makes use of a special range camera technology which was initially developed by a company named Prime Sense [1]. The sensor they developed could interpret a wide range of gestures, making the hands-free interaction of a person with the computer possible by using an infrared projector and a camera along with a microchip in order to track 3D movement. The 3D scanner was called

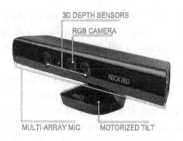

Fig. 1. Kinect features and build

'Light Coding' and it employed a sort of 3D reconstruction based on images. As it can be seen in Figure 1, the sensor features a motorized base which provides the device's tilt and pivot. Another feature is the RGB camera which functions at different resolutions, mainly 640x480 pixels, @30Hz or 1024x720 pixels but at a lower frame rate. It also features two 3D depth sensor cameras which function at 640x480 @30Hz at most. These two 3D depth sensor cameras provide full body 3d motion capture and facial recognition to some degree. One last strong point of the device is the multi-array microphone which runs proprietary software and allows for voice recognition commands [14].

The most useful feature, the depth sensor is comprised from an infrared projector and a monochrome CMOS (Complementary Metal-Oxide Semiconductor) sensor, which, when combined, can collect the 3D data in front of the Kinect regardless of the lighting conditions. The way it works is that the infrared projector blasts the entire area in front of the device with infrared light which can, in turn, be interpreted by the CMOS camera. Because of this infrared blaster, objects which are too close to the device become too bright, therefore, not easy to distinguish, this narrowing the area which the device can see to a zone starting roughly at 0.5 meters in front of the device and ending at roughly 5 meters from the device. The device's microphone array allows the computing of acoustic source localization and ambient noise suppression, thus capturing sound clearly, making voice recognition and chatting between people possible without the need of an additional device. The microphone array is comprised of four microphones that can isolate the voices of the player from other background noise.

The depth sensor video stream is monochrome and has a VGA resolution with 11-bit depth. It provides 2048 levels of sensitivity and can also stream the image from the infrared camera prior to it being converted into a depth map. The video camera complements the depth sensor in identifying colors, thus providing all the information required for tracking things like facial features.

The piece of hardware requires an area of roughly 6 square meters in order for it to function optimally. It has an angular field of view of 57 degrees horizontally and 43 degrees vertically, the motorized pivot allowing the tilt of the sensor up to 27 degrees either up or down.

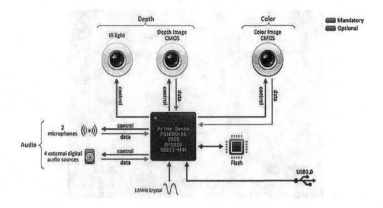

Fig. 2. Prime Sense diagram explaining how their reference platform works [1]

2.2 Depth Field Data Collection

Machine vision is the area of research aimed at observing and measuring physical objects using a video camera. It is usually associated with manufacturing and detecting defects in different objects that are being manufactured. Computer vision is the area of research aimed at teaching a computer its physical surroundings via the use of image sensors.

In both cases, 3D image sensors like Microsoft's Kinect have a huge impact as they solve an array of issues associated with traditional 2D cameras such as perspective distortion (the distortion of objects as they get further from the camera), all at a very low cost.

There is a wide range of methods by which one can measure depth with a camera. The Kinect 1.0 makes use of triangulation in order to achieve this. Triangulation is the process used by stereo-imaging systems, such as the human sight. It works by capturing the image information from two perspectives and generating a 3D image based on the resulting image.

Even though the Kinect 1.0 sensor does make use of triangulation, it is not exactly the same type of triangulation as the human eyes, since it does not make use of two cameras in order to perform the triangulation. The device actually relies on the triangulation between a near-infrared camera and a near-infrared laser source in order to create the process called structured-light. This process is one of the first methods for 3D scanning and it features a single light stripe which sweeps across a target object. A complete 3D surface can be constructed from the collection of images taken as the light stripe swiped across the object.

An important module of the SDK is the Microsoft Face Tracking Software Development Kit for Kinect for Windows (Face Tracking SDK) which, along with the Kinect for Windows Software Development Kit (Kinect for Windows SDK), allows developers to create applications that can track human faces in real time.

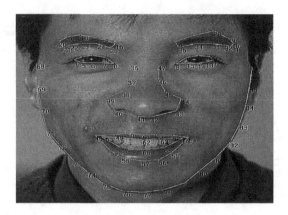

Fig. 3. The tracked 2D points

This Face Tracking SDK features a face tracking engine that analyzes input from a Kinect camera and computes the head pose and facial expressions, making the information available to an application in real time. The data gathered gives the developer information regarding a tracked user, such as the tracking status, 2D points and 3D head pose. The SDK can track 87 2D points indicated by figure 5. These points are returned in an array and are defined in the coordinate space of the RGB image, thus making for a fairly easy debug system. There are 13 additional points which are not shown in the figure, such as the center of the eye, the corners of the mouth and the center of the nose.

3 Tongue Detection

Tongue detection was done with the help of the Kinect SDK and the Face Tracking SDK using the Kinect 1.0. It is written in C# using Windows Presentation Foundation framework, in which the data collected by the Kinect is taken and displayed as a webcam stream would. On top of that video stream, certain points of interest are also displayed.

When starting to work with the Face Tracking SDK, it became quickly obvious that while it does provide a lot of information and it can be tailored to suite our needs, it wasn't exactly made to track intricate details and soft movements, as tongue tracking process would require. This is because of the technical limitations that exist, as explained in previuos section. The Kinect tracks groups of depth points and merely estimates the depth between those points, thus not allowing for very fine tracking or very subtle movement detection.

Also, the Kinect SDK can, as presented in the earlier section, detect several features of the face out of the box. Upon closer inspection of how the face tracking module works however, we noticed that a lot of the information displayed is just an approximation and not only that, but a lot of it was obtained by reflection. It did not in fact capture each individual point, instead, it captured an array of points which it tracked correctly and placed the others where they would need to be, forming the symmetrical shape of the face.

For the tongue detection we began by identifying the exact needs of an application which could assist a therapist for speech recovery sessions, namely, being able to implement a way to not only detect that the tongue is pointing out but also the movement of the tongue. The exercises that needed to be implemented required for a pretty good grasp of the location of the tip of the tongue. We started researching what the Kinect SDK provided in terms of information regarding the captured and tracked data, only to quickly find out that it does not provide any sort of support for the detection of the tongue. We also checked to see whether someone else had done this before, and, if so, to what extent. We found a couple of solutions (none of them described but only presented in some demo videos) that were nowhere near the level of accuracy that we knew we needed in order for the exercises to be a success. With that in mind, we started to develop an algorithm from scratch.

While we could retrieve the information regarding the depth of the pixels in front of Kinect device, because of the technical implementation, often it may prove that the depths in question were more or less guess-work. This made it clear that besides just using the depth field to capture the movement, we would need to implement something on top of it that not only follows the tongue movement but smooth's out the entire process. This was because of the fact that the depth field was very jittery and spastic, making the smooth and precise tracking of a certain point a pretty difficult endeavor.

The first iteration of the solution followed a pretty simple logic: to make use of a combination of information that the Kinect made available, the depth field and the facial points that are tracked. By using the two, the idea was to track the depth field strictly in the area of the mouth, thus making it so that the lowest depth value (closest to the Kinect device) would be considered the tip of the tongue. The solution had come to fruition and yielded decent results such that, in a controlled environment and with one of us as a test subject, it could be presented as a very early proof of concept. There were many issues though, it was too jittery, it would easily lose track of the tip of the tongue and, worst of all, for some reason, it only worked on one of us and no one else. It was very unreliable and we knew that it was mostly because the depth field the Kinect draws is a pretty rough representation of reality.

In the second iteration we went back to the drawing board, knowing that the results shown by the initial solution were not nearly good enough to be used in a post-stroke recovery application reliably. What we eventually came up with is a system which follows a few rules:

a. As soon as the application starts up and the video and depth streams are loaded it locates the points belonging to the mouth as seen in figure 4, 0 - top lip, 1 - bottom lip, 2 - left of mouth, 3 - right of mouth

b. Once these points are located it narrows down the search area as seen in figure 4. The ellipse represents the mouth. The search area is narrowed down to the zone covered horizontally by the area of x_0, x_1 and x_2 and vertically by

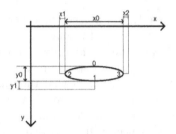

Fig. 4. An explanation of the area of search

y_0 and y_1. The added values to the left, right and bottom are there in order to take into account the fact that the tongue may move slightly outside the points marked by the lips. The top part of the mouth does not get a bigger zone of capture because of the risk that the Kinect might detect the nose as the closest point.

c. With the area narrowed down, it searches for the point of minimum value in the depth field for the area computed by the second rule. This point should represent the tongue tip. Because of the rough state of the depth field, this point cannot be used as a reliable reading for the tip of the tongue though.

d. Once the point considered to be the tip of the tongue is determined, a new point is created. This point will start off where the initial tip of the tongue is detected. We will call it 'TT' (from tongue tip), and we will use 'DVP' (depth value point) for the point representing the minium depth value in the computed area.

e. With this new point becoming known, the application narrows down area of the depth field that will be used for keeping track of the tip of the tongue even more. This needs to be done precisely because of the fact that the Kinect 1.0 only knows the true depth of certain groups of points. Therefore it only estimates the depth of the pixels in between those points, giving off rough interpretations of depth. By narrowing down the area even more, the chance of getting an off-reading becomes even smaller. The new area is roughly 1 cm horizontally to the left and right of the TT (2 cm in total), and the same vertically. That zone is further restricted by a set of maximum outer bounds. For example, as the TT reaches the left extreme of x_1, if the distance between TT and the left extreme of x_1 is less than 1 cm, the new limit for the left of the TT becomes x_1. This applies to the right extreme with x_2, the bottom extreme with y_1 and for the top extreme, the top of y_0.

f. In order to keep the interpretation of the TT smooth and for it to not jump around all over the place because of the roughness of the depth field, the TT does not move in the same pace that the DVP does. Considering that the application recalculates the DVP 30 times a second, not all 30 of the readings will be accurate because some of them are only estimations having fallen between the points whose depth value are calculated properly. Because of this, if the DVP would be the point that decided the area that will be taken into consideration, the reading would be all over the place and not accurate at all, having the possibility to drift off far from the tongue and not to return. In order to avoid this from happening, the TT is the point that decides the area that is taken into consideration, and in order to not fall in the same pitfalls as the DVP, the TT actually only has a movement allowance of roughly 1 mm per frame in the direction that the DVP is pointing. This means that if the DVP were to wonder off on some incorrect readings, the TT would not move along at the same rate (as the DVP might give reading differences between two frames of even 2 or 3 cm) and instead, it would only make a slight movement in the wrong direction, not allowing the detection area to drift off to incorrect coordinates. Because of this, the chances that the next reading of the DVP are also very far off become much more negligible, as the DVP could even fail, for example, 5 frames and as long as the next few frames it detects the correct position, the TT would still follow the correct reading. This system makes for a very smooth and accurate reading of the position of the tip of the tongue in space.

With these new rules in place, the application gets a very smooth reading. So smooth in fact, that it could be used as a mouse cursor for people with disabilities. It is not yet perfect, admittedly, as in some situations it may lose track of the tip of the tongue, but only for a short period and it gets back on track (based on our tests in 10 minutes the system lost track the tip of the tongue 3 times in average).

With the tongue detection module out of the way, we developed a variation of a pretty popular game concept which follows a few simple rules and showcases the wide range of movement pretty well. The game's idea was that the player represent a red dot. There is a rectangular playing field in which the dot can move. In this playing field, there are a number of blue dots which move around randomly, at random speeds and random directions, bouncing off the walls. The red dot is not allowed to be hit by these blue dots. The objective is to capture a slightly bigger, orange dot in order to claim points. The red dot is controled by using the players tongue in order to decide in which direction you move (figure 7). This game was created just as a proof of concept, and it fits very well to that end because of the fact that it tests the ability to control a dot by using the tongue, allowing for movement in any direction.

In a future implementation, we aim to make the data capture as reliable as it can get, eliminating any quirks that might exist currently. Another aspect we wish to implement is on the game side, the direction that the player is moving can be computed by translating the vector between the DVP and the TT to the coordinates of the player dot, in order for the dot to move in the same direction that the DVP to TT vector is pointing at. This will allow for a much greater area of movement and will allow for a much smoother process in dealing with future implementations, such as using the tongue movement in order to move the mouse cursor.

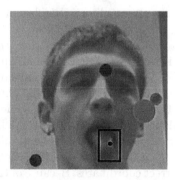

Fig. 5. The tongue detection game in action

4   Conclusions

This paper covers an array of topics, namely, how the Kinect device works, how its software makes use of the data that the hardware collects and how the SDK allows developers to make use of the features it provides. It also goes over the results of our original work, and explains the tongue detection module in detail and goes over all the difficulties encountered while developing this module.

While there are other applications which make use of some concepts present in this article, like tongue detection, none of them were developed for the same purpose as this application, and even if they would, they would fall short as the accuracy of those applications isn't as precise or as smooth. This article brings originality through the use of the tongue detection module in areas of medicine where technology wasn't to its full efficiency. The application developed, sMilestone, not only brings originality in the field, but also innovation, as it makes the recovery process much easier on the patient, being non-invasive and making use of occupational therapy, while also keeping a constant exercising environment available. The patient isn't the only one benefitting from the application, as doctors can constantly monitor patients with the reports and statistics tracked by the application. The application saves the patient's time, the doctor's time, and, even though the technology is complex, it is also expensive, also saving money as opposed to other treatments that are invasive as well.

In the future, the tongue detection module can, and will be used towards providing people with disabilities another way of interacting with the computer. With the Kinect 2.0 being on the way, having explained all the improvements it brings, the application can only move forward in becoming incredibly reliable and useful for patients all over the world.

References

1. Inon Beraca: PrimeSense Supplies 3-D-Sensing Technology to, Project Natal. Microsoft News Center (2010),
   http://www.microsoft.com/en-us/news/press/2010/mar10/
   03-31primesensepr.aspx
2. Davaasambuu, E., Chiang, C.C., Chiang, J.Y., Chen, Y.F., Bilgee, S.: A Microsoft Kinect Based Virtual Rehabilitation System. In: Proceedings of the 5th International Conference FITAT 2012, pp. 44–55 (2012)
3. Hayes, A., Dukes, P., Hodges, L.F.: A Virtual Environment for Post- Stroke Motor Rehabilitation. Clemson University, Clemson (2012)
4. LaBelle, K.: Evaluation of Kinect Joint Tracking for Clinical and In-Home Stroke Rehabiliatoin Tools. Undergraduate Thesis, University of Notre Dame (2011)
5. Microsoft: Xbox 360 + Kinect. Accesible (2011),
   http://www.xbox.com/en-US/kinect
6. Pogrzeba, L., Wacker, M., Jung, B.: Potentials of a low-cost motion analysis system for exergames in rehabilitation and sports medicine. In: Göbel, S., Müller, W., Urban, B., Wiemeyer, J. (eds.) GameDays 2012 and Edutainment 2012. LNCS, vol. 7516, pp. 125–133. Springer, Heidelberg (2012)
7. Robertson, C., Vink, L., Regenbrecht, H., Lutteroth, C., Wünsche, B.C.: Mixed Reality Kinect Mirror Box for Stroke Rehabilitation. Image and Vision Computing New Zealand, 231–235 (2013)
8. Royal College of Speech and Language Therapists: Policy statement: The specialist contribution of speech and language therapists along the care pathway for stroke survivors. Accessible (2007),
   http://www.stroke-in-stoke.info/otherfiles/policynov07.pdf
9. Stone, E.E., Butler, M., McRuer, A., Gray, A., Marks, J., Skubic, M.: Evaluation of the Microsoft Kinect for screening ACL injury. In: 35th Annual International Conference of the IEEE EMBS, Osaka, Japan, pp. 4152–4156 (2013)
10. Tingfang Du: Upper Body Motion Analysis Using Kinect for Stroke Rehabilitation at the Home. Electrical Engineering Masters Thesis, Arizona State University (2012)
11. Stephen Totilo: Natal Recognizes 31 Body Parts, Uses Tenth Of Xbox 360 Computing Resources (2010),
    http://kotaku.com/5442775/natal-recognizes-31-body-parts-uses-tenth-
    of-xbox-360-computing-resources
12. World Health Organization (WHO): Global burden of stroke (2014),
    http://www.who.int/cardiovascular_diseases/en/
    cvd_atlas_15_burden_stroke.pdf?ua=1 (accessed on August 8, 2014)
13. Bao, X., Mao, Y., Lin, Q., Qiu, Y., Chen, S., Li, L., Cates, R., Zhou, S., Huang, D.: Mechanism of Kinect-based virtual reality training for motor functional recovery of upper limbs after subacute stroke. Neural Regeneration Research 8(31), 2885–2974 (2013)
14. Zhang, Z.: Microsoft Kinect Sensor and Its Effect. IEEE Computer Society, IEEE MultiMedia 19(2), 4–12 (2014)

Organizational Culture and Innovation: An Industrial Case Study

Raluca Alexandra Ciuciu[1], Veronica Mateescu[1], and Ioana Ciuciu[2]

[1] Babes-Bolyai University, Cluj-Napoca, Romania
[2] University Joseph Fourier, Grenoble, France
Raluca.Ciuciu@gmail.com

Abstract. The paper proposes the study of the perception of the relationship between the organizational culture and innovation. More precisely, we propose to identify those features of the organizational culture that affect (determine or inhibit) innovation and elaborate on these observations. The methodology used in this approach is rooted in knowledge management theory and based on a questionnaire applied in the Engineering Department of a newly established multinational in the automotive industry in Romania. The observed relationship is exemplified with a real-world case study from the automotive industry.

Keywords: organizational culture, innovation, business environment, values, creativity, social interactions.

1   Context and Motivation

"Innovate or die". This expression characterizes today's world, be it in areas such as the automotive industry, the high-tech, art or lifestyle. We find these words in many works of literature and organizational studies have recognized that in the world of business, it is a slogan that underpins any business idea. In the academic world, the concept of innovation is widely discussed and many attempts have been made to define it. Its meaning, however, is fully highlighted if placed in the context of a particular company and related to its organizational culture. No less discussed is the concept of organizational culture (OC). In order to succeed, the innovation process needs support and this may come from the OC features characterizing an entity.

The present work proposes to study the two concepts and their relationship and interactions. More precisely, we propose to identify those features of the OC that determine or inhibit the innovation and will elaborate on these observations. We exemplify with a real-world case study from the Romanian automotive industry. Since the Romanian business environment is a relatively new one, where many investors from abroad are present, an analysis on the development of the OC of a young company, with constituents both Romanian and foreign, gives us a hopefully relevant picture of how this development takes place in our country (where there is currently no specific OC proper to the corporate landscape) at the micro level, involving people and their knowledge.

R. Meersman et al. (Eds.): OTM 2014 Workshops, LNCS 8842, pp. 514–518, 2014.
© Springer-Verlag Berlin Heidelberg 2014

2   Perspectives on the Concept of Organizational Culture

There are two major theoretical perspectives of the OC: the positivist perspective and the constructivist perspective. The first one assumes the stable nature of the OC and the possibility to precisely analyze it, while the second one assumes a continuous, changing process which constitutes the creation of the OC [1].

The concept takes shape around a famous study led by Elton Mayo[1] regarding the interaction between people at work and its effect in the organization. In 1982, the work of Peters & Waterman [2] demonstrates that the success of an organization is tightly related to the OC of that organization. Moreover, the authors conduct other studies that show the importance of the human factor for the success of the business world. Regarding the success of the Japanese organizations, it is rooted in the mix between corporate values and the Japanese traditional beliefs [3].

Schein [4] defines the OC as being *"A pattern of shared basic assumptions that was learned by a group as it solved its problems of external adaptation and internal integration, that has worked well enough to be considered valid and, therefore, to be taught to new members as the correct way to perceive, think, and feel in relation to those problems"*. Schein identifies three main levels of study for the OC of a company: (1) the artifacts; (2) the beliefs and values shared by its members; and (3) the basic assumptions of the individuals, considered to be the DNA of the OC.

A European perspective, closer to the anthropology, is given by Bernoux [5], which considers that the OC is a construct rooted in symbols and myths. Morgan defines the organizations based on metaphors, as instrument of creation and understanding [6]. He creates eight metaphors of the organizations: the organization as: *machine, organism, brain, culture, political system, psychological prison, system of change and flow, instrument for domination*. The most important of which is the metaphor of the *organization as culture*. Organizations are seen as mini-societies with a certain model of culture and sub-culture. Morgan considers that the best way to study the culture of an organization is to observe it on a daily basis. Another study rooted in anthropology is that of Wright [7]. For Wright, the OC is transformed in an instrument for the management control. The use of OC as instrument of the management in order to achieve certain goals, together with the OC seen as a process are two basic visions of the application of the concept. Weick [8] develops the concept of "sense making" in the analysis of the OC as a process. This implies the creation by the members of an organization of the reality in which they live consciously and consensually. This is why the OC inside that organization becomes a continuous process formed by its members.

3   Perspectives on the Concept of Organizational Innovation

The actual society employs the term *innovation* in a multitude of aspects of our lives, often associated with the technological domain. We will attempt to define innovation, and show the underlying processes and its effects in the business world.

---

[1] *The Hawthorne effect*, [http://www.economist.com/node/12510632], 2008, 30.03.2014.

Organizational innovation is defined in the *Oslo Manual*[2] as: "*the implementation of a new or significantly improved product (good or service), or process, a new marketing method, or a new organizational method in business practices, workplace organization or external relations*". The *Manifesto for Creativity and Innovation in Europe*[3] discusses the importance of the concept, underlining the fact that innovation needs to be a key factor for the modern society. The study *Towards a multidisciplinary definition of innovation* [9], analyzes 60 definitions of the innovation from various domains, proposing an integrated definition: "*the multi-stage process whereby organizations transform ideas into new/improved products, service or processes, in order to advance, compete and differentiate themselves successfully in their marketplace*"[9]. The authors stress that innovation is a dynamic concept, and therefore the definition changes over time.

Regarding the **analysis levels** of the innovation, one can identify three levels: (i) individual level; (ii) group level; and (iii) organizational level. Risk taking at group level is observed to be higher than at individual level, which could be an advantage for the innovation process [10]. Also at group level, new ideas generation is higher due to a higher degree of diversity. There are two ways for **innovation development** in a company: *top-down* innovation (characterized by a vision and a mission of the company which define what the company seeks to produce) and *bottom-up* innovation (fed by the individual ideas from any department of the company).

Concerning the **classification of the innovation**, the most common types are the *product innovation* and *process innovation,* referring to a new (or improved) product and to a new way to create a product respectively. Technical innovation defines new processes, products and services, while administrative innovation defines new procedures and rules [11]. A special type of innovation is the business concept innovation, referring to the creation of a business, a totally new company from an existing one[4]. Innovation inside a company can be either *sustainable*, implying gradual changes, or *disruptive*, implying sudden and total changes.

Very often, innovation is confounded with **creativity**. The difference between creativity and innovation lays firstly in the capacity of measuring the two features. Creativity means freeing that potential from the individual's mind which generates new ideas [12]. Innovation represents the introduction of change in a relatively stable system. Innovation results after creativity and is a multi-stage process[5].

4   Organizational Culture and Innovation: A Case Study

Methodology. Based on theoretical aspect presented in previous sections, we created a questionnaire to quantitatively analyze the desired aspects. The questionnaire is

---

[2] http://www.keepeek.com/Digital-Asset-Management/oecd/
science-and-technology/oslo-manual_9789264013100-en#page47,
01.08.2014.

[3] http://europa.eu/rapid/press-release_IP-09-1702_en.htm?locale=en,
01.08.2014.

[4] http://thegentleartofsmartstealing.wordpress.com/
types-of-innovation/, 01.08.2014.

[5] http://thenewcreativity.com/creativity-vs-innovation-yes-there-
is-a-difference/, 01.08.2014.

composed of 23 questions of three types: (i) identifying the type of OC and its features inside the company; (ii) quantifying the innovation process and its features; and (iii) capturing the perception on the influence of the OC and innovation. The questions are either single-choice, or allowing a free text answer.

The questionnaire was applied within the Engineering Department of the volunteering company, composed of 11 persons with an age interval between 25-32. Out of the 11 persons, 10 are males and 1 female. Regarding education, 10 of the participants have completed superior studies, 2 have ongoing superior studies, while 1 has other type of studies. Their positions in the company range from engineer, junior engineer, to department manager. Seniority inside the department is as follows: 2 persons - less than 6 months; 2 persons - between 6 months and 1 year; 2 persons - between 1 and 1.5 years; 5 persons - between 1.5 and 2 years.

Values and Beliefs inside the Company. The first OC elements we observed inside the company were directed towards the *values and beliefs of its members*, as follows: development (54%), responsibility (50%), efficiency (45%), professionalism (36%), integrity, quality, flexibility, enthusiasm, relationship with the team (less than 40%). Being asked which of the values are predominant in the company, 55% of the answers indicated the values that were gained during time. Regarding the *values related to social interactions*, communication is the most common value (0.54%), followed by correctness (0.36), assertiveness and empathy, friendship and good mood (0.18). Applying Morgan's model, we came to the conclusion that most of the participants (55%) see the organization as an organism, 27% see the organization as a machine and 18% see the organization as a domination instrument. Being asked to enumerate three dominant characteristics of OC of the company, most of the volunteers opted for employee development, followed by customer orientation. Regarding the *international nature* of the working environment, the multinational character of the company and the fact that this is part of a global structure, but situated at long distance from the headquarters largely determine the OC. Studying how the *informal (friendly) aspect of the group* affects its productivity, asking the participants to indicate, on a 1 to 5 scale (1 – very little; 5 – very much), their relationship with their colleagues at work from an informal point of view, we obtained the following: 55% chose level 4, 27% - level 3, 9% - level 2 and 9% - level 1. Therefore, a considerable part of the participants feel comfortable at work from an informal point of view. However, as the organization grows, it is possible that it becomes more formal.

Innovation inside the Company. Regarding the *role of the management* in the innovative process, the participants were asked if they consider their work environment to be beneficial for their productivity and development. A number of 9 answered positively, 5 of which consider that the management involvement in this sense is important, and 4 of which consider it to be non-relevant. When there are *new proposals* coming from the employees, 64% of the participants answered that they are appreciated, but rarely adopted, 9% considered them to be appreciated and adopted, while 27% considered they were not appreciated nor adopted. The majority of employees consider that a higher *autonomy* concerning the realization of a task would contribute positively to achieving the objective, since they would feel more creative.

Trying to identify the *type of innovation* within the company from product innovation and process innovation, 91% of the participants answered that process innovation is mostly present in their organization; only 9% considered that product innovation is predominant. Regarding the *way* in which innovation happens, gradually or suddenly, 65% say that in their organization innovation takes place gradually, with small steps during a longer period, while 36% consider the process to happen suddenly. Regarding the idea that the development of the company is tightly related to the professional development of the employees, 73% of the participants indicate that innovation is averagely stimulated compared to the professional development of the employees; 19% - weak and 9% - strong. In our case, the answers indicating that the time allocated for the process to take place was not sufficient are at a rate of 82%.

5   Conclusion. Diagnosis and Recommendations

The diagnosis must take into account the nature of the participating company: 2 years old start-up, part of a foreign multinational. The observed characteristics of the OC describes it as being a young culture, with a medium degree of fragility, but with a tendency towards development and a certain ambition of its members to make a strong culture out of it. In this context, innovation plays an important role since, being in the formative phase, the company can benefit from the innovative process. Being a start-up company, the degree of innovation can be high, but it needs to be supported by the management in a higher degree, as seen from the participants' answers. This type of OC can be an advantage towards innovation in the sense that if the openness towards it would be high and its members would be more aware of its importance, it could have beneficial results. However, this could also represent a disadvantage due to the young nature of the company.

Since this is the first study realized inside the company and due to its start-up nature, as future research directions, we consider that a comparative study must be taken into account which can offer a diagnosis at a regular time interval, through which the organization is able to survey its evolution and to improve its strengths.

References

1. Mateescu V.: Cultura organizațională, Aspecte teoretice și practice, Editura Fundației pentru Studii Europene Ideea Europeană, Cluj-Napoca (2009)
2. Peters, T.J., and Waterman, R.H. Jr.: In Search of Excellence (1982)
3. Drucker, P.F.: What We Can Learn from Japanese Mgt. Harvard Business Review (1971)
4. Schein, E.: Organizational Culture and Leadership, Jossey-Bass, San Francisco (2004)
5. Bernoux, P.: La Sociologie des Organisations. Fiche de lecture, Univ. Paris XII (2008)
6. Morgan, G.: Images of Organizations. SAGE Publications (2006)
7. Wright, S.: The Anthropology of Organisations, Routledge, Londra (1994)
8. Weick, K.E.: Sensemaking in Organizations, SAGE Publications (1997)
9. Baregheh, A., Rowley, J., Sambrook, S.: Towards a multidisciplinary definition of innovation. Management Decision 47(8), 1323–1339 (2009)
10. McAdam, R., McClelland, J.: Individual and Team-based Idea Generation With Innovation management: Organisational and Research Agendas (2002)
11. Racolța-Paina, N.D.: Cultura inovației, Aspecte teoretice și practice, Editura Fundației pentru Studii Europene Ideea Europeană, Cluj-Napoca (2009)
12. Marshall, D.: There's a Critical Difference Between Creativity and Innovation, Business Insider (2013)

MSC 2014 PC Co-Chairs Message

The rapid progress of the Internet as new platform for social and collaborative interactions and the widespread usage of social online applications in mobile contexts have led the research areas of mobile and social computing to receive a widespread interest from academic and research institutions as well as from private and public companies.

Mobile computing plays an important role in many social and collaborative activities, predominantly in those activities where having the right data at the right time is a critical issue. Challenging activities that have been conducted in mobile computing include wireless mobile networks, ad-hoc networks, smart user devices, mobile computing platforms, and location-based and context-aware mobile services.

Social computing deals with the design and application of information and communication technologies (ICTs) in social contexts. In this scenario the emerging technologies are stimulated and stimulate social evolution, considering that they will be used by very heterogeneous people according to their social, cultural and technological features. Social computing addresses many challenges, such as increasing interactive collaboration, understanding social dynamics of people, socially constructing and sharing knowledge, helping people to find relevant information more quickly.

Social networking is one of the most important topics of social computing. Social networking technologies bring friends, co-workers and other social communities together. Challenging problems of social networking are robustness, vulnerability, privacy, security access, content management in large-scale collections, context awareness, multimedia search and retrieval, social graph modelling, etc.

To discuss such research topics, the International Workshop on Mobile and Social Computing for collaborative interactions (MSC'14) was organized in conjunction with the OTM Federated Conferences. The workshop, held in Amantea, Italy, 27-28 October 2014, provides a forum for discussing about artificial social systems, adaptive open socio-technical systems, mobile computing, social computing, networking technologies, human-computer interaction, and collaborative environments.

This year, after a rigorous review process, seven papers were accepted for inclusion in the workshop proceedings. Each of these submissions was rigorously peer reviewed by at least three experts. The papers were judged according to their originality, significance to theory and practice, readability, and relevance to workshop topics.

The selected papers have addressed the areas of social networking, human-computer interaction, and social intelligence.

Social networking papers have discussed the problems of integrating services of social networking from different fields, the privacy and social rights in social networks, as well as the emergence of a mixed offline-online community space paradigm in virtual communities.

Human-computer interaction papers have addressed the building process of an Italian multimodal corpus and the design of usable Web interfaces for collaborative editing among blind users.

Finally, social intelligence papers have addressed the creation of an experimental tool for event-specific information extraction from news headlines and the definition of a multidimensional ontology model for semantic search of academic resources.

The success of the MSC14 workshop would not have been possible without the contribution of the OTM 2014 organizers, PC members and authors of papers, all of whom we would like to sincerely thank.

September 2014   Fernando Ferri
                                                        Patrizia Grifoni
                                                        Arianna D'Ulizia
                                                        Maria Chiara Caschera

Towards Social Networks Services Integration

Tiziana Guzzo, Alessia D'Andrea, Fernando Ferri, and Patrizia Grifoni

Institute for Reaserch on Population and Social Policies (IRPPS)
National Research Council (CNR)
00185, Rome, Italy
{tiziana.guzzo,alessia.dandrea,
fernando.ferri,patrizia.grifoni}@irpp.cnr.it

Abstract. The paper provides a framework that allows integrating services of Social Networking in different fields. In particular, its use by companies, healthcare professionals, teachers, tour operators, travel agencies and scientific researchers professionals and consumers in general are discussed. Within the framework users can select topics of interest (business/marketing, health, learning, tourism and/or scientific research) according to their profile (professional or consumer). The framework offers users the opportunity to share information knowledge and services related to their professional field.

Keywords: Social Network, Business/Marketing, Health, Tourism, Scientific Research.

1   Introduction

In the contemporary society, where each person cannot know everything even about specific topics, sharing information and cooperating is becoming more and more important for the advance of individuals as well as of society in the different fields. Complex tasks often require the combined contribution of different kinds of specialized knowledge and, often, also require a sharing and collaborative issue. Social networks (SNs) are providing a concrete opportunity for sharing professional knowledge to create conditions for ongoing collaboration. SNs in the last years have improved the possibilities of creating patterns of self-organizing behavior that is a crucial issue for addressing participatory and knowledge sharing approaches of communities. The popularity of SNs combined with the widespread diffusion of mobile technologies has also given rise to the phenomenon of mobile SNs. Mobile SNs allows easy sharing and updating information when it is born and when it becomes valid [1]. The diffusion of mobile devices is more and more amplifying the social networks use even for people that always refused to use a personal computer. In fact, SNs are increasingly used in people daily life mainly as tools for interpersonal communication, for the sharing of experiences, ideas, information and interests that are necessary for the increasing knowledge and competitiveness. Beyond these positive impacts there are also some risks for novice and even experienced users. For example, users share personal information on the networks but they are very often not aware of the consequences of leaving information openly available on SNs. Other possible risks are related to the violation of users personal information, to identity

R. Meersman et al. (Eds.): OTM 2014 Workshops, LNCS 8842, pp. 521–530, 2014.
© Springer-Verlag Berlin Heidelberg 2014

theft and stalking. Another important risk is addiction. Some users especially teenagers use social networks as a showcase creating an idealized profile to be accepted by groups spending several hours per day on SNs [2]. Despite these risks, SNs are more and more frequently used by professionals to bring people together to collaborate and learn from each other, creating and sharing new knowledge. SNs represent a complete change for communication among professionals and between professionals and consumers, because they enable people not only to access and browse contents, but also to create and share them. The availability of a wide amount of information and services, however, can produce problems for their real retrievability and accessibility by users, underlining the need to have a framework adopting an ecosystemic approach that quickly assembles web resources, knowledge, services, making they available in a unified manner. Starting from these considerations, the paper analyses different uses and services of the SNs in different professional fields: business/marketing, health, learning, tourism and scientific research and proposes the experience of a Framework that provides the holistic version. The paper is organised as follows. Section 2 provides some related works on the professional use of SNs in different fields. In Section 3, a framework that integrates all services of different professional fields is provided. Finally, Section 4 concludes the paper.

2   Background

The term SN, refers to a group of people who share their ideas, experiences and other information related to specific topics of interest [3]. SNs are widely used in different fields. On considering the business/marketing field the real advantages of SNs can be exploited in the possibility for companies to individually and interactively address consumers this allows understanding better their target and providing new products and services in fulfilling their needs [4]. In health field SNs enable patients to interact in a virtual space with people having similar experiences. SNs also allow physicians to participate in continuous medical education at a time and location convenient for them, [5]. With respect to the learning field, SNs allow the sharing of learning practice by capturing, developing, sharing and maintaining learning knowledge inside a community. [6]. In tourism field SNs are becoming more and more a relevant reference and indispensable resource in the tourism field both for customers and companies [7]. Finally, in research field SNs are increasingly used to collaborate on professional issues and to share experiences, ideas and interests and to disseminate knowledge and scientific information widely and quickly. Starting from these considerations in the following sections an analysis of the use of SNs in business/marketing, health, learning, tourism and research fields is provided.

2.1   Business/Marketing Field

Business and marketing strategies are relevant for each company, they enable companies to address consumers in their choices of products and/or services that satisfy their needs; these include the processes of informing, persuading and removing all barriers for consumers to possess products and/or services [8]. SNs do not alter this ultimate objective [9]. Due to its unique range of creative possibilities, SNs are attracting significant interests and benefits for companies and consumers [10]. Many companies have begun to integrate SNs into their business strategies in search of different benefits such as: more effective market segmentation [11], support new product development efforts [12], stronger brands [13], positive word-of-mouth [14], increased website traffic [15], increased sales [16]. There is a growing body of literature that underlines the consumers attitude to exchange personal information with a company on SNs [17], this allows to create stronger relationships between companies and their consumers and to enhance the consumers desire to participate in SNs. So the benefits of SNs in business process can be view on considering the companies as well as the consumers point of view [18]. From the companies point of view the most important benefit that a SN can offer is the possibility to build a trustful relationship with customers. The interactive nature of SNs provides the opportunity to build a personal environment for customers, each one considered as an individual in addressing promotional viral marketing messages [19], providing products/services diffusion, testing and redesign and social influence and knowledge sharing among consumers [20]. The possibility to individually and interactively address customers, allows companies to better understand their target and to provide new products and services promotion in fulfilling the customer's needs [21]. From consumers' point of view the key useful characteristics of a SN to consider are: (i) inter-activity: (ii) aggregation of services: (iii) deliverability: a SN is delivered in real time 24 hours a day, and 7 days a week.

2.2   Health Field

The literature indicates a SN in healthcare field as "a website where consumers may be able to find health resources at a number of different levels. Services may range from a basic tier of emotional support and information sharing to questions and answers with physicians to quantified self-tracking to clinical trials access" [22]. Some examples of SNs in health domain are Doctors.net.uk, PatientsLikeMe, MedHelp, Forum Salute etc. These SNs represent an unprecedented opportunity for patient self-education. This is due to the simplicity of use and to the fact that access and age barriers are rapidly disappearing and patients express their needs in using SNs to develop: (i) consumer-oriented health care models; (ii) the increase of health information; (iii) actions that increase the possibility to access to best care [23]. The interaction and social support that patients receive from people who suffer of the same pathology play a relevant role in positively influencing their well being [24]. Patients, thanks to Web, can share the same illness with people all over the world and feel themselves less alone. In addition according to 2008 study people have more trust in "a person like me " than business, government and media [25]. Similarly, doctors can share ideas and debate treatment options, and they can produce a collective decision to improve quality of cares [26]. According to [27] In a SN people can be organised according to three main kinds of communities: (i) the community of healthcare professionals who actively seeks each other and share authentic information; (ii) the community of patients that share common health problems (e.g. cancer, infertility, neurodegenerative diseases, etc); (iii) the hybrid communities made both healthcare professionals and patients that share opinions and medical information every time and everywhere [28].

2.3   Learning Field

The communication and the collaboration in SNs are efficiently supported by the use of technology results and the development of more efficient forms of education. The use of technological media and tools is focal in SNs due to the fact that have the purpose to provide virtual education that refers to instruction in a learning environment where teachers and learners are separated by time and/or space [29]. This learning environment must allow learners to engage each other intentionally and collectively in the transaction or transformation of knowledge. It is not enough that material is presented to people and they interact with it. It is not enough that the learners interact with instructors to refine their understanding of material [30]. SNs provide also important opportunities and challenges to complex concerns such as environmental issues because they allow to inform and raise awareness at all level of society supporting building of coalitions and, in particular, they carry peer-to-peer learning. They enable people to learn from each other and experts to share data and information and to participate in all places and at any time throughout the lifecycle of policy development and implementation. This has the potential to make the decision making process more democratic [31]. Some important topics in E-learning are to make learners able in the virtual learning environments to feel the social presence of others and don't feel alone in their problems and tasks, allowing them to achieve higher level of knowledge and improve the learners problem-solving abilities [32]. In the last years, E-learning is rapidly evolving into a Blended Learning method, which blends online learning with more traditional learning. This method blending to the new collaborative tools of Web 2.0 allows cohesion and interaction among learners and between learners and moderator by improving collaboration and social relationships [33].

2.4   Tourism Field

The tourist product is for its own nature an "experience good"; indeed consumers will be able to completely estimate it only after s/he has taken advantage. This aspect is very important because the consumer searches information and advices by real travelers to select the best option in carrying out their own choice [34]. Moreover, this allows tour operators to control the moods and customer satisfactions and to better manage their market strategies. In [35], the authors analysed how the information quality and consequently the travel quality are improved in on line tourism communities compared to traditional paper guidebooks. Traditional travel agencies are today offering their services on SNs thanks to the great potential to serve ubiquitous information and communication needs. SNs allow also a more participative action also involving the local communities living in particular places of interest. For example in [36] a framework that involves different Social Media able to promote and develop sustainable tourism has been provided. The framework considering both the needs of "consumers" (tourists) and "producers" (local communities). The opportunity of business is both, for local administration because can develop the economy of territory and, local people who will participate to sustainable and economic development of their country. An important concept that is introduced by the use of SNs in tourism field is the word-of-mouth (WOM). This represents the most significant benefit of SNs because allows travel agencies to multiply the popularity through consumers who spread the message. Among the most famous and visited international travel SNs there are: Tripadvisor, Virtualtourist, Gusto, TripIt. Some evolutions of these networks are systems based on visualization. In [37], a dynamic visualization of the travel SNs has been introduced. It allows to visualize people on a map according to the landscape metaphor; to visualize the spatial locations and interests of each user in a map; to provide a visual representation of the temporal evolution of the people interests. SNs can be also used as a tool for charity donations and social contribution/participation. According to [38] when people travel they have a chance to see real problems and electronic support may give them an occasion (even after return home) to participate in social help/support or projects developed in places already visited or in locations where the tourists plan to go.

2.5   Scientific Research and Professional Field

In the last years is growing the interest in the use of SNs for scientific research and professional use. Awareness, by researchers and professionals in general, of its potentialities for scientific research and business, is rising. Today SNs are frequently used by professionals to collaborate and learn from each other, to create new knowledge, to share the same topics, knowledge objectives, documents, experiences and links. Many studies underlined that the use of SNs was very useful for professional purposes. In [39] the authors found that Facebook gives a lot of benefits to web worker such as: to look for old co-workers and current connections, join groups related to business interests, ask questions, look for events, and edit profile and security settings. In [40] the authors found that the IBM employees use Facebook to maintain contacts in their workplace, awareness among colleagues, build relationships within the organization, keep in touch with college friends. Similarly, in [41] the authors found that Microsoft employees use Facebook to build stronger working relationships and for professional information-gathering. It is necessary to recognize SNs' power also in professional field and in particular in communicating advancements in the scientific research both among professionals and population. A good communication can be made only by using the channels in which the general public is currently engaged [42]. Facebook is increasingly used both from researchers and professionals in all the research fields, because of its potentialities for an efficient and effective information delivering and knowledge sharing, for establishing professional contacts and collaboration on common aims, for facilitating the organisation of events, conferences, professional courses and the creation of debates and discussions [43]. In this context, to analyse the evolution of the scientific interests of researchers, [44] proposed a method based on SNs visualization to analyse the social networking evolution in the scenario of a scientific seminars cycle.

3   A Framework to Incorporate SNs in Different Professional Fields

Starting from the previous analysis of the SNs' uses in different professional fields in this section a framework that allows integrating all services of such field is provided.

In particular the framework can be used by companies, healthcare professionals, teachers, tour operators, travel agencies and scientific researchers professionals and consumers in general. Within the framework the user, according to his/her profile (professional or consumer) have the possibility to select the field of interest (business/marketing, health, learning, tourism and/or scientific research). As illustrated in Figure 1 the framework provides user all the services for managing the different kind of activities related to their field of interest.

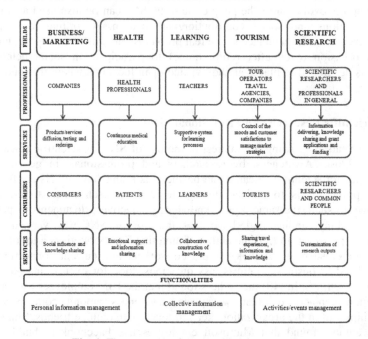

Fig. 1. The structure of the provided framework

In particular with respect to the business/marketing field the framework allows companies to build a trustful relationship with customers and provide products/services diffusion, testing and redesign according to the consumers needs. While from consumers' point of view the framework allows social influence and knowledge sharing among them. In the health field the framework offers the healthcare professionals the possibility to participate in continuous medical education at a time and location convenient for them, along with useful communication. In a virtual space physicians collect observations from their daily practice and then challenge or collaborate each others' opinions. Concerning patients, the framework enables them to provide and receive emotional support as well as information concerning treatments, health insurance or particular medical problems. Information shared between users includes reports on how the disease had been contracted and how it affects daily life. On considering the learning field the framework can be used by teacher as supportive system for learning process. In particular the teachers have the possibility to provides course content through course management applications, multimedia resources, videoconferencing etc. This learning environment must allow learners to engage each other intentionally and collectively in the transaction or construction of knowledge. In the tourism field the tour operators travel agencies can use the framework for controlling of the moods and customer satisfactions to manage market strategies. This allows to multiply the popularity through consumers who spread the message. Moreover the framework allow tourist to share their travel experiences, information and knowledge. Finally in the research/professional field the framework represent an important tool for professionals to collaborate and learn from each other, to create new knowledge, to share the same topics, knowledge objectives, documents, experiences and links. This allows the information delivering, knowledge sharing and dissemination of research outputs but also the increasing of possibilities for grant applications and funding information. In order to access the services summarised in Figure 1 the framework offers users the following kinds of functionalities: *personal information management, collective information management* and *activities/events management. The personal information management* functionality implies: personal information, media and social tools. The personal information allows the user to add or to change her/his personal information, i.e. the profile photo, and personal data. The media functionality enables users to manage websites, articles and galleries connected with the user's personal interests. Finally the social tools offer the possibility for members of the community to explore their contacts, their messages or their Facebook profiles or to search for new contacts. *The collective information management* functionality involves: tools, unified access to Facebook, LinkedIn and Twitter. Tools allow collecting and sharing different kinds of resources like guidelines, libraries of documents, databases, etc. with the community to facilitate daily work. They also allow exploring, adding new web resources or searching for web resources on Google. The Facebook, LinkedIn and Twitter unified access offers the possibility to explore user resources; adding new members or companies by selecting a heading, adding an address and a description and choosing a category. Finally, *the activities/events management* functionality involves: search activity, personal activity, joined activities and public activities. These functionalities allow sharing the organization of activities/events by each member of the community, from the personal to the collective perspective. The described framework provides a holistic vision that integrates the different SNs functions with web resources, information, activity management and services according to both personal and collective perspective.

4   Conclusion

The paper, starting from an analysis of the SNs' uses in different fields such as business/marketing, health, learning, tourism and/or scientific research, provides a framework that allows integrating all services of such field. In particular with respect to business/marketing field, the framework allows companies building a personal environment for customers that can seeking information, testing the product and proceeding to place order for products. In the health field, the framework provides a cheap, fast and reliable mode of sharing relevant information or knowledge among physicians who often find it difficult to schedule and to attend conferences or courses in order to keep themselves up to date. Moreover the framework can provide patients information concerning treatments, health insurance or particular medical problems allowing to easily establish contacts and having a mutual knowledge that is much more sound. With respect to the learning field, the framework provides learners and teachers an environment to perform courses content through course management applications, multimedia resources, videoconferencing, and other computer mediated communication systems. In the tourism field, the framework enables both tourists to share travel experiences, information, knowledge and tour operators and travel agencies to control the moods and customer satisfactions to manage market strategies. Finally in the research/professional field, the framework allows information delivering, knowledge sharing and dissemination of research outputs but also the increasing of possibilities for grant applications and funding information.

References

1. Wojciechowski, A., Siek, K.: Barcode Scanning from Mobile-Phone Camera Photos Delivered Via MMS: Case Study. In: Object-Oriented and Entity-Relationship Modelling/International Conference on Conceptual Modeling / the Entity Relationship Approach - ER(OOER), pp. 218–227 (2008)
2. Guzzo T., Ferri F., Grifoni P., Social Network's Effects on Italian Teenager's Life. Journal of Next Generation Information Technology (JNIT). AICIT, Vol. 4, N. 3, pp. 54-62, 2013.
3. Boyd, D.M., Ellison, N.B.: Social networks: Definition, history, and scholarship. Journal of Computer-Mediated Communication 13(1) (January 5, 2009), http://jcmc.indiana.edu/vol13/issue1/boyd.ellison.html
4. Dholakia, U.M., Bagozzi, R., Pearo, L.K.: A social influence model of consumer participation in network- and small-group-based virtual communities. International Journal of Research in Marketing 21(3), 241–263 (2004)
5. Ferguson, T.: Digital doctoring-Opportunities and challenges in electronic patient-physician communication. Journal of the American Medical Association 280 (1998)
6. Pea, R.: Learning Science Through Collaborative Visualization over the Internet. In: Nobel Symposium (NS 120), Virtual Museums and Public Understanding of Science and Culture, Stockholm, Sweden, May 26-29 (2002)
7. Ferri, F., Grifoni, P., Guzzo, T.: Social Aspects of Mobile Technologies on the Web Tourism Trend. In: Unhelkar, B. (ed.) Handbook of research on mobile business: technical, methodological and social perspectives, pp. 293–303. IGI Global (2008)
8. D'Andrea, A., Ferri, F., Grifoni, P.: Virtual communities in marketing processes: A marketing framework. Book of Customer Centric Marketing Strategies: Tools for Building Organizational Performance. IGI Publishing (2012)
9. Bouras, C., Igglesis, V., Kapoulas, V., Tsiatsos, T.: A web-based virtual community. Int. J. Web Based Communities 1(2) (2005)
10. Arnone, L., Colot, O., Geerts, A., Pozniak, L.: Company managed virtual communities in global brand strategy. Journal of Business Research. Journal of Business Research 4(2), 97–113 (2010)
11. Armstrong, A., Hagel, J.: Real profits from virtual communities. The Mckinsey Quarterly, vol. 3, pp. 126–141 (1995) (retrieved October 01, 2004)
12. Moon, J.Y., Sproull, L.: Turning Love into Money: How some Firms may Profit from Voluntary Electronic Customer Communities, Workingpaper, Stern School of Business, New York, NY (2001)

13. McWilliam, G.: Building stronger brands through online communities. Sloan Management Review 41(3), 43–54 (2002)
14. Bickart, B., Schindler, R.M.: Internet forums as influential sources of consumer information. Journal of Interactive Marketing 15(3), 31–40 (2001)
15. Bughin, J., Hagel, J.: The operational performance of virtual communities: Towards a successful business model. Electronic Markets 10(4), 237–243 (2000), http://www.electronicmarkets.org (retrieved)
16. Brown, S.L., Tilton, A., Woodside, D.M.: The case for on-line communities. The Mckinsey Quarterly, 1 (2002), http://www.mckinseyquarterly.com (retrieved)
17. Schoenbachler, D.D., Gordon, G.L.: Trust and customer willingness to provide information in database driven relationship marketing. Journal of Interactive Marketing 16(3), 2–16 (2002)
18. D'Andrea, A., Ferri, F., Grifoni, P.: SNeM2S: a Social Network Model for Marketing Strategies. International Journal of e-business development (2012)
19. Grifoni, P., Ferri, F., D'Andrea, A.: An integrated framework for on-line viral marketing campaign planning. International Journal of Business Research, Toronto (2013)
20. Ferri, F., D'Andrea, A., Grifoni, P.: IBF: An Integrated Business Framework for Virtual Communities. Journal of Electronic Commerce in Organizations (2012)
21. D'Andrea, A., Ferri, F., Grifoni, P.: A Business Model Framework for Second Life. In: Hugh, M. (ed.) E-Novation for Competitive Advantage in Collaborative Globalization: Technologies for Emerging E-Business Strategies, IGI Publishing (2011)
22. Swan, M.: Emerging Patient-Driven Health Care Models: An Examination of Health Social Networks, Consumer Personalized Medicine and Quantified Self-Tracking. Int. J. Environ. Res. Public Health 6, 492–525 (2009), http://www.mdpi.com/1660-4601/6/2/492/
23. D'Andrea, A., Ferri, F., Grifoni, P.: Social impacts of mobile virtual communities on healthcare IGI Global, Hershey (Stati Uniti d'America). In: Handbook of Research on Mobile Business: Technical, Methodological and Social Perspectives (2009)
24. Leimeister, J.M., Krcmar, H.: Patient-oriented Design of Online Support Communities Marco, Helmut. In: Proceedings of the 11th International Conference on Human-Computer Interaction (HCI International (January 2005)
25. Edelman.: Edelman Trust Barometer (2008), http://www.edelman.com/trust
26. Surowiecki, J.: The Wisdom of Crowds. Anchor Books, New York (2005)
27. D'Andrea, A., Ferri, F., Grifoni, P.: E-health prospectives in the internet age: the social networking development. In: 9th National Conference ICT in pediatria, nell'assistenza domiciliare e nel supporto alla disabilità diagnostica per immagini ed ingegneria clinica, Trieste, IT (2008)
28. D'Andrea, A., Ferri, F., Grifoni, P., Guzzo, T.: Multimodal social networking for healthcare professionals. In: MIMIC 2010: Fourth International Workshop on Management and Interaction with Multimodal Information Content, Bilboa, ES (2010)
29. Kurbel, K.: Virtuality on the Students and on the Teachers Sides: A Multimedia and Internet Based International Master Program (ICEF). In: GmbH, B. (ed.) Proc. on the 7th International Conference on Technology Supported Learning and Training. Online Educa, pp. 133–136 (2001)
30. Caschera, M.C., D'Andrea, A., Ferri, F., Grifoni, P.: Knowledge access and interaction evolution in virtual learning communities IGI Global. Hershey (Stati Uniti d'America) in Technologies and Practices for Constructing Knowledge in Online Environments: Advancements in Learning (2010)

31. Grifoni, P., Guzzo, T., Ferri, F.: Environmental Sustainability and Participatory Approaches: the Case of Italy. Journal of Sustainable Development. Canadian Center of Science and Education 7(3), 1–12 (2014)

32. D'Andrea, A., Ferri, F., Fortunati De Luca, L., Guzzo, T.: Mobile Devices to support advanced forms of e-Learning. In: Grifoni, P. (ed.) Handbook of Research on Multimodal Human Computer Interaction and Pervasive Services: Evolutionary Techniques for Improving Accessibility, pp. 389–407. IGI Global (2009)

33. Guzzo, T., Ferri, F., Grifoni, P.: Social Aspects and Web 2.0 Challenges in Blended Learning. In: Anastasiades, P.S. (ed.) Blended Learning Environments for Adults: Evaluations and Frameworks, pp. 35–49. IGI Global (2012)

34. Dall'Ara, G.: Il fenomeno degli alberghi diffusi in Italia. Palladino (2005)

35. Schwabe, G., Prestipino, M.: How tourism communities can change travel information quality. In: 13th European Conference on Information Systems, ECIS (2005)

36. Guzzo, T., D'Andrea, A., Ferri, F., Grifoni, P.: A Framework to Promote and Develop a Sustainable Tourism by Using Social Media. In: Proceeding of the International Workshop on SOcial and MObile Computing for collaborative environments (SOMOCO 2013), Graz, Austria, September 9-13 (2013)

37. Caschera, M.C., Ferri, F., Grifoni, P., Guzzo, T.: Multidimensional Visualization System for Travel Social Networks. In: 6th International Conference on Information Technology: New Generations ITNG 2009, Las Vegas, April 27-29, pp. 1511–1516. IEEE Computer Society (2009)

38. Wojciechowski, A.: Models of charity donations and project funding in social networks. In: Meersman, R., Herrero, P., Dillon, T. (eds.) OTM 2009 Workshops. LNCS, vol. 5872, pp. 454–463. Springer, Heidelberg (2009)

39. Sohn, J.: 12 Ways to Use Facebook Professionally (2007),
http://gigaom.com/collaboration/12-ways-to-use-facebook-professionally/ (accessed June 5, 2011)

40. DiMicco, J., Millen, D.: Identity management: multiple presentations of self in Facebook. In: Proceedings of the International Association for Computing Machinery (ACM) Conference on Supporting Group Work Group 2007, New York (2007)

41. Skeels, M., Grudin, J.: When social networks cross boundaries: a case study of workplace use of Facebook and LinkedIn. In: Proceedings GROUP 2009, pp. 95–104. ACM Press (2009)

42. Van Eperen, L., Marincola, F.M.: How scientists use social media to communicate their research. Journal of Translational Medicine 9, 199 (2011)

43. Ferri, F., Grifoni, P., Guzzo, T.: New forms of social and professional digital relationships: the case of Facebook. Social Network Analysis and Mining Journal 2, 121–137 (2012)

44. Caschera, M.C., Ferri, F., Grifoni, P.: SIM: A dynamic multidimensional visualization method for social networks. PsychNology Journal 6(3), 291–320 (2008)

How to Create Mixed Offline-Online Community Spaces? A Behavioural Science Position Paper

Tamas David-Barrett

Department of Experimental Psychology, University of Oxford
tamas.david-barrett@psy.ox.ac.uk

Abstract. Humans are exceptionally social, irrespective whether they are online or offline, a trait that is present in every society, irrespective of cultural variation. Both urban planners and evolutionary anthropologist have long recognized that the more frequently we have meaningful social contact with the members of our social network, the closer we feel to them, and the stronger our communities end up. The received wisdom in sociology is that communities fall apart when members of the community get involved in the majority of their social life outside the group, a phenomenon that has been thought to automatically happen with the rise of new online sociality-servicing technologies. However, in internet-based social networking most online interaction is local, supplementing rather than replacing local off-line interaction. Furthermore, much of dyadic interaction online is essentially identical to its offline nature, despite the fact that the manifestation can radically differ. Yet, it is very difficult to generate lasting online communities which are truly online only. Online communities tend to be similar to offline hobby clubs in their structure, and in almost all cases that are to last, after a while the need emerges to meet off-line. In these occasions people usually choose to engage in natural group bonding activities that release endorphins and create social bond in a literally *natural* way. As a consequence, current day human societies are heading towards social existence in which they are neither entirely off-line, but nor are entirely online. An integrated design for urban and digital sociality space would allow the natural rise of healthy and robust human communities.

Keywords: Online communities, urban communities, human sociality, internet science.

1 Introduction

Sociologists and anthropologists used to regard modern communication technologies as the curse of human communities. The received wisdom in these disciplines is that previously robust and healthy communities become shallow, fragile, and slowly disappearing the moment the new technologies enter. Although this observation used to be certainly true en large, the trend has been changing at least for the past few years. The deep penetration of 'traditional' social networking sites into our societies, well beyond the tech savvy, highly educated youth, as well as a host of new technologies have resulted in a surprising result: much of the online social behaviour is local.

R. Meersman et al. (Eds.): OTM 2014 Workshops, LNCS 8842, pp. 531–536, 2014.
© Springer-Verlag Berlin Heidelberg 2014

For designers of both urban and digital spaces this creates two questions: are some frameworks, online and offline ones, more likely to generate real human communities than others; and, perhaps even more importantly, is the integrated design, one that organically brings together the urban and digital space approaches, better in generating healthy communities.

This position paper first introduces some key features of human communities from an evolutionary anthropology point of view. Second, it argues that much of dyadic human sociality, albeit altered in its manifestation, is unchanged in its nature, as it migrates from offline to online. Third, it observes that unlike the dyadic aspect of human sociality, community structure can be, and indeed often is, dramatically different online compared to offline. Fourth, the paper points out that the need for being physically present makes it unlikely that human communities will, at least in the foreseeable future, be entirely online, while the spread and penetration of the new sociality technologies also make any luddite no-technology, offline only community be a utopia. Hence, lastly, the paper asks if there is a way to integrate online and offline design of social, community spaces.

2   The Problem of Online-Offline Spaces for Sociality

To design online spaces which generate and strengthen rather than weaken and destroy offline communities, we need to re-examine a very basic human behavioural trait: the urge to form a community with others.

Our species is an exceptionally social species. It is difficult to find any other animal that is characterized by individuals being reliant on others to the same extent. We learn from society: what to eat, where to find food, we process food in a very social way, we share it and receive a share from others. Even in hunter-gatherer societies, access to food is typically collective to a very large extent. We live in shelter, houses that we build together with others. We raise our young together, we teach them our technologies together. We defend our families against predators, and sometimes more importantly from other human groups in a very social, communal way. In short, humans are dependent on society in almost every aspect of their lives.

Not surprisingly, every human is an evolved sociality machine. We make friends, keep track over distant relatives, and take into account what others think of our mates when we choose someone to have children with. These traits are universal human features: they are present in every society, irrespective of the remarkable cultural variation around the world.

The fact that people feel comfortable in natural communities also means that when these communities are not there, for any reason, people are stressed and the society they form becomes unstable. This creates a society-engineering problem for the disciplines that are focused on generating frameworks in which human communities would naturally emerge. In particular, urban planners have been facing the question of how to create urban spaces in which natural human communities would emerge without external intervention [1-3]. It has been long observed that urban spaces in which the frequency of meaningful social contact among the individual members of a particular population is high tend to generate healthier communities [4].

Evolutionary anthropology has also recognized this feature (the need for repeated reinforcement of the relationships) of human sociality. In a ground-breaking study [5] showed that emotional closeness is dependent on frequency of meaningful social contact in both the cases of relatives, and friends. The more frequently we have meaningful social contact with the members of our social network, the closer we feel to them, the more we trust them, and the more they can trust us. One of the big questions with the rise of new forms of interactions (from messengers, to letters, to telegrams, to telephones, to one-way broadcast, to electronic mail, and then the Internet with its multitude of different ways of allowing human social interaction) is whether this will change communities in any significant way [6].

People are born to be automatically members of local communities, but after a while they have access to technologies that will allow them to have meaningful contact with other people who are not present locally. The received wisdom in sociology is that communities weaken when members of the community get involved in sociality outside the group. This would suggest that the new technologies that the Internet offers will necessarily, unavoidably, and irreversibly break up existing communities, and impede the formation of new ones. However, with the rise of Internet-based social networking, a new and interesting phenomenon emerged. Most online interaction is local, and thus they supplement rather than replace local off-line interaction [7].

To illustrate the mechanism behind this phenomenon, let us use the case of laughter as an example. We know that shared sense of humour is very important in building and maintaining all forms of dyadic social relationship [8, 9]. We are more likely to make friends with people with whom we laugh at the same jokes. This is especially important in maintaining close friendships: shared laughter for instance is the characteristic of smaller group sizes than shared conversation. [10].

A very simple experiment can show that this effect of shared laughter is similar off-line and online. If we initiate a Skype conversation with someone we have never met, and at first we can only hear the other rather than see the other, then we tend to be a bit tense. Once both sides switch on the computer cameras and can see each other they immediately (and automatically) laugh. The quality of the social contact has changed instantaneously. This can be replicated in experimental setting: when shared laughter occurs in digital communication, it does trigger very similar effect to offline shared laughter [11]. The important difference however between off-line and online communication is that the frequency of laughter is much lower in the case of the latter than the former. Similar to laughter other features of human sociality, such as, choosing partners to have children with, maintaining our kin relationships, interacting with acquaintances are remarkably similar online and off-line.

This lack of dissimilarity between online and offline dyadic relationships translates to community level consequences. For instance, the human limitation to the maximum number of psychologically meaningful social contacts [12, 13] is also present in online world [6, 14]. This suggests that the early popular belief that the Internet would entirely change our societies and human communities was, simply put, just wrong. It seems that humans will build online communities in very similar ways to the way they build off-line communities [6].

Yet, up to now, it has been difficult to generate lasting online communities which are truly online only. Similar to an offline hobby clubs, members of an online community need to have a strong interest and a continuous opt-in for them to stay involved, and thus for the community to last. This is very different from off-line communities. For instance, members of a hunter gatherer tribe do not constantly and continuously choose to be members of that group. For them, their community is just given, they cannot leave it. If they do leave, there has to be a very strong reason, given how very dangerous it is to be left alone. (Not surprisingly, one of the harshest punishments in tribal societies is ostracism.) In online communities, even in single interest communities, after a while the need tend to emerge, in a natural way, to meet off-line. And in these occasions people usually choose to engage in natural group bonding activities: they tend to eat together, drink together (often alcohol), they tend to do some shared activity together, often something that involves physical activity. All of these release endorphins and create social bond in a literally natural way.

In short, current day human societies are heading towards social existence in which they are neither entirely off-line (as people are engaging in online social activities), but nor are entirely online (as so far no technology has been able to replace real face-to-face contact).

Humans are not the only species for whom the nature of dyadic bonds result in structural consequences for their social networks. Physical proximity (sharing the same space, bumping often into each other, seeing and smelling each other) has been shown to offer proxy signals for genetic relatedness in many other species [15]. The recognition of kinship in such a way can then result in the emergence of a social network structure which is characterized by a set of high density communities that are interconnected only sparsely, a pattern that can emerge from initially panmictically connected populations [16].

The importance of locality, shared geographical space for a medium-sized group of people has been long recognized by cultural anthropologists [17-21]. In an urban space in which the social contact is unavoidable high density communities naturally emerge, usually associated with a locality, a neighbourhood. These local communities then are characterized by strong community spirit, an emerging local culture, and often strong norms concerning social interaction and behaviour [17].

A good example that highlights this effect is that of cul-de-sacs. These create a spatial delineation for the possible limits of social neighbourhood. The fact that a cul-de-sac creates a naturally high density social network tends to result in the emergence of more robust communities than the other street communities in the wider neighbourhood. This has had a positive effect on people who are living in these neighbourhoods. For instance, adults who had been raised in cul-de-sac communities tend to have better education, better health, higher earning, and more stable marriages when grown up [22-24]. The community support that works for hunter-gatherer societies, also works for urban neighbourhoods.

3   Designing the Framework for Online-Offline Communities

This leaves us with two very interesting questions.

First, would it be possible to learn from the urban experience when comparing communities in thoroughfares versus cul-de-sacs? Would it be conceivable to re-create natural boundaries for an online social network cul-de-sac (or walled garden) to emerge in the case of the latter as well? Perhaps, a platform that enforces social contact among a group of people who already know each other online, in a way that they cannot easily opt out would re-create the social forces that work in close knit communities.

Second, when integrating the approaches of urban design and evolutionary behavioural science, would it be possible to design new spaces that are prone to generate local communities that are characterized by both online and off-line dyadic relationships? Could what we know about the nature of human communities under the disciplinary umbrella of behavioural science, create tools for urban designers that would allow the inevitable online interaction among members of a community to strengthen rather than weaken these communities?

4   Conclusions

Designers of social networking sites and urban spaces have faced the same devilishly difficult task: to design spaces in which people will naturally form stable, robust, healthy communities. This social engineering problem is amplified by the recognition that communities in the foreseeable future will not belong to only one of the two domains. Apart from occasional isolationist attempts, there will not be communities that will be based entirely on offline social interactions, and until Internet interfaces will be able to increase the dimensionality of human interaction substantially, and in a way that it is relevant to the human psychology, the vast majority of online communities we also require offline interaction. In other words, the subject matter of social network site design and urban space design will be merged into one: to generate frameworks for future social communities, designers will have to recognize the mixed online-offline nature of them.

References

1. Jacobs, J.: The death and life of great American cities. Cape, London (1961)
2. Katz, P., Scully, V., Bressi, T.W.: The new urbanism: toward an architecture of community. McGraw-Hill, New York (1994)
3. Pendola, R., Gen, S.: Does "Main Street" promote sense of community? A comparison of San Francisco neighborhoods. Environ Behav 40, 545–574 (2008)
4. Oxley, D., Haggard, L.M., Werner, C.M., Altman, I.: Transactional Qualities of Neighborhood Social Networks - a Case-Study of Christmas Street. Environ Behav 18, 640–677 (1986)

5. Roberts, S.G.B., Dunbar, R.I.M.: The costs of family and friends: an 18-month longitudinal study of relationship maintenance and decay. Evolution and Human Behavior 32, 186–197 (2011)

6. Dunbar, R.I.: Social cognition on the Internet: testing constraints on social network size. Philosophical transactions of the Royal Society of London. Series B, Biological sciences 367, 2192–2201 (2012)

7. Pollet, T.V., Roberts, S.G., Dunbar, R.I.: Going that extra mile: individuals travel further to maintain face-to-face contact with highly related kin than with less related kin. PloS one 8 e53929 (2013)

8. Curry, O.S., Dunbar, R.I.M.: Sharing a joke: The effects of a similar sense of humor on affiliation and altruism. Evolution and Human Behavior 34, 125–129 (2013)

9. Dunbar, R.I., Baron, R., Frangou, A., Pearce, E., van Leeuwen, E.J., Stow, J., Partridge, G., MacDonald, I., Barra, V., van Vugt, M.: Social laughter is correlated with an elevated pain threshold. Proceedings. Biological sciences/The Royal Society 279, 1161–1167 (2012)

10. Dezecache, G., Dunbar, R.I.M.: Sharing the joke: the size of natural laughter groups. Evolution and Human Behavior 33, 775–779 (2012)

11. Vlahovic, T.A., Roberts, S., Dunbar, R.: Effects of Duration and Laughter on Subjective Happiness Within Different Modes of Communication. Journal of Computer-Mediated Communication 17, 436–450 (2012)

12. Dunbar, R.I., Shultz, S.: Evolution in the social brain. Science 317, 1344–1347 (2007)

13. David-Barrett, T., Dunbar, R.I.M.: Processing power limits social group size: computational evidence for the cognitive costs of sociality. P R Soc B 280 (2013)

14. Goncalves, B., Perra, N., Vespignani, A.: Modeling users' activity on twitter networks: validation of Dunbar's number. PloS one 6, e22656 (2011)

15. Ohtsuki, H., Hauert, C., Lieberman, E., Nowak, M.A.: A simple rule for the evolution of cooperation on graphs and social networks. Nature 441, 502–505 (2006)

16. Skyrms, B., Pemantle, R.: A dynamic model of social network formation. Proceedings of the National Academy of Sciences of the United States of America 97, 9340–9346 (2000)

17. Hirschon, R.: The social institutions of an urban locality of refugee origin in Piraeus. pp. iii, 381 leaves, 326 leaves of plates (383 folded). University of Oxford (1976)

18. Suttles, G.D.: The social order of the slum: ethnicity and territory in the inner city. University of Chicago Press, Chicago (1968)

19. Suttles, G.D.: The social construction of communities. University of Chicago Press, Chicago (1972)

20. Soja, E.W.: The political organization of space. Association of American Geographers, Commission on College Geography, Washington (1971)

21. Gold, J.R.: Territoriality and Human Spatial-Behavior. Prog Hum Geog 6, 44–67 (1982)

22. Brown, B.B., Werner, C.M.: Social Cohesiveness, Territoriality, and Holiday Decorations - the Influence of Cul-De-Sacs. Environ Behav 17, 539–565 (1985)

23. Hochschild, T.R.: Cul-de-sac kids. Childhood 20, 229–243 (2013)

24. Mayo, J.M.: Effects of Street Forms on Suburban Neighboring Behavior. Environ Behav. 11, 375–397 (1979)

Socio-Political Event Extraction Using a Rule-Based Approach*

Vera Danilova[1,2] and Svetlana Popova[2,3]

[1] Autonomous University of Barcelona, Spain
[2] ITMO University, Saint-Petersburg, Russia
maolve@gmail.com
[3] Saint-Petersburg State University, Saint-Petersburg, Russia
svp@list.ru

Abstract. News reports are currently one of the most studied data sources in the field of information extraction. Event descriptions that come from these sources are controversial, complementary and reflect relationships between the participating entities. The aim of the present work is to test a group of predefined patterns and rules to obtain sets of automatically filled scenario templates for socio-political events (case study: protests) and to apply clustering algorithms. At this stage the information is extracted from Russian news titles. The results of the pattern quality assessment and clustering are presented.

Keywords: information extraction, linguistic patterns, event extraction, text clustering, short text clustering.

1 Introduction

Transforming unstructured text into quantitative data is a key application for scientists. The researchers of civil unrest in Russia claim that the social protest phenomenon has not been exhaustively explored, and the study of motives, factors and potential causes of protest events in Russia still needs to be performed [1]. These data can be extracted from news reports, as it was done before within the framework of the global studies of civil unrest in [2][3], and the existing event extraction methods are applicable, because they provide a structured representation of happenings and their attributes that are encoded in the diversity of the natural language. Automatic event extraction tools assist analysts in the daily event monitoring (PULS: http://puls.cs.helsinki.fi/static/index.html, European Media Monitor: http://ec.europa.eu/dgs/jrc/). Also, they supply data for populating event registries and ontologies that can be further scrutinized by the analysts and researchers (NetOwl project: http://www.netowl.com/, Xlike project: http://xlike.org, Societal Stability Protocol: http://www.clinecenter.illinois.edu /research/speed.html).

* This work is partially financially supported by the Government of Russian Federation, Grant 074-U01 and by research work 414648 "Development of monitoring system for socio-cultural processes in cyberspac".

R. Meersman et al. (Eds.): OTM 2014 Workshops, LNCS 8842, pp. 537–546, 2014.
© Springer-Verlag Berlin Heidelberg 2014

Our aim is to create an experimental tool for event-specific information extraction from news headlines as an application to sociological studies of civil unrest in Russia. Further we plan to add multilingual functionality (Spanish, Catalan, Polish, Bulgarian, English). The extracted slots will be used for domain ontology population at the next step of our work.

The intuition of selecting headlines as the analysis units is that they tend to contain short descriptions of events. As it was observed in [4], according to the "5W rule" that determines the press article structure, answers to Who, What, Where, When and Why have to be given in the top of documents. In [5], it was proved that in 80% of cases the noun in the title of a press article is the main argument of an event. Also, in [6] it is observed that processing titles has a number of advantages: there is no need to analyse coreference, because relevant facts are often summarized in a single sentence, and superficial patterns that are closer to the real data can be applied.

Also, clustering is a very important issue in the task of news feeds processing. It allows to group the crawled texts according to topic similarity. The topics of the largest clusters can be identified. Performing the automatic grouping of news headlines makes us face the problem of short-text clustering, which is considered one of the difficult tasks in the corresponding domain [7][8].

The present study consists of two stages. Firstly, we perform a manual analysis of a large collection of news titles and propose a set of linguistic patterns for the extraction of slot data for the social protest scenario (event type, event origins, participants, location) from news headlines and social network posts (LJ: http://livejournal.com). At the second stage we evaluate the quality of pattern-extracted data and study the possibility of using slot patterns to improve the performance of topic-based clustering.

2 Related Work

2.1 Pattern Construction for Event Extraction Systems

Currently most of the event extraction systems rely on patterns and knowledge bases (ontologies, gazetteers etc.). Each domain requires manual or semi-automatic pattern construction. Pattern-based techniques, machine learning-based methods and hybrid approaches are described in [9].

Up-to-date systems for processing domain-specific events [6][12][13][14] apply JAPE-based rules (the GATE Rule Transducer component: https://gate.ac.uk /gate/doc/plugins.html) that consist of a left-hand side (LHS) that describes pattern constraints and a right-hand side (RHS) containing annotation commands. There are two stages of event extraction in such systems: first, basic named entities, unnamed person groups, values, dates and other attributes are detected using morphological analysers and gazetteer look-up; second, patterns that include event anchor and its arguments are matched using parsers and ontologies.

The authors of [6][12] develop language-independent technologies for event detection. NEXUS system extracts events for border security and crisis monitoring. It processes only titles and a few sentences of the articles in an event cluster. Event triggering patterns are acquired via weakly supervised machine learning and are based on JAPE and XTDL, a SProUT platform formalism (http://sprout.dfki.de/). They include 1/2 slots (semantic roles with string attributes) and match simple syntactic constructions. In [15] a system for civil unrest events extraction from English texts is described. Stanford dependency parser is used to identify verb phrases for pattern dictionary bootstrapping. The main pattern components are agents (participants, nouns) and purpose (verb).

In event extraction systems with Russian language module a limited number of scenarios is covered. In [16] a methodology for building templates to extract business events from news articles is described. The use of Chomsky free-context grammars and I.A.Melchuk's model "Meaning text" allows to obtain complete sets of templates. TextMARKER (http://uima.apache.org/) is used for rule representation and text annotation. Template tuples include event indicators and arguments.

In [17][18] the Russian module of PULS is presented, which monitors security and health-related events and processes full-length news texts. The applied patterns use morphological, syntactic and semantic constraints and consist of a regular expression and an action code. Most of them include two elements (verb/object, verb/subject) and match five syntactic constructions. Morphological and syntactic analysis is performed using the AOT (Automatic Processing of Text) project tools (http://aot.ru). An event is triggered, when a pattern is associated with a concept in the domain ontology.

We contribute to the present research by creating and evaluating patterns for socio-political events, one of the previously undescribed domains in the context of Russian event extraction. At this stage we examine the advantages of two-layer lexico-syntactic patterns. The top layer is based on the press language behaviour and reflects the distributional properties of information blocks within news headlines. The lower layer uses gazetteer lookup and PoS tagger results. The advantage of this approach consists in the possibility of simultaneous extraction of slot data, based on the discourse properties of short text, such as news headline.

2.2 Short Text Clustering

Due to the wide spreading of data in the form of short texts across the network, the processing of such texts has become an important issue. Such data as short news, social network posts, blog entries and academic abstracts qualify as short texts. News titles are very short, and their length often amounts to 10-15 tokens. It has been observed that short text clustering makes us face the problem of high data sparseness and difficulties in statistical data collection [7][8][19]. Term selection techniques also play an important role in this task and need further development [8]. Short-text clustering becomes more challenging, when texts belong to the same domain and have significant lexical overlap [7][8]. A number of works have been dedicated to the study of short-text clustering problem, however, they do not consider the use of linguistic patterns for text representation. We have investigated the possibility of the latter in the present work.

3 Experiment Description

3.1 Scenario Slots

The structure is logically divided into two blocks. The first one lays emphasis on the extraction of data specific of the protest-related news titles, the second one deals with topic-based clustering of news headlines.

In order to extract data from news titles we selected protest scenario slots with the notation as follows. Manual inspection of the data reveals that there are regularities in the semantic composition of the news titles. The most mentioned are such components as event location, origin, participants, and the event trigger or indicator. Basing on the set of these semantic components, the list of slots for the protest scenario template is prepared.

T - Event trigger. The What of the event: the protest gazetteer includes keywords like "protest", "march", "piqueting", etc. for this slot.

NE - Governing authorities. The Who of the event (governing authorities, law enforcement): the protest gazetteer includes keywords like "Moscow City Hall", "National Court", "police", etc. for this slot.

AG - Animated group. The other Who of the event (participants, victims): the protest gazetteer includes keywords like "feminists", "neonationalists", "islamists", etc. for this slot.

R - Event reason. The Why of the event: the protest gazetteer includes keywords like "in support of", "in defence of", "against", etc. for this slot.

L - Location: the Where of the event: the protest gazetteer includes city names, country names, keywords like "bridge", "road", "wall", "city centre", "street", "avenue", etc. for this slot.

3.2 Lexico-Syntactic Patterns

For each of the slots a set of patterns and rules is built, based on Part-of-Speech tags, gazetteer lookup or both.

The pattern sets use the subsequent notation: w - any word/word group from the lexicon W; A - Adjective; N - Noun; P - Preposition; V - Verb; C - a word starting with a capital. Round brackets denote the facultative nature of a component: a pattern like (A) + N actually spans two patterns A + N and N. The symbol * stands for multiple repetition (0 or more times), for in-stance: w* matches word sequences of any length from the lexicon W. A pattern can match a sequence within exactly one sentence, it cannot start in one sentence and end in another.

Patterns for the slot T. A word (word sequence) is selected as a T value if it is in lexicon W1 ={"demonstration", "advocate for", "strike", "mass gathering", "protest", "action", "hunger strike", "march", "civil disorder", "riot", "piqueting", "parade", etc.}.

Patterns for the NE slot. A word sequence is selected as a NE value if it matches the patterns [A + N + N], [A + N], [N], [N + N], and contains words from the set W2 = {"Moscow governmental authorities", "Moscow City Hall", "pro-governmental political party", "court", "police" etc.}.

Patterns for the AG slot. A word sequence qualifies as an AG value, if it matches the patterns [N], [V], [A + N], [N + N], [A + N + N], [N + A], [N + A + N], and the following conditions are satisfied: 1) the pattern starts with a word like "strike", "mass gathering"; 2) the pattern contains at least one token from the set W3={"neonationalists", "opposition", "radicals", "activists", "workers", "oil workers", "demonstrators", "protesters", "detained people", "those, who gathered", etc.}. Furthermore, the slot value sequence is selected (independently of the patterns) that starts at the beginning of the sentence or after location (look slot L) and ends with a word from the following lexicon W4={"to advocate for", "to protest", "to express", "to go out", "to hold", "to encourage", "to support", "to block", etc.}. The algorithm processes past, present and future tense forms of the listed verbs.

Patterns for the R slot. A word sequence qualifies as a value for the R slot if it matches the pattern w5 + (w6*), where W5 = {"in support of", "in honour of", "against", "on the occasion of", "with the requirement of", "in defence of", "on the occasion of the events", "in commemoration of", "on the occasion of", etc.}, W6 includes the general lexis of the Russian language.

Patterns for the L slot. A word sequence qualifies as a value for the L slot if it matches the pattern w7 + (w6*) + (w8) + C, where W7 = {"on", "in", "near", "across", "close to"}, W6 any word from the general lexis of the Russian language, W8={"centre", "wall", "prospect", "street", "square", "region", "channel", "town", "building", "metro station", etc.} denotes a physical setting, where an event takes place.

Output duplicates removal stage. For each scenario slot, the extracted subsequences that partially coincide with the main extracted sequence are removed. For instance, if the list of sequences for the slot AG output is "protest of neonationalists", "protest of neonationalists on Sunday", than the maximum length sequence is selected.

3.3   Clustering

At the present stage we check the possibility of improving the quality of topic-based clustering of news titles using slot-related word sequences for document representation. The intuition of these experiments is that slot data is a concise representation of the main topic-defining content: participants (protesters), location, origins (against/in support of what). Our assumption is that clustering performance can be enhanced through filtering out less relevant data. We apply several clustering strategies together with two ways of document representation, such as using 1) all headline tokens, or 2) scenario slot-related tokens.

Two clustering algorithms that are well-known in the Information Retrieval domain are applied: k-means [20] and hierarchical clustering (Single-Link, Complete-Link, and Average-Link). Both methods are exhaustively described in [21]. K-means is distinguished by its fast run-time performance, while hierarchical clustering techniques can ensure better results. For the purpose of our experiments, Weka library (http://www.cs.waikato.ac.nz/ml/weka/) implementations of both algorithms are used. 1-cos(a,b) is selected as a distance measure, where a and b are vectors that represent the corresponding documents. The feature space contains all tokens that fall within at least one text. In order to evaluate features in each text we applied the TF-IDF measure.

4 Test Collections

4.1 Annotated Dataset

For the present experiments we crawled a collection of unique news titles in Russian language from several news portals (mk.ru, ria.ru, interfax.ru, gazeta.ru, fontanka.ru, lenta.ru, forbes.ru, ng.ru, livejournal.ru) and divided it into three sets. The first set contains 1000 units and was manually analysed to create event extraction templates, patterns and experimental lexicons for protest event detection. As we mentioned earlier, titles are special text units that aim to capture user's attention and, therefore, commonly tend to provide a sufficient description of an event. Crawlers are built within the Python-based Scrapy web crawling framework (http://scrapy.org) and are able to extract news titles and, optionally, the text body, date, time and source of the messages. Headlines are added to the list in case of mutual presence of key-words from two keyword sets.

The resulting collection (the second set) covers mass demonstrations, strikes, symbolic protest acts, marches, verbal expressions of protest and related events (acts by governmental initiators, politically motivated attacks, etc.) that took place in Russia, Ukraine and other countries in the years 2013-2014. The gold standard includes 72 event reports. Expert-annotated slot values for each sentence are colon-separated and are listed in a predefined order. Each slot contains word sequences exactly as they are in the source text.

4.2 Clustering Dataset

The third set of the collection (71 headlines) is manually processed and the units are grouped according to topic similarity. The resulting collection properties are as follows: it contains a large amount of topics and few documents per each group. 22 topical groups are defined. The main characteristics of the dataset are: 8 clusters with size 1 document, 4 clusters with size 2, 1 cluster with size 3, 2 clusters with size 4, 2 clusters with size 5, 2 clusters with size 6, 2 clusters with size 7, 1 cluster with size 8; examples of topics: "violation of the civil rights", "against corruption", "liberty of expression and Internet censorship", "street protest actions in Egypt", "strikes in Greece" etc.

4.3 Performance Evaluation

Pattern Quality Evaluation. For each slot of the top layer (T, NE, AG, R, L), the quality of extracting data from news headlines is evaluated on the basis of the corresponding patterns. We test the full matching of the automatically extracted data and expert-annotated slots. It should be noted that the gold standard contains only one correct word sequence per slot, while the output of the automatic processing may include several sequences per slot. For this reason we apply 2 evaluation measures. The first one calculates the number of documents for which at least one of the automatically extracted sequences corresponds to a given slot. Second measure calculates the precision of slot data extraction and takes into account the total amount of retrieved sequences for a given slot: $Precision = \frac{|G \cap C|}{|G|}$, where G is the number of sequences that were extracted from all the documents for a given slot, C is the amount of documents for which among all the retrieved sequences there is a string that coincides with the expert annotation of the same slot.

Clustering Quality Evaluation. Clustering quality evaluation was performed using the combined information on precision and recall of the resulting clusters [22][23]:

$$F = \sum_i \frac{|G_i|}{|D|} \max_j F_{ij},$$ (1)

where: $F_{ij} = \frac{2 \cdot P_{ij} \cdot R_{ij}}{P_{ij} + R_{ij}}$, $P_{ij} = \frac{|G_i \cap C_j|}{|G_i|}$, $R_{ij} = \frac{|G_i \cap C_j|}{|C_j|}$, $G = \{G_i\}_{i=1,...,n}$ - is an obtained set of clusters, $|D|$ - the number of documents, $C = \{C_j\}_{j=1,...,n}$ - is set of classes, defined by experts.

5 Experiments

Block of experiments 1: scenario slot data extraction. At this stage, we extract word sequences from the test collection that correspond to scenario slot patterns. The preprocessing (PoS tagging) is performed using the Yandex API Mystem (http://api.yandex.ru/mystem/doc/). Upon extraction, the quality of the retrieved data is evaluated by comparing the obtained results to the expert annotation.

Block of experiments 2: using scenario slot data to improve clustering. At the present stage we apply k-means and hierarchical clustering strategies together with two ways of document representation, such as using 1) all headline tokens, or 2) scenario slot-related tokens. Only the slot T has not been used in the clustering task, because it contains only the general event type (demonstration, piquet, boycott, protest, strike, hunger strike) and does not provide event-specific data (cause, participants, location, etc.). In order to evaluate the clustering quality, the k-means algorithm was run 500 times on the basis of which the best (max), the worst (min) and the average (avg) results were selected.

6 Results and Discussion

Table 1 presents the quality evaluation results for the slots extracted using patterns from the test dataset. It shows the number of documents per each correctly extracted slot, and the evaluation of the extracted sequences using Precision measure for 72 documents that have been processed. In case the gold standard annotation for a given slot is empty (the headline does not provide the necessary data), than, if the automatically extracted slot is also empty, the system output is considered to be correct.

Table 1. Extraction performance for the protest scenario slots

Slot labels	Slot description	Number of documents per correctly extracted slot (total 72 documents)	Precision
T	Event trigger	43	0.54
R	Action reason	44	0.62
AG	Animated group	33	0.40
L	Location	47	0.54
NE	Governing authorities	69	0.96

High extraction performance for the slot NE is due to the absence of the corresponding data in the test set. During the automatic processing of the test set we obtained the same result (no sequence corresponding to the NE slot).

It should be also noted that the sequence for a given slot is correct, only if it is a full match of the expert annotation. Consequently, if the sequence contains one word more or one word less, the output is deemed invalid, although the necessary data is partially present. For this reason the L extraction quality is rather poor, the extracted sequences are longer than the gold standard. The Precision value 0.61 can be obtained, if we leave the minimum length L sequences out of all extracted variants in output duplicates removal stage.

Table 2 presents the headline clustering performance. The implementation of clustering algorithms upon lemmatization (Yandex MyStem was used) outperforms preprocessing-free clustering, therefore, we show only the results that take into account lemmatization step. In Table 2, "original" means that the document is represented by the whole set of tokens, and "w.p."(with patterns) denotes the document representation using pattern-extracted slot sequences.

Table 2. The results of test dataset clustering

	K-means Clustering			Hierarchical Clustering		
	avg result	min result	max result	Average-Link	Complete-Link	Singl-Link
original	0.55	0.42	0.68	0.68	0.72	0.44
w.p.	**0.59**	**0.46**	**0.71**	**0.74**	0.67	**0.58**

The obtained results show that in most cases clustering using patterns ensures better results due to the fact that the irrelevant data is discounted: pattern-based document representation allows to leave the most prominent features of an event (Who participated, Where it took place, Why it happened, etc.).

7   Conclusion

In the present paper, we describe the experiments in processing news headlines related to the protest activity and crawled from several Russian news portals and a social network (LiveJournal). We have studied the possibility of extracting exact string values for certain template scenario slots: event trigger, governing authorities, event purpose, location and animated group (participant, victims). For this purpose, we proposed a set of linguistic patterns that combine specialized lexicons of words and collocations and Part-of-Speech tags upon having manually analysed a group of headlines. The results show that pattern-based document representation allows to improve the performance of news headlines clustering.

References

1. Dementieva, I.N.: Theory and methodology of social protest study. Journal of Public Opinion Monitoring 4(116), 3–12 (2013)
2. Braha, D.: A Universal Model of Global Civil Unrest. PLoS ONE 7(10) e48596 (2012)
3. Hayes, M., Nardulli, P.F.: SPEEDs Societal Stability Protocol and the Study of Civil Unrest: an Overview and Comparison with Other Event Data Projects (white paper). Cline Center for Democracy. University of Illinois at Urbana-Champaign (2011)
4. Lejeune, G.: Structure patterns in Information Extraction: a multilingual solution? In: Advances in Method of Information and Communication Technology, AMICT 2009, Petrozavodsk, Russia, vol. 11, pp. 105–111 (2009)
5. Wunderwald, M.: Event Extraction from News Articles (Diploma Thesis), Dresden University of Technology. Dept. of Computer Science (2011)
6. Piskorski, J., Tanev, H., Atkinson, M., van der Goot, E., Zavarella, V.: Online news event extraction for global crisis surveillance. In: Nguyen, N.T. (ed.) Transactions on CCI V. LNCS, vol. 6910, pp. 182–212. Springer, Heidelberg (2011)
7. Pinto, D., Rosso, P., Jiménez, H.: A Self-Enriching Methodology for Clustering Narrow Domain Short Texts. Comput. J. 54(7), 1148–1165 (2011)
8. Pinto, D.: Analysis of narrow-domain short texts clustering. In: Research report for Diploma de Estudios Avanzados (DEA), Department of Information Systems and Computation, UPV (2007)
9. Hogenboom, F., Frasincar, F., Kaymak, U., de Jong, F.: An Overview of Event Extraction from Text. In: Workshop on Detection, Representation, and Exploitation of Events in the Semantic Web (DeRiVE 2011). CEUR Workshop Proceedings, vol. 779, pp. 48–57 (2011)
10. Grishman, R.: Information Extraction: Capabilities and Challenges. In: Notes for the 2012 International Winter School in Language and Speech Technologies. Rovira i Virgili University. Tarragona, Spain (2012)
11. Piskorski, J., Yangarber, R.: Information Extraction: Past, Present and Future. Survey. In: Poibeau, T., et al. (eds.) Multi-source, Multilingual Information Extraction and Summarization?, Theory and Applications of Natural Language Processing, Springer, Heidelberg (2012)
12. Atkinson, M., Piskorski, J., Van der Goot, E., Yangarber, Y.: Multilingual Real-time Event Extraction for Border Security Intelligence Gathering. In: Wiil, U.K. (ed.) Counterterrorism and Open Source Intelligence. LNS, vol. 355, Springer, Wien (2011)

13. Hogenboom, A., Hogenboom, F., Frasincar, F., Schouten, K., van der Meer, O.: Semantics-based information extraction for detecting economic events. Multimed Tools Appl 64, 27–52 (2013)
14. IJntema, W., Sangers, J., Hogenboom, F., Frasincar, F.: A lexico-semantic pattern language for learning ontology instances from text. Web Semantics: Science, Services and Agents on the World Wide Web 15, 37–50 (2012)
15. Huang, R., Riloff, E.: Multi-faceted Event Recognition with Bootstrapped Dictionaries. In: Proceedings of NAACL-HLT, pp. 41–51 (2013)
16. Solovyev, V., Ivanov, V., Gareev, R., Serebryakov, S., Vassilieva, N.: Methodology for Building Extraction Templates for Russian Language in Knowledge-Based IE Systems. In: HP Laboratories Technical report. HPL-2012-211 (2012)
17. Du, M., von Etter, P., Kopotev, M., Novikov, M., Tarbeeva, N., Yangarber, R.: Building support tools for Russian-language information extraction. In: Habernal, I., Matoušek, V. (eds.) TSD 2011. LNCS (LNAI), vol. 6836, pp. 380–387. Springer, Heidelberg (2011)
18. Pivovarova, L., Du, M., Yangarber, R.: Adapting the PULS event extraction framework to analyze Russian text. In: At ACL: 4th Biennial Workshop on Balto-Slavic Natural Language Processing, Sofia, Bulgaria (2013)
19. Errecalde, M., Ingaramo, D., Rosso, P.: ITSA*: An effective iterative method for short-text clustering tasks. In: García-Pedrajas, N., Herrera, F., Fyfe, C., Benítez, J.M., Ali, M. (eds.) IEA/AIE 2010, Part I. LNCS, vol. 6096, pp. 550–559. Springer, Heidelberg (2010)
20. MacQueen, J.B.: Some Methods for classification and Analysis of Multivariate Observations. In: Proceedings of 5-th Berkeley Symposium on Mathematical Statistics and Probability, vol. 1, pp. 281–297. University of California Press, Berkeley (1967)
21. Manning, C., Raghavan, P., Schutze, H.: Introduction to Information Retrieval. Cambridge University Press (2009)
22. Zu Eissen, S.M., Stein, B.: Analysis of clustering algorithms for web-based search. In: Karagiannis, D., Reimer, U. (eds.) PAKM 2002. LNCS (LNAI), vol. 2569, pp. 168–178. Springer, Heidelberg (2002)
23. Stein, B., zu Eissen, S.M., Wißbrock, F.: On Cluster Validity and the Information Need of Users. In: Hanza, M.H. (ed.) 3rd IASTED Int. Conference on Artificial Intelligence and Applications (AIA 2003), Benalmádena, Spain, pp. 216–221. ACTA Press, IASTED (2003)
24. Hogenboom, F., Frasincar, F., Kaymak, U., de Jong, F.: An Overview of Event Extraction from Text. In: Workshop on Detection, Representation, and Exploitation of Events in the Semantic Web (DeRiVE 2011), CEUR Workshop Proceedings, vol. 779, pp. 48–57 (2011)

Semantic Search of Academic Resources in a Mobile Computing Platform

Maricela Bravo, Lizbeth Gallardo, and Henoch Cruz

Systems Department, Autonomous Metropolitan University
Azcapotzalco, DF, CP 02200, Mexico
{mcbc,glizbeth}@correo.azc.uam.mx,
henochcruz@gmail.com

Abstract. The rapid development of wireless communication technologies and the easy access to mobile computing devices has generated an increase in the development of innovative applications to leverage the benefits of these mobile technologies. Also, over the last decades new platforms and paradigms for intelligent data processing have gained much attention from practitioners and researchers: mobile computing, use of ontologies and Web services for the rapid information processing: In this article, we present an approach for semantic search of academic resources based on the integration of a multi-dimensional ontology model with inference facilities for query answering, and the deployment of Web services for supporting a mobile application. The approach was evaluated based on a set of general competency questions which were translated into a rule-based query language. Results show that the overall solution approach is technologically viable and promising.

Keywords: mobile computing, web services, ontologies.

1   Introduction

Searching of data and information in academic environments is one of the most common tasks performed in any educational institution. Considering that currently the majority of students, teachers and in general all the staff working in academic institutions have easy access to telecommunication technologies, it is clear that new data and information search mobile applications should be developed. Semantic search refers to the incorporation of semantic Web technologies (ontologies, reasoner engines and rule languages) to support the intelligent recovery and precise delivery of information based on ontology models for the representation of data.

In this article, a semantic search engine for academic resources based on the integration of a multi-dimensional ontology model with adaptable and extendible ontology modules, the incorporation of reasoning and inference facilities for query answering, and the deployment and invocation of Web services for attending mobile user demands. As a result, the approach reported in this paper offers an innovative contribution for dynamic and changing mobile environments. The mobile computing platform was implemented and evaluated based on a set of general competency

R. Meersman et al. (Eds.): OTM 2014 Workshops, LNCS 8842, pp. 547–556, 2014.
© Springer-Verlag Berlin Heidelberg 2014

questions which were translated into a rule-based query language. Results show that the overall solution approach is technologically viable and promising.

The rest of the paper is organized as follows: in Section 2, related work is described; in Section 3, the Mobile Computing Platform is presented; in Section 4, the multidimensional ontology model is described; in Section 5, the evaluation is presented; and finally in Section 6, conclusions are presented.

2   Related Work

Concerning the approach reported in this work three research topics are of particular interest: use of ontology models for query answering support, deploy and invocation of Web services for attending mobile user demands, incorporate a semantic Web service model and use reasoning and inference facilities for query answering.

Weißenberg et.al [1] presented FLAME2008, a platform for service customization through the use of information based on individual situations and personal demands of users. This proposal tries to determine the most appropriate set of web-based information and services through the semantic descriptions of situations and services. Among the main differences with the semantic search reported in this paper, is that the ontology is populated manually, because the information represented will not be dynamically changing, such as the geographical data. Sheshagiri et.al [2] presented myCampus, a project where users subscribe with a set of task-specific agents to develop different tasks. These agents require the knowledge of contextual attributes of users. The sources of contextual information are modeled as Semantic Web Services that can be automatically discovered by agents. The static knowledge about users is stored in the form of rules that map contextual attributes into service invocations, in this way the ontology can identify and activate the resources in response to the context of the users. FLAME2008 and MyCampus were two of the first projects that incorporated a semantic Web service approach by using OWL-S. However, the main drawback of OWL-S model is that it makes difficult the automatic incorporation of existing Web services (legacy WSDL files) requiring their semantic extension with OWL-S. Gu et.al [3] presented SOCAM, one of the first ontology-based models to represent contexts; SOCAM includes person, location, and activity and computer entity. SOCAM provides support for discovering, acquiring, interpreting and accessing context information. Although SOCAM uses the concept of services, these are not implemented in WSDL. Kim et.al [4] described a framework to search products and services through the use of a real-time ontology mapping mechanism between heterogeneous ontologies and taxonomies. This proposal is based on Web services and Semantic Web and is composed of: service client, service providers and search agent. The main component of this proposal is the Service Search Agent, which is responsible of harvesting the service providers through the use of a semantic web robot. This framework has a disadvantage, it requires services providers to describe their services using their own ontologies, leaving aside the use of interoperable Web service description languages.

Dickson et.al [5] presented the use of Multi-Agent Systems, Semantic Web and Ontologies (called MAIS) for the implementation of an ubiquitous touristic service. Their objective was to provide coordination and integration of information and service resources anytime anywhere and provisioning personalized assistance to tourists. In the MAIS architecture tourist inquiries are sent to an ontology, results are produced according to the requirements and preferences of users. Through the use of the ontology the system can propose tour plans, formulate itinerary plans and connections between transport routes. Amel Bouzeghoub et.al [6] presented a context aware semantic recommender system. Recommendations are based on a multidimensional ontology which models persons, buildings, events and available resources. The recommender system was implemented for mobile users in a campus environment. Cadenas et.al [7] described mIO, an ontology network to represent knowledge related to context. The mIO ontology consists of a core ontology which interlinks different ontology modules needed for modeling context. They introduce the concept of modularization for ontologies. Their ontology network contains ten modular ontologies: User, Role, Environment, Location, Time, Service, Provider, Device, Interface and Network. Authors also propose using context logs for better recommendation results. Despite the use of an ontological model in Dickson [5], Bouzeghoub [6], and Cadenas [7] projects, their main drawback is that they do not incorporate semantic representation and reasoning. Sousa [8] presented ICAS, an architecture that allows creation of context aware services, and SeCoM, a semantic model to represent contexts. SeCoM model consists of six main ontologies and six supporting ontologies. Main ontologies are: Actor ontology, Time ontology, Temporal Event ontology, Space ontology, Spatial Event ontology, Device ontology, and Activity ontology. Secondary ontologies are: Contact ontology, Relationship ontology, Role ontology, Project ontology, Document ontology and Knowledge ontology. Woerndl and Hristov [9] described an approach for personal information management in mobile devices, using a recommender system based on ontologies. The system recommends documents and articles considering time and location context and the user personal ontology. Authors implemented a PDA Semantic Desktop (SeMoDesk). Liiv [10] describe SMARTMUSEUM, a platform for recommendations in the cultural domain of a museum. SMARTMUSEUM uses a combined approach based on rules, collaboration and content personalization, where content is semantically enabled by an ontology. Recommendations are about cultural objects allocated in the museum and content related with those objects. User profile includes abilities and interests of user, and a log of visited places. Gómez-Pérez presented SEEMP [11] a project which consists of an ontology network which describes employs and employees from human resource perspective. SEEMP reference ontology consists of the following ontologies: Job Seeker Ontology, Job Offer Ontology, Compensation Ontology, Driving License Ontology, Economic Activity Ontology, Occupation Ontology, Education Ontology, Geography Ontology, Labour Regulatory Ontology, Language Ontology, Skill Ontology, Competence Ontology, and Time Ontology. Gómez et al [12] presented an ontology for surveillance and ubiquitous systems, which is based on semantic levels for modeling the context and the situation and an ontology of semantic technologies, to enable inference by rules.

These reported proposals are based on similar technological mechanisms, such as ontologies, Web services and mobile computing. However, the main difference between related work and the approach described in this paper, is the implementation of a multi-dimensional ontology model with adaptable and extendible ontology modules; and the invocation of Web services that support mobile application development.

3   Mobile Computing Platform

In this Section we describe the Mobile Computing Platform (MCP) that was designed and implemented to support the semantic search of academic issues. The MCP uses a Client - Server architecture (see Figure 1). The aim of this MCP is to provide the flexibility to implement and deploy mobile applications compatible with Android, from which any user that has a mobile device can search for scholarly information. The mobile client-side of the MCP comprises the following layers: *User layer*, this layer consists of the graphical user interface through which the interaction between the end user and the mobile search application on Android is done; *Query layer*, this layer consists of a set of client-side programming interfaces which create call objects to specific query Web services, depending mainly of the user input data; *Web service invocation layer*, this layer consists of a set of calling objects that are triggered to invoke specific Web services to gather information from the ontology model allocated into the server; *Mobile connection layer*, this connection is executed through the use of SOAP over HTTP protocol. The SOAP protocol encapsulates the Web service message request into an XML-encoded envelope and sends the message to the server-side provider of Web services. The server returns the answer as an XML-response message.

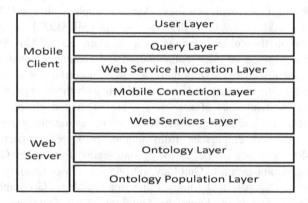

Fig. 1. General architecture of the mobile computing platform

The server side of the MCP comprises the following layers: *Web services layer*; this layer consists of a set of published Web service descriptions that are deployed to be invoked and provide particular responses of information that is asserted and inferred into the ontology model; *Ontology layer*, this layer consists of the set of ontologies that together integrate the ontology system; *Ontology population layer*, this layer consists of a set of modules that allow the instantiation of individuals, object properties and data properties into the ontology model.

4   Multidimensional Ontology Model

In this Section we present the multidimensional ontology model that represents the academic entities and semantic relationships which are the support of the semantic searcher. The architecture depicted in figures 2 and 3 show the multidimensional ontology model. Representing multiple dimensions of semantic information using ontologies is a promising trend from the area of knowledge representation that has proven good results. An important benefit of using multi-dimensional ontologies is the feasibility of maintaining each ontology and the possibility of exchanging and extending parts of the model.

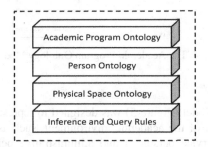

Fig. 2. Multidimensional ontology model

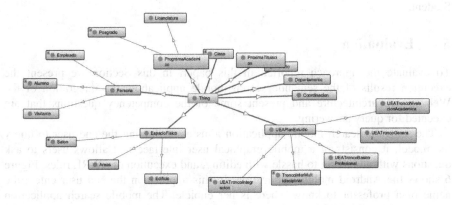

Fig. 3. Main classes and sub-classes of the ontology model

The multidimensional ontology model is integrated by three independent ontologies: the Academic Program Ontology, the Person Ontology, and the Physical Space Ontology.

4.1 Academic Program Ontology

The Academic Program Ontology model was designed to represent the academic programs offered at the Autonomous Metropolitan University. Figure 4 shows the main classes and semantic relationships between classes on this ontology. In particular, this ontology model represents academic programs, which is sub-classified into Bachelor and Postgraduate programs. The postgraduate program is sub-classified into Master and PhD academic programs.

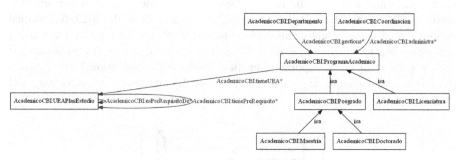

Fig. 4. The Academic Program Ontology Model

4.2 Person Ontology

The Person Ontology Model (Figure 5) was designed to represent any kind of person individuals that are part of the academic environment, such as: employees, visitors, academic personnel, service personnel and administrative personnel. Of particular interest are the following semantic relationships (object properties): is supervisor (es asesor), which is used to establish a semantic relationship between a Professor and a Student.

5 Evaluation

To evaluate the approach reported in this paper, in this Section we present the execution results of the semantic search mobile application, the integration of the Web service architecture and present some of the competency questions that are executed for query answering.

The semantic search mobile application aims at facilitating the end user to query the model, it consists of a mobile graphical user interface that allows users to ask questions without having to hassle with editing, and execution of SWRL rules. Figure 6 shows the Android mobile application. In this application the end user enters the name of a professor to know where is her cubicle. The mobile search application connects and calls a Web service method, which in turn generates and returns the answer; finally, the returned response is displayed on the mobile client application.

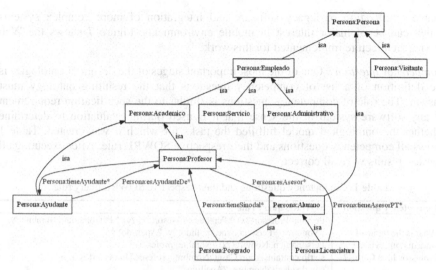

Fig. 5. The Person Ontology Model

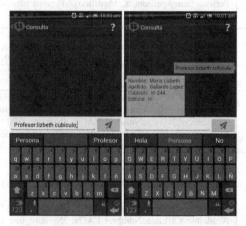

Fig. 6. Semantic search mobile application

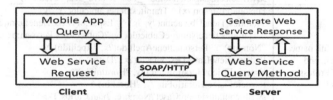

Fig. 7. Web service architecture

The *Web Service-oriented architecture* represents an important technological trend for distributing software resources around the world. Web services are software component interfaces based on a set of XML-based standards, languages and protocols and are executed through the exchange of XML messages. Web services enable reutilization of legacy software and integration of more complex systems which can be of major interest in mobile environments. Figure 7 shows the Web service architecture implemented for this work.

Competency questions. One of the most important stages of the design of ontologies is the definition of a list of competency questions that the resulting ontology must answer. The role of competency questions is similar to the specification requirement of any software system in the sense that it is used during evaluation to determine whether the ontological model fulfilled the tasks for which it was created. Table 1 shows all competency questions and their respective SQWRL rule. After executing all queries, results were all correct.

Table 1. Competency questions and their respective SQWRL query rule

Competency question	SQWRL query rule
What is the name of students supervised by Professor Juan Carlos?	Persona:Profesor(?x) ^ Persona:esAsesor(?x, ?y) ^ Persona:tieneNombre(?y, ?Nombre) ^ Persona:tieneApellido(?y, ?Apellido) ^ Persona:tieneNombre(?x, ?Nombre_profesor) ^ swrlb:containsIgnoreCase(?Nombre_profesor,"Juan Carlos") -> sqwrl:select(?Nombre, ?Apellido)
What is the name of the students who are developing their final project?	Persona:Licenciatura(?x) ^ Persona:tieneAsesorPT(?x, ?y) ^ Persona:tieneApellido(?x, ?Apellido) ^ Persona:tieneNombre(?x, ?Nombre) -> sqwrl:select(?Nombre, ?Apellido)
What is the name of the students who are over 18 years?	Persona:Licenciatura(?x) ^ Persona:tieneEdad(?x, ?y) ^ swrlb:greaterThan(?y, ?anios) ^ Persona:tieneApellido(?x, ?Apellido) ^ Persona:tieneNombre(?x, ?Nombre) -> sqwrl:select(?Nombre, ?Apellido)
How many students are over 18 years?	Persona:Licenciatura(?x) ^ Persona:tieneEdad(?x, ?y) ^ swrlb:greaterThan(?y, ?anios) -> sqwrl:count(?x)
What is the key and credits of the subject Differential Calculus?	AcademicoCBI:UEAPlanEstudio(?x) ^ AcademicoCBI:tieneClaveUEA(?x, ?Clave_uea) ^ AcademicoCBI:tieneCreditosAsignados(?x, ?Creditos) ^ AcademicoCBI:tieneNombreUEA(?x, ?Nombre_uea) ^ swrlb:containsIgnoreCase(?Nombre_uea,"Calculo Diferencial")" -> sqwrl:selectDistinct(?Nombre_uea, ?Clave_uea, ?Creditos)
What is the name, code and credits of the subjects that are prerequisite of the subject Differential Calculus?	AcademicoCBI:UEAPlanEstudio(?x) ^ AcademicoCBI:tienePreRequisito(?x, ?y) ^ AcademicoCBI:tieneCreditosAsignados(?y, ?Creditos) ^ AcademicoCBI:tieneClaveUEA(?y, ?Clave_uea) ^ AcademicoCBI:tieneNombreUEA(?y, ?Nombre_uea) ^ AcademicoCBI:tieneNombreUEA(?x, ?Nombre_uea_x) ^ swrlb:equal(?Nombre_uea_x,"Calculo Diferencial") -> sqwrl:selectDistinct(?Nombre_uea, ?Clave_uea, ?Creditos)
What is the full name, data, location, and schedule of Professor Juan Carlos?	Persona:Profesor(?x) ^ Tramites:tieneCubiculo(?x, ?y) ^ Tramites:TieneUbicacion(?y, ?g) ^ EspacioFisico:TieneLetra(?g, ?Edificio) ^ Tramites:tieneNombreCubiculo(?y, ?Cubículo) ^ Persona:tieneNombre(?x, ?Nombre) ^ Persona:tieneApellido(?x, ?Apellido) ^ Persona:tieneDatosDeContacto(?x, ?Datos) ^ EspacioFisico:HorarioInicio(?y, ?HoraInicio) ^ EspacioFisico:HorarioFin(?y, ?HoraFin) ^ swrlb:containsIgnoreCase(?Nombre,"Juan Carlos") -> sqwrl:select(?Nombre, ?Apellido, ?Datos, ?Cubículo, ?HoraInicio, ?HoraFin, ?Edificio)
How many students fit in the classroom E309?	EspacioFisico:Salon(?x) ^ EspacioFisico:Cupo(?x, ?Cupo) ^ EspacioFisico:NumSalon(?x, ?Numero_salon) ^ EspacioFisico:NomSalon(?x, ?Nombre_salon) ^ swrlb:containsIgnoreCase(?Numero_salon,"E309") -> sqwrl:select(?Nombre_salon,?Numero_salon,?Cupo)

Table 1. (*continued*)

What is the name and registration number of the student José Enrique?	Persona:Licenciatura(?x) ^ Persona:tieneNombre(?x, ?Nombre) ^ Persona:tieneMatricula(?x, ?Matricula) ^ Persona:tieneApellido(?x, ?Apellidos) ^ swrlb:containsIgnoreCase(?Nombre, "Jose Enrique") -> sqwrl:select(?Nombre, ?Apellidos, ?Matricula)
What is the full name of the student with registration number 1234?	Persona:Licenciatura(?x) ^ Persona:tieneNombre(?x, ?Nombre) ^ Persona:tieneMatricula(?x, ?Matricula) ^ Persona:tieneApellido(?x, ?Apellidos) ^ swrlb:equal(?Matricula, ?numero_matricula) -> sqwrl:select(?Matricula, ?Nombre, ?Apellidos)
What are the documents required to obtain a graduate degree?	Tramites:Tramites(?x) ^ Tramites:TieneNombre(?x, ?Nombre_tramite) ^ Tramites:TieneDocumentos(?x, ?Documento) ^ swrlb:containsIgnoreCase(?Nombre_tramite, "Titulo de posgrado") -> sqwrl:select(?Nombre_tramite,?Documento)
Who is responsible for receiving and processing the documents for a graduate degree?	Tramites:Tramites(?x) ^ Tramites:TieneNombre(?x, ?Nombre_tramite) ^ swrlb:containsIgnoreCase(?Nombre_tramite, "Titulo de posgrado") ^ Tramites:TieneDocumentos(?x, ?y) ^ Tramites:TieneResponsable(?x, ?encargado) ^ Persona:tieneNombre(?encargado, ?Nombre_encargado) ^ Persona:tieneDatosDeContacto(?encargado, ?Datos) -> sqwrl:selectDistinct(?Nombre_tramite, ?Nombre_encargado, ?Datos)
Which is the guide to obtain a graduate degree?	Tramites:Tramites(?x) ^ Tramites:TieneNombre(?x, ?Nombre_tramite) ^ Tramites:TieneGuia(?x, ?Guia) ^ swrlb:containsIgnoreCase(?Nombre_tramite, "Titulo de posgrado") -> sqwrl:select(?Nombre_tramite,?Guia)
What is the full name and contract number of teacher assistants of Professor Juan Carlos?	Persona:Licenciatura(?x) ^ Persona:esAyudanteDe(?x, ?y) ^ Persona:tieneNombre(?x, ?Nombre_ayudante) ^ Persona:tieneApellido(?x, ?Apleiido_ayudante) ^ Persona:tieneApellido(?y, ?Apellido_profesor) ^ Persona:tieneNombre(?y, ?Nombre_profesor) ^ swrlb:containsIgnoreCase(?Nombre_profesor,"Juan Carlos") ^ Persona:tieneNumeroEconomico(?x, ?Número_economico) -> sqwrl:select(?Nombre_ayudante, ?Apellido_ayudante, ?Número_economico)
What is the class schedule of E309?	OntologiaRed:Clase(?x) ^ OntologiaRed:tieneUea(?x, ?Uea) ^ AcademicoCBI:tieneNombreUEA(?Uea, ?Nombre_uea) ^ OntologiaRed:impartidaPor(?x, ?profe) ^ Persona:tieneNombre(?profe, ?Nombre_profesor) ^ Persona:tieneApellido(?profe, ?Apellido_profesor) ^ OntologiaRed:tieneSalon(?x, ?y) ^ EspacioFisico:NumSalon(?y, ?Num_salon) ^ swrlb:containsIgnoreCase(?Num_salon, "E309") ^ OntologiaRed:HoraInicio(?x, ?Hora_inicio) ^ OntologiaRed:HoraFin(?x, ?Hora_fin) -> sqwrl:selectDistinct(?Nombre_uea,?Nombre_profesor,?Apellido_profesor,?Hora_inicio, ?Hora_fin)
What are the names of the departments of the Division of Basic Science and Engineering?	AcademicoCBI:Departamento(?x) ∧ AcademicoCBI:tieneNombreDepartamento(?x, ?Nombre) → sqwrl:selectDistinct(?Nombre)
What are the subjects taught by Professor Juan Carlos?	Persona:Profesor(?x) ^ OntologiaRed:Clase(?y) ^ OntologiaRed:impartidaPor(?y, ?x) ^ OntologiaRed:tieneUea(?y, ?uea) ^ AcademicoCBI:tieneNombreUEA(?uea, ?Nombre_uea) ^ Persona:tieneNombre(?x, ?Nombre_profesor) ^ swrlb:containsIgnoreCase(?Nombre_profesor,"Juan Carlos")→ sqwrl:select(?Nombre_uea)

6   Conclusions

This paper describes a semantic search mobile application, which incorporates various technological paradigms: Web services, mobile computing and ontologies. The main objective of integrating these technologies was to support the development of more complex and intelligent mobile search applications. The use of multidimensional models implemented with ontologies offers significant advantages: the ability to exchange, expand, extend and maintain the individual ontologies. The type of questions that the multidimensional ontology model is capable of answering concern academic issues; location of people, buildings, roads. Ontologies represent a key enabler for mobile search applications, as they enable concept and knowledge sharing while providing a model reasoning and query answering. The incorporation and exploitation of Web services through ontological models is a clear trend that promises to improve the automatic selection and invocation of legacy and new Web services. All these technologies together (Web services and ontologies) are key facilitators for the wise management of search-based systems based on mobile computing.

References

1. Weißenberg, N., Voisard, A., Gartmann, R.: Using ontologies in personalized mobile applications. In: Proceedings of the 12th Annual ACM International Workshop on Geographic Information Systems, pp. 2–11. ACM (2004)
2. Sheshagiri, M., Sadeh, N., Gandon, F.: Using semantic web services for context-aware mobile applications. In: MobiSys 2004 Workshop on Context Awareness (2004)
3. Gu, T., Pung, H.K., Zhang, D.Q.: A service-oriented middleware for building context-aware services. Journal of Network and computer applications 28(1), 1–18 (2005)
4. Kim, W., Lee, S., Choi, D.: Semantic web based intelligent product and service search framework for location-based services. In: Gervasi, O., Gavrilova, M.L., Kumar, V., Laganá, A., Lee, H.P., Mun, Y., Taniar, D., Tan, C.J.K. (eds.) ICCSA 2005. LNCS, vol. 3483, pp. 103–112. Springer, Heidelberg (2005)
5. Chiu, D.K., Yueh, Y.T., Leung, H.F., Hung, P.C.: Towards ubiquitous tourist service coordination and process integration: A collaborative travel agent system architec-ture with semantic web services. Information Systems Frontiers 11(3), 241–256 (2009)
6. Bouzeghoub, A., Do, K.N., Wives, L.: Situation-aware adaptive recommendation to assist mobile users in a campus environment. In: International Conference on Advanced Information Networking and Applications, AINA 2009, pp. 503–509. IEEE (2009)
7. Cadenas, A., Ruiz, C., Larizgoitia, I., García-Castro, R., Lamsfus, C., Vázquez, I., ... Poveda, M.: Context management in mobile environments: a semantic approach. In: Proceedings of the 1st Workshop on Context, Information and Ontologies, p. 2. ACM (2009)
8. Paulo Sousa, J., Carrapatoso, E., Fonseca, B., da Graça Campos Pimentel, M., de Freitas Bulcão-Neto, R.: Composition of context aware mobile services using a semantic context model. International Journal on Advances in Software 2(2 and 3), 275–287 (2009)
9. Woerndl, W., Hristov, A.: Recommending resources in mobile per-sonal information management. In: Third International Conference on Digital Society, ICDS 2009, pp. 149–154. IEEE (February 2009)
10. Liiv, I., Tammet, T., Ruotsalo, T., Kuusik, A.: Personalized context-aware recommendations in SMARTMUSEUM: combining semantics with statistics. In: Proceedings of the 2009 Third International Conference on Advances in Semantic Processing, pp. 50–55 (2009)
11. Suárez-Figueroa, M.C., Gómez-Pérez, A., Villazón-Terrazas, B.: How to write and use the Ontology Requirements Specification Document. In: Meersman, R., Dillon, T., Herrero, P. (eds.) OTM 2009, Part II. LNCS, vol. 5871, pp. 966–982. Springer, Heidelberg (2009)
12. Gómez, A.H.F., Martínez-Tomás, R., Tapia, S.A.A., Zamorano, M.R.: Using semantic technologies and the OSU ontology for modeling context and activities in multi-sensory surveillance systems. International Journal of Systems Science 45(4), 798–809 (2014)

An Italian Multimodal Corpus: The Building Process

Maria Chiara Caschera, Arianna D'Ulizia, Fernando Ferri, and Patrizia Grifoni

Institute of Research on Population and Social Policies (IRPPS),
National Research Council (CNR)
00185, Rome, Italy
{mc.caschera,arianna.dulizia,fernando.ferri,
patrizia.grifoni}@irpps.cnr.it

Abstract. During the design of multimodal interaction environments, the use of a corpus of multimodal sentences is very important in order to achieve various tasks of multimodal interaction. In last decade, several researchers addressed the creation of multimodal corpora for English, French, and various other languages. However, from the analysis of these multimodal corpora, there clearly is a lack of multimodal corpora for Italian. This paper describes the building process of an Italian multimodal corpus. Starting from the manual analysis of multimedia dialogues, this process extracts different multimodal data, i.e. speech and gestures, which are used to generate grammar rules and to train the multimodal interpreter in order to set the framework for the multimodal corpus building. Following that, the set framework is used to annotate semi-automatically multimodal information, such as syntactic roles and semantics, on new dialogues to be included in the corpus.

Keywords: Multimodal interaction, Multimodal corpus, Italian Multimodal corpus.

1 Introduction

Multimodal corpora are necessary for various tasks of multimodal interaction. In fact, they are useful during the combination of information (fusion), the interpretation, as well as the presentation (fission) phases. Specifically, they are necessary in order to create the grammar, to train and test the interaction system for the correct interpretation of multimodal inputs, and to produce outputs according to the grammar rules, the semantics and pragmatics defined in the corpus. In the last years, many multimodal corpora aiming at this were built [1, 2, 3, 4, 5, 6]. They were recorded in various languages, mainly English [2, 3, 4] and French [1] [5]. NESPOLE! [6] is the only multilingual and multimodal corpus that addresses the Italian language; however, it is not freely available to the research community. The building of a freely available multimodal corpus for the Italian language is the first challenging objective that is faced in this paper.

Another important research topic concerns the automation of the annotation process. Generally, during the construction of a multimodal corpus, it is indeed necessary to specify a standardized way of representing and extracting multimodal

R. Meersman et al. (Eds.): OTM 2014 Workshops, LNCS 8842, pp. 557–566, 2014.
© Springer-Verlag Berlin Heidelberg 2014

information from the recorded material in order to give access to large multimodal corpora. All the aforementioned multimodal corpora were annotated using a heavy and time-consuming manual procedure, which is generally long, at least as much as the recording itself.

The aim of this paper is to gather the two challenges that are described above by proposing a methodology for building an Italian multimodal corpus that semi-automates the annotation of multimodal data, which speeds up this process. To demonstrate our methodology, we applied it to a set of 60 freely available YouTube video recordings of Italian dialogues. These multimedia data were manually annotated and syntactic, temporal and conceptual information were extracted from them. The edited data were used as examples to generate the grammar rules and to train the multimodal interpreter in order to set the multimodal corpus building framework. Following that, this framework was used to extract semi-automatically the associated syntactic and semantic information from new dialogues to be included in the corpus.

The remainder of this paper is structured as follows: Section 2 provides an overview on multimodal interaction and multimodal corpora. Section 3 introduces the proposed methodology for building an Italian multimodal corpus. Finally, Section 4 concludes the paper and discusses future works.

2   Related Works

2.1   Multimodal Interaction

In multimodal systems, two of the main steps of the interaction process are the information fusion and interpretation [7]. An overview of multimodal systems is provided in [8], where they are analyzed by considering the main features to combine modal inputs. In those systems, different data types, which are defined by different input modalities, are combined and fused by imposing temporal, syntactic and semantic constraints. Therefore, the fused information is correctly interpreted by considering different features, such as available interaction modalities, conversation focus, and context of interaction, and by simultaneously considering semantic, temporal and contextual constraints [9]. During the fusion, interpretation and fission phases, data-driven methods can be applied, and, for these methods, the use of multimodal corpora is fundamental. Moreover, the correct interpretation of multimodal inputs implies the management of modal (e.g. sketch ambiguities [10]) and multimodal ambiguities [11]. To address this purpose, several data-driven methods were developed, such as in [12]. More specifically, multimodal corpora are crucial to: define the rule to combine and to fuse the modal inputs and outputs into multimodal ones; train the methods to correctly interpret multimodal inputs; test methods developed for the correct multimodal interpretation.

Considering the fusion of multimodal inputs, several multimodal grammatical frameworks use multimodal corpora to generate grammatical rules. In fact, multimodal interaction requires that several alternative or simultaneous inputs, coming from various modalities, are opportunely integrated and combined into a sentence [13, 14], i.e. a multimodal fusion process has to occur. In the literature, various approaches to the fusion process have been proposed [15]. One of the most promising approaches is the grammar-based fusion strategy, in which the different unimodal inputs are integrated into a unique multimodal input by using the multimodal grammar specification [16, 17]. This approach is indeed more coherent with the human-human communication paradigm, in which the dialogue is seen as a unique and multimodal communication act [18]. These considerations lead to the need of multimodal corpora in order to infer multimodal grammar specification as in [19, 20, 21, 22, 23, 24, 25].

Regarding the training phase, multimodal corpora impact on methods that need a learning step in order to correctly interpret multimodal inputs. These methods are based on probabilistic approaches and, as a consequence, they need a data set in order to build and train the model. Therefore, corpora are used in order to acquire the needed information to make learned the model. In the recent literature, several efforts were made to develop those methods, and an overview of methods used to correctly interpret multimodal inputs is presented in [26]. It is interesting to note that researches are moving towards the development of methods that shift the cognitive load from the user to the system by defining probabilistic approaches that can learn the main features using data extracted from corpora, such as in [27, 28, 29, 30, 31, 32].

Considering the testing phase, a key role is played by multimodal corpora. As an example, [33] uses a multimodal corpus to evaluate a gaze estimation approach. In [34], a multimodal corpus has allowed evaluating the accuracy of a method that was developed to classify multimodal ambiguities in order to provide a correct interpretation of the multimodal user's input.

2.2   Multimodal Corpora

As stated in [35], "a multimodal corpus is a digitized collection of language and communication-related material, drawing on more than one modality". In recent years, a growing interest in the creation of multimodal corpora is emerging [1, 2, 3, 4, 5, 6]. The process of collecting this material is not a trivial task, and several challenges must be faced. The first challenge concerns the identification of modalities that must be recorded and, consequently, the choice of features that must be extracted from the acquisition systems (e.g. sensors, cameras, microphones, etc.). Depending on the next use of the corpus, different modalities need to be considered and a tailored extraction process of features must be designed. Secondly, the choice of the language and the communication-related material to be collected is a further challenge that strictly depends on the future use of the corpus. For instance, if the corpus will be used for human-computer interaction purposes, the material should contain human-computer interaction dialogues. However, if it will be used to analyse human-human communication, multimodal dialogues between two or more people are more suitable. This challenge implies that interaction scenarios can be used in order to observe and collect multimodal dialogues. Finally, the annotation of the multimodal registrations is a challenging task that implies the choice of meaningful information, which has to be extracted from multimodal dialogues. Since verbal and nonverbal communications are culturally conditioned, multimodal dialogues are affected by cultural issues, as described in [36]. Therefore, the annotation process of multimodal corpora mines different meaningful information according to the languages of the people who interact.

Several multimodal corpora have mainly been developed for English, but also for French, German and other languages. The literature analysis highlights a lack of multimodal corpora for the Italian language. NESPOLE! [6] is a multilingual and multimodal corpus that also addresses the Italian language; however, it is not available for free. On the other hand, various linguistic corpora have been developed for the Italian language (natural language). A list of the most important corpora of spoken Italian collected and published since 1965 is provided by BADIP (Banca Dati dell'Italiano Parlato – Database of Spoken Italian) [37]. Currently, this database contains the link to approximately thirty developed Italian linguistic corpora.

In this paper, the building process of a free-available multimodal corpus for the Italian language is faced.

3   The Semi-automatic Building of a Multimodal Corpus for the Italian Language

The development of a multimodal corpus for the Italian language is realized using the multimodal corpus building framework, proposed in our previous work [38]. Figure 1 shows the general architecture of this framework.

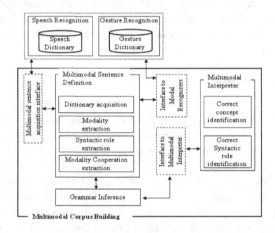

Fig. 1. Multimodal corpus building framework

The development of the multimodal corpus is organized into the following steps:

- Data acquisition: this step includes the selection of multimedia material containing multimodal dialogues and the extraction of modal information from these dialogues;
- Multimodal corpus building framework setting: in this step, the grammar inference and the multimodal interpreter training will be performed in order to have the grammar rules and the trained interpreter for the semi-automatic annotation;
- Semi-automatic multimodal annotation: this step performs the semi-automatic extraction of multimodal information from new dialogues.

In the following sections, each one of the cited steps will be illustrated in detail.

3.1   Data Acquisition

The first step of the creation of a multimodal corpus for the Italian language consists in selecting suitable multimedia material for this purpose. As we needed multimodal dialogues, we started by searching online multimedia files containing dialogues between two or more people who interact with each other using more than one modality. We chose the video data which were available in the project L-Pack [39]. The peculiarities of these multimedia contents are listed below:

- 60 short videos of dialogues, related to everyday life, and freely available on YouTube;
- the videos contain speech and gestural interactions during colloquial dialogues;
- the audio tracks of the videos and the written texts of the dialogues are respectively available in mp3 and pdf.

After the multimodal dialogues are downloaded, the next step is to extract the metadata (i.e. the syntactic role, the modality, the value, and the kind of cooperation), which are associated with modal information and needed as inputs for the following steps. The involved modalities are speech and gesture. The video files were annotated using Anvil [40]. The videos were segmented into meaningful frames and the gestural interpretation was extracted and annotated (see Fig. 2b). Moreover, metadata on the audio tracks synchronization with the video frames, along with the syntactic role, the value, and the modality cooperation of each word were extracted and annotated (see Fig. 2b).

Six people were involved in this extraction process, all native Italians. They were instructed to use Anvil to extract all the elements of the dialogues and associate the aforementioned modal information.

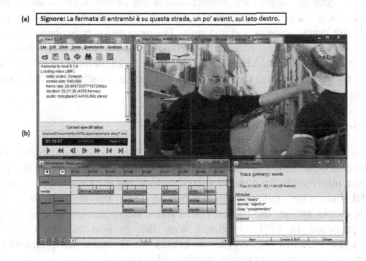

Fig. 2. An example of dialogue and modal information extraction

As an example, we considered the excerpt of dialogue written in Fig. 2a. The video of this dialogue was annotated considering the information on synchronization with the corresponding audio track. Moreover, the gestures of the arm were codified with the corresponding meanings (e.g. "Avanti" (ahead), "lato destro" (on the right), "questa strada" (this road)) as shown in Fig. 2b. Following this, syntactic roles, values and kinds of modality cooperation were extracted. The standard nomenclature of the ISDT Treebank (Italian Stanford Dependency Treebank) [41] is used to represent the syntactic categories.

3.2   Multimodal Corpus Building Framework Setting

The setting of the Multimodal corpus building framework consists in: generating the grammar rules through the Grammar Inference module and training the Multimodal Interpreter module.

Considering the Grammar Inference module, all the modal information extracted in the previous phase is used to generate a linear sequence of elements of multimodal sentences. Indeed, the linearization takes place according to the previously extracted kinds of modality cooperation and syntactic roles. More in detail, modalities cooperation allows determining whether some elements of the dialogue convey information that has some relation with the information conveyed by the other elements, while syntactic roles allows determining whether elements can be considered close together in syntax. At the end of this process, each sentence of the dialogue is linearized in a sequence of annotated elements. The set of linearized multimodal sentences is input to the grammar inference algorithm, defined in [42]. The algorithm generates the production rules, expressed in MAG notation [19], which will be used by the interpreter in the following step. Fig. 3 shows the grammar rules generated for the example of dialogue in Fig. 2a.

Since the Multimodal Interpreter module uses an HMM-based approach, it needs to be trained in order to support the correct annotation of the multimodal corpus. The training process is supported by examples of multimodal sentences that are correctly associated with syntactic roles and concepts. The association between an element and the correct syntactic role is obtained by considering the knowledge given by the Grammar Inference module. The association between an element and the associated concept is given by the knowledge of the conceptual structure of the context, as described in [38].

3.3   Semi-automatic Multimodal Annotation

The annotation process has been achieved by using the multimodal corpus building method described in [38]. This method allows to automatically extract the syntactic and semantic information from multimodal data by using the knowledge of the trained Multimodal Interpreter module. As defined in [38], the method to annotate a multimodal corpus applies the trained HMM-based interpretation and disambiguation approach proposed in [27], combined with the method to detect multimodal ambiguities provided in [34], in order to extract the semantic interpretation and the correct syntactic roles to annotate the multimodal corpus.

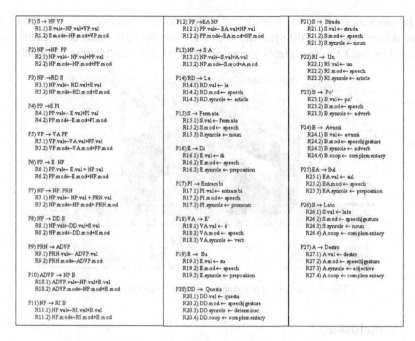

Fig. 3. Grammar rules generated for the example

The trained Multimodal Interpreter module, as described in Section 3.2, was applied to the video data available in the project L-Pack [39]. The multimodal sentences are acquired during the data acquisition step, described in Section 3.1. During the semi-automatic multimodal annotation step, the Multimodal Interpreter module observes the acquired data and it associates to each element of the multimodal sentence the correct syntactic role in the sentence and the referred concept. Data of each video are divided in sessions: one session for each sentence that composes each dialogue. As an example, the session that concerns with the sentence corresponding to audio track

"Guardi"(look), "ce ne"(there), "è" (is), "una" (one), "proprio" (just), "all'" (at the), "angolo" (corner))

and the gestures of the arm *("sinistro" (left))* is annotated with the corresponding syntactic roles and meanings. Fig. 4 shows the xml file containing the annotation of this sentence.

```
<?xml version="1.0"?>
<input>

    <mminput mod="speech" ts="01:25:40" te="01:26:05" conc="guarda" synt="V"/>
    <mminput mod="speech" ts="01:26:29" te="01:26:32" conc="ce" synt="B"/>
    <mminput mod="speech" ts="01:26:38" te="01:26:44" conc="ne" synt="B"/>
    <mminput mod="speech" ts="01:26:49" te="01:26:55" conc="è" synt="V"/>
    <mminput mod="speech" ts="01:26:69" te="01:26:95" conc="una" synt="N"/>
    <mminput mod="speech" ts="01:27:10" te="01:27:56" conc="proprio" synt="B"/>
    <mminput mod="speech" ts="01:27:25" te="01:28:65" conc="all'" synt="EA"/>
    <mminput mod="speech" ts="01:26:58" te="01:28:70" conc="angolo" synt="S"/>
    <mminput mod="gesture" conc="sinistro" synt="A"/>

    <nlsentence sent="guarda ce ne è una proprio al angolo sinistro"/>

</input>
```

Fig. 4. Example of XML that contains information for multimodal input annotation

The annotation of the audio track and gestures of the example is shown in Fig. 5, where information about the syntactic roles and concepts of the sentence elements are provided by the XML file (Fig.4) generated by the Multimodal Interpreter module.

Fig. 5. Example of automatic multimodal input annotation

4   Conclusions

The main purpose of this paper has been to provide a building process for the development of a multimodal corpus for the Italian language. The building process has been achieved by three main steps: the selection of the multimedia material and the extraction of modal information; the framework setting by defining the grammar rules and by training the interpreter for the semi-automatic annotation; and the multimodal annotation by the semi-automatic extraction of multimodal information from new dialogues. Starting from an existing multimedia corpus, this process was applied in order to annotate multimodal information, such as syntactic roles and semantics. As future work, the multimodal corpus building framework will be tested in order to evaluate the accuracy of the annotation process.

References

[1] Ringeval, F., Sonderegger, A., Sauer, J., Lalanne, D.: Introducing the RECOLA Multimodal Corpus of Remote Collaborative and Affective Interactions. In: 2nd International Workshop EmoSPACE (2013)

[2] Inoue, M., Hanada, R., Furuyama, N., Irino, T., Ichinomiya, T., Massaki, H.: Multimodal Corpus for Psychotherapeutic Situations. In: International Workshop Series on Multimodal Corpora, Tools and Resources, pp. 18–21 (2012)

[3] Melvin, R.S., May, W., Narayanan, S., Georgiou, P.G., Ganjavi, S.: Creation of a Doctor-Patient Dialogue Corpus Using Standardized Patients. In: LREC (2004)

[4] Fleury, A., Vacher, M., Portet, F., Chahuara, P., Noury, N.: A multimodal corpus recorded in a health smart home. In: Proceedings of the LREC 2010, pp. 99–105 (2010)

[5] Vacher, M., Lecouteux, B., Chahuara, P., Portet, F., Meillon, B., Bonnefond, N.: The Sweet-Home speech and multimodal corpus for home automation interaction. In: LREC 2014, pp. 1–8 (2014)

[6] Costantini, E., Burger, S., Pianesi, F.: NESPOLE!'s Multilingual and Multimodal Corpus. In: LREC (2002)

[7] D'Ulizia, A., Ferri, F., Grifoni, P.: Toward the Development of an Integrative Framework for Multimodal Dialogue Processing. In: Meersman, R., Tari, Z., Herrero, P. (eds.) OTM 2008 Workshops. LNCS, vol. 5333, pp. 509–518. Springer, Heidelberg (2008)

[8] Caschera, M.C., Ferri, F., Grifoni, P.: Multimodal interaction systems: information and time features. International Journal of Web and Grid Services 3(1), 82–99 (2007)

[9] Caschera, M.C., Ferri, F., Grifoni, P.: An Approach for Managing Ambiguities in Multimodal Interaction. In: Meersman, R., Tari, Z. (eds.) OTM-WS 2007, Part I. LNCS, vol. 4805, pp. 387–397. Springer, Heidelberg (2007)

[10] Avola, D., Caschera, M.C., Ferri, F., Grifoni, P.: Ambiguities in Sketch-Based Interfaces. In: HICSS 2007, p. 290. IEEE Computer Society (2007)

[11] Caschera, M.C., Ferri, F., Grifoni, P.: Ambiguity detection in multimodal systems. In: Advanced Visual Interfaces, AVI 2008, pp. 331–334. ACM Press (2008)

[12] Avola, D., Caschera, M.C., Grifoni, P.: Solving ambiguities for Sketch-Based interaction in mobile environments. In: Meersman, R., Tari, Z., Herrero, P. (eds.) OTM 2006 Workshops. LNCS, vol. 4277, pp. 904–915. Springer, Heidelberg (2006)

[13] D'Ulizia, A., Ferri, F.: Formalization of multimodal languages in pervasive computing paradigm. In: Damiani, E., Yetongnon, K., Chbeir, R., Dipanda, A. (eds.) SITIS 2006. LNCS, vol. 4879, pp. 126–136. Springer, Heidelberg (2009)

[14] Ferri, F., D'Ulizia, A., Grifoni, P.: Multimodal Language Specification for Human Adaptive Mechatronics. JNIT 3(1), 47–57 (2012)

[15] D'Ulizia, A.: Exploring Multimodal Input Fusion Strategies. In: Handbook of Research on Multimodal Human Computer Interaction and Pervasive Services: Evolutionary Techniques for Improving Accessibility, pp. 34–57. IGI Publishing (2009)

[16] D'Ulizia, A., Ferri, F., Grifoni, P.: A Hybrid Grammar-Based Approach to Multimodal Languages Specification. In: Meersman, R., Tari, Z. (eds.) OTM-WS 2007, Part I. LNCS, vol. 4805, pp. 367–376. Springer, Heidelberg (2007)

[17] D'Ulizia, A., Ferri, F., Grifoni, P.: A Survey of Grammatical Inference Methods for Natural Language Learning. Artificial Intelligence Review 36(1), 1–27 (2011)

[18] Manchón, P., Pérez, G., Amores, G.: Multimodal Fusion: A New Hybrid Strategy for Dialogue Systems. In: Proceedings of ICMI 2006, pp. 357–363. ACM (2006)

[19] D'Ulizia, A., Ferri, F., Grifoni, P.: Generating Multimodal Grammars for Multimodal Dialogue Processing. IEEE Transactions on Systems, Man and Cybernetics, Part A: Systems and Humans 40(6), 1130–1145 (2010)

[20] Shimazu, H., Takashima, Y.: Multimodal Definite Clause Grammar. Systems and Computers in Japan 26(3), 93–102 (1995)

[21] Johnston, M., Bangalore, S.: Finite-state multimodal integration and understanding. Nat. Lang. Eng. 11(2), 159–187 (2005)

[22] Reitter, D., Panttaja, E.M., Cummins, F.: UI on the fly: Generating a multimodal user interface. In: Proceedings of Human Language Technology Conference (2004)

[23] Pereira, F., Warren, D.H.D.: Definite Clause Grammars for Language Analysis - A survey of the Formalism and a Comparison with Augmented Transition Networks. Artificial Intelligence 13(3) (1980)

[24] Baldridge, J., Kruijff, G.J.M.: Multimodal combinatory categorial grammar. In: Proceedings of the 10th Conference of the European Chapter of the ACL, pp. 211–218 (2003)

[25] D'Andrea, A., D'Ulizia, A., Ferri, F., Grifoni, P.: A Multimodal Pervasive Framework for Ambient Assisted Living. In: Proceedings of the PETRA. ACM Digital Library (2009)

[26] Caschera, M.C.: Interpretation methods and ambiguity management in multimodal systems. In: Handbook of Research on Multimodal Human Computer Interaction and Pervasive Services: Evolutionary Techniques for Improving Accessibility, pp. 87–102. IGI Publishing (2009)

[27] Caschera, M.C., Ferri, F., Grifoni, P.: InteSe: An Integrated Model for Resolving Ambiguities in Multimodal Sentences. IEEE Transactions on Systems, Man, and Cybernetics: Systems 43(4), 911–931 (2013)

[28] Avola, D., Caschera, M.C., Ferri, F., Grifoni, P.: Classifying and resolving ambiguities in sketch-based interaction. Int. J. Virt. Technol. Multimedia 1(2), 104–139 (2010)

[29] Caschera, M.C., Ferri, F., Grifoni, P.: Personal sphere information, histories and social interaction between people on the Internet. In: Meersman, R., Tari, Z., Herrero, P. (eds.) OTM 2008 Workshops. LNCS, vol. 5333, pp. 480–488. Springer, Heidelberg (2008)

[30] Rabiner, L.R.: A tutorial on hidden Markov models and selected applications in speech recognition. Proc. IEEE 77(2), 257–285 (1989)

[31] Makhoul, J., Starner, T., Schwartz, R., Chou, G.: On-line cursive handwriting recognition using hidden Markov models and statistical grammars. In: Proc. Workshop Hum. Lang. Technol., pp. 432–436 (1994)

[32] Jelinek, F.: Robust part-of-speech tagging using a hidden Markov model. Comput. Speech Lang. 6(3), 225–242 (1992)

[33] Li, N., Busso, C.: Evaluating the robustness of an appearance-based gaze estimation method for multimodal interfaces. In: ICMI 2013, pp. 91–98 (2013)

[34] Caschera, M.C., Ferri, F., Grifoni, P.: From Modal to Multimodal Ambiguities: a Classification Approach. JNIT 4(5), 87–109 (2013)

[35] Allwood, J.: Multimodal Corpora. In: Lüdeling, A., Kytö, M. (eds.) Corpus Linguistics. An International Handbook, pp. 207–225. Mouton de Gruyter, Berlin (2008)

[36] Caschera, M.C., D'Ulizia, A., Ferri, F., Grifoni, P.: Multiculturality and Multimodal Languages. In: Multiple Sensorial Media Advances and Applications: New Developments in MulSeMedia, pp. 99–114. IGI Global Publishing (2012)

[37] http://badip.uni-graz.at/it/lista-di-corpora

[38] Caschera, M.C., D'Ulizia, A., Ferri, F., Grifoni, P.: Methods for dynamic building of multimodal corpora. In: LTC 2013, pp. 499–503 (2013)

[39] https://www.youtube.com/user/L2pack

[40] http://www.anvil-software.org/

[41] Bosco, C., Montemagni, S., Simi, M.: Converting Italian Treebanks: Towards an Italian Stanford Dependency Treebank. In: ACL Workshop (2013)

[42] D'Ulizia, A., Ferri, F., Grifoni, P.: A Learning Algorithm for Multimodal Grammar Inference. IEEE Transactions on Systems, Man, and Cybernetics - Part B: Cybernetics 41(6), 1495–1510 (2011)

Collaborative Editing: Collaboration, Awareness and Accessibility Issues for the Blind

Maria Claudia Buzzi[1], Marina Buzzi[1], Barbara Leporini[2],
Giulio Mori[2], and Victor M.R. Penichet[3]

[1] IIT-CNR, via Moruzzi 1, 56124 Pisa, Italy
{claudia.buzzi,marina.buzzi}@iit.cnr.it
[2] ISTI-CNR, via Moruzzi 1, 56124 Pisa, Italy
{barbara.leporini,giulio.mori}@isti.cnr.it
[3] Computer Systems Department, University of Castilla-La Mancha, Albacete, Spain
victor.penichet@uclm.es

Abstract. Collaborative tools enable teachers and students to easily create and share knowledge as well as edit content in a cooperative way anytime, anywhere, and with various devices. However, technical barriers increase difficulties for users with special needs if interfaces are not designed with accessibility in mind. Blind people in particular may experience great accessibility and usability issues when using collaborative editors via screen reader, with consequent difficulty of inclusion at school or work. In this paper, we discuss the design of usable Web interfaces for collaborative editing, especially focusing on how blind users interact with them. Google Docs was chosen as a case study of a collaborative tool in order to analyze the accessibility of its main collaborative features. Based on the results, five guidelines are proposed for supporting collaborative editing, including "accessible awareness" for blind users.

Keywords: Collaborative editing, Google Docs, blind users, screen reader.

1   Introduction

Collaborative editing environments via Internet are particularly interesting and useful since they allow people to work together in a simple, economic and efficient way. These tools can greatly empower a team's work, and should be accessible and easy to use for all, including people with disabilities. One of the most popular collaborative suites is Google Docs. Unfortunately, it still presents difficulties and obstacles for blind people, making collaboration a challenge. In a previous study we carried out an initial accessibility inspection describing all the accessibility issues encountered when interacting via the JAWS screen reader [1].

The World Wide Web Consortium (W3C) defined the new version of the Web Content Accessibility Guidelines (WCAG) in 2008. WCAG 2.0 enhances the previous version by incorporating usability for improving user satisfaction. Four general principles, detailed in 12 guidelines, drive the web interface design. In March 2014, the W3C published WAI-ARIA (Accessible Rich Internet Applications), a recommendation that defines how to make dynamic Web content more accessible [http://www.w3.org/TR/wai-aria/].

R. Meersman et al. (Eds.): OTM 2014 Workshops, LNCS 8842, pp. 567–573, 2014.
© Springer-Verlag Berlin Heidelberg 2014

This study explores the accessibility of collaborative aspects and awareness features in the Google Docs environment: it is inspired by the personal experience of one the authors, totally blind since childhood, who experienced some difficulties that made it impossible to use this collaborative tool with her colleagues.

Our methodology starts with gathering user requirements carried out by inspection via screen reader of Google docs from all authors of this paper. For the main interaction problems detected we propose basic techniques for removing the accessibility issues. Last, generalizing problems from the specific case study, we suggest some basic guidelines for designing collaborative editing environments accessible for blind people.

2   Related Work

Collaborative Web applications offer a way to control access to information, manage different versions of the documents, ease publication and protection processes, support advanced searches, provide mechanisms to approve documents, and so on. Awareness is a very important factor that can determine the success of this kind of application: it is crucial for a user to know what other users are doing in the system and what is going on. Since systems and interfaces change, awareness must be kept up-to-date over time.

Few studies have specifically analyzed the accessibility of collaborative environments and tools [1, 2, 3, 4]. Khan et al. [3] performed a usability study with four novice and four experienced users on ThinkFree, a collaborative writing system. Although ThinkFree proved effective for the proposed tasks, efficiency and availability of resources were more limited than in Google Docs. The use of groupware systems by a blind user usually requires considerable technical skill. For simplifying access to a popular groupware system (Lotus Notes), Takagi et al. developed a self-talking client to allow blind people to access main groupware functions efficiently and easily, masking the user from the complexity of the original visual interface [4].

Kobayashi developed a client application (Voice Browser for Groupware systems) enabling visually impaired people to interact with a popular Japanese groupware system. The browser intercepts pages generated by the server, and converts them on-fly to a suitable format [5].

Recently, Schoeberlein and Wang [6], created a Microsoft Word plug-in to simplify interaction for blind people (in revision mode). This study is very useful since it tackles problems of information delivery to the screen reader and content contextualization; however, at this time Word still offers limited functions, allowing one to exchange documents with revisions, while tools such as Google Docs enable a greater degree of collaboration, allowing a group to write a document collaboratively in real time.

3   Google Docs as a Case Study

Google Docs offers a free Web-based word processor, spreadsheet, presentation, and form application. The Google Docs functionality for word processors is Google Documents. Google Documents relies heavily on visual features and dynamic changes of the user interfaces. If the screen reader does not detect them, they are inaccessible for blind users.

For the evaluation, we first selected a set of main functionalities to consider when editing a document in a collaborative way, and then tested them via screen reader. The visual interface functions were compared with those perceived by the blind author of the paper. The analysis was performed using the screen reader JAWS v. 14 (http://www.freedomscientific.com/), and the browsers Internet Explorer (IE) v. 11, Firefox v. 27.0.1 and Google Chrome (GC) v. 35. We summarize the issues here, described in detail in our previous work [1]:

Fig. 1. A Google document screen shot

- **Inviting People.** Main accessibility issues for the "share" function are: 1. The document checkbox is not selectable and the menu appearing for the checked document is inaccessible (not announced by the screen reader); 2. The "Share" pull-down menu is not properly accessible since it is not possible to exit from the editing area when pressing the ESC key.
- **Email as Attachment, Send Message to Collaborators.** 1. The "Attach as" label in the "Email as attachment" window is not announced by JAWS and not selectable; 2. Both windows sometimes lose the focus; 3. An error message appears when collaborators' addresses are not inserted, but even when text is announced by JAWS, the button "Ok" is not selectable via keyboard, causing user disorientation and frustration. It is difficult to insert email addresses in the "Email as Attachment" window.
- **Seeing Who Is Accessing.** Google Docs highlights who is working on the document at the same time only visually, not conveying this information to the screen reader. Furthermore, the collaborators' icons are placed in the toolbar that is not accessible from the editing area.
- **Publishing as a Web Page.** The function "Publish" is not accessible via keyboard and screen reader. Similarly, interactive elements of the Publish interface are inaccessible.
- **File Upload.** The upload functionality is not accessible. Using IE, the upload menu (showing type of file to upload) appears after pressing the related button, but the menu items are not announced by JAWS, while when using Firefox and GC the menu does not even appear.
- **Revision History.** The document "Revision History", available through the menu "File", cannot be reached via screen reader. Accessing the list of the revised

document versions, the screen reader announces only the date and names of the people involved. When a version is selected, the editor shows visually the old version of the document with changes -- very intuitive for sighted users, but very difficult and incomprehensible for a blind person.

- **Comments.** The function is inaccessible from either the menu or the toolbar. Furthermore, a screen reader is unable to detect the comment content. Neither keyboard nor screen reader command is available to go back to the main content when the comment has been edited.

3.1   Combining Collaboration, Awareness and Accessibility

In a collaborative environment it is crucial to perceive the features related to other collaborators, such as a) *see who is accessing*, b) *see revision history* and c) *comments*. It is fundamental not only to perceive the presence of the other collaborators clearly, but also to be aware of what other collaborators are doing (or have done) and where.

Unfortunately, at the moment Google Docs does not support awareness for users operating via screen reader, although in the recent version some WAI-ARIA attributes have been applied (July 2014). We suggest possible techniques that can help blind users access or better perceive each awareness aspect.

3.1.1   Seeing Who Is Accessing

Awareness of who is logged in the collaborative environment and is working on the same document in real time is important. For a user to be aware of the login/logout status of another collaborator, ascending/descending tone can be associated with the login/logout event, or a voice announcing the name and status of the collaborator can be used (for instance: "John is entering").

Using the voice is probably clearer and more immediate than a sound, since the name of the collaborator provides immediate comprehension. If the number of collaborators is high, a different sound associated with each collaborator could be confusing, or many announcements, using the voices, could be invasive, interrupting the user during her/his work. A WAI-ARIA live region may be a better solution for informing the user about the change of the state of a collaborator. The live region allows one to regulate the frequency of the announcements or disable the vocal/sound notifications by means of attributes. A setting page could allow the user to customize the preferred announcing level and type (sound or voice).

3.1.2   Revision History

In recent versions of Google Docs changes in the documents, text selections, and cursor positions of collaborators are emphasized by different colors, allowing a sighted user to better understand the editing actions of each collaborator. However, this is not compliant with accessibility guidelines: the use of colors, a visual feature, is not an accessible solution for blind users. This aspect could be adapted using sounds or vocal tags, in a two-level exploration, to improve blind users' awareness and accelerate the reading process:

1. Detect document changes (Perception): It is important for a blind user to quickly scan a document to understand whether a paragraph or section contains some changes instead of reading the entire document sequentially via screen reader.
2. Understand changes made by other collaborators (Comprehension): to understand in detail the changes and know their authors.

Possible solutions for implementing these functionalities are discussed:

Check for Document Changes: It would be important to have an area/page of the editor interface containing the list of doc changes, composed of links, directly connected to the beginning of the updated section or paragraph.

Furthermore, to improve the "visibility" of blind users it would be important to know the position of each paragraph containing the collaborators' changes in terms of the percentage of the entire document length, such as a radar view of the editing workspace. Awareness of this information may influence user actions and decisions.

Other useful information is the percentage indicating the current focus position of the blind user within a document. Both them could be inserted within a *live region*. In alternative, an accessible vertical slider bar (Javascript using the WAI-ARIA slider role) could be a solution for managing document navigation and announcing the user's position inside the document.

Check for Changes by Other Collaborators on a Paragraph: For document changes, it is important to know both the author and where these changes occurred. The support for opening and closing tags wrapping each changed block would be an important facility for designing accessible interfaces.

For example the <ins></ins> and <del></del> opening/closing tags of HTML 5 visually define whether a text has been inserted (usually browsers underline inserted text) or deleted (browsers strike a line on text) in a document, but these solutions are not sufficient for auditory interaction. To facilitate blind user interaction, these tags should provide the same information vocally. In addition, these opening/closing tags should support some customizable attributes. For example, the attributes could be used for the author's name or other useful information (such as the authors' status). This would allow the screen reader to announce the tag embedded information via sound or/and voice.

3.1.3 Comments

Being able to read comments is important because they inform every collaborator about particular notes. WAI-ARIA provides the role *tooltip* as a solution for an accessible pop-up with a description of a user interface (UI) element when the focus is on it. A blind user should be able to perceive document comments, and be aware of their authors and any other useful information.

3.2 Basic Accessibility Guidelines for Collaborative Editing UI

Inspired by the four general principles already introduced in [1], five guidelines are herein proposed for improving the blind user experience in a collaborative environment. In short, the following are the four principles leading the proposed guidelines:

- **Editing Operable:** All editing functions must be operable via keyboard. The edited text has to be explorable with different granularity: char-by-char, word-by-word, and line-by-line. The focus should be easily movable between the main areas, toolbars and menu or interactive items. It would be possible to skip from one UI logical section to another, relieving the user from the sequential navigation.
- **Awareness Perceivable:** Information about the on-line users (status and actions) should be appropriately delivered to assistive technologies: who is online, or what they are doing and where.
- **Changes Understandable:** When more users are contemporary working on the same document, information on updated text should be adequately provided to the assistive technology, so that the blind user can quickly be aware of which parts have been modified.
- **Dynamic Messages and Prompt Feedback Sizeable:** Feedback and alerts, triggered by user actions, should be clear and easy to perceive. Alerting should be promptly provided to the assistive technology to readily inform the user. Short sounds and audio feedback can communicate main events (failure or success, collaborator login/logout, etc).

In addition to the standard general accessibility guidelines (W3C, ISO, usability experts) and the recommended principles for the collaborative editing environments, mentioned before, we can suggest some specific guidelines:

1. "Provide buttons grouped according to editing functions, made operable also via shortcuts."
2. "Make immediately perceptible the editing points where collaborators are working on"
3. "Mark properly the modified document parts, by indicating changes and authors".
4. "Inform the user about the status of the collaborators, when they are coming on-line and off-line, or working on the document".
5. "Make available the information on the current version of the document, such as the relative current position, the last changes (in short who, when and the percentage modified), the sections revised, etc."

Each guideline may be implemented by using different techniques. For instance, the guideline 3 could be applied using different solutions, such as the tags available from the markup language, or via hidden labels, given markers (e.g. specifics symbols or characters), ad-hoc regions, etc.

4   Conclusions

In this paper we considered obstacles encountered by blind people when interacting with Google Docs via screen reader, especially regarding co-editing. We suggested potential ways to inform blind users about who is seeing or modifying a document, and of any changes appearing on the user interface, enabling them to move more rapidly to the point of interest while providing a contextualization for comments and reviews.

Visual features and dynamic changes of the user interface need to be delivered to the assistive technology and thus to the user. WAI-ARIA and the use of HTML 5 features could help make UI elements and actions accessible, simplify interaction and make it more rapid and satisfying. In this perspective, we have outlined potential solutions in order to overcome several issues. Thus, basic guidelines for accessibility of collaborative editors have been herein proposed.

Many problems still remain, and blind users will truly benefit from accessible groupware environments only if browsers, screen readers and Web developers focus on a common accessibility goal.

References

1. Mori, G., Buzzi, M.C., Buzzi, M., Leporini, B., Penichet, V.M.R.: Collaborative editing for all: The google docs example. In: Stephanidis, C. (ed.) Universal Access in HCI, Part IV, HCII 2011. LNCS, vol. 6768, pp. 165–174. Springer, Heidelberg (2011)
2. Schoeberlein, J.G., Wang, Y.: Accessible collaborative writing for persons who are blind: a usability study. In: 14th International ACM SIGACCESS Conference on Computers and Accessibility, pp. 267–268 (2012)
3. Khan, M.A., Israr, N., Hassan, S.: Usability Evaluation of Web Office Applications in Collaborative Writing. In: First International Conference on Intelligent Systems, Modelling and Simulation, pp. 147–151 (2010)
4. Takagi, H., Asakawa, C., Itoh, T.: Non-Visual Groupware Client: Notes Reader. In: Center on Disability Technology and Persons with Disabilities Conference, California State University (2000)
5. Kobayashi, M.: Voice Browser for Groupware Systems: VoBG - A Simple Groupware Client for Visually Impaired Students. In: International Conference on Computers Helping People with Special Needs, pp. 777–780 (2008)
6. Schoeberlein, J.G., Wang, Y.: Providing an accessible track changes feature for persons who are blind. In: Stephanidis, C., Antona, M. (eds.) UAHCI 2013, Part III. LNCS, vol. 8011, pp. 389–398. Springer, Heidelberg (2013)

OnToContent 2014 PC Co-Chairs Message

Ontology content creation and use became a topic of utmost relevance in a world increasingly in the need to make sense of floods of data and information. Although the ontology engineering field is well established and produced useful results for practice, the creation and use of ontology content in the real world lacks theoretical and empirical knowledge, needing more research effort. Furthermore, the study of ontology content is a challenging research area because of its inherent multidisciplinarity: the object of study is socio-technical and the contexts of its use are socially determined.

The OnToContent workshop aimed to debate the current and future challenges of ontology content creation, use and management in aspects such as methodologies and tools concerned with developing ontology content, ontology content evaluation, ontology content management and ontology governance. Special attention was given to the impact of ontologies and their content in real life domains such as business, employment, healthcare, community development, and participatory government.

This edition of the workshop was organised as a venue of experts, and was part of the On The Move Federated Conferences 2014. It resulted also in an opportunity for identifying new directions in applications of ontologies that can be developed in future research projects.

We would like to thank to the Program Committee members for their availability, in particular the ones who served as reviewers. The deadlines were tight, the time for review very short and, in despite of that, all the reviews were insightful and helpful.

The accepted papers, published in this chapter, addressed several of the proposed topics from a more theoretical focus to a more practical orientation. Public administration, biodiversity management, and chemical-pharmaceutical industry are examples of the real world applications proposed.

September 2014

António Lucas Soares
Carla Sofia Pereira
Mustafa Jarrar

Applying Foundational Ontologies in Conceptual Modeling: A Case Study in a Brazilian Public Company

Stefane Melo and Mauricio B. Almeida

Universidade Federal de Minas Gerais, Belo Horizonte, Brazil
stefanems@ufmg.br, mba@eci.ufmg.br

Abstract. Information Systems (IS) should be based on consistent representations of the reality. Poor modeling results in problems throughout the IS development. Ontologies are key instruments for the improvement of conceptual modeling since they are able to provide well-defined semantics. This paper discusses the application of foundational ontologies in conceptual modeling, presenting partial results of a case study in which real UML diagrams were assessed according to ontological principles. Our findings indicate that violations of ontological restrictions of part-whole relations are somehow usual in modeling practices. In order to cope with this, we make a proposal for using part-whole relations based on ontological constraints, with the aim to seek for improvements in the practice of conceptual modeling.

Keywords: Conceptual modeling, Foundational ontology, Part-whole relations, Interoperability.

1   Introduction

Information Systems (IS) should be based on consistent representations of a knowledge domain, with the aim to meet the requirements for which they were planned, as well as to ensure the quality of the system according to the user´s perspective. In this context, conceptual modeling has a significant role, even though a desirable modeling is often neglected insofar as time and financial restrictions arise. For the long term, lack of interoperability between systems has been caused by ad-hoc models, which result in inadequate representations of reality and cause problems for communication.

Within the realm of IS, ontologies can be used to describe the meaning of symbols, which are employed according to a particular view of the world [7]. Indeed, ontologies share some features with conceptual models. However, ontologies are supported by strong theoretical foundations, which enable them to work as a kind of meta-model, or a kind of reference. This characterization as a reference allows ontologies to express a shared conceptualization for a community of users in a very rigorous way and without ambiguities. Nowadays, the ontology approach is being considered and debated in context of the Software Engineering and the Business Applications communities, mainly for its proximity to the (conceptual and business) modeling fields, to the UML language and the fields of software component re-use and integration.

R. Meersman et al. (Eds.): OTM 2014 Workshops, LNCS 8842, pp. 577–586, 2014.
© Springer-Verlag Berlin Heidelberg 2014

This paper describes research carried out in the scope of an on-going project within a Brazilian public company, which involves modeling and development of a large-scale IS. We present a case-study that describes the partial results of the application of a foundational ontology to activities of conceptual modeling. Throughout our research, we have evaluated the matching between conceptual models developed in the company and ontological standards. We have found so far that certain semantic relations between entities of the models, which has been established by system analysts involved in the project, do not meet ontological criteria.

2   Theoretical Background

In this section, we provide an overview of the important concepts that represent a required background to understand our research.

2.1   Ontology for Information Systems

Ontologies are an interdisciplinary matter, since it is subject of study in several research fields [1]. In the scope of computer science, ontologies can be used as software engineering artifacts applied to several contexts. For example, they can be used for the IS modeling, as a kind of meta-model and the applied in knowledge representation [6].

Ontologies has been applied in modeling insofar as they can aid in the selection of the modeling grammar for domain representation, in the understanding of phenomena represented by diagrams and in the definition of the meaning of entities with the aim of reducing ambiguity [15]. Foundational ontologies have been used to seek of better level of quality in modeling [17].

Since the late 80s, it could be observed an increasing interest in the application of foundational ontologies for evaluation processes and reengineering of conceptual modeling languages. Examples of foundational ontologies are: the Basic Formal Ontology [16], the Descriptive Ontology for Linguisitics and Cognitive Engineering (DOLCE) [5], the General Formal Ontology (GFO) [10] and the Unified Foundational Ontology (UFO) [9] and the Enterprise Ontology [4].

2.2   Foundational Ontologies for Conceptual Modeling

The pioneering research on ontologies applied to information systems is a result of extension of the theory of Bunge [20]. The Bunge approach resulted in a realistic philosophical ontology, which considers the possibility of objective human knowledge, which is based on scientific method [18]. Bunge-Wand-Weber ontology (BWW) is a proposal that provides a theoretical basis for evaluating modeling practices and capacity of representation languages. Wand and Weber [19][20] describing criteria, called ontological completeness and ontological transparency, made possible the mapping between the constructs of a modeling language and ontological constructs defined by BWW.

One initiative that makes use of BWW is the Unified Foundational Ontology (UFO). UFO is a foundational ontology developed to support the activities of both conceptual and organizational modeling. UFO is the result of a merge of GFO [10], parts of DOLCE and principles of OntoClean methodology [8]. The UFO is composed by three levels, which reflect the world stratification: (i) UFO-A (endurants), an ontology of objects; (ii) UFO-B (perdurants), an ontology of events; (iii) UFO-C (social and intentional entities), an ontology of social entities including linguistic aspects [9]. In order to make possible the activity of conceptual modeling via UFO, it was proposed a conceptual modeling language that uses the ontological constraints of UFO-A as modeling primitives. Such language, which is named OntoUML, was specified above the UML 2.0 meta-model, namely, the Meta-Object Facility (MOF) [14]. The goal was to ensure the mapping between MOF and UFO-A structure [9].

2.3   Part-Whole Relation as Semantic Relation

In the context of conceptual modeling, a domain is represented by the identification of relevant concepts in that domain and by the relations among them. Research on semantic relations is extensive, but it is possible to identify some important semantic relations. One of the most important of them for purposes of conceptual modeling is the so-called part-whole relation [1], [3], [11], [12].

The standard language for modeling, known as Unified Modeling Language (UML) [14], one of the most widely used notations for the development and modeling of IS, encompasses the following semantic relations [2]: generalization/specialization, association, aggregation, composition. To develop conceptual models is important to treat the relation as the base of the domain being represented. In this paper, we focused on the application of part-whole relations in conceptual modeling of IS.

The part-whole relations in the scope of UML are specified in aggregation or composition relations [14]. In first case, an aggregation is represented by a whole and a part where the existence of these elements separately makes sense. In second case, a composition is represented by the relation between a whole and a part where the existence of these elements does not make sense when separated as a strong form of aggregation.

In the context of relations that compose UFO defined by [9], we highlight the meronymic relations, referring to the part-whole relations. In particular, there are two meta-properties associated to this relation: is-essential (isEssential) and is-inseparable (isInseparable). The first implies that only the whole is existentially dependent of part, and the second implies that the part and the whole do not exist separately. These two concepts refer to the concepts of aggregation and composition in UML, which also addresses the coexistence between parts and wholes.

According to [9], UML defines only two types of part-whole relations, the aggregation and composition. That's because the UML metamodel considers only single general definition for objects, being indifferent to the ontological distinctions between entity types. In order to cover this gap, the UFO considers four types of part-whole relation, based on types of entities that compose the meronimyc relations, called: subQuantityOf, subCollectionOf, memberOf and componentOf (Fig. 1).

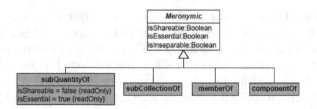

Fig. 1. Types of part-whole relations in UFO [9]

The Fig. 2 illustrates the types of individuals addressed in the four part-whole relations in UFO: Collective, Quantities and Functional Complexes.

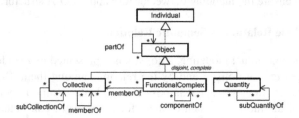

Fig. 2. Types of entity in part-whole relations [9]

1. Quantities: Always refer to the amount of matter. For example, water, sugar, wine, etc. The subQuantity of matter always refers to the same type of matter. Any subQuantity of water remains water (Fig. 3).

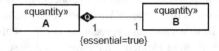

Fig. 3. Part-Whole relation among quantities - subQuantityOf [9]

2. Collectives: They may have parts which are not of the same type, such as tree and forest. In this case, a whole it is not infinitely divisible, i.e., a forest is not can be composed by only of a tree, but a set of trees. This element can be represented in the memberOf relation, when dealing with the relation between singular and plural entities or subCollectionOf, when dealing with the relation between plural entities. The Fig. 4 and Fig. 5 represents these two types of relationships mentioned.

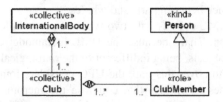

Fig. 4. Example of memberOf relation [9]

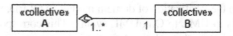

Fig. 5. Example of SubCollection relation [9]

3. Functional complexes: Differently of the collectives, in the functional complexes each element may have a specific role. For example, among a fleet of ships may exist defense ships, storage ships. The complexes are composed of parts that play multiple roles in the context of a whole. The parts of a complex have in common that they have a functional link with the whole complex. In other words, all parts contribute to the functionality (or behavior) of the whole (Fig. 6).

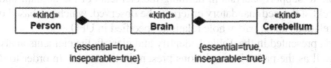

Fig. 6. Example of componentOf relation between complexes [9]

The classification of entities through the types defined by [9] represents a step forward in the understanding domains even before its representation in a diagram.

3   Case Study

The case study described in this paper focuses on real activity of conceptual modeling through UML, in the scope of a IS development project in a large Brazilian public company. This project is oriented to business process management and contains many business processes related to public management in their scope. It is in this context that our research has been performed.

The study consists of steps that compose the evaluation of domain models and a proposal for improvement for the conceptual modeling based on Unified Foundational Ontology (UFO). Our ongoing research is nowadays in the stage of testing a proposed methodology for the evaluation of semantic relations. We present here this proposed methodology and the partial results.

3.1   Methodology

The first stage of the research corresponds to the evaluation of domain models made during the development of the project. Then a proposal for improvement to the modeling was carried out according to our findings.

The methodology used for evaluation consists of the following steps: i) Examination of domain models; ii) Selection of models to be evaluated; iii) Mapping the UML models to OntoUML; iv) Verification of the models adherence to the ontological pattern of UFO through the OLED[1] tool v) Proposal of correction of models through the ontological criteria and retest in OLED until the elimination of errors.

---

[1] OLED - OntoUML Lightweight Editor.
http://code.google.com/p/ontouml-lightweight-editor/

In order to perform the verification of domain models in OLED, we needed a mapping of the original models in UML to OntoUML syntax. This corresponds to the classification of concepts and relations through the definitions documented in the project specification requirements and the types of elements contained in the UFO. Then, the mapped models were submitted to verification in OLED. In the cases in which the OLED tool accused modeling errors during the tests, the model was then rebuilt according to the requirements, experts working on the project and UFO's specification. The model was tested and rebuilt again and again until the tool no longer points out modeling errors. From preliminaries results obtained, it was possible to note that some relations have not been well defined by business analysts involved in the project, mainly our focus, that is, the part-whole relations. In order to solve this particular situation, it was proposed a checklist table to support analysts in defining the elements of the domain under modeling. This checklist defined mandatory criteria to be observed, which are based on types of entities and relations about part-whole relations specified in UFO.

The criteria presented in the Table 1 identify and classify the elements analyzed in the domain, as well as the part-whole relations present in the model. In order to do this, we compare each element of the domain to the list of criteria. At the end of the modeling activity, more consistent mappings were defined among concepts and relations.

Table 1. Table of criteria

Criteria	Sub-criteria	Description of criteria/sub-criteria
C1		Quantity always relates to amount of matter and sub quantity (part) is the same kind of matter of the quantity (whole). If a term defined for the domain representing a quantity or a sub quantity, probably exists a part-whole relation.
C2		Collectives and Functional Complexes refer to objects. So, it is worth classifying the elements are objects in domain and verify the existence of collective or functional complexes. If there are such objects of these types, can be a signal of part-whole relations.
	SC1	Collectives may be a subset of individuals, with same kind of objects in parts and wholes like in subCollection relation, or may be represented by different types of individuals, like in memberOf relation.
C3		Functional Complexes are composed by parts that play multiple roles in the context of the whole. Then, objects with this characteristic should be observed throughout the domain context. The existence of this type of object in domain indicates a possible part-whole relation, like aggregation or composition, for example.
	SC2	All parts of a complex must have a functional link with the whole, because they all contribute to functionality (or the behavior) of the complex.
	SC3	The dependence attributes is essential, when the whole is existentially dependent of part, and is inseparable, when the part and the whole do not exist separately, can determine relations as aggregation or composition.

3.2   Experiment

Our research adopted a population of twenty three domain models available at time of this research. In this population, we selected randomly, by draw, a sample of ten models for testing, in order to obtain results that can represent the project in question (at this stage, we did not intend to represent the entire set of models available in the company). For size limitations of this article, we selected one model from the sample, in order to illustrate the proposed methodology. The selected model is named State Administration.

The first step of the experiment performs a mapping of the UML model to the OntoUML language, to ensure that tests are possible in OLED. Then, the model rewritten in OntoUML is tested in the OLED. From the result returned by the OLED, we verified the requirements and ontological criteria. The model is re-done and re-tested until no more errors were found.

3.3   Results

The Fig. 7 presents the original model of State Administration, made by the analyst's team (mod.1). Then, the mod.1 was rewritten in OntoUML language (mod.2, Fig. 8) and finally imported in OLED for the tests.

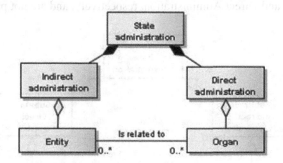

Fig. 7. State Administration domain model (mod.1) made in UML

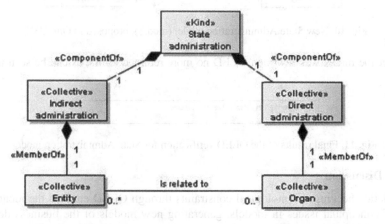

Fig. 8. State Administration domain model (mod.2) rewritten in OntoUML

OLED returned problems in tests of mod.2, as seen in Fig. 9. So, the model was rewritten and tested again, until the elimination of problems.

ERROR: The model is not valid sintatically. The following error(s) where found:

[unnamed] (<<memberof>>) - The sum of the minimum cardinalities of the parts must be greater or equal to 2

[unnamed] (<<componentof>>) - componentOf relates individuals that are functional complexes (part)

[unnamed] (<<memberof>>) - The sum of the minimum cardinalities of the parts must be greater or equal to 2

[unnamed] (<<componentof>>) - componentOf relates individuals that are functional complexes (part)

Model verified in 21.345 ms, 4 error(s) found

Fig. 9. Results of the OLED verification of the State Administration model

In the State administration model, we observed that the relationships identified as part-whole relations actually are specialization and association relations (mod.3, Fig. 10). According to the business processes, the requirements and UFO criteria, the Indirect and Direct Administrations are types of State Administration and are not parts of it. So, the same criteria can be observed for Entity and Organ, which are actually types of Indirect and Direct Administration, respectively, and are not parts.

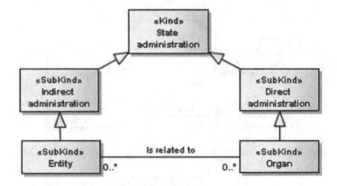

Fig. 10. New State Administration model (mod.3), proposed in OntoUML

After the model was rewritten OLED no more returned errors, as can be seen in Fig. 11.

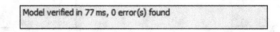

Model verified in 77 ms, 0 error(s) found

Fig. 11. Final results of the OLED verification for State Administration model

3.4   Discussion

Automatic checking of ontological constraints through OLED enabled the identification of conceptual issues in models, generating new models of the business domain under evaluation.

With the results of tests in OLED, we observed that the decisions of analysts represented in models did not meet UFO ontological constraints, revealing modeling problems in the original model.

Ontologies can help analysts to better understand the semantics of the business domain in which they are involved. However, it is known that the own understanding of ontologies is not simple or trivial. With the intention to make this understanding easier, for those who are not involved with ontologies, we propose a preliminary table of ontological criteria.

4   Final Remarks

This paper discussed the application of foundational ontologies in conceptual modeling of IS and aimed to present partial results of a case study that evaluates real domain models in a software development project. We make use of UFO-A ontology in order to propose improvements to the conceptual modeling activity. Until now we obtained empirical results that indicate issues in modeling within the project analyzed related to part-whole relations. During the process of rewritten the models, it was necessary the review the business processes and the corresponding specification requirements. We could observe that for this aim it is essential that business processes and requirements are clearly defined and mapped, which does not always happen. From these findings and from studies on ontology, we proposed improvements.

This case study has not exhausted the verification of adherence to the ontological domain models to UFO patterns. In the next research steps will be proposed templates for types of part-whole relations described in the criteria table (Table 1), as a more practical way to support modeling. We also intend to analyze some questions about the test results for the entire sample of ten models such as: percentage of models that have part-whole relations; percentage of models with part-whole relationship that contains errors; percentage of the most common errors. This analysis will allow us an assertive inference about the use of part-whole relations in the context of population of models analyzed.

References

1. Almeida, M.B., Baracho, R.M.A.: A Theoretical Investigation about the Notion of Parts and Wholes: Mereological and Meronymic Relations. Information Retrieval Today (forthcoming, 2014)
2. Booch, G., Rumbaugh, J., Jacobson, I.: The Unified Modeling Language User Guide, 2nd edn. Addison Wesley (2005)
3. Dahlberg, I.: Teoria Do Conceito. Ciência Da Informação. Rio De Janeiro 7(2), 101–107 (1978)
4. Dietz, J.: Enterprise Ontology: Theory and Methodology. Springer, Berlin (2006)
5. Gangemi, A., et al.: Sweetening Ontologies with DOLCE (2002)
6. Gruber, T.: What is an ontology (1993)
7. Guarino, N.: Formal Ontology in Information Systems. In: Proceedings of FOIS 1998. IOS Press, Amsterdam (1998)

8. Guarino, N., Welty, C.: Evaluating ontological decisions with OntoClean. Communications of the ACM 45(2), 61–65 (2002)
9. Guizzardi, G.: Ontological Foundations for Structural Conceptual Models (2005)
10. Herre, H., et al.: General Formal Ontology (GFO): A Foundational Ontology Integrating Objects and Processes. Part I: Basic Principles. University of Leipzig (2006)
11. Hjørland, B.: Fundamentals of Knowledge Organization. Knowledge Organization 30(2), 87–111 (2003)
12. Khoo, C., Na, J.C.: Semantic Relations in Information Science. Annual Review of Information Science and Technology 40, 157–228 (2006)
13. Mylopoulos, J.: Conceptual Modeling and Telos (1992)
14. OMG - Object Management Group Infrastructure. Unified Modeling Language (OMG UML), V2.1.2 (2012), http://www.omg.org/docs/formal/07-11-04.pdf
15. Shanks, G., Tansley, E., Weber, R.: Using ontology to validate conceptual models. Communications of the ACM 46(10), 85 (2003)
16. Smith, B., Grenon, P.: SNAP and SPAN: Towards Dynamic Spatial Ontology (2004)
17. Smith, B., Welty, C.: Ontology: Towards a new synthesis (2001)
18. Bunge, M., Ontology, I.: The furniture of the world. Dordrecht: Reidel, 376 p. (Treatise on basic Philosophy, v. 3) (1977)
19. Wand, Y., Weber, R.: An ontological evaluation of systems analysis and design methods. In: Falkenberg, E., Lingreen, P. (eds.) Information System Concepts: An In-depth Analysis, pp. 79–107. Elsevier Science, North-Holland (1989)
20. Wand, Y., Weber, R.: Mario Bunge's ontology as a formal foundation for information systems concepts. In: Studies on Mario Bunge's Treatise, pp. 123–150. Radopi, Amsterdam (1990)

An Identification Ontology for Entity Matching

Stefano Bortoli[1], Paolo Bouquet[1,2], and Barbara Bazzanella[2]

[1] Okkam SRL
via Segantini 23, I-38121 Trento, Italy
[2] University of Trento - DISI
via Sommarive, 14 I-38123 Povo di Trento, Italy
bortoli@okkam.it, bouquet@disi.unitn.it, barbara.bazzanella@unitn.it

Abstract. In this context we present the Identification Ontology, as an application ontology for a knowledge-based solution to the entity matching problem in the context of the Semantic Web. The Identification Ontology has a threefold role: (1) represent a selection of attributes that are relevant for identification (or entity matching) of a set of entity types; (2) supporting the definition of a set of contextual ontological mappings to ease the problem of semantic heterogeneity affecting entity matching in the Semantic Web; and (3) represent meta-properties of the considered features to highlight their roles in the definition of a knowledge-based entity matching solution. The Identification Ontology taxonomy is defined refining and extending the Okkam Conceptual Model, as a top level ontology modeling the *identity and reference* domain. Furthermore, it defines also a set of top-level entity types and relative features relying on a methodology that combines results from cognitive studies and a survey of existing vocabularies available through Linked Open Vocabulary initiative. The Identification Ontology is currently used as part of the Okkam Entity Name System matching framework, which was successfully tested in entity matching experiments and used in large-scale (industrial) linkage tasks to enable data integration for applications dealing with tax assessment and credit risk analysis.

1 Introduction

The problem of entity matching has been known for many years in the context of information science under different names (e.g. record linkage, entity disambiguation, duplicate detection). The task consists in comparing two records (or descriptions) to establish whether they refer to same real word entity. In the context of the Semantic Web [5], a relevant amount of Linked Data [6,8] is being produced and made available online. The growth of the linked data cloud as a Global Giant Graph [7], raises interest in the exploitation of such enormous data pool to create new applications and foster the development of the data economy. The decentralized and independent production of structured data presents several degrees of heterogeneity. The most basic is related to the definition and usage of different vocabularies (or ontologies) to model data. Fortunately, best practices related to ontology engineering (e.g. [13]) push for the reuse of terms

R. Meersman et al. (Eds.): OTM 2014 Workshops, LNCS 8842, pp. 587–596, 2014.

and classes, creating a linked vocabulary eco-system[1] and reducing useless multiplications of terms and classes. Another element of heterogeneity affecting the Linked Data is the policy related to the creation of URIs for entities. When it comes to real world entities, the guidelines suggest to create new identifiers (i.e. URIs) whenever required, and then rely on the definition of *owl:sameAs* statements to reconcile the identities defined in different RDF graphs. These settings produce a relevant amount of ambiguity [18], inherently complicating the consumption of Linked Data. Several tools were defined to resolve the problem of entity matching matching on the Linked Data, among others consider [19,22,24,20]. However, an analysis of the *owl:sameAs* statements showed that these are not suitable for a reliable consumption of the Global Giant Graph [17].

Under these premises, in [9] we propose the definition of a knowledge-based solution for the entity matching problem in the context of the Semantic Web (or Linked Data). The main idea underlying the solution is to define an entity matching solution relying on a combination of bottom-up machine learning techniques and top-down formal ontology tools to define robust and dependable entity matching solution. One of the pillars of such knowledge-based solution is the definition of an Identification Ontology, which has the twofold role of defining explicitly the features that are relevant for the entity matching problem, and providing the point of reference for the definition of an extensible set of contextual mappings [11] to support *semantic harmonization* of relevant features. A graphical view of the the representation of the matching process and the role of the Identification Ontology is presented in Figure 1. Furthermore, we intend to use the ontology to represent a new set of meta-properties of the features result of formal ontology analysis to highlight how these can be employed along the solution of entity matching tasks.

2   Meta-properties for Identification

As mentioned in the introduction, we intend to rely on a set of meta-properties to explicitly highlight special properties of features when involved in the entity matching processes. Hence, we propose to rely on a top-down ontological analysis to extend the identification ontology attempting to compensate, or integrate, the ontology with meta-properties that may be useful to declare properties that have special roles in the matching process. The idea is to apply concepts and principles that are proper of formal ontological analysis (e.g. [16]) to support the definition of matching, or non-matching, constraints. It is important to keep in mind that in formal ontology identity cannot be defined in general as sufficient condition, and what can be defined are actually some sort of information constraints providing necessary condition for identity [15].

As previously mentioned, in the definition of identity criteria OntoClean [16] proposed to consider the distinction between *Synchronic* versus *Diachronic* identity criteria. Synchronic identity criteria allow to establish identity between entities at the same instance of time. Formally, p is synchronic if $\exists t \forall x, y (t > t_0 \rightarrow$

---

[1] Linked Open Vocabulary `http://lov.okfn.org/dataset/lov/`

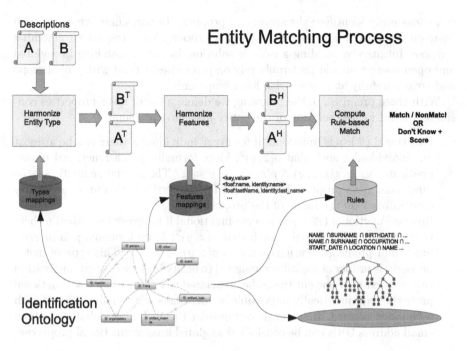

Fig. 1. A view of a knowledge-based matching process with Identification Ontology

$(p(x, y, t_0) \rightarrow p(x, y, t)))$ with t_0 denoting the first time y was assigned to x as the value of the property p. Diachronic identity criteria imply the notion of persistence of the identity criteria through time. Formally, p is a diachronic if $\forall t, x, y(t > t_0) \rightarrow (p(x, y, t_0) \rightarrow p(x, y, t)))$. Namely, they do not change with time, and thereby represent essential properties of the identified entity. In Onto-Clean, the individuation of identity criteria is essential to annotate concepts in a taxonomy, and thus evaluate its soundness according to this methodology. However this distinction may become useful also in the context of entity matching problem.

In fact, the solution of the entity matching problem in an open and wide context such as the Web requires preference to diachronic identity criteria have to be preferred with respect to the synchronic ones. Indeed, the Web, as global information space, has to be interpreted as intrinsically asynchronous with respect to the real world entities mentioned and described in it. Thereby, assume synchronicity of properties for entity matching solution may lead to problems.

The solution of the entity matching problem in the context of the web is affected by over-specification. Namely, descriptions could contain attributes that can be interpreted correctly only within a specific context, as for example a *student id number*. These properties are very likely to be inverse functional in the context of a university information system. However, there is no guarantee that two systems independently do not assign the same id to different students in different universities. Thereby, there is also a further dimension to be considered con considering identifier: the scope of a property. In particular, we distinguish between local scope and global scope of a property with respect to matching purpose. Intuitively, building a reliable solution for entity matching in a global and open context should preferably rely on properties defined with global scope and treat carefully attributes with local scope only.

With these premises, in the following we define a list of meta-properties considered useful for the solution of the entity matching problem:

- Functional ($\mathcal{F}$): p is functional if for every individual x there can be at most one individual y such that $p(x, y)^2$. More formally, p is a functional binary predicate: $\forall x, y, z(p(x, y) \land p(x, z) \rightarrow y = z$. The official semantic of the functional meta-property is a shortcut for properties with a max cardinality constraints 1 on the range of the property.
- Inverse Functional (IF): p is inverse-functional if for every individual y there is at most one individual x such that $p(x, y)^3$. More formally, p is inverse-functional predicate: $\forall x, y, z(p(x, y) \land p(z, y) \rightarrow z = x$. This type of meta-property is proper of identifiers assigned to entity in some context, and within that context only one entity can be associated to it. Global inverse functional properties are practically impossible as identifiers are usually assigned with a bounded context. However, if we consider the Web as a global space then email address URIs can be considered as global inverse functional properties.

Here we define a set of meta-properties for identification properties, taking into consideration time and scope dimensions. In particular we define:

- Functional Diachronic ($\mathcal{FD}$): p is functional diachronic if and only if it is both functional and diachronic as identity criteria. Namely the range of this property must have cardinality maximum 1, and its value does not change in time for any reason. An example of properties that are functional diachronic for a person are the date of birth and the birthplace.
- Inverse Functional Diachronic (IFD): p is inverse-functional diachronic if it is both inverse-functional and diachronic as identity criteria. Namely, given a property p and a value y, the domain of p must have cardinality maximum 1, and furthermore the value does not change in time.

In the following sections we will describe the process of extending backbone taxonomy produced starting from the OCM with the set of features considered relevant for the identification process.

3   The Identification Ontology

In the definition of a knowledge-based solution, it is necessary to draw boundaries to the domain represented in the ontology. The Okkam Conceptual Model (OCM) described in [12] provides an optimal starting point to define the Identification Ontology as model the solution proposed in [9]. Indeed, besides modeling

---

² http://www.w3.org/TR/owl2-syntax/#Functional_Object_Properties
³ http://www.w3.org/TR/owl2-syntax/#Inverse-Functional_Object_Properties

the relation between entities and identifiers, the OCM embeds a simple taxonomy of top level, disjoint, categories. These categories are defined with the goal of providing an initial set of disjoint types covering large part of interesting entities consistently with other top level ontologies such as DOLCE[4] [14], Yago[5] [23] and OpenCyc[6] [21] and presented in [4,3]. Quite intuitively, the types considered are: Person, Organization, Location, Event, Artifact Type and Artifact Instance and a bulk category Other. The Okkam Conceptual Model was carefully designed, but no formal ontology method was ever applied to validate its soundness with respect to the the rigidity of the classes in the taxonomy and the possibility of defining formal Identity Criteria for each of them. Therefore, we analyzed the OCM relying on the OntoClean methodology [16], with the goal of validating the backbone taxonomy and remove inconsistencies, if any. The details of the types defined and a precise contextualization of the interpretation of these types is presented in [9]. The exercise performed along the analysis of the Okkam Conceptual Model guided the process of dissecting concepts and properties that intuitively appear easy to handle, but that present many subtleties when analyzed in detail with respect to clear identity criteria. The main result of this process with respect to this work is the a further confirmation that the OCM taxonomy is an optimal starting point to define the model the knowledge base supporting the proposed solution. A view of the taxonomy labeled according OntoClean methodology is presented in Figure 2.

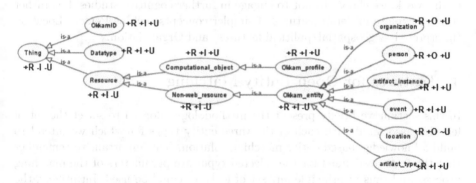

Fig. 2. Identification Ontology backbone Taxonomy obtained by the Analysis of the Okkam Conceptual Model

As mentioned in the introduction, the identification ontology is conceived not only to describe what types of entities are considered, but also what features are considered relevant for the matching task for each of the considered types. Thereby, the identification ontology will present as OWL 2 Classes the considered types,and OWL2 Datatype properties ($\mathcal{DP}$) and Object properties ($\mathcal{OP}$) the

---

[4] http://www.loa.istc.cnr.it/DOLCE.html
[5] http://www.mpi-inf.mpg.de/yago-naga/yago/
[6] http://www.cyc.com/platform/opencyc

features for each of the considered types. Furthermore, besides the properties associated to considered types, we also declare specific meta-properties of these properties that can be useful to support the matching purposes. As we will show in Section 2, it would be necessary to extend the set of meta-properties for properties defined in OWL 2 in order to accommodate the level of expressiveness required. However, as supporting scalable model-theoretic reasoning is not the goal of the identification ontology, we believe we can take the license to introduce interpret differently some properties without feeling the need of exploring in depth the implications of formally extending OWL. The problem may be considered in future developments of the method, but in this work we limit our analysis to the creation of specific properties we use to classify other properties. A detailed list of features used for three of the considered types, together with the results of the ontological analysis, is presented in section 4.

The taxonomy depicted in figure 2 is used as core component of the Identification Ontology underlying the knowledge-based solution for open entity matching. In particular, the part that is more interesting for the goal of this work is the part of the taxonomy specifying the Okkam Entity subclasses. The pragmatic philosophical approach used to analyze concepts like Event or Artifacts in the application of the OntoClean methodology can hardly be used to define an explicit knowledge-based solution without relying on cognitive studies unfolding the implication of the definition of explicit identity criteria. An attempt in this direction was proposed in [2]. However, given the time available and the scope of this work, we choose to not to engage in further cognitive studies, but rather start to explore in detail features of simpler concepts such as Person, Location (interpreted as geospatial/political features) and Organization.

4   Features for Open Entity Matching

In this section we briefly present the methodology adopted to select the set of features associated with each of the three entity types for which we intend to build a knowledge-based entity matching solution. It is important to remember that the features defined for the selected types are parameters of the matching process, and thus in principle any set of features could be used. Intuitively, the broader the set of features, the broader the set of sources that can be matched precisely. However, a large set of features requires also a large training set to learn their relevance in the matching process. Furthermore, the larger the set of attributes the larger and cumbersome is the maintenance of the contextual mappings towards the identification ontology.

In the following sections, we present a set of features obtained relying on different sources and methodologies. Their combination will produce the set of features associated with each of the types considered. The first set of considered features is the result of a cognitive science experiment aimed at eliciting through experiments with people what are the most discriminative attributes for several entity types [2,3,1]. The attribute proposed were then ranked based on the estimation of semantic relevance, and attributes below a certain threshold were not

Table 1. A tabular view of the features for Person, Location and Organization

		person	location	organization
DP	FD	birth date date of death first name last name middle name gender eyes color	longitude longitude degree longitude second longitude minute longitude direction latitude degree latitude direction latitude minute latitude second latitude	dissolution date foundation date
	IFD	email address email address hashcode website public institutional id fax nr phone nr picture url	geocoordinate coordinate geometry picture URL	email address email address hashcode website public institutional id fax nr phone nr picture url
		nickname description domain tag height nationality occupation postal code street address title	location type description domain tag location name elevation area postal code street address timezone	activity sector description domain tag activity start year color longitude latitude name offers organization type postal code start date end date street address slogan
OP	FD	birthplace deathplace country of residence city of residence	first level administrative parent second level administrative parent third level administrative parent forth level administrative parent	has foundation place
		affiliation involved in member of participant in author	city contains country contained by	associated with city controlled by controls country founded by geocoordinate has key people has members has parts is part of has location involved in

considered [2]. The results of this work are also used in [22] to weight the relevance of attributes to compute entity matching similarity. The set of properties defined is surely relevant, but unlikely to be complete due to its specific focus on 'searching' rather than matching.

In order to extend this first set of properties we surveyed for existing vocabularies and extracted the features the most generic features associated to the considered entity types. Given the large varieties of existing vocabularies presenting similar properties for the the same type of entity, we propose to adopt an approach aiming at clustering shared (similar) properties towards general properties that could encompass all their instantiations. In fact, in generalizing these properties, we considered *sub-property* as a relation supporting clustering of existing properties. Consider for example the properties that provide information about a person belonging to some group, or organization. For a politician, a property indicating the political party of reference could be *dbpedia:party*, whereas for a musician, the band could be indicated with *dbpedia:musicalBand*. It is clear that representing all possible domain-specific variants of this property would lead quickly to an unmanageable vocabulary. Thereby, we decided to cluster these properties to the more generic property: *member_of*. In principle, clustering properties has the important advantage of reducing sparsity in the data, but may also introduce some noise. Experimental evaluation will show whether the positive effects of generalization compensate the lost of specificity.

The Linked Open Vocabularies[7](LOV) listed 319 vocabulary spaces, providing classifications for and properties for many different types of entities. LOV is a very useful entry point for gathering types and properties related to them, as it provides a formal SPARQL interface. Given the large space of vocabularies available only in the Linked Data initiative, we limited our analysis to a best effort exploration of the properties associated to concepts considered relying on the LOV search and browsing services. The complete exploration of the vocabularies space will be pursued in future work. The features (or properties) defined for the entity type Person, Location and Organization are presented in table 1.

5   Concluding Remarks

The aim is to collect a first set of properties that can be used to identify an entity of type Person, Location and Organization. Nevertheless, the approach based on generalization allows to cover a wide set of properties in existing ontologies and define a wide set of mappings. Hence, we choose pragmatically to stop extending the set of feature considered, relying on the fact that future application of the method will lead us towards incremental specialization of the vocabulary.

The set of property proposed is quite extensive and provides an initial baseline to future improvements. Future evolutions of the identification ontology types, or specific application scenarios may need further deep analysis related to the level of granularity of the features described so far. In the future, we may consider also to represent compound attributes. It is important to remark that the ontology serves as a tool to mediate among vocabularies dealing with data represented at different levels of granularity and precision. This implies that, for example, the management of properties dealing with the containment of a location must consider both the *administrative level* (used by Geonames) and the *contained by* features (used by DBpedia). In this work we presented the Identification Ontology as central element in the definition of a knowledge-based entity matching solution. The Identification Ontology was designed starting from the Okkam Conceptual Model, relying on OntoClean methodology to produce a formal validation of the backbone taxonomy. In this paper we described a preliminary definition of the features that are considered relevant for the matching of entities of the type Person, Organization and Location. Furthermore, an ontological analysis was performed, aiming at extending the set of meta-properties available in OWL 2. The identification ontology, available online at http://models.okkam.org/identification_ontology.owl, was successfully applied along a set of entity matching experiments (see [9], and is currently employed to support *semantic harmonization* tasks as part of the

---

[7] http://lov.okfn.org/dataset/lov/

Okkam Entity Name System[8] matching system [10]. Around the current version of the ontology were collected several thousands of mappings from the vocabularies listed at the Linked Data Initiative (LOV), which are and will be available through the Okkam Synapsis web application[9].

Future development of the ontology will further expand the set of feature available for the analyzed types, and will explore feature for other types of entities such as Events and Artefacts. Furthermore, our experience in the solution of the entity matching problem in an open context will continuously stimulate the definition and refinement of the meta-properties of the identified features.

References

1. Bazzanella, B., Bouquet, P., Stoermer, H.: A cognitive contribution to entity representation and matching. Technical report (DISI-09-004) University of Trento (2009)
2. Bazzanella, B.: Uniqueness in Cognition. PhD thesis, Doctoral School in Physicological and Education (2010)
3. Bazzanella, B., Bouquet, P., Stoermer, H.: Top level categories and attributes for entity representation. Technical report, University of Trento (2008)
4. Bazzanella, B., Chaudhry, J.A., Palpanas, T., Stoermer, H.: Towards a general entity representation model. In: SWAP (2008)
5. Berners-Lee, T., Hendler, J.A., Lassila, O.: The Semantic Web. Scientific American (May 2001), http://www.sciam.com/2001/0501issue/0501berners-lee.html
6. Berners-Lee, T.: Design issues- linked data. Published online (May 2007), http://www.w3.org/DesignIssues/LinkedData.html
7. Berners-Lee, T.: Giant global graph. Decentralized Information Group - (2007), http://dig.csail.mit.edu/breadcrumbs/node/215
8. Bizer, C., Cyganiak, R., Heath, T.: How to publish linked data on the web (July 2007) (online tutorial)
9. Bortoli, S.: Knowledge Based Open Entity Matching. PhD thesis, International Doctoral School in ICT of the University of Trento, Italy (2013)
10. Bouquet, P., Stoermer, H., Niederee, C., Mana, A.: Entity Name System: The Backbone of an Open and Scalable Web of Data. In: Proceedings of the IEEE International Conference on Semantic Computing, ICSC 2008, no. CSS-ICSC 2008-4-28-25, pp. 554–561. IEEE Computer Society (August 2008)
11. Bouquet, P., Giunchiglia, F., van Harmelen, F., Serafini, L., Stuckenschmidt, H.: C-OWL: Contextualizing ontologies. In: Fensel, D., Sycara, K., Mylopoulos, J. (eds.) ISWC 2003. LNCS, vol. 2870, pp. 164–179. Springer, Heidelberg (2003)
12. Bouquet, P., Palpanas, T., Stoermer, H., Vignolo, M.: A conceptual model for a web-scale entity name system. In: Gómez-Pérez, A., Yu, Y., Ding, Y. (eds.) ASWC 2009. LNCS, vol. 5926, pp. 46–60. Springer, Heidelberg (2009)
13. Gangemi, A., Presutti, V.: Ontology Design Patterns, pp. 221–243. Springer, Heidelberg (2009)
14. Gangemi, A., Guarino, N., Masolo, C., Oltramari, A., Schneider, L.: Sweetening ontologies with DOLCE. In: Gómez-Pérez, A., Benjamins, V.R. (eds.) EKAW 2002. LNCS (LNAI), vol. 2473, pp. 166–181. Springer, Heidelberg (2002)

---

[8] http://api.okkam.org

[9] http://api.okkam.org/synapsis

15. Guarino, N.: The role of identity conditions in ontology design. In: Freksa, C., Mark, D.M. (eds.) COSIT 1999. LNCS, vol. 1661, pp. 221–234. Springer, Heidelberg (1999)
16. Guarino, N., Welty, C.: An overview of ontoclean. In: Staab, S., Studer, R. (eds.) The Handbook on Ontologies, pp. 151–172. Springer (2004)
17. Halpin, H., Hayes, P.J., McCusker, J.P., McGuinness, D.L., Thompson, H.S.: When owl:sameAs isn't the same: An analysis of identity in linked data. In: Patel-Schneider, P.F., Pan, Y., Hitzler, P., Mika, P., Zhang, L., Pan, J.Z., Horrocks, I., Glimm, B. (eds.) ISWC 2010, Part I. LNCS, vol. 6496, pp. 305–320. Springer, Heidelberg (2010)
18. Hayes, P.J., Halpin, H.: In defense of ambiguity. International Journal on Semantic Web and Information Systems. Vol. 4(2), 1–18 (2008)
19. Hogan, A., Polleres, A., Umbrich, J., Zimmermann, A.: Some entities are more equal than others: statistical methods to consolidate linked data. In: Proceedings of the Workshop on New Forms of Reasoning for the Semantic Web: Scalable & Dynamic, NeFoRS 2010 (2010)
20. Hogan, A., Harth, A., Decker, S.: Performing object consolidation on the semantic web data graph. In: i3: Identity, Identifiers, Identification. Proceedings of the WWW2007 Workshop on Entity-Centric Approaches to Information and Knowledge Management on the Web, Banff, Canada, May 8 (2007)
21. Matuszek, C., Cabral, J., Witbrock, M., Deoliveira, J.: An introduction to the syntax and content of cyc. In: Proceedings of the 2006 AAAI Spring Symposium on Formalizing and Compiling Background Knowledge and Its Applications to Knowledge Representation and Question Answering, pp. 44–49 (2006)
22. Stoermer, H., Rassadko, N., Vaidya, N.: Feature-based entity matching: The FBEM model, implementation, evaluation. In: Pernici, B. (ed.) CAiSE 2010. LNCS, vol. 6051, pp. 180–193. Springer, Heidelberg (2010)
23. Suchanek, F.M., Kasneci, G., Weikum, G.: Yago: A large ontology from wikipedia and wordnet. Web Semantics: Science, Services and Agents on the World Wide Web 6(3), 203–217 (2008)
24. Volz, J., Bizer, C., Gaedke, M., Kobilarov, G.: Discovering and maintaining links on the web of data. In: Bernstein, A., Karger, D.R., Heath, T., Feigenbaum, L., Maynard, D., Motta, E., Thirunarayan, K. (eds.) ISWC 2009. LNCS, vol. 5823, pp. 650–665. Springer, Heidelberg (2009)

Beyond INSPIRE: An Ontology
for Biodiversity Metadata Records

João Rocha da Silva[1], João Aguiar Castro[1], Cristina Ribeiro[2], João Honrado[3],
Ângela Lomba[3], and João Gonçalves[3]

[1] Faculdade de Engenharia da Universidade do Porto/INESC TEC
{joaorosilva,joaoaguiarcastro}@gmail.com
[2] DEI—Faculdade de Engenharia da Universidade do Porto/INESC TEC
mcr@gmail.com
[3] CIBIO—Centro de Investigação em Biodiversidade e Recursos Genéticos
{jhonrado,angelalomba}@fc.up.pt, joaofgo@gmail.com

Abstract. Managing research data often requires the creation or reuse
of specialised metadata schemas to satisfy the metadata requirements
of each research group. Ontologies present several advantages over metadata schemas. In particular, they can be shared and improved upon more
easily, providing the flexibility required to establish relationships between
datasets and concepts from distinct domains. In this paper, we present
a preliminary experiment on the use of ontologies for the description of
biodiversity datasets. With a strong focus on the dynamics of individual species, species diversity, biological communities and ecosystems, the
Predictive Ecology research group of CIBIO has adopted the INSPIRE
European recommendation as the primary tool for metadata compliance
across its research data description. We build upon this experience to
model the BIOME ontology for the biodiversity domain. The ontology
combines concepts from INSPIRE, matching them against the ones defined in the Dublin Core, FOAF and CERIF ontologies. Dendro, a prototype for collaborative data description, uses the ontology to provide an
environment where biodiversity metadata records are available as Linked
Open Data.

1 Introduction

Research data are often unique and valuable beyond the time frame of individual projects, but their long-term preservation depends on the existence of
associated metadata records [5]. Many metadata schemas have been proposed in
the past for different domains, often sharing elements with similar or matching
meanings [8,11]. However, their combination or co-existence is not easy, often
requiring translation or crosswalk operations [1].

Ontology languages are general-purpose knowledge representation technologies and can be adopted for capturing the nature of metadata records. They
convey not only the syntactic rules that enforce the correctness of a metadata

R. Meersman et al. (Eds.): OTM 2014 Workshops, LNCS 8842, pp. 597–607, 2014.

record but also the meaning of each descriptor used in a record—in a machine-processable way. They are essential for the description of resources on the Semantic Web [4]. The Linked Data principles rely on a unique identifier, or URI, for each resource on the web, on the existence of links between those resources, and on the ability to retrieve resources linked to a particular one, all of them being represented using standard formats (e.g. RDF, OWL) and queryable via standard languages (e.g. SPARQL). Generalizing these guidelines to data that is publicly accessible yields the concept of Linked Open Data (LOD) [3].

Biodiversity information is rich and has many facets to take into account, from very specific ones such as taxonomies of species or community types, ecosystem process typologies or habitat descriptions, spatial and temporal resolution, to more general ones such as geo-referencing, institutional context, time of collection, methods and instruments applied to data collection, and the people involved in it [13].

We are focused here on the representation of biodiversity datasets, providing enough information to make them searchable and understandable by domain experts and relying on researchers to provide a minimal set of dataset-level descriptors. Moreover, we integrate biodiversity dataset description in Dendro [19,20], a prototype collaborative research data management platform. Dendro is ontology based, and takes advantage of the set of basic descriptors for biodiversity captured in BIOME, an ontology that includes the relevant properties of data collected by researchers focused on the patterns and dynamics of biodiversity and ecosystems. Conforming to previous work [18], we have incorporated in BIOME concepts from INSPIRE, an European Commission directive for representing geospatial metadata, to test its applicability in a data management and metadata creation scenario.

Using Dendro and the BIOME ontology, researchers can collaborate in the creation of metadata records that have all the advantages of a fully linked open data representation [20], including SPARQL querying and metadata record representation in formats suitable for LOD de-referencing (e.g. JSON, RDF or OWL).

2   About Biodiversity Data

Worldwide, environmental changes are acknowledged by their contribution to the increasing rates of biodiversity loss [7,17,18]. Understanding and assessing environmental and ecological change is thus essential if the baseline of natural capital is to be defined, in the context of monitoring schemes and long-term ecological research [17,18]. However, even though the production of spatially-explicit biodiversity data has been increasing, such assessment has been recurrently constrained by incomplete spatial and taxonomical indicator coverage [17].

Biodiversity data often refer to several taxonomic groups, community types, typologies of ecosystem processes, or habitat descriptions across distinct time periods, and are usually collected by distinct groups of researchers. Furthermore, assets of spatially-explicit data related to biodiversity have recently increased significantly, even if they present important differences regarding e.g. their source and methodological development, time of acquisition, and spatial resolution [15,18]. As a result, there is a pressing need towards the development of common and collaborative networks and tools towards the harmonisation and sharing of data from different sources and scales under common standards and languages [15,18].

Attempts to tackle such challenges have already been made in the context of specific research projects e.g. the European projects EBONE[1] and BIO_SOS[2], in the context of broader initiatives e.g. the Group on Earth Observation Biodiversity Observation Network (GEO BON)[3]. Specifically, in the case of BIO_SOS project, a geo-portal has been developed so that all researchers from distinct partners and countries could share metadata concerning the datasets produced in the context of the project. The cornerstone of the implementation of this geo-portal was the definition of a metadata profile, built on the INSPIRE core profile, that each of the researchers would fill in during the data gathering stages. This then allowed the evaluation of the fitness of each dataset for the specific intended uses, using a methodology based on the metadata entries, that was itself embedded in the geo-portal [18]. This approach has been used by the CIBIO team in recent projects, as a standard toolkit for data management and quality assessment.

The INSPIRE directive 2007/2/EC[4] aims to create an European Union spatial data infrastructure, enabling the sharing of environmental information among public sector organisations to facilitate public access to spatial information across Europe [2].

The metadata elements specified in the INSPIRE recommendation include the identification of the resource, classification, geographic and temporal references, statements related to the quality and validity of the datasets, conformity with implementing rules on the interoperability of spatial data sets and services, constraints related to access and use, and the organisation responsible for the resource. Information about metadata records themselves is also necessary to ensure that records are kept up to date, and for identifying the organisation responsible for their creation and maintenance.

The INSPIRE directive also considers the possibility of users and systems providing a more detailed description of their resources. This allows them to use additional elements if these are prescribed by other international standards or working practices in their community.

3   The BIOME Ontology

We now introduce BIOME, an ontology that reuses concepts from the INSPIRE directive 2007/2/EC[5], grouped according to the sections of the INSPIRE

---

[1] http://www.wageningenur.nl/
[2] http://www.biosos.eu/
[3] http://www.earthobservations.org
[4] http://eur-lex.europa.eu/legal-content/EN/ALL/?uri=CELEX:32008R1205
[5] http://inspire.ec.europa.eu/index.cfm/pageid/48

Geoportal Metadata Editor[6] and complemented by others specified in the BIO_SOS metadata quality guidelines [13].

INSPIRE specifies more than just the metadata representation and exchange formats, it also details how software infrastructures and web services must be designed, for example. Thus, building an ontology for the representation of the entire INSPIRE directive is a very complex task. This model in no way conflicts with other initiatives aimed at capturing the INSPIRE directive in a more fine-grained detail. This is one of the main advantages of modelling with ontologies, the ease with which different approaches can be combined and the incremental development of models at different granularity levels.

All the concepts created for this ontology were given annotations specifying their `rdf:label`s and `rdf:comment`s. This is important because a natural language description of the concepts is essential to ensure their interpretation by humans [6], and is a good ontology modelling practice overall. Moreover, it is actually necessary to specify these annotation properties to use the ontologies with Dendro, as the platform uses their values to build its dynamic resource description interfaces.

The metadata elements recommended by INSPIRE comprise many categories, including information about the metadata records themselves. This way, metadata are kept up to date and the organisation responsible for their creation and maintenance can be easily identified. The directive also considers the possibility of users and systems providing a more detailed description of their resources. This allows them to use additional elements if these are required by other international standards or the working practices in their communities.

The BIOME ontology is designed for ease of use. It is simple enough to be both easily processable by machines and easily managed by data curators. We have minimized the number of object properties, focusing the model on some core classes and data properties and dispensing with constraints and axioms. The classes capture high-level concepts that represent both data and metadata, while the data properties correspond to the descriptors used in the description of the resources. Resources are therefore captured as instances of the defined classes.

Ontologies that follow this approach have been termed "lightweight ontologies". The Dublin Core (DC) ontology[7] and the Friend of a Friend (FOAF) are examples of two widely used lightweight ontologies [10]. We also promote the reuse of concepts from other ontologies, namely DC, FOAF and CERIF[8]. All the relations that we established between BIOME and the Dublin Core

---

[6] http://inspire-geoportal.ec.europa.eu/editor/

[7] A OWL version of the Dublin Core metadata schema can be found at http://bloody-byte.net/rdf/dc_owl/

[8] The Common European Research Information Format (CERIF) Ontology Specification provides basic concepts and properties for describing research information as semantic data. An OWL representation of CERIF is available at http://www.eurocris.org/ontologies/cerif/1.3/

ontology were based on the "INSPIRE implementing rules for metadata and Dublin Core" [9].

3.1 Classes

The first step in the development of the BIOME ontology was to select the concepts to be represented as *classes*. The following concepts were considered essential to capture the top entities in the domain.

1. **Keyword**
   The *Keyword* class captures the concept of a keyword, a special term which can be associated to a resource; the keywords from a specific controlled vocabulary are examples of instances of the *Keyword* class.
2. **GeographicLocation**
   In BIOME this class is defined as a sub-class of the Dublin Core element *Location*, which is in turn a subclass of the *LocationPeriodAndJurisdiction* in Dublin Core as well.
3. **TemporalReference**
   This concept captures the temporal dimension of the data. The INSPIRE directive defines that at least a temporal reference must be provided.
4. **ResponsibleParty**
   The responsible party is an organisation responsible for the establishment, maintenance and distribution of the spatial data and services.

3.2 Properties

Table 1 shows the concepts proposed for the BIOME ontology. It illustrates the categories that aggregate the descriptors under the heading **Group**, while presenting the **Properties** in each category—second column. The third column has the **Label** (rdf:label) for each property. The label facilitates the interpretation of the property name by users at the time of metadata creation in the data management platform interface. Table 2 shows the additional concepts that were drawn from GeoCoMaS[9] and ISO 19115 respectively. In the table, mandatory properties are marked with a ∗ symbol. A − (dash) symbol before the property names in a sequence of properties indicates that the property immediately above them is used as a prefix; this is the case for *title*, *referenceDate* and *dateType* with respect to *originatingControlledVocabularyTitle*. In case there is a subsumption (⊑) or equivalence (≡) relationship between a property in BIOME and another from a different ontology, the relationship is expressed in parentheses. For example, *resourceLocator* is equivalent to the identifier property in the DC ontology, so they are marked with (≡ dcterms:identifier) in their table line.

---

[9] GeoCoMaS is a normative system of good practices used by the CIBIO research team for managing files in their internal repository.

Table 1. Descriptors drawn or adapted from INSPIRE

Category	Property	Label
Identification	resourceTitle(*)	Resource title
	resourceAbstract(*)	Resource abstract
	linkage	Linkage
	identifierNamespace	Identifier namespace
	identifierCode(*)	Identifier code
	resourceLanguage	Resource language
	resourceLocator ($\equiv$ `dcterms:identifier`)	Resource locator
Classification	topicCategory* ($\sqsubseteq$ `dcterms:subject`)	Topic Category
Keyword	keywordINSPIRE(*)	Keyword INSPIRE
	keywordValue(*) ($\sqsubseteq$ `dcterms:subject`)	Keyword Value
	originatingControlledVocabulary:	Originating controlled vocabulary:
	-title*	-title
	-referenceDate*	-reference date
	-dateType*	-data type
Geographic Location	geographicBoundingBox(*)	Geographic bounding box
Temporal reference	temporalExtentStartingDate(*)	Temporal extent starting date
	temporalExtentEndingDate(*)	Temporal extent ending date
	dateOfCreation* ($\equiv$ `dcterms:created`)	Date of creation
	dateOfLastRevision ($\equiv$ `dcterms:modified`)	Date of last revision
	dateOfPublication ($\equiv$ `dcterms:published`)	Date of publication
Quality & Validation	lineage	Lineage
Spatial Attributes	spatialRepresentationType	Spatial representation type
	spatialResolution	Spatial resolution
	spatialResolutionEquivalentScale	Spatial resolution equivalent scale (part of a spatial resolution record)
	spatialresolutionDistance	Spatial resolution distance (part of a spatial resolution record)
Conformity	conformityDegree(*)	Degree of conformity
	specification	Specification
	conformityDate	Conformity date
	conformityDateType	Conformity date type
Constraints	limitationsOnPublicAccess ($\sqsubseteq$ `dcterms:accessRights`)	Limitations on public access
	conditionsApplyingToAccessAndUse ($\sqsubseteq$ `dcterms:rights`)	Conditions applied to access and use
Responsible party	organizationName(*)	Organisation Name
	responsiblePartyEmail(*)	Responsible party e-mail
	responsibePartyRole(*)	Responsible party role
Metadata on Metadata	organizationName(*)	Organisation name
	metadataPointOfContactEmail(*)	Metadata point of contact email
	metadataLanguage(*)	Metadata language
	metadataDate ($\sqsubseteq$ `dcterms:date`)	Metadata date

Table 2. Descriptors drawn from ISO 19115 and GeoCoMaS

Group	Property	Label
GeoCoMaS	projectName	Project name
	version	Version
	diagnosticAndUsability	Diagnostic and usability
ISO19115	distributionFormatName	Distribution format name
	geographicExtentCode	Geographic extent code
	spatialRepresentation	Spatial representation
	referenceSystem:	Reference system:
	-authority	-authority
	-identifier*	-identifier
	-identifierCode*	-identifier code
	-identifierCodeSpace	-identifier code space

For the purpose of providing information about the metadata record itself, the properties *metadataLanguage*, *metadataDate* and *metadataPointOfContactEmail* were created. Resource identification is done using the properties *resourceTitle*, *resourceAbstract*, and *resourceLanguage* defined in the ontology. A *linkage* property was also created as a way to record the *resourceLocator* in the form of a URL, along with the *identifier*. The classification of spatial data and services can be described by a *topicCategory* property, that can assist users in finding a resource based on a topic search. The *Keyword* class can be described by a *keywordValue*, that assumes free-text values to represent "a commonly used word, formalised word or phrase to describe the subject"[10], contrasting with the *keywordINSPIRE*, that represents a INSPIRE thematic category, and whose valid values are found in the Gemet Thesaurus[11]. The *originatingControlledVocabulary* specifies valid *Keyword* values and must be "a formally registered thesaurus or a similar authoritative source of keywords"[12], as captured in the *title, referenceDate* and *dateType* of the corresponding controlled vocabulary. For representing the geographic location of the resource, we included the *geographicBoundBox* property, that must express the westbound and eastbound longitudes and the southbound and northbound latitudes of the intended location. On the other hand the *TemporalReference* class is described with values related to the *temporalEntextStarting/EndingDate*, the *dateOfCreation*, *dateOfPublication* and the *dateOfLastRevision*. We derive most of the temporal and geographical concepts from the DC classes *Location* and *PeriodOfTime*.

To address process history record-keeping and the overall quality of the dataset, along with the *spatialResolution* referring to the level of detail of a dataset, the *lineage*, *resolutionDistance*, and the *equivalentScale* properties were included. To register conformity of the dataset with implementing rules, or other specifications, we define the *conformityDegree* property to represent the degree of metadata conformity, the *specification* it conforms to, the *conformityDate* and the *conformityDateType*.

The constraints related to the access and use are stated via the *conditionsApplyingToAccessAndUse* and by the *limitationsOnPublicAccessAndUse*. Finally, the entity that holds responsibility over the resource must be described using the *organizationName*, the *responsiblePartyEmail* and a *responsiblePartyRole*.

To account for the possibility of a more detailed annotation, which is in compliance with the INSPIRE directive, the BIOME ontology also includes extra elements prescribed by the ISO 19115 [12]. These elements are intended to describe the spatial reference system used in the dataset (*referenceSystemCode*, *referenceSystemAuthority*, *referenceSystemIdentifier*), the digital mechanism used to represent spatial information (*spatialRepresentation*), the description of the geographic area through identifiers (*geographicExtentCode*) and the format in which the data is to be distributed (*distributionFormatName*).

---

[10] As described in the INSPIRE online documentation.

[11] http://www.eionet.europa.eu/gemet/en/themes

[12] See footnote 10.

The metadata records created by the researchers in this domain are complemented by elements from the GeoCoMaS fields, and must include a *version* of the resource, the identification of the project where the resource originated from (*projectName*), its domain expressed as a CERIF *Project*, which is in turn a subclass of the FOAF's *Project* class. A summary of data characteristics, quality and usability is specified in *diagnosticAndUsability*.

4   Ontology-Driven Data Description

Dendro is a prototype data management platform currently under development at the University of Porto, built for LOD compliance from the ground up and complete with a SPARQL endpoint [19,20]. Its data model relies on the existence of publicly available ontologies (such as Dublin Core or FOAF) that can be loaded directly into the database layer of the system. As a result, the Dendro system is built on a fully graph-based model capable of representing every entity in the research data management environment, as well as the relationships between these entities, using explicit semantics [21]. The model can also be expanded by directly loading additional ontologies into the underlying graph database (using a SPARQL LOAD operation in Dendro's graph database interface), thus providing the flexibility that is expected of a cross-domain data platform. After loading an ontology, its properties become available as descriptors for files and folders.

Like a metadata schema, an ontology can be developed by a data curator, a data management role that may be assumed by either a domain expert or an information science expert. However, ontologies are advantageous to drive data description when compared with metadata schemas because they can be used to express not only the syntactic rules for metadata record compliance but also the semantics of metadata descriptors, in a machine-processable way. They can also be directly integrated into the data model, as an information representation and exchange format—in fact, Dendro cannot operate without first loading some ontologies that provide the metadata descriptors that allow the platform to work.

Figure 1 shows the different stages involved in the description of a dataset using Dendro. The BIOME ontology is based on the analysis of the INSPIRE directive, a relevant standard and the analysis of the metadata records that CIBIO researchers already produce (1). After loading BIOME into Dendro (2), its user interface (3) allows the creation of metadata records that include the same descriptors used in the original metadata sheets (see 1A and 3A), but with an ontology-based representation.

4.1   Dendro as a Description Platform for Biodiversity Datasets

Figure 2 shows a possible integration scenario between the current CIBIO information systems and Dendro. Data files and metadata continue to be created and loaded using the geo-portal, with Dendro being regarded as a project-centered data description platform. Metadata records in the geo-portal can be exported to Dendro for inclusion in a new project, initiating a process of collaborative description. At any time, the metadata records in Dendro can be imported back on

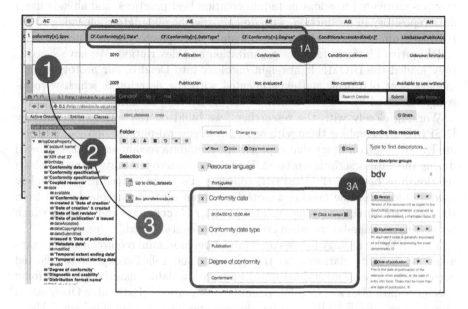

Fig. 1. Creating ontology-based metadata records in Dendro

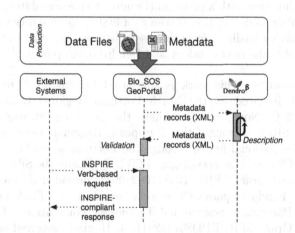

Fig. 2. Integrating the current data management platforms of the CIBIO team

the geo-portal, where they are queried and retrieved using INSPIRE-compatible web services.

5   Conclusions

In this paper we have presented BIOME, a lightweight ontology designed for the management of datasets in the biodiversity science domain. The research group is motivated to adopt metadata creation best practices, and already has a data repository in production, with domain-specific metadata conforming to the INSPIRE directive. Their goal its to couple the repository with a project-level collaborative platform for data organization and description. We have successfully loaded the BIOME lightweight ontology into Dendro, our prototype data management platform, and experimented with the descriptors which were already validated by the researchers in the biodiversity domain.

Working closely with the researchers, we build on the concepts defined by INSPIRE and combine them with others from general-purpose ontologies to create BIOME—an ontology that captures the metadata recommendations followed during the data description process. We promote interoperability by establishing relationships between the INSPIRE concepts and those defined in other widely used ontologies, while making annotations about all the concepts derived from the INSPIRE directive (using `rdf:label` and `rdf:comment`) and defining which properties are mandatory when creating a metadata record.

The BIOME ontology focuses on establishing minimum requirements for managing biodiversity datasets, so the concepts and relationships were selected accordingly. More fine-grained ontologies are available, namely for describing specimen data (Darwin Core[13]), scientific observations (Extensible Observation Ontology or OBOE [16]) and other domain-specific concepts (Ecological Metadata Language or EML [14]). While still needing validation, this work is a first step in a path where, rather than starting with a very rich ontology, simpler ones are used in conjunction with a platform (Dendro) to manage datasets from their creation and minimal description is seen as a first stage in dataset preservation and sharing. Further feedback from the researchers as they start to manage their datasets will guide the next ontology and Dendro developments.

Acknowledgements. This work is supported by project NORTE-07-0124-FEDER000059, financed by the North Portugal Regional Operational Programme (ON.2-O Novo Norte), under the National Strategic Reference Framework (NSRF), through the European Regional Development Fund (ERDF), and by national funds, through the Portuguese funding agency, Fundação para a Ciência e a Tecnologia (FCT). J. Rocha da Silva is also supported by research grant SFRH/BD/77092/2011, provided by the Portuguese funding agency, Fundação para a Ciência e a Tecnologia (FCT). A. Lomba is supported by the Portuguese Science and Technology Foundation (FCT) through Post-Doctoral Grant SFRHBPD807472011. J. Honrado received support from FCT and COMPETE through project grant IND_CHANGE (PTDC/AAG-MAA/4539/2012).

References

1. Baca, M.: Practical Issues in Applying Metadata Schemas and Controlled Vocabularies to Cultural Heritage. Cataloging & Classification Quarterly April 2014, 37–41 (2003)

---

[13] http://rs.tdwg.org/dwc/

2. Bartha, G., Kocsis, S.: Standardization of Geographic Data: The European IN-SPIRE directive. European Journal of Geography, 79–89 (2011)
3. Berners-Lee, T.: Linked Data—Design Issues (2006)
4. Berners-Lee, T., Hendler, J., Lassila, O.: The Semantic Web. Scientific American 284(5), 34–43 (2001)
5. Borgman, C.: The conundrum of sharing research data. Journal of the American Society for Information Science and Technology 63(6) (2012)
6. Brickley, D., Guha, R.V.: RDF Schema 1.1 W3C Recommendation (2014)
7. Butchart, S., Walpole, M., et al.: Global Biodiversity: Indicators of Recent Declines. Science 328(5982), 1164–1168 (2010)
8. Chan, L.M.: Metadata Interoperability and Standardization - A Study of Methodology Part I. D-Lib Magazine, 1–34 (2006)
9. European Commission. State of progress in the development of guidelines to express elements of the INSPIRE metadata implementing rules using ISO15836. Technical report, European Commission (2008)
10. Corcho, O.: Ontology based document annotation: trends and open research problems. International Journal of Metadata, Semantics and Ontologies 1(1), 47–57 (2006)
11. Day, M.: Integrating metadata schema registries with digital preservation systems to support interoperability: a proposal. In: International Conference on Dublin Core and Metadata Applications, DC-2003 (2003)
12. International Organization for Standardization. ISO 19115:2003 Geography Information - Metadata. Technical report (2003)
13. Honrado, J., Alonso, J., Castro, P., et al.: The BIO_SOS metadata geoportal and the external quality of pre-existing datasets. Deliverable 4.5 of the FP7 project BIO_SOS. Appendix 1. Technical report (2010)
14. Jones, M.B., Berkley, C., Bojilova, J., Schildhauer, M.: Managing scientific metadata. IEEE Internet Computing 5(5), 59–68 (2001)
15. Lomba, A., Guerra, C., Alonso, J., Honrado, J., Jongman, R., McCracken, D.: Mapping and monitoring High Nature Value farmlands: Challenges in European landscapes. Journal of Environmental Management 143C, 140–150 (2014)
16. Madin, J., Bowers, S., Schildhauer, M., Krivov, S., Pennington, D., Villa, F.: An ontology for describing and synthesizing ecological observation data. Ecological Informatics 2(3), 279–296 (2007)
17. Pereira, J., Brummitt, H.M., et al.: Global biodiversity monitoring. Frontiers in Ecology and the Environment 8, 459–460 (2010)
18. Pôças, I., Gonçalves, J., Marcos, B., Alonso, J., Castro, P., Honrado, J.: Evaluating the fitness for use of spatial data sets to promote quality in ecological assessment and monitoring. International Journal of Geographical Information Science (June), 1–16 (2014)
19. Rocha, J., Castro, J., Ribeiro, C., Lopes, J.C.: Dendro: collaborative research data management built on linked open data. In: Proceedings of the 11th European Semantic Web Conference (2014)
20. Rocha, J., Castro, J., Ribeiro, C., Lopes, J.C.: The Dendro research data management platform: Applying ontologies to long-term preservation in a collaborative environment. In: Proceedings of the iPres 2014 Conference (2014)
21. Rocha, J., Ribeiro, C., Lopes, J.C.: Ontology-based multi-domain metadata for research data management using triple stores. In: Proceedings of the 18th International Database Engineering & Applications Symposium (2014)

OntoCleaning the Okkam Conceptual Model

Stefano Bortoli[1], Paolo Bouquet[1,2], and Barbara Bazzanella[2]

[1] Okkam SRL
via Segantini 23, I-38121 Trento, Italy
[2] University of Trento - DISI
via Sommarive, 14 I-38123 Povo di Trento, Italy
bortoli@okkam.it, bouquet@disi.unitn.it, barbara.bazzanella@unitn.it

Abstract. The way people define and use identifiers to refer to entities has been under (philosophical) investigation for a long time. This problem gained attention also in the context of the Semantic Web, where the Identity Crisis has threatened one of the cornerstones of the proposed vision: the unambiguous identification of Resources. In this paper we present the application of OntoClean as a formal methodology to formally validate the Okkam Conceptual Model that was proposed to address the problem of identity and reference. In performing such analysis, we unfold some of the philosophical problems affecting the representation of several types of real world entities, presenting a literature review and arguing in favor of some interpretation. This is done with the twofold purpose of contributing to the ongoing debate, and fostering the definition of a shared vision about the problem that will support further advancements in development of the Semantic Web vision. Furthermore, we argue in favor of the adoption of the Okkam IDs as globally persistent and rigid identifiers as a sound solution to the problem of the Identity and Reference in the context of the Semantic Web.

1 Introduction

The way people defines and uses identifiers to refer to entities has been under (philosophical) investigation for a long time, among others [23,25,24,19,21]. At this regards, we are assisting to a phase of transition where criticism proposed by Kripke [23] to the widely adopted *theory of description* [27] are well received, but at the same time no alternative solution gained consensus. Recent developments in the context of the Semantic Web (see [1]) are fostering further investigation about particular aspects and practical issues related to the problem of "Identity and Reference", aiming to find solution to the problem known in this context as "identity crisis" [14,22,17,18,6]. The focus of the problem is in the way URIs[1], adopted as syntactical solution for the representation of "names", should be used to refer to entities, and how naming and reference through URIs should fit the architecture of the Web. With respect to this, two main complementary approaches emerged: (1) Linked Data approach [2], the Okkam approach [9].

---

[1] Uniform Resource Identifiers, RFC3986.

R. Meersman et al. (Eds.): OTM 2014 Workshops, LNCS 8842, pp. 608–617, 2014.
© Springer-Verlag Berlin Heidelberg 2014

The Linked Data initiative, promoted by the W3C, endorses the approach supporting the fact that names for entities are equivalent to description. Thereby, in this context the creation and definition of URIs must always be associated to a description of the entity identified. This solution has appreciable practical advantages as it fits the current architecture of the Internet. In fact, the supporters of the Linked Data initiative suggest to adopt URL[2] as identifiers for entities [4]. This solution has the advantage of defining globally unique identifier that are also de-referenceable into documents containing a description for the entity [5]. This mechanism allows the definition of the Web of Data, relying on existing infrastructures and protocols defined for the Web. The main drawbacks of this approach are two: first, there is no lookup system to find and reuse names referring to entities and this has the side effect of causing a proliferation of names limiting effective data integration; second, the equivalence between URIs managed through "OWL sameAs" statements is disputable and requires the computation of transitive closure along the Global Giant Graph [3].

Okkam was a large scale integration project co-founded by the European Commission aiming at the definition and development of an Entity Name System (ENS) as backbone service handling the process of assigning and managing the lifecycle of globally unique identifiers for entities in the WWW [9]. These identifiers are global, with the scope of persistently identifying entities across system boundaries. The Okkam approach can be seen as orthogonal and complementary with the Linked Data one. In order to promote the role of the ENS as means for smooth and frictionless data integration, entity profiles present Web of Data URIs as alternative identifiers for Okkam entities they co-refer to. More information about the ENS can be found in [8,7].

2   The Okkam Conceptual Model

To make explicit the role of the Entity Name System as a solution to the identity crisis, a conceptual model describing the domain of entities and their relation with URIs as their identifier on the Semantic Web was defined [10]. This model, named Okkam Conceptual Model (OCM[3]) was first defined to provide an explicit representation of domain in which the ENS was proposed as infrastructural element, and to support and justify technical solution implemented within the ENS.

The conceptual model for Okkam is aimed at providing an explicit representation of "the world of entities and their identifiers", extending and adapting the model proposed in [17,18]. In particular the model describes how entities are represented and identified in the context of the (Semantic) Web. In this context, the founding pillars are the concepts of Resources and URI. The definitions of Resources and URI (RFC 3986[4]) are circular, and make the two things dependent from each other. Indeed, essentially the definitions say that *"a Resource is*

---

[2] Uniform Resource Locators, RFC1738.

[3] An OWL implementation of the OCM:
   http://models.okkam.org/ENS-meta-core-vocabulary.owl

[4] http://www.ietf.org/rfc/rfc3986.txt

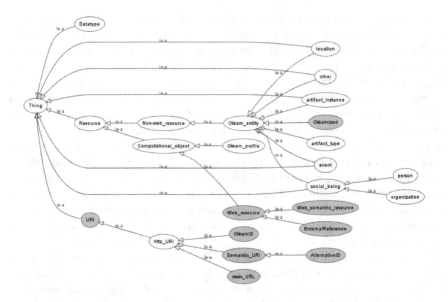

Fig. 1. The taxonomy backbone of the Okkam Conceptual Model

anything that can be identified by a URI" and *"a URI is an identifier for a Resource"*. These two types are then dissected into sub-classes, defining more fine grained classes to represent specific types of Resources and URIs. A graphical view of the backbone taxonomy of the Okkam Conceptual Model is presented in figure 1.

3   OntoClean Meta-properties Annotation

The first important step of the OntoClean methodology is to analyze the backbone taxonomy and label each property (or concept) with specific marks representing its evaluation with respect to Rigidity (R), Identity (I) and Unity (U). In the following, each paragraph presents a description summarizing the analysis leading to the assignment of each meta-property for the most relevant concepts. A definition of the concepts can be found in the online model available at http://models.okkam.org/ENS-meta-core-vocabulary.owl.

According to the standard definition[5], a RESOURCE *"is anything that can be identified by a URI"*. It is important to notice that this definition is circular with respect of what a URI is. However, if something can be identified, it is possible to define sufficient own identity criteria. Thereby, a resource supplies identity criteria (**+O**). The concept of RESOURCE is so broad and it involves potentially any other concept with different unity criteria. For this reason, this concept has no-unity property (**-U**). Intuitively, *being a Resource* is an essential property of all resources so, RESOURCE has rigidity property (**+R**).

---

[5] Definition of URI in RFC3986, http://tools.ietf.org/html/rfc3986

A NON-WEB RESOURCE essentially it includes anything but computational objects. A NON-WEB RESOURCE inherits identity criteria from RESOURCE (+I). *Not being a computational object* is a rigid property of Non-Web Resource (+R) and does not present clear unity criteria (-U).

An OKKAM ENTITY refers to all particulars and concrete entities, including events but excluding all abstract entities and concepts. Intuitively, being an Okkam Entity is a rigid property of all its instances (+R), inherits identity criteria from Resource (+I) and has no clear unity criteria as the varieties of possible instances makes impossible to imagine common unifying relations defining wholes (-U). An EXTERNAL REFERENCE is a Web Resource providing further information about a resource without being a Web Semantic Resource. Being an External Reference does not appear to be neither essential nor rigid property of a Web Resource, so the this property is anti-rigid (~R). On the other side, External references inherits both unity (+U) and identity criteria (+I) from Web Resources.

A WEB SEMANTIC RESOURCE is a Web Resource forming the Web of Data promoted by the Linked Data initiative. The property of *being a Web Semantic Resource* does not appear to be rigid with respect to the computational object realizing them. A Web Semantic Resource is a computational object representing a set of semantically annotated information that is accessible on the Web. Thus, as for Web Resources, also Web Semantic Resources are anti-rigid (~R). Web Semantic Resource property inherits identity criteria from (+I) Web Resources, and present clear unity property as any computational object (+U).

A SOCIAL BEING is anti rigid property (~R) as a "status acknowledged within a social system" can be interpreted as an agent having some role recognized by in a social system. Thus, assuming that we could remove a whole social system apart from one of its element, for example due to a terrible disease or a nuclear disaster, this element would exists *without being a social being* anymore as there would not be a society acknowledging it. *Being acknowledged by a society* does not allow to define commonly shared identity criteria (-I) nor define precise unity condition (-U). It is important to notice this problem is due to the fact that social being is quite a vague concept.

The property PERSON has been widely analyzed in other works such as [20], thus referring to that work can easily realize that the property of *being a person* is rigid with respect to all its instances, and that this property has clear unity (+U) and its own identity criteria (+O).

Also the property ORGANIZATION has been analyzed in [20], and following the intuition of the authors we can say that being an organization is a rigid property (+R), presenting identity (+O) and unity criteria (+U). Finding a common unity criteria defining an organization as a whole seems to be possible relying on the functional notion of unity. Namely, an organization can be seen as a whole as it functions as whole, not only because of the mereological sum of its part.

A LOCATION is rigid with respect to all its instances (+R). A location seems to have its own identity criteria (+O) as, intuitively, it seems to be possible to determine equality between two location by analyzing their mereological extension [19]. However, this type of criteria seems to be suitable only to establish synchronic identity, but it would create problems along time. From an ontological perspective, it seems that a location does not have a clear unity criteria, indeed it is impossible to establish uniform unifying relation between the parts of a location ($\sim$U) to form a whole without depending on unity criteria of other entities. The concept of EVENT is under the lenses of philosophers for many years, but no shared agreement over their nature was ever found. Despite this, an analysis of some literature was performed with the aim of finding some evidences of approaches that could be applied dealing with 'events' in the context of the Okkam Entity Name System. The first paper considered was a famous work of Davidson [16] which attempts to give a definition of events on base of 'cause and effects'. Quine in [26] pointed out that the identity criteria given by Davidson suffers from some kind of circularity. Kellenberg in [21] criticizes the approach of Lowe [25,24], and proposed a pragmatic definition of identity criteria as "*doing that, if successfully performed, pick out only single entities of the kind in question from all single and all pairs of entities relevant in the domain*". Unwin [28] proposes a schema in which sortal terms should fit to be recognized as events. Cleland [15] proposes to use changes (or concrete phases) as basic individuals for the identification of events; finally, Carlson [11] proposes a linguistic analysis where thematic roles would have a conceptual role in the individuation of events starting from the principle that 'an event has at most one entity playing a given thematic role'. The pragmatic approach to the definition of identity criteria proposed by Kellenberg could be used to define events in the context of the Entity Name System (+I). Furthermore, one could argue that 'concrete phases' [15] could be proper unity criteria for events, and thus we would be tempted to say that events do have unity criteria (+U). Furthermore, if we consider the a unique set of entities with specific thematic role participating in an event, thus having a precise effect on the world, we can see also an event as whole from a 'cause-effect' or functional perspective.

An ARTIFACT TYPE is a rigid property (+R)(similar conclusion are also in [12]). Artifact types have the property of being unique, or being the unique models for an arbitrary number of instantiation copies. Intuitively, it seems then that artifact types have their own intrinsic diachronic and synchronic identity criteria as two different models will be realized in different types of artifacts. Adopting a pragmatic approach as proposed by Kellenberg in [21], it seems reasonable to conclude that artifact types do have identity (+O) and unity criteria (+U). However, artifacts are still under the lens of philosophers (e.g. [13]) and works as [12] ended up with different conclusions.

An ARTIFACT INSTANCE is a rigid property of every artifacts (+R). A possible identity criteria could be the fact that artifacts can said to be the same if the they are composed of exactly the same components and exactly by the same matter (+I) even thou someone may not agree [12]. Most artifact instances have intuitively clear unity criteria, but there are types of artifacts (e.g. wine) that do not have clear unity property, if not depending from others. Thus it seems reasonable to state that not all artifact instances present unity criteria (-**U**).

The property OTHER defines *"the class of things which do not fall under any other predefined class of OKKAM entities"*. This property has to be intended as a utility to represent all those entities that cannot be classified according to the main set of class analyzed but an it is disjoint from them. Nevertheless, being a other is not a rigid property ($\sim$**R**), and does not define identity (-**I**) and unity criteria (-**U**).

The definition of URI (Uniform Resource Identifier) is given in RFC3986, http://tools.ietf.org/html/rfc3986. According to this definition, a URI has its own identity criteria as explicit identity (+**O**) property are defined and proper of all URIs. The combination syntax, encoding, size constrains seems to suggest that a URI has also unity criteria (+**U**). According to the definition of URI, a URI is such only if it is associated as identifier of a resource. This fact seems to suggest that *being a URI* is not an essential property of all the strings respecting the URI syntax, and thus the property of being a URI is anti-rigid ($\sim$R). Indeed, at some extent, the definition of URI seems describing a role with respect to the RESOURCE it is attached to. Intuitively, it is impossible to understand if a URI *per se* identifies any resource at all. The only rigid property of a URI is the syntactic one, so at worst we could define the class of "URI-like" strings as rigid.

HTTP URI makes implicit reference to the HTTP protocol as mean to dereference a resource identified by a URI. Similarly to URI, the property of *being an HTTP URI* has unity (+**U**) and identity properties (+**I**). Also in this case, intuitively an HTTP URI does not guarantee *per se* that there is a resource de-referenceable related to it. Thereby, being an HTTP URI is an anti-rigid property ($\sim$**R**).

OKKAMID similarly to URI, has unity (+**U**) and identity properties (+**I**). As to rigidity the class of OkkamId requires a more detailed analysis. First of all, any OkkamId is generated just and only when a new Okkam Entity is Okkamized, namely it is assigned an OkkamId. This means that since its generation, and OkkamId is necessarily tied to an Okkam Entity. Furthermore, in principle no Okkam Entity should be removed by the Entity Name System, and thus for all its existence, even along the lifecycle of the Okkam Entity, and Okkam Id is rigidly tied to an Okkam Entity. This principles of persistence and consistency gives, in our opinion, rigidity property to an Okkam ID. Namely, every OkkamID is necessarily tied to the Okkam Entity for all its existence. An OkkamId does not have merely the role of de-referencing objects, but to be a rigid and shared name for entities. Thus, according to our intuition we affirm that being an OkkamId is a rigid property (+**R**).

A SEMANTIC URI, similarly to URI, has unity (+**U**) and identity properties (+**I**). The automatic de-referentiation mechanism underlying the existence of Semantic URIs suffers from the same lack of rigidity as regular HTTP URI. Indeed, in principle a Semantic URI does not guarantee *per se* that there is a Semantic Resource de-referenceable related to it. Thereby, being a Semantic

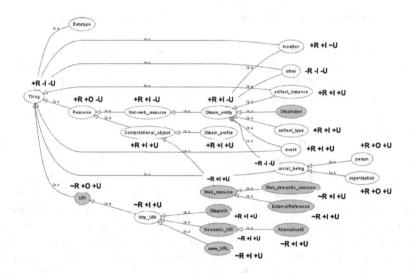

Fig. 2. Okkam Conceptual Model Labeled with OntoClean metaproperties

URI is an anti-rigid property (∼**R**). Similar analysis can be done for the class of WWW URL.

3.1   Constraints Violation in Backbone Taxonomy

A view of the taxonomy labeled according to the analysis described in section 3 is presented in Figure 2. An analysis of this taxonomy with respect to the metaproperties assigned helps highlighting problems or misconception in the definition of the model.

The first constraints check is about the rigidity meta-property. As shown in Figure 2, many properties included in the model as classes are anti-rigid. These classes anyway are clearly part of the domain the Okkam Conceptual Model wants to represent. In particular, the properties presenting constraints violation to be removed from the taxonomy are: SOCIAL BEING and OKKAMID. Both the properties break the OntoClean constraint (+R ⊄∼R). Thereby, the relation between SOCIAL BEING and properties PERSON and ORGANIZATION should not be represented by subsumption, but should be represented by a disjunction. That is, if something is a SOCIAL BEING, then it is either a PERSON or an ORGANIZATION. Analyzing the taxonomy it seems clear the intent of finding a common ancestor for person and organization as social agents. However, we believe that a better way to model this would be to model legal agent as a role, and state that persons and organizations play the role of social agents. Regarding OKKAMID property, it seems that this cannot be in subsumption relation with URI, but rather it is constituted by a URI and inherits its syntactic characteristics. Anyway, as we concluded that an OKKAMID is rigid property with respect to its property of being about an OKKAM ENTITY, then we have to remove OKKAMID from the subsumption relation with the URI.

Another subsumption that violates an OntoClean constraint is the one between OKKAM ENTITY and OTHER. This property is too vague to be maintained in the taxonomy and subsumption relation with OKKAM ENTITY violates the (-I ⊄ +I) constraint. OKKAM ENTITY has identity property, but the property OTHER seems not to have it, and incompatible identity criteria are sign that the properties are disjoint.

The taxonomy defined by rigid classes does not present particular inconsistencies with the constraints defined by the OntoClean methodology.

According to the methodology, the first stage after considering rigidity, is to individuate the so called phased sortal. A phased sortal is a property that changes identity criteria along its existence, while remaining the same entity. Analyzing the taxonomy, potential candidates for being phased sortal could be WEB RESOURCES, URI and their subclasses. Nevertheless, these classes don't change their identity criteria along their existence and thus, we can conclude that there are no phased sortal in the taxonomy.

The next step is analyze the presence of roles. Performing this task we can identify a set of classes that seems to play some role, in particular: WEB RESOURCE, WEB SEMANTIC RESOURCE, EXTERNAL REFERENCE. All these classes seems to share the same kind of problem with respect to rigidity. In particular all of these are computational objects that happen to be accessible on the Web, and thus depend on two things: the host server and the URI that is resolved in the specific location of the host. Without these two essential elements, no computational objects can play the role of being a web resource of any type. The property URI and its subclasses do not seem to play a role. One could think that they play the role of being the identifiers of resources, but in my opinion this is not a role. URIs are properties following specific syntactic constraints that can be employed in the system of the web to identify/locate resources. Their existence is independent from the resources they refer to. Indeed, nobody would deny that

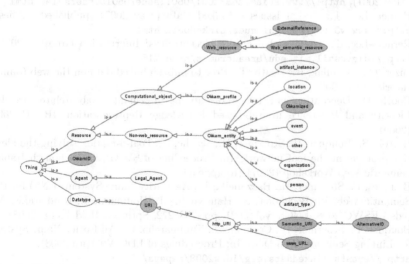

Fig. 3. Okkam Conceptual Model taxonomy modified to remove constraint violation.

a string representing a URL is not a URL despite no computational object can be retrieved resolving it according to any of the HTTP protocols. In my opinion, URIs are particular data types, more specifically strings that respect a defined grammar (URI), declare specific protocols for its resolution (HTTP URI), follow specific conventions (WWW URL, Semantic URI), or present some common pattern (OkkamID). A view of the taxonomy modified to remove constraint violation is presented in Figure 3.

4   Concluding Remarks

In this paper we presented an analysis of the Okkam Conceptual Model using the OntoClean methodology. The purpose of such analysis is to formally validate the model defined, and remove inconsistencies. In doing so, we performed a survey of the literature dealing with slippery problems such as the definition of unity and identity criteria for entity types such as Events and Location. Presenting this work, we believe we contribute to the debate concerning the problem of ' 'identity and reference" ' on the Web, arguing in favor of the adoption of the Okkam Entity Name System as a tool to support the creation and reuse of globally unique persistent identifiers. We also argued that the concept of OkkamId is by definition a conceptually useful tool in this context, as it goes beyond the concept of URI which we interpret as a mere Datatype. In particular, we believe that the OkkamId is suitable to be used as a global and reusable name for real world entities, representing an entailment and reification of the vision of Kripke in its analysis of Naming and References [23].

References

1. Berners-Lee, T., Hendler, J.A., Lassila, O.: The Semantic Web. Scientific American (May 2001), http://www.sciam.com/2001/0501issue/0501berners-lee.html
2. Berners-Lee, T.: Design Issues – Linked Data (May 2007) (published onlines), http://www.w3.org/DesignIssues/LinkedData.html
3. Berners-Lee, T.: Giant global graph. Decentralized Information Group - (2007), http://dig.csail.mit.edu/breadcrumbs/node/215
4. Bizer, C., Cyganiak, R., Heath, T.: How to publish linked data on the web (online tutorial July 2007)
5. Booth, D.: Denotation as a two-step mapping in semantic web architecture. In: Identity and Reference in web-based Knowledge Representation, IR-KR 2009 (2009)
6. Bortoli, S., Bouquet, P., Stoermer, H., Wache, H.: Foaf-o-matic - solving the identity problem in the foaf network. In: Proceeding of SWAP 2007 - Fourth Italian Semantic Web Workshop (2007) (to appear)
7. Bouquet, P., Stoermer, H., Bazzanella, B.: An Entity Name System (ENS) for the Semantic Web. In: Bechhofer, S., Hauswirth, M., Hoffmann, J., Koubarakis, M. (eds.) ESWC 2008. LNCS, vol. 5021, pp. 258–272. Springer, Heidelberg (2008)
8. Bouquet, P., Stoermer, H., Cordioli, D., Tummarello, G.: An Entity Name System for Linking Semantic Web Data. In: Proceedings of LDOW (April 2008), http://events.linkeddata.org/ldow2008/papers/23-bouquet-stoermer-entity-name-system.pdf

9. Bouquet, P., Stoermer, H., Niederee, C., Mana, A.: Entity Name System: The Backbone of an Open and Scalable Web of Data. In: Proceedings of the IEEE International Conference on Semantic Computing, ICSC 2008, no. CSS-ICSC 2008-4-28-25, pp. 554–561. IEEE Computer Society (August 2008)

10. Bouquet, P., Palpanas, T., Stoermer, H., Vignolo, M.: A conceptual model for a web-scale entity name system. In: Gómez-Pérez, A., Yu, Y., Ding, Y. (eds.) ASWC 2009. LNCS, vol. 5926, pp. 46–60. Springer, Heidelberg (2009)

11. Carlson, G.: Thematic roles and the individuation of events. In: Rothstein, S. (ed.) Events and Grammar, pp. 35–51. Kluwer Academic Publishers (1998)

12. Carrara, M., Giaretta, P., Morato, V., Soavi, M., Spolaore, G.: Identity and modality in ontoclean. In: Varzi, A., Vieu, L. (eds.) Formal Ontology in Information Systems, IOS Press (2004)

13. Carrara, M., Vermaas, P.E.: The fine-grained metaphysics of artifactual and biological functional kinds. Synthese 169(1), 125–143 (2009)

14. Clark, K.G.: Identity Crisis (September 11, 2002)

15. Cleland, C.: On the individuation of events. In: Synthese, vol. 86, pp. 229–254. Springer (1991)

16. Davidson, D.: The individuation of events. In: Essays on Actions and events, Claredon Press (1980)

17. Gangemi, A., Presutti, V.: Towards an OWL Ontology for Identity on the Web. In: Semantic Web Applications and Perspectives, SWAP 2006 (2006)

18. Gangemi, A., Presutti, V.: A grounded ontology for identity and reference of web resources. In: i3: Identity, Identifiers, Identification. Proceedings of the WWW2007 Workshop on Entity-Centric Approaches to Information and Knowledge Management on the Web, Banff, Canada, May 8 (2007)

19. Guarino, N., Welty, C.: Identity, unity and individuality: Towards a formal toolkit for ontological analysis. In: ECAI-2000: The European Conference on Artificial Intelligence (2000)

20. Guarino, N., Welty, C.: An overview of ontoclean. In: Staab, S., Studer, R. (eds.) The Handbook on Ontologies, pp. 151–172. Springer (2004)

21. Kellenberg, A.: Identifying criteria of identity. Ontology Metaphysics 10, 109–122 (2009)

22. Kent, W.: The Unsolvable Identity Problem. In: Extreme Markup Languages (2003)

23. Kripke, S.: Naming and Necessity. Basil Blackwell, Boston (1980)

24. Lowe, E.J.: Kinds of Being. A Study of Individuation, Identity, and the Logic of Sortal Terms. Blackwell (1989)

25. Lowe, E.J.: What is a criterion of identity? The Philosphical Quarterly 39, 1–21 (1989)

26. Quine, W.V.: Events and reification. In: Lepore, E., McLaughlin, B. (eds.) Actions and Events: Perspectives on the Philosophy of Davidson., Blackwell (1985)

27. Russell, B.: On denoting. Mind 14(56), 479–493 (1905)

28. Unwin, N.: The individuation of events. Mind 105, 315–330 (1996)

Ontology-Driven Public Administration Web Hosting Monitoring System

Francesca Fallucchi[1], Elena Alfonsi[2], Alessandro Ligi[2],
and Massimiliano Tarquini[2]

[1] Guglielmo Marconi University, Rome, Italy
[2] 4IT Solution S.r.l, Rome, Italy
f.fallucchi@unimarconi.it,
{e.alfonsi,a.ligi,m.tarquini}@4itsolution.it

Abstract. The Public Administration (PA) is constantly on the look-out for new solutions to improve its performance. The ICT-enabled public sector innovation and the open government approach are needed to provide new data-driven services to improve the public governance. The challenge is how to organize the public information so that it can be easily used by users and PA itself. To support such needs, research is proposing new approaches. Among these approaches, semantic technologies are becoming predominant. We realized an innovative Ontology-driven system that automates the processes of data collection, knowledge extraction, and representation using different and heterogeneous sources. In particular, we show how this approach can be profitably used for automatic monitoring and systematic review of the web hosting service in PA. This paper is a report on a proof of concept demonstrating how our system can be successfully used to provide relevant information about PA scenarios and how such information can be used to lead PA decisional processes.

Keywords: Ontology-driven, knowledge acquisition, open governance, public sector.

1 Introduction

The new challenges posed by the evolution of the company and the financial crisis renewed the impetus towards the modernization of the public sector, which has begun more than a decade ago. Indeed authoritative studies show that the public sector has a responsibility also on competitiveness and economic growth of a country. The European Digital Agenda, sets targets for growth in the European Union to be achieved by 2020. In order to meet new demands and growing expectations from citizens and businesses, it is necessary that the government should review its organization, administrative procedures and processes through information and communication technologies.

The ICT-enabled public sector innovation and the open government approach are needed to provide new data-driven services to improve the public governance. The goal of this reorganization is to improve the efficiency of the public sector

R. Meersman et al. (Eds.): OTM 2014 Workshops, LNCS 8842, pp. 618–625, 2014.

which is an important factor, even to the degree of competitiveness and opportunities for development of the national economy.

The activity of administrative simplification as the aim to implement the reorganization of the public sector to provide more efficient and effective services to citizens, businesses and the public administration itself. To achieve it, the "Italian Digital Agenda", contains a list of urgent actions involving the massive use of innovative information and communication technologies, in order to improve the quality of the public spending (spending review policy).

The process of information retrieval and entities correlation using different data sources in the context of Public Administration, is definitely one of the most interesting and challenging activity. It needs algorithms to correlate entities from heterogeneous sources and methodologies to introduce an abstraction layer that allows to define how the elements that are found in structured and unstructured sources (like web pages) can be transformed into information stored in a knowledge base. This paper describes the approach used to provide a unified view of data collections gathered from different sources and how to perform a semantic enrichment with continuous automatic tools devoted to knowledge acquisition. The proposed approach is based upon an ontological paradigm to process, organize and represent information from public sector. In particular, we show how this approach can be profitably used for automatic monitoring and systematic review of the web hosting service in public administrations.

The rest of the paper is organized as follows. After the related work (section 2), we firstly give a general idea of our approach in section 3, then we present the domain ontology that we have used for the public sector (section 4) and our ontology-driven web mining system for the PA web discovery (section 5). In section 6 we report a proof of concept demonstrating how our system can be successfully used to provide information about PA web discovery. Finally, we draw some conclusions and we plan the future work (section 7).

2   Related Work

The need to combine vast amount of archived data in PA domains gives a very interesting test-bed for testing semantic technologies. Recently, the emphasis is put on the modelling of PA domain and application of the semantic web technologies for integration of eGovernment systems. The challenge is how to organize the public information so that it can be easily used by users and PA itself. To support such needs, research is proposing new approaches. Among these approaches, knowledge acquisition systems are becoming predominant.

Public administration is still not sufficiently modelled, partly due to its size and complexity, and consequently there are no widely accepted representations/ models/definitions describing the domain.

Many efforts have been made to describe the public sector with an ontological approach. ONTOGOV service ontology [3] is an eGovernment domain-specific service ontology while DIP eGovernment Ontology [4] is an extensive Ontology

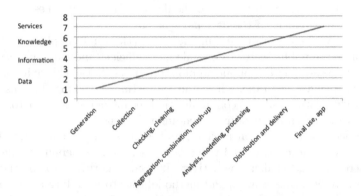

Fig. 1. Stages of value creation with public data

that models a wide range of eGovernment and community services and information. WebDG Ontologies [5] are ontologies used to organize government information in order to make automatic composition feasible while GEA PA [6,7] is a generic Public Administration domain ontology.

Also other systems have been proposed to improve the public sector. For example, the framework is used to add a semantic web layer to legacy organizational information in different use cases provided by the Italian National Research Council (CNR) intraweb [8]. In [9], the first industrial experience of a comprehensive OBDA project of Treasury of the Italian Ministry of Economy and Finance is presented. The work [10] is of help for the public sector to explore the perceived usefulness of the knowledge discovered through the knowledge discovery in database (KDD) in the decision making process of government agencies.

Many other approaches, methods, and systems have been proposed to use semantic technologies in order to improve the use of ICT in italian public administration systems but they are not esaustive and generalized for all the specific PA domains, e.g. the PA web hosting domain.

3   Approach

Public sector information is a strategic resource, holding great potential for a number of beneficiaries including public sector agencies, private businesses, academia, citizens and civic organizations. Government data can offer a significant contribution of to the public service value chain [2] using the stages shown in Fig. 1.

The opening of the data is a complex process that requires serious evaluation and quality review. In most cases, the data are made available in tabular formats more or less using open standards (such as Excel or CSV), and published on the corporate website of the owner of the data subject. Each used data-source has specific characteristics, but generally they can be divided into two main categories:

- General domain: sources that take a census of the entities belonging to the public administration regardless of specific domain they belong. Examples of sources are the index compiled by the ISTAT (National Institute of Statistics), the Index contained in IPA (Index of the Public Administration) and the web.
- Specific domain: sources that take a census of a subset of entities belonging to the public administration related to a particular domain of interest, such as government agencies, hospitals, educational, etc. They are specific sources of domain where indexes are prepared by a public entity on its own in order to perform its job and to provide services relevant to its duty.

Therefore, it is clear that the challenge is to establish mechanisms for the entity correlation of data coming from various sources, and the need of an abstraction layer to define how entities that are found in structured sources can be successfully represented into a knowledge base.

Information integration is the approach used to provide a unified and transparent view of the collections of relational data stored in different, independent, and heterogeneous sources. The domain ontology obtained with this approach is populated with an Ontology-driven system that automates the processes of data collection, knowledge extraction, and representation using different and heterogeneous sources. The module presented in this work starts from a Web Mining activity performed on the PA Web sites. We report a proof of concept demonstrating how the web crawled data can be successfully mashed up with the proposed Ontology-driven system in order to provide an enriched vision of PA scenarios and to show how such information can be used to lead PA decisional processes.

4 Domain Ontology for the Public Administration Sector

The universe of Public Administration is made up of as many domains as the areas in which they carry out the various activities and as many domains as the number of entities carrying on such activities.

The scale and complexity of functions and domains in the public administration and the lack of a precise definition of the concept of authority belonging to the public administration represent the major difficulty in designing a global schema that includes all the concepts and relations related to these domains.

Although many organizations already use a taxonomy to organize information, this is often insufficient. In fact, a single taxonomy or a single ontology is not very appropriate because not suitable to describe exhaustively all domains of interest; working with many ontologies, instead, increases the precision and the wealth of information in the phase of the description of the domains. The use of different ontologies, as we did in our approach, provides a terminology that is

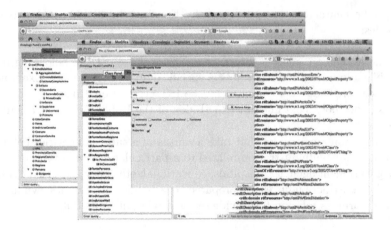

Fig. 2. PA ontology browsing in Semantic Turkey

accessible to all the figures that deal with a particular domain, and also offers the capability to create different views of the same domain.

Semantic Turkey [1], a Semantic Web extension for the popular Firefox web browser, is used as information visualization/semantic browsing and Ontology editing tool. The Fig. 2 reports a part of ontology used in this work related to some classes of the Italian Public Administration.

5   Ontology-Driven PA Web Hosting Monitoring System

We realized an Ontology-driven PA web hosting monitoring system that automates the processes of data collection, knowledge extraction, and representation using different and heterogeneous sources. A specific component, allows the operator to collect data mining the Web sites of the PA. The collected information represents new knowledge used to populate the reference ontology. The "Web Mining" component is made of: a discovery component; a software module which has as its main objective the identification of the addresses of sources of information that are useful for populating the knowledge base; connectors which are software components written ad-hoc with the aim of extracting data from target information sources. Combining the use of such components, the system is capable of: discovering new websites in the domain of the PA; finding the mail exchanger of the PA, and geting information about web hosting, mail and network providers. The discovery component is made of the following sub-components:

- *KB:* it is the knowledge base containing the above described domain ontology. It provides input for and receives output from the discovery process.
- *Discovery Site:* by means of a heuristic applied to the results produced by the Google search engine, it is able to discover sites, domains, and subdomains hosted by a PA web site;

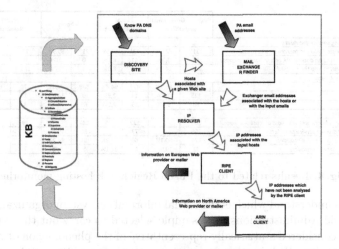

Fig. 3. Workflow of Web Hosting Discovery

- *Mail Exchanger Finder:* it uses a Domain Name System (DNS) to look for the mail exchangers starting from an hostname;
- *IP Resolver:* it uses a DNS to reverse naming lookup of the URLs producing a list if IPs;
- *Ripe Client:* it is connected via a web service to the RIPE database[1]; it is used to collect information about European server providers hosting PA sites, and about networks they are connected to.
- *Arin Client:* it is connected via a web service to the ARIN database[2] Used to collect information about America server providers hosting PA sites, and about networks they are connected to. More specifically ARIN provide information about providers from Unites States, Canada, North Atlantic Islands, Caribe.

The whole process is organized as a workflow, as described in Fig.3. The output from a component can be used as input for the next one. Workflow can be dynamically changed. Finder and the three components (IP Resolver, Ripe Client, Arin Client) continuously inject knowledge populating the reference ontology presented in section 4.

6   Results

This paper is a report on a proof of concept demonstrating how our system can be successfully used to provide relevant information about PA scenarios and how such information can be used to lead PA decisional processes. The purpose of this report is to assess the effectiveness and usefulness of a system for automatic monitoring and systematic review of the web hosting service in PA domain. This

---

[1] https://www.ripe.net
[2] https://www.arin.net

	Regional Government and Offices		Local Government		Schools		University and Researche	
Web Hosting service providers								
Web site hosted into commercial service providers	1311	82,5%	421	83,5%	759	99,3%	10	5,7%
Web site hosted on another PA or a in house company	53	3,3%	41	8,1%	0	0,0%	0	0,0%
Web site hosted into the PA Itself	226	14,2%	42	8,3%	5	0,7%	165	94,3%
Geographic Areas								
ITALY	1379	86,7%	477	94,8%	588	77,0%	171	97,7%
EUROPE	125	7,9%	14	2,8%	107	14,0%	1	0,6%
EXTRA EU	86	5,4%	13	2,6%	69	9,0%	3	1,7%
Web Servers								
Numbers of subnetworks who host at least one website	266		122		131		19	
Number of distinct service providers:	156		77		86		14	
- Commercial service providers	125	80,1%	60	77,9%	81	94,2%	7	50,0%
- Public service providers	31	19,9%	17	22,1%	5	5,8%	7	50,0%

Fig. 4. Results related to the Puglia Region web hosting monitoring

is useful to understand which is the actual information system organization models in Public Administrations. The sample selected to carry out the experiment cannot be considered statistically representative of the phenomenon of web hosting. Nevertheless, Web hosting monitoring activities provides useful information (i.e. services providers, consortium of administrations that offer web services , supplier market shares, etc) about the IT services organization inside PA, that is useful to evaluate ex post which are the effects of decisions.

The presented results, however, are significant. They allow to evaluate the potential usefulness of a system monitoring web hosting services, in order to study other phenomena in connection with it. We chose a Region as a sample because it represents many organizations ruled by a common set of rules (regional laws). In particular, this document reports the experimentation activities on the Puglia Region. Specifically, the object of the monitoring of web hosting service covers 4 sub-sectors of the Puglia Region: Regional government and offices, local government (as Provinces, municipalities, unions and associations of municipalities, mountain communities), schools, University and Research.

For each one of the said sub-sectors, the following analyses have been made:

- Location (hosting): individuation of the service provider for each PA website either at home or hosted by another public entity (in-house company , participated company, public consortium, other administration) or hosted by a private operator;
- Geographical location: Italy, Europe or outside Europe;
- IP subnets locations and legal entities that maintaing domain records (market players or public companies).

We surveyed 1590 websites for the Regional Government sector. More than 80% of the sites is managed by market operators (99% for the schools). Another interesting fact is that the 94% of University and Research manages websites in their own facilities.

In the average, the 86% of the sample sites is hosted in Italian service providers, the 8% in European service providers, and the 6% in non European service providers.

With the same system, it is possible to extract information related to the IP subnet of websites. For example, the 1590 websites of the considered sample are hosted in 266 distinct IP subnets. These subnets are registered by 156 distinct service providers, 125 managed by market operators and 31 managed by PAs.

7 Conclusion and Further Work

Defining strategies int the PA have to determine the possible alternative actions and to measure the results to improve its performance.

The system we present is able to develop and manage a qualified knowledge concerning entities of the PA from open data sources. It can be successfully used to provide relevant information about PA scenarios and the obtained knowledge can be used to lead PA decisional processes. Th adoption of semantic technologies simplified the comparison and integration between collected data from different heterogeneous and evolving sources allowing a continue monitoring service.

The Puglia Region use case presented in this paper is just a pilot example. The system can be used in general to collect and organize new knowledge for monitoring different aspects of the PA, for improving the PA activities, and for supporting the PA tasks through semantic technologies.

References

1. Pazienza, M.T., Scarpato, N., Stellato, A., Turbati, A.: Semantic Turkey: A Browser-Integrated Environment for Knowledge Acquisition and Management. Semantic Web Journal 3(2) (2012)
2. Ubaldi, B.: Open Government Data. In: Towards empirical analysis of open government data initiatives OECD Working Papers on Public Governance, vol. 22, OECD Publishing (2013)
3. Apostolou, D., Stojanovic, L., Lobo, T.P., Thoenssen, B.: Towards a semantically-driven software engineering environment for eGovernment. In: Böhlen, M.H., Gamper, J., Polasek, W., Wimmer, M.A. (eds.) TCGOV 2005. LNCS (LNAI), vol. 3416, pp. 157–168. Springer, Heidelberg (2005)
4. Nagypal, G., Lemcke, J.: D3.3: A Business Data Ontology. DIP project deliverable (2004)
5. Medjahed, B., et al.: Infrastructure for EGovernment Web Services. IEEE Internet Computing Magazine 7(1), 58–65 (2003)
6. Peristeras, V.: The Governance Enterprise Architecture - GEA - for Reengineering Public Administration, in Business Administration, University of Macedonia: Thessaloniki (2006)
7. Goudos, S.K., Loutas, N., Peristeras, V., Tarabanis, K.A.: Public Administration Domain Ontology for a Semantic Web Services EGovernment Framework, pp. 270–277. IEEE Computer Society Press (2007)
8. Gliozzo, A.M., Gangemi, A., Presutti, V., Cardillo, E., Daga, E., Salvati, A., Troiani, G.: A collaborative semantic web layer to enhance legacy systems. In: Aberer, K., et al. (eds.) ASWC 2007 and ISWC 2007. LNCS, vol. 4825, pp. 764–777. Springer, Heidelberg (2007)
9. Antonioli, N., Castan, F., Civili, C., Coletta, S., Grossi, S., Lembo, D., Lenzerini, M., Poggi, A., Fabio Savo, D., Virardi, E.: Ontology-Based Data Access: The Experience at the Italian Department of Treasury. CAiSE Industrial Track 9-16
10. Bani-Hani, I.: Knowledge Discover in The Government Decision Making Process: A Study of Swedish Government Agencies and Public Owned Companies. LAP Lambert Academic Publishing, Germany (2012) ISBN: 3848403854, 9783848403851

Establishing Conceptual Commitments in the Development of Ontologies through Competency Questions and Conceptual Graphs

Cristóvão Sousa[1,2], António Lucas Soares[2,3], Carla Pereira[1,2], and Samuel Moniz[2]

[1] CIICESI - ESTGF, Polytechnic Institute of Porto,
Rua do Curral - Casa do Curral-Margaride, 4610-156, Felgueiras-Portugal
[2] INESC Porto, Rua Dr. Roberto Frias, s/n 4200, Porto-Portugal
[3] FEUP, University of Porto, Rua Dr. Roberto Frias, sn 4200-465 Porto, Portugal
{cpsousa,asoares,csp,Samuel.moniz}@inescporto.pt

Abstract. The process of establishing the ontology objectives by the stakeholders is fundamental for the ontology success. This process is unstructured by nature, being a continuum from the initial discussion of the purpose to the first agreed conceptual representation. The inherent (inter) subjectivity of the process and their outcomes together with an excessive informality are perhaps the reasons for being overlooked in the literature. This paper proposes an approach integrating competency questions (CQ) and conceptual graphs to the support of domain experts and knowledge specialists in defining the purpose and fundamental conceptual commitments of the ontology to be developed. The approach was experimented and validated with experts in a project in the chemical-pharmaceutical industry.

Keywords: Collaborative ontology development; Competency Questions. Conceptual Graphs.

1   Introduction

Ontology engineering (OE) is a multipurpose scientific domain [1] concerned with the means to produce a well-defined account of a shared understanding (an ontology), typically used to promote knowledge management (KM) and facilitate knowledge sharing in networked environments. In order to develop ontologies is necessary to capture, organize, code and store domain relevant information in a systematic way. To cope with that, several methodologies have been developed [2]. Recently [3], there has been a paradigm shift, focused on collaboration and in the early stages of ontology development (the conceptualization phase), wherein domain experts (DE) assume a leading role producing semi-formal ontologies - here called lightweight ontology (LO) [4, 5]. LOs, allow poor computational processing and it only have non-inferable constructs, which means there is not a complete axiomatic definition of domain concepts and relations. To fully axiomatize a LO there is the need to formalized it using OWL and using Description Logic (DL), which is not affordable for a DE. They can only provide the relevant conceptual knowledge. Moreover, the need for a formal

R. Meersman et al. (Eds.): OTM 2014 Workshops, LNCS 8842, pp. 626–635, 2014.

ontology, in the sense of being fully axiomatized, is not the case in many situations (e.g. for structuring and maintaining knowledge bases information). So, the problem tackled in this paper might be posed as follows: how to assist DE to produce useful and reusable LO? This encloses two challenges: 1) the LO must conform to the intended needs and; 2) the LO must be rigorously defined, which means computational-ready and well-formed (compliant with a well defined representation scheme). Typically, the exact statement of the particular needs to be satisfied by the LO, might be addressed by the concept of competency questions (CQ). In fact, several research works have been investing on *CQ-based* approaches not only for ontology validation but also for building them from scratch [6, 7, 8, 9, 10]. Despite of valuable, they tend to focus on knowledge engineers or ontologists rather than DE [6][7], or it requires previous knowledge of specific semi-formal knowledge representations [8]. Others [9], beyond focusing on the ontology axiomatization, are using CQs but in an ad-hoc manner (using natural language). Some works share our vision that CQs "can have a clear structure and relatively simple syntactic pattern" [10], however their approach is too focused on creating OWL ontologies and are deeply committed to this particular application, violating one of the grubber's conceptualization principles [11].

Our CQ based approach can be distinguished from others in 4 main aspects: 1) CQs are used not only for LO specification and validation, but as an aid to its initial building; 2) the formulation of the CQ itself, is keyword-based rather than natural language-based. The experts are invited to, wittingly, think about the more appropriate keywords to formulate the questions (typically associated to candidate concepts and relations), rather writing CQs according to his own writing standards (or habits) and interpretations. A CQ catalog was implemented where a mapping between CQ's structure and the underlying semi-formal conceptual representations was defined based on the conceptual relations that each CQ type comprises; 3) CQs are "internally" represented according to the conceptual graphs (CG) structure [12], and; 4) the achieved CQ's conceptual representations, which define the LO, are further extended towards its completion by means terminological methods.

The paper is structured as follows: i) section 2 depicts the overall process of building LO driven by CQ; ii) section 3 discusses the evaluation of the current approach, ending with some short conclusions.

2   Build-to-Reuse Lightweight Ontologies

For an ontology to be useful and reusable is necessary to find a tradeoff between its commitment with the real world and the experts vision, in order to avoid either its under specification or over specification [11].   In other words, building useful ontologies means that they should be specified at the knowledge level [13] and represent what was initially intended to. Furthermore, for ontologies to be reusable they should not be too complex or overcommitted to a particular application [14] and its structure should be rigorously defined.

On pursuing straightforward mechanisms to stimulate DE involvement in the process of ontologies construction, the following approach was designed (Fig. 1), aiming at producing (re)usable ontologies for knowledge organization purposes (e.g. to capture, organize, categorize and maintaining knowledge bases information).

Due to space constraints, we will focus mainly on the inception phase of the process (the specification).

Generically, the process runs as follows: 1) CQs are formulated by means of the set of templates available in the CQ catalog and; 2) a transformation operation occurs, in order to convert CQs into semi-formal conceptual representations; 3) DE validate and the CQ's graphical representations, which are then represented (internally) under the CG formalism. After the formulation of the CQs and its acceptance by DE, the resulting conceptual structures can be extended with more concepts and relations by means terminological services, namely: i) extracting relevant terms from a previously organized corpus and; ii) retrieving contextual information according to existing concepts and queries (using the corpus). This aims at discovering new concepts and/or conceptual relations through specific lexical patterns [15].

2.1   Structured Formulation of Competency Questions

From our experience in previous projects, CQs should be easy to specify and clear to understand. Thus, in order to commit the experts to the task of specifying the goals for the ontology, fostering the development of concept-based queries, we followed a template-based approach to assist the formulation of each objective, based on typical query types and underlying patterns [16]. The identified patterns, can be associated to the form of the following query types: i) what; ii) why; iii) how and; iv) where. For each query type, one or more formulation patterns can be derived, corresponding to a typical abstract syntactic structure through which a CQ statement is obtained. The set of these patterns are made available through a CQ catalog in the form of templates used by DE experts to provide the fundamental keywords instead of a complete formulation of the CQ. This allows building simpler and unambiguous CQ sentences. From the CQ analysis is possible to establish a connection between query types and conceptual relation types, which each CQ purpose encloses [17].

Table 1. Query type vs. query purpose vs. conceptual relation (CR) type

Query type	Purpose	CR type	Examples of CR [18, 19]
What (which)	Used to represent or claim about the **'types and sub-types'** or **'parts and wholes'** of an entity that has a certain interaction with another specific entity.	Generic/specific relation or containment relation	type of, part of included, in, etc.
How	Used to represent or claim about what might be **used** to accomplish an action or function.	Usage relations	used by
Why	Used to represent or claim about what might be the **cause** (reason or motivation) through which some entity (or agent) accomplish/realize some action/function.	Causal relations	result of, caused by, etc.
Where	Used to represent or claim about what might be the local where a specific interaction between two entities occurs	Spatial relations	located at, next to, in, etc.

Furthermore, for each query type it was identified its typical structure - here called pattern - and the corresponding formal representation by means of conceptual graphs.

Types of competency questions (CQ)

The *"what/which"* query type, has the following pattern:

- **What/Which *<entity> <objectProperty | 'part of'>* <entity>*,** where: a) all information presented between "< >" is provided by domain expert when formulating the CQ; b) objectProperty – refers to a possible relation phrase, linking the object to another object. Typically corresponds to a verbal form. Users may choose from a predefined set of linking phases; c) entity - refers to an entity of the domain of the discourse. Typically corresponds to a noun; d) the "*" symbol means mandatory input and; c) the "|" symbol means a logical or. That is, either the user provides an arbitrary *objectProperty*, or it chooses specifically the "part of" label;

The typical CG representation of the what/which pattern is depicted bellow (Fig. 1, and it can be read as follows: which kind of *entities* interact by means of *objectProperty* with a specific domain entity?

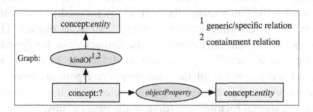

Fig. 1. The CQ What/Which pattern represented as a CG

In a CG linear form (textual) and according to the information provided by the DE, the "what/which" pattern may assume other two conceptual structures:

a) [concept:?] → (*Kind of*) → [concept: *entity*] → (*part of*) → [concept: *entity*], and read as follows: which kind of parts (*entity*) a whole (*another entty*) holds?

b) [concept:?] → (*Kind of*) → [concept: *entity*], and can be read as follows: what subtypes an *entity* holds?

Due to space restrictions, all the remaining CQ types patterns and conceptual structures are synthesized in the table bellow.

Table 2. CQ patterns and conceptual structure

Query type	Pattern	(Conceptual) Structure
How	Pattern	How <*'many'*	*'much'*> <*entity*> <*objectProperty*	*dataProperty* >* <*entity*>*
	CG form	[concept:?] → (*usage-relation*) → [concept:*] → (*objectProperty*) → [concept: *entity*]; [concept:?] → (*usage-relation*) → [concept:*entity*] → (*objectProperty*) → [concept: *entity*];

Table 2. (*continued*)

	Pattern	**Why <entity> <objectProperty >* < entity >***
	CG	[concept:*] → (*objectProperty*) → [concept:entity] → (*causal-relation*)
Why	form	→ [concept: ?];
		[concept: entity]→(*objectProperty*)→[concept: entity]→(*causal relation*)
		→ [concept: ?];
	Pattern	**Where < *entity* > <objectProperty >* < *entity* >***
	CG	[concept:?] → (spatial-relation) → [concept:*] → (objectProperty) →
Where	form	[concept: entity];
		[concept:?] → (spatial-relation) → [concept: entity] → (objectProperty)
		→ [concept: entity];

From the preceding table and the depicted patterns it is possible to derive five patterns for "how" CQ type. The "how much" variant, for instance, is related to an amount of something, regarding its value or importance, whereas the inclusion of a dataProperty is related to a specific characteristic of an entity. Thus, these three variants were disregarded once they intend to represent knowledge "out" of the domain conceptual level, that is, the identification and representation of concepts and they relationships. As for the "how many, its intention is focused in counting the number of specific concepts of the most generic concept (named as object). The interest of this variant is focused on the after conceptualisation activities for typical search purposes. Its interest as a competency question to define the goals of the conceptual model is limited. Furthermore, all the aforementioned patterns have an exception, which occurs when the objectProperty token encloses itself to a usage relation, a causal relation or a special relation according to the pattern "how", "why" or "where", respectively. In those cases the pattern reverts a "What/Which pattern" in its simpler form: [concept: object] → (objectProperty) → [concept:?]

2.2   CQ Graph Structure Formalization

As mentioned earlier a CQ can be represented as a CG and thus, described in a formal way.

Definition 1 - (CQ Vocabulary). CQ vocabulary is composed as:

- a single concept type designated by the term : concept;
- a set of conceptual relations (TR) corresponding to CRRM;
- a set of unordered query types , TQ = {"what", "how", "why", "where"};
- a set of conceptual markers I = {$t_1, t_2, ..., t_n$}, whose elements correspond to specific domain terms that can be used to designate specific concepts.

Definition 2 - (Assignment Relation). Assignment relation is a *surjective* relation given by function θ, which associates types of conceptual relations (r) to types of CQ queries (q), such as $\theta: T_R \longrightarrow T_Q$, where: $\forall q \in T_R, \exists r \in T_Q, \theta(q) = r$

Definition 3 - (Competency Question). A competency question (CQ) is a CG corresponding to a 4-tuple (C, R, E, ⋏), where:

- C, is triple of concept nodes {c1, c2, c3};
- R, is a tuple of relations {r1, r2};
- E, is a set of edges {e1, e2, e3, e4} connecting two disjoint sets C and R;
- λ, is a labeling function;

A concept node c is labeled as: (type(c), marker(c)), where type(c) is always "concept" and marker(c) corresponds to: i) the specific concept[1] we are focused in, in case of concept c1, and; ii) a domain term from I, in case of c2 and c3, where c3 is explicit indicated by experts and c2 may be any term from domain terminology represented by a generic concept.

A relation r is labeled as λ $(r) \in T_S \subseteq T_R$ (which is the same as type(r)), according to a source query q, whose type is given through the label function λ $(q) \in T_Q$ (which is the same as type (q)), where:

$$\forall q, \exists r_1, r_2 : \theta(\lambda(r_1)) = \begin{cases} GENERIC_{SPECIFIC\ TYPE}, & if\ \lambda(q) = WHAT_{TYPE} \\ CONTAINEMENT_{TYPE}, & if\ \lambda(q) = WHAT_{TYPE} \\ USAGE_{TYPE}, & if\ \lambda(q) = HOW_{TYPE} \\ CAUSE_{EFFECT\ T_{TYPE}}, & ,if\ \lambda(q) = WHY_{TYPE} \\ SPATIAL_{TYPE}, & if\ \lambda(q) = WHERE_{TYPE} \end{cases} \wedge \lambda(r_2) \in T_R;$$

An edge labeled i between a relation r and a concept c is denoted (r, i, c).

The conceptual structure is given by the edge labeling function and the underlying edge orientation, which depends, by its turn, on the CQ type and the underlying CG form (c.f. table 2).

3   Empirical Evaluation

3.1   Case Study Description and Research Design

A group of researchers, whose high level of expertise is well known in the domain of production planning and scheduling, was conducting a study towards the development of a decision-making tool for the chemical-pharmaceutical industry. The development of a tool to support planning is considered very challenging because of the complexity of the decision making process. In particular, the tool must integrate data sourced from distinct departments such as Sales, Research and Development, Procurement, and Production Planning, posing problems of information organization and retrieval. Information (or knowledge) organization models need thus to be understood and used in the same way by all the stakeholders of the decision-support tool. Due to the complexity of the decision and information models involved, decision-makers (DEs from our perspective) ended up spending a significant amount of time trying to understand and explain each other (several companies involved) the concepts and idiosyncrasies of the decisions and methods. This required some sort of representation of the concepts associated with the problem solving methods i.e., a conceptual model that could

---

[1] Represented graphically a question mark (?).

be used for the DEs to understand what methods are more suitable for a given planning problem. In research terms, we saw the opportunity to face this particular modeling challenge together with DEs by applying the approach described in this paper. The general goal was twofold: first, to identify the relations between concepts, structuring the concepts and developing a common comprehension of the existing knowledge. Second, to harmonize concepts targeting the generalization of the data structures to be used by the tool. DEs of this domain have been involved and validated the approach. To accomplish that, a participatory action-research [19] method was followed.

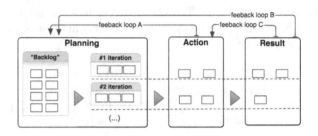

Fig. 2. Adopted action research scheme

Fig. 3 outlines how this study was structured and carried out. We call it an (agile) action research approach, comprising a planning phase, as well as, the action and result phase. During the planning phase it was defined how and when the group (DE and the researchers) would interact. The objectives were collected and introduced into the planning structure. Thus, the "backlog" contains the guidelines for the development of this case study, wherein each "backlog" item corresponds to a specific goal. Later the "backlog" items are reorganized and distributed by several iterations (or sprints). Each interaction contains one or more tasks in order to fulfill one or more goals. Either the "backlog" or the iterations can be readjusted according to the performance of the team during the action phase or the analysis of the results. This updates are represented by feedback loop A and B respectively. Feedback loop C occurs within each iteration. In this case, the researcher, as an observer, is able to perceive if the specialist feels some resistance or difficulty on performing his actions. Thus, it is provided, immediately, some additional information to unblock the process.

Three main goals were set for this real world experiment: 1) to validate the CQ query patterns; 2) to validate the transformation rules that convert semi-informal assertions into semi-formal conceptual representations, and; 3) to ascertain whether the designed method approach is capable of guiding experts onto the specification and production of conceptual representations from scratch. In order to evaluate these goals, four iterations were planned. In the first iteration the DE tried to formulate "what/which" CQs through a simple user interface. During the second iteration the DE were invited to formulate more complex questions such as "how" and "why" CQs. In both iterations, for each formulated CQ, a conceptual representation (in the form of concept map) with a short textual description was provided. It was the domain expert function to accept or reject the CQ after the analyses of the visual representation. This encloses a double check validation of the formulated queries. In a third iteration, the DE was confronted with the network of concepts created by the CQs raised by themselves. As the CQs complement each other, it was possible then to start forming a network of concepts. At this stage, the DE validates or rejects the proposed CQs interlinking.   The final iteration comprised the creation of a domain corpus with a short sample of documents (mainly scientific articles). Afterwards, terminological methods were used to: i) extract domain relevant terms and; ii) extract the contextual information for each concept within the network, in order to identify and retrieve possible concepts and conceptual relations to complete the ontology.

3.2   Research Results

During the real world experiment case study, it was produced about a dozen of CQs, of which a small subset is listed bellow (c.f. table 3).

Table 3. Sub-set of the formulated CQ

CQ type	Formulated query
What/which	Which kind of Characteristics are part of Planning Problems?
	Which are the types of Planning Problems?
How	How Industry addresses Planning Problems?
Why	Why MILP Methods ensure Optimal Solutions?
Where	Where Construction Industry uses MILP Methods?

After the CQ formulation, only one was rejected when the DEs were invited to check CQ's visual conceptual representations. This is an indicator that the transformation rules are correct and aligned with the structure of the different CQ types. Fig. 4 depicts a subset of CQ conceptual representations using the concept map notation. Note that the "which question" (e.g. "which means?") designating some of the concepts in the next images, refers to a placeholder to be substituted by the DEs.

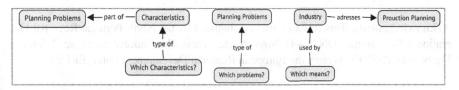

Fig. 3. Sub-set of CQ conceptual representations (concept map notation)

Having formulated all the CQs, the common terms were identified and merged forming a network of concepts. The DEs made no rejections at this stage. Finally, DEs proceeded to complete the conceptual model by retrieving the appropriate terms to designate the concepts initially represented by placeholders (e.g. *Which Characteristic?*). Terminological methods supported DEs to find occurrences, within domain corpus, that might indicate new concepts and/or conceptual relations to be included in the model. The result is evidenced in the picture bellow (Fig. 5), where the dashed boxes represent the concepts, whose designations were retrieved form corpus, indicating types of characteristics.

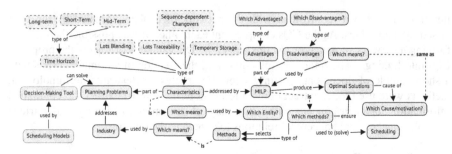

Fig. 4. Subset of the final conceptual representation

4   Conclusions

The approach presented in this paper proposes competency questions to support do-main conceptualization driven by domain experts. Considering the challenge on how non-knowledge engineers model a knowledge area in a standard and intuitive way, current preliminary results, showed evidence that our approach contributes for a sys-tematic manner of guiding experts on establishing conceptual commitments in the development of ontologies. In this action-research experiment we could observe that the semi-informal specification of CQs can be effective in overturning the initial bar-rier to build an ontology. This CQ-approach guides specialists through the know-ledge-level of a conceptualization, towards the development of "well-defined" lightweight ontologies. At the end almost all CQ queries were answered and domain experts knew exactly what was needed to complete the LO. Once the CQs, as well as the resulting conceptual representations are build and formalized into CG graph struc-tures, it is possible to apply well-defined CG operations [12] for reasoning and reus-ing purposes. Hereafter, new experiments will be designed in order to involve DE from other domains and to evaluate to which extent inference and CQs complemen-tarity rules support the evolvement of the ontology.

Acknowledgments. This research was co-financed by the North Portugal Regional Op-erational Programme (ON.2 – O Novo Norte), under the National Strategic Reference Framework (NSRF), through the European Regional Development Fund (ERDF).

References

1. Uschold, M., Gruninger, M., Uschold, M., Gruninger, M.: Ontologies: Principles, methods and applications. Knowledge Engineering Review 11, 93–136 (1996)
2. Corcho, O., Fernández-López, M., Gómez-Pérez, A.: Methodologies, tools and languages for building ontologies. Where is their meeting point? Data & Knowledge Engineer-ing 46(1), 41–64 (2003)
3. Pereira, C., Sousa, C., Soares, A.L.: Supporting conceptualisation processes in collabora-tive networks: a case study on an R&D project. International Journal of Computer In-tegrated Manufacturing 26(11), 1066–1086 (2013)

4. Chi, Y.L.: Elicitation synergy of extracting conceptual tags and hierarchies in textual document. Expert Systems with Applications 32(2), 349–357 (2007)
5. Giunchiglia, F., et al.: Lightweight Ontologies (2007)
6. Bezerra, C., Freitas, F., Santana, F.: Evaluating Ontologies with Competency Questions, pp. 284–285 (2013)
7. Zemmouchi-Ghomari, L., Ghomari, A.: Translating Natural Language Competency Questions into SPARQLQueries: A Case Study. Presented at the WEB 2013: The First International Conference on Building and Exploring Web Based Environments (2013)
8. Fernandes, P.C.B., Guizzardi, R.S.S., Guizzardi, G.: Using Goal Modeling to Capture Competency Questions in Ontology-based Systems. JIDM (3) (2011)
9. Malheiros, Y., Freitas, F.: A Method to Develop Description Logic Ontologies Iteratively Based on Competency Questions: an Implementation. In: ONTOBRAS, pp. 142–153 (2013)
10. Ren, Y., Parvizi, A., Mellish, C., Pan, J.Z., van Deemter, K., Stevens, R.: Towards Competency Question-Driven Ontology Authoring. In: Presutti, V., d'Amato, C., Gandon, F., d'Aquin, M., Staab, S., Tordai, A. (eds.) ESWC 2014. LNCS, vol. 8465, pp. 752–767. Springer, Heidelberg (2014)
11. Gruber, T.: Collective knowledge systems: Where the Social Web meets the Semantic Web. Web Semantics: Science, Services and Agents on the World Wide Web 6(1), 4–13 (2008)
12. Sowa, J.F.: Conceptual graphs as a universal knowledge representation. Computers & Mathematics with Applications 23(2), 75–93 (1992)
13. Uschold, M.: Knowledge Level Modelling: Concepts and Terminology. Knowl. Eng. Rev. 13(1), 5–29 (1998)
14. Shotton, D., Catton, C., Klyne, G.: Ontologies for Sharing, Ontologies for Use. Ontogenesis, http://ontogenesis.knowledgeblog.org/312
15. Sousa, C., Pereira, C., Soares, A.: Collaborative Elicitation of Conceptual Representations: A Corpus-Based Approach. In: Rocha, Á., Correia, A.M., Wilson, T., Stroetmann, K.A. (eds.) Advances in Information Systems and Technologies. AISC, vol. 206, pp. 111–124. Springer, Heidelberg (2013)
16. Cao, T.H., Mai, A.H.: Ontology-Based Understanding of Natural Language Queries Using Nested Conceptual Graphs. In: Croitoru, M., Ferré, S., Lukose, D. (eds.) ICCS 2010. LNCS, vol. 6208, pp. 70–83. Springer, Heidelberg (2010)
17. Nuopponen: Concept Relations: An update of a concept relation classification. Presented at the 7th International Conference on Terminology and Knowledge Engineering
18. Sousa, C., Soares, A., Pereira, C., Costa, R.: Supporting the identification of conceptual relations in semi-formal ontology development. In: ColabTKR at LREC (2012)
19. Baskerville, R., Myers, M.D.: Special issue on action research in information systems: making is research relevant to practice–foreword. MIS Q. 28(3), 329–335 (2004)

CoopIS 2014 PC Co-Chairs Message

CoopIS represents one of the most qualified and well-established international conferences positioned in a scientific area focusing on the engineering of information systems with a strong characterization on "Cooperation". It is then characterized by the cross fertilization of several disciplines, from information systems to service oriented architectures, from business processes and workflows to monitoring and application systems assessment.

CoopIS 2014, being part of the Federated Conferences "On The Move", this year has attracted 68 submissions that have been carefully evaluated by a massive review process that involved more than 80 PC Members who have produced more than 250 review reports. After the evaluation process we were able to select 24 full papers (with a selection rate of 35%), plus 2 short papers and 2 posters.

CoopIS 2014 has continued attracting important research results, amongst which the most represented research area is related to business process modeling and management covering various aspects, from the design phase and the process enactment (7 full papers) to behavioral similarity analysis (4 full papers). Connected to the latter, a group of 3 papers are concerned with process alignment. The second most popular topic concerns services and service-oriented computing (7 full papers), followed by methods for monitoring and assessment of processes (3 full papers). Other topics concern event-management and cooperative applications. Also the 3 short paper are concerned with process analysis. We believe that such a rich scientific program will provide an inspiring showcase of top researches going on in the mentioned areas.

Once more we wish to recall that the rich scientific program offered by CoopIS 2014 has been possible primarily thanks to the authors and their high quality papers, by the dedicated work of the Program Committee, and, last but not least, by the intense work of the OTM organization, in particular of Daniel Meersman and Jan Demey, with the wise supervision of Robert Meersman. We wish to recall that the scientific program is complemented by the Industrial Program chaired by Hervé Panetto.

September 2014

Michele Missikoff
Lin Liu
Oscar Pastor

A Workflow Execution Platform
for Collaborative Artifact-Centric Business Processes

Sira Yongchareon[1], Kan Ngamakeur[2], Chengfei Liu[2], Sivadon Chaisiri[3], and Jian Yu[4]

[1] Department of Computing and Information Technology
Unitec Institute of Technology, New Zealand
sira@maxsira.com
[2] Faculty of Science, Engineering and Technology
Swinburne University of Technology, Australia
{kngamakeur,cliu}@swin.edu.au
[3] School of Information Technology, Shinawatra University, Thailand
sivadon@ieee.org
[4] Auckland University of Technology
School of Computing and Mathematical Sciences, New Zealand
jian.yu@aut.ac.nz

Abstract. To execute an artifact-centric process model, current workflow execution approaches require it to be converted to some existing executable language (e.g., BPEL) in order to run on a workflow system. We argue that the transformation can incur losses of information and degrade traceability. In this paper, we proposed and developed a workflow execution platform that directly executes a collaborative (i.e., inter-organizational) workflow specification of artifact-centric business processes without performing model conversion.

1 Introduction

An artifact-centric process modeling approach has emerged to provide an alternative approach for specifying a business process. The approach focuses on describing how business-relevant key data entities, known as "*artifacts*", evolve in a business process [7]. IBM [5, 7] has developed an operational modeling framework which consists of three components: *artifacts*, *services*, and *associations* (between artifacts and services) and proposed a Guard-Stage-Milestone (GSM) approach to modeling artifact-centric processes [12]. Current workflow execution approaches require an artifact-centric model to be transformed to an executable activity-centric process language (e.g., BPEL) in order to run on existing workflow systems (e.g., in [9, 15, 17]). We argue that the model conversion incurs losses of information and affects traceability and monitoring ability of workflow [16], especially in a collaborative environment where the workflow span across multiple inter-business entities. We found several technical challenges such as executable model specification, workflow coordination, and data access/management that need to be addressed when developing a system to support execution of artifact-centric models in a distributed environment.

R. Meersman et al. (Eds.): OTM 2014 Workshops, LNCS 8842, pp. 639–643, 2014.
© Springer-Verlag Berlin Heidelberg 2014

To address the challenges, we developed an artifact-centric workflow execution platform for collaborative artifact-centric processes based on using view-based artifact-centric approach [2, 4] on service-oriented and event-driven architectures.

2   Artifact-Centric Collaboration Execution Framework

An artifact-centric process model can be constructed using *artifacts, their life cycles* and *interactions* [4]. To achieve goals of a collaborative process, all organizations in the collaboration must develop and agree on a mutual contract for them to progressively operate towards the goals [3]. Here, we model artifact-centric processes by using the *Artifact-Centric Collaboration Model* [2] and the view-based approach presented in [1]. Two types of artifacts are used to model collaboration or the contract: (1) *local artifact* and (2) *shared artifact. Local artifacts* are owned and accessed by one organization to support the coordination between its local business processes and the inter-organizational processes. *Shared artifacts* are defined as a contract between participating organizations where it contains business stages to capture progress of the process toward the completion of the collaborative process. We illustrate architecture of our Artifact-Centric Collaboration (ACC) Execution Framework and its platform in Fig. 1 and Fig. 2, respectively.

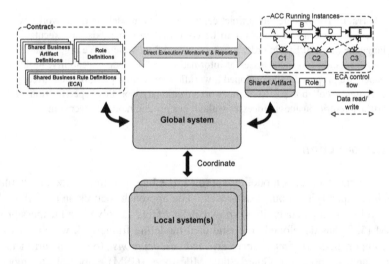

Fig. 1. Artifact-Centric Collaboration (ACC) Execution framework

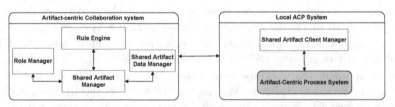

Fig. 2. Architecture of workflow execution platform for ACC

The platform utilizes event-driven and service-oriented architectures to design and implement the centralized controller to support distributed execution across organizations based on using a set of shared artifacts and shared business rules to govern interaction between organizations [2, 4, 13]. The platform comprises of an *Artifact-centric collaboration (ACC)* system and *local ACP* system(s). The local ACP system is designed to run in each participating organization. The ACP system is extended from the system presented in [8, 16] with a *Shared artifact client manager* to support execution of shared artifacts in a collaboration. The ACC system acts as a central controller and it consists of four components: *shared artifact manager, rule engine, role manager,* and *shared artifact data manager*. *Shared Artifact Manager* provides management functionality to ensure each contract running in the execution is created, managed and updated correctly. *Rule Engine* is to deliver functionality of rule evaluation. The rule engine serves as a central controller to coordinate internal and external operations of each component in the platform. *Role Manager* is to handle a task that is allocated to each role involved in a particular business process. *Shared Artifact Data Manager* performs a task of updating these shared artifacts. In a local ACP system, *Shared Artifact Client Manager* is designed to address communication between the central controller and local systems. Its main functionality is to receive and pass messages issued by the controller to a local system and also detect status of process execution of the local system and notify the controller regarding completion of a task or a session of the local system in a synchronized manner. A *coordination contract* is implemented in the ACC system for correct and consistent coordination between the global system and all local systems. Our platform is available at [19].

3   Related Work Discussion and Conclusion

This paper proposed a platform for executing collaborative artifact-centric business processes. Cohn and Hull [7] illustrated that IBM has used BELA tool to map an artifact-centric process model into an executable model (e.g., BPEL) that can run on IBM's WebSphere Process Server. Cohn et al. [10] proposed a system called Sienna to support execution of Finite-State-Machine lifecycles for artifacts. Barcelona [18] supports the execution of artifact models with Guard-Stage-Milestone (GSM). Sienna and Barcelona require ACSI Interoperation Hub [6] to support interoperation between enterprises. However, both of their systems are not publicly available at this stage, therefore we are not able test and evaluate them. G. Liu et al [9] proposed an artifact-centric workflow model, namely ArtiFlow, with a technique to translate ArtiFlow to a BPEL specification to run on a BPEL engine. Their prototype was developed and presented in [15, 17]. To support a dynamic runtime modification, Xu et al. [11] developed a hybrid model called EZ-Flow based on the ArtiFlow to gain advantages of both declarative and procedural natures. Compared with our approach, we execute an artifact-centric model without converting the model to an activity-centric model. Moreover, our system can record all running artifacts as specified in the artifact-centric model, therefore tracking can be achieved not only at the process level but also at the artifact level. Marinoiu et al. [14] developed AXART system to manage the updates of Active XML (AXML) models with embedded function/Web service calls.

Compared with our work, artifacts, rules, and services are defined as separate components. Thus, those components are less coupled and can be more effectively managed. Russo et al. [20] proposed Data Centric Dynamic Systems to execute data-centric processes. The system uses a business rule engine to control an action that updates the state of data. However, their concept of the life cycle is not incorporated and there is no discussion on execution of inter-organizational processes.

In the future, we will improve our system prototype in several areas, e.g., run-time verification, exception handling, and change management.

References

1. Yongchareon, S., Liu, C.: A Process View Framework for Artifact-Centric Business Processes. In: Meersman, R., Dillon, T.S., Herrero, P. (eds.) OTM 2010. LNCS, vol. 6426, pp. 26–43. Springer, Heidelberg (2010)
2. Yongchareon, S., Liu, C., Zhao, X.: An Artifact-Centric View-Based Approach to Modeling Inter-organizational Business Processes. In: Bouguettaya, A., Hauswirth, M., Liu, L. (eds.) WISE 2011. LNCS, vol. 6997, pp. 273–281. Springer, Heidelberg (2011)
3. Van Der Aalst, W.M.P., Lohmann, N., Masuthe, P., Stahl, C., Wolf, K.: Multipart Contracts: Agreeing and Implementing Interorganizational Processes. The Computer Journal 53(1), 90–106
4. Yongchareon, S., Liu, C., Yu, J., Zhao, X.: A View Framework for Modeling and Change Validation of Artifact-Centric Inter-Organizational Business Processes. To appear in Information Systems (2014), doi:10.1016/j.is.2014.07.004
5. Bhattacharya, K., Hull, R., Su, J.: A data-centric design methodology for business processes. In: Handbook of Research on Business Process Modeling (2009)
6. Hull, R., Narendra, N.C., Nigam, A.: Facilitating Workflow Interoperation Using Artifact-Centric Hubs. In: Baresi, L., Chi, C.-H., Suzuki, J. (eds.) ICSOC-ServiceWave 2009. LNCS, vol. 5900, pp. 1–18. Springer, Heidelberg (2009)
7. Cohn, D., Hull, R.: Business artifacts: A data-centric approach to modeling business operations and processes. IEEE Data Engineering Bulletin 32(3), 3–9 (2009)
8. Yongchareon, S., Liu, C., Zhao, X., Xu, J.: An Artifact-Centric Approach to Generating Web-Based Business Process Driven User Interfaces. In: Chen, L., Triantafillou, P., Suel, T. (eds.) WISE 2010. LNCS, vol. 6488, pp. 419–427. Springer, Heidelberg (2010)
9. Liu, G., Liu, X., Qin, H., Su, J., Yan, Z., Zhang, L.: Automated Realization of Business Workflow Specification. In: Dan, A., Gittler, F., Toumani, F. (eds.) ICSOC/ServiceWave 2009. LNCS, vol. 6275, pp. 96–108. Springer, Heidelberg (2010)
10. Cohn, D., Dhoolia, P., Heath III, F., Pinel, F., Vergo, J.: Siena: From PowerPoint to Web App in 5 Minutes. In: Bouguettaya, A., Krueger, I., Margaria, T. (eds.) ICSOC 2008. LNCS, vol. 5364, pp. 722–723. Springer, Heidelberg (2008)
11. Xu, W., Su, J., Yan, Z., Yang, J., Zhang, L.: An artifact-centric approach to dynamic modification of workflow execution. In: Meersman, R., et al. (eds.) OTM 2011, Part I. LNCS, vol. 7044, pp. 256–273. Springer, Heidelberg (2011)
12. Hull, R., et al.: Introducing the guard-stage-milestone approach for specifying business entity lifecycles (Invited talk). In: Bravetti, M., Bultan, T. (eds.) WS-FM 2010. LNCS, vol. 6551, pp. 1–24. Springer, Heidelberg (2011)
13. Yongchareon, S., Liu, C., Zhao, X.: A Framework for Behavior-Consistent Specialization of Artifact-Centric Business Processes. In: Barros, A., Gal, A., Kindler, E. (eds.) BPM 2012. LNCS, vol. 7481, pp. 285–301. Springer, Heidelberg (2012)

14. Marinoiu, B., Abiteboul, S., Bourhis, P., Galland, A.: AXART – Enabling collaborative work with AXML artifacts. In: Proc. VLDB Endowment (2010)
15. Zhao, D., Liu, G., Wang, Y., Gao, F., Li, H., Zhang, D.: A-Stein: A prototype for artifact-centric business process management systems. In: BMEI 2011, vol. 1, pp. 247–250 (2011)
16. Ngamakeur, K., Yongchareon, S., Liu, C.: A Framework for Realizing Artifact-Centric Business Processes in Service-Oriented Architecture. In: Lee, S.-g., Peng, Z., Zhou, X., Moon, Y.-S., Unland, R., Yoo, J. (eds.) DASFAA 2012, Part I. LNCS, vol. 7238, pp. 63–78. Springer, Heidelberg (2012)
17. Zhao, D., Liu, G., Jiang, Y., Gao, F., Wang, Y.: The execution and detection of artifact-centric business process. In: IEEE International Conference on Computer Science and Automation Engineering, vol. 4, pp. 491–495. IEEE Press, Shanghai (2011)
18. Heath III, F(T.), Boaz, D., Gupta, M., Vaculín, R., Sun, Y., Hull, R., Limonad, L.: Barcelona: A Design and Runtime Environment for Declarative Artifact-Centric BPM. In: Basu, S., Pautasso, C., Zhang, L., Fu, X. (eds.) ICSOC 2013. LNCS, vol. 8274, pp. 705–709. Springer, Heidelberg (2013)
19. Ngamakeur, K., Yongchareon, S.: ACC & ACP systems prototype (2014), https://sites.google.com/site/maxsirayongchareon/artifact-s
20. Russo, A., Diag, S., Mecella, M., Patrizi, F., Montali, M.: Implementing and Running Data-Centric Dynamic Systems. In: The 6th IEEE International Conference on Service-Oriented Computing and Applications, pp. 225–232 (2013)

Towards Simple and Robust Automation of Sustainable Supply Chain Communication

Gregor Grambow, Nicolas Mundbrod, Jens Kolb, and Manfred Reichert

Institute of Databases and Information Systems
Ulm University, Germany
{gregor.grambow,nicolas.mundbrod,jens.kolb,manfred.reichert}@uni-ulm.de
http://www.uni-ulm.de/dbis

Abstract. In supply chains, companies are forced to produce in a more sustainable way. Amongst others, this involves the reporting of various sustainability indicators to legal entities. To gather necessary data from their suppliers, companies must employ long-running, cross-organizational data collection processes. Being dependent on many companies and contextual factors such processes imply great variability, are manually managed, and tend to be tedious and error prone. This paper proposes an approach for automated contextual process configuration that also supports humans with lightweight, correct modeling and execution of configurable processes.

Keywords: Process Configuration, Business Process Variability, Data Collection, Sustainability, Supply Chain.

1 Introduction

In many domains of modern industry, sustainability has become increasingly important. Companies are forced by legal regulations and customer demands to a more sustainable production. This involves the reporting of various sustainability indicators, such as the amount of lead in a certain product. However, in a supply chain, this becomes a challenge as most products are the result of the collaboration of multiple companies. Consequently, reporting companies must employ long-running, cross-organizational data collection processes to obtain required indicators from their suppliers as well. Furthermore, as sustainability is an emerging topic, most companies do not have a standardized approach to such reporting. Thus, the latter still is tedious and error prone.

In the SustainHub[1] project, we have identified a set of core challenges for such data collection processes by investigating use cases from companies in the electronics and automotive domain. The first challenge concerns the selection of the parties involved. As reporting is manually managed, it is often not clear, which suppliers or service providers need to be involved for retrieving a certain

---

[1] SustainHub (Project No.283130) is a collaborative project within the 7th Framework Programme of the European Commission (Topic ENV.2011.3.1.9-1, Eco-innovation).

R. Meersman et al. (Eds.): OTM 2014 Workshops, LNCS 8842, pp. 644–647, 2014.
© Springer-Verlag Berlin Heidelberg 2014

indicator. Furthermore, as different companies employ different approaches, data formats, and reporting tools, getting access to the data is often problematic. Being dependent on a myriad of contextual influences, each data collection process is almost unique. Thus, usually, many variants of the same request exist usually that cannot be reused. Moreover, the meta data, on which these variants depend, is mostly managed implicitly and thus obscure (see [1] for more information on these challenges).

2   A Process-Based Approach for Data Collection

In the SustainHub project, we are developing an approach to support such data collection in a semi-automated fashion. As basis for this approach, we realize the data collection processes through explicitly modeled processes enacted in a PAIS (Process-Aware Information System). Thus, a set of issues can already be dealt with as the processes are now explicit and repeatable, and the PAIS automatically manages the different manual and automatic activities involved. However, still many open issues remain. Therefore, we build a system comprising additional components as illustrated in the upper part of Fig. 1.

The central component of our approach is a *process configuration component* that extends pre-defined base processes with pre-defined process fragments. To enable this in alignment with the context and meta data of the respective situation, we add a *context mapping component* as well as a comprehensive data model. Thus, it becomes possible to map various contextual factors into the SustainHub system and use them as parameters for process configuration to automatically generate process instances matching the properties of the respective situation.

However, to enable such a flexible automated approach, users must be able to pre-model many aspects involved in process configuration as illustrated in the lower part of Fig. 1. This comprises concepts for the context mapping: we apply *context factors* to capture contextual data. In turn, these can be mapped via *context rules* to a stable set of *process parameters* used as input for process configuration. The process configuration component employs *bases processes* and *process fragments*. The former are used as basis for a data collection process, while the latter are applied to extend that process situationally (see [2] for more details).

All entities based on these concepts have to be modeled correctly by users. To support this, we have introduced comprehensive correctness checks and put focus on keeping our approach as simple as possible. The first building block to achieve this is keeping the modeling of both base processes and process fragments directly in the PAIS. So the modeling is understandable and the processes can be checked by the PAIS automatically. In addition, users only have to model entities based on the three introduced context mapping concepts a small number of other entities for process configuration that govern where exactly to insert the fragments into the base processes. For both parts, we have also added correctness checks to ensure that only correct models come to execution.

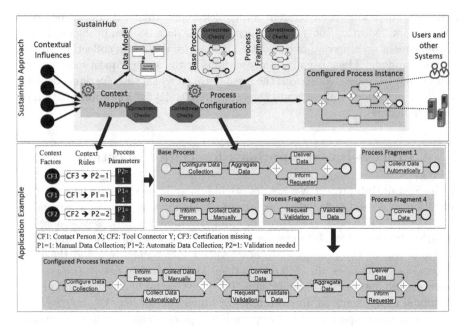

Fig. 1. Configurable Data Collection Approach in SustainHub

The lower part of Fig. 1 shows a simplified example of such a configuration use case from the industry: An automotive company wants to collect sustainability data relating to the quantity of lead contained in a specific product. This concerns two of the companies suppliers that deliver parts of that product. One is a bigger company with a dedicated system for managing sustainability data in place. The other is a smaller company with no system and no dedicated responsible for sustainability. For the smaller company, a service provider is needed that will validate the manually collected data ensuring its compliance with legal regulations. The system of the bigger company has its own data format that has to be explicitly converted in order to be usable. As depicted in Fig. 1, we apply three context factors to model that situation. These are mapped to values for two process parameters leading to the selection of four process fragments. Two of these are used for automatic and manual data collection while the two others enable external validation and data conversion. All fragments are integrated automatically into the base process to obtain a configured process instance. The latter first executes the data collection activities for both companies in parallel. After that, again in parallel, the data of one company is converted, while the data of the other company is validated externally.

3 Related Work

Various approaches for process variability exist. One aspect is the extension of process modeling languages to enable configurable process models [3]. Other approaches like [4] target meta-modeling of various different aspects for process variability. Process fragments and their modeling, in particular, have been the focus of research, as in [5]. Finally, the automated composition of executable processes from pre-defined process fragments has also been shown in approaches like [6]. These approaches cover many areas of the process variability topic comprehensively. However, none of them has taken the context and users as our approach into account. The latter not only enables automated contextual process composition but also easy and error free modeling.

4 Conclusion

In this paper, we have sketched an approach for automated contextual process configuration. The latter not only enables the automatic processing of context data and the automatic composition of executable processes, it also puts focus on the users interacting with our system. Thus, we have created a lightweight way of modeling all necessary concepts and integrated a comprehensive set of correctness checks to support them. We have further applied this approach for complex data collection processes to supply chain communication in two domains. As part of future work we plan to extend our approach with runtime variability features and applying it in a comprehensive industrial evaluation.

Acknowledgement. The project SustainHub (Project No.283130) is sponsored by the EU in the 7th Framework Programme of the European Commission (Topic ENV.2011.3.1.9-1, Eco-innovation).

References

1. Grambow, G., Mundbrod, N., Steller, V., Reichert, M.: Challenges of Applying Adaptive Processes to Enable Variability in Sustainability Data Collection. In: SIM-PDA 2013, pp. 74–88 (2013)
2. Grambow, G., Mundbrod, N., Steller, V., Reichert, M.: Towards Configurable Data Collection for Sustainable Supply Chain Communication. In: CAiSE 2014 Forum. CEUR Workshop Proceedings, CEUR-WS.org (June 2014)
3. Ayora, C., Torres, V., Weber, B., Reichert, M., Pelechano, V.: Vivace: A Framework for the Systematic Evaluation of Variability Support in Process-Aware Information Systems. Information and Software Technology (May 2014)
4. Saidani, O., Nurcan, S.: Business Process Modeling: A Multi-perspective Approach Integrating Variability. In: Bider, I., Gaaloul, K., Krogstie, J., Nurcan, S., Proper, H.A., Schmidt, R., Soffer, P. (eds.) BPMDS 2014 and EMMSAD 2014. LNBIP, vol. 175, pp. 169–183. Springer, Heidelberg (2014)
5. Eberle, H., Leymann, F., Schleicher, D., Schumm, D., Unger, T.: Process Fragment Composition Operations. In: Proceedings of APSCC 2010, pp. 1–7. IEEE Xplore (December 2010)
6. Murguzur, A., De Carlos, X., Trujillo, S., Sagardui, G.: Context-Aware Staged Configuration of Process Variants@Runtime. In: Jarke, M., Mylopoulos, J., Quix, C., Rolland, C., Manolopoulos, Y., Mouratidis, H., Horkoff, J. (eds.) CAiSE 2014. LNCS, vol. 8484, pp. 241–255. Springer, Heidelberg (2014)

ODBASE 2014 PC Co-Chairs Message

We are delighted to present the proceedings of the 13th International Conference on Ontologies, DataBases, and Applications of Semantics (ODBASE) which was held in Amantea (Italy) 27-31 October 2014. The ODBASE Conference series provides a forum for research and practitioners on the use of ontologies and data semantics in novel applications, and continues to draw a highly diverse body of researchers and practitioners. ODBASE is part of the OnTheMove (OTM 2014) federated event composed of three interrelated yet complementary scientific conferences that together attempt to span a relevant range of the advanced research on, and cutting-edge development and application of, information handling and systems in the wider current context of ubiquitous distributed computing. The other two co-located conferences are CoopIS'14 (Cooperative Information Systems) and C&TC'14 (Cloud and Trusted Computing '14). Of particular relevance to ODBASE 2014 are papers that bridge traditional boundaries between disciplines such as databases, social networks, mobile systems, artificial intelligence, information retrieval, and computational linguistics.

This year, we received 47 paper submissions and had a program committee of 40 dedicated colleagues, including researchers and practitioners from diverse research areas. Special arrangements were made during the review process to ensure that each paper was reviewed by 3-4 members of different research areas. The result of this effort is the selection of high quality papers: fifteen regular papers (32%), ten short papers (21%), and four posters (9%). Their themes included studies and solutions to a number of modern challenges such as querying and management of linked data and RDF documents, ontology engineering, semantic matching and mapping, social network analysis, semantic web services, and streaming data. The scientific program is complemented with a very interesting keynote speech by Domenico Saccà on Mining and Posting Big Data on the Web.

We would like to thank all the members of the Program Committee for their hard work in selecting the papers and for helping to make this conference a success. We would also like to thank all the researchers who submitted their work. Last but not least, special thanks go to the members of the OTM team for their support and guidance.

We hope that you enjoy ODBASE 2014 and have a wonderful time in Amantea!

September 2014

Alfredo Cuzzocrea
Timos Sellis

PerGO: An Ontology towards Model Driven Pervasive Game Development

Hong Guo, Hallvard Trætteberg, Alf Inge Wang, and Shang Gao

Department of Computer and Information Science,
Norwegian University of Science and Technology
Trondheim, Norway
{guohong,hal,alfw,shanggao}@idi.ntnu.no

Abstract. Model Driven Software Development (MDSD) & Domain Specific Modeling (DSM) are means to overcome software development challenges like increased software complexity and shortened development cycle in many domains. However, in the computer game domain it is not widely and successfully applied yet since it is not easy to understand the complex domain knowledge and use the knowledge to develop qualified DSM solutions. These difficulties can be alleviated by a deep and thorough domain analysis. In our research, we proposed an ontology to structure and accelerate the domain analysis process. To make our work more concrete, we focus on the emerging pervasive (computer) game genre.

Keywords: MDSD, DSM, Ontology, Domain Analysis, Pervasive Game.

1   Introduction

The Model Driven Software Development (MDSD) field has given birth to Domain Specific Language (DSL) which formally represents domain solutions using high level concepts which are close to the problem domain. DSL development usually takes four stages (decision, analysis, design, and implementation)[1]. Among them, domain analysis provides crucial information for the DSL construction, but has not received as much attention as consequent stages. Few DSLs (only four out of 39 as evaluated in [1]) utilized more formal domain analysis such as FAST (Family-Oriented Abstractions, Specification, and Translation) [2] and FODA (Feature Oriented Domain Analysis) [3]. The formal domain analysis showed good language design result but the usage of these approaches are still limited [4, 5]. Researchers investigated Ontology Based Domain Analysis (OBDA) [4] considering ontologies are closer than its original domains and provide effective way to reuse the domain knowledge in traditional domain engineering [6]. In this paper, we present our trial in model driven game development domain. To make our work more concrete, instead of general computer games, we focus on pervasive (computer) games. Such kind of games are emerging and attracting more and more interests recently due to the involvement of physical and social elements in the virtual game world as well as development in sensor and mobile technology. Well known pervasive games are like

R. Meersman et al. (Eds.): OTM 2014 Workshops, LNCS 8842, pp. 651–654, 2014.

"Epidemic Menace [7]", and "Capture the Flag [8]". Typical pervasive games have features such as location awareness, using physical user interfaces, mobility and long lasting. In this paper, we introduce an ontology for pervasive games (PerGO), and a procedure based on it to structure and accelerate the domain analysis process.

2   Pervasive Game Ontology (PerGO) Formalism

PerGO is designed to serve for a structured and efficient domain analysis. The motivation behind PerGO is to pre-define a number of commonly used concepts (as well as the relationships among them) within the pervasive game domain, and provide a structured way to use these concepts to produce domain analysis outputs, and construct DSM artefacts afterwards. We choose UML class diagram as the language [9] to formalize our ontology. This is primarily because our ontology will be further used to construct DSL meta-models which are often based on class diagrams as well. And UML class diagram contains all the standard hierarchical relations [10] (classification, aggregation, generalization and association) that we need to describe relationships among concepts.

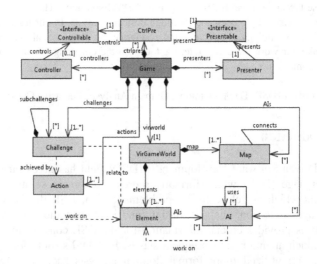

Fig. 1. Core Part of PerGO

There are in total more than 100 concepts in PerGO, and they are organized in 6 perspectives which focus on different aspects of game software separately. These perspectives are identified based on the useful channels to find DSL concepts [11] and our current research focus. These perspectives are Gameplay (challenges and actions), Artificial Intelligence (AI), Virtual Game World, Control, Presentation, and CtrlPresentation (abstraction for logic which is in charge of flexible user interfaces like physical user interfaces). On the other hand, there are two kinds of concepts within PerGO: high-level concepts which are common to all computer games and low-level concepts which are specific to pervasive games (primarily used or often used by pervasive games). While high level concepts constitute the core part of PerGO (as shown in Figure 1), low level concepts are derived from the high level concepts and constitute the pervasive part of PerGO. For instance, Figure 2 presents the pervasive game concepts in Presentation perspective. These concepts are about how to present the game world status outwards to the players and the physical world. For example, MakeCall which derives from PhyPre means making a phone call physically.

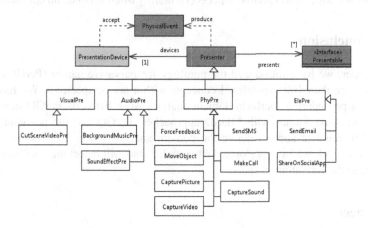

Fig. 2. Pervasive Game Concepts in Presentation Perspective

3 Domain Analysis Procedure Based on PerGO

A four steps (domain analysis) procedure is proposed in order to produce outputs of domain analysis based on PerGO. There are three major outputs that are usually produced by domain analysis: a domain vocabulary, commonality space, and variability space. Table 1 is used for us to collect such information.

Table 1. Domain Analysis Table

Perspective	Concept	Commonality Details	Variability Details

The four steps are proposed as:

1. Quickly identify perspectives that are related to current domain, and record them in the first column;
2. Go through the perspectives in the first column. For each of them, consider corresponding common game design, then select useful concepts from PerGO or derive more specific concepts for the domain based on PerGO to stand for these design. Record the concepts in the second column and more detailed information like some attributes in the third column if there are;

3. Similar to step 2), go through the perspectives in the first column. Consider about variable game design that may be used in different game samples and add new concepts (within PerGO or newly invented) that are needed in the second column;
4. Go through all the concepts in the second column, write attributes or relationships that can be used to support the variable game design in the last column.

The four steps help analyzers to consider in a reasonable order: from general aspects (perspectives) to concrete aspects (concepts, attributes, and relationships), and from common aspects to variable aspects (variability often depends on commonality).

4   Conclusion

In this paper, we have introduced the ontology for pervasive games (PerGO) which contains more than 100 pre-defined concepts within six perspectives. We have also proposed a procedure to perform domain analysis work based on PerGO in order to develop pervasive games with MDSD approaches. PerGO and the procedure were designed to regulate and accelerate the domain analysis work. To demonstrate and evaluate our work we have performed case studies and will report the results in future work due to the limitation of space.

References

1. Mernik, M., Heering, J., Sloane, A.M.: When and how to develop domain-specific languages. ACM Comput. Surv. 37(4), 316–344 (2005)
2. Pohl, K., Böckle, G., Van Der Linden, F.: Software Product Line Engineering, vol. 10, pp. 3–540. Springer (2005)
3. Kang, K.C., Cohen, S.G., Hess, J.A., Novak, W.E., Peterson, A.S.: Feature-Oriented Domain Analysis (FODA) Feasibility Study (November 1990)
4. Tairas, R., Mernik, M., Gray, J.: Using ontologies in the domain analysis of domain-specific languages. Springer (2009)
5. Ceh, I., et al.: Ontology driven development of domain-specific languages. Computer Science and Information Systems 8(2), 317–342 (2011)
6. Falbo, R.d.A., Guizzardi, G., Duarte, K.C.: An ontological approach to domain engineering. In: Proceedings of the 14th International Conference on Software Engineering and Knowledge Engineering, ACM (2002)
7. Lindt, I., et al.: A report on the crossmedia game epidemic menace. Computers in Entertainment (CIE) 5(1) (2007)
8. Cheok, A.D., et al.: Capture the flag: mixed-reality social gaming with smart phones. IEEE Pervasive Computing 5(2), 62–69 (2006)
9. Denny, M.: Ontology building: A survey of editing tools. In: XML.com (2002)
10. Krogstie, J.: Model-based development and evolution of information systems: A Quality Approach. Springer (2012)
11. Kelly, S., Tolvanen, J.-P.: Domain-Specific Modeling Enabling Full Code Generation. John Wiley & Sons, Inc. (2008)

Toward an Arabic Ontology for Arabic Word Sense Disambiguation Based on Normalized Dictionaries

Nadia Soudani[1,2], Ibrahim Bounhas[1,3], Bilel ElAyeb[4,5], and Yahya Slimani[1,6]

[1] LISI Laboratory of Computer Science for Industrial Systems, INSAT, Tunisia
[2] Faculty of Sciences of Tunis (FST), University of Tunis El Manar, Tunisia
Nadia.soudani@gmail.com
[3] Higher Institute of Documentation (ISD), University of Manouba, Tunisia
Bounhas.Ibrahim@gmail.com
[4] RIADI Laboratory, National School of Computer Science (ENSI),
Universiy of Manouba, Tunisia
[5] Emirates College of Technology, P.O. Box: 41009. Abu Dhabi, Émirats Arabes Unis
Bilel.Elayeb@riadi.rnu.tn
[6] Higher Institute of Multimedia Arts of Manouba (ISAMM), University of Manouba, Tunisia
Yahya.Slimani@fst.rnu.tn

Abstract. In this paper, we propose an approach for constructing Arabic Ontology based on normalized dictionaries. This approach mainly consists in transforming non structured Arabic dictionaries into LMF (Lexical Markup Framework) based-normalized ones. We are basically exploiting Arabic dictionaries of Hadith for experimentation. Then, from an Arabic normalized dictionary of Hadith, an ontology will be constructed. It represents hidden knowledge in Hadith texts. It will be next integrated into an information retrieval and navigation system. We will take advantage of it to semantically disambiguate Arabic terms of both the formulated user query and/or the Arabic texts with application on texts of Hadith.

Keywords: Arabic language-Arabic Dictionary-LMF-Arabic Ontology- Word Sense Disambiguation-Query Reformulation- Information Retrieval System.

1 Introduction

Arabic Language is characterized by its richness in different levels of Automatic Natural language Processing [4]. It is agglutinative, derivational and inflectional. This makes the NLP of Arabic linguistic Resources so difficult because of Arabic terms ambiguity. In addition, the NLP of the Arabic Language is suffering from the lack of linguistic resources as Corpus, Dictionaries, Ontologies and Standards of Test [4,5,6][8]. Nevertheless, the existing resources as electronic dictionaries aren't exhaustive and non standardized. Also, Arabic linguistic resources are rich with hidden knowledge. However, interrogated resources aren't mined and they aren't deeply explored by Information Retrieval tools to extract and use hidden knowledge. These problems are especially recognized with the advent of the semantic web.

R. Meersman et al. (Eds.): OTM 2014 Workshops, LNCS 8842, pp. 655–658, 2014.
© Springer-Verlag Berlin Heidelberg 2014

Among these important resources, we detect Corpus of Hadith. They are characterized by a complex structure rich with hidden knowledge. Their exploit by Information retrieval tools is still insignificant. Then, research tools based on these Corpus, don't consider the semantic aspect of text of Hadith for both the query and the documents of Corpus. This is what we aim in our actual work. A need for use of Arabic dictionaries of Hadith is remarkably noticed to identify and treat senses of terms of Hadith. In this paper, we propose a generic approach for the process of normalization of these dictionaries leading to ontology to be integrated in the search tool for Arabic Word Sense Disambiguation. This work is still in progress.

2   Machine Readable - Dictionaries of Hadith

To determine the concepts of the ontology and which are corresponding to the terms of Hadith, it is necessary to use dictionaries of Hadith. The following list describes the principle dictionaries of Hadith from the existing ones and which are in a machine readable format:

- المعجم المفهرس لألفاظ الحديث النبوي (Al-MuâjaAl-Mufahres Li-Alfadh Al-Hadith Al-Nabawi)
- الفائق في غريب الحديث للزمخشري (Al-Faiq Fi-Gharib Al-Hadith for Zamakhchari)
- النهاية في غريب الحديث والأثر (Al-Nihaya Fi-Gharib Al-Hadith wAl-Athar)
- معجم لغة الفقهاء (Muaâjam   lughat Al-Fuqahaâ)
- إعراب ما يشكل من ألفاظ الحديث النبوي (Iârab Ma Yuchkal Men Alfadh Al-Hadith Al-Nabawi)

We have chosen both the two dictionaries « النهاية في غريب الحديث و الأثر» (Al-Nihaya fi Gharib Al-Hadith w Al-Athar) and معجم لغة الفقهاء (Muâjam Lughat Al-Fuqahaâ). But, we first process our experimentation on « النهاية في غريب الحديث و الأثر» (Al-Nihaya fi Gharib Al-Hadith w Al-Athar).

3   Generic Proposed Approach

This proposed approach draws a general schema to follow. It represents a linear process where all its steps interact by input and output flows. Figure 1 illustrates this approach.

The basic idea of this approach consists in benefiting from dictionaries of Hadith to convert them into a format which is unified, reusable and exploitable for interrogation and for knowledge extraction to be used finally for AWSD. Four principle phases characterize our approach: Specification, Conceptualization, Formalization and Operationalization. Proposal is inspired from Mhiri work [10] and current primitive searches in MIRACL Laboratory [2,3] [9].

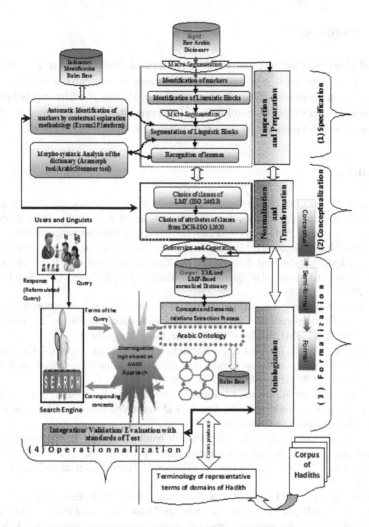

Fig. 1. Generic Approach of Normalization and Ontology Construction for Arabic Dictionaries

Specification phase consists in an inspection of the raw dictionary and the preparation of the needed data to normalize it. The second phase of Conceptualization is essentially an abstraction of the structure of the dictionary basing on LMF format [7] and its transformation into a normalized one. The phase of Formalization is a complete work of an ontology construction. Finally, the last phase of Operationalization consists in integrating this ontology into the information retrieval tool to be used by the AWSD Approach engine to disambiguate Arabic terms. Then validation of results and assessment of performance and quality with use of a Standard of Test will be at this level of the approach. We only process the two first phases by accomplishing our experimentations on (Al-Nihaya fi Gharib Al-Hadith w Al-Athar) dictionary.

4   Conclusion

A general idea about our research work was presented. We promote to achieve different objectives. The main goal is to propose a generic normalization approach for Arabic dictionaries and especially for dictionaries of Hadith as a first step before passing to the construction of the ontology of Hadith and its integration into an information retrieval and navigation system, which is our semantic portal of Hadith.

References

1. Alrahabi, M.: EXCOM-2: plateforme d'annotation automatique de catégories sémantiques. Applications à la catégorisation des citations en Français et en Arabe. Thèse de doctorat, sous la direction du Prof. Jean Pierre Desclès, Université Paris-Sorbonne (2010)
2. Ben Amar, F.B., Gargouri, B., Ben Hamadou, A.: Towards a generation of domain ontology from LMF standardized dictionaries. In: 22nd International Conference on Software Engineering and Knowledge Engineering (SEKE 2010), Redwood City, San Francisco Bay (2010)
3. Ben Amar, F.B., Gargouri, B., Ben Hamadou, A.: Domain ontology enrichment based on the semantic component of LMF-standardized dictionaries. In: Wang, M. (ed.) KSEM 2013. LNCS, vol. 8041, pp. 404–419. Springer, Heidelberg (2013)
4. Bounhas, I., Elayeb, B., Evrard, F., Slimani, Y.: Organizing contextual knowledge for arabic text disambiguation and terminology extraction. Knowledge Organization Journal. Ergon Verlag of Würzburg 38(6), 473–490 (2011)
5. Bounhas, I., Elayeb, B., Evrard, F., Slimani, Y.: ArabOnto: Experimenting a new distributional approach for Building Arabic Ontological Resources. International Journal of Metadata, Semantics and Ontologies, IJMSO (2011)
6. Bounhas, I.: Construction et intégration d'ontologies pour la cartographie socio-sémantique de fonds documentaires arabes guidée par la fiabilité de l'information. Thèse de doctorat en informatique, Faculté des Sciences de Tunis, Université de Tunis El Manar, Tunisie (2012)
7. Francopoulo, G.: LMF Lexical Markup Framework. Wiley-ISTE, Etats Unis (2013)
8. Jarrar, M.: Building a Formal Arabic Ontology Methodology and Progress. In: Proceedings of the Experts meeting on Arabic Ontologies and Semantic Networks, Alecso. Arab League, Tunis, Tunisia (2011)
9. Khemakhem, A., Elleuch, I., Gargouri, B., Ben Hamadou, A.: Towards an automatic conversion approach of editorial Arabic dictionaries into LMF-ISO 24613 standardized mode. In: 2nd International Conference on Arabic Language Resources and Tools (MEDAR), Cairo, Egypt (2009)
10. Mhiri, M., Gargouri, F., Benslimane, D.: Détermination automatique des relations sémantiques entre les concepts d'une ontologie. In: Proceedings of INFORSID 2006, pp. 627–642 (2006)

Ranking Object under Team Context

Xiaolu Lu[1], Dongxu Li[1], Xiang Li[1,*], and Ling Feng[2]

[1] School of Software, Nanjing University
{mf1232050,mf1332027,lx}@software.nju.edu.cn
[2] Department of Science and Technology, Tsinghua University
fengling@tsinghua.edu.cn

Abstract. Context-aware database has drawn increasing attention from both industry and academia recently by taking users' current situation and environment into consideration. However, most of the literature focus on individual context, overlooking the team users. In this paper, we investigate how to integrate team context into database query process to help the users get top-ranked database tuples and make the team more competitive. We review naive method and propose an optimized query algorithm to select the suitable records and show that they output same results while the latter is more computational efficient. Extensive empirical studies are conducted to evaluate the query approaches and demonstrate their effectiveness and efficiency.

1 Introduction

Millions of users take portable devices in the palm of their hands. It leads to the rapid development of context-aware database whose users have great expectations of getting suitable query results based on their ambient environment. Meanwhile, context-aware query has been widely explored to tackle with the many-answers problem due to overwhelming information. Essentially, these applications keep context information to predict users' preferences. Researches in context-aware query have mainly focused on contexts from sensors and user profiles rather than the users' organization-level context i.e the team context until recently proposed *qualitative* and *quantitative* approaches. However, most of them are based on the individual context. In [2], group context is taken but the group cannot change during the query process.

In this paper, we propose the problem of ranking under team context(RTC). Differ from others, we taking the whole organization background into consideration which can provide answers in different level of organization as shown in Fig.1(a). In an effort to handle the excessive I/O overhead, we introduce an I/O-efficient approach RTC*, based on NN search and prove its correctness. The rest of the paper is organized as follows: Section 2 describes related work with a comparison. Section 3 define the RTC problem and Section 4 propose our method a review of baseline method. Section 5 presents the experiments with analysis of the results. Section 6 is conclusion and future work.

---

* Corresponding author.

R. Meersman et al. (Eds.): OTM 2014 Workshops, LNCS 8842, pp. 659–662, 2014.
© Springer-Verlag Berlin Heidelberg 2014

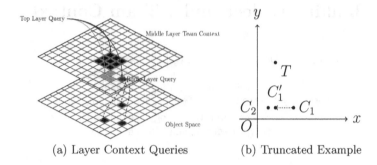

(a) Layer Context Queries   (b) Truncated Example

2 Related Work

Researches in field of context-aware query can be roughly divided into two categories: *qualitative* and *quantitative*. Qualitative way often use score functions to decide users' preference [3,5] while quantitative strategies hard coded logic rules to database system for inferring users' preferences [7].

But group or team context is overlooked until [6], Stefanids *et al.* generalized their previous work on hierarchical context model to tackle the needs of a group. Li and Feng proposed several methods to meet most of the people's preferences in a group [2]. However, all these work consider group as a union of individuals and solve the problem entirely.

3 Prelimilaries

Consider an example in NBA, teams ranked as top 10 in regular seasons can enter play-offs. To the end, team leaders of 11st~20th teams often exchange one player in the team with another bought. We refer the problem of finding the bought one as Ranking under Team Context(RTC).

Given a d-dimensional object space $\mathbb{O}$ and a dataset $\mathcal{D} \in \mathbb{O}$. Team context(TC) $\mathbf{C}(c_1, c_2, ..., c_d)$ is formed by m objects $\{O_1, O_2, .., O_m$ in $\mathcal{D}$. If $\mathbf{C}$ wants to supersede its target T, the best way is to shorten the distance on dimensions where $c_i < t_i$ ($i \in [1, d]$), denoted as $\widetilde{\text{Dis}}_{\mathbf{C},\mathbf{T}}$ henceforth. Formally, our problem is:

Problem 1. Ranking under Team Context (RTC Problem). Given a swap-out object R, the problem is to find a swap-in object P which makes $\text{Min}_{\widetilde{\text{Dis}}_{\mathbf{C'},\mathbf{T}}}$.

4 Model Analysis and Solution

Usually, we measure the difference between contexts(or objects) by weighted Euclidean distance, i.e, the case $\{C_2, T\}$ in Fig.1(b). However, positive distance yields to represent the overall conditions of a TC, especially the case $\{C_1, T\}$ shown in Fig.1(b). In this case, we just calculate distance between C_1' and T, which we referred to as *truncated Euclidean distance*. In calculating distance, dimensions weigh differently. We adopt the Kendall's tau(τ) coefficients as the weight parameter. For a clear expression, we define a 0-1 truncating vector $\overrightarrow{TV}(tv_1, tv_2, ..., tv_d)$ where $tv_i = 0$ if $c_i \geqslant t_i$.

Denote swap-out object $R(R \in C)$ and swap-in object $P \in \mathcal{D}$, therefore, truncated distance we need to minimize is:

$$\widetilde{dis} = \sqrt{\sum_{i=1}^{d} (t_i - (c_i - r_i + \frac{\lambda_r}{\lambda_p} p_i)) \times \overrightarrow{TV})^2} \tag{1}$$

To solve the problem, we define a virtual object $V(v_1, v_2, ..v_d)$ as:

$$v_i = \frac{\text{diff}_i + r_i}{\lambda_r} \times \overrightarrow{TV_2}(i) \tag{2}$$

where λ_r is a context-aware parameter and $\overrightarrow{TV_2}$ is a truncating vector of V and r_i is the value of swap-out object R on dimension i.

Corollary 1. *Assume $\forall w_i \in W(w_1, w_2, ..., w_d), w_i > 0$, denote the truncated distance between objects as $\widetilde{\text{oDis}}$. The nearest neighbours of virtual objects measured by $\widetilde{\text{oDis}}$ is the top-ranked ones who can make C become closer to T.*

Proof. Suppose we can find a nearest neighbor P of V, $P \in \mathcal{D}$, using $\widetilde{\Delta}'$ to represent truncated distance between P and V. Thus, $\widetilde{\text{diff}}'$ is:

$$\widetilde{\text{diff}}_i' = (\frac{\text{diff}_i + r_i}{\lambda_r} - p_i) \times \overrightarrow{TV_3}(i) \tag{3}$$

where $\overrightarrow{TV_3}$ is truncating vector, so $\widetilde{dis}'$ can be also as:

$$\widetilde{dis}' = \sqrt{\sum_{i=1}^{d} (w_i((v_i - p_i)\overrightarrow{TV_3}(i))^2} = \widetilde{\text{oDis}} \tag{4}$$

$\square$

So RTC can be mapped into object space. Which is, by considering nearest neighbors of virtual objects under current team context.

5   Experiments

We implement the experiments based on iDistance [1] and perform on machine with Intel Core(TM) i3 CPU and 4 GB RAM. **Real dataset** is the statistic data of NBA regular season 2011 to 2012 of both teams and players[4] and the **synthetic dataset** is generated based on real dataset with 1.07×10^6 records of 69MB size in total.

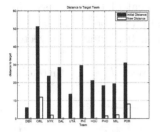
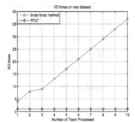
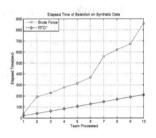

Fig. 1. Distance Compare   **Fig. 2.** Distance Change   **Fig. 3.** Distance Change

Distance change of both RTC* and brute force method is equal which reveals correctness of RTC* as shown in Fig.1.

As shown in Fig.2, only one I/O will be performed using RTC* as long as we had set up the indexing based on virtual player while brute force varies depending on the data. Time cost on synthetic dataset in Fig.3 indicates RTC* is better than brute force due to the lower cost of I/O operation.

6   Conclusion and Future Works

In this paper, we introduce the RTC problem, which is quite practical in improving the team or organization's competence. We propose an I/O efficient algorithm RTC* based on NN-indexing and prove its correctness. We would like to extend our work from two directions in our future work. First, due to the fact that the probabilistic database tuples are not uncommon, we plan to do probabilistic object selection. Second, query the database objects based on the teams' temporal contexts.

References

1. Jagadish, H.V., Ooi, B.C., Tan, K.-L., Yu, C., Zhang, R.: idistance: An adaptive b$^+$-tree based indexing method for nearest neighbor search. ACM Trans. Database Syst. 30(2), 364–397 (2005)
2. Li, X., Feng, L.: Context-aware group top-k query. In: ICDIM, pp. 149–154 (2012)
3. Li, X., Feng, L., Zhou, L.-z.: Contextual ranking of database querying results: A statistical approach. In: Roggen, D., Lombriser, C., Tröster, G., Kortuem, G., Havinga, P. (eds.) EuroSSC 2008. LNCS, vol. 5279, pp. 126–139. Springer, Heidelberg (2008)
4. Sports Reference LLC. Player season finder (November 2013),
   http://www.basketball-reference.com/play-index/psl_finder.cgi
5. Stefanidis, K., Pitoura, E., Vassiliadis, P.: Adding context to preferences. In: ICDE, pp. 846–855 (2007)
6. Stefanidis, K., Shabib, N., Nørvåg, K., Krogstie, J.: Contextual recommendations for groups. In: ER Workshops, pp. 89–97 (2012)
7. van Bunningen, A.H., Fokkinga, M.M., Apers, P.M.G., Feng, L.: Ranking query results using context-aware preferences. In: ICDE Workshops, pp. 269–276 (2007)

Fact-Based Semantic Modeling
in the Information and Behavioural Perspectives

Peter Bollen

Department of Organization & Strategy, Maastricht University
P.O. Box 616, 6200 MD, The Netherlands
p.bollen@maastrichtuniversity.nl

Abstract. Many dialects in the fact-based approach (NIAM, ORM, CogNIAM) provide modeling constructs for the information perspective in semantic modeling. In this paper we will define a number of modeling constructs that allow us to model 'behavioural perspective' semantics in a way that is compatible with the existing fact-oriented semantic modeling constructs in the information perspective.

1 Introduction

In order to define the fact-based modeling constructs for the event perspective, we will formalize the definition of derivation rules as they are currently used in fact-based modeling languages (e.g ORM [1]). The derivation rules that constitute an application's process base can be fully formalized whenever an appropriate references structure for the (static) information grammar has been put in place. We note how the pre-condition references the object types that are specified in the process argument and possibly references the (ingredient) fact types that must be contained in the application information grammar. We note that the post-condition specifies what the result will be of the execution of the derivation rule, whenever the pre-condition evaluates to true. The *create* operator is defined as follows: a fact instance that will be 'created' has subsequently to be inserted to the application's information base. If the projected information base after the proposed insert transaction will violate the application's conceptual schema or information grammar, a created fact will **not** be added to the application's information base. The rule-body of the derivation rule contains the explicit derivation logic that 'computes' the value(s) for the 'derived' role for the fact instance(s) that will be created.

Dr1:   **Derive Credibility Status <(arg1, customer)>**

IF	There exists an instance of Ft2 SUCH THAT FT2.R2 = 'arg1'
AND	There exists at least one instance of Ft3 (where ' FT3.R1' is SUCH THAT there exist an instance of Ft2 SUCH that Ft2.R2 =' arg1') [pre-condition]

THEN	Create an instance of fact type Ft1 SUCH THAT Ft1.R2= 'arg1' AND Ft1.R1= DRbody1 [post-condition]

R. Meersman et al. (Eds.): OTM 2014 Workshops, LNCS 8842, pp. 663–666, 2014.
© Springer-Verlag Berlin Heidelberg 2014

DRbody1:=	IF there exists at least one instance of Ft3 SUCH THAT Ft3.R2 = 'bad' THEN ' not credible' ELSE 'credible' [rule body]

2   The Extension of ORM with Event-Condition-Action (ECA) Modeling Constructs

Although the execution of the derivation rule is constrained by the *pre-conditions* and *post-conditions*, there still remain degrees of freedom with respect to *when* and in *what sequence* these derivation rules or *information base update processes* (IBUPs) can be executed. Therefore, an additional modeling construct is needed, to specify *when* the instances of derivation rules from the *conceptual schema* will be executed. These 'rule' executions will be triggered by events. For example the occurrence of an event instance that an *insurance application* is created will 'trigger' the derivation rule: *derive customer credibility*:

```
ON     insurance application is created
THEN   derive customer credibility
```

Definition 1. An *event type* is a set of events in the application subject area, each of these events can lead to the execution of one or more derivation rules.

Definition 2. An *event type argument set* of a given event type specifies all occurrences of object types, instances of which should be supplied for an event instance of the event type.

An *event* can start the execution of a derivation rule or IBUP (in some cases) under (a) condition(s) on the information base. In the population constraints from the application information model we have modeled the 'invariant' business rules that must hold for every information base state. For example the business rule that states that *every insurance application must state the insurance type*. In the pre-condition of the derivation rule(s), the business rules are modeled that specify what ingredient fact instances should be available in order to 'compose' or 'derive' the resulting fact instance(s) in the derivation rule [2: p.1519]. In the event perspective we will model the business rules that contain the knowledge under what condition (on the application information base) an event of an event type will trigger a specific derivation rule or IBUP. An example event description for the insurance application example will look as follows:

```
ON E1:insurance application is created (arg1:application)
THEN   derive customer credibility (arg1:customer)

ON E2: new day(arg1: date, arg2: month)
IF C1: (E2.arg1= '1' AND E2.arg2= 'january')
THEN    derive customer credibility (arg1:customer)
```

Definition 3. A *guard condition* is a proposition on the information base.

The proposition in the guard condition can contain a reference to one or more instances of the event argument.

3   The Impulse Mapper

In many cases the derivation rules are executed by users from different user groups in the same organization. The *external schema* for the event perspective for such a user group might contain *compound impulses*. This means that an event will trigger two or more derivation rules at the same time. In order to abstract from externally imposed "ways of working" we will have to atomize these *compound impulse types*. Each *atomic impulse* containing exactly **one** (primitive) *event* [3], exactly **one** *derivation rule* or *IBUP* and the condition under which the derivation rule or IBUP will be executed. We will call the effect of an event occurence into the execution of one derivation rule or IBUP (eventually under a condition on the information base) an *impulse* (instance). It is this definition of an impulse that allows us to look at an impulse as a specific type of 'business constraint' (see the discussion in [4: p.112-113]) without having to worry about run-time implementation issues like *code generation* [5], *message sending* [3: p.132] and *software components* (e.g. *event handler* [6]).

```
Algorithm 1:Fact-based behavioral modeling procedure
BEGIN    Take the first user group in application subject area
  WHILE    still user groups left in
         Take the first derivation rule or IBUP from conceptual schema
         WHILE    still derivation rules/IBUP's in conceptual schema.
         Ask the users in the Sphere of Influence what event type(s)
         invoke such a derivation rule or IBUP
         Check whether such an event type is already listed.
         IF event type not listed
          THEN For each event type determine the event type argument
          ELSE For each event type that evokes such a process:
              determine the condition on the IB and event
              argument under which the der. Rule is instantiated.
              IF the condition is different from an existing
                 condition on the same event type and derivation
                 rule/IBUP
              THEN Make a combined condition which contains the
                    old condition type and the new condition type
              ELSE the impulse is already defined.
              ENDIF
              For each (relevant) impulse determine the impulse mapper
              IF parts of such an impulse mapper can not be determined
              THEN redefine the part of the event argument such that an
                    impulse mapper can be defined
              ENDIF
              For each impulse define the event-condition
                and the condition-process trigger type (if relevant)
          ENDIF
           take next derivation rule/IBUP
        ENDWHILE
         take next user group in sphere of influence
    ENDWHILE
END
```

Events that do not have the potential to 'trigger' derivation rules from the application's conceptual schema or IBUP's are not relevant for the description of the behavioural perspective in a given application subject area [7 : p.3]. We can now classify all impulses that have the same *event type*, the same *derivation rule or IBUP* and the same *condition type* into a set of impulse instances that belong to the same *impulse type*. An impulse type contains an event type, a condition type, and a derivation rule (or a conceptual process type in general) or IBUP.

Definition 4. An *impulse mapper* is a construct that transforms values of event type arguments and fact instances from the application information base into instantiation values for the *argument set(s)* for the derivation rule or IBUP.

Example:

Event type	*Et1: insurance application created (arg1: application).*
Derivation rule	*Dr1: determine customer credibility (arg1:customer).*
Guard Condition type	*C1 : Ft4.R1 ='car' (where FT4.R2='E1.arg1')*
Impulse mapper	*Dr1.arg1:=Ft2.R2 (where Ft2.R1='E1.arg1'*

In algorithm 1 the modeling procedure for deriving the business rule model in the behaviour-oriented perspective is given.

4   Conclusion

In this article we have proposed a set of fact-based semantic modeling constructs and the methodology for instantiating those constructs for the event perspective in an application subject area. We have thereby explicitly referenced the application conceptual schema for the models in the data and process perspectives. The basic modeling constructs for the behavioral perspective is the event (type). The event type interacts with the data perspective in the form of the impulse-condition, and subsequently it interacts with the process-oriented perspective by referencing the derivation rule(s) or IBUP(s) that must be executed whenever the impulse-condition is true.

References

1. Halpin, T., Morgan, T.: Information Modeling and Relational Databases: from conceptual analysis to logical design, 2nd edn. Morgan Kaufmann, San Francisco (2008)
2. Bollen, P.: Conceptual process configurations in enterprise knowledge management systems. In: Applied computing 2006, ACM, Dijon (2006)
3. Bassiliades, N., Vlahavas, I.: Processing production rules in DEVICE, an active knowledge base system. Data & Knowlege Engineering 24, 117–155 (1997)
4. Bollen, P.: On the applicability of requirements determination methods, in Management and Organization. University of Groningen, Groningen. p. 219 (2004)
5. Dietrich, S.W., et al.: Component adaptation for event-based application integration using active rules. Journal of Systems and Software (in press)
6. Pissinou, N., Makki, K., Krishnamurthy, R.: An ECA object service to support active distributed objects. Information Sciences 100, 63–104 (1997)
7. Paton, W. (ed.): Active rules in database systems. Monographs in Computer Science. Springer, New York (1999), Gries, D. (ed.)

Author Index